THE
KINSEY
INSTITUTE
NEW REPORT
ON SEX

*What You Must Know
to be Sexually Literate*

THE
KINSEY INSTITUTE
NEW REPORT
ON SEX

*What You Must Know
to be Sexually Literate*

JUNE M. REINISCH, Ph.D.
DIRECTOR

with RUTH BEASLEY, M.L.S.

Edited and compiled by
DEBRA KENT

ST. MARTIN'S PRESS
NEW YORK

The Kinsey Institute "K" symbol stamped on the front cover of this book was designed by Enock, Inc., New York, New York.

Publisher's Note: The ideas, procedures, and suggestions contained in this book are not intended as a substitute for consulting with a physician.

Book design by Bea Jackson
Jacket design by Ruth Kolbert / Bea Jackson

Library of Congress Cataloging-in-Publication Data

Reinisch, June Machover.
    The Kinsey Institute new report on sex : what you must know to be
sexually literate / June M. Reinisch with Ruth Beasley: edited and compiled by Debra Kent
        p.   cm.
    Includes bibliographical references and index.
    ISBN 0-312-05268-5
    1. Sex. 2. Sex customs—United States. I. Beasley, Ruth. II. Kent, Debra
III. Kinsey Institute for Research in Sex, Gender,
and Reproduction. IV. Title.
HQ21.R415   1990
306.7'0973—dc20   90-41444
                                                                         CIP

First Edition: October 1990

10 9 8 7 6 5 4 3 2 1

Dedication

Chancellor Herman B Wells

President of Indiana University (1936-1964)

Teacher, Scholar, Leader, Diplomat, Sage, Visionary, and Humanitarian

There would be no Kinsey Institute without Herman B Wells. His courage and vision more than fifty years ago has sustained the past, current, and future work of the Institute. Nor would this book have been possible without him.

Preface

I would like to share a few of my thoughts about this book with its readers. During the process of writing the book, accuracy and sensitivity have been my main objectives. Every fact has been checked and each is supported by scholarly or research data. However, because science and medicine are constantly growing and changing, I would expect some of the information in this book to become outdated. There certainly is some particular information which I hope will have to be updated very quickly, such as the development of a cure for and vaccine against AIDS. Further, when there is disagreement in the scientific or scholarly communities about any particular issue, I have chosen to provide the perspective with which I agree but have also attempted to indicate that controversy exists and in many cases have presented other points of view.

Human sexuality is a domain of knowledge and experience that is not only of scientific, scholarly, and personal human interest, but it also has political, legal, and religious significance in many societies. The Kinsey Institute's mission has been for fifty years and continues to be to provide scientific and research-based facts so that individuals can make informed decisions regarding their personal lives based upon the most current information available. The institute does not take political positions with regard to sexuality, except when it involves nonconsensual sex. This book has been written in service of this long-standing tradition. It is up to each reader to decide how best to integrate this information into the context of his or her own personal values.

The first draft of this book was literally four volumes long and it was obvious that many important issues could not be included in the detail I wished and with the thoroughness they deserve. Solely due to space limitations, I was forced to limit the discussion of such topics as pregnancy, infertility, and sexual violence among adults—these topics as covered in this book include only those questions most asked of The Kinsey Institute and those directly related to sexuality. Other topics, such as the sexual abuse of children and incest are too sensitive to be addressed without a full and complete discussion, and thus no questions about these topics are included. All of these important and complex concerns require entire books to properly and fully explain the issues involved and to comment on the relevant research. Although I regret not being able to cover such topics thoroughly or at all, I have provided, wherever relevant, the titles of some books related to these issues so that readers can find the information they need.

The letters included in this book are taken from thousands received by The Kinsey Institute. We have tried to maintain the inherent character of each writer. As you will see, people who are happy with their sex lives don't write to us as often as those who are not, but the letters highlight the lack of basic information reaching the public.

You will find some repetition. Information and recommendations are repeated because I don't expect all readers to sit down and read the book cover to cover in the order in which it was organized and written. As with Alfred Kinsey's books, many people may use the table of contents and the index to find the topics of greatest personal interest; they will start their reading there, moving on to the other sections in the order of their interests. Thus I've tried to design each section to read as an accurate and responsible whole, with references to other related sections. It is my hope that people will return to this volume for information again and again, as new questions arise, rather than reading it once and setting it aside.

One final comment: An important source of institute funding is donations by those who support our work and income generated by publications. Purchasers of this book will contribute to this tradition because, like Kinsey, all my royalties for this book are being paid directly to The Kinsey Institute in support of its research, education, and archival functions.

June Machover Reinisch, Ph.D.
Director and Professor
The Kinsey Institute for Research
  in Sex, Gender, and Reproduction
Indiana University
Bloomington, Indiana

February 2, 1990

Acknowledgments

During the three years we have been working on this book, many individuals have contributed their expertise. My apologies to anyone inadvertently omitted from this list of public acknowledgments. I wish to thank Dr. Craig Hill, Dr. Stephanie Sanders, and Mary Ziemba-Davis for their major contribution to the analyses of The Kinsey Institute/Roper Organization Survey data, and these researchers plus J. Susan Straub for their involvement in the final editing process; Sandra Stewart Ham for additional editing and compiling; Dr. Leonard Rosenblum for data consultation and editing; Jana Wilson, Margaret Bullers, and Brad Braunecker for library and information service research; Joseph Becherer for art curatorial consultation and assistance in the writing of art captions; Thomas Albright and Roman Frackowski for computer support; Stacey Waltman for organizing the illustration materials; Lyndall Bass for her beautiful and sensitive original art work; Eva Enderlein for photographs of the art from The Kinsey Institute Collections; H. L. Kirk for his fine copy editing; David Hendin and Hana Lane of Pharos Books; indexers Mary and George Neumann; from the Roper Organization, Bud Roper and Harry O'Neill; Harriet Pilpel, Esq., the Institute's legal counsel; The Kinsey Institute Board of Trustees and our Science Advisory Board.

I also extend my gratitude to the individuals who read and commented on the manuscript: Dr. John Bancroft, Prof. Eugene Eoyang, Lillian Reinisch, Dr. Marian Dunn, Dr. Harold Lief, Sherry Hackett, Margaret Harter, Carolyn Kaufman, Jane Kelley, Petra Miskus, Elizabeth Roberge, Janet Rowland, Kim Sare, Terry Sare, Scott Schurz, Jean Seger, Abner Sheffer, and Diane Meyer Simon.

I want to express my deep appreciation and thanks to the scientists and scholars who have generously provided their expertise whenever asked or whose publications have been heavily relied upon: Drs. Gloria Bachmann, Wendy Baldwin, Frank Beach, Joseph Bellina, Philip Blumstein, John Boswell, Ed Brecher, Eli Coleman, Winnifred Cutler, Julian Davidson, David Eschenbach, John Goodheart, Julia Heiman, Gilbert Herdt, Preban Hertoft, King Holmes,

Virginia Johnson, Robert Jones, William G. Karow, Robert Kolodny, Prakash Kothari, Peter Lee, Jere Levy, Sandra Lieblum, Harold Lief, Joseph LoPiccolo, William Masters, Andrew Mattison, Vickie Mays, David McWhirter, John Money, Ronald Nadler, Margaret Nichols, Raymond Rosen, Raul Schiavi, Leslie Schover, Patricia Schreiner-Engel, M. Fini Schulsinger, Pepper Schwartz, George Semel, Michael Shernoff, Barbara Sherwin, Terry Tafoya, Bruce Voeller, Gorm Wagner, Jeffrey Wolin, Gail Wyatt, and the hundreds of other researchers, scholars, and clinicians whose work has been used throughout this book. The following government agencies and private institutions have also provided information: AASECT, Abbott Laboratories, American Fertility Society, The Alan Guttmacher Institute, The National Institute of Allergy and Infectious Diseases, The National Institute of Child Health and Human Development, Planned Parenthood, SIECUS, Stone Belt Council for Retarded Citizens, United Cerebral Palsy Association, and the U.S. Centers for Disease Control.

The following agencies have provided grant support to The Kinsey Institute research projects and programs: The National Institute of Allergy and Infectious Diseases, The National Institute of Child Health and Human Development, The National Institute on Drug Abuse, The National Institute of Mental Health, and The Fund for Human Dignity.

My deepest gratitude to my mentors Drs. John Money, Brian Sutton-Smith, and Herbert Birch and the loving support of my husband, Dr. Leonard Rosenblum; parents, Lillian (Machover) and Mann B. Reinisch; daughter, Karen Reinisch, and stepchildren Gianine and Doug Rosenblum; Rich Hall, Jennifer Beasley, Jeannette Fisher, and Doshia Hall for their loving support of Ruth Beasley.

Finally, appreciation and thanks to the thousands of individuals from the United States and around the world who have written to The Kinsey Institute with their questions about sex, gender, and reproduction; the 1,974 Americans who most generously participated in The Kinsey Institute/Roper Organization Sex Knowledge Survey; and the citizens of Bloomington, Indiana, who helped us to pilot that survey.

                                                                    J.M.R.

Contents

If you would like to volunteer to be part of The Kinsey Institute's research projects on sexual behavior, knowledge, and attitudes, please send us a postcard with your name, mailing address, age, and sex. We will mail you a questionnaire. Your responses will be anonymous (no name is required on the questionnaire) and completely confidential. All reports are written on groups of respondents not on individuals. Mail the postcard to The Kinsey Institute, 313 Morrison Hall, Indiana University, Bloomington, IN 47405.

Your participation will be invaluable in helping the institute to advance scientific knowledge of human sexuality and will provide data relevant to many of the problems and concerns included in this book.

Sex and The Kinsey Institute

An Introduction

I'm a virgin and I'm planning to get married. Will my first sexual intercourse be painful?

I'm 70 years old and I'm having trouble getting an erection. Is this just a normal part of old age? Is this the end of my sex life?

Can masturbation make me sterile?

I think I may have VD. What can I buy at the drug store to cure it?

My wife and I desperately want a child and have sex every other day, but we're having trouble becoming pregnant. Is there any way we can increase our chances?

This may seem dumb, but what does a homosexual do sexually that's different from other people?

It seems that answers to questions like these should be fairly easy to find. Sexual issues are standard fare on television and radio talk shows; bookstores have entire sections devoted to titles on sexuality; and many popular magazines have monthly columns on sexual health. However, the thousands of questions The Kinsey Institute receives each year and the national survey reported in Chapter 1 make it evident that most people still do not have a source of accurate information about sex, gender, and reproduction upon which to base decisions about their personal lives and health. Even though "sex" seems to be everywhere in the media, much of the information is superficial, focuses on the more sensational aspects, relies on sources of questionable accuracy, or is confined to one person's opinion or experience.

Our mail shows that many people are still confused about sexual issues and are particularly concerned about whether their own bodies, sexual feelings, and sexual activities are "normal." This book presents many of these basic questions and provides answers based on the latest scientific studies.

The situation was different in 1938, the year the Association of Women

Students at Indiana University petitioned the administration for a course in human sexuality for students who were either engaged, married, or considering marriage. Certainly, accurate sexual information was almost impossible to obtain. Materials with explicit sexual passages or even contraceptive information were illegal to import into the United States or to send through the U.S. postal system. As often happens with such bans, a booming underground distribution system supplied erotic materials to those who knew where to look for these illicit items and who could afford to buy them.

The university asked a well-respected professor of zoology to coordinate the course and felt that Dr. Alfred C. Kinsey, a Harvard-trained scientist known for his biology textbooks and exhaustive research on gall wasps, would provide a scholarly perspective to this sensitive subject.

As he set out to gather materials for his curriculum, Kinsey soon discovered that few scientific data were available on human sexual behavior. The little that did exist was in general either distorted by personal bias or based on studies of small numbers of clinical patients. Accustomed to basing his lectures on fact, Kinsey began to collect basic data from his students in confidential interviews by getting answers to questions like: Were you a virgin when you got married? How often do you have intercourse? How many sexual partners have you had? Have you ever had an extramarital affair? When did you begin to masturbate and how often do you do so? Soon Kinsey was interviewing residents of Bloomington, Indiana, and eventually he took his research to many cities and towns around the country.

By 1941 Kinsey's pioneering work had earned the financial support of the prestigious National Research Council, at that time funded by the Rockefeller Foundation. Recognizing that the controversial nature of Kinsey's work made it vulnerable to outside attack from political and religious forces, in 1947 university president Herman B Wells suggested that Kinsey establish the Institute for Sex Research as a not-for-profit private corporation affiliated with Indiana University. This new status helped guarantee absolute confidentiality to the people interviewed and provided permanent sanctuary for the growing collection of interview data.

Kinsey had a clear vision for the institute: to supply accurate research-based information with which individuals and society could make informed decisions about sexual behavior. As he became aware of their existence, he also began to collect a wide range of literary materials, art objects, commercial items, and other materials depicting human sexual behavior from diverse cultures and periods of history for scholarly use.

In 1948 Kinsey's first book, *Sexual Behavior in the Human Male*, was published; it included data collected from individual interviews with more than 5000 males of all ages. For the first time, Americans would be able to find out precisely what went on behind bedroom doors other than their own. They learned, among other things, that more than 90 percent of the males questioned said they had masturbated and more than a third said they had had at least one sexual experience with another male since puberty.

The book was published by W. B. Saunders, a publisher of medical textbooks. The information was presented in dry, academic style and was accompanied by detailed data tables. On the assumption that the sole purchasers would be

Illustration No. 1. This portrait appeared on the cover of *Time* magazine for August 24, 1953. Flowers, birds, and a bee surround Kinsey; the mirror-of-Venus female symbol decorates his bow tie. In the cover story Alfred Kinsey was acclaimed "the Columbus of Sex."

BORIS ARTZYBASHEFF. *Alfred Kinsey.* Watercolor on paper. 1953. 15″ x 11-⅔″. The Kinsey Institute Collections.

scientists and physicians, only a few copies were printed initially. The book became a best-seller almost overnight.

In 1953, the institute released *Sexual Behavior in the Human Female*, and the public learned that half of the nearly 6000 women interviewed said they had not been virgins when they married and 25 percent reported they had engaged in extramarital sex. This volume, also a best-seller, caused much clamor in the press, among the clergy, and in Congress. Although most Americans in the early 1950s were willing to accept the fact that men were sexually active beings, few were ready to believe that women engaged in sex for anything other than procreation.

The public was obviously greatly interested in the information these books contained, but other forces were at work to halt Kinsey's scientific inquiry. Some members of the clergy declared that he was doing the devil's work. McCarthyism was in full swing by the time the second volume was released, and one Congressman insisted that studying human sexual behavior was paving the way for a Communist takeover of the United States. Kinsey and his research became the subject of a special investigative committee of the House of Representatives. Responding to pressure from Congress, the Rockefeller Foundation withdrew financial support after many years as the major source of Kinsey's funding.

Even in this difficult time, the institute continued its work, surviving on book royalties and protected by Indiana University President Wells and its status as a not-for-profit corporation affiliated with the university. But the scrutiny, criticism, and harassment took an emotional and physical toll on the institute's founder. In 1956, Alfred Kinsey died at the age of 62, never to know that less than a decade later he would be considered one of the most influential figures of the twentieth century. Moreover, the early staff's collection of 17,500 interviews remains the largest data base of sexual histories; it is still the most frequently cited source of data on human sexual behavior. Even in 1986, this data base was used by the National Academy of Science as the sole source of sex information from which to predict estimates of the spread of the AIDS virus.

Scarred by the attacks during the 1950s, the institute scrupulously avoided the spotlight for the next two and a half decades. Anthropologist Dr. Paul Gebhard, a member of the original Kinsey research team, became director after Kinsey's death and the institute's primary efforts for several years were directed toward analyzing and publishing the unique body of data already accumulated.

One book, *Pregnancy, Birth and Abortion*, published in 1958, revealed that one out of every ten women reported becoming pregnant before marriage. Of these women, three-quarters had had an abortion, which was illegal at that time. Similarly, *Sex Offenders: An Analysis of Types*, published in 1965, provided definitive evidence for the first time that most voyeurs are not incipient rapists and that most exhibitionists are not physically dangerous to others. Both books were important works, yet these and other research findings that emerged during this era received little public attention.

New research studies were begun in the 1960s and 1970s, many of them focused on homosexual behavior. The institute also began training programs on human sexuality for physicians, therapists, and counselors. But the low public profile was maintained.

As Gebhard neared retirement, the university formed a search committee for a new director, stipulating that the institute needed to broaden its scope to include the more biomedical aspects of sexuality. They also wanted the institute to achieve a more prominent public role. Dr. June Machover Reinisch, a psychobiologist, was hired as director in 1982 and changed the name of the Institute for Sex Research to The Kinsey Institute for Research in Sex, Gender, and Reproduction to reflect its expanded scope and to honor its founder. Because most scientific research, including that done at The Kinsey Institute, is financed by public funds, it was agreed that there was an ethical imperative to provide research-based information directly to the people who pay for it. Thus, among many new goals, Reinisch was charged with finding ways to provide the public with straightforward, scientifically-based information about sex, gender, and reproduction.

While it has always been vitally important that the institute's work be recognized by the scientific community through publication in professional journals and reports at scientific meetings, it was also important to provide a direct dialogue between scientists and the public. From the phone calls and letters the institute continually received and the questions people asked when Reinisch lectured, it was clear that many people still remained painfully ignorant about basic sexual issues despite the media's increasing coverage of sexual topics. The goal was to answer people's questions in a medium that was responsible, respectable, accessible, and relatively inexpensive.

The first result was the development of a research-based newspaper column, where answers would be derived from authoritative research, not opinion. Based on Alfred Kinsey's philosophy, the column would not tell people what to do, but rather would provide scientific information from which individuals could draw their own personal conclusions and make informed decisions about their sexual lives, health, and behavior, within the context of personal values and individual circumstances. This book follows the same philosophy.

Producing *The Kinsey Report* column has involved many members of the institute staff in addition to Reinisch. It could never have been brought to press without the dedication of Kinsey researchers and librarians and access to our extensive collection of scientific materials. Ruth Beasley, formerly assistant director of the Institute, was a key researcher and co-writer for the first five years. Jana Wilson, publications research associate, assumed those responsibilities in August 1988. All column proceeds go directly to support The Kinsey Institute's research and educational activities.

Some people are opposed to public dissemination of sex information, believing that if people want answers to their questions on sex, they can go to parents, teachers, family doctors, or the public library. If only that were true! It would be best if children and teenagers felt comfortable asking their mothers and fathers about sex, and the institute often encourages them to do so. The reality is that many kids don't and their parents are uncomfortable discussing the subject. Instead, children ask their friends, and more often than not the answers they get are both incorrect and scary.

It would also help if school systems in all regions of the country had solid sex education programs in place, beginning with the earliest grades, but this is not the case either, despite the fact that a 1988 national poll indicated that 89 percent of U.S. adults endorse sex education in the public schools. Although it is known that sexual responses begin even before birth and sex behavior is evident throughout childhood, many people still assume that if the topic is not mentioned, children will never think of it by themselves.

This book is not meant to take the place of a doctor's appointment, and readers are frequently told why they *must* see a physician. But it is clear from many of our letters that people either are too embarrassed to approach their family physicians with questions about sex or their physicians are just as embarrassed and won't—or can't—answer their patients' questions. Even those family doctors who are willing to discuss sexuality have not usually had training in sexual medicine or sexology, nor are they always up-to-date on the latest findings, specialized tests, or treatment methods.

In the best of all possible worlds, sex education would begin at home. Parents would teach their children about how their bodies develop, how reproduction takes place, the emotions involved in forming, maintaining, and ending relation-ships, and their personal values about managing the sexual aspects of life. In the same way good parents teach their children that they can get burned if they put their hands on a hot stove, parents would tell children about sexually transmit-ted diseases and how to prevent them.

Some parents are fearful that sex education itself may propel children into sexual exploration. However, the research available shows that this widespread belief is not true. Sex education does *not* promote increased sexual activity among young people, and a young person's attitudes about sexual behavior do not change to become either more or less liberal after sex education. In fact, a study of school-based clinics that provided both sex education and contracep-tives found that these services *delayed* the age of first intercourse and significantly *reduced* teen pregnancies.

The purpose of this book is to compile in one source the factual information that is desperately needed but not readily available elsewhere.

Further Readings

Christenson, C. V. *Kinsey a Biography*. Bloomington, IN: Indiana University Press, 1971.

Pomeroy, W. B. *Dr. Kinsey and the Institute for Sex Research*. New York: Harper & Row, 1972.

America Fails Sex
Information Test

Each year The Kinsey Institute receives thousands of letters and telephone calls from a wide variety of people seeking accurate, up-to-date answers to questions about sex. We began to wonder whether these questions reflected both the general concerns and a lack of information among Americans at large. To find out, in the fall of 1989, The Kinsey Institute tested the basic sexual knowledge of a statistically representative group of 1,974 American adults.

Unfortunately, Americans failed the test.

This poll, conducted during a face-to-face interview by The Roper Organization, shows that Americans either don't have the facts or are misinformed about a range of sexual topics, including AIDS, contraception, homosexuality, erection problems, infidelity, and menopause.

Of American adults taking our eighteen-question test, 55 percent failed (see Table 1, America's Report Card.) That means the majority could correctly answer only half the questions or fewer. Another 27 percent of respondents received Ds, a grade requiring only 56 to 66 percent correct answers. Fourteen percent obtained Cs. There were only five A students (less than .5 percent) and only sixty-eight people (4 percent) received Bs.

Who passed the test? These people tended to be 30-44 years old; with at least some college education; from higher income groups; with no religious affiliation; from the Midwest or West; politically liberal; single, married, divorced or separated but not widowed; and from more densely populated urban areas.

Who failed? They were more likely to be 60 years of age or older; to have no high school diploma; to come from lower income groups; to have a religious affiliation; to live in the South or Northeast; to be politically conservative or moderate; widowed; and to come from less densely populated or more rural areas.

Given the fact that those who failed outnumber those who passed, it is clear that the American public is not getting accurate sexual information. Whether in campaigns for preventing AIDS, guidelines for avoiding unplanned pregnancy, discussions of intimate sexual problems, or information about sex and aging, the

AMERICA'S REPORT CARD

Grade	Number of correct answers required to receive this grade	Number of participants receiving this grade	Percent of participants receiving this grade
A	16 - 18	5	<1
B	14 - 15	68	4
C	12 - 13	239	14
D	10 - 11	463	27
F	1 - 9	936	55

Note: Of the 1,974 survey participants, 263 (13%) completed ten or fewer of the 18 test items and were not included in the computation of these overall test scores. However, all those answering a question were included in the item-by-item analyses.

Table 1

facts are not reaching the majority of Americans. Educators, physicians, public health officials, and the media must provide more sexual information to the public.

We knew at the outset that asking Americans about sex would pose some challenges; surveys about sex-related topics are often difficult to conduct in a way that ensures accurate responses that are relatively free from bias. For example, if the interview procedure is not properly set up, respondents may feel awkward or embarrassed by the subject matter. This situation becomes even worse if interviewers themselves feel uncomfortable with the material.

We are confident that the responses to this survey reflect those of the adult American population because they are based on a nationally representative sample. The high level of response on all of our questions gives us further confidence in the accuracy of these findings. In the end, only an average of 9 percent of people refused to answer any particular question, which is very low compared with other sex surveys. We believe that our high response rate is due to The Kinsey Institute's reputation as an authoritative source for research-based sexual information, its fifty-year history of maintaining confidentiality, and the expert assistance with question construction and sampling provided by The Roper Organization, which has had more than five decades of experience in surveying the American people. Also, more people probably agreed to answer these questions because this was a test of knowledge, not personal experience.

The remainder of this chapter is organized as follows: First, the survey questions and response options are presented so that you can take The Kinsey Institute/Roper Organization National Sex Knowledge Survey yourself. Then you are given the answer key and told how to score your test. Next, we discuss each question's answer in detail telling you how different groups (divided by sex, age, education, and so on) responded. This is followed by a description of which groups did best on the overall test. We also asked the survey participants about where they went for information about sex when they were growing up and where they would go now if they had a question about sex and we tell you what they said. We then take a brief look at how going to these different sources of information related to performance on this test.

THE KINSEY INSTITUTE/ROPER
ORGANIZATION NATIONAL SEX KNOWLEDGE TEST

Instructions: Circle one answer after reading each question carefully.

1. **Nowadays, what do you think is the age at which the *average* or *typical* American *first* has sexual intercourse?**

a. 11 or younger	e. 15	i. 19
b. 12	f. 16	j. 20
c. 13	g. 17	k. 21 or older
d. 14	h. 18	l. Don't know

2. **Out of every ten married American men, how many would you estimate have had an extramarital affair—that is, have been sexually unfaithful to their wives?**

a. Less than one out of ten	g. Six out of ten (60%)
b. One out of ten (10%)	h. Seven out of ten (70%)
c. Two out of ten (20%)	i. Eight out of ten (80%)
d. Three out of ten (30%)	j. Nine out of ten (90%)
e. Four out of ten (40%)	k. More than nine out of ten
f. Five out of ten (50%)	l. Don't know

3. **Out of every ten American women, how many would you estimate have had anal (rectal) intercourse?**

a. Less than one out of ten	g. Six out of ten (60%)
b. One out of ten (10%)	h. Seven out of ten (70%)
c. Two out of ten (20%)	i. Eight out of ten (80%)
d. Three out of ten (30%)	j. Nine out of ten (90%)
e. Four out of ten (40%)	k. More than nine out of ten
f. Five out of ten (50%)	l. Don't know

4. **A person can get AIDS by having anal (rectal) intercourse even if neither partner is infected with the AIDS virus.**

True   False   Don't know

5. **There are over-the-counter spermicides people can buy at the drugstore that will kill the AIDS virus.**

True   False   Don't know

6. Petroleum jelly, Vaseline Intensive Care, baby oil, and Nivea are *not* good lubricants to use with a condom or diaphragm.

   True   False   Don't know

7. More than one out of four (25 percent) of American men have had a sexual experience with another male during either their teens or adult years.

   True   False   Don't know

8. It is usually difficult to tell whether people *are* or are *not* homosexual just by their appearance or gestures.

   True   False   Don't know

9. A woman or teenage girl can get pregnant during her menstrual flow (her "period").

   True   False   Don't know

10. A woman or teenage girl can get pregnant even if the man withdraws his penis before he ejaculates (before he "comes").

    True   False   Don't know

11. Unless they are having sex, women do not need to have regular gynecological examinations.

    True   False   Don't know

12. Teenage boys should examine their testicles ("balls") regularly just as women self-examine their breasts for lumps.

    True   False   Don't know

13. Problems with erection are most often started by a physical problem.

    True   False   Don't know

14. Almost all erection problems can be successfully treated.

    True   False   Don't know

15. Menopause, or change of life as it is often called, does *not* cause most women to lose interest in having sex.

    True   False   Don't know

16. Out of every ten American women, how many would you estimate have masturbated either as children or after they were grown up?

    a. Less than one out of ten   d. Three out of ten (30%)
    b. One out of ten (10%)   e. Four out of ten (40%)
    c. Two out of ten (20%)   f. Five out of ten (50%)

g. Six out of ten (60%)
h. Seven out of ten (70%)
i. Eight out of ten (80%)

j. Nine out of ten (90%)
k. More than nine out of ten
l. Don't know

17. What do you think is the length of the average man's *erect* penis?

a. 2 inches
b. 3 inches
c. 4 inches
d. 5 inches

e. 6 inches
f. 7 inches
g. 8 inches
h. 9 inches

i. 10 inches
j. 11 inches
k. 12 inches
l. Don't know

18. Most women prefer a sexual partner with a larger-than-average penis.

True   False   Don't know

SCORING THE TEST

Each question is worth one point. So, the total possible number of points you can get is 18. Using this chart, score each item and then add up your total number of points. When a range of possible answers is correct, according to currently available research data, all respondents choosing one of the answers in the correct range are given a point.

Question number	Give yourself a point if you circled any of the following answers	Circle the number of points you received
1	f,g	0 1
2	d,e	0 1
3	d,e	0 1
4	False	0 1
5	(any answer, everyone gets a point as explained in discussion of question)	1
6	True	0 1
7	True	0 1
8	True	0 1
9	True	0 1
10	True	0 1
11	False	0 1
12	True	0 1
13	True	0 1
14	True	0 1
15	True	0 1
16	g,h,i	0 1
17	d,e,f	0 1
18	False	0 1

Total Number of Points: _____

Now look up the grade you received.

If you got this number of points	You receive this grade
16-18	A
14-15	B
12-13	C
10-11	D
1-9	F

DISCUSSION OF EACH QUESTION

We will now discuss the answer to each of the questions and tell you how the participants in the national sample did. We also analyzed how people did on each question and on the overall test according to various demographic characteristics such as sex, age, and education. Some of the significant findings are described in the discussion of the answers to questions. In order to best understand the findings reported in this chapter, you should now look at *Table 2, Demographic Characteristics.* This shows how the groups were divided and how many people in our national sample fell into each group.

1. **Nowadays, what do you think is the age at which the *average* or *typical* American *first* has sexual intercourse?**

Correct answer: *16-17 years old*

Most studies report that the average American has intercourse for the first time between the age of 16 and 17. Based on the answers of our survey respondents, this may be older than what you thought. This is an average—many start at younger or older ages. It is important to note that in the United States a teen gets pregnant every thirty seconds. And every thirteen seconds an American teen gets a sexually transmitted disease (STD). If we are to change this, young people need to get accurate information on sex, including discussions of parental and community values regarding sexuality, *before* they become sexually active so that they will be better prepared to make responsible choices about their behavior *(see Chapters 11 and 12).*

Only about one in four of our participants got this one right. Who did best?: Midwesterners, political moderates, the more highly educated, and those in the top income group.

But the vast majority (76 percent) did not answer this question correctly. Apparently most people—especially Southerners, liberals, and those separated or divorced—believed that intercourse begins a lot earlier. Most of those who answered incorrectly *underestimated* the age; in other words, most believed that the average age of first intercourse is 15 or younger, and some even believed it occurs at 11 years old or younger. When women underestimated, they thought the average age was 13 years or younger. Men were a bit more conservative believing that first intercourse usually happens at age 15.

Older people (60+), on the other hand, tended to *overestimate*; they were twice as likely as everyone else to say that typical Americans start having intercourse at 18 or older.

2. Out of every ten married American men, how many would you estimate have had an extramarital affair—that is, have been sexually unfaithful to their wives?

Correct answer: *Three to four out of ten (30%-40%)*

Based on a comprehensive review of the major studies published over the last forty years, The Kinsey Institute estimates that *37 percent* of married men have had at least one extramarital affair. Only one in four answered correctly, leaving a hefty 75 percent with the wrong answer.

Just as more Americans think teenagers begin having sex earlier than they really do, people seem to think that affairs are more common than they actually are. Half of the respondents thought that at least five out of every ten married men were doing this. Women (much more than men) believed that at least *70 percent* of married men have had an extramarital affair.

One particularly interesting finding: People who were divorced or separated, followed by singles, were more likely than the married or widowed to overestimate the number of men who have been unfaithful. Although this was a survey of knowledge, not experience, it is possible that the responses of the separated or divorced group were influenced by their personal experience, while singles' overestimates reflected their concerns and fears (we often get letters from single women, particularly those engaged to be married, who worry that their future husbands inevitably will have an affair).

In 1990, two widely publicized national surveys reported very different estimates of extramarital activity. One, conducted by telephone, reported that only 1 out of 10 (10%) of 657 currently married men and women said thay had had affairs since the day they were married. Respondents were only asked about their current marriage. It is also impossible to know whether a spouse was in the room which might have affected people's answers to this question. The second survey also did not ask about extramarital activity over the lifespan. However, by comparing the number of partners since age 18 with the number of marriages, it was estimated that 70% of men are not "chaste" which was then interpreted as a measure of "unfaithfulness." Since neither study collected data directly on lifetime extramarital experience these two surveys could not be included in the Kinsey Institute estimates of extramarital activity *(see Chapter 5)*.

3. Out of every ten American women, how many would you estimate have had anal (rectal) intercourse?

Correct answer: *Three to four out of ten (30%-40%)*

Nearly 80 percent of the public got this question wrong. Only 21 percent

DEMOGRAPHIC CHARACTERISTICS

Demographic characteristic	Groups	Number of survey participants in each group	Percent of survey participants in each group
Sex	Male	940	48
	Female	1034	52
Age	18-29 years old	453	23
	30-44 years old	698	35
	45-59 years old	351	18
	60+ years old	470	24
	Age not reported	2	*
Education	No high school diploma	411	21
	High school graduate	675	34
	Some college	886	45
	Education not reported	2	*
Income	Less than $15,000	387	20
	$15,000 - 24,999	329	17
	$25,000 - 34,999	372	19
	$35,000+	542	27
	Income not reported	344	17
Race	White	1586	80
	Black	211	11
	Hispanic	114	6
	Other	21	1
	Race not reported	43	2
Marital Status	Married	1189	60
	Single	399	20
	Separated/Divorced	199	10
	Widowed	186	10

Table 2

correctly knew that three to four out of every ten American women had tried anal intercourse.

There is a longstanding and strongly held myth in our culture that only homosexual men (male-male couples) have anal intercourse. The fact is that not all homosexual men engage in anal sex while many heterosexual (male-female) couples *do*, according to a Kinsey Institute paper published in *American Psychologist* (November 1988). Also a Kinsey Institute survey of a Midwestern university found that one out of four of these college students (25 percent) had tried anal sex at least once *(see Chapter 7)*.

DEMOGRAPHIC CHARACTERISTICS (cont'd)

Demographic characteristic	Groups	Number of survey participants in each group	Percent of survey participants in each group
	Marital status not reported	1	*
Religious	Protestant	971	49
Affiliation	Catholic	607	31
	Jewish	66	3
	Other	147	8
	None	158	8
	Don't know	9	*
	Religion not reported	16	1
Political	Conservative	819	42
Philosophy	Moderate	629	32
	Liberal	462	23
	Political philosophy not reported	64	3
Region of the	Northeast	440	22
United States	Midwest	518	26
	South	652	33
	West	364	19
Population size	1 (most urban)	796	40
of hometown	2	625	32
	3	309	16
	4 (most rural)	244	12

Note: For a more detailed description of these demographic breakdowns see Methodology, pp. 25-26.
* Less than .5%

Nearly all the letters we receive at the institute on this subject are from heterosexual couples concerned about the association between anal intercourse and AIDS *(see discussion of Question 4)*.

Unlike the questions on first intercourse (Question 1) and extramarital affairs (Question 2), in which people often overestimated sexual activity, there was a strong tendency to *underestimate* on this question about anal sex. Almost 37 percent of American adults thought that only one or two out of ten women have had anal sex, while only 15 percent actually overestimated, thinking that at least half of all women had tried it.

Perhaps the most striking finding was the dramatic number of American adults—28 percent—who simply answered "Don't know" rather than venture a guess, possibly underscoring the perception of anal intercourse as a particularly taboo topic in our culture. (Many of these respondents were in the 60-plus age group.)

More men than women knew the answer to this question, and people aged 18 to 44 were *three and a half times* as likely to get it right than those 60 and older. The college-educated, the higher income groups, and those who were single, separated or divorced were all more likely than others to answer correctly.

4. **A person can get AIDS by having anal (rectal) intercourse even if neither partner is infected with the AIDS virus.**

Correct answer: *False*

Research has shown that unprotected anal intercourse (without a condom or other barrier) with an *infected* partner is the sexual behavior most likely to transmit the AIDS virus *(see Chapter 19)*. But many Americans mistakenly believe that anal intercourse itself can cause AIDS.

The fact is that anal sex itself does not cause AIDS. Just as a woman will not get pregnant unless sperm are available to impregnate her, a person cannot develop AIDS unless he or she has been infected by the AIDS virus (HIV). So, unless one partner is infected with the AIDS virus (HIV), there is no risk of developing AIDS as a result of anal intercourse or any other sexual behavior.

Half of America answered this question incorrectly, a lack of knowledge also reflected in the letters we receive at the Institute from heterosexual, often sexually exclusive, couples who have anal intercourse but now fear developing AIDS as a result.

Education made a difference—college-educated Americans were twice as likely to answer correctly.

Women 30-44 years old outscored everybody else. Among men, the 60+ age group was least likely to get it right. More than half of Americans with religious affiliations answered incorrectly. In contrast, only about 30 percent of those with no religious affiliation answered incorrectly. And significantly more liberals than conservatives knew that anal sex by itself does not cause AIDS.

The false idea that AIDS can spontaneously develop as a result of a particular behavior in the absence of infection may be rooted in the taboo about anal sex, bias against homosexuality, and the belief that sexually transmitted diseases (STDs) are the inevitable consequence of engaging in "bad" sexual behavior.

One final note: Keep in mind that you cannot tell by appearance whether a person or sexual partner is infected with the AIDS virus (HIV). It can take many years from infection with the virus until symptoms of AIDS appear, so a person can seem healthy and still have the virus and be capable of transmitting it to others. (*See Chapter 19 for more information on STDs and safer sex techniques that can help you reduce your chances of becoming infected with the AIDS virus or any other STD organism.)*

5. **There are over-the-counter spermicides people can buy at the drugstore that will kill the AIDS virus.**

Correct answer: *True*

Many nonprescription, over-the-counter spermicides (substances that kill sperm and are used to prevent pregnancy) contain nonoxynol-9. Nonoxynol-9 is a chemical which has been shown in laboratory tests to kill the AIDS virus (HIV) as well as many other STD organisms. Therefore, many health care professionals and organizations such as the U.S. Centers for Disease Control's STD hotline and the National AIDS hotline suggest that using a condom together with a spermicide containing nonoxynol-9 may protect you even more than a condom alone against transmission of the AIDS virus. Read the labels on spermicides or ask your pharmacist to help you find the ones that contain nonoxynol-9. *(For more information, see Chapter 19.) NOTE:* In mid-1990 new research data suggested that use of spermicides may increase the risk of vaginal and urinary infections for some women *(see Chapter 17)*.

Only 5 percent of our sample answered correctly. We decided to give everybody a point toward their overall test score regardless of what they answered, because some people might have misunderstood this question, thinking that the statement meant that there is a *cure* for AIDS. On the other hand, if the people taking this test knew about the effects of spermicides on the AIDS virus and other STD organisms they would not have misinterpreted this question.

Because nonoxynol-9 can kill the AIDS virus (HIV) in the laboratory does not mean that there is a cure for AIDS. Condoms and substances that contain nonoxynol-9 can help *prevent* transmission of the AIDS virus from an infected person to a sexual partner. They do this by blocking the virus or killing it *before* the virus has had an opportunity to infect the partner. But once a person has been infected with the AIDS virus (HIV) these things cannot be used as a cure.

Here again, making a comparison to pregnancy and birth control may help. Condoms and spermicides can be used to help prevent pregnancy by preventing sperm from getting into the vagina and by killing sperm in the vagina, respectively. However, once a woman is pregnant, condoms and spermicides can not undo the pregnancy. Also, a man cannot ingest these spermicides to kill sperm that he is producing.

Five percent answered true, 84 percent answered false, and 11 percent said they did not know. Information on nonoxynol-9 and messages about the difference between preventing transmission of the AIDS virus and curing the disease are obviously not reaching the public. This lack of information cuts across both sexes, all ages, religious affiliations, marital-status groups, and levels of education and income.

Everyone did poorly on this question. However, it appears that liberals did better than conservatives. We can also point out that 60-year-olds were more likely than other groups to say they didn't know. The positive side to responding "Don't know" is that people who are aware that they *don't* know something may be more open to learning the facts.

Unlike performance on most other questions, people in the Northeast and South were *more* likely to be correct than those from the Midwest and West. People from urban areas did better than those from rural areas. These results may reflect differences in the quality and scope of AIDS education campaigns in different regions, and the U.S. Centers for Disease Control's relative success in educating populations in the cities with the highest prevalence of reported AIDS cases. Eight of the cities with the highest number of AIDS cases are in the South (Houston, Washington, D.C., Miami, Atlanta, Dallas) and Northeast (New York, Newark, and Philadelphia). These findings indicate that additional, broader, more intense, longer duration national education campaigns by the Centers for Disease Control are likely to have a more profound effect on the American public. Such efforts deserve strong support so that a larger portion of Americans will be informed about how to protect themselves against HIV and other STD infections.

6. **Petroleum jelly, Vaseline Intensive Care, baby oil, and Nivea are *not* good lubricants to use with a condom or diaphragm.**

Correct answer: *True*

Petroleum jelly, Vaseline Intensive Care, baby oil, Nivea, or any other oil-based cream, lotion, or jelly will erode a condom or diaphragm and should *not* be used as a lubricant. Within sixty seconds these products can make microscopic holes in condoms or diaphragms big enough for the AIDS virus and other STD organisms to pass through and soon afterward the holes are big enough for sperm to penetrate *(see Chapter 16)*.

This is crucial information, yet half (50 percent) of American adults did not know it. Those who did know were more likely to be women, younger people, and those who are single, separated or divorced. As with the information on nonoxynol-9 in question 5, people in cities and suburbs (urban areas) did better than those in more rural areas.

One of the major goals of public health agencies in the United States is to encourage the use of latex condoms to protect against STDs, including AIDS. Success is dependent on proper use. The fact that half of our respondents believed that it was OK to use an oil-based lubricant with a condom or diaphragm indicates that a significant number of people may be seriously decreasing the effectiveness of these latex products. Based on these data, The Kinsey Institute has suggested that condom manufacturers provide a warning label on each individual condom wrapper, which might read:

> **WARNING: Do not use with any lubricant containing oil, such as petroleum jelly, baby oil, or handcream. Microscopic holes in this latex product will result within 60 seconds after contact. Ask your pharmacist about water-based lubricants.**

Lubricants that can be used safely with latex contraceptives include water-based products such as K-Y Jelly and Lubrin inserts. Read the label. If you have any questions, ask your pharmacist. Remember, just because a lubricate washes off easily DOES NOT mean it is water-based and therefore SAFE to use with a condom or diaphragm.

7. **More than one out of four (25 percent) American men have had a sexual experience with another male during either their teens or adult years.**

Correct answer: *True*

According to a Kinsey Institute review of the research (published in *American Psychologist*), at least 25 percent of all American men have had a sexual experience with another male as teenagers or adults. (This is actually a conservative estimate—the data suggest that it is probably closer to one out of three American men.) Therefore, having had a same-sex experience is not unusual for men, even for those whose behavior is entirely heterosexual throughout the rest of their lives. The majority of these men think of themselves as heterosexual.

Data such as these are important in that they highlight the fact that regardless of what people call themselves—that is, heterosexual or homosexual—or what their current sexual behavior patterns are, you cannot assume that they accurately reflect behavior across the lifespan (*see Chapter 7*). There is concern about "hidden" bisexual behavior as it relates to the AIDS epidemic (*see Chapter 19*). It is important for people to understand that it is a person's sexual behavior pattern, not group membership (heterosexual or homosexual), that determines risk for infection with the AIDS virus (HIV).

Only 21 percent answered correctly: men were more likely than women to do so. Seventy-nine percent of Americans got this one wrong, with no differences among regions, religions, or areas of different population density.

Forty-two percent believed that fewer than one out of four men (25 percent) have had this experience. This may reflect a general belief that same-sex activity is rare and taboo. Similarly, American adults also generally underestimated on the questions about anal intercourse (Question 3) and masturbation (Question 16). It is interesting to note, however, that they appear to believe first intercourse occurs earlier (Question 1) and more men have had an extramarital affair (Question 2) than research indicates.

8. **It is usually difficult to tell whether people *are* or are *not* homosexual just by their appearance or gestures.**

Correct answer: *True*

Homosexual men can be extremely masculine, average, or effeminate in their appearance and gestures. They can be football players, hairdressers, truck drivers, stockbrokers, or have any other type of occupation. Likewise, homosexual women can be extremely feminine, average, or masculine and hold any job. Thus, a person's appearance, gestures, and occupation are not accurate indicators of sexual orientation. Almost 59 percent of American adults answered correctly. But another 31 percent did not; these people thought that indeed it is not difficult to tell if a person is homosexual merely by looking at him or her. Another 10 percent said they didn't know.

Conservatives and moderates, people living in the South and Northeast, those who didn't graduate from high school, people living in households with incomes less than $15,000, and older people (60+) were more likely than others to believe that you *can* usually identify a homosexual by his or her appearance or gestures.

One noteworthy finding: Americans in less populated areas actually did better on this question than people in or near metropolitan areas. This could be because respondents living in less populated areas are more likely to believe they have never met a homosexual, and thus simply are not sure what one might look like. On the other hand, urban areas often have visible gay communities. So people in these areas may have met homosexuals whose appearance and gestures fit the stereotype and for this reason may believe that most homosexuals look or act a certain way *(see Chapter 7).*

9. **A woman or teenage girl can get pregnant during her menstrual flow (her "period").**

Correct answer: *True*

The Institute receives many letters which reveal a surprising lack of information about the basic facts of reproduction *(see Chapter 15)*. Although a woman's chances of becoming pregnant during her period are not as high as at other times, it can and does happen. A woman may menstruate and ovulate irregularly, particularly during adolescence, and sperm can live for up to eight days in a woman's reproductive tract. This means that even if a woman only has sex during her period, there is a chance that sperm may still be present in her reproductive tract a week later to fertilize an egg should ovulation occur at this time. For these reasons, it is certainly possible for pregnancy to occur as a result of sexual intercourse during the menstrual flow. Having unprotected sex during the menstrual flow probably contributes to the number of pregnancies that occur every year for those using the rhythm or "natural" methods of contraception.

While 51 percent of Americans knew that it is possible to get pregnant during the menstrual flow, another 49 percent did not. It appears that the people who are most likely to get pregnant were more likely to answer correctly: Women outscored men. Those 18-to-29-year-olds did better than older participants; and the single, separated, and divorced did better than the married and widowed. Those with at least a high school diploma were more likely to be correct than those who didn't finish high school.

10. **A woman or teenage girl can get pregnant even if the man withdraws his penis before he ejaculates (before he "comes").**

Correct answer: *True*

Sixty-five percent of the American public correctly answered that withdrawal is not a very effective method of contraception. In fact, the drop of clear fluid that sometimes appears at the tip of the penis during arousal may contain enough sperm to fertilize an egg *(see Chapter 16)*. Yet one in four American adults believed a girl or woman could not get pregnant this way, while another 10 percent did not know the answer.

As in Question 9 about conception during menstruation, women were more likely than men to get this right, highlighting the fact that women generally shoulder the responsibility for preventing pregnancy. Younger Americans were more likely to answer correctly, whereas those over 60 were three times as likely to say they didn't know.

There was a profound difference between college-educated respondents and those with fewer years in school. Those with fewer years in school were also generally older. They therefore may have been less likely to receive any sex education because they did not have as much schooling and also attended at a time when there was even less sex education in the schools than there is today. Nearly 73 percent of those with some college knew about the risk of pregnancy using withdrawal, while 65 percent of high school graduates knew; and only 50 percent of those who hadn't finished high school thought there was a risk of pregnancy when relying on withdrawal as a contraceptive method.

11. **Unless they are having sex, women do not need to have regular gynecological examinations.**

    Correct answer: *False*

    Whether or not they are having sex, *all* women should have annual gynecological examinations beginning at age 18—or before that if they are sexually active—and continuing throughout their lives even after menopause *(see Chapter 17)*. The overwhelming majority of American adults—85 percent—answered correctly. Unfortunately, knowing that you should do something and doing it are two different things. The Kinsey Institute receives hundreds of letters from women each year who are not seeing a gynecologist regularly.

    Women, regardless of their age, were much more likely to get the correct answer than men. Single people, incidentally, scored lowest of all marital groups. This is of special concern since it is more likely that people who are single and sexually active have had several partners. These women in particular need regular gynecological examinations because they are at greater risk for catching STDs and developing pelvic inflammatory disease (PID), which can reduce fertility if not treated early *(see Chapter 19)*.

12. **Teenage boys should examine their testicles ("balls") regularly just as women self-examine their breasts for lumps.**

    Correct answer: *True*

    Most common between the ages of 20 to 34, testicular cancer is found in about four of every 100,000 white men each year, and at lower rates in men of other races. Detecting lumps or changes early is important for successful treatment, so it is vitally important that men of all ages beginning at puberty check their testicles every month, just as women should examine their breasts *(see Chapter 17)*.

The good news is that a large majority of Americans (73 percent) answered this one correctly. Like women, men may know that regular self-examination is a good idea, but that does not mean they are doing it or have been taught how to do it correctly. Many men we have talked to about testicular self-examinations said they had never even heard of it. In fact, the men in this survey were more inclined than women to say that teenage boys do not need to examine their testicles. The high percentage of correct answers on this question, as with Question 11 about gynecological exams, may reflect America's recent increased health consciousness.

13. Problems with erection are most often started by a physical problem.

Correct answer: *True*

Until recently many experts believed that erection problems were primarily psychological, not physical. We now know that most erection difficulties start with some physical factor including diseases such as diabetes, drug or alcohol use, or a wide range of medications *(see Chapter 8)*. Only 35 percent of America correctly believed that most erection difficulties begin with physical problems.

Only 30 percent of the college educated respondents answered correctly, compared with 43 percent of those who did not graduate from high school. Similarly, people with lower incomes outscored the top income group. Perhaps Americans with more education did not answer this question correctly because they are the ones most likely to have been exposed to explanations about psychological causes of physical problems.

This was also one of the few questions on which older and widowed Americans outperformed all the rest. Compared with all other age groups, twice as many people over 60 knew that most erection problems are physical in origin, while the youngest age group was least likely to know this. Although the majority of erection problems begin with a physical or health-related cause, psychological factors often worsen or perpetuate the problem. Therefore even when the physical cause is identified and taken care of, erectile dysfunction often continues until the psychological issues are resolved through sex therapy.

14. Almost all erection problems can be successfully treated.

Correct answer: *True*

Although a minority of American adults believed that most erection problems start with a physical problem, many more believed that erection problems are generally curable *(see Chapter 8)*. Sixty-four percent of the public responded correctly.

Women 60 and older were least likely of both sexes in all age groups to know that most erection problems are treatable—a finding strongly supported by the letters we receive from older women who tell us how their marriages have suffered as a result of their husbands' erectile failure. Women 30 to 44, on the other hand, did better than all other women. The married, separated, and divorced outscored those who were single and widowed.

Interestingly, the two groups that did best on Question 13 about the causes of erection problems—less educated, lower-income Americans— were least likely to get this one correct. So, even though they knew that most erection difficulties are caused by physical problems, they were not aware that most erection problems are treatable. This may mean they would be less likely to go for help and more likely to give up on working toward a solution.

15. Menopause, or change of life as it is often called, does *not* cause most women to lose interest in having sex.

Correct answer: *True*

Nearly 30 percent of America answered incorrectly—believing that most women *do* lose interest in sex after menopause (literally, the "last menstrual flow"). We know from research data, and from many older women who write to us, that for most women menopause does not mean an end to interest in sex. Although *some* women do experience a lowered sex drive at this time, this can often be helped with hormone replacement therapy *(see Chapter 9)*. The point is that most people over 50, including menopausal women, continue to have a healthy and active sex life.

Who did best? Not surprisingly, more women than men got this one correct. Moreover, women 30 and older outscored younger women and men of all ages. Younger women were most likely to say they didn't know whether menopause affected sex drive, which could reflect a lack of knowledge or a view that sexuality in older individuals is not important. Looking at the scores among men, those over 45—perhaps due to their own experience— were also more likely than younger men to know that menopause does not necessarily affect most women's interest in sex.

16. Out of every ten American women, how many would you estimate have masturbated either as children or after they were grown up?

Correct answer: *Six to eight out of ten (60 to 80%)*

Like anal sex, masturbation is generally seen as a forbidden topic, especially for girls and women. As our test scores reveal, most American adults don't know that 60 to 80 percent of females have masturbated. Only 18 percent answered correctly. A considerable number underestimated: 47 percent thought that no more than 50 percent of girls and women have masturbated. An additional 22 percent simply didn't know. Only 13 percent of Americans actually overestimated, thinking that 90 percent or more of females have masturbated.

Even though this was a question about women, more men than women tended to get it right. Surprisingly, women were more likely than men to say they didn't know the answer.

These findings raise some intriguing questions. First, since masturbation is relatively common among women, why didn't more women answer correctly? One possible explanation is that a woman or girl who masturbates may believe that her behavior is unusual. We get scores of letters from females ranging from 14 years old to older than 80 who masturbate and worry that they are different from other women.

But why were men more likely than women to get this question correct? Perhaps their answers were influenced by the fact that almost all men have masturbated or perhaps they have had more frequent exposure to depictions of female masturbation in sexually explicit movies, men's magazines, or erotic books *(see Chapter 6)*.

17. What do you think is the length of the average man's *erect* penis?

Correct answer: *5-7 inches*

Because this is the second-most-asked-about topic by men writing to The Kinsey Institute, our survey wouldn't have been complete without a question on penis size. The Kinsey research as well as an analysis of data by sexologist Dr. John Money indicate that the average erect penis measures five to seven inches in length. Nearly 60 percent answered correctly, a high proportion compared to most of the other questions. But about 30 percent of American men got this question wrong; presumably these men are representative of the ones who write us concerned about the size of their penises *(see Chapter 4)*.

Who did the best overall? Men were more likely than women to know the correct answer, and younger people (18-44) among both sexes did better than those 60 and older.

It was especially interesting to observe the types of errors made by those who answered this question incorrectly. These American adults were almost *twice as likely* to overestimate penis size as to underestimate. About 12 percent said that the average erect penis is eight to twelve inches long, while approximately 7 percent believed that the erect penis measures only two to four inches long.

Given men's concern that their penises aren't big enough, it should be pointed out that American women were almost twice as likely as men to think that the average erect penis is four inches or less or to say they simply didn't know the answer.

Who was most likely to say that eight to twelve inches was the average penis size? People 29 and younger; women 18 to 29; the less educated; single, separated, or divorced; liberals; and Northeasterners were all more inclined to overestimate.

18. Most women prefer a sexual partner with a larger-than-average penis.

Correct answer: *False*

As already noted, men who write to us about this issue are often worried that their penises are too small and wonder whether they are big enough to "satisfy" a woman. However, studies indicate that women generally don't have a preference in penis size. In fact, the letters we receive suggest that when women are concerned about this issue, it is more often because they think that their partner's penis is too large, not too small.

Even so, only four out of ten Americans knew that most women don't have a preference for a larger penis. Another 27 percent believed that women do prefer larger-than-average penises, while the rest said they didn't know. Although women were just as likely as men to get this one right, they were more likely to answer "Don't know." It may be that most women don't even think about this issue because it is not important to them (see Chapter 4).

Americans 30 to 44 years of age did better than all other age groups, while older people were the most likely to say they didn't know the answer. The more highly educated and those with higher incomes outscored those who hadn't finished high school or made less than $15,000 a year. Moreover, married Americans were more likely than single, separated or divorced, and widowed individuals to answer correctly that most women don't prefer larger penises.

HOW DIFFERENT GROUPS DID ON THE TEST

What follows is a closer look at how the different groups of adult Americans scored. Bear in mind as you read that the vast majority failed this test. So even when women outscored men, for example, or when young people did better than their elders, those who answered correctly were dramatically outnumbered by all those who answered incorrectly.

• DIFFERENCES AMONG AGE GROUPS. Older and widowed people of both sexes consistently scored lowest of all. This finding isn't all that surprising considering that the older people were born and raised in a profoundly different time, an era when syphilis was often a fatal disease and the only choices for reliable contraception were barrier methods (see Chapter 16), if you could find them— and even condoms and diaphragms were outlawed in some states. Post-World War I America was a different place, not just sexually but in all the ways that affect public access to information. Sixty years ago there were no televisions, no talk shows, no national newspapers, fewer libraries, few telephones, and no airplane travel for the average American. Sex education in schools was essentially nonexistent for this Depression-era generation, and straightforward discussions about sex at home were likely to be just as rare. Sex information and erotic materials were illegal.

There were, however, a few significant exceptions to the survey's general trend: More women 60 and older rightly believed that one usually can't tell by gestures or appearance if a person is homosexual. More older women also knew that most postmenopausal women don't lose interest in sex. And older Americans correctly answered that difficulties with erection usually begin with a physical problem.

Although older Americans generally didn't get many right answers, at least they *knew* what they didn't know. In other words, when they didn't know the right answer they said so, while younger people were confident in their ignorance—much more sure they were right even when they were not.

Women 18 to 44 years old (55 percent passed) and men 30 to 44 (52 percent passed) scored higher than all other age groups (only 37 percent passed). One possible explanation for these findings is that these Americans came of age sexually during an era characterized by the women's movement, the Pill, and books about female sexuality such as *Our Bodies, Ourselves*. Women were beginning to believe that they had a *right* to sex information, and there was greater access to higher education for both sexes.

• DIFFERENCES BETWEEN MEN AND WOMEN. Women and men were about equal in their knowledge, or lack of it. Men were generally more correct on questions relating to sex behavior (specifically anal sex, masturbation, and extramarital sex), as well as about penis size and treatment of erection problems. Women did better on questions about female sexual health care and contraception (which isn't surprising, since women traditionally have had to shoulder the responsibility for contraception). Responses on the rest of the test cut across sex, with both men and women equally correct or incorrect on questions relating to homosexuality, AIDS, and women's preferences in penis size.

• THE MORE EDUCATION, THE HIGHER THE SCORE. In question after question, the top scorers were those with at least a few years of college (57 percent passed), followed by those with a high school diploma (41 percent passed), who in turn scored higher than Americans with fewer years of school (24 percent passed). Income reflected the effect of education, probably because education is a major factor in salary.

• RELIGIOUS AFFILIATION. Among people indicating a religious affiliation, Catholics (46 percent) were more likely to pass than Protestants (42 percent). Sixty percent of those who did not have a religious affiliation passed.

• WHICH REGIONS DID BEST? Anyone who thinks Northeasterners are more knowledgeable and sophisticated about sex need only take a look at our regional analysis. People from the Northeast and South (40 percent passed) scored consistently lower than Midwesterners (55 percent passed) and those from the West (47 percent passed).

• POLITICAL PHILOSOPHY. Liberals (51 percent passed) obtained higher scores than conservatives (44 percent passed) and moderates (45 percent passed).

• WHO DID NOT ANSWER (NOT EVEN INDICATING "DON'T KNOW")? Though this survey had a higher participation rate for all questions than the typical sex survey, it is interesting to see which people were most likely not to answer some of the questions.

Older respondents were more likely not to answer any given question, with people 60 and older doing this most often. Other groups likely not to answer were those without a high school diploma, people whose income was less than $15,000, Northeasterners, and the widowed.

HOW AMERICA LEARNS ABOUT SEX

Now that we know some of what Americans don't know about sex, let's see where they received their information in the first place. We asked our partici-

Sources of Sex Information

Where they got their sexual information while growing up		*Where they would go for answers now*	
Mother	29%	Mother	10%
Father	12%	Father	5%
Grandmother	2%	Grandmother	*
Grandfather	1%	Grandfather	*
Sister	8%	Sister	4%
Brother	6%	Brother	3%
Other relative	6%	Other relative	4%
Friend	42%	Friend	19%
Boyfriend or girlfriend	17%	Boyfriend, girlfriend, or spouse	14%
Doctor or nurse	4%	Doctor or nurse	44%
Health center or family planning clinic	1%	Health center or family planning clinic	11%
Therapist or counselor	*	Therapist or counselor	7%
Sex education	14%	Sex education	5%
Teacher	5%	Teacher	1%
Member of the clergy	1%	Member of the clergy	3%
Books	22%	Books	26%
Magazines	13%	Magazines	4%
Newspaper columns	1%	Newspaper columns	1%
Television	5%	Television	1%
Movies	6%	Movies	1%
Radio	1%	Radio	*
Did not use any source	3%	Would not use any source	4%
Don't remember	2%	Don't know	3%

Note: Respondents could choose up to three choices for each time period about which we asked. Twelve percent of the sample did not answer these questions.
* Less than .5% indicated this source

Table 3

pants to tell us where they had gone for information about sex when they were growing up, and where they would go if they had a question now. Each participant was given a chance to choose three sources for each of these time periods. The possible choices and the proportion who picked them are summarized in Table 3.

Before taking a closer look at the sources Americans turned to for information about sex, remember that the majority of Americans failed our knowledge test; thus, no matter where they went, the sources of sex information available to Americans while they were growing up were probably inadequate. That said, let's examine the most common information sources of our participants more closely.

When you were growing up, where did you go for information about sex?
(Responses are listed in order of most to least popular.)

• FRIENDS. Forty-two percent of America turned to their friends for sex information when they were growing up. Males were more likely than females to do so. People 60 and older and those who hadn't completed high school were *least* likely to name friends as a source.

• MOTHER. About 29 percent said they asked their mothers about sex when they were growing up. Many more females (40 percent) did so than males (18 percent). Among religious affiliations, Protestants (33 percent) were more likely to have gone to their mothers than Catholics (26 percent).

• BOOKS. About 22 percent of American adults said they read books when they were growing up and needed information about sex. Interestingly, 30-59-year-olds were more likely to have turned to books than either the youngest (18-29) or the oldest (60+) of our respondents. Perhaps this is the case because books with sexual information were generally unavailable to the American public growing up prior to the publication of Kinsey's first volume in 1948, whereas the 18-29-year-olds grew up in an era when the media dramatically increased their coverage of sexual issues.

Who else was most likely to use this source? Protestants, those with no religious affiliation, and—not unexpectedly—more-educated Americans cited books.

• BOYFRIEND OR GIRLFRIEND. About 17 percent of American adults said they turned to a boyfriend or girlfriend when they were growing up to get answers about sex. Just as older Americans (60+) did not go to their friends for information when growing up, only 9 percent of them listed boyfriend or girlfriend as a source. People from the Midwest (one of the two regions that did best on the test) were more likely than those from all other regions to talk to boyfriends or girlfriends when they needed sexual information.

• SEX EDUCATION. A slim 14 percent of all respondents said they received information from sex education classes when they were growing up. As expected, the youngest age group was most likely to name this source, reflecting the fact that these classes have only recently become a part of some school curricula.

Americans from the Midwest and West were more likely to have gotten their information from sex education classes than those in the Northeast and South. Since the Midwest and West did better than the other two regions on our test, this finding highlights the importance of sex education in schools. Those who had not completed high school and the politically conservative were least likely to say they had had a sex education course when growing up. Since the vast majority of Americans failed this test, there is obviously a need for better and more widely available sex education programs.

• MAGAZINES. About 13 percent of American adults said they had gotten sex information from magazines when they were growing up. In adulthood, only 4 percent said they would go to a magazine. More than twice as many men as women named this source, and men 44 years old and younger were most likely to have gotten their sexual information from magazines. (*Playboy* was first published in 1952).

Those with some college education were more inclined than less educated Americans to say they read magazines. People from rural areas were the most likely (in contrast to those from urban areas) to have turned to magazines.

• FATHER. About 12 percent said they went to their fathers when they needed information about sex while growing up. Three times as many men (19 percent) as women (6 percent) said they turned to their fathers. Women were nearly seven times as likely to consult their mothers, as compared to their fathers, about sex; whereas men were equally likely to go to mother or father.

• NO SOURCE. Three percent of our respondents said they did not use any source for sexual information when they were growing up. Significantly, those 60 and older were more likely than any other age group to report they had no source; they were six times as likely to say this than Americans 18 to 29 years old. Similarly, the widowed were seven times as likely as single people to say they had no source for sex information. (It is not surprising, then, that older and widowed people were least likely to know the answers to the test.)

If you had a sexual question now, where would you be most likely to go for answers?

• DOCTOR OR NURSE. Adult Americans were most inclined to consult medical professionals—44 percent said they would go to a doctor or nurse with questions about sex. Only 4 percent listed this as a source while growing up.

• BOOKS. Twenty-six percent of American adults said they would refer to books if they have questions about sex. Men were just as likely as women to choose this source.

As with other sources of information, Northeasterners (who did poorly on this test) chose books less frequently than people in all other regions.

• FRIEND. About 19 percent of Americans would turn to friends if they had questions about sex. Younger people were most likely, while the two oldest groups were least likely, to choose this source.

• BOYFRIEND, GIRLFRIEND, OR SPOUSE. About 14 percent of the public would take questions about sex to a boyfriend, girlfriend, or spouse. This choice was most popular among younger Americans and least popular among those 60 and older, a finding supported by the letters we receive from older people who say they find it difficult, if not impossible, to discuss sexual issues and problems with their spouses.

• HEALTH CENTER OR FAMILY PLANNING CLINIC. Approximately 11 percent of Americans would turn to health centers or family planning clinics, whereas only 1 percent did so while growing up.

• MOTHER. Even as adults, some Americans would turn to their mothers if they had questions about sex. While people were growing up, mothers were the second most frequently chosen source of sexual information. In adulthood, mother is the sixth most frequently cited source, with 10 percent saying they would still turn to her.

Just as when they were growing up, more women than men (13 percent versus 6 percent) would ask their mothers sexual questions. Younger women (25 percent) more often said they would consult with their mothers than women in the older age groups (10 percent).

• THERAPIST/COUNSELOR. About 7 percent of American adults would turn to therapists or counselors if they have questions about sex. Not unexpectedly, college-educated and higher-income Americans would be most likely to do this, while those who didn't graduate from high school and whose incomes were less than $15,000 would be least likely to consult a therapist or counselor—possibly because they cannot afford it.

• NO SOURCE. About 7 percent of American adults—primarily those 60 and older and people in the lowest income groups—said if they had a question about sex they would not use any source for information or they did not know where they would go.

HOW SOURCES OF SEX INFORMATION
RELATED TO TEST PERFORMANCE

Sources of sex information throughout one's life appear to be a factor in whether a person passed or failed The Kinsey Institute/Roper Organization National Sex Knowledge Test. More of those who passed this test (compared with those who failed) got their sexual information while growing up from the places most likely to provide the facts: books and sex education classes, and a few went to health centers or family planning clinics. Those who failed were more likely to say they had no source at all.

The only other sources of information while growing up that were associated with the likelihood of passing were asking friends and reading magazines. Although asking friends or reading magazines may not have been the most reliable sources of accurate sexual information, this finding suggests that openness to communicating and talking about sexual issues and actively seeking information is related to eventually getting "the facts" about sex.

As adults, the people who passed this test would also consult sources most likely to provide accurate information about sex. For instance, 39 percent of those who passed said they would refer to a book, compared with only 22 percent of those who failed. About 15 percent of Americans who passed our test would consult a family planning clinic or health center, while only 10 percent of those failing chose this source. Those who scored passing grades would also be more likely to consult a doctor or nurse, and twice as likely to turn to a therapist or counselor. Once again, more people who *failed* than passed said they did not know where they would go for sexual information or said they had no source at all.

Another noteworthy observation: Compared with Americans who failed the test, the people who did better would be more likely to go to a boyfriend, girlfriend, or spouse for answers to their sexual questions. Although these sources are not always the most accurate, this finding suggests that the people who passed are more willing to *communicate* with their partners about sex. And while it may not always yield correct answers, this willingness and ability to talk about sex with your partner helps eventually unearth accurate information.

The results of this survey highlight the need for and effectiveness of sex education. The majority of Americans who participated in The Kinsey Institute/ Roper Organization National Sex Knowledge Survey failed the test. Yet our analyses reveal the positive effect of education (including specific sex education classes) and the availability and use of accurate sources of sex information. Sex-related information that is important to health and well-being is not reaching the American public in sufficient amounts and in effective messages. In light of the current problems facing our country in terms of teen pregnancy and STDs, including AIDS, it is imperative that Americans encourage and support the development of high-quality public education campaigns and sex education programs.

METHODOLOGY

Between October 14 and October 20, 1989, The Roper Organization in face-to-face interviews surveyed a nationwide cross section of 1,974 women and men 18 years of age and older, comprising a representative sample of the population of the continental United States but not including institutionalized segments of the population (nursing homes, prisons, military bases, and the like). Six questions were asked by the interviewer and twelve were on a questionnaire completed in the presence of the interviewer who could provide clarification or read items aloud if necessary. Respondents were instructed to place their completed unsigned questionnaire in the envelope provided, seal it, and return it to the interviewer.

The Kinsey Institute/Roper Organization National Sex Knowledge Test appeared in the middle of a larger survey on nonsexual issues (such as the environment), so we can assume that the responses to our test were not significantly affected or influenced by the preceding questions.

• EDUCATION. A person with any college education (including those with graduate degrees) was listed in the "some college" category. (Trade school or secretarial school did not count as college.) Anyone who was a high school graduate was labeled as such. Anyone with an eleventh-grade education or less was included in "non-high school graduate." Since these are self-reported education levels, they may be subject to some exaggeration.

• INCOME. Income was reported as total family income.

• POLITICAL PHILOSOPHY. This was based on how people regard their own political/ social outlooks: conservative (very or moderately so), moderate (middle-of-the-road), or liberal (very or moderately so).

• GEOGRAPHIC AREAS. The survey findings are divided into four geographic regions consistent with the U.S. Bureau of the Census: the Northeast, the South, the

Midwest, and the West. (The Roper Organization uses the same geographic delineation as the U.S. Bureau of the Census.)

The **Northeast** includes New England and the Middle Atlantic states, specifically Connecticut, Maine, Massachusetts, New Hampshire, New Jersey, New York, Pennsylvania, Rhode Island, and Vermont.

The **South** refers to the West South Central, East South Central, and South Atlantic states: Alabama, Arkansas, Delaware, District of Columbia, Florida, Georgia, Kentucky, Louisiana, Maryland, Mississippi, North Carolina, Oklahoma, South Carolina, Tennessee, Texas, Virginia, and West Virginia.

The **Midwest** includes the West North Central and East North Central states: Illinois, Indiana, Iowa, Kansas, Michigan, Minnesota, Missouri, Nebraska, North Dakota, Ohio, South Dakota, and Wisconsin.

The **West** refers to the Pacific and Mountain states, which include: Arizona, California, Colorado, Idaho, Montana, Nevada, New Mexico, Oregon, Utah, Washington, and Wyoming.

• POPULATION DENSITY (MARKET SIZE *[see Table 2]).*The most densely populated areas (1) were all counties comprising the 25 largest metropolitan areas. The second most densely populated areas (2) were those that either individually have a population of 150,000 or more or form part of a metropolitan area with an aggregate population of that size. Less densely populated, or more rural, areas (3) have an individual population of 35,000 or more or are part of a metropolitan area with a population of that size. All the remaining counties fall in the category of the most rural, least densely populated, areas (4).

ALL GROUP DIFFERENCES REPORTED IN THIS
CHAPTER ARE STATISTICALLY SIGNIFICANT

2

The Adult Female: Outside and Inside

Lack of accurate basic information about the female sexual organs—external and internal—is surprisingly widespread. For many women and even more men, female reproductive and sexual anatomy remains shrouded in mystery and clouded by outdated attitudes of shame or embarrassment.

This kind of ignorance is not good for women—or their partners. A woman who does not know what the healthy vulva looks like cannot recognize the early signals of an unhealthy one. The man who doesn't know where the clitoris is located has a diminished chance of giving his partner sexual pleasure. And the woman who understands the function of her clitoris will be less likely to become concerned or distressed if she doesn't achieve orgasm through sexual intercourse alone.

EXTERNAL GENITALIA

Most noticeable of the physical differences between adult females and males is the fact that male genitals are in full view, but the most important parts of the female external genitalia can be seen only if the woman spreads her legs wide (Illustration 2).

The entire area of the external female genital anatomy is called the **vulva**. Beginning at the top of the illustration, the **mons** is an area of fatty tissue that forms a soft mound over the pubic bone. (The Latin *mons veneris* means "mound of Venus," the Roman goddess of love.) The mons is covered by skin and pubic hair.

The **labia majora** (often called the outer lips) extend down from the mons to below the vaginal opening. These include a fold of skin on each side filled with fatty tissue, sweat and oil glands, and nerve endings. Pubic hair grows on the outside of the outer lips. The two outer lips usually meet and cover the urinary and vaginal openings unless a woman is sexually aroused or her legs are spread apart.

The **labia minora** (the inner lips) are inside the outer lips and extend from

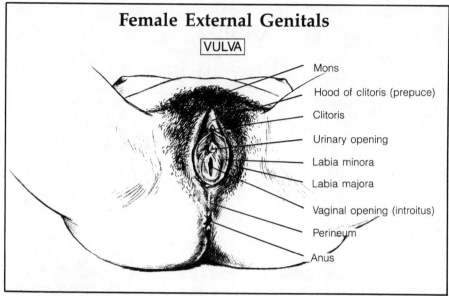

Female External Genitals

VULVA

- Mons
- Hood of clitoris (prepuce)
- Clitoris
- Urinary opening
- Labia minora
- Labia majora
- Vaginal opening (introitus)
- Perineum
- Anus

Illustration No. 2. **Female External Genitals (Vulva)**

just above the clitoris to below the vaginal opening. These two folds of skin are thinner and do not have pubic hair or fatty tissue, but they have more nerve endings than do the outer lips. Even though often called inner, it is not unusual for them to protrude beyond the outer lips. The color varies among women (pink, red, purple, black are all normal) and may change during sexual arousal.

The head (glans) of the **clitoris** is just below where the top of the inner lips meet and indeed can often be seen only when a fold of skin (called the prepuce) is gently pushed up. Not much of the shaft of the clitoris is visible because it is also covered by the labia and extends inside the body to the region of the pubic bone. (Before birth the clitoris is formed from the same tissues that would have become the glans and upper shaft of a penis if the embryo had been exposed to "male" hormones). It, like a penis, is highly sensitive to stimulation and swells somewhat with sexual arousal. Unlike a penis, however, it does not carry urine out of the body. The sole known function of the clitoris, in fact, is to receive and focus sexual stimulation.

Just below the clitoral glans is the very small **urinary opening** and below that is the **vaginal opening** (often called the *introitus*, Latin for "entrance"). Seeing that these two openings are so near each other makes it easier to understand why many women experience urinary infections after having sex (*see Chapter 17*).

Below the vaginal opening and where the labia meet is a small area of smooth, usually hairless skin called the **perineum**, and below that is the **anus** (the opening through which the bowels empty). This entire perineal area is sensitive to sexual stimulation. Women should always wipe from front to back (following the order of Illustration 2, from top to bottom) after using the toilet to avoid having fecal matter transferred near the vaginal and urinary openings, one common cause of vaginal and urinary infections. It is important for women to do regular self-examinations of their external genitals. How to do this is explained in Chapter 17.

I think that quite a few men (and maybe some women) do not understand and appreciate the function of the clitoris. Would you please write about that "organ?"

The clitoris is located toward the front or top of a woman's external genitals (see Illustration 2). The head of the clitoris, about the size of a small pea, is often visible or can be seen by gently pushing up the skin covering it. The size and appearance of the clitoris vary among women. Most of it is inside and not visible.

As a woman becomes sexually aroused, the clitoris pulls back against the pubic bone and the labia swell so that the head is protected from direct touch. Shortly after orgasm, the clitoris resumes its unstimulated position.

Contrary to popular myth, the head of the clitoris is not some type of "magic button" for all women and, in fact, direct stimulation is uncomfortable or even painful for some. A touch that contributes to sexual responsiveness for one woman can be painful to another woman—an example of why communication between sexual partners is necessary.

I am 54 years old and up until recently have never heard of the trigger or "G" spot in a woman. There was even a lengthy story in *Playboy* which I just read. Truthfully, is there such a thing, and, if so, where?

There has been considerable debate over the existence of the G spot or Gräfenberg spot, named for Ernest Gräfenberg, the German gynecologist who first described it. The results of studies on the G spot vary widely. Some researchers have found no evidence of it, while others report finding a highly sensitive spot on the vaginal wall of some women that has the characteristics of the G spot.

The G spot is said to be a small mass of tissue (the size and shape of a small bean) about 2 inches inside the vaginal opening on the front wall of the vagina (the side toward the belly button). This area is reputed to be highly sensitive to sexual stimulation, during which the area becomes larger, about the size of a dime.

Many experts feel more research is necessary before the existence of the G spot can be established, but there is no question many women notice that some areas of the vagina are more sensitive to erotic touch than others.

I am 65. After intercourse, what happens to the semen that remains in my body? Is that dangerous? Should I douche? This has troubled me for a long time.

The semen does not stay in your body. It gradually runs out of the vagina after intercourse. A healthy vagina cleans itself naturally, as secretions work their way to the external genitals. This means that carefully washing and rinsing the folds of the external genitals each day is all the cleaning most women need.

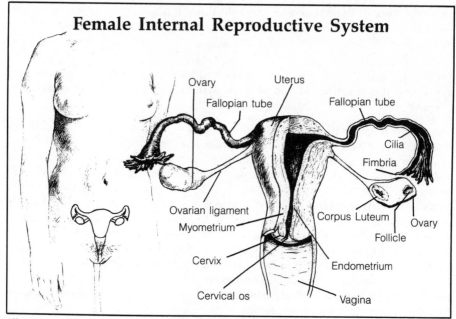

Female Internal Reproductive System

Illustration No. 3. **Female Internal Reproductive System.** The drawing on the left shows where the internal organs are located inside a woman's body. The drawing on the right provides more detail; the cutaway right half reveals what they look like on the inside.

INTERNAL GENITALIA

Most of the female's reproductive system is inside her body, as shown in Illustration 3. The two **ovaries**, which produce eggs and hormones, are each about the size of a grape (approximately 1 inch by 1/2 inch). At birth, each ovary contains approximately 200,000 immature eggs. Each egg is surrounded by a thin tissue envelope called a **follicle**. Each ovary is attached to one end of an **ovarian ligament** (a band of fibrous tissue). The other end of each ligament is attached to the uterus.

One common misconception is that the ovaries are also attached to the **Fallopian tubes** (named for the Italian anatomist who first described them), since an egg released by an ovary must travel through one of the Fallopian tubes to reach the uterus. Indeed, one end of each Fallopian tube (about 4 inches long and about as big around as a piece of spaghetti) is attached to the top area of the uterus, but the other end simply dangles near an ovary. The outer ends are formed somewhat like a funnel-shaped flower with fringelike extensions called **fimbria**. When an egg is released from an ovary the fimbria wave about, surround the ovary, and draw the egg into the Fallopian tube near that ovary. The inside of each Fallopian tube is lined with **cilia**, tiny hairlike structures that also move. Conception occurs when an egg and sperm meet inside one of the Fallopian tubes, which is where the embryo begins to grow.

The **uterus** (also called the womb) is about the size and shape of a pear (about 3 inches long and 2 inches wide) but much flatter. It is made of muscle (the outer layer called the **myometrium**) and has a special inner lining (the **endometrium**), which first builds up and then leaves the body as menstrual flow in each reproductive cycle when conception does not occur. If conception does occur, the fertilized egg travels through a Fallopian tube into the uterus, where it implants in the endometrium and uses the nutrients of the lining for the early stages of embryonic development *(see Illustration 28 in Chapter 15)*. It is quite remarkable that the small uterus can expand over the course of nine months to accommodate a full-size newborn.

The bottom part of the uterus is called the **cervix** (Latin for "neck"). The cervix is connected to and protrudes into the upper end of the **vagina**. In the center of the cervix is a small hole, the **os** ("mouth" in Latin), through which menstrual flow passes from the uterus to the vagina. It is also through the os that sperm must swim from the vagina into the uterus and then into the Fallopian tubes to meet an egg. During labor, the os greatly enlarges (dilates) for passage of the newborn.

The **vagina** is a small tube (about 3 to 4 inches long) made of muscle and covered on the inside walls with a mucous surface similar to the lining of the mouth; this surface produces vaginal lubrication. Unless a woman is sexually aroused, the sides of the vagina touch each other. When a woman becomes sexually aroused the walls of the vagina produce a slippery liquid and balloon open so that a penis will fit inside. It can open even further to permit passage of a fully grown newborn.

Annual pelvic examinations and Pap tests are necessary for all women from age 18 (or earlier if they begin having sex before that age). *(See Chapter 17.)*

I am a 20-year-old woman who occasionally has a white jellylike vaginal discharge. The texture is very much like gelatin. It is not the usual yellow or white creamy discharge. This occurs about once every two months. What is this? Is it anything to be alarmed about?

What you have noticed is probably either normal cervical mucus or vaginal lubricating fluid. If you have no other symptoms (such as vaginal itching, soreness, or pain), the changes you've seen probably are normal. Ask about this during your next annual pelvic exam so the physician can check the condition of your cervix or take samples of secretions for analysis.

The appearance and texture of vaginal secretions vary throughout each monthly reproductive cycle as conditions inside the vagina respond to changes in hormonal levels. This is especially true of the mucus secreted by the cervix.

Cervical mucus usually appears in greater quantities midcycle, around the time the egg is released, and color and texture then differ from vaginal secretions during the rest of the month. This special mucus facilitates the journey of the sperm through the cervix into the uterus. In addition, the lubricating fluid produced by the vagina during sexual arousal also looks different from other vaginal secretions.

I have a problem I had never heard of before. Ever since having my second child, I sometimes pass wind through my vagina. This is very embarrassing to

The Female Reproductive Cycle

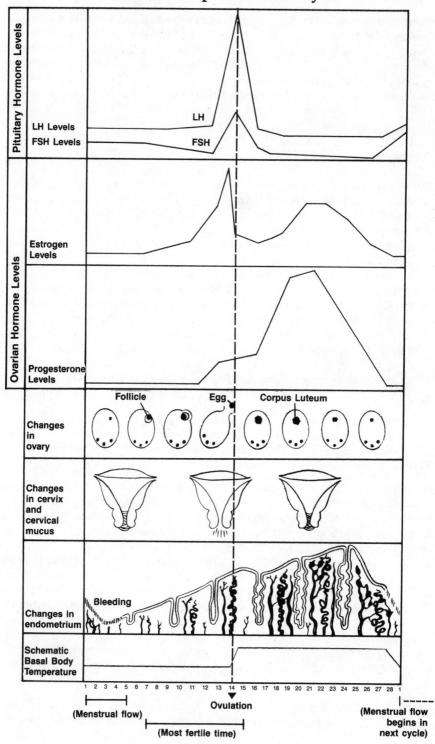

me, especially during sex. Have you ever heard of this before? What causes it? How can it be cured?

Although there are no data on how many women experience this, it is not uncommon for air to become trapped in the vagina and then be released with "embarrassing" sounds.

At your next regular pelvic examination, ask if there are any indications of vaginal hernias or prolapse (when the top end of the vagina bulges back down into the lower end). Some physicians consider this air problem an early sign of relaxation of the pelvic support muscles. (*For more information on these conditions see Chapter 17.*)

If there are no physical problems, you should find it reassuring to know that the sounds probably indicate good sexual responsiveness. As a woman becomes sexually aroused, the top section (the inside end near the cervix) of the vagina "tents" or balloons open. As the man thrusts, air can be expelled.

The few clinicians who have written about this situation advise patients and their partners to find reassurance in this signal of healthy sexual responsiveness, have a sense of humor about it, and, if it continues to be embarrassing, turn on music to mask the noise.

THE FEMALE REPRODUCTIVE CYCLE

Between puberty and menopause healthy women menstruate on a cyclic basis. Although most people are aware only of the days of a woman's menstrual flow (usually calling it her period), these days are only the most obvious stage in the complete reproductive cycle. A cycle begins on the first day of a menstrual flow and ends when the next cycle's flow starts.

Each reproductive cycle is a complex set of interactions among the brain, the pituitary gland, the ovaries, and the uterus. Messages are sent and received among these organs to change the levels of various hormones that cause an egg to mature and be released from an ovary and the uterus to build up and then shed its lining. The purpose of each cycle is to mature an egg in the ovaries (presenting an opportunity for conception) and to prepare a woman's body for a pregnancy if conception does occur.

Some of the most important features of a single reproductive cycle are included in Illustration 4. The **menstrual flow** is the best place to begin keeping track of cycles because it is the only part of a cycle most women notice. Beginning with the first day (called Day 1) of menstrual flow, the levels of most of the hormones involved are low.

The low level of **estrogen** causes the hypothalamus in the brain to send a message to the pituitary gland to secrete **FSH** (follicle stimulating hormone) into the bloodstream. The ovaries react to the increased FSH level by beginning the maturation process of an egg inside the follicles of the ovaries. As the **follicle** begins to grow, it produces the hormone estrogen. The presence of estrogen

Illustration No. 4. **The Female Reproductive Cycle.** This drawing illustrates the interacting biological changes occuring in brain chemicals, hormones, the uterus, and the ovaries during one full reproductive cycle.

causes the cells in the **endometrium** (the lining of the uterus) to multiply and the lining gradually becomes thicker.

As the follicle develops, the estrogen level continues to rise for around ten days, until it is high enough to stimulate the pituitary gland to release **LH** (leutinizing hormone). This sudden rise in LH acts on the ovaries and triggers release of the mature **egg** from inside a follicle. The rising estrogen level also causes changes in the cervix and the cervical mucus.

Called **ovulation**, this egg release occurs about halfway between the start of one menstrual flow and the next and means that an egg is available for fertilization if sperm are present in the woman's reproductive tract. This is also the point at which FSH and LH levels are at their highest, but the estrogen level falls for two or three days after ovulation.

After an egg is released, the cells that had lined the ovarian follicle change shape and color to become a **corpus luteum** ("yellow body"). The corpus luteum produces both estrogen and **progesterone**, another hormone. The level of progesterone, therefore, is higher after ovulation and the level of estrogen also rises again. The increase in progesterone causes a woman's body temperature to rise.

By this point in a cycle the lining of the uterus is already five to ten times thicker than it was just after the woman's last flow stopped. But with the addition of progesterone from the corpus luteum, the lining changes to form distinct layers with tiny blood vessels, nutrients, and other features which will be needed to support a pregnancy if the egg is fertilized.

The presence of progesterone also causes the level of LH and FSH to drop gradually. When the level of LH is low enough, the corpus luteum is no longer stimulated and gradually stops producing progesterone and estrogen. This drop in progesterone and estrogen causes the uterus to shed its lining as the menstrual flow—which is Day 1 of the next cycle. The low level of estrogen also signals the hypothalamus and the pituitary gland to start secreting more FSH again, thereby beginning the next reproductive cycle. (If conception does occur, the progesterone level remains high and the uterine lining remains to support the fertilized egg.)

For questions about menstrual cycles, see Chapter 17.

3

The Adult Male: Outside and Inside

The major components of the male reproductive system are visible on the outside of the body. Because their genitals are more obvious, easily accessible, and easily stimulated most males discover at an earlier age than females that their genitals can be a source of special pleasure. Because males urinate through the penis and therefore must handle it to free it from clothing, they face fewer social prohibitions against touching their genitals than do females. (Unless they are masturbating, in which event young boys may be told to stop touching their genitals in that *particular* way, but they are not forbidden to continue all touching.)

Despite the fact that a male sees his penis at least several times each day, he probably does not examine the other parts of his external genitals closely and most males remain as uninformed as females about their internal reproductive organs and how they work. *(See Illustration 5)*. The questions we receive confirm this lack of information. Males most frequently ask about the appearance of the penis and testicles and about erections, ejaculation, and the prostate gland.

EXTERNAL GENITALIA

One important difference between the male and female genital areas is that males have two openings, one for passing urine and semen through the tip of the penis, and the anus located behind the scrotum. Females, on the other hand, have three openings: the urinary opening, the opening into the vagina, and the anus.

The most obvious feature of the male external genitalia is the **penis,** which consists of the shaft and the head or glans. Inside the shaft is the **urethra** (the tube that carries urine and semen from the inside to the outside of the body) and three cylinders of spongy tissue. The skin covering the shaft of the penis is movable, permitting it to expand during erection and to slide on the shaft.

The cylinder located on the bottom side of the length of the penis is called the **corpus spongiosum;** when the penis is erect the bulge of the corpus spongiosum can be seen and feels like a ridge. The urethra runs through the center of this

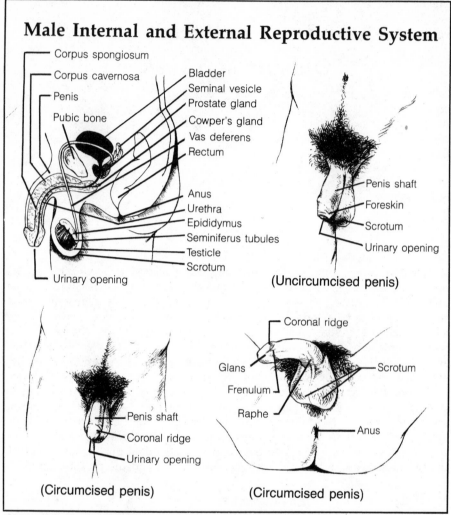

Male Internal and External Reproductive System

Corpus spongiosum
Corpus cavernosa
Penis
Pubic bone

Bladder
Seminal vesicle
Prostate gland
Cowper's gland
Vas deferens
Rectum

Anus
Urethra
Epididymus
Seminiferus tubules
Testicle
Scrotum

Urinary opening

Penis shaft
Foreskin
Scrotum
Urinary opening

(Uncircumcised penis)

Coronal ridge
Glans
Frenulum
Raphe
Scrotum
Anus

(Circumcised penis)

Penis shaft
Coronal ridge
Urinary opening

(Circumcised penis)

Illustration No. 5. **Male Internal and External Reproductive System.** The top-left cross-section drawing shows the location of the internal organs. The other drawings show male genitals from the outside.

cylinder. The other two cylinders (the two **corpora cavernosa**) fill the rest of the shaft along the sides and lie close together on the top side of the penis.

All three cylinders are filled with many small blood vessels and tissues that act like sponges, swelling as they fill with blood. This swelling of the cylinders causes the penis to enlarge and lengthen during **erection**. Each cylinder is surrounded by a thin membrane that holds the blood inside the cylinder and contributes to the rigidity of the penis during erection.

The head, also called the **glans**, of the penis is also filled with spongy tissue.

The **urinary opening** (or meatus) is in the glans. Between the shaft and the glans is a ridge of tissue (the **coronal ridge**). On the bottom side of the penis is an area of skin (the **frenulum**) that extends from the skin on the penile shaft to the glans. The glans, coronal ridge, and frenulum are all filled with nerve endings and are highly sensitive to touch.

On the bottom side of the shaft there is a ridge or seam in the skin; this is called the **raphe** and was formed before birth when the skin that would have covered the labia in a female grew together in response to exposure to male hormones. In uncircumcised men, the skin covering the shaft extends to also cover, but is not attached to, the glans. This retractable skin is called the **foreskin**.

Although not visible from the outside, the structures of the penis continue inside the body. The urethra runs through the center of the prostate gland to the bladder, and the spongy cylinders continue into the pelvic area and are attached to blood vessels, pelvic muscle, and bone.

The same tissues that form the glans and upper shaft of the penis in male embryos (in response to exposure to male hormones before birth) form the glans and shaft of the clitoris in female embryos. These structures are similar for both sexes in that they respond to stimulation by filling with blood and swelling, then returning to the nonstimulated state after orgasm.

Many males are convinced that their penis is smaller than it should be. *(For more on this concern see Chapter 4.)* Because this is such an important issue for many men, one would expect that scientists would have done a great deal of research on penis size, but surprisingly this is not the case. What few data are available are based on small numbers of men or involved having volunteers measure their own penises at home, without the direct supervision of scientists. The possibility exists that men with smaller penises did not volunteer, that measurements were not done according to instructions, or that some men simply rounded up to the next highest number when they reported the measurement back to the scientists. Keep the limitations of such studies in mind as you read the following information.

The average length of the *flaccid* (nonerect) adult penis is approximately 4 inches (measured along the top from the pubic bone to the tip of the penis). This means that many flaccid penises will be somewhat shorter and many will be somewhat longer. A number of factors can affect the apparent size of a flaccid penis, including excess body fat, cold temperatures, and stressful situations. Moreover, the pioneering research on sexual functioning by Drs. William Masters and Virginia Johnson has established that these differences in length while flaccid often disappear during erections—men with shorter-than-average flaccid penises have a larger percent of size increase during erection while larger-than-average flaccid penises increase relatively less with erection. Therefore, based on the data available and the reservations stated above, it is our estimate that during *erection* the majority of men have a penis that measures between 5 and 7 inches in length. Again this means that many men will have erect penises that are somewhat shorter and many will be somewhat longer.

Hanging below the penis is the **scrotum**, a bag of loose skin with a thin layer of muscle. When exposed to cold, physical exercise, or sexual stimulation, the muscles of the scrotum contract, pulling the **testicles** (or testes) inside the scrotum closer to the body. This movement of the testicles, closer to or farther away from the body, is very important because the testicles must be kept at a temperature lower than body temperature. If they are too warm or too cold, the production of sperm is reduced. If they stay too warm for long periods of time (as happens with an undescended testicle), fertility may be permanently reduced and the risk of changes leading to cancer of the testicle are increased. An undescended testicle is a testicle that remains in the abdomen where it developed rather than moving into the scrotum before birth.

The two testicles are oval and each measures approximately 1.5 inches long and 1 inch wide (similar to a large grape). It is normal for one testicle to hang lower in the scrotum than the other. Inside the testicles are Leydig cells, which produce testosterone, the hormone necessary for male development and sexual functioning and responsible for many masculine characteristics such as facial hair growth. Also inside the testicles are the **seminiferous tubules** in which the Sertoli cells continuously produce new sperm from puberty until death.

Each testicle is attached to the body by a spermatic cord that extends into the pelvic area through the inguinal canal (the passageway in the lower abdomen through which the testicles descended into the scrotum before birth). Inside each spermatic cord are blood vessels (which is one way testosterone enters the bloodstream) and the **vas deferens** (through which sperm travel from the testes to the urethra).

The **anus** (through which the bowel empties) is behind the scrotum.

Why is the hair around the genitals called public when in a sense it is very private?

The hair in question is called *pubic* (rhymes with cubic), not *public*. Dictionaries note that the phrase "pubic hair " is related to both the pubic bone (which is under the hair) and puberty (the time of development when the hair first appears on the genitals.)

I am 19 years old. My problem is that when I have an erection, my penis gets a slight curve in it and it can be very embarrassing when I get into sexual situations. I was wondering if there is a special physician I could see for this problem or a special procedure that can be done to correct my problem.

It is not unusual for an erect penis to have a slight curve. Asked about the angle and shape of their penis, about 20 percent of men said it points straight out from the body when erect, 5 percent said it points down, and the rest said it points upward. Some reported that the angle became more downward as they got older. More than half of men said their erect penises are centered in relation to their bodies, about 30 percent said the penis aims to the left, and about 6 percent reported that it aims to the right. However, if the curve is severe enough to make sexual penetration difficult or if having an erection is painful, you should consult a urologist.

A few men do have more severe curves. Some are born with penile structural problems, such as a short urethra that can cause the penis to severely bend (called chordee, this is discussed on page 48). A different type of penile curve that suddenly appears much later in life can be a symptom of Peyronie's disease *(see Chapter 9).*

As a very much younger man I tore my "G" string and I've wondered since exactly what it was that I tore. The short membrane, or cord, that holds the foreskin forward. Would you give me the anatomical nomenclature of this important presence?

From your description it sounds as though the name you're looking for is *frenulum preputii*, the fold of skin (frenulum) that passes from under the glans of the penis to the skin covering the penis shaft.

The human body has many such folds of skin. (There is one between the undersurface of the tongue and the bottom of the mouth and another beneath the upper lip, between the lip and gum.) Tearing the frenulum you refer to is not unusual.

Such a tear may produce a great deal of blood, but it usually heals spontaneously. These tears require surgery only if any scar tissue that forms hinders movement of the penile skin or causes discomfort. Most men find this particular frenulum especially sensitive to erotic touching.

As an uncircumcised male, I've found that I have pain during intercourse, occurring at the first stage of penetration. Also, I'm unable to pull back my foreskin. I'm sure these two conditions are interrelated. Is circumcision the answer?

Circumcision may not be necessary. Check with a physician, preferably a urologist, to determine why your foreskin is not moving freely and if this is related to your pain during intercourse. If the problem is an infection, antibiotics may correct the problem. Or the foreskin opening can sometimes be surgically enlarged so that it will more easily permit retraction. *(For more information on infections of the foreskin see Chapter 17.)*

I have a problem that has frustrated me for years. Could you please answer these questions: What is a normal size of a man's testicle? And is there any way that they can be enlarged?

In adult males each testicle measures about 1.5 inches long and about an inch wide (although one testicle may be *slightly* larger than the other). If your testicles do not measure near this normal size range, consult a urologist. Significantly smaller testicles can be one sign of a health problem, such as a tumor of the pituitary gland, and enlarged testicles can also signal a serious health problem. If your testicles measure near the normal size range, yet you are bothered by the *idea* that they are small, consult a psychologist or counselor. Many men have the mistaken idea that larger testicles are a sign of being more manly or more fertile; this is not true.

I know of no way to increase testicular size unless the condition is due to a specific medical problem. If the underlying problem is corrected, then the size of the testicles may change in response to treatment, especially for a young man who has not yet finished going through puberty.

Is it normal for one testicle to hang lower in the scrotum than the other testicle? The right one is almost always near the base of the penis while the left one is always lower, touching the bottom of the scrotum. Is this normal for all males?

Yes. This helps keep the testicles from being squeezed when a man's legs are together. In most men, the left testicle is lower than the right testicle. In left-handed men, the opposite is often true.

If a man has been castrated, can he ever again be sexually active? What actually happens to the body in such a case?

Research has shown that a few men can have erections and sexual relationships following castration (surgical removal of the testicles). But they would not be capable of impregnating a woman because sperm are produced only in the testicles. And because the testicles produce testosterone, the man's body would gradually show the effects of the lack of this hormone (facial hair growth would slow, for example) unless it was replaced by taking synthetic hormones.

INTERNAL ORGANS AND
MALE REPRODUCTIVE SYSTEM

A male continuously produces new sperm in the seminiferous tubules inside each of the two testicles from puberty until death. When sperm leave a testicle they enter one of the **epididymis** (a curved structure about one-half inch long located on the back side of each testicle). Inside each epididymis is a thin, tightly coiled tube (about 20 feet long) where, as the sperm move through, they undergo a maturation process which gives them the ability to swim in a forward motion (*see Illustration 5*).

Then sperm enter one of the **vas deferens**. Each is a tube about 20 inches long which leads from one testicle, up into the body through the inguinal canal, loops around the bladder, and comes back down toward the inside end of the urethra. There it is attached by an ejaculatory duct to the urethra. It is at this interior end of the vas deferens that sperm collect and wait to be expelled out through the urethra at ejaculation.

On each side of the urethra at the ejaculatory duct, each vas deferens joins with the opening of a **seminal vesicle**, and the seminal vesicles connect to the urethra. These seminal vesicles produce a fluid that is alkaline (important in overcoming the acidity of the vaginal secretions) and contains fructose (a type of sugar which is a nutrient for sperm).

Next, surrounding the urethra like a small doughnut, is the **prostate gland**. The prostate gland also produces an alkaline fluid, which flows at emission into the urethra through ducts near the ejaculatory ducts of the vas deferens and seminal vesicles.

Further down the urethra, nearer to where the penis leaves the body, are another pair of ducts. These lead to the two pea-sized **Cowper's glands**, which produce a mucuslike fluid.

During the time the sperm are traveling from the testicles to the ducts near the urethra they are moved along by cilia (small hairlike structures) and contractions of the tubes. Sperm do not begin to swim on their own until after ejaculation. This entire process from development of sperm in the testicles, maturation in the epididymis, and travel through the vas deferens takes about seventy days.

During male sexual arousal the Cowper's glands secrete their fluid, which lubricates the urethra. This can happen close to the time of actual ejaculation, so sperm may already be present in this clear pre-ejaculatory fluid.

At **ejaculation** the opening between the bladder and the inside end of the urethra closes. At the same time the sperm, fluid from the seminal vesicles, and fluid from the prostate gland mix together as **semen** and enter the urethra to be forced out of the opening in the head of the penis by the muscle spasms of orgasm.

The total volume of semen in each ejaculate is around one teaspoon and contains 120 to 600 *million* sperm. But even this enormous number of microscopic sperm is extremely small in volume, equivalent to less than a tiny drop of semen. All the rest of the semen is fluid from the prostate gland (about one-third), the seminal vesicles (about two-thirds), and other internal glands. (This explains why the volume of a man's ejaculate is not noticeably reduced after a vasectomy, since only the sperm are then missing.)

The color of semen varies, normally shades of white, yellow, or gray. The texture is usually creamy, sticky, and thick immediately after ejaculation. The semen then becomes more liquid but eventually dries after exposure to air.

Any time a man has difficulty urinating or ejaculating, or if his semen changes, he should consult a urologist.

I would like to know the breakdown of semen. That is, of just what is it composed, the chemical composition, by percentage perhaps?

The chemicals in human semen vary somewhat, depending on the man's diet, health, and frequency of ejaculation, but the average ejaculate chemically consists mostly of protein, citric acid, fructose (a complex sugar), sodium, and chloride.

There are smaller amounts of ammonia, ascorbic acid, acid phosphatase, calcium, carbon dioxide, cholesterol, prostaglandins, creatine, other minerals, and numerous other chemicals.

I'm confused. A friend of mine told me he was sterile, but he also brags about his sexual activities. How can his stories be true if he can't have sex?

A man can be sterile, or infertile, and still have an active sex life. One condition does not necessarily affect the other. Having or not having sperm has nothing to do with whether a man can have erections, orgasms, or ejaculations of semen.

Millions of men have opted to have a vasectomy (a surgical procedure in which the vas deferens are cut) to avoid having children; this can be thought of as becoming sterile. I seriously doubt that vasectomies would be popular if one of the results was to interfere with future sexual activity.

I am a 70-year-old male. I hear more and more about cancer of the prostate gland. Where is the prostate and what is its function?

The prostate is shaped something like a small doughnut surrounding the first inch of the urethra nearest the bladder (*see Illustration 5*). During puberty the increase in testosterone stimulates the prostate to grow to its adult size, which is approximately an inch thick and 1.5 inches across.

The prostate makes a fluid that mixes with the sperm and fluids from other male reproductive organs. These fluids come out of the male urethra and are called the ejaculate or semen. About one-third of the ejaculatory fluid is from the prostate. Researchers think the prostatic fluid, which is alkaline, plays a role in reproduction by reducing the high acidity of vaginal secretions. Sperm are not as motile (do not actively swim forward) in an acidic environment as in one that is more chemically neutral.

Even though scientists do not think the prostate plays an active role in the hormonal system, it is certainly affected by changes in other organs and hormone levels. For example, the prostate will decrease in size if testosterone levels drop or estrogen levels rise.

The prostate, the opening of the bladder, and the tubes that carry sperm and other fluids to where they mix for ejaculation are located at the inner end of the urethra. The prostate can be felt through the wall of the rectum, especially if it is enlarged for any reason. One symptom of an enlarged prostate is difficult urination (a swollen prostate gland may squeeze around the urethra and slow or block the flow of urine).

A physical that includes a manual examination of the prostate every year after the age of forty is important to detect any changes in the prostate gland early (*see Chapter 17*).

4

Body Image and
Self-Esteem

Now we turn to an important *psychological* aspect of sex, gender, and reproduction: How does a person *feel* about his or her own body and physical appearance? For many people, their view of themselves has as much impact on their ability to form intimate, loving relationships as does their actual physical condition—in some cases more.

Embarrassment about some physical flaw (real or imagined) can stand in the way of even nonsexual pursuits such as playing sports (because it involves undressing in a locker room) or forming friendships (fearing the relationship might eventually progress to sexual activity). A person can become so strongly convinced of the abnormality or repulsiveness of some physical feature that it prevents him or her from seeking a medical evaluation. And those who do gain the courage to finally ask a physician if something is wrong are often unconvinced by the doctor's assurance that everything is normal.

A person's view of his or her own physical appearance is called *body image*. People who have strong negative body images, such as those who wrote the letters included in this chapter, can help resolve their concerns by learning to accept their appearance through psychological counseling, or by getting appropriate medical help if something is truly wrong and can be corrected or improved.

A positive body image is an important part of *self-esteem*, and having high self-esteem is vital to establishing intimacy with others. It is the belief that one is valuable and deserving of loving relationships. More simply put, it means feeling good about yourself. It also means being secure enough to risk having a lover find out that you are not completely perfect.

The pain and anguish caused by having a negative body image is clearly evident in this small sample of the many letters received on the topic.

GENITAL APPEARANCE

More men than women worry about whether their genitals look normal. Questions about penis size, shape, and appearance are in fact the second most frequently asked questions by men who write to the institute. (The topic most frequently asked by men is about problems with getting or keeping erections.) Some women also write about the appearance of their genitals.

The details in each of the following letters are different, but the idea is essentially the same: Many men feel their penises are too small.

I am 22 years old and have a problem that I am sure many other men have. The size of my penis is very small, in the flaccid state and when erect.

At one time I could have accepted this. But no longer. I have seen my doctor about it. He just laughed and said it was small, but that there was nothing he could do that he knows of.

Now I have become a loner, not having anything to do with girls. I live alone and keep to myself. I am writing to you to see if there is anything that can be done, since I am at the end of the line.

————

I am a 25-year-old man. I have a small "penis." It's about 5 1/2 inches. Actually I am getting shy when I make love with women. Do you think there is a way that can help me?

————

I'm 24 years old. My problem is that my penis is only 6 1/2 inches when it's erect. And I know that's average size, but I want it bigger.

So one time I was looking at a men's magazine and I saw an ad about a pump that will make your penis bigger so I sent for it. But it didn't work. I want to know if there really is a way you can make your penis bigger? If so, please send details.

————

I know that those magazine ads for penis enlargers are worthless, but are there any medical treatments (such as hormones or surgery) that will work? What kind of doctor do I go to for help—a urologist? If there is no hope, tell me so that I will not waste my time or suffer the embarrassment of asking.

————

When not erect, my penis is smaller than my 12-year-old grandson's. When erect, it at least triples in size and is fully functional, but this does not reduce the embarrassment I've always felt in public locker rooms, showers, etc. What can I do?

————

Can hypnosis increase the size of the human male penis? If so, what is the usual increased amount?

Not hypnosis, exercises, pills, creams, pumps, vitamins, injections, or any other of the hundreds of products or services advertised at the back of magazines or through direct mail—will increase the size of the adult penis. What's more, some of these products can have a harmful effect. Pump devices, for instance, have been known to damage fragile erectile tissue.

The vast majority of men measure within the average genital size range and have a penis that is approximately 5 to 7 inches long when erect, a length that is more than adequate for sexual functioning. Actual difficulties with sexual functioning or reproduction, in fact, rarely occur unless the *erect* penis is less than 2 inches long. In general, at erection smaller flaccid penises lengthen by a greater percentage than do larger flaccid penises. In other words, the size of a penis when it is flaccid does not predict what its size will be when erect. *(See also Chapter 3.)*

From what they describe, nearly all the men who write about this worry are well within the normal size range, yet they are convinced that their penises are too small for a satisfying sexual life. Some judge themselves against the genitals depicted in erotic films and magazines, where men are usually hired precisely because they have larger-than-average penises.

Many men assume—just as women do about breasts—that the opposite sex prefers a large penis. In one study, when men were asked to list what they thought women find sexually attractive, they gave very high priority to large genitals. But the women surveyed preferred firm muscle tone, well-groomed hair, a clear complexion, and white teeth. (The nonphysical factors women rated as important were a willingness to share emotions and thoughts, a good sense of humor, and dependability.)

Penis size is no more a measure of manhood, sexual capacity, or the ability to please a partner than is the size of a man's feet. Although some men worry that penis size is essential to being a good lover, the female genital organ most important to sexual arousal and orgasm is the clitoris, not the vagina, and it is more easily stimulated by touching with a hand than by thrusting with a penis.

As for intercourse, there is *no scientific research* suggesting that women generally prefer large penises, but there *is* research showing that most women *do not care* about their sexual partner's penis size. A vagina can feel stimulation in the 2 inches or so nearest the vaginal opening, so physiologically a penis that reaches this area is adequate for vaginal stimulation. A man who wants to learn more about lovemaking techniques can consult Chapter 8, or talk with a sex counselor or therapist.

Some of these concerns may derive from the way men visually compare their own penises to those of other men. A man should realize that his own penis may look smaller than those of other men because of the viewing angle. Looking down at one's penis, it appears shorter than when viewed from the side or front, the way one might see the genitals of other men in locker rooms or public toilets.

During puberty there is an additional problem with such observations because not all boys' genitals begin to grow at the same age nor do they grow at the same rate *(see Illustrations 26 and 27 in Chapter 12)*. However, by adulthood, the boys who developed later or more slowly catch up. Unfortunately, many young men have made unfavorable comparisons before they've reached full growth and the *thought* that they're "small" stays in their heads even after they've reached a fully mature average size. Because it is also during adolescence that we begin to interact with others and practice the social skills we need to function healthily in adult relationships, men should seek counseling help when they *first* begin to feel inadequate, rather than postponing it.

Even in early childhood, a young boy is likely to compare his penis to his father's and begin worrying about smallness. Parents can take steps to stop these worries before they even start *(see Chapter 11)*.

If an adult is concerned and finds upon measuring his penis that it is 2 inches or less when erect, he should have an evaluation by a urologist to see if there is a correctable problem involved.

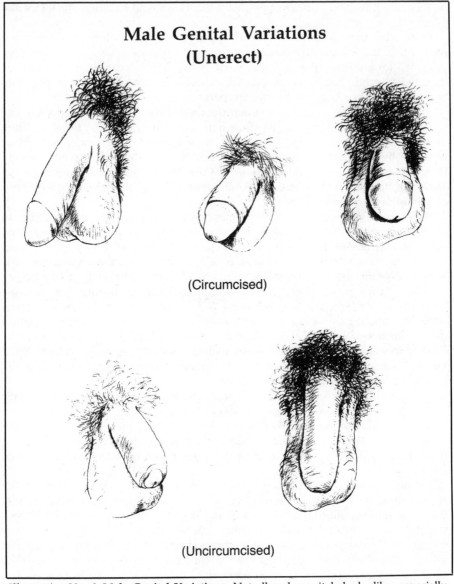

Male Genital Variations
(Unerect)

(Circumcised)

(Uncircumcised)

Illustration No. 6. **Male Genital Variations.** Not all male genitals look alike, especially when the penis is not erect (flaccid). In this state the penis can be short or long, thin or fat, with a head that looks wider or narrower than the shaft. The scrotum can hang lower or higher than the end of the penis. All these "variations" are normal.

But any man who feels self-conscious, humiliated, frustrated, depressed, embarrassed, anguished, angry, or suicidal because he thinks his penis is too short—whatever the size actually is—should talk with a counselor, psychologist, or psychiatrist. Although there is no product to increase the size of the penis, therapy can indeed boost a man's self-esteem and help him understand that his body is just fine the way it is.

I have read that you shouldn't use vacuum devices advertised to enlarge the penis, because they can damage erectile tissue.
If such damage has already occurred to penile tissue, can it be surgically repaired, or is the damage irreversible? This affects me directly. What action should be taken? This is very frustrating. Your answer will help put an end to my mental and physical suffering.

Repair depends on exactly what is wrong with the penis. You will have to consult a specialist in male sexual functioning *(see Appendix)* who is skilled in assessing male genital problems resulting from trauma or injury to the penis. The specialist, usually a urologist, can evaluate your condition and discuss treatment options.

It is very important that you explain precisely what happened. If you still have the device, take it with you so the physician can better understand all the factors involved. Most urologists have heard about these vacuum pumps and treated injury caused by them, so don't feel too embarrassed to seek help.

I know that women get silicone injections to enlarge their breasts—it makes them look better and is a great psychological boost to them as well. Why can't the same method be applied to a man's penis? I have recently learned about a clinic that specializes in what they call "male enhancement." The problem is that the clinic is in Mexico and I have heard many negative things about people going south of the border for drug treatment and surgery because they can't get it in the U.S. Do you think silicone injections are safe?

Absolutely not. It is not safe to inject liquid silicone into the penis, the breasts, or any other part of the body. Moreover, in the United States, it is *illegal* to inject liquid silicone into breast tissue, and some states have laws against injecting it into penile tissue too.

Liquid silicone does not stay where it is injected but tends to move around and harden into clumps. We have been told about cases where men had this procedure done, but—as the silicone migrated—found themselves with a penis that resembled a baked potato.

My question may seem very strange and odd, but I am curious about this. Concerning the size of penises: What is the largest size penis on record?

The blue whale reportedly has the largest penis, approximately 10 feet long. The longest erect human penis on record was 13 inches, documented early in the twentieth century by Dr. Robert L. Dickinson, a physician interested in sex research.

I am a 20-year-old man who is having trouble having sex with young ladies because I have an overly large penis. It seems to hurt them too much. Have you ever heard of this problem? What can be done?

Are you sure the size of your penis is the problem here? Before assuming you're too large, consider some other possibilities. Maybe your partners weren't fully aroused before you attempted penetration. When a woman is sexually excited, her vagina becomes lubricated and expands, making intercourse more comfortable, so that insertion and thrusting are not painful. For most women adequate foreplay is an essential part of lovemaking.

In addition to not penetrating until your partner is fully sexually aroused, you might want to try positions in which the woman can control the depth of penetration and movements. This means having your partner on top or being side-by-side. Whatever position you choose, ask whether your partner is ready to begin intercourse and let her control insertion so she can use an angle that's comfortable for her. If she feels discomfort or pain, stop deep or hard thrusting. Many women find shallow and gentle thrusting more pleasurable. If her pain persists, withdraw and continue with techniques that don't include intercourse, discussed in Chapter 7. If trying different techniques doesn't work, consult a sex counselor, who can offer suggestions that are specific to you and your partner.

I am a 19-year-old male and have normal sexual desires, but I have never been able to have intercourse because of trouble getting and maintaining an erection. This has caused a lot of problems with self-esteem and wonderment about my future. I have symptoms of something called chordee (downward curve of erection), but information about this is difficult to obtain.

I really have a hard time accepting this and I find myself lying to my friends about why I don't pursue relationships with girls. Could chordee be causing my problem? Can it be corrected with surgery?

Many normal, healthy men have slight penile curves up, down, or to one side during erection but more severe curves do rarely occur.

You may or may not have chordee (severely curved, often painful, erection of the penis). Chordee occurs when the urethra (the tube in the center of the penis, which carries urine from the bladder to the outside) is shorter than the penis. This makes the penis bend, especially when erect. Severe chordee is often diagnosed at birth or during childhood. When the condition is less severe (when the urethra is almost, but not quite, as long as the penis), chordee is not so obvious until a young man's penis grows during puberty. Chordee can usually be surgically corrected.

Probably you haven't had a thorough medical evaluation of your genitals. Only a urologist can accurately answer your questions—after examining your penis.

Your erection problems may well be caused by your concern about the appearance of your penis. You don't say how your penis works when you masturbate, but feeling self-conscious about your penis is certainly a factor that can cause erection difficulties with a partner.

Look for a urologist who specializes in treating male sexual dysfunctions (see Appendix). This physician can evaluate your physical condition, arrange for surgery if necessary, and recommend an experienced counselor who can help you become more confident about your ability to function sexually.

(A different kind of problem, which causes the appearance of a curve in the erect penis in adulthood, after a man's penis has been just fine for years, can be the result of Peyronie's disease; this is discussed in Chapter 9.)

I'm in my late 30s. In my teens I had an unsuccessful operation for an undescended testicle. Now I hear of an operation for an artificial testicle. I feel this would improve my sex life (self-image). I have always covered up at showers after swimming. Please tell me if you think this operation would help me.

Testicular implants of silicone gel enclosed in an inert covering (like implants for breast enlargement) are now routinely available for men who lack a testicle. Most men who request implants have had an undescended testicle that couldn't be surgically lowered into the scrotum, as in your case, or have lost a testicle from an accident or disease. Implanting the artificial testicle is a simple operation; ask your physician to refer you to a plastic surgeon with experience in this procedure. *(For more information on testicular implants, see Chapter 18.)*

When you consult a specialist about the artificial testicular implant surgery, also ask how he or she will assess the condition of your undescended testicle.

I'm writing to you about something I've never seen discussed. My labia minora are extremely large. They protrude outside the outer labia and the outer edges are a purplish color. I have had this problem since the onset of puberty. I feel like a freak, but I'm too embarrassed to bring this problem up with my doctor.

My doctor has never said anything about it but my boyfriend has. I just want to feel normal, which I don't.

You are fine. Your description of the appearance of your genitals is quite normal. It is not unusual for the inner folds to protrude beyond the outer folds.

Women's external genitalia vary greatly in size, shape, and color (pale pink to purplish black). The appearance changes during puberty, especially with the normal growth of the labia minora (the inner genital lips). There are also changes in shape and color during sexual arousal. Since most women do not have the opportunity to see the wide variation in other women's external genitalia they often believe that their own are unusual.

I'm a woman who has had a very bad problem with yeast infections, but I won't see a doctor. When my last baby was born my vaginal opening was torn upward toward my clitoris and left that way. I am very ashamed of this, and this is why I won't go to the doctor.

It is extremely important for your health that you have annual pelvic examinations and Pap smears, whether or not you are having vaginal infections. Gynecologists and obstetricians have seen vaginal tearing before, so you should not be embarrassed about having a physician see this. Many vaginal tears can be repaired; the physician you consult can advise you about surgically correcting this problem and recommend a surgeon experienced in plastic surgery of the vulva.

If you cannot bring yourself to make an appointment with a physician, first see a counselor who is trained to help women bolster their self-esteem and assertiveness. You have a right to competent and supportive health care, and a counselor can help you make sure you get it. Most towns have a community mental health clinic that can help you find such a counselor.

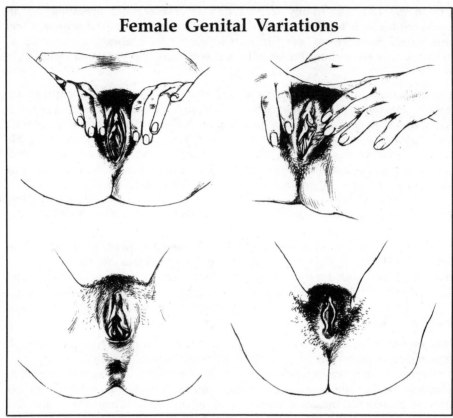

Female Genital Variations

Illustration No. 7. **Female Genital Variations.** Not all female genitals look alike. The labia can have many folds or be smooth, and both sides of the labia do not have to match. The labia can look closed or more open and their color can vary, especially during sexual arousal. The inner lips can fit inside the outer ones or protrude beyond them. All these variations are normal.

I am 22, female, and a virgin. Although I'm not ready to share my body with my boyfriend, we have discussed sex.

He and I disagree about one aspect of female anatomy. He claims that any female who has had a lot of sex, and all women who have had a baby, have outward-turning or contorted labia (majora and minora). Although my labia are inward or smooth, most of my girlfriends have labia that are not.

Is such unfolding of the labia automatic proof of sexual intercourse or childbirth?

No, it isn't. Even an experienced physician conducting a pelvic examination cannot determine a woman's history of sexual activity from the appearance of her genital lips. Prominent size, protrusion of the inner lips (labia minora) beyond the outer lips (labia majora), or having folds in the labia are not proof of either prior sexual intercourse or childbearing.

BREASTS

If men worry about genitals, women worry about breast size.

I'm flat-chested, 31-A, but wear bras that at least make me look bigger. Well, when I got married I never mentioned to my husband I was flat, not intentionally deceiving him. I never really thought about it and he never brought the subject up either. On our wedding night I could see he was surprised and I asked him if he was disappointed but he said no. But then and to this day, he never pays any attention to my breasts and when we're at the beach, his eyes are taking in all the nicely endowed women.

I've questioned him about being unhappy with my breasts. He still says no, but now I'm so self-conscious about them I cry to myself at least once a day! I even wear shirts now when we make love just so he can't see my small breasts any more. It really hurts when you think your husband is comparing you to other women. What should I do?

I'm very flat-chested and am seriously considering breast augmentation surgery. How much does it cost? Who is a good doctor in my area? How big could the surgeon make my breasts or is there a limit?

Every time I lose weight my breasts go first, and I cannot afford surgery. In the back of many women's magazines there are ads for pills and creams that enlarge breasts. Has there been any proof that pills and creams work effectively—especially the ones with hormones? If so, which one can I use?

My breast size really bothers me. When I'm with my husband I'm very conscious of this and our sex life has become a problem. Please help me. I'm only 26 and desperate.

I'm one of the unfortunate women who are very small-breasted. My bra size is 32A. I've tried programs such as nutritive powder drinks that promised increased bust size, but to no avail.

Now I'm thinking of using a cream containing 25,000 units of estrogen. Is it safe? What do you suppose is the matter with my breasts?

Is it possible to increase bust size through exercise? And if so, how much? My bust is 30A, Age 27, Height 5'5", Weight 112-118 lbs.

Whether women bind their breasts, enlarge them, or accept them as they are varies among cultures and has varied throughout time. In American society, for instance, during the 1920s the idealized shape of a "flapper" included a small bosom, and many women bound their breasts tightly to achieve that fashionable look. In the late 1940s a fuller silhouette was popular, so for the next decade or so women wore bras that were constructed to push the breasts up and out. Then effective surgical techniques became more available and some women chose to increase their breast size by this permanent method. And now the fashionable shape seems to be going toward having smaller proportioned breasts on a lean, athletic body. Throughout history the fashion in breast shape has also changed; in some eras ideal breasts were supposed to be rounded and in others to come to a sharp point.

Like men who pine for a larger penis under the illusion that all women desire this in a partner, many women believe bigger breasts are very important to the opposite sex. But research on what men find desirable about women's bodies has shown that only 50 percent mentioned breasts at all, and that half of these said that *small* breasts were most desirable.

No cream or lotion, with or without hormones, has been proven effective for increasing the size of women's breasts. And no cream containing estrogen has been approved by the Food and Drug Administration (FDA) as safe and effective for increasing bust size. Pumps are also ineffective. The FDA has also prohibited the use of liquid silicone injections into the breast because of serious health hazards. Only enclosed silicone gel implants are approved for breast enlargement. Readers can call the FDA to report problems with silicone injections or implants (1-800-638-6725).

No exercise will increase the amount of breast tissue, so it is not possible to increase actual breast size with special exercises or exercise equipment. What can be changed are the muscles under the breasts; exercises designed to strengthen and firm the pectoral (chest) muscles may slightly increase the *measurement* around the bust, but the breasts themselves, made up primarily of fatty tissue, cannot be enlarged through exercise. Improved posture (back straight and shoulders held down and back) may also help give the illusion of larger breasts.

Cosmetic surgery (called *augmentation mammoplasty*) to insert forms filled with silicone gel remains the only effective way of increasing breast size. An estimated 72,000 women in the United States have this surgery done each year. The surgery consists of placing a soft silicone gel-filled implant under the breast tissue, either outside or inside the muscles of the chest wall.

An incision about 1.5 inches long is made in the crease where the bottom of the breast meets the chest. The surgeon forms a pocket beneath the breast tissue, then inserts and positions the implant. The incision is closed with stitches. Done properly, only a thin light scar will remain but this is hidden by the way the breast hangs on the chest. Some surgeons use a similar procedure but make the incision around the edge of the areola (the darker skin surrounding the nipple). This incision site may be less desirable because there is more risk of damaging the milk-producing glands, milk ducts, and nerves.

In general, breast implant surgery done by a skilled cosmetic surgeon experienced in this procedure should not interfere with breast-feeding or sensation from the nipple area (important to many women's sexual functioning). Also, most physicians believe the silicone gel implants should not interfere with monthly breast self-examinations or X-rays of the breast (mammograms) to detect cancer or other diseases. Research on different types of breast implants, for example containing peanut oil, are in process with animals and if proven safer and more effective may be available for women by 1992.

Costs vary from one geographic area to another and also vary from one patient to the next, depending on the exact type of surgery appropriate for the individual. Check with your insurance company; many will not cover this type of optional surgery. It is vitally important to select the best surgeon you can find. (Write to the American Society of Plastic and Reconstructive Surgeons, 233 N. Michigan Avenue, Suite 1900, Chicago, IL 60601, or to the Aesthetic Society at the same address for help in finding a qualified and experienced surgeon in your area.)

You may want to consult with two or three different surgeons to compare their recommendations on the amount of increase appropriate for your body, surgical techniques, and costs. Often there is no charge for these initial interviews. Ask to see pictures of former patients, and ask to be put in touch with those who had their mammoplasty one or two years ago so you can find out if they are satisfied with the long-term results. How much to increase breast size depends on your wishes, how much your breast skin will stretch, and the recommendations of the surgeon.

Reputable surgeons will clearly explain about possible negative outcomes such as excessive scarring, infections, and capsular contraction (in which the capsule that develops around the implant as part of the body's healing process squeezes the implant, making it too firm or misshaping it). Some 25 to 33 percent of women will have a feeling of tightness in the breast, and in a few cases the capsule will harden to the extent that the breast becomes distorted or painful. This can be corrected surgically but tends to recur.

It is important to remember that this procedure carries all the risks of any major surgery that involves general anesthesia, whether done in a hospital or in a well-equipped office. There is a risk of one death per 10,000 anesthesia procedures.

Although rare, hemorrhage can occur if a blood vessel is not repaired during surgery; a second surgery is then required to correct the problem. Infection is also rare, but can happen. Starting antibiotics 48 hours before surgery can lower the risk of infection. If antibiotics are ineffective at treating an infection, the implant must be surgically removed. There are also a few reports of implants being ruptured by a hard blow to the chest, requiring surgical correction. Since silicone gel implants have been used for only about twenty years, no one is certain yet about any longer-term health risks.

Even though learning to accept one's body as it is will always be the safest option, many women are extremely pleased with the results of breast augmentation.

You will be asked why you want the surgery done, and some surgeons also do a psychological assessment to make sure you don't have unrealistic expectations about the effect of surgery on your life. Are you doing it to please someone else? Do you believe bigger breasts will change your life, pull you out of depression, attract men, land you a better job, save your marriage, or turn you into a beauty queen? If the answer to any of these questions is yes, consider seeing a counselor, psychologist, or psychiatrist before consulting a cosmetic surgeon. If there is such a thing as a good candidate for breast augmentation surgery, it would be someone with high self-esteem who doesn't expect bigger breasts to change anything but her silhouette.

I'm thinking of having breast enlargement through surgery. I heard a story on the radio long ago that a young woman had this surgery and after hugging her boyfriend closely, one of the breasts popped. Could this be true?

The horror story you recall may have been about a type of inflatable implant that is no longer used. That implant was a silicone envelope which was filled with a sterile saline (salt water) solution after being placed in the breast. There were reports of leakage and breakage under pressure with this type of implant during the 1960s.

I am 42 and have asymmetrical breasts (my left breast is larger than my right breast). It has been this way for most of my life since my breasts developed, but the older I get the worse it becomes. It's now to the point that it is difficult to find clothing that doesn't make me look lopsided. Do I have any medical recourse other than breast augmentation to correct the unevenness or is this a stumper doctors know nothing about?

You have four options: augmentation mammoplasty surgery to increase the size of the smaller breast; reduction mammoplasty to reduce the size of the larger breast; camouflage the size difference with clothing and by padding one bra cup; or have counseling to learn to accept your body as it is. If you elect surgery, find a good, qualified, experienced cosmetic or plastic surgeon.

Most women's breasts are at least somewhat uneven, and many women imagine that differences between their breasts in size or shape are much more noticeable than they really are. A conscientious physician will discourage surgery if it is not necessary for the improvement of your appearance.

I am 23, wear a 32A bra, and have nipples that measure nearly three inches across. Although I have fair skin, they are dark brown. This has prevented me from wearing nice bikinis and low-cut gowns.

Is there any surgery that would reduce the size of my nipples without reducing the limited fullness of my breasts?

I am too embarrassed to discuss this with my personal physician. Am I unusual? I have never seen other women, even those with large breasts, who have nipples of this size.

Both nipple size and the size of the darker-colored area around the nipples (the areola) vary greatly from one woman to the next. Even in the same woman, the areola on one breast can be larger than on the other. This circle of darker, more wrinkled skin extends an inch or more outward from the nipple itself, so a 3-inch total across would not be unusual.

Talk with a counselor about your feelings first. Then, if you are not reassured, consult a plastic or cosmetic surgeon. Surgically removing part of the areola is technically possible, but be sure to ask if this surgery will cause any reduction in the sensitivity of the nipples or if it will affect future breast-feeding. Also, ask about scars. All surgery leaves some scarring, so you should be given a clear idea of where and how noticeable the scars will be.

[NOTE: The institute also receives letters from many women who say their areolae are similar and they are proud of them; some men write that they *prefer* large areolae.]

I am very self-conscious about my breasts. I can accept the fact that they are small, but the real problem is that I have inverted nipples. Is there anything I can do to make them come out? I'm really embarrassed because they do not become erect when I'm excited. Is there any possibility that when I become pregnant they will come out permanently?

Variations in Appearance of Female Breasts

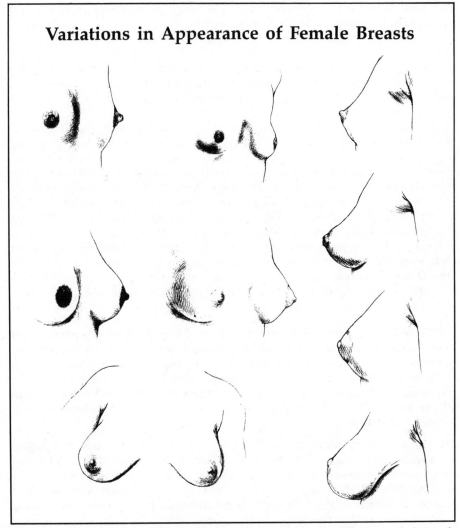

Illustration No. 8. **Variations in Appearance of Female Breasts.** The size and shape of women's breasts vary greatly. Some stand out from the chest wall and others are more rounded. Some nipples are pointed, some are flat, and others fold inward. Often the two breasts or the two nipples do not match. All of these characteristics are normal.

Nipple structure varies greatly, from very prominent to flat to inverted. Many women have flat nipples, and some have inverted ones (the center of the nipple pulls inward and is folded inside the breast skin). A few women have one inverted nipple with the other flat or prominent.

Inverted nipples are caused when the milk ducts inside the breast are shorter than the breast thickness, pulling the nipples inward. Although present from birth, this condition usually isn't noticeable until the breasts begin to grow during puberty. (Men can also have inverted nipples, but they are usually not as self-conscious about them as women are.) There are no serious difficulties associated with having inverted nipples, although more careful washing and drying may be necessary to clean away secretions.

If, however, a person's nipples have always turned outward and one or both begin to invert in adulthood, it is important to see a doctor immediately since this type of nipple change after puberty can be a sign of serious breast disease.

Most women with inverted nipples can successfully breast-feed their babies and, for a few, pregnancy makes inverted nipples stand out, temporarily or permanently.

To help women with inverted nipples prepare for breast-feeding, some physicians recommend Hoffman's Exercise, a technique that involves stretching the skin around the areola with the fingers. Because breast tissue is so sensitive, ask your physician for instructions on doing this exercise properly if he or she thinks it's safe and appropriate in your case. Also, the La Leche League can tell you about a special shield that is worn during pregnancy to help prepare inverted nipples for breast-feeding. You can contact them by writing to P.O. Box 1209, Franklin Park, IL 60131-8209 or call 312-455-7730.

None of the surgical procedures proposed to correct inverted nipples appear widely effective. In some cases, the nipples have inverted again after surgery; in others, surgery severed the milk ducts, preventing breast-feeding.

If the appearance of your nipples is interfering with feeling good about yourself and your attractiveness, consult a counselor.

I'm 13 and my problem is I have stretch marks on both of my breasts. My mother says it's from laying on my belly when I sleep. One of my friends who has them almost as bad as I do said it's from growing too fast.

Either way, it's getting very embarrassing, especially since I don't know any way to avoid taking showers with my gymmates at school. I'm hoping you can tell me how I got these stretch marks and how I can get rid of them real quick before school starts.

The exact cause of stretch marks hasn't yet been established, but they appear where skin tissue at some time has been stretched, as when breasts are growing. This causes the tissues to separate. Another example of this process is the appearance of stretch marks during pregnancy as the breasts and abdomen enlarge. Similar marks can also appear on both men and women after gaining and losing weight on the arms, breasts, stomach, and hips.

Hormones may also be involved. Some experts think the high level of progesterone during pregnancy makes the marks appear more readily than after simple weight gain and loss. Therefore the fluctuations of hormones during puberty could be involved for women your age.

Nothing in the research literature, however, indicates that stretch marks could result from any type of temporary pressure, such as a sleeping position. Regardless of cause, however, there's not yet a way to prevent or get rid of stretch marks. They usually fade after a time and become less noticeable.

Stretch marks are fairly common. It may be that you notice yours more because they're yours or because they are more recent (and hence darker) than those of your classmates.

I'm a 19-year-old woman who jogs. Will it cause my breasts to sag if I run without a bra?

Some physicians believe that exercising without a bra can damage the breast's supportive ligaments, but research on women athletes has not clearly established that the damage is permanent. If you don't wear a bra and/or elastic binding, you may experience short-term soreness. The larger the breasts, the greater the likelihood of discomfort.

It's probably a good idea to wear a bra if you experience any discomfort. In one study, women athletes mentioned the following elements as important bra-design features: absorbent fabric, seamless cups, absence of irritating clasps, and shoulder straps that stay in place during vigorous movement. Sometimes bras with these special features are called sports bras.

I am a woman in my early 50s. My breasts are very large and heavy. I have deep ridges in my shoulders from bra straps. Also, my right breast is considerably larger than my left. How successful is surgery to make them smaller?

First, find a reputable plastic or cosmetic surgeon. Reduction surgery is more complicated than surgery to enlarge the breasts, so make sure you clearly understand what is involved.

Breast-reduction surgery (removal of some of the fatty glandular tissue) does leave some visible scars; however, this usually is considered a small price to pay by those women whose heavy breasts cause back or shoulder pain and interfere with athletic activities.

Some insurance companies cover breast-reduction surgery when it is recommended by a physician as treatment for physical discomfort.

I am a male, 67 years old, and I have wondered about the following: America is obsessed with big breasts in our advertising, clothing industry, choice of TV actresses, etc. But are women with large breasts really sexier? Many women who are not as well endowed seem to be genuinely sexier, better lovers, better able to obtain climax, etc.

Any assumptions linking breast size to sexual capacity are a matter of cultural and individual preference and there appears to be no formal research correlating breast size with sexual behavior or responsiveness. Preferences differ from one culture to another, change from decade to decade, and differ among men. The present cultural ideal appears to be shifting in favor of more athletic-appearing, smaller-breasted women.

I'm a 62-year-old man. I weigh 190 pounds and am 6 feet tall. Basically, I'm built quite well except I have large breasts. It's most embarrassing when I wear tight shirts. For many years I've hoped I could do something about this problem. But I've never done anything. Please send any information that would be helpful. PS: I'm trying to tell you that I'd like to have my breasts made smaller, some way, so that I could wear tight shirts without embarrassment. Please help.

Enlargement of the male breast (gynecomastia) is not unusual and can have many causes, each with appropriate treatments. Make an appointment with an endocrinologist to evaluate your condition. *(See Appendix.)*

Researchers estimate that between 30 percent and 40 percent of all men over age seventeen have breast enlargement great enough to warrant the medical label of gynecomastia.

It is important to have a physical examination to rule out major problems such as tumors of the adrenal glands and the testicles, which can alter hormone levels. Some diseases such as cirrhosis of the liver (from excess alcohol consumption) and kidney failure, as well as malnutrition, can cause breast enlargement in men, as can a number of drugs (including reserpine, digitalis, and spironolactone).

When a disease is found and treated or a suspected drug is changed, the condition lessens for some men, but not for all. If an endocrinologist finds that you are generally healthy and you truly want to have your breasts reduced, then ask to be referred to a plastic or cosmetic surgeon who specializes in breast reduction. The results can be quite natural-looking with nipple sensitivity retained and minimal scarring.

Any man who notices sudden breast enlargement should consult a physician promptly. While simple gynecomastia may be involved, in other cases breast tumors can be the cause. Since men, like women, can develop breast cancer, every man should regularly examine his breasts for lumps or changes.

A final related point: Many newborn male babies have breast enlargement for a few weeks (probably because of exposure to the mother's estrogen) and about 60 percent to 70 percent of boys experience temporary breast growth during puberty due to fluctuations in the levels of androgens and estrogen.

HAIR

I am a 17-year-old girl and am extremely hairy. I have sideburns, a mustache, hair on my chin and excessively hairy arms, toes, and stomach. I've got more hair on my body than most guys. I'm of Greek descent, which I'm sure has a lot to do with it—but my mother, who's Greek, doesn't have this problem.

Is there any medication I can get to resolve this problem? I can't stand myself any longer and feel disgusted whenever I look in the mirror. Is there any hope for me that I'll be able to get rid of this hair (and not shaving and electrolysis—they don't work for me). I would think that if they can give someone a new heart, they should be able to help me, too.

Many women with a Southern European background have more dark, coarse body and facial hair than other ethnic groups. A large percentage of the women who seek treatment for hirsutism (excessive facial and body hair) are perfectly healthy women whose natural appearance doesn't match the current American cultural image of hairlessness for females.

You do not mention your pubertal development or menstrual status. If you have not menstruated or if you menstruate irregularly, you should be tested to determine if the hair is related to high levels of androgenic hormones (males usually have more of these hormones than females). Another key question will be whether the body hair is coarse or fine-textured, since hormonal problems are more often associated with coarse body and facial hair.

Have you asked your physician or a specialist in endocrinology about this? (See Appendix.) It may take a number of blood tests, X-rays, or other procedures to diagnose any hormonal or other health problems. However, once a medical cause is diagnosed, appropriate treatment can resolve the problem and reduce the hirsutism. Treatment differs for each possible medical condition, so no single drug can be recommended. There also is no drug that "cures" hirsutism in healthy women.

Nearly all physicians who evaluate women for hirsutism know that worries about appearance can have a devastating impact. Most can recommend a counselor who is experienced in helping women achieve a better appearance and a better outlook on life. Counseling is combined with teaching how to remove or disguise unwanted facial and body hair. These techniques include the use of pumice, waxing, chemical depilatories, bleaching, shaving, electrolysis, and make-up.

I am a male, 37 years old. But I look like I am 25-26 years of age. My problem is that I have no body hair. Is there a drug which causes hair to grow? I am in excellent health. Should I consult a doctor?

If you want to have a hairier body because you assume women find it sexually attractive, you may be mistaken. Research has shown that most women rank hairiness low when rating physical components of male sexual attractiveness. I know of no effective drug approved to make body hair grow.

I'm 18, male, and about to enter my freshman year in college. My problem is excess body hair. Since I was 14 or 15 I've had a lot of hair on my legs and arms. Now I see hair darkening on my shoulders, back, and upper arms. I hate to think how I'll look in two years. I dread the onset of summer. I'll stay in our apartment and won't go out in shorts or a T-shirt. I go in and out of deep depression because of this and once I almost killed myself. I feel like an outcast. Being a student, I cannot afford electrolysis. Do those "hair-away" solutions work? Being a male, I'd like some body hair but if it seems like my choice is between too much or none at all, in a *second* I'd choose having none at all.

To top it off, I read that "research has shown most women rank hairiness low when rating the physical components of male sexual attractiveness." What can I do?

The anxiety you feel is reason for more concern than what you believe to be excessive hairiness. Feeling intensely self-conscious can cause severe distress, especially during adolescence and early adulthood, and it is not easy to resolve these feelings on your own. Talk to a therapist or counselor about this problem. If you can't afford one, call your local mental health unit and ask for help. Free or low-cost counseling should be available.

Your quote from an earlier letter is accurate, but you've misinterpreted it. The question was from a man seeking a drug that would grow more body hair because he assumed it would make him more attractive to women; many men think women are attracted to a hairy body and I cited research to disprove that notion. It's not that women find hairlessness more or less appealing, but that the amount of body hair is not important *one way or the other* to most women questioned about what makes men sexually attractive.

Beyond physical characteristics, women have said they are most attracted to a man's willingness to be open about emotions and thoughts. They also rate highly a good sense of humor and dependability. A counselor can help you emphasize those aspects of your personality and reduce your concerns about your body hair.

Depilatories may work for you, assuming you're not allergic to the chemicals they contain. Some women use them on legs, arms, bikini lines, and underarms with good results. Waxing by a professional cosmetician is also very effective and lasts longer, but is more expensive. There are also several new hair removal appliances that pull hair out which might work for you.

I am a female, 34 years old. I've been meaning to ask if the hair surrounding the nipples of my breasts is normal or unusual. When I nursed my first baby, the hospital nurse advised that I clip the hair so as not to annoy the baby. (I did not.) Does this hair, if not typical of most females, indicate a greater-than-normal amount of testosterone in my chemical make-up?

Many women have hair on their breasts. The amount of hair and its distribution on the body is controlled by several factors, the main one being heredity: Some people simply are hairier than other people, and darker hair shows up more than lighter hair.

Blood tests could determine if your hormone levels are within the normal range for women your age. Hair on the female chest area, however, is rarely associated with higher-than-normal levels of androgens ("male" hormones).

Is it harmful to pluck hair from around the nipples?

No, but it can be painful and it's not a permanent solution. Hair will grow back after plucking. Nearly everyone has at least a few hairs around his or her nipples.

I have a problem with excessive pubic hair. It runs down the inside of my legs about two inches below my bathing suit. I've tried shaving, but when the hair starts to grow back I develop a lot of whiteheads. This is very painful and unsightly. In the summer I always end up wearing shorts when I would really like to be in a bathing suit. Please help! Summer is just around the corner.

There are only a limited number of ways to manage unwanted hair, and because the inner thighs are a tender area, keeping it both hairless and comfortable is particularly challenging.

Shaving with a razor and shave cream removes the hair for only a few days, although it's the least expensive and time-consuming solution. You might want to consult a dermatologist about the whiteheads and ask if a medication could prevent or reduce the skin problem.

Depilatories are lotions or creams that dissolve hair just below the skin surface; the hair takes seven to ten days to grow back. Make sure the product is labeled for use on the "bikini" area. Before applying it to your thighs, put a small amount of the depilatory on the inside of your wrist and wait 24 hours. If no redness or irritation appears, then follow package instructions.

Waxing, in which a coat of wax is applied to the skin and pulled off, will keep you hairless for about three weeks when you first start, then for four weeks after you've been doing it awhile. It is painful, particularly the first few times. Check the phone book for salons offering this service and find a cosmetician who is experienced in waxing bikini lines.

The only permanent method of hair removal is electrolysis, which is the most costly in time and money and should be done by a certified professional.

You might want to consider bleaching the hair to make it appear lighter rather than removing it. Check with a hairdresser experienced with hair bleaching first because dark, coarse pubic hair may not bleach evenly.

I am 18. I have very thick pubic hair, which my boyfriend wants me to shave. I hate the idea. I think of it as protection and fear I will feel funny and naked without it. What's the role of pubic hair? If I shave it, will it grow back again?

Pubic hair doesn't have a known biological function at this point in human history. But one theory holds that before people covered their bodies with clothing, pubic hair served to distribute pheromones (chemicals that carry specific messages to other members of the same species). These messages may have signaled, for instance, that a female was in her fertile stage.

Growing a new crop of pubic hair after shaving can be very uncomfortable. It takes quite a while to get beyond the stubble stage, which can be itchy for you and irritating for your partner. But the best reason of all for not shaving it off is that you say you hate the idea. If you don't want to shave your pubic hair, don't. Your boyfriend should understand and respect your desire to leave your body the way it is.

I am a 29-year-old male who's had a very active sex life since a teenager. For the last 2½ years, I've noticed my head hair is thinning. Could the amount of sexual activity have anything to do with this?

It is highly unlikely that sexual activity would cause a man to lose his head hair, and there is also no research to either support or reject the widespread notion that bald men are "sexier."

Sudden hair loss can be a sign of a condition called alopecia areata (a scalp condition when hair falls out leaving bald patches), which requires diagnosis and treatment by a physician. Also, some diseases accompanied by high fevers can cause hair loss, but in these cases the hair nearly always grows back. Other types of reversible hair loss include damage from hair products such as permanents or bleaches or by such drugs or medical treatments as cortisone, X-rays, or chemotherapy.

The vast majority of balding men have simply inherited the tendency to develop male-pattern baldness. About 12 percent of all men exhibit this type of gradual hair loss by age twenty-five, and nearly half of all men have significant hair loss by age forty-five.

Despite the many ads that promise growth of new hair, no drugs, lotions, vitamins, or other "miracle cures" have been shown to effectively reverse this type of hair loss in most men. One prescription drug—Rogaine (minoxydil)—helps some men. Before you consider using it, talk with your physician and make sure you understand the possible side effects, that it takes several months for this medication to begin to show results, and that if you stop using the medication any new hair will fall out.

There are also ways to camouflage a receding hairline or a bald spot, among them hairpieces, hair weaving, and hair plug transplants. When hair loss is viewed as a traumatic experience or has a negative effect on a man's ability to cope with life, counseling may be needed.

SKIN

I am a 38-year-old single male. Although I have had sex with over 30 women in my life, I have had trouble lately forming a sexual relationship with a woman. Along with suffering from low self-esteem, I have had psoriasis on my penis for about four years. During the one- to three-week outbreaks, there are red rashlike spots on the head and under the glans. The psoriasis is not contagious and does not reduce the ability to have sex, but I fear that women will be repulsed. Also, sex (both intercourse and masturbation) seems to worsen the condition.

Although some, if not most, of my problems with forming sexual relationships stem from my unexciting life-style, which can be changed, the psoriasis is a real, observable condition that won't go away. Since my dermatologist tells me that this condition is not rare, other men are probably experiencing some of the same fears too. What can you suggest I do?

An estimated 2 percent (two out of a hundred people) of the U.S. population has psoriasis, a skin condition that can erupt as reddish lesions or areas of scaling anywhere on the body. Your dermatologist is correct: Both men and women can have psoriasis in the groin area and on the penis or the labia majora. As you've discovered yourself, friction on the affected area will worsen or cause an outbreak for many psoriasis patients.

As yet, there is no permanent cure. Current treatments focus on increasing the length of time between attacks. Treatments for psoriasis on the genitals include hydrocortisone creams or sulfur-based pastes. Less sensitive areas of the body can be treated with other methods, including tar preparations and ultraviolet light. Several medications under investigation may prove effective at limiting psoriasis outbreaks; check with a dermatologist regularly to see if any new treatments have been approved for use on genital skin and mucous membranes.

Meanwhile, you may want to talk with a counselor or therapist about your concerns. Individuals who have obvious physical problems can learn various ways to handle tense social situations. For example, you might practice exactly what explanation you'll give to a potential sexual partner, and at what point in the relationship. This can free you to focus on meeting new friends and building other social skills without being so concerned about the appearance of your penis.

When you do tell a sexual partner about the psoriasis, you should emphasize that even though it can appear on the genitals, psoriasis is not a sexually transmitted disease. It should be much easier to reveal your condition and your concerns if you have developed a good friendship and emotional openness before the relationship becomes sexual.

I'm a 35-year-old woman and get more pimples now than I did as a teenager. It gets pretty bad and is embarrassing for me. I seem to get them a couple of days before my period and a few days later. They last for a week. I try to let them go away on their own, but they stick out so far that sometimes I pop them.

I haven't changed my make-up or my soap. Why is this happening even though I'm not a teenager?

Your pimples may be acne, and you may be having trouble now for the same reason teenagers do: hormonal changes.

Even though most people associate it only with puberty, acne can be a symptom of hormonal changes at any point in life. For women, this can mean during each menstrual cycle (many women report acne the week before menstrual flow), during pregnancy, when taking hormonal contraceptive pills or after stopping them, and around menopause.

Mention this to your gynecologist during your annual pelvic examination and Pap test. It may be time to monitor the level of estrogen and other hormones you are producing, since the level of these hormones may gradually begin to change or drop several years before actual menopause occurs.

Or you could consult a dermatologist, who can advise you about effective acne treatments such as using an ointment with an antibiotic or taking low doses of tetracycline daily (both of which require a prescription). In the meantime, resist the temptation to squeeze pimples because of the risk that skin bacteria, which can cause an infection, may make the pimple last longer or lead to scarring.

HEIGHT AND BODY SHAPE

Is it true that women prefer tall men?

This may be true to some extent: Women do seem to prefer partners taller than they are. When all other physical factors are equal, most women will choose the tallest male among several equal rivals. But one study of college women showed that, given a choice among all physical factors, most would choose handsomeness over tallness in their male partners.

However, in those studies that have included both physical and nonphysical factors the most highly valued attributes of a partner are personality and intelligence.

What is the real story on steroids? I suspect they work because of all the furor. And, if they work for Olympic-caliber athletes, why wouldn't they be great for ordinary guys?

Steroids are powerful substances that reduce normal hormone production and shrink the sex glands—reason enough for "ordinary guys" to avoid them. Research has documented many negative physical and psychological effects from these drugs.

There are many kinds of steroid hormones. The kind used by athletes for body building are called *anabolic* steroids, which are forms of synthetic testosterone made from plants. Anabolic steroids have two effects on the body: anabolic (muscle- and bone-building) and androgenic (masculinizing).

The anabolic, body-building effect changes the balance of chemicals in the body, which often results in increase of muscle size and weight. For this reason, anabolic steroids are sometimes prescribed for short-term medical treatment to slow down the withering of muscles in surgical or burn patients and to speed weight gain in premature babies. Any muscle-building or weight-gain effects disappear when the drug is stopped; prolonged use may permanently reduce the normal muscle-building process and risk future muscle and bone growth and development.

The androgenic effects of adding anabolic steroids to a system that already produces a normal level of these hormones are negative. For men, high dosage or long-term use can result in shrinkage of the testicles, a decrease or discontinuance of sperm production, an increase in breast size, and erection problems. Steroids may also enhance the growth of existing tumor tissue in the prostate, an alarming effect since death from prostate cancer is second only to death from lung cancer in men older than seventy-five.

My husband is a walking example of the changes caused by anabolic steroids. Grossly large muscles and an overall swollen look. I've also read they cause liver damage and other such things.

My questions are some that my husband and I have argued about for a very long time. He is very moody, irritable, and no longer his easygoing self. I compare him to a woman with PMS. He's used Anavar, Deca-durabolin, and testosterone, both orally and by injection. Can these be affecting him mentally? Please respond to this. My marriage could depend on this!!!

Anavar and Deca-durabolin are brand names for synthetic testosterone. Research on the behavioral effects of this hormone on aggressiveness in adult males has reported conflicting results. However, reports on athletes who took anabolic steroids noted that the athletes thought these hormones increased their feelings of competitiveness, which some researchers equated with aggression, and it is clear that they do have dramatic negative effects on other aspects of mental health.

In one study of a group of forty-one body builders and football players who had used anabolic steroids, 34 percent (one in three) had serious emotional or psychiatric responses while taking these hormones. These men exhibited severe psychiatric symptoms, including hallucinations, paranoia, delusions, major depression, and some had at least one manic episode.

Examples of manic behaviors while on steroids included buying expensive sports cars for which the individual did not have the money; driving a car deliberately into a tree while having a friend videotape the event; and smashing another driver's windshield because his directional signal was flashing but he did not make a turn. All these manic symptoms disappeared within a few weeks of stopping the anabolic steroids. So, yes, the emotional changes you've described could be a side effect of these hormones.

Another possibility is that your husband might be irritable because he doesn't feel well, especially since you say he looks swollen. Edema (retention of fluids in body tissues) is also a possible side effect of taking anabolic steroids. Your information about liver damage is correct too, and worthy of serious concern. There are various reports of changes in liver function and liver tissue, deaths from liver failure, and cases of cancer of the liver associated with steroid use. It is not clear whether stopping use of these drugs reverses these physical side effects.

How does your husband get these drugs? They require a prescription by a physician, and the manufacturers advise doctors to check the patient's liver function regularly and to discontinue the drug immediately if side effects are found. If he hasn't been tested in the last month, encourage him to consult an endocrinologist, who will check both his liver function and his hormone levels.

Further Readings

Fisher, S. *Development and Structure of the Body Image*. 2 vols. Hillsdale, NJ: Lawrence Erlbaum Associates, 1986.
(An academic text which addresses such topics as what is known about body image; how males and females differ in their body perceptions; and how children integrate their body experiences.)

5

Attraction, Love, and Commitment

This chapter explores elements of interpersonal relationships: attraction, love, and commitment. Even though most concerns and problems with intimate relationships don't surface until we've matured physically, the way in which we interact with others takes root in early childhood. And sexual attraction, even serious love, can occur in adolescence.

During childhood, interactions with parents and other adults help determine whether we view ourselves as male or female and masculine or feminine—only two of the important concepts that develop during this period. The way we interact with our peers helps determine which characteristics we will eventually find desirable in a partner and which desirable traits we want for ourselves. We are also influenced by messages about desirability from books, TV, movies, magazines, and other sources. As puberty begins, most of us also become aware of our own feelings of sexual attraction and notice that we are more likely to become aroused by specific types of people or situations, while other people or situations have little or no effect on us. All of these learning experiences help us determine which people we eventually will be attracted to and then, in some cases, fall in love with. These experiences also affect the content of our sexual fantasies and the pattern of our sexual behavior because we tend to imagine or seek out partners or situations that are arousing to us and ignore or avoid those that are not.

Dr. John Money, one of the world's most respected sex researchers and theoreticians, has called these internalized patterns for a person's particular sexual interests and behavior lovemaps. He believes these lovemaps begin to take shape early in our lives and become fixed as we go through experiences that more clearly define what contributes to sexual arousal. Most people from similar backgrounds end up with essentially similar maps in which only the details differ. For example, most men will be attracted to women within a few years of their own age whose physical characteristics, like height and weight, are more or less within average range, but each may prefer or be drawn to particular characteristics—including hair, eye, and skin color; body shape; or personality type. A few people are only aroused by individuals with very specific or rare features or attributes, as discussed in Chapter 7.

Adult relationships are also affected by the interactions with others experienced during infancy and early childhood. When we develop the ability to give and accept affection and trust others, we are better equipped to form close friendships later in life. And if our experiences with friendships have helped us learn that we can be loved and accepted just as we are (warts and all), we begin to let ourselves be vulnerable, which is an important element in experiencing feelings of love and forming long-term commitments to others. Allowing oneself to risk being vulnerable, and thus open to another person, is one aspect of intimacy, and shared intimacy is essential in the establishment of fulfilling, loving long-term relationships.

Love and sex within committed relationships provide a special sense of emotional security that is valuable to a person's sense of well-being, happiness, and perhaps even physical health. All mutually caring, committed relationships (heterosexual, homosexual, married, or not) involve the same elements of love and provide positive benefits for the partners. This is not to say that less committed or short-term intimate relationships are always negative—they too can contribute to an individual's healthy development by, for example, bolstering a person's self-esteem and providing opportunities to learn about oneself and others. But without mutual affection, trust, and caring, there is a risk that one or both partners may be hurt by a sexual relationship.

One further point: Some people do not fall in love or form pair-bond relationships. They are quite happy and satisfied to be by themselves at various times in their lives or even for an entire lifetime, deriving much pleasure from nonsexual friendships, family, work, and other sources. People who have made this choice are no less mentally healthy than those who choose to love and have sex with and commitment to another person.

ROMANTIC LOVE AND COMPANIONATE LOVE

Accounts of romantic love are found in many cultures and periods of civilized history, but not everyone experiences or every culture acknowledges this particular emotion. Research on feelings of love typically divides them into two categories: passionate and companionate.

Specific characteristics often associated with *passionate love* (also referred to as "being in love") include thinking about the other person constantly, having a strong need for the other person to reciprocate the love, being blind to any faults or flaws of the loved one, and having your own moods dependent upon the other person's actions. Some people studied reported that their work or grades in school suffered while they were "in love," but others said their productivity increased because they felt so good about themselves. As many people will testify, it can be difficult for friends or family to understand the behavior of a person experiencing passionate love.

Some researchers have speculated that passionate love may have a genetic component, having evolved in humans as a way of keeping couples together long enough to protect pregnant women and nursing mothers. Others believe that "being in love" is a specific chemical reaction of the body similar to other strong emotional states such as fear.

One researcher has even argued that the thrilling feelings of love may be due to a specific chemical in the brain, phenylethylamine, which has effects similar to drugs that cause euphoria and increase energy. If this is true, it may help explain why when lovers break up, the feelings are often described as being similar to drug withdrawal—and why chocolate (which is high in phenylethylamine) is so popular.

Also, there is speculation that as a relationship moves from passion to a more companionate love, higher amounts of other brain chemicals are produced (similar to narcotics) that make a person feel tranquil.

As a relationship continues over a period of time, new and different feelings about partners and the relationship tend to emerge. These include a growing sense of intimacy and a commitment to staying together, a type of love often referred to as *companionate love*.

Often as passionate love fades, we are suddenly aware of previously overlooked flaws in our loved one or the relationship. Or the relationship may lose its spark and sizzle, becoming more like a business partnership devoted to running a household or raising children.

The most satisfying relationships are those that retain some aspects of passionate love while growing to include mutual trust, a desire to see our partner lead a fulfilling life even if it doesn't always involve us (going back to school, for example, or building a career), and a realistic assessment of our partner's attributes without the idealization that accompanies the early stage of passionate love—in other words, the best aspects of deep friendship.

Building and maintaining a companionate love relationship is not always easy. For one thing, couples must reconcile their differences about basic sexual issues—unfortunately this usually happens just when partners are most overwhelmed with real-life demands like raising children, earning a living, and other time-consuming and intrusive matters.

This new type of love requires a willingness to be flexible and the motivation to work out disagreements. Talking together about feelings, being honest without being hurtful, listening carefully to our partner's expression of needs, and negotiating mutually acceptable compromises are all necessary. If doing this as a couple doesn't produce results, consulting a marriage, family, or sex counselor can be helpful.

Companionate love doesn't exclude an exciting and satisfying sex life. Quite the contrary. As we learn more about the things that produce arousal and orgasm in our partner, sex can become even more satisfying at this stage of a relationship. But again, attaining this level of sexual satisfaction includes telling your partner what turns you on and what turns you off, listening and responding carefully to each other's preferences, and giving importance to the sexual aspects of the relationship. Lovers, no matter how long they've been together, are not mind readers.

Each relationship makes rules that both partners are expected to follow. One of the prime relationship "rules" is sexual exclusivity—in the sense of having sex only with each other. Unless partners explicitly verbalize those rules and

Illustration No. 9. "The Lesson" is the first of twelve three-dimensional sliding panels that depict a romantic, then intimate, relationship between a young man and woman.

Lacquer box with sliding panels. Chinese, about 1850. Wood, black lacquer, inlaid colored jade, mother of pearl, and ivory, 7¼" x 11¼" x ⅖". The Kinsey Institute Collections.

expectations (for instance, "I won't have sex with anyone besides you, and you won't have sex with anyone else except me"), problems can occur and trust be threatened or destroyed.

Whatever love's definitions, types, or duration, it deserves more scientific study, if only to help those people who experience severe distress when love ends. One study reported that 17 percent of 400 people questioned had either contemplated or attempted suicide when their love was rejected or a love relationship ended. This is why love at any age should be taken seriously by family and friends, since the person may need special help and support if the relationship does not go well.

I'm a 17-year-old girl and think I'm in love, but my parents say I don't know what real love is. What is love and how can I tell if I'm really in love?

Poets will tell you one thing, philosophers will tell you another, and your parents will have their own opinion as well. But you're probably looking for the scientific community's definition of love.

Only a few researchers have attempted to investigate love. What's more, many policymakers, funding agencies, and some scientists feel that love *shouldn't* be a subject of research. They feel that love should remain a mystery. Thus, we have less scientific information about the meanings of love or how feelings of love affect our lives than is necessary to fully answer your questions.

There do appear to be several different types of love, including the love of parents for their children, love between best friends, and love of country or generalized ideals. But passionate love for a particular person clearly appears to be a different type of love. This strong emotional experience can occur at any age and can last for a few days, many years, or a lifetime—although the average duration appears to be two years.

Researchers have noted some factors that are involved in liking a particular person. These include having similar beliefs and values, physical attraction, and having your feelings reciprocated.

Talk with your parents and discuss the various types of love scientists know exist and that passionate love can exist at any age. Perhaps they will understand that there is not just one type of love.

I'm a 15-year-old high school freshman. This year I met a 17-year-old senior boy. I really love him a lot, but he wants me to have sex with him. How old do you think a girl should be before she has sex?

The feelings of being "in love" are very real and there is a temptation to be swept away by those emotions, but it's possible to have a loving relationship that does not include sexual intercourse. No single age is right for everyone to begin sexual activity, and it would be impossible to tell you which age is right for you.

The average age of first intercourse in the United States is between 16 and 17. This means that many individuals begin at both older and younger ages. However, factors other than statistical averages are more important. A person must be mature enough to be able to feel confident that having intercourse is the right thing to do based on his or her own personal values, ethics, and feelings of love and trust between the partners, regardless of age.

A person should also have correct information about sex and be ready to accept the responsibilities of becoming sexually active, which include having annual pelvic exams (for females) and avoiding sexually transmitted diseases and unplanned pregnancies. This is a decision you must make for yourself without being pressured by your boyfriend. It sounds as if you have under-standable reservations about having sex right now.

It is common for young people to feel pressured about having sex. Boys are pressured by their peers (many of whom haven't had sex, in spite of all the big talk) to have sex with girls. In turn, the boys pressure the girls, often using the line "If you love me, you'll do it" or "If you were grown-up you'd do it." Girls can respond with "If you loved me, you wouldn't ask or pressure me when I'm not sure" or "Being grown-up is making responsible decisions about what is right for me." Both boys and girls also feel a kind of physiological pressure; puberty brings sharp increases in hormonal levels and these are linked to increased sexual feelings, fantasy, and desire.

There are real dangers to having sex during adolescence. You've probably already been warned about teenage pregnancy. An unplanned pregnancy can seriously affect your future by limiting your options for schooling and a career. And the risk of sexually transmitted diseases is also high among teenagers: Current statistics show that a teenager contracts a sexually transmitted disease every thirteen seconds. Sexually transmitted diseases can damage your repro-ductive organs, which may prevent you from becoming a parent later.

But even when pregnancy or disease is not involved, there are other risks. Once you've had sex, breaking up with your boyfriend can be more emotionally devastating and may make it more difficult to trust other boys and form new relationships. There are less risky ways to feel better about yourself and your value as a person. These include achieving educational, career, or other personal goals and having a loving relationship without having sexual intercourse. Moreover, intercourse is not the only physical way to express your sexuality and achieve sexual satisfaction (*see Chapter 7*).

If you've decided not to have intercourse just yet, you may find it difficult to discuss that decision with friends. Find someone to talk with; some schools, community mental health centers, churches, and family planning centers (like Planned Parenthood) have counselors skilled at helping adolescents articulate their concerns. And of course, if possible, you should try discussing this issue in a general way with your parents. You may be pleasantly surprised to hear their perspective.

I would like to know if it's all right to have a live-in boyfriend at my age. I am 55. I've been a widow for six years, and have been living with my boyfriend for nearly a year. My daughter says I'm too old to have a live-in friend, but she's 33 and also lives with a man.

We won't get married because I'm retired and it would hurt our income. We have a good sex life. He cares for me, and I care for him. Am I doing wrong? I don't know what to tell my daughter when she calls me nasty names.

You might tell your daughter that 55 (or 75, or 95) years old is not too old for love, sexual desire, sexual activity, or companionship. Each person decides what is correct behavior based on his or her needs and values. It's not unusual for children to have a hard time accepting or understanding the sexuality of their parents—or of older people in general.

It might interest you to know that the 1980 U. S. Census found that unmarried-couple households had more than tripled since 1970, to 1.6 million couples. Among men and women age 45-64 living in unmarried-couple households, 13 percent of the men and 10 percent of the women had been married previously.

In a 1984 study of older Americans, 29 percent of the unmarried men and 14 percent of the unmarried women reported they were living with a sexual partner. Sixty-two percent of the men and 52 percent of the women said they hardly ever felt lonely, and many reported also enjoying life more than ever. Being in a mutually caring relationship and enjoying life is important regardless of age, and it also may be important to living longer.

Monogamy, having only one sexual mate, has long been advocated by religions and sometimes by laws. But isn't this an unnatural behavior? Aren't humans, especially males, the only animal that is expected to try to reach this idealized state by repressing their natural instinct to have sex with many partners?

The word *monogamy* is defined as marriage with only one person at a time, but in our society the term is also used to indicate that a couple has sex only with each other, having formed a sexually exclusive relationship.

Many, but certainly not all, human groups expect married couples to maintain sexually exclusive relationships. Sometimes, societal rules about limiting sexual partners apply only to one sex (for example, a woman may have sex with only her husband, but a man may have sex with many others) or to one type of partner (for example, a person may have sex with single, but not with other married people).

In many cases, these rules have more to do with establishing a clear pattern of inheritance (so that property passes only to a mother's or father's genetic children) than with moral, religious, or cultural ideals. In fact, historically the concept of formal marriage was based on economic or political relationships among families or groups—not on the current Western concept of being "in love."

Contrary to your assumptions, some animals do maintain sexually exclusive bonds. About 3 percent of mammalian species, a smaller percentage of fish, and more than 90 percent of birds practice some form of sexual exclusivity. Any limitation on sexual partners varies from one species to another; for example, sexual exclusivity may last only for a single breeding period or it may be for an entire lifetime. Sexually exclusive animals include two species of primates— gibbons and marmosets—whose members pair for life. Other examples include geese, swans, angelfish, beavers, and soldier beetles.

Among nonhumans, exclusive relationships include many aspects of life, not just the sexual—building a home, feeding offspring, and scaring off predators. Without the exclusive bond, the species would not be able to survive.

In some species, both sexes share the same tasks, such as taking turns at gathering food to bring back to the offspring while the other mate guards the young. In other species, tasks are divided by sex. Among owl monkeys, for example, males rear the infants while females find food.

Lifelong exclusive pairs often exhibit extensive, long-term responsibilities to their offspring. For example, one species of gibbon (a type of ape), which produces offspring every other year, lives together as a family group. As each male offspring reaches maturity (around eight years of age), the parents help him select and defend his own patch of territory. Without this support, the young male has little chance of establishing himself and finding a mate.

Many species have extended periods of courtship before committing to a sexually exclusive bond. Some birds "keep company" for several seasons before beginning to breed. Beavers often choose each other during adolescence and live together for at least six months before sexual maturity and mating occur. Scientists speculate that prolonged courtship may be a testing period during which the couple makes sure that each mate can fulfill his or her parental and partnership roles before offspring are produced.

It is simplistic, however, to equate animal behavior with human behavior, no matter how many interesting parallels may be found. Although many humanlike examples of sexual exclusivity can be found in nature, we shouldn't attempt to explain animal behavior in terms of human emotions or ideals. For example, a species of bird that pairs for life is no more "moral" than a species that pairs for only one breeding season. They are simply following the most effective reproductive strategy for that species.

Among human groups, lifelong sexual exclusivity may be as "natural" for some people as it is "unnatural" for others and can occur for a wide variety of reasons (religion, economic factors, social status, rearing offspring, etc.). Certainly one good reason to be sexually exclusive is to avoid the risk of sexually transmitted diseases such as AIDS.

I'm planning to get married, and already I find myself feeling insecure. My question is, are there any marriages in which the male spouse is totally faithful to the wife? I find myself getting angry at him because of my own insecurities. He never knows what causes me to become so upset. I just worry about him being unfaithful. What I want to know is, are there any truly faithful marriages?

Our recent analysis of six different studies yielded the estimate that only 37 percent of husbands had at least one sexual partner outside the marriage, and analysis of nine studies of wives showed 29 percent had had extramarital sex at least once. (*There is more information in Chapter 1.*)

Concerns about faithfulness and worry that an extramarital affair could damage or destroy a marriage are quite common. In one study of 6000 couples, the vast majority of spouses felt sexual exclusivity should be a goal, but there was less agreement on what would happen if one or both partners didn't live up to that ideal. Some felt that if there was sex outside the marriage there would be no effect on the primary relationship, while others felt that even one incident of infidelity would be the end of trust, love, commitment—and the relationship.

What turned out to be important were the "rules" a couple made about their relationship. There were some couples whose rules included the idea that sex with other partners would not detract from their commitment or their feelings about each other. In contrast, the rules for most other couples entailed severe consequences for unfaithfulness.

In any case, you and your fiancé should discuss your personal values concerning fidelity, preferably *before* getting married. Express your values and expectations clearly so that there is no chance of misunderstanding. What often happens, however, is that a couple agrees to be sexually exclusive, then if extramarital activity occurs, it is handled by deception rather than by discussion and reconsideration of the rules of the relationship.

Worrying in advance of the wedding may be a signal of low self-esteem on your part. Perhaps you feel you don't deserve a husband who would limit his sexual and affectional activities to you alone. If this is the case, discussion with a therapist can help. Beginning a marriage with these kinds of feelings and doubts can cause problems which won't go away by themselves.

I hate it when my husband says he's going out with his buddies. He says they go fishing, but I can't help thinking he may be lying, although he doesn't lie about other things. He says he's not involved with anyone else and I'm just being insanely jealous. I can't stop worrying every time he's gone. It really upsets me. What should I do?

It's not clear from your letter exactly what's going on. Does your husband participate with you in other activities? Do you have friends with whom you spend time without including your husband?

These are the types of questions a marriage counselor would ask to help you sort out the issues involved.

Researchers define jealousy as an emotion experienced when a person thinks that another person (either real or imagined) poses a threat to their relationship with their partner. Jealousy seems to consist of two factors: desiring an exclusive relationship and feelings of inadequacy and low self-esteem.

When asked how they would react if they felt jealous, men said they would get angry whereas women were more likely to say that they would get depressed. Moreover, for men jealousy seems to involve threats to their status, but for women it involves threats to the relationship.

Remember the old saying about husbands and the "seven-year-itch"? Is it true that most husbands have an affair during the seventh year of marriage?

This is certainly one of our accepted cultural myths, but—like so many other myths—it does not appear to be based on fact. Alfred Kinsey reported in 1948 that around 40 percent of the more than 2000 married men he interviewed had at least one instance of sex with another woman during his first marriage and that most had begun such extramarital sex before the fifth year of marriage.

Kinsey also found around 20 percent of married women had at least one incident of sexual intercourse outside their marriage—a figure that created a furor when published in 1953—and more than half of these women had also begun such behavior before the seventh year of marriage.

Therefore, the data suggest that extramarital sex is more likely to occur in the fourth or fifth year than in the seventh.

Is having a bad sex life the major cause of divorce?

Based on divorce data, no. Dissatisfaction with marital sex is not a major cause of divorce. Disagreements about money, family and personal goals, how to spend nonwork hours, and other nonsexual conflicts are the most commonly stated causes of divorce.

But tension and conflict over these aspects of marital life frequently erode a couple's feelings of affection for one another, thus leading to sexual problems. If a husband and wife feel unfriendly toward each other and their sexual enjoyment is reduced, sex can become yet another topic for argument. In that way, sex can be a major contributing factor in divorce.

There is one way sex may directly cause divorce: extramarital sex. Some studies place the incidence of divorce caused by infidelity or adultery at around 20 percent of all divorce cases.

Even more enlightening are reports of research among couples who described themselves as happily married and who had never sought marital counseling or sex therapy. In one study of 100 of these self-defined "happy couples," 77 percent of the wives and 50 percent of the husbands reported sexual difficulties. It appears that when other aspects of a marriage are going well, a couple can tolerate a high level of sexual dissatisfaction without seeking a divorce.

Further Readings

Berscheid, E., and Walster, E. H. *Interpersonal Attraction* (2nd ed.). Reading, MA:
Addison-Wesley, 1978.
(A more scientifically oriented book, but one that is a classic in the field of
research on attraction.)

Blumstein, P., and Schwartz, P. *American Couples: Money, work, sex*. New York:
William Morrow and Company, 1983.
(An interesting, easy-to-read description of the results from a study of more
than 7,000 American couples including married couples, cohabiting opposite
sex couples, gay male couples, and lesbian couples.)

Huston, T. L. *Foundations of Interpersonal Attraction*. New York: Academic Press,
1974.
(A more scientifically oriented book, but one that is a classic in the field of
research on attraction.)

Kelley, H. H.; Berscheid, E.; Christensen, A.; Harvey, J. H.; Huston, T. L.;
Levinger, G.; McClintock, E.; Peplau, L. A.; and Peterson, D. R. *Close
Relationships*. New York: W. H. Freeman, 1983.
(A collection of papers on research in close relationships by leading scientists
in the field.)

Lee, J. A. *The Colors of Love: An exploration of the ways of loving*. Ontario, Canada:
New Press, 1973.
(Describes different types of romantic love, a framework which was the basis
for more recent research on love and relationships.)

Money, J. *Love and Lovesickness*. Baltimore: Johns Hopkins University Press, 1980.
(Covers a wide range of topics in human sexual development, ranging from
the determination of "maleness" and "femaleness" to the development of
pair bonding among individuals. Written for the educated layperson.)

Money, J. *Lovemaps: Clinical concepts of sexual/erotic health and pathology, paraphilias,
and gender transposition in childhood, adolescence, and maturity*. New York:
Irvington Publishers, 1986.
(Explains the development and importance of lovemaps.)

Tennov, D. *Love and Limerence: The experience of being in love*. New York: Stein &
Day, 1979.
(A book about the experience of falling in and being "in love" written in a
popular style.)

Walster, E., and Walster, G. W. *A New Look at Love*. Reading, MA: Addison-
Wesley, 1978.
(An earlier book which provided the basis for much research in the field of
love and close relationships.)

6

The Sexual Adult

Sexuality plays a profound role in our lives and has done so throughout human history. Although certainly essential to the reproduction of our species, sex also affects a person's day-to-day existence and has an important impact on society as a whole.

THE ROLE OF SEX

What is the purpose of sexuality? What does sex actually do? Sex researcher Dr. John Bancroft of the Centre for Reproductive Biology, Edinburgh, Scotland, has speculated that the nonreproductive functions of sex include strengthening of pair-bonding (a satisfying sex life may encourage a couple to stay together and raise a family), fostering intimacy between partners (important to emotional security), providing pleasure, bolstering self-esteem, and reducing tension and anxiety. In benefiting the individual and the couple, these positive functions of sex benefit society as well.

But not all functions of sex are positive. For example, while sex can be a way of positively demonstrating one's masculinity or femininity, it can become a problem if a person is bound or oppressed by rigid sexual stereotypes such as that women are not supposed to enjoy sex or that they mean yes when they say no, and that men are always supposed to initiate sex or be ready to have sex at any time. Sex is also more detrimental than beneficial when a person uses it to express hostility toward or to manipulate another, or when it is used for material gain (such as when sex is used by one partner for material gain while allowing the other partner to think it is an expression of love).

In humans, is sexual release (whether from having sex or masturbation) necessary for physical and mental well-being?

Sexual release may be psychologically necessary for some people, but abstaining from sexual activity, including masturbation, carries no known physical health risks. Some people are quite satisfied to go without sexual release for extended periods of time or even their entire lives, while others find lack of regular sexual release unsatisfactory, frustrating, or even impossible. Both reactions are considered normal in humans.

But even when a person consciously decides to forgo sexual activity, the body can create outlets for sexual release on its own. Some men and women have orgasms during sleep. For men past puberty, this is called a nocturnal emission (or wet dream); for women and for boys before puberty it is called a nocturnal orgasm.

I heard on a TV game show about a survey in which physicians were asked if it was unhealthy to go without having sex with someone for a year, and 18 percent said, yes, it was unhealthy.
Is that true? How could not having sex damage your health?

There is no scientific evidence to support the idea that abstaining from sex will make you sick, although some evidence suggests that, for many people, some type of regular sexual outlet or orgasm may be a basic element of good health. Post-menopausal women who either masturbated to orgasm or had regular sexual intercourse had much healthier external genitals, vaginal tissue, and urinary tracts than did women who had no sexual outlet at all.

Also, many physicians who treat prostate problems suggest that "feast or famine" patterns of sexual activity can increase the likelihood of prostate problems; therefore, they sometimes recommend that men have orgasms or ejaculations on a more regular basis. Of course, the prostate doesn't know whether it is being emptied by sexual intercourse with a partner or by masturbation.

It is not clear what rate of sexual activity is the "most" healthy, but it probably varies greatly from one person to the next, and for some people it may be zero.

Is having sex a good way to lose weight?

Sexual activity expends around 6.4 calories per minute during the highest preorgasmic stage and the stage immediately after orgasm. If you're seriously overweight it's probably faster to lose weight by eating a well-balanced low-fat diet and doing regular aerobic exercise.

READINESS FOR SEX

Masters and Johnson have discussed the concept of readiness for love, but I feel this idea can be expanded to include readiness for sex. A person who feels that sex is a distraction, for example, or a waste of time better spent on furthering one's career or some other pursuit, is less likely to be ready to experience the positive aspects of sex. Even a person who wants sexual release may not be ready to invest the time and effort necessary for love or commitment.

Unless a person has thought about sex and found a place for it in his or her personal system of values and ethics, there is the risk of conflict, guilt, jealousy, and other negative feelings that may outweigh the benefits of sex. Having sex with someone besides one's committed partner, for example, carries such risks unless the couple has agreed that sex with others is acceptable.

Being ready for sex includes not just knowing the facts and taking the responsibilities, but also being committed to sending and receiving messages about what is pleasurable and what is not. These messages can be carried by words or nonverbal signals—sighs, moans, winces, or moving a partner's hand away from or toward a specific place.

Before becoming sexually active, a person should have accurate information about sexually transmitted diseases and how to prevent their spread (*see Chapter 19*). Being ready for sex for heterosexuals also means being informed about how reproduction takes place (this includes knowing the effectiveness of various contraceptive methods, how to use them correctly, and *using* them if pregnancy is not desired; see Chapter 16).

Even though many of the physical responses of sex are considered automatic (male fetuses begin to have erections in the womb), other aspects of sex require some degree of learning. Learning to have orgasms and enhancing sexual satisfaction takes practice. Moreover, a person must be able to recognize the physical sensations of her or his own arousal. For many, this learning is acquired gradually during adolescence as relationships begin to include hugging, kissing, and body caresses.

Often a person who feels physically ill does not want to have sex, but may still desire nonsexual physical expressions of affection; receiving affection itself may foster recovery. People with emotional problems or depression may also be incapable of, or not interested in, sexual activity; but they too may need and benefit from nonsexual expressions of affection and love.

Other elements important to satisfying sexual interactions include personal cleanliness, comfort with one's own appearance, and a sense of self-esteem and self-worth.

Sexual readiness can also vary from one time or situation to another for the same person. These changes may have physical causes (such as fluctuations of the hormone cycle) or psychological causes (the stress of meeting a deadline at work).

How can I become more lovable? To me, sex is dirty. My boyfriend can't understand me.

You need to find someone besides your boyfriend to help you sort out your feelings about sex. Most communities have a mental health center; call and ask for an appointment with the person most experienced in treating sexual aversion or sexual inhibition.

You don't give your age or any information about your personal situation, so it is impossible to suggest what might be involved in your negative feelings about sex. However, the types of problems that can be related to such feelings range from parental teachings that sex is bad to prior physical or sexual abuse during childhood or by a partner (rape).

Do you enjoy physical closeness, such as hugging and kissing, at all? Do you remember ever feeling sexually aroused? The answers to these and similar questions will permit a skilled counselor to determine the extent of your negative feelings about sex and how best to help you to manage these feelings.

The goal of counseling isn't to make you have sex. The goal is to help you

Illustration No. 10. This painting of sexual intimacy is one of Paul Becat's illustrations for a 1930s edition of John Clelland's eighteenth-century erotic novel *Fanny Hill*. Face-to-face intercourse with the male on top is commonly known as the missionary position (see page 123).

PAUL BECAT. Illustration for *Fanny Hill*. 1930s. Gouache, 5¹⁄₁₀″ x 3½″. The Kinsey Institute Collections.

discover why you feel the way you do and then to decide how best to manage sexuality given your personal situation and values. For example, it may be that having sex with this particular boyfriend right now conflicts with other nonsexual goals such as going to school or seeking a better job. Or maybe all you need is accurate information about sexual functioning so you'll know that experiencing sexual feelings is a normal, physical process.

When you do decide you're ready to engage in sexual activity, behavior therapy has proved helpful at gradually decreasing a person's negative reactions in cases of sexual aversion. Whatever is involved in your particular case, see a professional counselor or therapist: It's unlikely that you can solve this on your own.

I've always heard that men's "sexual peak" is at age 18, while women's "sexual peak" is age 35. Is this true? And if so, is there a biological reason for this?

I've often suspected this is a myth used by younger men as an excuse for "sowing their wild oats." And besides, I'm 35 and don't see any "sexual peak" happening to me and my friends.

If you're counting orgasms, there is scientific evidence to support the idea that women's sexual peak is later than men's. Most young men during adolescence and their early twenties report more frequent orgasms than men in older age groups. This includes orgasms from all sources—nocturnal emissions, masturbation, and intercourse. These younger men also have very short refractory periods, in some cases requiring only a few minutes between one orgasm and the next.

Women in general, on the other hand, experience their highest numbers of orgasms from their mid-twenties to mid-forties.

But neither of these statistics says anything about how often a man or woman would like to have sex or how much they are enjoying it. In fact, women often have intercourse more frequently in their early twenties (theoretically, because it's more often initiated by their male partners) than they do in their forties, but they have more orgasms in their older years. That's because they're more likely to be easily orgasmic after they've had more sexual experience.

There has been much speculation as to why this apparent orgasmic difference between the sexes exists. The idea that orgasm rate is governed by hormonal levels doesn't explain the difference because at puberty hormonal levels are high in both sexes, but only males exhibit higher orgasmic frequencies compared to later in life.

It appears that orgasm rates for women may be related more to psychology than to biology. Many women must learn how to have orgasms and might reach high frequencies only when they feel secure about their sexuality and relationships. And most Western cultures don't encourage women to lose their sexual inhibitions during their youth or to practice having orgasms.

As women become older and learn more about their sexual capacity, the sexual patterns of those with older male partners may also change to include longer periods of stimulation before erection and more thrusting before ejaculation. This slowing in male arousal and response patterns may increase the likelihood of orgasm for some women due to longer foreplay and intercourse.

It is important to understand that individual men and women may have orgasm patterns that are very different from the averages reported for large surveys of men and women.

SEXUAL RESPONSE

One might suppose that sexual response would be simple: breathless excitement, followed by an explosive orgasm, and finally a tranquil afterglow. But sexual responses in both females and males are actually a complicated, and easily disrupted, process involving many different psychological factors and physical processes. (*See Illustrations 11 and 12.*)

We've already discussed ways in which a person must be in a state of readiness for sex. The next phase of sexual response is called **sexual arousal** or **excitement** (often called feeling "turned on" or "hot.")

A type of sexual appetite (similar to being hungry for food) must exist or be created for arousal to take place. Sexual appetite may be the result of thinking about sex; encountering the smells, sights, or touches a person interprets as sexual; or receiving or giving a signal that sex is desired.

Physical changes accompany mental arousal. The nervous system sends messages to certain centers of the brain, causing measurable changes in the body. For example, blood pressure rises and heartbeat and breathing rates alter.

Messages also send blood to the genitals, alter muscle tension, and increase skin sensitivity, among other physical changes. A person's ability to sense and identify these physical changes as signs of sexual arousal actually contributes to the arousal process.

As the level of sexual arousal increases in females, vaginal lubrication begins, the inner two-thirds of the vagina expands, the outer lips of the vulva open, the inner lips enlarge, and the clitoris swells. In males, the penis fills with blood and becomes erect and the testicles draw closer to the body. In both sexes these physical changes are due to vasocongestion (increased blood in the tissues of the genitals and the female breasts). Nipples may also become erect in both sexes.

Much of the research on sexual responses has been done by Masters and Johnson (and many of the details in this section come from their book *Human Sexuality*). They call the next stage of response the **plateau phase**. Arousal intensifies, and sexual and muscular tension increases. In both sexes heart rate, breathing rate, and blood pressure increase. A "sex flush" that looks like a rash sometimes appears on the skin covering the chest, neck, or other areas of the body.

In females, the outer one-third of the vagina swells and narrows the opening (the physiological reason that penis size is not important; if arousal is high enough, the vagina will grip even a shorter or thinner-than-average penis). The inner two-thirds of the vagina tents or balloons up, lifting the uterus and cervix away from the end of the vagina. The clitoris pulls closer to the pubic bone and is often covered by the enlarged labia. The inner lips may become two or three times thicker than when not sexually aroused and a darker or brighter color. The areolae surrounding the nipples may swell, sometimes making nipples look less erect, and the breasts may increase in size.

The plateau stage in males may include an increase in the size of the head of the penis and the testicles. The head of the penis may also deepen in color. The testicles move closer to the body and rotate, so they press close to the area beween the scrotum and anus. Clear fluid may appear at the tip of the penis (pre-ejaculatory fluid).

If nothing interferes with this physiological process (for example, if the phone doesn't ring, the baby doesn't cry, no pain or discomfort occurs, guilty or frightening thoughts don't pop into mind, or the partners don't start worrying about whether or not they are going to have orgasms) and each person feels secure enough to "let go," **orgasm** will usually occur.

Orgasm lasts only a few seconds (in contrast to the other stages, which can last for minutes or even hours) and consists of rhythmic muscular contractions. The mind focuses on experiencing these pleasurable sensations and the person may appear briefly to "black out" or lose consciousness; brain-wave patterns have been shown to change during orgasm. Involuntary vocal sounds and changes in facial expression may also occur.

The intensity of orgasm differs from person to person and from one time to the next for the same person. Muscular contractions, for example, can range from a slight throb in the genitals to involuntary thrashing or rigidity of the entire body. What counts is how a person *feels* about the orgasm. If a person feels pleasure and satisfaction by a less dramatically obvious orgasm, that's just fine. Comparisons, or seeking "better" orgasms, may only result in dissatisfaction or even disruption of the natural physical progress to orgasm.

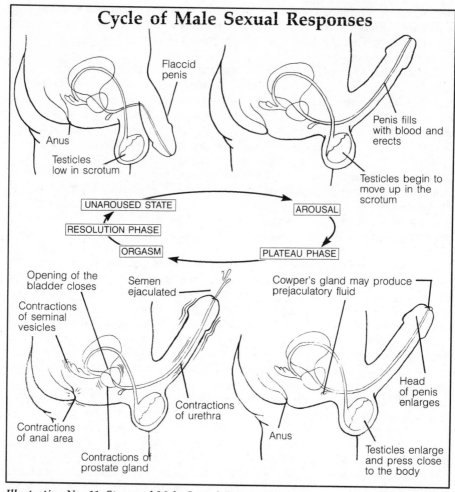

Cycle of Male Sexual Responses

Flaccid penis

Anus

Testicles low in scrotum

Penis fills with blood and erects

Testicles begin to move up in the scrotum

UNAROUSED STATE

AROUSAL

RESOLUTION PHASE

ORGASM

PLATEAU PHASE

Opening of the bladder closes

Contractions of seminal vesicles

Semen ejaculated

Cowper's gland may produce prejaculatory fluid

Contractions of anal area

Contractions of urethra

Contractions of prostate gland

Anus

Head of penis enlarges

Testicles enlarge and press close to the body

Illustration No. 11. **Stages of Male Sexual Response.** These four side views of a man's external and internal organs show the changes that take place during the four stages of sexual response.

For females, orgasm consists of three to ten muscular contractions (less than one second apart) of the outer one-third of the vagina, the uterus, and the anal area. Pleasant sensations may be felt in the clitoris and throughout the genital and pelvic area.

In males, orgasm includes two separate and distinct events, even though in many men they occur at the same time. First, the prostate and other internal glands (*see Illustration 11*) contract and force their fluids into the base (the inside end) of the urethra; this is sometimes called "emission". Once this has occurred, ejaculation is inevitable and cannot be stopped. Several seconds later, orgasm involving contractions of the penis and the urethra force the semen out through

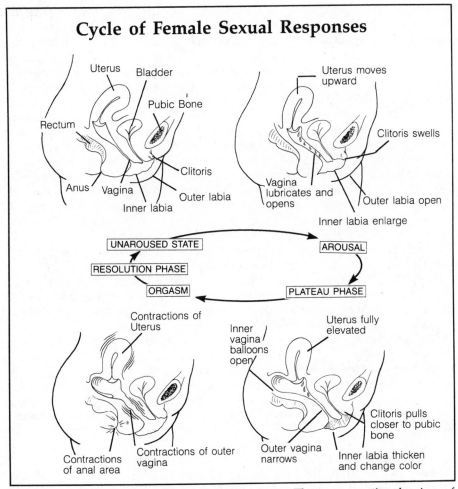

Cycle of Female Sexual Responses

Illustration No. 12. **Stages of Female Sexual Response.** These cross-section drawings of a woman's external and internal organs show the changes that take place during the four stages of sexual response.

the tip of the penis in spurts. As in females, these contractions are less than one second apart, also involve muscles surrounding the anus, and may be felt in other genital or pelvic areas.

The final phase of sexual response is called the **resolution phase.** This immediately follows orgasm and consists of the time it takes for the body to return to its **unaroused state.** Blood leaves the genital area and organs gradually shift back to their original positions, size, and color. Any "sex flush" disappears; sweating may occur; heart rate and breathing slow; and blood pressure returns to the normal level. The length of time required for the resolution phase varies.

There are differences between males and females during the resolution phase.

If stimulation and sexual interest continue after orgasm, some females have the potential to reenter the plateau stage and have another orgasm; this may happen more than once and is referred to as multiple orgasms. But just because the theoretical capacity for multiple orgasms exists does not mean that trying to have them should be a goal or a measure of "good sex" for either the woman or her partner. In fact, many women find continued stimulation of the genitals after one orgasm uncomfortable.

In contrast, after orgasm most males enter a "refractory period." This may last only a few minutes or much longer; and even though penile erection may remain, another orgasm is usually not possible until the refractory period ends. A very recent study of a small group of men has, however, documented that at least some males may be similar to females and be able to have multiple orgasms, and sometimes multiple ejaculations, if stimulation continues after the first orgasm. The length of the refractory period varies greatly from one man to another, and had been thought to increase to hours or even to days as a man aged. The new study also brings this issue into question, since half the men in the study began having multiple orgasms (and hence no refractory period) after age 35. More research is needed on male orgasm.

The sexual responses described above occur in males and females whether the activity that produces them is masturbation, interaction with an opposite-sex or same-sex partner, or stimulation by hand, mouth, tongue, or other activity.

[NOTE: The above descriptions of sexual responses should not be used as a "check list" against which to measure your own sexual performance or that of partners. Moreover, the descriptions are about what happens physically when everything is working perfectly. Distractions, fatigue, or being insufficiently aroused (among many other factors) can contribute to having a less-than-perfect sexual response. And, in fact, even these experiences can be very satisfying if the person or his or her partner doesn't demand or expect perfection every time.]

I am a healthy male, 29, with no apparent sexual problems. However, I do not produce any pre-ejaculate fluid during arousal, erection, or foreplay. Is this normal in some males and not in others? Is it possible to encourage my body to produce this?

Kinsey found that around 30 percent of men did not have pre-ejaculatory fluid at all; around 25 percent made one drop, 10 percent two drops, and the rest made a bit more. It seems that having fluid appear before ejaculation is normal and that *not* having this fluid appear is also normal.

This fluid comes from the Cowper's glands (two small glands the size and shape of peas located near the prostate gland—see Illustration 5 in Chapter 3) and maybe from other nearby glands. Their secretions enter the urethra (the tube that carries urine and semen through the penis) near the base of the penis. During arousal, fluids from various sex organs are pooled near the prostate and become mixed together. Presumably, men who do not have any pre-ejaculatory fluid still make fluid in their Cowper's glands but it mixes with the other components of semen at the time of ejaculation and doesn't leave the penis in advance.

I'm not sure why you think it's important to have this fluid, unless you hoped it would contribute to lubrication for sexual intercourse. If that's the case, try putting a small amount of a water-soluble lubricant on your penis just before penetration, or prolong foreplay so that your female partner has adequate time and stimulation to produce more vaginal lubrication.

Why is it necessary for the female to have an orgasm? The male orgasm is an important step in reproduction, implanting the sperm in the vagina. How does female orgasm fit into reproduction?

As yet, there is no complete answer. Some researchers say that the rhythmic vaginal contractions of female orgasm may make it more likely that sperm will swim through the cervix, the pathway between the upper end of the vagina and the uterus. This theory, however, is disputed by other researchers. (Remember that, contrary to myth, a woman can become pregnant whether or not she has an orgasm.)

Other experts suggest a more subtle connection between female orgasm and reproduction. They speculate that if a woman enjoys intercourse as a result of having orgasms, then she and her partner will have intercourse more frequently, thereby increasing the chances of pregnancy.

As for your idea that the male orgasm is an important step in reproduction, understand that ejaculation and orgasm are two separate events and only the ejaculation relates to reproduction. A man can experience ejaculation without orgasm and orgasm without ejaculation. It's possible that the theory explaining the female orgasm's relationship to reproduction can also be applied to the male orgasm: If it feels good, it's an experience worth repeating, which increases the chances of conception.

Is it true that if a female doesn't have an orgasm before her first period, she may never be able to have one?

No, it is not true. There is no established age at which women must experience their first orgasm; nor is there any age past which a first orgasm is not possible.

About 23 percent of women have experienced their first orgasm by age 15 and 90 percent by age 35. These figures include orgasm from masturbation, a partner's manual and/or oral stimulation of the genitals, nocturnal dreams, fantasy, and other sources—not just intercourse.

Please explain what happens when a woman has an orgasm, what her body does and how she can tell if she has ever had one?

There are still no standard measures or descriptions of the feeling of having an orgasm. (Some people use *climaxing* or *coming* instead of orgasm.) In many cases it is difficult to decide if a woman is describing an orgasm or a preorgasmic state.

Even though researchers can measure and document various physiological changes associated with arousal and orgasm, only the woman herself can interpret when those changes become an orgasm. That's because the mind is still the best indicator of sexual fulfillment. If a woman thinks she has had an orgasm and is satisfied with her sexual life, there's no reason for her to see a sex therapist for verification just because she doesn't experience, for example, a skin flush or nipple erection.

I have read that women must learn how to have orgasms. I am 36 and began to have orgasms spontaneously in my early teens. (By spontaneously I mean waking up having an orgasm from a dream. The dream didn't even have to be overtly sexual.) I masturbated to orgasm during high school and was a virgin until my second year of college.

I've never really discussed this with other women, but I'd always assumed that becoming sexually responsive and experiencing orgasms was just a normal part of puberty. I certainly was never "taught" to have orgasms or felt that any teaching was necessary. Am I abnormal, or are the researchers off the wall?

Neither. When sex researchers talk about orgasm as a "learned response" they mean that each individual goes through a learning process. This begins when a person notices which physical and psychological stimulation cause sexual arousal and orgasm. If that first orgasm is pleasurable, he or she repeats the activities that produced the orgasm, which explains why masturbation techniques differ from one person to the next.

It is precisely because orgasm is a learned response that therapy programs can successfully treat many sexual dysfunctions. Women who have never had an orgasm, for instance, can learn about their bodies' responses to various types of stimulation and increase their ability to have orgasms. Similarly, men who experience orgasm too quickly can learn to monitor their arousal more closely and slow their orgasmic response.

Many women report experiences similar to yours; among orgasmic women, nearly 60 percent report that they "discovered" orgasms by themselves. The first orgasmic experience often occurs during puberty but can also happen earlier or later.

Only about 25 percent of boys, however, discover orgasm by themselves. Seventy percent find out about masturbation and orgasm when the experience is described by others, usually friends. Boys are likely to talk about this topic among themselves, while most girls do not.

Why do some women's legs shake and then get weak during climax?

For the same reason that some men's legs do. Muscle tension that is gradually built up during sexual arousal is released suddenly at orgasm, followed by muscular relaxation.

Each person exhibits and experiences these muscular responses differently. In some, the tension in the legs is more noticeable and may include trembling or spasmodic jerking. People can't consciously control these physical reactions, especially near or at orgasm, and many are not even aware of their reactions at this time.

Is it normal for a female having a climax to giggle? It is so bad that you are afraid the children, or neighbors, will hear you. When I have a climax I laugh the whole time.

Although there are no data on how many people react this way, we do know it's not unusual for women and men to involuntarily vocalize (moaning or calling out, for example) during orgasm. Giggling would also be included in this category of normal involuntary behavior.

For many years now, when I experience a particularly intense orgasm, when I feel a certain tenderness from and toward the person I am making love to, when the orgasm has subsided, I often cry. I thought I had read about the phenomena called "homo triste," but no one I've told this to, and no books I have ever read discuss this.

Do you know of other women to whom this happens? I don't particularly think this is a problem: I always explain it to the person that I am with, that this is likely to happen and it in no way reflects on the experience or the person. In fact, I'm not even sure this experience comes from a place of sadness. Am I the only woman who does this?

Homo triste comes from an anonymous writing often attributed to Galen, a second-century Greek physician and writer: *Post coitum omne animal triste* ("All animals are sad after intercourse"). But crying also can be associated with joy, so it isn't correct to assume tears indicate sadness either about the sexual experience or a partner.

The Kinsey Institute library could find no studies investigating crying after orgasm, but there are clinical reports about the wide range of emotions experienced after sexual climax, which can include joy, sadness, peacefulness, and relief. Intense emotion, including laughing or crying, can be a sign of an especially wonderful sexual climax.

If emotions after sex pose any problem at all, it's when two partners have different ideas about what should happen next. It can diminish sexual satisfaction if, for example, one person falls asleep or goes to get something to eat while the other person wants to cuddle or to be close.

All this only underscores the fact that sexuality is more than a mechanical coupling between two bodies: In sexual satisfaction, the mind plays the most important role.

Generally after having sexual relations I sleep for two to four hours. Why?

Probably because you're tired or relaxed. Many people go to sleep after sex; others feel more energized. Several variables are involved: People who have sex just before their usual bedtime are more likely to go to sleep than those who have sex at some other time of day, and people who have an orgasm are more likely to sleep than those who do not.

Another factor may be each individual's history of masturbation. People who have used masturbation as a form of relaxation before falling asleep may also be more likely to fall asleep after having sex with a partner.

The point is that falling asleep after sex is neither "right" nor "wrong." It's just another area of normal differences among people.

Maybe I haven't read enough sex manuals, but it seems the subject of women's ejaculations is rarely discussed. I ejaculate in perhaps one out of ten orgasms,

most often during masturbation. I should add that I am a 62-year-old woman, and this has been occurring only for the last eight or ten years. These orgasms are more intense by far than my nonejaculatory ones. Is this unusual? Have you any data on the percentage of women who ejaculate?

It is not clear how many women expel fluid at orgasm. Some researchers report that nearly 40 percent of women questioned had at least one ejaculation at orgasm, while others have found a much smaller percentage.

There is also disagreement over the source of this fluid and whether it is urine or a specialized secretion from vaginal glands. But regardless of what scientists eventually decide, it is important to realize that what happens to you is normal for you and does happen to other women. There is nothing to be uncomfortable about when this happens—just bring a towel to bed and reassure your partner that it's normal for you.

While researchers debate about female ejaculation, writers of erotic stories continue to emphasize the wonders of female ejaculation as they have done for centuries. Although female ejaculation is a frequent theme in sexual fiction, it isn't as common as one might conclude from such stories, and when it does happen the amount of fluid isn't as copious as these tales would have us believe.

INDIVIDUAL SEXUAL BEHAVIORS

Involuntary Sexual Behavior

Some sexual behaviors involve only oneself and no one else. These include automatic, or involuntary, behaviors—ones a person cannot consciously control. For example, episodes of arousal (including vaginal swelling and lubrication in females and erection in males) occur several times each night (approximately every 90 minutes), usually but not always during one specific stage of sleep called REM (Rapid Eye Movement). Ejaculation (in males past puberty called a nocturnal emission or "wet dream") and orgasm (called a nocturnal orgasm in females and in males before puberty) can also occur automatically during sleep.

I read that the clitoris functions on the same principle as the penis. Does that mean it goes through nocturnal episodes as does the male organ?

Yes, both males and females exhibit physical signs of sexual arousal during certain periods of sleep. Although the clitoris does swell during REM sleep, researchers studying sleep arousal in women usually measure vaginal lubrication instead, a more easily documented sign of arousal. Neither males nor females have direct control over these automatic responses during sleep.

I would like to know the physiology aspects of "wet dreams" for women. Even though I'm a 55-year-old woman, I admit there are many things I don't know or understand about my body.

I haven't engaged in intercourse for more than five years, because I have no partner, but from time to time I enjoy the most intense nocturnal orgasms. I wake up extremely aroused, sexually, and my clitoris and genitals very sensitive. Yet I know I have not actually touched myself physically during the experience.

These orgasms during sleep seem more intense than any I ever experienced during intercourse and I have wondered how the thought and the brain can produce such a pleasant phenomenon.
PS: I do not dream of intercourse when this occurs.

Nobody is yet sure how or why the brain and body produce the signs of sexual arousal and sometimes orgasm during sleep, but it is estimated that 80 percent of men and 40 percent of women have had at least one such nocturnal orgasm, with peak rates for men occurring in their twenties and for women in their forties.

Some sexual responses (erection in men, vaginal swelling and lubrication in women) occur regularly during sleep and may or may not involve a sexual dream. One theory is that these responses are simply a check to make sure a person's brain, nervous system, and genitals are healthy and in good working order.

I understand that most physically normal men have two to five erections a night during the REM stage of sleep. My husband and I are both 23. I began watching my husband on some nights when he slept.
You were definitely right. My husband and I have a good sex life, so that's not the problem. But I've begun getting bugged about all this because it seems to me that my husband would have to be dreaming of sex or other situations, possibly with other women, to cause the erections.
Well, to be honest with you, my sexual desires have been dampened. I've spoken with my husband and he says he can't remember his dreams. But if this is really an involuntary reflex, why does it only occur during the dreaming stage?

You're wrong to assume that your husband is dreaming about sex. In clinical studies, men were awakened during periods of sleep while they had erections and asked the content of their dreams. Only rarely did the men report erotic or sexual dreams. So even if your husband did recall a dream, it is not likely that it would involve sexual activity.

A man can't always control his erection reflex even when he's awake and has no control at all over his erections during sleep. Erections require a combination of events in the brain, nervous system, blood system, muscles, and body chemicals. In animals scientists have noted that electrical impulses to certain sections of the brain trigger a reflex erection. They theorize that a similar link between brain and genital reactions exists in humans.

Measurements of brain activity taken during sleep show bursts of various types of brain waves occurring during REM periods. These are accompanied by measurable changes in the body, including increased pulse and breathing rates, changes in eye movement, and changes in the skin's electrical resistance. All these signals indicate arousal of the nervous system.

Researchers have found the same kind of arousal responses in women by measuring changes in the genitals during sleep. Are you aware of having sexual dreams during these automatic, regular, and natural periods of genital changes in your sleep?

One other finding might be of interest to you. Some scientists wondered if the number or intensity of nocturnal erections increased if a man had not recently had intercourse or said he was not satisfied with his sexual outlets. They found that sleep erections were not related to the frequency, amount, or quality of sexual intercourse.

So there's really no need to feel jealous. Your husband's sleep erections are probably not related to sexual dreams but are simply a sign that his brain and body are healthy. And even if they were related to sexual dreams, people can't consciously control their dreams, either. But they can control their jealous impulses—perhaps that's what you should be focusing on. If you think your jealousy is related to feeling insecure about yourself or your marriage, perhaps counseling would be reassuring.

I'm in my 30s. Almost every morning when waking up I have a strong erection. It's kind of bothering me, especially if I don't have time to "cool down" before going out. Is there anything I can do to stop this?

No, or at least there is no safe way to prevent morning erections that wouldn't jeopardize your sexual functioning at other times.

Until the 1970s it was thought that morning erections were caused by a full bladder, since they frequently disappear when the man awakens and urinates. Subsequent research has shown that these morning erections result from abrupt awakening during the last cycle of REM sleep and are simply the last erection of the night's sleep. If your morning erections really bother you that much, consider using an alarm clock with a "snooze" option, which may allow your brain time to reduce the erection before you are fully awake.

Look at the positive side: Waking up with an erection is one sign of a man's general good physical and psychological health. In fact, men who are ill or under a great deal of psychological stress have greatly reduced amounts of erection time during sleep, and men with serious erectile problems caused by diseases such as diabetes may have no sleep erections. The reduced or absent erections during sleep, as verified in a sleep laboratory, are indications that a man's erection problems are probably caused by physical, not psychological, factors.

We also know that the time most men have their highest levels of testosterone (a hormone necessary for sexual functioning) occurs during the early morning hours, which also may contribute to these morning erections. Theoretically, you could probably do away with your morning erections by taking hormones that counteract the effect of testosterone, but the likely result would also be that you would have a reduced sex drive and few, if any, erections at all. There are other possible negative side effects as well.

I am a 24-year-old male. Admittedly, I have been under pressure recently in my work and my sex life has been next to nonexistent lately. Given these factors, why do I often have "wet dreams"? I find it hard to believe that this is normal.

It is not yet clear what causes nocturnal emissions, but we do know that they are normal for many boys and men (Kinsey found that 83 percent of males had at least one such experience), and they cannot be consciously controlled.

But you are not alone in your concern. In a 1983 study of male reactions to nocturnal emissions, many of the college men surveyed felt that this experience represented a loss of control over their sexual behavior, was sinful, or was psychologically traumatic. The study found that these men had never been told that nocturnal emissions are a part of normal, healthy functioning, and some of them had unsuccessfully tried to stop themselves from having them.

There has been much speculation about what factors may increase or decrease nocturnal emissions. Researchers theorized that having other sexual outlets (such as orgasms from masturbation or intercourse) might reduce the rate of nocturnal emissions. This appears to be true for some men, but not for all.

Sexual Fantasy

Another type of sex behavior that can be considered involuntary to some extent is having sexual fantasies. Although some people can consciously control when they fantasize and the content of these thoughts, others cannot. There are a few instances when the fantasy itself becomes powerful enough to control or affect a person's behavior. Not everyone has sexual fantasies, but researchers have generally reported that both men and women do have them.

Sexual fantasies have several beneficial functions. They can provide a type of safe rehearsal for sexual behavior one has not yet experienced (imagining what one might do or say if a sexual opportunity presented itself may be of great importance to adolescents, for example) or a safe way to experience sexual situations that an individual would *never* actually do.

Fantasies can be a type of daydreaming, permitting a brief escape from the demands of real life, or they can be used to increase sexual arousal before and during masturbation or sex with a partner. They may also act as a type of safety valve to release tensions caused by questions, doubts, or guilt about sex behavior.

Sexual fantasies can be deliberately conjured up or may simply pop into one's mind with or without being related to a specific sexual stimulus.

The content of sexual fantasies varies enormously and often includes imagining activities, sexual partners, or situations that a person has never experienced. Some men report that they might try their "unusual" fantasies (such as sadomasochistic sexual encounters) if the opportunity presented itself, but most women say they would not want to carry out their more unusual fantasies. The person literally acts as the "director" of these types of fantasies, and thus can give every "story" a satisfying ending or stop the fantasy if it becomes disturbing.

Some people repeat the same fantasy "plot" again and again (perhaps having learned that it can be depended upon to increase sexual arousal or to move from the plateau stage to orgasm). Others change the content of their fantasies quite often (perhaps because novelty enhances arousal for them).

Sexual fantasies are private, enhancing, safe experiences for most people. A few individuals, however, become quite anxious or fearful because they believe that having a specific fantasy is some type of warning that they may actually act out the behavior in real life or be mentally ill. Because many fantasies involve behaviors a person would normally condemn as illegal, dangerous, or outside their value system, it is easy to understand why some people might feel guilt and concern about their fantasies. Nevertheless, having any particular fantasy is, by itself, generally not seen as an indication that a person has a psychological problem or personality disorder.

Some psychologists and psychiatrists believe that having erotic fantasies can, in some few cases, interfere with relationships or produce sexual difficulties, for example when a specific fantasy becomes absolutely necessary for sexual arousal and a person can no longer respond to his or her real-life partner or situation. Psychological counseling can help a person "turn off" distressing fantasies or resolve problems created if fantasies begin to intrude into real life.

I'm a 40-year-old married man who often thinks about sex—and by often I mean every few minutes (at the grocery store, watching TV, wherever and whenever). I'm happily married and wouldn't act on any of these thoughts, but is it normal to think about sex so often?

If I do it this much, how often does a teenage boy (with a higher sex drive) have these thoughts?

The few impressionistic studies which asked a handful of males about this topic found that many think about sex at a surprisingly regular frequency. And there does seem to be a decline with increased age.

When asked if sex had "crossed their mind" in the last five minutes, 51 percent of 16- and 17-year-old males studied said yes, as did 20 percent of males aged 40 to 55. For 14 percent of the 16- and 17-year-old males and 4 percent of the 40- to 55-year-old men, sex had been the central focus of their thoughts in the preceding five minutes.

In another study, males aged 12 to 19 estimated they thought about sex every five minutes; 40- to 49-year-old men said they thought about sex every half-hour.

I'm a sexually active male and would like to know if it's OK to fantasize during masturbation. Since childhood I've been taught to love and respect women, but seem to get much pleasure arousing myself while looking at photos of nude females in magazines. I also enjoy very intense orgasms if I masturbate while looking at nude photographs of movie and TV actresses which are sometimes included in the pictorials.

I'm sure there are many other male readers who share this dilemma.

The vast majority of both men and women have had erotic fantasies, so you are not alone. Erotic fantasies are most common during masturbation, but many people also fantasize while they are having sex with a partner. In one study, 71 percent of men and 72 percent of women said they had fantasized while with partners to enhance sexual arousal.

The content of sexual fantasies is wide-ranging but, generally speaking, the most common fantasies involve sexual activity one has never engaged in or sexual partners other than one's own. You'll be reassured to find out that celebrities are often reported as favorite fantasy partners. Masters and Johnson reported that heterosexuals often fantasize about homosexual encounters and vice versa and that this reflects curiosity rather than a suppressed desire to change the sex of one's real-life sexual partners. Most people state clearly that they have no desire to act out their sexual fantasies.

I'm a woman who considers myself to be quite secure, confident, and assertive in my dealings with others. My husband and I still have a mutually exciting

and satisfying sex life after nearly 20 years together. I am not hesitant about hinting when I'd like to have sex or about making the first move, but during intercourse itself I usually fantasize that I am being forced to have sex with a gangster, pirate, or other intimidating sort of man—which I end up enjoying.

Does this mean that I secretly want to be raped? I'm especially worried because this story line matches what I've read is supposed to be a common male myth—that women who are raped secretly enjoy it.

No, the fantasy you describe does not mean that you want to be raped, and is actually quite common among women. This kind of fantasy can be particularly distressing to women who value equality in relationships.

Several researchers have pointed out that fantasies that include elements of force may be one way of absolving oneself from the responsibility of initiating sex. It can also be a way to avoid feeling guilty about enjoying sexual pleasure. Some men also report fantasies of being forced to have sex against their will.

Many males do report fantasies that involve forcing a woman to have sex but are quite clear in their minds that in real life they would not commit rape.

Is it true that all men have some homosexual desires? At age 58, I started to get homosexual fantasies. Four years later I still have them, even though I have never had a relationship with a man. As each year passes, it keeps getting stronger and stronger—the desire, that is. Trying to research this subject, I came up with a blank. Is this something that happens to older men? I still have sex with my wife, so why am I having these homosexual desires?

One research project investigating men's sexual fantasies reported that fantasies about homosexual activities are among the most common fantasies revealed by heterosexual males. Also, most people have no intention of acting out their fantasies; they simply use them to induce or intensify sexual pleasure. Perhaps this is what you are experiencing.

Much of the research on homosexuality reports that most homosexual men recognize their attraction to partners of the same sex before or during adolescence. Recent data, however, reveal that for some men, sexual interest in other men does not emerge until adulthood. This awareness of same-sex attraction at older ages is more common among female homosexuals (lesbians).

If your feelings are causing guilt or anxiety that intrude on your ability to live a happy life, talk with a counselor or a therapist who is trained in dealing with human sexuality (see Appendix). These professionals can help clients sort out feelings and determine whether their thoughts are just sexual fantasies or are related to their sexual partner orientation.

I am a 34-year-old widower with a 14-year-old daughter. I lost my beloved wife two years ago; our marriage was nearly perfect in every way. I have not had a sexual partner since her death, but do masturbate about once a month when the sexual tension becomes unbearable.

My daughter and I are extremely close and she is very affectionate. About once a week we try to spend an entire day together of pure, glorious fun, with things like going to the beach, hiking, or skiing, or whatever.

Invariably that same night I will have a wet dream involving my daughter.

This sounds very, very sick, I know. However, I do not ever think of her in a sexual way during waking hours. I swear this is true.

What can I do to stop this? I'm aware I have guilt feelings about sex because around age 14 when I began to have wet dreams, my mother discovered the dried semen and accused me of masturbating. This was traumatic and it was not until much later that I was told that wet dreams are normal and natural.

Your experience is not unusual and it shouldn't be cause for alarm. Nearly all men and about 70 percent of women are thought to have sexual dreams. It is also not unusual for the content to contain acts or sexual partners that the person would never consider when awake. Often a daytime feeling like affection will acquire a sexual portrayal in a dream.

Nocturnal emissions (more commonly referred to as wet dreams) are also common, especially for young men and previously married men with no other sexual outlet. The emissions cannot be consciously controlled any more than one can control the content of a dream.

Because this distresses you and because sorting out feelings about sex can be very complicated, you might consider talking with a psychologist or psychiatrist who has experience in the area of guilt about sexual feelings. This person can reassure you that these dreams are not an indication that you want to or might commit incest.

But there's another reason to seek help: It may be important to your daughter's healthy psychosocial development as well. Children have an uncanny ability to perceive the emotions of adults. It is possible your concerns have caused you to unconsciously change your behavior toward your daughter, by becoming less affectionate, for example. She may interpret this to mean that you care for her less or disapprove of her in some way.

For this reason, the therapist may want to talk with your daughter and check whether she may need a little extra support as well. Adolescence can be an emotionally difficult time even with two loving parents.

I'm a male in my 20s and need some information about an unusual fantasy that worries me. For some time I've had the desire to be diapered like a baby. I swear this is all true. The thought of wearing diapers and even rubber pants is a turn-on.

I've never told anyone about this because I'm afraid of what they'll think, but my worst feeling is that I'm the only person who has these thoughts.

Has anyone else ever had this fantasy? Is this a problem? I don't know where else to ask these questions.

No one is certain how many people have which particular fantasies or why, but yours would not be seen as a problem unless it is interfering with your ability to establish relationships or to function sexually.

If you change from fantasizing about wearing diapers to actually needing to put on diapers to become aroused to have sex, then the behavior would be characterized as a fetish. (*Fetishes are discussed in Chapter 7.*)

Masturbation

The most important things to know about masturbation are that the vast majority of people do it and that, unless a person uses an extraordinarily rough or violent technique, masturbation does not cause any kind of physical harm. Letters to the institute indicate the main problems associated with masturbation are psychological: the guilt and anxiety among some people who masturbate and then struggle with feelings that masturbation is harmful in some way. If that's the case for you, consider talking with a counselor to help sort out your feelings.

Is masturbation bad for your health?
No. It might even be helpful.
Does masturbation cause pimples?
No.
Does masturbation affect your capacity to become a mother or father?
No.
Does masturbation cause insanity?
No.
Can masturbation permanently enlarge your penis size?
No.
Can masturbation permanently shrink or shorten your penis?
No.
Does masturbation change the shape or curve of your penis?
No.
Does masturbation permanently alter the size, shape, or color of any part of the female genitals?
No.
Does masturbation cause disease?
No.
Does masturbation as a teenager reduce your ability to respond sexually with a partner later in life?
No.
Is there anything wrong with *not* masturbating?
No.

I have a personal question to ask you. Is masturbation harmful to your health?

No, masturbation doesn't appear to be harmful to either physical or mental health.

Among the thousands of people interviewed by Kinsey during the 1940s and 1950s, 94 percent of males and 40 percent of females reported having masturbated to orgasm. More recent studies report that about the same percentage of males masturbate but that the percentage of females has increased to around 70 percent (or more, depending on the study).

Masturbation frequency varies greatly. Some people masturbate more or less frequently as circumstances in their lives change; others masturbate at the same rate regardless of whether they're also having other types of sexual activity. It also appears that no two people use exactly the same technique— which may explain why sexual adjustment for couples usually requires explaining one's own personal preferences about the types of stimulation that feel best and taking the time to learn about a partner's likes and dislikes.

There is some scientific evidence that women who have a history of masturbating to orgasm are more likely to more easily experience orgasm later in sexual activities with a partner. In fact, treatment programs for anorgasmic women (women who have never had an orgasm by any means) are structured around the concept of first learning how to masturbate to orgasm and then moving on to having orgasms in interactions with a partner.

On the other hand, some men and women develop habitual ways of masturbating (for example, squeezing the thighs together) on which they become dependent for orgasm. Then they may have a problem incorporating those techniques into lovemaking with their partners.

I've always had this problem of masturbation. I'm 23 years old and I've been masturbating ever since I can remember. I've never had a problem with women and I've always had a healthy sexual relationship with my girlfriends.

I'm very concerned now because I found out that heavy masturbation causes a male to become sterile and lack fertile sperm to reproduce after years of masturbation. I'm very worried because I always wanted a family. Is this true? If so, does this mean I'm sterile for life?

There are no data to support the notion that masturbation leads to sterility. This fear is based on the widespread *false* idea that a man is born with a fixed number of sperm and that if he has many ejaculations early in life he will use them up. *This is not true.*

Males begin to manufacture sperm when their testicles mature at puberty and continue to produce viable sperm, capable of fertilizing an egg, for the rest of their lives. No matter how many ejaculations a man has, his body continues to produce new sperm that will appear in later ejaculations.

There is only one temporary relationship between masturbation and reduced fertility. If a man ejaculates several times within a few hours, each ejaculation will have fewer sperm than were in the first ejaculation, but sperm count will return to normal within a day or two. So stop worrying!

I am an older woman and have what is probably a dumb question. How do people masturbate? When I was growing up we never had any information about sex, and were punished if we touched our private parts.

The ways to give oneself sexual pleasure differ greatly from one person to the next—and while some people use the same method each time, others vary their masturbation technique. Masters and Johnson reported that no two of the women they studied masturbated in exactly the same way and that there were wide variations in the timing and tempo of the genital stimulation used.

Most women stroke, rub, or apply pressure to the genital area while lying down, standing, or sitting. While most use their hands for stimulation, others rub against a pillow or other object or masturbate in the bathtub under flowing water. In one study of women age 18 to 35, 26 percent had used a vibrator for stimulation at least once.

Contrary to what many people assume, most women do not insert anything into the vagina when masturbating, and only a few include breast stimulation in their behavior.

Men have less diversity in their masturbatory behavior. Most rub or stroke the shaft of the penis. Some also stimulate the head of the penis, scrotum, or frenulum (the raised area of skin beneath the head of the penis on the bottom side).

Some men and women use a lubricant when masturbating.

In reference to celibacy practiced by both sexes in some religions, is it possible to go the entire span of life without masturbation? Isn't it imperative for the sperm to have some form of escape whether it be through masturbation or another method of ejaculation?

No to both your questions: many religions that require celibacy do not specifically prohibit masturbation, and sperm do not require any form of "escape."

Celibacy is properly defined as the state of being unmarried, but has come to mean not having sexual relations with others. Various religious and cultural groups have differing views on what constitutes celibacy, but many don't outlaw masturbation. Besides, it would be impossible to regulate orgasms during sleep, which are involuntary and not under a person's conscious control.

Sperm don't require an escape route. The male ejaculate is mainly fluid from the prostate and other internal glands and the volume of sperm in each ejaculation is just a tiny drop. Unejaculated sperm are readily absorbed by the man's body without any ill effects.

What percentage of single males masturbate? Does it differ by age?

The data collected by Kinsey during the 1940s and 1950s are still the most complete information available on this subject. More recent, smaller studies report similar figures, but few include as wide an age range.

At some point in their lives, nearly all men (94 percent) masturbate, but the percentage does vary by age, educational level, and other variables. Among single men who had a college education: 64 percent masturbated between puberty and age 15; 83 percent between 16 and 20 years of age; 84 percent between 21 and 25; 79 percent 26-30 years old; 74 percent 31-35 years old; 76 percent 36-40 years old; 65 percent 41-45 years old; and 60 percent 46-50 years old.

Another survey published in 1984 of more than 2000 men aged 50 and older found that 63 percent of unmarried men masturbated.

I'm in my 60s; I was never crazy about sex and don't really miss it, but now and then (about once a month) I get the urge. My husband is, however, impotent. I've read that a woman can stroke her coitus for relief. What's the coitus? Is it at the top of a woman's privates? I do this and it feels good. My husband doesn't know I do this. I feel guilty about it. Is it natural?

I think you're referring to *clitoris*, not coitus. (*Coitus* is the Latin word for sexual intercourse.) The clitoris is indeed located where a woman's labia meet at the top of the vulva (*see Illustration 2*) and, for most women, is the most sensitive part of the genitals.

A study of more than 4000 American men and women 50 and older reported that 62 percent approved of masturbation for older people and that 37 percent of the women in their sixties were currently masturbating. It's also not unusual for married individuals to masturbate, whether or not they're also having inter- course. Further, masturbation has been shown to help older women maintain the health of their genitals after menopause.

Your behavior isn't unusual. If knowing you are not alone doesn't help allay your guilt, consider talking to a counselor to discuss your feelings.

Why would a man who is regularly active with a partner masturbate? How can you tell if your partner is doing it? This has been heavy on my mind for quite some time. As you have probably guessed, I am the partner. My husband stated that he did masturbate before we got married. I would be so hurt if I knew he still did.

If your husband does masturbate, don't assume it means your marriage is lacking in sexual satisfaction or that you're somehow sexually inept or undesir- able. Even though people often think that's the case, there is no evidence to support this idea.

Many husbands and wives masturbate to orgasm as a pleasurable sexual activity distinct and separate from the pleasure they derive from intercourse. It is, in many ways, a *supplemental* activity rather than one that subtracts from their feelings about their partner or the quality of their marital sexual interactions. A study in the 1970s reported that 72 percent of husbands and 69 percent of wives masturbated.

One smaller study documented that although masturbation is common dur- ing marriage, marital partners frequently do conceal this behavior. Interviews with 24 married couples showed that all 48 spouses masturbated regularly, but 92 percent of the husbands thought their wives did not and 8 percent of the wives thought their husbands did not.

If your husband chooses to conceal it, there's no way to know whether or not he's masturbating. But if this continues to bother you, talk with him about it. Many spouses are surprised to find that activities they view as no more significant than showering or brushing their teeth are interpreted by their partners as a sign of personal rejection. So if you ask, understand that whether the answer is yes or no it is *not* likely to be a reflection on the quality of your sexual relationship with your husband.

Does a man need condoms to masturbate? A friend told me they do.

Although condoms are not necessary there are indeed reports of men using condoms to masturbate. Some say they use them because they like the feeling of the rubber; others because it more closely mimics the feel of intercourse. It's also neater, since the ejaculate is caught by the condom and doesn't have to be cleaned up afterward. And, since many condoms are lubricated this can reduce friction, making masturbation more pleasurable.

I'm 15 and have a heavy addiction to masturbating. I have to masturbate at least once a day. The problem is that I have a really unusual way of masturbat- ing. I do it by leaning my testicles and penis against the bathroom counter. I start and stop until I ejaculate. Is this abnormal?

Is what abnormal—the fact that you masturbate, the frequency, or your technique? Many men use pressure against their genitals, so your technique is not particularly unusual. Each person devises and uses methods that work best for him or her. You should, however, be aware that it is possible to damage the penis if it is pressed too roughly against a sharp object such as the corner of a countertop.

Once a day is not a "heavy addiction" to masturbating, by the way. It is considered a normal frequency at your age.

When I masturbate I ejaculate in about 30 seconds. My friend told me it took him about three to four minutes, which is average or normal. I worry that I won't be able to satisfy my wife.

The way a person masturbates, or responds during masturbation, is not always an accurate predictor of how he or she will respond with a partner. Even the first sexual experiences with a partner don't predict how a couple will interact after they have become comfortable with each other sexually and learned more about each other's bodies, preferences, and responses.

As explained in Chapter 8 you might want to broaden your masturbation pattern, taking more time to sense the various stages of arousal in different parts of your body. Focus on the pleasurable sensations rather than just on orgasm. But don't worry too much about this until you are in a long-term sexual relationship. Then, if both you and your partner feel that your ejaculation happens too quickly, sex counseling can teach both of you techniques to successfully increase the length of time between insertion and ejaculation.

Further Readings

Friday, N. *My Secret Garden*. New York: Pocket Books, 1973.
(A book about the range and diversity of women's sexual fantasies written in a popular style.)
Masters, W. H.; Johnson, V. E.; and Kolodny, R. C. *Human Sexuality*. 3rd ed. Glenview, IL: Scott, Foresman and Company, 1988.
(A comprehensive, in-depth book on the field of human sexuality used as a textbook and interesting to any reader.)
Masters, W. H., and Johnson, V. E. *Human Sexual Response*. Boston, MA: Little, Brown and Company, 1966.
(A scientific book which first described the stages of sexual response from excitement to orgasm.)

7

Sex With A Partner

As one would expect, having sexual interactions with another person is even more complex than engaging in the solitary sexual behaviors discussed in the previous chapter. The basic physical responses involved remain the same, but now another's physical reactions, feelings, expectations, and values are involved as well. Other factors which should be considered when we interact with others are possible parenthood *(see Chapter 16)* and infection with a sexually transmitted disease *(see Chapter 19)*.

This chapter includes a wide range of sexual behaviors. Most readers expect to find some behaviors, such as heterosexual intercourse, in a book about sex. Others, such as being turned on by the smell of stockings, may surprise some readers. The behaviors included in this chapter are here not because of any particular statistical frequency of their occurrence among the population, but because they exist—and because we know that they can cause considerable confusion and concern for those individuals involved, especially when the behavior is felt to be unique or strange.

The purpose of this chapter is to provide information about the sexual behaviors, concerns, and fears expressed by those who have written to The Kinsey Institute for answers. As you will see, the range of human sexual behavior (and the worries about sex) is as varied as the human imagination.

AROUSAL AND FOREPLAY

The word *foreplay* is widely understood to mean activities before intercourse such as kissing and touching, but most sex therapists and researchers broaden its definition to mean all nonintercourse sexual pleasuring activities between partners. This also includes becoming psychologically aroused by looking at visual materials, fantasizing, or reading items an individual or couple finds sexually stimulating.

You've heard it before: Good communication between partners is as essential to sexual pleasure (and to good sex in general) as is any particular technique.

Your partner can't know what you like unless you tell or show him or her. And if there's something your partner does that you *don't* like, it's important to talk about that too. The best time to talk about sexual matters is not when you're ready to have sex, or during sex, but at some other time. Then your partner is less likely to perceive suggestions and information as criticism.

Another point about foreplay: Many people view it strictly as a preliminary activity, a kind of appetizer, with intercourse the main course. It doesn't have to be that way. Many couples enjoy satisfying sexual activity (including orgasm) that consists only of "foreplay activities," such as stimulation of the genitals by hand, tongue, or mouth. This shouldn't be seen as any less "valid" than intercourse, and it can be just as satisfying for both partners.

Similar exchanges of physical affection, such as kissing and hugging, are also important to many people *after* orgasm, when arousal is not the goal.

I'm a 32-year-old married man with two children. I love my wife; she's a model mother. On the surface we are happily married, but I feel a need to be held and loved. I have heard other men ask the same questions I do: Why does my wife refuse to talk about sex or even to joke about it with me?

Your wife may feel uncomfortable joking and talking about sex, or initiating sexual activity, because she was raised to believe that "nice" women don't do those things.

Attitudes about sex vary widely. In most societies, men have been encouraged to be more open about sex than most women. In fact, any man who reacts negatively to sexual jokes or "locker-room talk" may be thought of as less manly than his peers. It has not been generally acceptable in our society for women to joke or talk with men about sex or to initiate sexual activity. Those who do may risk being labeled immoral, loose, or unattractively aggressive.

If you feel that you're not getting enough physical or emotional affection from your wife, you need to tell her exactly that. You should realize that some women avoid being physically affectionate because their partners automatically interpret it as a signal of readiness to have sex, when in fact the woman only wanted to cuddle. If this is true for your wife, you'll need to assure her that you won't misinterpret her hugs to mean that she necessarily wants to have sex right then. You both have the right to, and the need for, physical expressions of affection as well as a satisfying sex life.

It is important that you tell your wife what you need to feel loved and it is also important that you listen to what she says she needs. If you can't do this by yourselves, a counselor can help a couple learn how to communicate about these crucial matters, and negotiate a *mutually* satisfying arrangement.

I have been happily married to my wife for 20 years and when we make love it's still as good as it was the first time.
But why must I always take the initiative? My wife initiates sex only very, very rarely. What would cause that? How could I change that?

Your wife's behavior is not unusual. Here is what the data show: In one study, 4 percent of the women questioned on this issue reported never initiating sex, 42 percent said they initiated sex sometimes, and another 44 percent said initiation was about equal with their male partners. Asked why they didn't take the first step in sexual encounters, some women said they would not because it isn't "feminine" or is something only "bad" women do.

Your feelings aren't unusual either. Eighty percent of the men asked about this issue said they were pleased when women took the sexual initiative, although one study on this question revealed differences among men based on age and education. Men 35 and older with lower education levels were more likely to think it was unacceptable for a woman to make the first move. Younger, college-educated men were more likely to find it both acceptable and desirable.

In some cases a woman may indeed be initiating sex, but in more subtle ways that the man doesn't notice. She might, for instance, pay more attention to her appearance or put on a particular nightdress as a signal that she would welcome having sex. In contrast, male initiating patterns are more obvious, such as asking to have sex or beginning to touch the woman's body.

If both partners learn to recognize each other's signals, then sexual communication is taking place: A message is sent and received, and its content is clear to both. When messages are not clear, couples must talk about the responsibility for initiating sex and agree on what the signals will be.

Perhaps you could agree on a nonverbal signal if she isn't comfortable with saying she wants to have sex, so that her desire to have sex is clear to you. One such example would be for her to turn on a special light. I know of a couple who keeps two figurines standing on the mantel; whichever partner feels like having sex lays one figurine on its side. If the other agrees, sometime during the evening the other figurine is laid down too. This type of signal works well because it permits both partners time to think about having sex, fantasize about sex, and look forward with anticipation to the evening. This type of anticipation and readiness for sex can increase arousal and have a positive effect on the sexual encounter.

After 19 years of marriage, how can I rekindle the sexual excitement that was present years ago? We have good communication and share intimacy, but our sex life could improve. We have both gained weight and need to lose. We are trying. Is it a good idea to have an affair?

Based on a study of 1000 couples, the conclusion was that having an extramarital affair is not a good idea. At worst, an affair can destroy a marriage, and at best it may interfere with the intimacy of the marital relationship.

Many clinicians suggest that couples should instead focus on revitalizing their sexual lives. Some techniques offered by experts include setting aside a special time and place to have sex, initiating romantic gestures (such as candlelight, music, or sexy nightwear), or trying different foreplay techniques or intercourse positions.

Even though you and your husband share good communication, make sure this extends to your sex life. Your husband will never know you are interested in (or turned off by) something unless you tell him.

The books listed at the end of this chapter should be available in bookstores or libraries. Try reading them together. If this doesn't help, find a sex counselor or sex therapist, who will be able to recommend strategies and techniques that have worked for many other couples.

I'm 23 years old and I have a question to ask you. This is probably really funny to you. What is a French kiss?

A French kiss is usually defined as mouth-to-mouth contact where the lips of both partners are open and the tongue of one person enters the mouth of the other or the tongues of both partners meet. Other commonly used terms for this type of kiss are soul kiss, deep kiss, or tongue kiss.

The mouth, lips, and tongue are among the several highly *erogenous* (sexually sensitive, capable of arousing sexual desire) areas of the body. French kissing often accompanies a change in a couple's relationship from friendship to a more emotional, intimate involvement. Couples usually kiss this way as the relationship progresses to a more advanced stage, or in an established partnership signaling existing sexual arousal or the wish to stimulate sexual arousal in the partner.

Kissing, especially for anything longer than a brief peck, appears to be a feature of only a few, mostly Western, cultures. Kissing is viewed unfavorably, for example, by many African and Asian cultures.

My husband and I have been married for 16 years and in all those years he has never been able to satisfy me sexually. The worst part is that when he kisses me on the lips, neck, or anywhere else, it tickles. I have to hold back my laughter. What do you make of this?

Anorgasmia (the condition of never having experienced an orgasm from any kind of stimulation) is a valid reason to see a sex counselor or therapist. Therapy teaches women how to have orgasms and is discussed in Chapter 8. Therapy can also help you learn to focus on other physical sensations and emotions besides the tickling. If your husband is willing to go along, ask for a therapist who works with couples. If you've had orgasms by masturbation or by other techniques, then you'll need to work on communicating to your husband what he can do to help you experience orgasm.

You need to stop spending energy on controlling your laughter and spend it instead on learning to communicate about what touches you like and to recognize pleasurable sensations during foreplay.

Many of my women friends and I have the same question. Why do some men shower or bathe only once or twice a week? Among the working class, this is quite common. It is very difficult, if not impossible, to get sexually excited by someone who is offending all the senses. Not to mention the health risks of having penetration by a dirty penis. Somehow these husbands think that marriage gives them the right to have sex with their wives under any circumstance. I wouldn't want to go to someone with a dirty and smelly body—and I don't!

How important is men's personal hygiene on women's sexuality?

Most women prefer that their partners be clean and smell clean. Research has shown that women are more sensitive to smells than are men.

This means that a man should shower or bathe daily if he wants to be attractive to sexual partners, especially before a sexual encounter, even if *he* is not aware of a noticeable body odor. Cleanliness doesn't require an array of deodorants, perfumes, or other products—just a thorough washing and rinsing with soap and water.

Although we've never received a letter complaining about women's body odor, in all fairness being clean is important for both sexes. Women should also shower or bathe daily and carefully wash all the external folds of the genitals. Wearing perfume will not mask body odors in an intimate encounter.

I've noticed that the odor of female genitalia is a sexual stimulant to me. Is this a normal reaction for most men? Are male odors stimulating to women?

There hasn't been a great deal of research on this question. However, one survey reported that around 40 percent of men found the natural female genital fragrance sexually arousing. There is no comparable research on women, but we do know that, in general, women have a better sense of smell than do men.

Chemicals made in the apocrine glands (which, in humans, are located primarily under the arms and around the genitals) are important to sexual signaling among many mammals. They also may play some role in signaling sexual interest and reproductive status among humans and are referred to as *pheromones*.

This possibility is reinforced by the fact that the apocrine glands are largest during the reproductive years, so that the body odors of children before puberty and of older people generally differ from that of young adults.

I become very stimulated when my partner fondles and sucks my breasts. Can this cause breast cancer or damage my breasts later in life? Sometimes I have an orgasm just from breast stimulation. Is this normal?

About 90 percent of women report receiving manual or oral breast stimulation from a partner during sexual activity. About 11 percent regularly stimulate their own breasts to enhance sexual pleasure during masturbation.

A much smaller number of women report having orgasms from breast stimulation alone (both Kinsey and Masters and Johnson found 1 percent in their research samples). But that doesn't make you abnormal; it only makes you lucky to have another route for having sexual pleasure and orgasm. Many men also enjoy having their breasts and nipples stimulated.

Some researchers have reported that only about 50 percent of women say they actually enjoy breast stimulation, with many more saying they do it because it brings pleasure to their partners. A few women always experience pain or discomfort when their breasts or nipples are stimulated, while others find it uncomfortable only during one stage of the reproductive cycle—often right before menstrual flow begins.

Perhaps many women who don't enjoy breast stimulation feel this way because of lack of communication. Their partners are doing what they think is *supposed* to arouse women, when in fact it often does not. Women must tell their partners what enhances their arousal and orgasm, how lightly or firmly to touch, and where.

There is no research that links breast stimulation with breast cancer or other breast problems. Since the average woman has a one-in-ten chance of developing breast cancer, while 90 percent (9 out of 10) of all women experience breast stimulation, there would appear to be little direct connection between the two. Assuming that this activity doesn't leave bruises or cause pain (in which case you should caution your partner and consult a doctor), follow the usual schedule of having your breasts examined when you have your annual Pap test and do self-examinations each month.

I am 64 and a woman who enjoys having sex with my mate. Sometimes I get so nervous before we make love that I get very wet. When he gets in the mood, he says, "You are wet, what happened? Have you been with someone else?" It makes me feel really hurt. I would never have sex with anyone else. He says he doesn't believe me.

It sounds as if just the anticipation of having sex with your partner is sexually arousing to you. He should be flattered, not jealous. In women, one sign of being sexually excited or aroused is the appearance of vaginal lubrication. This moisture seeps out of the vaginal walls and may flow out of the vagina. This response is an automatic physical response to sexual arousal. For some women, no direct stimulation or foreplay is needed to create lubrication—just thinking about sex produces it. It *cannot* be controlled or willed to stop.

Tell your partner that the wetness is a sign that you find him sexually arousing, and that the wetness comes from inside of you, not from another man. If he still insists that you've been with another man, and if his jealousy causes distress in your relationship, consider making an appointment to see a sex therapist or a marriage counselor who can explain normal female sexual responses to him.

I'm a 23-year-old woman involved in my first sexual relationship. My problem is that as of yet, I haven't achieved orgasm. There are times when I feel close, but then I tense up and quickly lose the feeling. I believe I'm afraid of losing control of my body's functions. How can I overcome this? Does this often occur with inexperienced women?

Don't panic. Fear of losing control is a common concern among women, and it isn't necessarily related to a lack of sexual experience. A woman may fear, for instance, that she will appear physically unattractive as a result of the normal muscle tension in the face and body preceding orgasm, that she may lose control of bladder or bowels, or she will be ridiculed by her partner. A woman who doesn't fully trust her partner is especially vulnerable to such fears.

Many women, particularly in their first sexual relationships, don't become orgasmic immediately. Women need to learn for themselves what arouses them and brings them to orgasm; they then can communicate this information to their partners. It can take some time to develop enough trust in a partner to feel secure enough to reveal such personal information.

You didn't mention whether you've had orgasms during solitary or mutual masturbation. If you have never had an orgasm by any means, you first might want to rule out any medical problems, such as diabetes, or the effect of drugs like barbiturates or alcohol, which can inhibit orgasm for some women. If no physical problems exist, then there are methods you can use to learn how to have an orgasm (see Chapter 8).

But if you have had orgasms in the past from masturbation, becoming orgasmic with your first partner may be as simple as using a new position during intercourse or trying a particular technique to increase clitoral stimulation. One way would be to have either you or your partner touch your clitoris during intercourse. You should know that more than half of all women, regardless of their previous sexual experience, do not have orgasms from thrusting alone. Some women don't have orgasms during intercourse because they focus on *trying* to have an orgasm rather than on enjoying the overall sensations. If experimenting on your own doesn't help, consult a sex counselor or therapist.

I am seeking suggestions about a relationship that has some annoying and irritating aspects to me. My friend, divorced, will not get into any intimacies when it is daylight. She insists on covering herself and makes a big deal about her privacy. I ascribe some of her hang-ups to her personal growing up and her culture.

Partners frequently disagree about what is and what is not normal or appropriate sexual behavior. Most researchers believe that differences in preferred activities are most likely due to differences in educational backgrounds and to sex differences.

Forty-five percent of men, for instance, prefer to have at least some light available during sex, while only 17 percent of women want this. Researchers have speculated that this may be because males have a higher need for visual stimulation for arousal, while women generally have a greater need for the physical stimulation derived from touching.

Some women feel so self-conscious about their bodies that they're uncomfortable being naked or making love in the light. In these cases a partner can help a woman improve her feelings about her body with compliments and reassurance about her attractiveness.

Regardless of what caused the disagreement, you and your partner will have to resolve the light question before it interferes with your relationship. Talk together about it. Both of you should explain your point of view without criticizing. If that doesn't lead to a solution, find professional help.

It's better for the relationship if a compromise (such as using a dim light, rose-colored bulb, or a candle) can be negotiated in such a way that both partners' values and feelings are carefully and fairly considered.

My wife refuses to wear the sexy clothing I've bought her, such as garter belts. I've heard other men complain that women won't do this because the women believe only prostitutes wear such clothes. How can I make my wife see she's wrong?

I'm not sure your goal should be to make your wife see she's "wrong." While it obviously isn't true that the only women who wear sexy clothes or garter belts are prostitutes, women who earn their living catering to men's sexual desires often do wear such items. This is not necessarily because they enjoy wearing these things, but because they know their customers want them to. So there is some basis for your wife's belief. However, there may be other reasons for her feelings: many women view such clothes as demeaning, sexist, obscene, or as promoting a feeling of subservience.

Men, more so than women, derive much of their sexual arousal through sight. And for some people (perhaps this is the case for you), seeing a partner wearing a specific type of clothing is both arousing and important to adequate sexual functioning. Their partners either go along with the request or refuse.

The partner's response is more likely to be negative if he or she feels insecure in the relationship, fears the loss of marital status, or thinks the request conflicts with his or her own self-concept or personal values. For example, perhaps she thinks she looks silly, finds the snap crotch uncomfortable, thinks she's not slim enough to wear a slinky nightgown, worries that you may only find her desirable when she's dressed this way, or feels this kind of clothing is immoral.

Since fears and disagreements about sexual practices are sensitive issues for both partners, this type of conflict is often best handled by a counselor or therapist who can act as an impartial arbitrator to help each partner understand the other's feelings. If a man can *only* get aroused by women in one particular type of clothing and can't function otherwise, therapy is definitely in order.

I find that watching X-rated videos is arousing to me, but my wife finds them to be a sexual turnoff. Are certain types of materials more arousing to one sex than to the other? What types of materials are arousing to females as opposed to males? Why does my wife react this way?

Have you asked her? There are several *possible* reasons why your wife doesn't respond sexually to the videos you find so arousing. She may think, for instance, that your interest in erotic videos is an indication that you don't find her attractive or you are not satisfied with your sex life with her. She also may feel that you are pressuring her to watch the videos, mimic what the actors do, or become immediately aroused regardless of what else is going on in her life that day.

People who do not feel secure about a relationship or their own sexual attractiveness may feel negatively about sexual videos for another reason. These videos usually use actors who are unusually physically attractive and "well endowed," so that any comparison between the actors and the bodies of average men or women can reinforce an insecure viewer's low opinion of her or his own body.

Many couples watch sexually explicit videos. But not everyone is aroused by the same movies or scenes, so it will never be possible to state that all women are aroused by one type of video while all men are aroused by another. Many heterosexual men, for instance, don't respond to a video of male masturbation, while others do. Moreover, males are likely to become aroused by visual stimulation (such as watching a video), while most females report becoming aroused more easily by touching or other types of stimuli.

One study found that when men and women were given the choice between watching soft-core films (which the study defined as depicting sex within the context of a loving relationship) or hard-core films (sex only, no love or affection), women were more likely to prefer soft-core films. They also were more likely than men to refuse to participate in the study at all.

You don't say whether your wife has had orgasms, but there is one study which suggests that anorgasmic women react negatively to erotic videos *regardless* of the content because they resist becoming sexually aroused. Another study found that women were least aroused when sexual scenes stirred guilt feelings. These women responded positively only to depictions of activities that they had experienced or that they viewed as natural, acceptable lovemaking between couples who were depicted in the story as married or emotionally committed.

If disagreements about these videos are intruding on your sex life together or on other aspects of your relationship, consult a sex therapist.

My problem is the people who are trying to rid us of pornography. I'm talking about magazines like *Playboy* and the films you can rent at your local video store, not kiddie porn. I consider myself a normal person— mother of four, wife, active in the community, etc.—but I feel my rights and my morality are being infringed upon by these groups (notably the Citizens for Decency here in Indiana).

I feel there are many people who enjoy an occasional pornographic movie, just as my husband and I do, but are too embarrassed to stand up and say so. Our local video stores say the movies are very popular with all ages and groups of people. My question is, how many people watch or read adult films or literature?

I've talked informally to a number of videostore owners around the country and they report that one out of three tapes rented is X-rated, but there isn't much scientific data available on how many people view or read explicitly sexual materials. The problem with many studies of consumers of erotica is that researchers look only at people who have gotten into some sort of legal difficulty (such as being arrested for public indecency or some other sex offense). If they then find that these people also viewed sexual materials, the temptation is to say that viewing sexual materials caused the sex crime rather than some other factor. Unfortunately, there are few studies of the people who enjoy such materials but have not broken any laws.

Your letter was from a city in Indiana so there are some data that may be of direct interest to you. In 1984 The Kinsey Institute asked the Indiana Poll at Indiana University to survey a random sample of Indiana residents about their experience with erotic materials; 54 percent reported having watched an X-rated movie or videotape at least once.

Even with a possible sampling error of 4 percent, the results show that approximately half the population of Indiana, age 18 and older, report having seen materials similar to those viewed by you and your husband. You are certainly not alone in your experience with such materials.

I have read that using a vibrator could help a woman become more aroused. Where can I obtain one? Could it hurt me if I used it?

One common misconception is that all vibrators are the size and shape of an erect penis. Some are, but others are not. Also, most people do not insert the vibrator inside the vagina, but use it only on the external genitals. If the vibrator will be used for stimulation of external surfaces, then a phallic shape is not necessary.

Because genital tissues and structures can be damaged by overly rough handling, normal cautionary warnings apply: Be gentle, start slowly, use a lubricant on your genitals if necessary, stop immediately if there is discomfort, and go to a physician if pain or discomfort persists or there is bleeding.

Most drugstores carry vibrators and they are also advertised in many mail-order catalogs. These are usually marketed as devices for massage, not sexual stimulation, so you should not be embarrassed about looking at them or asking questions about them.

I'm a 58-year-old man, in good health, and have regular checkups. Recently, I've been using a vibrator to enhance sexual stimulation. Is that safe? How many times a week can I use it? Does it change the normal way of climaxing? I enjoy this and want to preserve my sexual functioning as long as I can.

Although there are a few published reports of problems associated with vibrator use (such as tissue irritation) it appears that most men and women don't experience any problems. Follow the manufacturer's instructions, and discontinue use if you notice irritation or discomfort. If you are inserting the vibrator in the anus (the area around the anus and near the prostate inside the rectum is highly arousing for many men), use a water-soluble lubricant to avoid irritation.

Increasing stimulation may enhance sexual functioning for some people, and there is no indication that using a vibrator alters the actual physiological processes associated with arousal or orgasm. However, some clinicians have reported that some patients become dependent on the intense stimulation provided by a vibrator and find it more difficult to achieve orgasm from the less intense stimulation provided by other touches.

As for your desire to continue sexual activity throughout your lifetime, research has shown that men and women who were sexually active in their sixties, seventies, and eighties also had had a high rate of sexual activity during their forties and fifties—perhaps verifying the old adage "use it or lose it."

Some people use a lubricant called K-Y Jelly with their vibrators. What is it and where can you buy it? Is it the same as Vaseline? Is Vaseline safer?

K-Y Jelly and other brand-name water-based personal lubricants do not require a prescription and are available in nearly all drugstores and many large grocery or general stores. They come in the kind of rectangular boxes that resemble toothpaste packaging and are shelved near sanitary napkins and tampons, or near contraceptive foams and condoms.

I am not aware of any negative reports associated with use of water-based products but these are *not* the same as Vaseline. In fact, couples who rely on condoms or diaphragms for contraception should *never* use Vaseline, Vaseline Intensive Care, Nivea, baby oil, or any other petroleum- or oil-based product for lubrication. These can weaken or make holes in those birth control devices in just seconds. Most clinicians also point out that petroleum products can cause allergic reactions; since they're not water-soluble, they are difficult for the vagina to naturally cleanse out, don't wash off the genitals easily, and are thought to change the vaginal environment for some women. This could be a factor in some vaginal infections.

I'm a 50-year-old male. For quite a few years I've used various types of rings to maintain harder erections as well as to delay ejaculation. This has contributed to what I feel has been a great sex life.

But now I find I'm unable to have what I call a good erection unless I'm using a ring, and I also have blood in my ejaculation and in my urine after having used a ring.

Have I damaged the blood vessels in my penis? Will they repair themselves if I refrain from using a ring?

First, stop using the rings and see a physician (preferably a urologist who specializes in diagnosing male sexual dysfunctions). You must tell that physician about use of the rings, otherwise the relevant tests may not be done. Although having blood in the ejaculate is not always a symptom of a serious problem, it must always be checked by a physician.

There are clinical accounts of penile rings causing damage to the urethra (the tube that carries urine and semen through the penis). This could explain having blood in the ejaculate and urine. There are also reports of rings damaging one of the penile cylinders that normally fill with blood during an erection, and this can cause erectile difficulties.

You may be surprised to learn that the physician has seen other cases involving sexual devices. Unfortunately, patients often hesitate to reveal using so-called sexual aids, and this embarrassment can delay getting appropriate treatment. Take the ring you use to the appointment, since it may be helpful for the physician to see the dimensions and gauge its flexibility or rigidity.

Any device that forces blood into the penis or that traps blood in the penis by acting as a tourniquet (the way a ring works) may cause damage. A few physicians have conducted experiments using rings or similar devices to aid erections, but the patients involved also received a thorough medical examination before the experiment began and were very closely monitored for any signs of trouble. To date there is not enough evidence from these clinical trials to say whether the penis ring is an effective, safe way to increase erectile functioning or delay ejaculation for the majority of men.

Because problems of erection rigidity and too-rapid ejaculation can be treated successfully by other means without risking damage to genital structures, trying penis rings or other devices without a supervising physician is not a good idea.

What are the effects/dangers of using the liquids commonly referred to as "poppers" during sexual activity? These are sold in small bottles and one inhales or sniffs the aroma. I think they contain amyl or butyl nitrite.

Both amyl nitrite (sold as a prescription drug to treat some heart problems) and butyl or isobutyl nitrite have been used because of the belief that they enhance sexual response. There is no scientific data to support this belief. Physically, the nitrite vapors produce a brief drop in blood pressure and an increase in blood flow in the brain. Called "poppers," these nitrites have been popular among some groups, especially homosexual males and users of so-called recreational drugs.

Although no deaths have been reported with use of nitrite, temporary side effects such as headaches, dizziness, nasal irritation, and nausea are fairly common. But because of the rapid drop in blood pressure, they should probably not be used by persons with cardiovascular or cerebrovascular disease.

It also seems sensible to avoid using *any* drug, including alcohol, that might affect your judgment or impair your ability to act responsibly, remember safer sex guidelines (*see Chapter 19*), and use them effectively.

I am worried about a young friend of mine. She often has welts all over her throat and neck. She says her husband bites her during sex. This is his second marriage, but it's her first one and I wish we could help her. She's a quiet type and will take most any kind of abuse. Is there any way we could help her?

It is not uncommon for people to give gentle bites or suction kisses (often called "hickies") during foreplay or intercourse. These may leave reddish marks on the skin for a day or two. But whether or not to get such "love nips," as well as where they are placed and how intense they are, should be under the control of the *receiver*, not the giver.

Personal preferences about this vary. One survey reported that 44 percent of men and 41 percent of women found it arousing to receive gentle bites; the rest of the people surveyed did not like it at all. The only way to find out whether a partner likes this or not is to ask.

Perhaps your friend and her husband have already discussed this, and it is something she finds arousing but is too embarrassed to reveal to you. If this is the case, using make-up to conceal the red marks or confining them to areas that are covered by clothing will help keep her personal sexual preferences private.

Or, perhaps the man's first wife liked it and he is automatically repeating the activity with your friend, thinking that all women like it. If your friend doesn't like receiving these bites or kisses, she must tell her husband.

More troubling possibilities include the chance that your friend is being bitten against her will or that she experiences pain, not pleasure. In either of these situations, she is being sexually abused. Many abused women find it extremely difficult to reach out for help.

You can tell her that you will help her in any way that she needs, but the decision to ask for help (from, for example, a social agency), must be hers unless you are *certain* that abuse is taking place. Tell her about the local services available and how to contact them. Most telephone directories have a listing of such groups, generally in the Yellow Pages under Social Service Organizations.

If it's clearly abuse and she does not act to protect herself, call a social-service agency yourself and ask for advice on how best to proceed. Reporting procedures vary from one locality to another. You might consider first calling a group that specializes in assisting abused women. This may help ensure that her safety is the primary consideration if intervention is mandatory under your local laws.

I am a newlywed. My husband says I play too rough with his testicles and that I should not squeeze his testicles to wake him up while he is asleep. Is it true this can cause serious pain or damage to the testicles? Or is it that he doesn't love me enough to take a little pain?

Unwanted touches, and certainly unwanted pain, should not be a part of any relationship. Since everyone has his or her own idea of which kinds of touch are

pleasurable and which are painful, partners need to discuss their own preferences. It is important that limits about touching be set by the receiver, not the
giver. Some men, but certainly not all, like having their testicles gently touched,
stroked, or squeezed when sexually aroused; but the same type and degree of
touch can be painful when they are not aroused.

A very few individuals (often labeled masochists) need pain to become
sexually aroused or to be sexually satisfied, but the vast majority of people do
not need it or want it. Even masochists are quite clear about the degree of pain
they find arousing, and they work out agreements with partners before having
sex so that their pain limit will not be exceeded.

It sounds as though your husband has clearly communicated his preferences
about this type of touching: He doesn't like it. It is possible to damage the
testicles, but the important point is that a caring partner must comply with
requests to stop certain touching, regardless of whether or not physical damage
could result. Being able to receive pain is not an indication of love. If you
disagree with that idea, then you should talk with a therapist to clarify misconceptions about how love is caringly expressed.

VIRGINITY

**I'm a 14-year-old freshman in high school. I was wondering what exactly does
the word "cherry" mean. What's the medical word for it and how is it
supposedly "broke"? My mom and I are not close at all so I can't ask her and
my friends, well, I'd be too embarrassed to ask them.**

The word *cherry* usually means a man or woman hasn't had intercourse. A
phrase such as "he's still cherry" usually means a male hasn't yet had sexual
intercourse.

In the recent past, meaning your mother's generation, the word was generally applied only to women and referred specifically to the *hymen,* a thin membrane stretching across the vagina near the vaginal opening at birth. Most
people thought this membrane was solid until a woman had her first sexual
intercourse, at which point it would be "broken." According to myths, this
dramatic event was expected to be accompanied by some discomfort and
bleeding.

During some historical periods (even today in some cultures), a new bride's
family was required to publicly display the sheets used for the wedding night;
bloodstained sheets were considered the only proof of the bride's virginity.
Historical records suggest, however, that often the bride and/or groom used
animal blood or pricked their fingers to provide this proof.

Now we know that this membrane begins to disappear shortly after birth and
continues to erode gradually during childhood and adolescence. If the myth of a
solid hymen until the wedding night were true, no girl would begin menstruating until after she was married, because menstrual flow would be blocked by the
hymen! Lack of blood on the honeymoon sheets, or a pain-free first intercourse,
therefore, does not mean that a woman has had sexual intercourse before.

Parents can be a good source of information about sex, although many are too
embarrassed to answer their children's questions. Your local library should have

books that answer many of your questions. Some are listed at the end of this chapter.

I've been married for five years. On our wedding night, I discovered my wife was not a virgin. When I asked her about it, she said it was because she had been active in gymnastics in school, but she couldn't recall any specific accident when her hymen had been broken.

She assures me I'm the only man she has ever had intercourse with.

I love her and think she's a truthful person, but lately this question has been eating away at me. I'm depressed.

I've always assumed that penetration was required to rupture a hymen. Is it possible this could have happened without penetration?

Absolutely. The first act of intercourse for many women does not involve pain, bleeding, or any of the dramatic signs frequently thought to be associated with first intercourse. This is because the hymen has usually eroded. This natural process doesn't require penetration of any sort.

Even gynecologists doing pelvic examinations cannot usually tell if a woman is a virgin or not. And this can be true even when a hymen is found, since in some cases the tissue is so elastic it simply stretches during intercourse but does not tear. If a skilled physician who closely examines many women each day cannot usually establish virginity, it should come as no surprise that an untrained person cannot.

If you are truly depressed about this you should talk to a counselor, clergyman, or sex therapist. It's important to be able to trust your spouse, since many aspects of marriage must be based on trust.

This is probably a stupid question since I'm 20 years old and know all I need to know about sex, but is there a way to tell if a man is a virgin?

I'd like to know (other than just taking his word for it) because, if I've saved myself for marriage, I believe he should've done the same.

There's no way to tell if a man has had intercourse before. And, except in rare cases, there's also no way to be certain if a woman has had sexual intercourse before either.

When is a man not a virgin? I did not have any sexual contact with anyone until I was 64, and that was with another male. So am I a virgin or not?

Frankly, the word *virgin* is not very useful in scientifically describing exactly what any person has or has not done sexually.

The concept of virginity has historically been applied only to women, with most definitions based on whether she has had sexual intercourse or the hymen is still present. Basically each person defines his or her own status as virgin or nonvirgin depending on how he or she defines "virginity."

I read that it is impossible for some girl virgins to have sex and that girls should be checked for this before having sex. Is this true?

Only a very few young women (about one in every 2000) have a vagina that remains completely closed by a hymen (a thin membrane at the vaginal opening) at puberty. One early sign of this condition is that a girl does not begin menstruating around the same age as her mother, sisters, or friends, even though she has all the other signs of pubertal development. This condition (when the hymen prevents menstrual flow from coming out of the body) is easily diagnosed by a gynecological exam and treated by minor surgery in the gynecologist's office.

But more women have small pieces or remnants of hymenal tissue partially stretched across the vaginal opening or along the sides. These don't affect menstrual flow and may even permit use of tampons (so a young woman has no idea they exist), but they can make the first intercourse uncomfortable. This is one reason why it's a good idea to have a pelvic exam before having sex for the first time.

I have a problem so embarrassing that I hesitate to discuss it with the man I'm going to marry, much less with my family doctor who has known me since I was ten.

My fiancé and I plan to be married soon. I guess we're among the few couples who have decided to wait for sexual relations until after marriage. We were both raised with conservative, traditional standards and are strong in our determination to wait.

The problem is that I am 5 feet 2 inches, small-boned, and weigh 110 pounds. My fiancé is 6 feet 1 inch, weighs 190 pounds, and appears very virile. I am worried sick that his male organ will be too large for my vagina and that this problem will spoil our pleasure and damage our chance for marital happiness. I expect discomfort on our wedding night, when the hymen is broken, but I'm worried about beyond that.

What are we to do? I simply can't talk about this to anyone!

First, you need to know that no physical attribute of a man (such as height or weight) predicts the size of his erect penis. The vast majority of men have erect penises within a similar length of 5 to 7 inches.

Second, healthy women's vaginas are capable of expanding to fit nearly any penis, with adequate arousal. Remember that a vagina can expand to deliver a baby, and a baby's head is much larger than any penis.

Third, communication between partners is essential. Start now to talk with your fiancé about this worry, and keep on talking about what you find pleasurable, uncomfortable, or of concern after your marriage.

It's also important to hold realistic expectations about your wedding night. Remember that sexual arousal is normally impaired when a person is overly tired, under stress, or preoccupied by nonsexual thoughts—all conditions that exist after a wedding. Don't be surprised or disappointed if you (or your new husband) don't feel "sexy." Sometimes it's a good idea for newlyweds to just kiss, cuddle, and wait to have intercourse until they're more relaxed and rested.

In general, the advice to sexually inexperienced couples is to go slow, giving minds and bodies time to recognize the sensations of sexual arousal. It may take a while to learn what produces arousal and sexual satisfaction in both partners. It's important to communicate during this process, even if the most you can bring yourself to say is "I like it when you do that" in response to a touch, position, or other stimulus.

Remember, a lifetime's prohibitions against sexual thoughts and activities do not automatically disappear with a marriage license. If you and your husband have problems with sexual adjustment, don't delay seeking help after the first few months.

I am 20 and had my first sexual experience last month. I'm alarmed because my body did not react to foreplay the normal way. I was mentally ready (I had contraceptives) and I was very attracted to my lover. It hurt (which I expected), but I didn't have an orgasm.

A week later the same thing happened, although I did lubricate. Am I impotent (or whatever the word is for ladies)?

Even though there's been a great deal written about the first intercourse experience, little research has been done on what actually takes place and how men and women feel about it.

For a woman, experiencing an orgasm during sex is thought to usually require some experience during which she learns more about her body, her particular responses, and what types of stimulation she enjoys and needs. Then she has to communicate this knowledge to her partner. It is important to know that fewer than half of all women experience an orgasm during intercourse solely from thrusting, regardless of their level of sexual experience.

A study of college women reported on a number of reactions associated with first intercourse. Feelings of nervousness and fear were reported by more than half these women; neither is conducive to sexual pleasure. Only 39 percent described first intercourse as pleasurable, and few had an orgasm.

Factors found to be associated with a positive reaction to first intercourse included feeling that the partner was loving, tender, and considerate and having had more prior experience with intimate relationships.

It appeared that experience with sexual arousal (from masturbation or foreplay) and with nonintercourse activities (such as kissing and foreplay) were important predictors of a pleasurable first intercourse.

Although you're obviously giving sex a great deal of thought and being responsible about contraception, too much evaluation during the sex act itself can cause problems. Monitoring your physical responses and worrying about whether you will reach orgasm is often called "spectatoring." This disrupts the ability to feel the physical sensations necessary for adequate arousal and orgasm.

It is much too early in your sexual life to assume that you are not capable of orgasm. Rather than trying to reach such a specific goal, focus on learning what kinds of touching and other activities feel most arousing to you. If after several episodes of becoming fully aroused (one sign is vaginal lubrication) you still have discomfort or pain when intercourse is attempted, ask your gynecologist to check for vaginal infections and other physical problems.

If after several months of regular sexual activity you have not had an orgasm from masturbation, self or partner touching during foreplay, or self or partner clitoral stimulation during intercourse, then consult a sex therapist or counselor.

It sounds as though you may have expected too much too soon. Gaining sexual responsiveness is a gradual process. The learning experience along the way to becoming orgasmic during sex with a partner should be enjoyable.

Does the size and length of a man's penis have anything to do with the age at which he begins having intercourse or the frequency or infrequency of having sex?

Neither age at first intercourse nor frequency of sexual activity have anything to do with the size or length of a man's penis.

However, a man's erection size can vary from time to time, depending on his level of sexual arousal. When a man is highly aroused, his erect penis may measure slightly larger than it does when he is less aroused. But these slight size variations from one sexual encounter to another have no permanent effect on penis size.

I am a 26-year-old male who was a late bloomer sexually. All the women I've had sex with were sexually experienced, and had at least six or seven years of experience. Lately I've become curious and depressed about something I may have missed. Is sex with a virgin more pleasurable?

In the opinion of many, the most pleasurable sex is with a partner in a loving, committed relationship. Mutual love, caring, trust, acceptance, and emotional bonds are of more importance to a sense of pleasure than is the prior sexual experience of either partner.

In most cases, the concept of sex with a virgin being particularly pleasurable is sheer fantasy, since few males enjoy sex when their partners do not also experience pleasure—and most women do not report feeling great pleasure, and rarely report orgasm, during their first intercourse even though few experience pain. One reason a virgin's vagina may *seem* tighter is because an inexperienced woman may have more difficulty becoming aroused and lubricating, thereby making penetration more difficult.

However, there is a common myth that women who have never had sex before have tighter vaginas, and that this is somehow "better" for the male partner. The desirability of having sex with a "virgin" is part of the sexual myths of many cultures; some believed this could add longevity and health for older men. Because men have historically wondered about the mysterious pleasures and benefits of having sex with a virgin, the supply of this limited and sought-after commodity became an important attraction of the prostitution business in many countries. The institute's library holds many accounts of the various techniques employed by prostitutes to simulate virginity over and over again for customers.

As a woman goes through the stages of increasing sexual arousal (*see Chapter 6*), one of the physical changes is a tightening or narrowing of the outer one-third of the vagina. This makes the vagina feel tighter around a man's penis and contributes to pleasurable sensations for both partners.

HETEROSEXUAL INTERCOURSE

One of the most frequent questions the institute receives about heterosexual intercourse is "How often?" Everyone wants to know how often everyone else is having sex.

A role of The Kinsey Institute is to gather data from reputable studies and to present this information in our writings. The problem is that some people use the information to set performance goals. If they fall short of the averages reported, they become overly concerned, even depressed or panic-stricken. Or they use the numbers to pressure their partners into having more sex or less sex, as the case may be. Others, finding that their frequency of sexual intercourse is higher than average, worry about being too sexually active, imagining it is a detriment to their health.

Data about intercourse are important and can be fascinating. But the key thing to remember is this: If you and your partner are essentially in agreement about how, when, and how often to have sex, then those positions, situations, and rate are normal for you—regardless of the averages generated by surveys. These and many other concerns are addressed below.

My problem is that I'm a 21-year-old virgin. I have slept with a few men, but they can't enter me because it hurts so much. I've heard of "breaking the hymen" and wonder if that's what it may be. Or maybe the problem is caused by dryness, since I never seem to lubricate during sex.

If I went to my gynecologist, would he be able to prescribe something to ease the pain?

The best reason to go to a gynecologist is to find out what's causing the pain, not just for a prescription to mask it.

Some women do have tight hymenal rings or small pieces of the hymen at the vaginal opening which can be removed by a doctor. Inadequate vaginal lubrication or vaginal infections can also cause painful intercourse, as can problems with ducts and glands near the vaginal opening.

A thorough examination by a gynecologist experienced in treating women with dyspareunia (painful intercourse) usually identifies any physical problems. In a few women, no physical problem is found and a diagnosis of vaginismus (involuntary tightening of the muscles of the vaginal opening) may be made. It has been estimated that 9 percent of all women have vaginismus. In these cases, a gynecologist working with a sex therapist can teach the woman to relax the vaginal muscles (vaginismus is discussed in Chapter 8).

In addition, many clinicians believe that women and their partners who experience painful intercourse or pain that prevents penetration can benefit by an explanation of sexual arousal, the use of foreplay techniques which increase vaginal lubrication, and suggestions of sexual positions which put the woman in charge of when she is ready for penetration and the depth and rhythm of thrusting.

I'm a young woman who has had sex two times and it hurt both times. Is this normal? My friends say it doesn't hurt after the first time.

A common myth is that all women experience pain when they have their first intercourse and then have pain-free intercourse forever after. These beliefs are not necessarily true on either count.

In one study of women asked about their first intercourse, 25 percent had no pain at all, 33 percent reported having pain (called dyspareunia), and the rest

reported moderate discomfort. In another study of 500 women visiting a gynecologist's office, 40 percent said they had pain some or all of the time during sex,
although only 4 percent said the pain was the reason for their visit.

The truth is that experiencing pain during intercourse can occur the first time,
second time, hundredth time, all the time, some of the time (during one part of
the menstrual cycle, for instance), or not at all. Regardless of when it occurs,
pain requires medical diagnosis and treatment.

Pain during sex can be caused by a number of physical and psychological
problems. The vast majority of women who have pain during sex are found to
have a physical problem, which can be corrected.

Nonmedical problems that can cause sex to be painful include guilt about
having sex, fear of pregnancy, inadequate sexual arousal and nonsexual problems in the relationship (all of which can cause lack of lubrication).

A visit to a gynecologist is the first step, to find out if physical problems exist.
If nothing is found to explain the discomfort or pain, ask to be referred to a sex
therapist or counselor who is experienced in working with women who have
pain during sex. Often the problem is quickly and easily solved by receiving
accurate information about sexual functioning and learning how to increase
arousal.

**When my husband and I make love, it feels like he touches something if he
goes pretty deep. It hurts both of us. What is he touching? Is it my cervix? Is
this normal?**

Go now or ask your physician about this during your next annual gynecologic
exam (pelvic examination and Pap test). It is not unusual to bump the cervix (the
area surrounding the opening between the vagina and the womb or uterus),
which feels rigid and juts out into the softer, more elastic vagina. The cervix is
sometimes described as the place deep inside the vagina that feels like the tip of
your nose.

But there are other reasons a woman might experience pain with deep
thrusting, such as an ovarian cyst, which can be an early sign of a potentially
serious problem. That's why every woman should have annual pelvic exams and
why she should mention problems like this to her gynecologist.

**My fiancé and I use a lubricating gel every time we have intercourse—about
three times a week. Is such frequent use harmful? Even though I enjoy sex, it
seems I never lubricate enough naturally for comfortable penetration. Is this
normal? Do women have different degrees of lubrication?**

Yes, women differ in the amount of vaginal lubrication produced, and even the
same woman may produce different amounts at different times, such as at
certain stages of her menstrual cycle.

As long as you're not experiencing any adverse reactions, using an artificial
lubricant regularly should cause no problems as long as it is water-based (such
as K-Y Jelly or Lubrin inserts) and not a product containing oil, scents, flavors,
or other chemicals known to irritate the mucous membranes or skin of the
genitalia of some men and women.

However, there are some physical causes of low levels of lubrication (such as
a vaginal infection) that you might want to have checked by your gynecologist.

Because a lack of vaginal lubrication adequate for pain-free insertion can also be a sign of low sexual arousal, you and your partner might want to discuss your foreplay activities. Many therapists advise increasing the time of foreplay, trying different types of direct stimulation on various parts of the body, and including psychological stimulation such as erotic talk, fantasies, or viewing or reading erotic materials to increase a woman's arousal and, hence, her amount of vaginal lubrication.

My wife and I have noticed different amounts of vaginal secretions during intercourse at various times of her cycle. While we assume these variations are normal, it does, at times, cause a problem. When lubrication is heavy, friction is reduced and it's difficult for her (and sometimes me) to reach orgasm. Is there any way to safely reduce the quantity of lubrication?

Some perfectly healthy women simply produce a large amount of lubrication. However, your wife should have a thorough gynecological exam to rule out any medical problems. Vaginal infections, inflammation of the Bartholin's and Skene's glands, and problems with the cervix are some possible causes of excessive levels of vaginal lubrication. When excess lubrication is caused by one of these problems, the level is usually reduced when the problem is treated.

Once your wife has seen a physician to rule out health problems, she might try wiping the moisture away from the opening of the vagina with a towel, Tucks pads, or cotton ball before penetration. Some clinicians recommend inserting a tampon to dry up the lubrication before beginning sexual arousal and removing it before penetration, but others caution that this might produce irritation for some women by making the vagina too dry.

Normal fluctuations in the level of hormones—especially estrogen—can increase vaginal lubrication at different stages of a woman's menstrual cycle and for some women it's possible that oral contraceptives affect the amount of lubrication. Your wife might want to discuss with her doctor the possibility of using a progestin-only pill or switching to another method of birth control. She shouldn't, however, switch to contraceptive foam or gel; these add more moisture to the vagina. Lubricated condoms would also contribute to the problem.

I have noticed that I desire sex about once a month. I realized that my desire occurred when I ovulated. And what more appropriate time for sexual intercourse than when a woman is fertile?

There is no *definitive* scientific evidence establishing that women in general feel any more sexual desire around the time of ovulation than at any other time of their monthly cycle. Some studies do show heightened sexual interest for some women at midcycle, and others report greater sexual interest just after menstruation. In research that looked at other factors affecting female desire, more significant changes were related to the day of the week than to a woman's reproductive cycle; in other words, people (especially males) were more interested in sex on weekends, perhaps simply because they have more leisure time than on other days.

It is this type of research, which investigates biological, psychological, and sociological factors, that may tell us more in the future about what is involved in happy, satisfying sexual relationships.

Is there such a thing as a male hormonal cycle? I think there are times when I feel much more interested in sex that I do at other times. Sometimes I think my interest level matches my wife's hormonal and menstrual cycles. Is that possible?

It is possible that changes in female hormone levels may influence the level of sexual interest in some males. Studies of married couples have shown that frequency of intercourse sometimes follows a pattern that relates to the wife's menstrual cycle.

In one study, the frequency of sexual intercourse was highest around the time of ovulation (which is also when the wives had their highest levels of testosterone). Interestingly, the husbands initiated sex more often when the wives measured highest in receptivity during a cycle, and wives initiated sex more often when the husbands measured highest in both receptivity and testosterone levels.

A different study found that husbands reported more arousal during their wives' menstrual flow.

Is it possible or practical for a couple ages 53 and 41 to have sex 12 to 15 times per week? My understanding is that this would be impossible because the male needs time to build up a supply of semen in order to create sexual excitement.

That rate is certainly physically possible for some couples, but whether it is practical depends on many different variables besides physical ones. It would be a problem if having sex twelve to fifteen times a week interferes with other aspects of daily life, or if one partner feels coerced or forced into having sex more often than he or she would like. If both partners are satisfied with that rate of sexual activity and continue to lead full, productive lives, then there is no problem.

Most males have a refractory period, a period of time immediately following an orgasm when the body is not capable of responding to sexual stimulation. The length of this refractory period varies enormously from one man to the next, and from one time to the next for the same man. In some men it is only a few minutes, and erection is not lost between one orgasm and the next. In other men, the refractory period is several hours, or even days.

However, sexual arousal is not caused by an accumulation of semen; it is caused by psychological and physical stimulation of the mind and body and can occur whether or not a man has any semen to ejaculate.

Furthermore, desire, arousal, erection, orgasm, and ejaculation are all separate processes. This means that a man can be highly aroused, have an erection and several satisfying orgasms fairly close together, but ejaculate semen during only one orgasm. Many men can have entirely satisfactory orgasms without ejaculating at all.

I am 38 and happily married. My husband and I have always had beautiful and fantastic sex two or three episodes a week, but lately our rate has increased to each night and some mornings. We have been waking each other up in the early morning for sex. I thought people slowed down as they approached 40.

The other day a friend was griping to me that her husband wanted sex too often. When I said we had it every night and that I was always ready for sex, she said I wasn't normal and must be perverted. I didn't tell her that I also sometimes masturbate, or that my husband and I also fondle each other while watching TV so I nearly always feel ready, or that having sex is sometimes my idea.

Is there something wrong with me? Is this unhealthy? What caused this recent increase?

No, there's nothing wrong with you and no, your behavior is not mentally or physically unhealthy. As long as you and your husband are in general agreement about how and when to have sex, there is no problem.

It is often reported that after the first year or two of marriage, the "average" American couple has intercourse two or three times per week during their twenties and thirties and then gradually less often after that. But the range of actual frequencies reported is quite wide (some couples have no intercourse at all, while others have intercourse two or three times each day). Each rate is considered "normal" as long as both partners are satisfied about it, regardless of whether or not their rate is close to the statistical average.

There's nothing unusual about couples who become more sexually active as they get older, and there are several reasons why this may happen: couples often develop a better understanding of their own and each other's sexual responses, they achieve happiness or stability in other nonsexual aspects of the marriage, or find new freedom from the demands of child rearing or careers.

There is also nothing wrong with a woman taking the initiative sexually. In studies looking at factors involved in happy marriages, one important aspect was that both partners felt equally comfortable about initiating sexual activity and each had an equal right to decline to have sex. When sexual initiation and/or sexual refusal was one-sided, sexual satisfaction tended to be lower for both partners.

My husband and I used to have a terrific sex life but since we've both been working, it's fallen away until we hardly make love at all. Could this be due to both of us working?

It is certainly possible. There are lots of other possibilities as well, including new parenthood, grown children who've left home (empty nest syndrome), financial worries, and job-related stress.

Work may affect sexual functioning in many different ways. If a career enhances a person's self-esteem, his or her attitude toward sex often improves. Conversely, problems at work can be brought home and cause sexual problems. Couples who work different shifts have very little time together for sex. Women who work outside the home and also carry the majority of household and child-care duties may have little time or energy left for themselves or for sexual behavior. And some spouses feel threatened by the possibility of having the relationship disrupted if their partner is exposed to other, presumably more tempting, people at work.

Couples who say that they don't have time to make love simply must reserve time for it in their schedules. This means that they must make specific arrangements to be alone, not be interrupted, and focus only on each other and on being romantic.

Is it possible for a couple to "burn out" their bodies by too much sexual intercourse? My wife and I experience intercourse at least once a day. Is it better to rest your body sometimes rather than overdoing it? Both of us are healthy and at an above-average fitness level. At this frequency, is it possible to eventually reach a point where the body will no longer respond to sexual stimulation?

Quite the opposite seems to be true. Your current level of regular sexual activity may actually be one way of ensuring that you and your wife will remain sexually responsive and active into old age.

Until this century, some authorities assumed that people, especially men, were born with a fixed amount of sexual fluids in their bodies. This type of thinking led to dire warnings about squandering one's "vital fluids" too early in life.

We now know that men produce sperm and ejaculatory fluids continuously, beginning with puberty and throughout the rest of their lives, unless production is disrupted by illness or injury. Even though women cease producing eggs at menopause, with good health and regular sexual activity their genitalia can continue to function very well sexually.

You should also know that having intercourse once a day isn't particularly rare. Approximately 5 to 15 percent of people in their thirties report having intercourse every day.

What is the source of those statistics: "approximately 5 to 15 percent of people in their thirties report having intercourse every day"?

The figures are based on studies of intercourse frequency in 13 different books and articles from 1932 to the present. But resist the urge to compare your personal sexual pattern to statistical data like these.

Many people read such research data and interpret them to mean that they're not "normal." They conclude that they're having too much or too little sex. Other people use the data to set sexual performance standards for themselves and see themselves as failures if they don't match the data. Or they use this information to try to force partners into changing sexual behaviors, calling them "abnormal" if they won't comply.

Whenever you hear a statistic, try to think about the flip side of every finding. The flip side of this would be that 85 to 95 percent of people in their thirties have intercourse less often or more often. Also statistical results represent a mathematical average compiled from many individuals and do not necessarily match any particular person or couple in the study.

My wife needs sex frequently. Is she suffering from nymphomania? Actually, what is nymphomania?

Nymphomania is a commonly misused and misunderstood term (in Greek, nymphe means "bride" and mania means "madness" or "frenzy") that has been used to refer to a woman who has a persistently high sex drive *and* who rarely achieves satisfaction even if orgasm does occur. It may also involve having numerous partners. In men, the same characteristics have been called *satyriasis* or *Don Juanism*. A more scientific term for both conditions is *hypersexuality*.

Not a great deal of research on hypersexuality exists. Masters and Johnson define it as a condition in which an insatiable need for sex interferes with daily functioning. They also report that for these individuals there is little if any emotional intimacy with the sex act, and even if orgasm occurs, it is not satisfying.

Men who are threatened by a woman with a higher sex drive than their own often will use the term nymphomaniac in a derogatory manner, but in fact this term is completely inappropriate to describe a wife with a high sex drive. One common stereotype is that a man who has a high sex drive is to be envied, while a woman in the same situation is looked upon as "abnormal."

Go together to visit a sex therapist *(see Appendix)* so that you both have a chance to state what should be improved about your sex life.

What are the most popular positions for intercourse?

The most commonly used position in Western cultures is the so-called missionary position (lying down, man-on-top, face-to-face; *see Illustration 10*). There are many vaguely similar accounts about the origin of this term. One such story tells of a group of Pacific islanders who observed this sexual practice among Western missionaries and gave it that name, since it differed from their own usual position of having the woman on the top.

The woman-on-top position, with partners face-to-face and the woman either sitting up or lying down, is another common position for penile-vaginal intercourse. Others include face-to-face while lying side by side; and rear-entry positions, in which the man faces the woman's back while kneeling, sitting, standing, or lying down (also called the "spoon position"; *see Illustration 33 in Chapter 18*).

As with many other sexual activities, the choice of favorite intercourse position varies widely among individuals, couples, and even cultures. For example, the missionary position is among the most frequently used by couples in the United States, Japan, and some traditional groups in South America. Woman-on-top positions are more common than other positions among specific cultural groups in some of the South Pacific islands and sitting positions more common in tribal Australia. Various types of rear-entry positions are favored by couples of many groups, for example, the Marquesans in the Pacific.

I am 24 and have been happily married for 10 months. The other night my husband asked me to ride him while we were having sex. Fortunately he didn't make fun of me or laugh when I asked him what that meant and he just said, "Don't worry about it." Please tell me what this means. I want to please my husband.

The first recorded usage of this slang term was before A.D. 1250 and referred to any act of intercourse. But your husband may have been referring to a particular position, such as the woman sitting on top of the man. The only way to find out exactly what he means by this phrase is to ask him, because slang definitions vary among regions and subcultures.

Does one sexual position in particular provide the most clitoral stimulation and female orgasms in intercourse? I am informed that the clitoris is situated so that optimal stimulation occurs with the rear-entry "doggy style" position.
    Primitive societies were thought to have used this position before adapting to the male-on-top, woman-lying-down position, and most animals use this position naturally as well.

Your information is incorrect. In a rear-entry position, the clitoris receives almost no direct stimulation, unless during intercourse the male reaches around the woman's body and touches the clitoral area with his hand or if the woman touches her clitoris.

In fact, few sexual positions do provide direct stimulation of the clitoris. Instead, indirect stimulation is usually involved. All the nerves in the genital area and in the outer one-third of the vagina are sensitive to pressure and touch, with the clitoris being the most sensitive and also having the capacity to focus sexual arousal received by nearby areas. This is one reason that touching the clitoral area helps many women have orgasms regardless of the position she and her partner use for intercourse.

Women vary as to the position they find most pleasurable (and the most likely to produce orgasm). In general, however, woman-on-top positions are often suggested for women who have difficulty experiencing orgasm during intercourse. It allows a woman more freedom to adjust her body to increase stimulation on whichever areas she finds most pleasurable. It also permits her more control over the depth of penetration and the rhythm of thrusting, other factors often important in achieving orgasm.

The *Kama Sutra* (also spelled *Kaama Suutra* and generally translated "Rules of Love"), an Indian sex manual dating from approximately A.D. 200, describes 529 different positions for intercourse. Man-on-top positions are the most common among all societies studied by modern researchers, even though it is not seen in all cultures and a few do not approve of it.

Woman-on-top positions are found less frequently, but they are certainly depicted in art from ancient cultures, and so also are not "new." Although rear-entry positions are found in many cultures, these sometimes are labeled as too "animal-like" by some social groups. As you mentioned, many, but not all, animals use a rear-entry position.

It is up to each couple to experiment with different positions to see which they find most pleasurable and to change positions under certain circumstances. During pregnancy, for example, rear-entry positions are often the most comfortable, *(see Illustration 29 in Chapter 15)* and in some cases of arthritis, side-by-side positions may be best *(see Illustration 33 in Chapter 18).*

I'm seriously considering marrying a man who is a lot bigger than I am. How does sex work between two people who are so different?

Illustration No. 13. Sensual scenes of human sexuality are frequent in traditional Japanese art. In this page of a folding book that illustrates an erotic story, the woman is shown on top of the man during intercourse. Note the crumpled tissues near the man's arm; each signifies an orgasm experienced by the couple.

Page from a folding accordian book. Japanese. 1850. Colored woodblock print, 7½" x 5⅓". The Kinsey Institute Collections.

I'm unclear about what you're asking. Are you talking about height or weight differences?

If your question is about height, the two of you can experiment with various positions for intercourse, including side-by-side and those not involving lying down, such as sitting on a chair. Anthropological studies have shown that even when there are great differences in height, most of the difference is in the length of the legs, not length of the trunk. Therefore, intercourse between two people who are very different in height isn't as difficult as it might appear.

If your fiancé weighs a great deal more than you do, the same suggestions apply, although intercourse is difficult for some very obese people because the genitalia are nearly buried in fat.

In either case, positions that have the shorter or lighter person on top may provide better sexual functioning because the smaller person can adjust positions, depth, and speed to enhance his or her physiological response.

I'm a 32-year-old man who is somewhat heavyset (5-foot-10, 225 pounds). I also have bad knees. It's impossible for me to have sex in the missionary position and it's hard for me to find partners who don't think that any other position other than that is perverted.

Could you please discuss the mechanics of the sex act when a person is heavyset? I'm sure I'm not the only one in this position (pardon the pun).

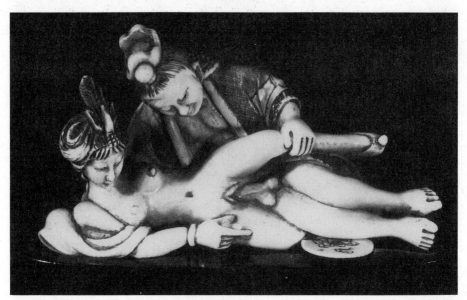

Illustration No. 14. Rear entry vaginal intercourse is depicted in this delicate Chinese ivory carving. The intricate detail and highly polished surface reflects the artistic value of the work, while the diminutive size suggests that it was originally intended for private display. The tiny fan shown near the couple's legs can be placed in the woman's hand to cover the genitalia.

Ivory Carving. Chinese, late 1880s. 1½″ x 3″ x 1¼″. The Kinsey Institute Collections.

Both men and women who have large abdomens, due either to obesity or, in the case of women, pregnancy *(see Illustration 29 in Chapter 15)*, may find it difficult to have intercourse in the missionary position.

An overweight man has several options, according to sex therapists. He can try rear-entry positions, use pillows to elevate his partner's pelvis, lie side by side with his partner at a right angle to him, or lie face up with his buttocks at the edge of a bed or other piece of furniture of the correct height, so that both his feet are on the floor while his partner straddles his body. It has been said that King Edward VII of Britain, who was very heavy, had a special table built so he could comfortably engage in intercourse. Perhaps you could lend copies of the books listed at the end of this chapter to a partner so she understands that special positions are often necessary and are not unusual.

But rather than build a special table or try to convince your partners that using a number of sexual positions is normal, you might consider losing weight. Those extra pounds may be bad for your sex life in other ways. Some researchers think obesity is related to erection problems, and exerting yourself during thrusting may cause you to become short of breath and distracted.

I hope you can give me an answer to a question that's puzzled me throughout my 27-year-marriage. My husband was never circumcised. Can this affect intercourse?

The doctor who gave me a premarital examination said that the penis should

come in direct contact with the clitoris during coitus, but this does not occur in our case, since the generous foreskin covers the vagina like a turtle neck.

Various positions have brought no success. I do not have orgasm during intercourse, but I do with manual stimulation. Either the problem of not having orgasms is due to his not being circumcised or I have been misled about what to expect from togetherness of climax.

You have been misled. Once the penis is inside the vagina it rarely contacts the clitoris which is near the top of the vulva. Moreover, during arousal a woman's clitoris is often covered as her labia swell. Although there aren't much data on this question, whether or not a man is circumcised doesn't appear to affect his partner's sexual functioning.

The advice you received twenty-seven years ago has been replaced by more accurate information. We now know that more than half of all women do not achieve orgasm from penile stimulation alone. Clitoral stimulation that results from penile thrusting is caused by the pulling of muscles surrounding the vagina or from the rubbing of the pubic areas, not from direct contact between the penis and clitoris. (*For more information about orgasms during intercourse see Chapter 8.*)

In our six years of marriage, my husband and I have never had simultaneous orgasms. I think we have a healthy sexual relationship, but I wonder if it could be better.

It is a myth that simultaneous orgasms should occur, that this is an important component of marital happiness, or that it is even desirable as a sexual pattern. Simultaneous orgasms are not common—and, in fact, probably not worth striving for. If by chance they happen, fine. However, clinicians point out that, for many people, an important part of sexual pleasure is watching and experiencing their partner's orgasm. This particular pleasure can be diminished if a person is fully absorbed in having and fully enjoying his or her own orgasm at the same moment.

I'm a 30-year-old male. I've noticed on occasion that my partner reaches orgasm before me, sometimes quite a while before. While I have received no complaints, I'm concerned about whether she's experiencing any pain, discomfort, or even boredom when I continue thrusting after she orgasms. If so what should I do to remedy this?

You have to ask her. She may enjoy continuing the thrusting, she may want thrusting to stop for a while, or she may want you to withdraw after her orgasm and then help you have your own orgasm using manual or oral stimulation. Moreover, she may not want to follow the same pattern each time you have sex. For example, sometimes she may want you to have your orgasm first, withdraw, and then help her have an orgasm using another technique.

Are you under the impression that couples must have their orgasms at the same time? During the 1950s and early 1960s, marriage manuals extolled the virtues of "simultaneous orgasm." This was one of the first widespread attempts to incorporate the idea of the importance of female sexual pleasure into our culture. Many people took this to mean that their sexual experience was somehow unsatisfactory if they didn't experience simultaneous orgasms. This misunderstanding was cleared up by Masters' and Johnson's publications in the 1970s, but then misinterpretations about the type, number, and timing of female orgasms surfaced, leading some people to think their sex lives weren't working correctly unless a woman had multiple orgasms.

Clearly, communication with your partner is far more important than matching research findings or mastering specific sexual techniques. Talk to your partner. Even though you say there are no major problems in your sex life, you may be surprised to discover that discussing such questions will enhance it even more.

Whenever my husband and I make love, I can never really tell or feel if he has climaxed and ejaculated. I can usually guess that he has because he relaxes, but the only way that I know for sure is by asking him. I don't like to do that too much. Could there be something physically wrong?

Are you asking if there's something wrong with you, or with your husband? If you both feel that other aspects of your life and your sexual functioning are satisfactory, then there is probably nothing physically wrong with either of you.

Men (and women) have remarkably varied responses at orgasm. Some make no sound and show no visible release of muscle tension; others scream or have dramatic, uncontrolled muscle spasms—and a few even lose consciousness for a brief time. Most fall somewhere between these extremes. A person's physical signs at orgasm also can differ from one time to the next, depending on mood, level of arousal, and many other factors. And the physical response does not necessarily indicate the amount of pleasure a person is experiencing.

It's unlikely that a woman could feel the ejaculate itself because there are few nerve endings in the inner two-thirds of the vagina. But there are other signs you could look for. The pulsing of the penis that usually accompanies ejaculation can sometimes be felt in the outer one-third of the vagina closest to the opening or by placing a hand near the base of the penis. You can also feel by touching when his testicles draw closer to his body at orgasm.

It sounds as if you and your husband find it uncomfortable to discuss your sex life. Couples who can talk openly about sex are more likely to be satisfied with their marriage and with life in general. Seeing a sex therapist once or twice can help get the conversation going.

I'm 24 and I've had the same boyfriend for five years. We have a great sex life. We have sex almost every day and I always have orgasms, usually through oral sex but sometimes during intercourse too. My best friend is always bragging about her multiple orgasms—10, 12, 16 orgasms in a row! I have never had more than one at a time and I'm beginning to wonder if there's something seriously wrong with my anatomy. Or is it psychological? After I come, my clitoris is too sensitive for any more stimulation. The times my boyfriend tried it, I had to push him away—no pleasure at all. What am I doing wrong? How can I have multiple orgasms too?

Kinsey's data from the 1940s and 1950s found that only 8 to 9 percent of women reported more than one orgasm, with most of these women having only two or three orgasms during one episode of intercourse.

Many women do not like stimulation after they have had an orgasm, just like you. Since it is impossible to objectively compare orgasms between women, there is no way to determine if one woman's experience is "better" or "worse" than another's. The only measure that counts is your satisfaction with your own lovemaking experiences.

I have a question I know a lot of men would like to know the answer to: Is there any way a man can tell if a woman has faked an orgasm? Is there some way her body reacts so she can't be faking an orgasm?

There is no way to be certain if orgasm has actually occurred short of having the woman wired to a huge array of physiological measurement instruments to monitor blood pressure, heart rate, vaginal contractions, brain activity, and all other indicators of arousal and orgasm. Of course you'd also need experts on hand to interpret the readings.

The real question is: Why are you concerned about this? And if you were to discover that a partner was faking orgasm, then what? Unfortunately, some men grade or measure their sexual prowess by whether or not their partner has an orgasm. Clinicians say that many of the women who admit to faking orgasms do it because they don't want to hurt their partner's feelings.

Remember that you don't "give" a partner an orgasm, nor can you "make her" have one. You can, however, learn what sparks and intensifies a partner's sexual arousal, as well as recognizing those things that dampen it. Encourage your partner to tell you, or show you, what she likes best. If you find it impossible to communicate this way, consider discussing these issues with a sex therapist or counselor.

I've been married for eight years and I think my husband and I have a problem. When we have sex it's over very quickly. I assumed that was normal until I read a magazine article about premature ejaculation. When I asked my husband about it, he said "Premature to what?" and said I was too slow, which may be true.

He says that when a man is ready there is no stopping him, and to criticize a man for that is like blaming him for having brown eyes. Books say only that "it varies," with no time given. What is the actual average time for intercourse? Are most men like my husband?

The truth is that the time between penetration and ejaculation varies not only from man to man, but from one time to the next for the same man. The appropriate length of intercourse for you and your husband would be the length of time it takes for you *both* to be mutually satisfied. If you need more intercourse to reach orgasm, then the answer to your husband's question ("Premature to what?") would be that he ejaculates premature to your being satisfied.

This is not to say that researchers have not asked people how long intercourse lasts, but it means that their answers were not linked to the issue of whether the couple was satisfied by that amount of time. For example, during the 1940s and 1950s Kinsey found that 75 percent of men ejaculated within two minutes of penetration. But he didn't ask if the men or their partners considered two minutes mutually satisfying. More recent research reports slightly longer times for intercourse.

Masters and Johnson speculated that premature ejaculation is the most common sexual dysfunction, even though more men seek therapy for erectile difficulties. That's because, although an estimated 15 percent to 20 percent of men experience difficulty controlling rapid ejaculation, most do not consider it a problem requiring help, and many women have difficulty expressing their sexual needs.

But more than half of all women have difficulty achieving orgasm through intercourse by itself no matter how long it lasts, and it is not useful to try to solve the problem by simply prolonging thrusting. Therapists suggest that couples use manual or oral stimulation as a means of increasing a woman's level of arousal before beginning intercourse, adding manual stimulation of the clitoris during intercourse, or combining these techniques with those that slow male orgasm. *(See Chapter 8 for more information.)*

It's important that you and your husband talk about these matters. Having an impartial person such as a trained sex therapist involved in discussions frequently helps. There are, for example, techniques for structuring conversations so that each person can say what he or she would like sexually without placing blame or arguing about whose "fault" it is.

I am an 18-year-old female college student who recently gave up my virginity to my fiancé. How can I strengthen the muscles of my vaginal wall? Is it possible to learn to control the tightening and loosening of these muscles? I've heard that this will increase his pleasure and strengthen his orgasms. Will it do the same for me?

Even though erotic stories often refer to women who have mastered control of their vaginal muscles to bring their male partners to orgasm, most sex researchers are less enthusiastic about this muscular potential than are the authors of these tales.

There is no question that some women do have stronger muscles in the pelvic area, greater awareness of these muscles, and a greater ability to consciously contract and relax them. What is not clear is whether the action of these muscles is directly involved in increasing a woman's sexual responsiveness or orgasms, or those of her partner.

And if strength and control of these muscles were found to be important, it is not clear whether specific exercises can be designed to increase strength and control. Research in this area has focused on the pubococcygeus (PC) muscle, which extends from front to back across the pelvic floor, supports the bladder, and surrounds the urinary, vaginal, and anal openings.

In general, researchers first measure the contraction strength of a woman's PC muscle, teach her a set of exercises to do for several weeks (Kegel exercises), and then remeasure the PC contraction strength after practice. Women answer questions about their sexual responses before and after doing the exercises. So far, these research projects have provided conflicting results. The differences may be due to inadequacies of existing measurement devices, the small numbers of women involved, the short duration of the experiments, or the adequacy of the training the women received.

It is also possible that these programs are destined to succeed (regardless of whether or not pelvic exercises are included) because they focus attention on a woman's sexuality, teach her more about her body, give her permission to sense specific sensations in her pelvis, and provide her a chance to ask questions about sex—all of which improve sexual functioning. *(More information about these exercises is in Chapter 8.)*

Perhaps these are the exercises you've heard about, but I must caution you that many people get themselves into difficulty by focusing on the mechanical aspects of sex and ignoring more important factors.

You also need to know that there is a difference between deliberate and involuntary vaginal contractions. A woman may indeed be able to control vaginal contractions during some phases of sexual response, but the contractions that accompany orgasm are involuntary. Attempting to control contractions at the point of highest arousal could block your ability to continue on to orgasm.

Nearly every time my boyfriend and I make love, I have to urinate. Sometimes I go to the bathroom before we have intercourse, but it doesn't alleviate my need to go afterwards. Is this normal?

Many women report feeling an urge to urinate during different stages of sexual activity. This is understandable, because the nerves and muscles involved in sexual responses are in the same area as those involved in urination. Moreover, during intercourse the penis can sometimes press against the bladder or friction can irritate the urethra (the tube that leads from the bladder to the urinary opening).

Try some different positions to see if a change affects the pressure on your bladder during intercourse.

It's a good idea to urinate after having sex, anyway. This is thought to rid the urethra and bladder of any bacteria that might have been pushed into the urinary tract during sex, reducing the risk of urinary infections.

After sex, I have a strong vaginal odor that I usually don't have. Does male sperm have an odor? My male friend tells me I am nuts. I am extremely clean regarding my body and am concerned about this.

Semen (not sperm) does have an odor; one urology textbook compares the smell to the blossoms of a chestnut tree. Perhaps what you notice is a combination of semen and your own vaginal fluids. Usually neither has a distinctive odor until they reach the external genitals and are exposed to air.

Careful and gentle daily washing of all the folds of the outer genitals (the vulva) during a bath or shower is generally all it takes to prevent vaginal odor. Gently wash all the folds of the outer and inner lips with mild soap and rinse thoroughly. In addition, some women report that gently wiping the genital area with a premoistened towelette (which does *not* contain fragrance or perfume), such as Tucks, is useful after having sex.

If vaginal or genital odor persists, see a gynecologist. Vaginal infections can change the smell of secretions—sometimes without causing other symptoms such as itching, swelling, or increased secretions.

ORAL-GENITAL SEX

Stimulation of the female genitals by a partner's mouth or tongue is called *cunnilingus,* and stimulation of the male genitals by a partner's mouth or tongue is called *fellatio.* These activities can be done as foreplay (to increase arousal before intercourse) or to orgasm.

Recently a friend and I were talking (he's a college grad, 78 years old) and he made a statement that really shocked me. He stated that nine out of ten women (all of them, young and old, single or married) will give a man oral sex. If that's true, I will have lost faith and respect for all of them.

I have never been a part of such an act. My wife of 50 years and I raised five children and not once in our lives did this question arise. To me, this is degrading to both parties. Please answer and tell me this is not true.

Your friend is not exactly correct, but this sexual activity is certainly quite common. People who engage in oral sex generally see it as a normal and pleasurable part of lovemaking, but you are not alone in your reaction. Oral sex is one of the topics some people find either incomprehensible or a subject too taboo for discussion.

Even when Kinsey asked his thousands of research subjects during the 1940s about fellatio and found that about half of husbands had received this, between 1 percent and 3 percent of the men interviewed volunteered the information that they were offended by even the idea.

A few states in the United States have laws against oral-genital sex (where it is often referred to legally as a form of sodomy or a "crime against nature"). Most states do not, however, and have replaced those outdated laws with so-called consenting adults legislation, in which any sexual activity conducted in private between consenting adults who agree on the behavior is not against the law.

Many married couples engage in oral-genital stimulation, and it's also an ancient and widespread sexual practice, not confined to our current U.S. culture.

One study reported that more than 90 percent of married couples younger than 25 had engaged in oral sex. Another study of more than 100 heterosexual couples of all ages reported a similar percentage.

This is a topic that's causing me much mental anguish and I need a few words from somebody (preferably a woman) about it. How does a woman get herself to the point of loving fellatio carried to conclusion? I have been told that 75 percent of all women like it, making me "not normal."

My reaction to a picture of a woman with an ecstatic look on her face, semen in her eyelashes and running down her face, is total repugnance. I've also been told it's men's favorite thing (and I have enough imagination to see why), but I cannot seem to get myself to have the "right" attitude about it.

Am I abnormal? How can I get to like this? What does it do for women?

Each person makes decisions about sexual behavior based on his or her own values, past experiences, knowledge or lack of knowledge. No one should be forced or coerced into doing anything she or he opposes, but people sometimes change their views—if they find they have believed inaccurate information, for instance, or when partners or circumstances change.

For example, a woman who had been opposed to oral activities throughout most of her life might decide to try it if she knew that was the only way her husband could have an erection or orgasm. It would not be unusual or abnormal for her to then report that she enjoyed this activity. One of the most important aspects of sex is the sharing. The feeling of enhancing a partner's pleasure often increases one's own pleasure, unless force or pressure is involved.

The information you've been given about how many women like fellatio is not correct. Although various studies show that 50 to 80 percent of women perform fellatio, only 35 to 65 percent of those find it to be pleasurable; the rest are indifferent (that is, they can take it or leave it) or do not enjoy it at all.

Talking with an experienced professional about this can help you understand your strong negative feelings about fellatio. Call your local mental health center and ask for an appointment with a female counselor. A counselor can help you examine why you feel as strongly as you do. She can explain that even within the context of a loving relationship, some other women do not like or do this, and provide support for your personal decisions about particular sexual activities. She can also practice with you how to explain your feelings about fellatio to a partner in ways that strengthen and preserve the relationship.

So many wives complain about elderly husbands being impotent and no book I've seen gives a clear, satisfactory substitute. I can't for the life of me understand why writers rarely suggest that men perform cunnilingus on their wives. The practice has worked well for me and my wife—and for many other couples, or so we've been told.

I'm glad to read that cunnilingus works for you and your wife. Oral and manual stimulation can be satisfying not only for women whose partners have erection difficulty, but for any woman who doesn't reach orgasm through intercourse. Also, fellatio can often stimulate to orgasm a man who has lost his ability to have erections.

Researchers also confirm what you've suspected all along: oral-genital stimulation is a common sexual activity for older couples. A recent study of Americans aged 50 and older reported that 56 percent of men said they gave oral stimulation and 49 percent of women said they received it; 95 percent of the men and 82 percent of women who engaged in this behavior reported enjoying it.

Although cunnilingus is effective and satisfying for many couples, some individuals and couples have a strong emotional bias against it. So while it works well for you and your wife, it's also true that some couples view oral-genital stimulation as taboo sexual behavior.

What is "69"? I'm sure it has to do with sex, but what does it mean?

It stands for the sexual position when a couple engages in oral-genital activity with each other at the same time. Look at the way the numbers 6 and 9 are shaped, imagine that the rounded parts are heads and the straight parts are the rest of a body of a stick figure, and then put them together—the result approximates a drawing of two people, each with their mouth on the other's genitals.

This position isn't always easy to do if the partners are of greatly different heights. And even though it can be an arousing type of activity, it's advisable to be quite familiar with each other's responses at orgasm before trying to have simultaneous orgasms in this position. A person cannot control any body jerking or facial clinching if he or she has that type of automatic response at orgasm, so this is an activity where it's sometimes advisable to take turns.

I'm a woman who wants to know how many calories there are in a single sperm ejaculate of the average male.

There are approximately five calories in the amount of semen usually ejaculated.

I wonder if during oral sex, is it dangerous to swallow so many sperm at one time?

There is no evidence that swallowing semen (the fluid ejaculated by men at orgasm, which includes the sperm) is harmful to your health—unless the semen comes from someone who carries a disease that can be sexually transmitted. Diseases that can be transmitted by semen include gonorrhea, chlamydia, hepatitis B, and possibly the AIDS virus. Moreover, just having oral contact with the genitals (without swallowing semen) can transmit herpes, syphilis, and human papillomavirus if these organisms are present. You should follow safer sex guidelines (described in Chapter 19) with partners unless you are certain they do not have an active stage of these diseases.

If a man takes medications for high blood pressure and a heart condition (post bypass surgery), are there residues of these drugs in his semen? If so, could this affect his partner's health if they have oral sex?

Unfortunately, there has been little research on the passage of various drugs into semen, but it is known that some drugs taken orally can be found in semen. For example, tetracycline (an antibiotic) has been found in semen shortly after the drug is ingested.

But the chance that any drug residue will have an impact on the health of the partner is slight. First, the amount of semen ejaculated each time is small (about one teaspoon) and so the amount of any drug in an ejaculation would be extremely small. Secondly, although tiny amounts of drug traces or by-products might exist, any effects would be further diminished by the process of being metabolized in the partner's body.

My boyfriend and I are talking about becoming sexually active and we're exploring our different birth control options. There's something I've been wondering about. If we used spermicide, will it drip and interfere if my boyfriend were to kiss my genital area?

Any spermicide which comes from the vagina can be wiped away before having oral sex. Keep a damp washcloth or a packet of premoistened fragrance-free towelettes beside the bed. But make sure you carefully follow the directions for using spermicides effectively. Most should be inserted shortly before inter-course. Prolonged foreplay or oral sex may reduce the effectiveness of spermicides by the time a couple begins intercourse.

Illustration No. 15. The depictions of anal intercourse on this ancient Peruvian painted clay vessel and others in the Kinsey Institute Collections suggest that this behavior was known and commonly practiced in this and other cultures.

Stirrup vessel. Mochican/Pre-Columbian, 400 B.C.–A.D. 700; 5½" x 9". The Kinsey Institute Collections.

ANAL SEX

Anal sex is exactly what it sounds like, sexual activities that include stimulation of the anorectal area.

My wife and I are in our 50s. She enjoys anal sex. We would like to know if there is any danger to this.

Depending on the study being cited, between 20 percent and 43 percent of married women have tried anal intercourse. Of the 43 percent mentioned above, around 40 percent of those women found it pleasurable—so your wife's experience is not unusual. Furthermore, in two studies which asked this question, 13 percent of women (in one study) and 9 percent (in the other study) reported that they engaged in anal intercourse regularly.

Unlike the vagina, the rectum produces no natural lubrication. Therefore, tissues are more prone to damage or irritation and thus more prone to infection. A lubricant should be used, insertion must be gentle, and thrusting may need to be slower or more shallow than with vaginal intercourse. After anal contact it is very important that the penis be washed thoroughly before using it to stimulate or penetrate your wife's vagina, or rectal bacteria may be transferred to the vagina, which can cause infection.

I have long wondered why so few expressed disgust about lesbianism and anal sex, and now I've read that about 40 percent of women have "experienced" anal intercourse.

Did this percentage include women who "experimented" only once or those who practice this regularly? What percentage of married couples do this regularly? What percentage do this as a method of birth control? I suggest it is important to elaborate on the statistics you use.

In the study you refer to, of the 43 percent of women who had tried anal intercourse, 22 percent had done this once, 19 percent had anal sex occasionally, and 2 percent did it often. All the women in that magazine survey were married. In two other scientific studies, which reported that 3 percent and 9 percent of women had anal intercourse regularly, it was not clear how many of the women were married.

I haven't seen any research that reports how many married couples use anal intercourse for contraception, but among white middle-class Americans (unfortunately the only group for which there are enough data to draw any conclusions on this topic) this behavior is apparently done more frequently for sexual pleasure than for avoiding pregnancy.

The study data you questioned were based on a random sample drawn from 100,000 married women surveyed by *Redbook* magazine; of the 43 percent of women who had tried anal intercourse, 40 percent found it somewhat or very enjoyable, 49 percent didn't like it, and 10 percent had no particular feelings one way or the other. Although this is not a carefully controlled scientific survey, it is still useful because there is little research on this question and the more carefully controlled studies generally survey fewer people. This study clearly shows that regardless of the exact percentage, a great number of married heterosexual women have engaged in anal intercourse, many do it more than once, and many enjoy it.

The connection between lesbians and anal sex you implied in your letter is confusing. With the possible exception that both behaviors may be considered unacceptable by some people, women who have sex with other women rarely use any type of anal penetration.

With all the articles I have read regarding the AIDS controversy, I am still confused and worry about anal intercourse. Is it possible for a man and a

woman who are not infected by the AIDS virus to become infected during anal intercourse? Or does one of the partners have to be infected for the virus to spread?

You're not the only one who is confused. Survey results included in the first chapter of this book show that half of Americans think that a person can get AIDS by having anal intercourse even if neither partner is infected with the AIDS virus.

Anal sex does *not* cause AIDS or any other sexually transmitted disease (STD) if neither partner is infected with HIV (the virus that causes AIDS) or any other infectious organism. If neither partner has the virus, the risk of AIDS— regardless of the specific sexual activity engaged in—is zero.

However, anal intercourse appears to be the sexual activity which most easily transmits the AIDS virus *if* it is present, perhaps because the anal and rectal tissues are more likely to be damaged, thereby providing easy access into the body.

I am a young woman, 26 years old. I have been going out with the same man of 44 for about five years. There is something that I don't seem to adjust too well to, and I would like to present it to you: I wonder if it is normal to have rectal relations in a heterosexual relationship. I don't like it. Also, I was once told that the man might have a homosexual tendency. Is it true?

Not all males who practice anal intercourse are homosexual or bisexual. There are some data that suggest that some bisexual men enjoy anal sex, but so do some totally heterosexual men. The Kinsey Institute reviewed seven studies and surveys conducted over the past 40 years to derive an estimate of the number of women who have experienced anal intercourse at least once. Our conservative estimate is that 39 percent—or more than one in three—have done so. In a recent study by The Kinsey Institute of college students at a Midwestern university, almost 24 percent of the women and 27 percent of the men reported having tried anal intercourse at least once.

Studies which asked if homosexual males engaged in anal intercourse report that between 59 percent and 95 percent had done so. As you can see, not all homosexual men engage in anal intercourse, and a reasonably large percentage of heterosexuals have tried it.

But, regardless of how widespread this practice may be, no one should be forced to perform any sexual activity that he or she does not want to do.

My boyfriend has expressed a keen interest in anal sex. We have tried it several times, but have not succeeded in penetration because I find it too painful. Is there any way to make anal intercourse less painful? What type of lubricant is best for this kind of intercourse?

In addition to using a lubricant (which must be water-based, have no oil at all, if you are using condoms), other suggestions for reducing discomfort and increasing pleasure during anal sex include making slight adjustments to the angle of entry and experimenting with different body positions, such as the woman lying on her back with her knees pulled to her chest, or the woman kneeling on her knees and hands. Pushing out with the rectal muscles as penetration is started may also help.

Even though some women enjoy anal sex, don't do it if you don't want to.

Does anal penetration cause anal cancer?

Anal cancer affects one man out of every 100,000 per year (aged 20 to 79). The incidence in women is higher, estimated as 1.6 women per 100,000 per year.

Causes of anal cancer are not yet clear. Penile penetration can cause small tears in the rectum and several STDs have been found in the rectum. Of particular concern with regard to rectal cancer is the human papillomavirus. This virus is now suspected of being involved in the early stages of some other types of cancer, such as cancer of the cervix (*see Chapter 19*). There has been speculation that sexual activity involving the anus *might* increase the risk of cancer *if* there are certain STDs present, but there are no data to support or refute this idea.

HOMOSEXUALITY AND BISEXUALITY

Homosexuality is a sexual orientation label that describes romantic attraction to, sexual desire for, or sexual behavior with a person of one's own sex (in Greek *homo* means "same"). Today many persons who are erotically attracted to and/or have sex with persons of the same sex prefer use of the word *gay*. Although I acknowledge there are valid reasons for avoiding the use of a term which has negative connotations, this book will continue to use the technical term *homosexual* traditionally employed in medicine and science. It will apply to both men and women except when we need to distinguish between the sexes; then the word *homosexual* will apply to males and the word *lesbian* to females. Bisexuality means sexual responsiveness to both sexes (in Latin, a meaning of *bi* is "two").

Science has not yet identified what determines sexual orientation—what causes a male or a female to be heterosexual (sexually attracted to people of the opposite sex), homosexual, or bisexual. What *has* been established, however, is that simple explanations (such as having a domineering mother) do not hold true for most homosexuals. Homosexuals and bisexuals come from as many different backgrounds as do heterosexuals.

We also now know that homosexuality is not "catching" or "contagious." Studies of children raised by homosexual parents show that they are no more likely to grow up to be homosexual than children raised by heterosexuals.

Moreover, there is now strong evidence that sexual orientation is not necessarily determined by the early social/cultural environment. One good example is a tribe in New Guinea where all young boys by approximately age eight begin to live in all-male groups. This tribe believes that in order to grow into a man, the younger boys must regularly ingest semen which the older boys directly provide (homosexual fellatio). However, at about age 17, 95 percent marry and add heterosexual fellatio to their behavior, and after the wife's first menstrual flow begin also to have heterosexual intercourse. After the birth of the first child, homosexual activity stops and 95 percent of these males engage in only heterosexual activities for the rest of their lives. The remaining 5 percent, whether married or not, continue homosexual behavior.

Finally, it is clear that people do not necessarily maintain the same sexual orientation throughout their lives. Some people have consistent homosexual orientation for a long period of time, then fall in love with a person of the opposite sex; other individuals who have had only opposite-sex partners later fall in love with a same-sex partner.

These changes are not a matter of "choice," just as a person can't will or force himself or herself to "fall in love" with some particular person. Just like heterosexuals, homosexual men and women fall in love and form lasting, loving, caring, and committed relationships.

This may seem like a dumb question, but what exactly is a homosexual? And what does a homosexual do (sexually) that's different from other people? I'd think they wouldn't have the right anatomy for sex with each other.

Generally speaking, homosexuals are people who feel sexual attraction to, and desire for, persons of the same sex. In other words, homosexual men are attracted to or fall in love with men; homosexual women are attracted to or fall in love with women.

The only major difference between homosexual and heterosexual sex activities is that homosexuals can't engage in penile-vaginal intercourse with a member of the same sex. All other sexual feelings and activities can occur, including kissing, caressing, hugging, nipple stimulation and other nongenital touching or foreplay, and oral-genital, hand-genital, and anal-genital activities. As with heterosexuals, homosexuals use a variety of positions to achieve sexual satisfaction; not all couples participate in or enjoy all possible behaviors.

Orgasm for homosexual men is most frequently achieved by fellatio or mutual masturbation. Orgasm for homosexual women is most frequently a result of mutual masturbation.

Contrary to popular myth, not all male homosexuals engage in anal intercourse. Another common myth is that all female homosexuals insert phalluslike objects into the vagina; research shows that only some engage in this activity.

Research comparing the sexual responses of homosexuals and heterosexuals has established that the basic physiology of sexual response is the same for both groups. This means that all men have the same pattern of desire, arousal, orgasm, ejaculation, and resolution whether they have sex with a male or a female. And the sexual response cycle for women is also the same, whether their sexual partners are female or male. Homosexual men and women also can have the same problems with relationships and the same problems with sexual functioning as do heterosexuals.

What percentage of the U. S. population is homosexual?

It depends on how you define "homosexual." It helps to distinguish between a person's sexual-orientation label (how you identify yourself—as heterosexual or homosexual), and his or her actual behavior (who you had sex with this week, last year, ten years ago). For example, research indicates that between 62 and 79 percent of men who label themselves homosexual have had sex with women. Thus the label a person chooses may not accurately describe or predict all sex behaviors and partners across the lifespan.

Approximately one-third of all males are thought to have had at least one same-sex experience leading to orgasm since puberty. The Kinsey data reported that about 8 percent of U. S. males had had exclusively same-sex partners for at least a period of three years at some point in life. Only about 4 percent of men were exclusively homosexual throughout their entire lives.

Among U. S. females, Kinsey found that around half of college-educated women and approximately 20 percent of non-college-educated women had at least one same-sex erotic contact past puberty; only 2 or 3 percent of these women were exclusively homosexual their entire lives.

Although these figures are taken from data collected by Kinsey in the 1940s and 1950s on primarily white middle-class subjects, they still provide the best estimates available. But the actual incidence of homosexual orientation may not be as important as understanding the fact that whether researchers find that 3 percent or 10 percent of people primarily engage in homosexual behavior, the actual *number* of people involved is quite large; given the current estimate that there are more than 250 million people in the United States, this means that a minimum of 7.5 million people in the United States alone are homosexual.

Do you agree that there are degrees of one's sexuality? That there are seven degrees ranging from 0 completely heterosexual to 6 completely homosexual and around 3 being bisexual? Is that scale to determine sexual orientation or simply measure sexual behavior? And is there in fact a difference between sexual orientation and behavior?

That scale, called the "Kinsey scale," was devised by Kinsey and has been widely used by sex researchers for more than 40 years. The scale classified persons with *only* heterosexual behavior as 0, only homosexual behavior as 6, and persons with mixtures of male and female sexual partners as 1, 2, 3, 4, or 5.

We too wondered if the scale continued to be useful for current research purposes. In 1986 The Kinsey Institute hosted a symposium for 50 of the world's most eminent researchers from many disciplines (including anthropology, biology, history, medicine, psychiatry, psychology, and sociology) and asked them the same question. Their opinions are compiled in *Homosexuality/Heterosexuality: Concepts of Sexual Orientation*, volume 2 in The Kinsey Institute Series published by Oxford University Press.

There was general agreement that the scale, while still useful, is enhanced by including separate scales for factors such as love, sexual attraction, fantasy, and self-identification. Another major point was that an individual's rating can change over time. In other words, the Kinsey scale should not be seen as a series of rigid, fixed descriptions that necessarily describe all behaviors or predict future behavior.

To use your question as an example, if a person had sex *only* with opposite-sex partners but fantasized about having sex with same-sex partners, on the original scale that person would be a 0. On the more complex scale, the 0 rating would remain on the partner scale, but the person would be a 1-6 on the fantasy scale, depending on what proportion of his or her fantasies included same-sex partners. In fact, researchers have discovered that one of the most common fantasies among heterosexuals is having sex with a same-sex partner, which can be reassuring to people who worry about future behavior when the content of their fantasies doesn't match their current behavior.

Thoughtful scientists have come to question whether labels such as homosexual or bisexual tell us very much about the way a person actually behaves sexually. In many past studies, once a person described himself or herself as homosexual, the researcher did not ask any questions about behavior with the opposite sex, assuming these questions would not apply to a homosexual; they also did not ask people who called themselves heterosexual about same-sex partners. But in a recent Kinsey Institute study of a group of lesbians from across the United States, 43 percent of even the women who had *always* referred to themselves as lesbian had had sex at least once with a man since age 18; of the total group of lesbians, 74 percent had experienced heterosexual sex.

What causes homosexuality? I don't understand how, given the same upbringing, one boy turns out normal and his brother grows up to be a homosexual.

Before answering your question I must address the use of the word "normal." The use of that word can imply that if a person is homosexual then he or she is not normal in some way. Homosexuality is not an abnormality, illness, or disorder.

No one knows what "causes" homosexuality. For that matter, no one knows what "causes" heterosexuality either. Many theories have been proposed, but so far most have not held up under careful scrutiny and none have been proven. In fact, scientists probably have a clearer idea of what does *not* cause a homosexual orientation. Children raised by gay or lesbian parents or couples, for instance, are *no* more likely to grow up to be homosexual than are children raised by heterosexual parents.

There also is *no* evidence that male homosexuality is caused by a dominant mother and/or a weak father, or that female homosexuality is caused by girls choosing male role models. There is evidence, in fact, that parents have very little influence on the outcome of their children's sexual-partner orientation.

It also is not true that people become homosexuals because they were seduced by an older person of the same sex in their youth. The childhood and adolescent sexual experiences of both homosexuals and heterosexuals are fairly similar, except that homosexuals recall later that they found opposite-sex encounters less satisfying than did heterosexuals.

Current theory is that there probably are many different developmental paths by which a person can come to be homosexual, bisexual, or heterosexual.

Please help! I just discovered that my 20-year-old son is gay. I carry this burden alone as my husband and older children are scornful of the whole homosexual scene. Why would a man "choose" to be gay when it is such a difficult life? Suicides must be high for these men.

You need help and support dealing with your feelings about your son. One source of support for many has been the national organization PFLAG (Parents and Friends of Lesbians and Gays). Write to Box 24565, Los Angeles, CA 90024.

First, your son did not "choose" to be gay in the way we usually think of the word *choice*, as in choosing to be a police officer or a physician, for example. And no scientist can tell you with certainty why your son's sexual-partner orientation is same-sex any more than why yours is opposite-sex. Perhaps part of the confusion about whether this is a voluntary type of choice comes from using words like preference instead of orientation.

Secondly, your worries about his mental health are likely to be unfounded. Questioning the earlier studies which used only men who had sought therapy, as early as the 1950s Dr. Evelyn Hooker (who became the chairperson of the 1967 National Institute of Mental Health Taskforce on Homosexuality) found that homosexual males not in or seeking therapy were no more neurotic than heterosexual males. More recent studies show that homosexuals can and do lead happy, mentally and physically healthy, lives. In the studies with more negative findings (for example, that 20 percent of homosexual men had made a suicide attempt as compared to 4 percent of a sample of heterosexual men), it appears that psychological problems may be more prevalent among only some types of homosexuals, just as they are among some types of heterosexuals.

Adolescent gays may be particularly vulnerable to suicide. Although there are few data on this issue, teenagers in general have a high rate of suicide and young gays may have an even higher rate. Feelings or fear about being rejected and isolated by family and friends are thought to be one major reason for suicide attempts by adolescent gays. PFLAG can help you find support for you and your son, if he is in psychological distress.

I desperately hope you'll answer my questions because I'm extremely unhappy and don't know where else to turn. I'm in my late teens and think I might be gay (or bisexual). I would rather not live if I have to live this life style. I know it's okay for some but not for me. I have several questions. First of all, where can one go to get counseling to "turn around" a gay person? Also, is this possible? Would injections of male hormones help? I've heard of a drug that disrupts all sexual desire. That might be my last hope.

It is not uncommon for people your age to feel confused about their sexual feelings, but the idea of using male hormone injections (testosterone) to "cure" homosexuality or other hormones to reduce sexual desire is not helpful. There is no evidence to support the notion that injecting any hormone or other medication has any effect on sexual orientation.

It's important to remember that sexual feelings aroused by a person of the same sex, fantasizing about same-sex activities, or even having sex with another male are not accurate predictors of your adult sexual orientation. In fact, approximately one out of three men has had at least one same-sex experience since puberty.

Stereotyped life styles don't exist for heterosexuals, homosexuals, or bisexuals. A wide range of behaviors and values exist within each of these groups, and some people change from one category to another at various points in their lives.

Find a center that specializes in counseling for adolescents and young adults so you can get the support and the information you need to help you resolve these issues (see Appendix).

I have just found out that one of my sons is gay. Can homosexuality be cured? How? Does a man who has had sex with men ever change and go "straight"?

The important question is how does your son feel about being homosexual? Sometimes well-meaning family members send homosexuals to therapists to have their sexual orientation changed. However, sexual orientation, whether heterosexual or homosexual, is not readily changed by any type of intervention.

According to the American Psychological Association and the American Psychiatric Association, homosexual orientation in and of itself is not a mental disorder. However, if an individual is unhappy about his or her orientation, then counseling may be helpful. A competent therapist will work with a client to ascertain the source of the unhappiness; many times it results from rejection by the family or stress from society's reactions.

A few researchers have reported on a small number of men and women who *voluntarily* came for therapy to change from same-sex to opposite-sex partners at some point in their adult lives because they were highly distressed by their sexual behavior. Evaluation of therapy programs designed to assist homosexuals who wish to function sexually as heterosexuals report varying success rates. It is not clear whether these individuals' orientation (which sex one falls "in love" with and is most aroused by) is actually changed or whether the only change is the ability to limit sexual behavior to opposite-sex partners.

In other words, the important issue is your son's happiness, self-acceptance, and whether he will be able to form loving relationships, regardless of the sex of his sexual partners.

Isn't it true that most people are bisexual—that there is some element of attraction to or love for members of one's own sex in everyone?

If you include attraction and love for individuals of both sexes in your definition of bisexuality, then yes: Many people could be labeled bisexual under those rules. However, if you count as bisexual only those people whose actual sexual activity is with partners of both sexes over a period of some years, then only 10 to 15 percent of the U.S. population can be labeled bisexual.

Some of those individuals would reject the bisexual label because they do not identify themselves in that way. Many prisoners, for example, have sexual activity with partners of the same sex only while they are incarcerated but continue to think of themselves as being heterosexual, not homosexual or bisexual. Both before and after being in prison, they have no sexual activity with partners of the same sex. Furthermore there is evidence that some people in the general population engage in occasional homosexual behavior yet think of themselves as heterosexuals.

At a Kinsey Institute symposium on the topic of sexual orientation, a researcher described a 65-year-old man who was happily married for 45 years but who, within a year of the death of his wife, fell in love with another man; this man reported that during his 45 years of marriage, he had never been attracted to or fantasized about another male. Another report involved a woman who first fell in love with a man, whom she married; ten years later, she fell in love with a woman and divorced her husband; but now, in her forties, she finds herself again sexually attracted to a man. These types of changes over the course of a lifetime (although probably not common) illustrate how complicated it can be to assign labels or categories to an individual solely on behavior at one period in his or her life.

I am a homosexual, 21 years old, and very interested in bisexuality. I have read a great deal about myself and my orientation, but am finding it very difficult to find any literature or books on bisexuality. This is interesting to me because several of my friends claim to be bisexual, and I am wondering about some possibly bisexual feelings within myself. Do all homosexuals have these feelings, or are homosexuals and bisexuals completely different?

There is an enormous number of ways to classify individuals based on actual sex behavior, attraction to specific partners, content of fantasies, or feelings of love. It wouldn't be unusual, for example, for a man to have sexual activity only with another man, but simultaneously have heterosexual fantasies and feel affection for and be attracted to women. A review of research studies shows that 62 to 79 percent of men who define themselves as homosexual have had sex with a woman, and that 74 to 81 percent of lesbian women have had at least one sexual encounter with a man.

There are very few individuals who are equally attracted to, can equally fall in love with, and have equal numbers of partners from both sexes. So the idea that to be bisexual means *equal* interest and activity is erroneous. It's probably better to talk about a person being "behaviorally bisexual" rather than using the label bisexual.

Many researchers no longer believe that people can be clearly divided into groups of homosexuals, heterosexuals, and bisexuals by simply asking about the sex of past or present sexual partners. When it comes to labeling one's sexual-orientation identity (not sexual behavior), the best judge is the individual himself or herself. And often you cannot predict behavior accurately from the label a person has selected.

This concept becomes increasingly important in terms of applying safer sex guidelines as individuals attempt to determine whether a potential sexual partner's past or present behavior places them at higher risk of infection with the AIDS virus (HIV). *(See Chapter 19.)*

Today, I again heard one of those preachers on TV say that the average homosexual has had more than 1000 sexual partners. As a gay man I find that hard to believe.

I have been monogamous for nine years with my first (and only) love. And, even though none of my gay friends has been lucky enough to find such a great relationship, none has had anywhere near 1000 partners. Are there any studies on this?

In one study during the 1970s, 574 male homosexuals were asked the number of sex partners they had had. About 40 percent reported having at least 500 sexual partners, but boasting or exaggeration may have been involved. Another survey from the same period revealed that three out of four male homosexuals (75 percent) reported more than thirty different partners during their lives.

In general, past research has shown that most homosexual men (but certainly not all) have a higher number of sexual partners than most heterosexual men. But some researchers speculate that many people in long-lasting homosexual relationships are missed when research data are collected because they are less likely to frequent gay bars or clubs, locations where most researchers enlisted their research subjects.

Moreover, recent studies conducted in San Francisco report that homosexual men have greatly reduced their number of sexual contacts, presumably because they have responded to educational information about the risk of AIDS rising with the number of sexual partners one has.

Are there data available on long-term male homosexual relationships? For example, what percentage of couples are together 5, 10, or 15 years?

A study of 156 male couples by Drs. David McWhirter and Andrew Mattison, a psychiatrist and a clinical psychologist, showed that many homosexual relationships do last for long periods. One of the couples they interviewed had been together for thirty-seven years. This study supports similar work by Masters and Johnson with homosexual couples. Their research found relationship patterns similar to those for heterosexual couples.

Even though some homosexual men have more sex partners than most heterosexual men, long-term relationships are not as unusual as the media might lead us to believe. In fact, a Kinsey Institute study published in 1981 found that nearly all of the several hundred homosexual men studied had had at least one steady relationship that lasted between one and three years. At the time of the interviews (well in advance of the current AIDS crisis), more than half the men were involved in such a long-term relationship.

Although long-term lesbian relationships have not been studied as intensively, in one survey of more than 1500 lesbian couples the average length of time as a couple was four years.

I am a 37-year-old gay male. My lover and I are monogamous. How much risk is there that either one of us will contract AIDS? We've been together six years, and our sexual activities are varied.

If neither of you is infected with the virus (HIV) that causes AIDS (which researchers believe has been prevalent since 1980) and neither is having sex with others or sharing needles with others, then your risk of getting infected with the AIDS virus (HIV) is as close to zero as anyone can get. If you are unsure about whether you were infected before your exclusive relationship— get tested.

The sole remaining risk would be infection through a contaminated blood transfusion, which has become very rare now that all blood is tested for HIV antibodies.

Your risk would be no higher than it is for sexually exclusive heterosexual partners. If the AIDS virus (HIV) is not present in one of the partners you cannot get AIDS regardless of which sexual activities you engage in. *(See Chapter 19.)*

Since yeast infections are caused by certain fungus and/or bacteria which are also present in the mouth as well as the vagina, can women transmit to other women by kissing? Or must they have oral sex to transmit this or other diseases?

Since women who relate sexually only to other women have relatively few problems with sexually transmitted diseases, please state how any infections and/or venereal diseases are transmitted between women.

There has been little research on health issues affecting lesbians and little is known about which diseases are sexually transmitted between them. Among sexually active groups, lesbians have the lowest rates of syphilis and gonorrhea, much lower than heterosexual women. To date, four reports of the AIDS virus being transmitted between lesbian partners have been published, but there is some question as to whether the methodology in these case studies was sound.

Researchers speculate that these low rates may be partly due to lesbian sexual behaviors, which often do not include penetration, and so the risk of exposure to infectious organisms via breaks in oral, vaginal, or anal tissues is reduced.

Another factor may be that most lesbians have fewer sexual partners than do other sexually active women. And female-to-female contact may simply be a less efficient way of transmitting an infectious organism than is male-to-female or male-to-male contact.

There are some other data that suggest why lesbians may have lower rates of vaginal Candida albicans infections (commonly called yeast infections) than other women. Possibly it is because few use birth-control pills (those with high estrogen content increase a woman's susceptibility to yeast infections). There are a few reports of Candida albicans infections of the throat, but these have been attributed to oral-genital contact, not to kissing.

Even though STD risks appear to be low, lesbians should still follow "safer sex" guidelines. Having sex with a woman who has had contact with men or who uses intravenous drugs increases risks. Don't assume that few lesbians have sex with men; in a recent Kinsey Institute study of lesbian women, 74 percent had had sex with a man at least once since age 18.

The few researchers who have studied STDs among lesbians all stress that women in their studies tend to neglect regular gynecological care. It is not clear whether this is because they hesitate to see male physicians or if they believe that as lesbians they are at lower risk for gynecological problems. One study of lesbian health reported that, on average, lesbians had not had a Pap test for twenty-one months, as compared to an eight-month interval since the last Pap test for the other women going to the same clinic.

Although STD risks are lower for lesbians, they have the same risks as other women for diseases of the reproductive system, and those who have not borne children may have an increased risk for breast and endometrial cancer. A homosexual woman must have annual breast and pelvic examinations and Pap tests, just like heterosexual or celibate women. If she objects to male physicians, she should find a female physician or a women's clinic and follow the recommended schedule for gynecological examinations, Pap tests, and mammograms (breast X-rays). (*For more information see Chapter 17.*)

I'm a 37-year-old gay male and frequently engage in anal sex (I'm the recipient). I recently read somewhere that cancer of the prostate is becoming more and more common and I'm curious to know whether or not anal penetration could have a detrimental effect on the prostate gland.

Anyone—male or female, heterosexual, bisexual or homosexual—who *receives* anal sex should have regular checkups that include examination of the anus and rectum. In females this means having that check done during the annual gynecological exam, and in males having an annual prostate exam (which all men should begin having at age 40).

The key is to find a physician one trusts for these exams, and then go once a year. Women should find a gynecologist and men a urologist for these annual checkups, if they are not comfortable talking to their family physician. Physicians who work in sexually transmitted disease clinics or who specialize in STDs are more accustomed to discussing sexual activities, so your search might start there.

As yet, there are no data that clearly establish whether or not being the recipient of anal sex is related to a higher risk of prostate cancer. This research is hampered by the fact that anal sex is a taboo subject for many and that most people don't reveal (and most doctors don't ask about) this sexual activity. Being the recipient of anal intercourse does appear to increase the risk of catching various STDs, including the AIDS virus, *if* the inserting partner carries the infectious organism. This is why it is prudent to follow safer sex guidelines if you are not in a sexually exclusive relationship in which both partners are disease-free. *(See Chapter 19.)*

I understand that some gay men wear a single earring in their right ear as a mark of recognition. Recently I've seen a few women wearing one or more earrings—but only in their right ear. Does this indicate that they, too, are gay?

Not necessarily. It probably just means that they are women who enjoy wearing one or more earrings in their right ear. Both men and women are doing this and it doesn't necessarily signify that the person is either heterosexual or homosexual. There are no specific types of clothing, hairstyle, or other "signals" by which one can reliably tell whether a person is homosexual or not.

This rather widespread notion about earrings and gays reminds me of a similar myth from my own youth about adolescent girls and circle-shaped pins. In that case, if your circle pin had a middle section, you were a virgin; if it didn't, you were signaling you had lost your virginity. These pins were extremely popular for several years and thousands of young women wore them for their fashion status, regardless of whether they had any history of sexual experience.

I am a 61-year-old male. I am also gay. Since I hold a responsible position with a large corporation I cannot publicize this fact. I am continually shocked by the depth and intensity of hatred that straights have for gays, as voiced by my associates. Many of these people are intelligent and educated. Some are very liberal in other respects.

Since most homosexuals mind their own business and have little if any impact on the larger segment of the population, this venomous hatred is difficult to understand. I understand that this prejudice has not always existed in all societies. What are the reasons for anti-gay attitudes in our society?

The causes of *homophobia* (fear, dislike, or hatred of homosexuals) are as unclear as the causes of many other prejudices. But there are studies which have compiled a long list of traits associated with this issue.

Those with antihomosexual views often think that they do not personally know any homosexuals; have peers who display negative attitudes toward homosexuals; are less educated; attend church more frequently; have rigid concepts about appropriate sex roles; and are highly authoritarian. People like this are often vocal in their opposition to homosexuals as a way of announcing to the world that they are most definitely heterosexual, want to be treated like one, and expect everyone around them to be heterosexual also.

In one national poll, only one-quarter of the adults responding said that they had a homosexual friend or acquaintance. Of course they could only respond about those they knew about! This means that three-quarters of American adults probably base their opinions about homosexuals on stereotypes.

Some common stereotypes are that all male homosexuals are effeminate; all female homosexuals are masculine; and all homosexuals are child molesters, mentally ill, or promiscuous. There is also a myth that homosexuality is somehow "catching" and that a child can catch it from a schoolteacher, for instance. None of these widespread misconceptions are true.

The initial idea that AIDS was spread only by homosexual activity may have also increased negative reactions to gays.

It is true that not all societies react negatively to homosexual behavior, especially by men. In some societies, sexual activity with members of the same sex is viewed as entirely normal under certain circumstances or during specific stages of life.

Changing negative feelings about homosexuality is thought to require exposure to homosexual persons in order to dispel stereotypes, knowledge that homosexuality does not threaten heterosexual sex roles, information that this orientation cannot be "caught" by associating with homosexuals, and reassurance that homosexuals do not rape or force their attentions on others, anymore often than do heterosexuals.

OTHER SEXUAL BEHAVIORS

This section discusses sexual behaviors which are often characterized as "sexually deviant"—meaning that a particular behavior differs from societal expectations or is statistically unusual.

Does the term "ménage á trois" mean three people having sex at the same time? Do many people actually do this?

The French phrase *ménage à trois* translates literally as "household of three" and is most often used to describe a married couple plus a third person who is the lover of one of the spouses. This type of consensual marital arrangement is thought to be fairly rare. Technically, the term does not imply that all three people have sex together, although the term is often used to suggest group sexual activity among three people.

About 3 percent of married men and 1 percent of married women report having engaged in sex with another partner while the spouse was present. The vast majority of those who reported this behavior also said that they did it only once. However, it is a favorite sexual *fantasy* of many men and women.

I have been told that sexual orgies are not unusual, but I find it hard to believe that very many people have been in an orgy.

Having sex simultaneously with multiple partners and/or in the presence of others is generally referred to as "group sex." One study of single unmarried people estimated that 24 percent of males and 7 percent of females have engaged in group sex, but most did this only once in their lives.

The word *orgy* is defined as "a wild, drunken, or licentious festivity or revelry," and historically included specific religious or traditional festivals in which dancing, drinking, and eating were the main activities, like the Bacchanalia in Roman times which was a kind of worship to Bacchus (the god of wine and revelry).

Festivals or rituals that included group sexual activity reputedly existed in many cultures, but often were restricted to a specific event (such as the annual harvest of a certain crop) or a particular setting (such as a temple which was presided over by women of high status and education who were regarded as sacred priestesses and who also had sex with male worshipers during religious festivals). The temple prostitutes or *hetairai* of Ancient Greece provide one well-known example.

I am a 34-year-old divorced career woman and mother of a 13-year-old girl. Recently I've begun to think a great deal about exploring my sexual options—bisexuality and group sex. I have even gone so far as to talk to a swinging group member.

I have several concerns, however. What types of people participate in such groups? How can I be sure I'm protected against venereal disease? How can I be sure my anonymity is protected? Could my interest in swinging be a sign that I am afraid of commitment and intimacy?

The little research that has been done on "swingers" or group-sex participants consists of small samples, so it's impossible to generalize about who is generally involved in these activities and why. Estimates are that around 2 percent of the U.S. adult population has tried swinging or group sex at least once, and perhaps one-half of 1 percent engages in this behavior on a regular basis.

Definitions of this behavior vary: Some researchers restrict the definition of swinging to mate-swapping by married couples, while others include unmarried individuals. Each group of swingers apparently devises its own rules as to who will be included and the types of sexual activity permitted. It is not unusual, for instance, for groups to allow sex between women but not between men. Any person who violates group rules is excluded from future gatherings, since information about these "parties" is usually passed by word-of-mouth invitations.

You're right to be concerned about sexually transmitted diseases. Studies reported a low incidence of gonorrhea, but found problems with crab lice and various vaginal and urinary infections. These reports, however, are from data collected before herpes and human papillomavirus were widely identified and before AIDS. Safer sex guidelines are a must. (*See Chapter 19.*)

Research on the psychological aspects of swinging are also limited. Some participants reported that swinging was seen as just another sexual activity and was "in addition to" a committed relationship. Members of one group were given a standard psychological test and some had "normal" scores, while others scored high on variables often associated with a need for psychological counseling. Researchers point out that some swingers may have problems with intimacy.

It's difficult to meet new people and make informed decisions about possible sexual contacts; meeting several new people at once increases both the complexities and the risks. You might want to consult a counselor to help you sort out your feelings about intimacy before considering getting involved in group sex.

Before my wife and I were married, a local nudist camp held an open house, which we attended. Her reaction was not favorable. Several times over the 24 years since that visit I have attempted to interest her in nudism. Each time I have been told it was not for her.

Recently I visited a nudist park alone. After the visit I told my wife. She said visiting these places was not healthy. She claims diseases are spread in those places, especially AIDS.

Is it normal for a 50-year-old man to want to enjoy the out-of-doors nude in the company of others who are also nude? Also, please tell me what is the propriety of visiting a nudist park without one's spouse?

Organized social nudism has had a small but loyal following in this country since it was introduced from Germany nearly sixty years ago.

One study of nudists found that most were young, middle-class, and families with children. The underlying reasons most went to nudist camps were, initially, curiosity and then included feelings of freedom, relaxation and being at one with nature, and interest in sunbathing. Interestingly, most women first become social nudists to please their husbands.

People who equate nudity with arousal or sexual behavior would be quite disappointed with a visit to a nudist camp. Most nudist behavior is very conservative, and camps have strict rules against staring, body contact, and use of drugs or alcohol.

In most camps, admittance requires approval of the owner or members. Sometimes character references are requested. In addition, many camps discourage unmarried individuals from visiting (especially males) or charge them higher rates. New people may be admitted on a temporary basis, gaining full membership only after demonstrating they are willing to follow the camp's rules.

In light of the strict codes against intimate contact at most nudist camps, however, there would be little reason to expect nudists to be at any greater risk than non-nudists for AIDS or other sexually transmitted diseases.

If you want to visit a nudist camp, contact the owner in advance and ask about policies and fees. Explain that your wife will not accompany you.

Why do men go to prostitutes? Is it just for coitus or because they can get other types of sex, such as oral sex? What kind of guy would go to a prostitute?

Men seek out prostitutes for many different reasons. According to Masters and Johnson, these reasons do include wanting certain sexual activities that the man's usual partner will not perform. Before World War II, intercourse was the most requested sexual activity. Today, fellatio is the number-one request. Anal intercourse and oral-genital stimulation preceding vaginal intercourse are also frequently requested.

Men also go to prostitutes when they're without a sexual partner due to travel

Illustration No. 16. In Western art the prostitute is often depicted as a morally degenerate temptress, as in this etching by the noted German artist Otto Dix.

OTTO DIX. *Prostitute and Sailor.* 1922. Etching, 19⅝" x 17⅛". The Kinsey Institute Collections.

or military service, when they want sex without emotional involvement, or when they want a sexual outlet that does not threaten their family relationships. Some men with physical handicaps find it difficult to find partners. And in some cultures, men seek prostitutes because it would be difficult to have sex with unmarried women without detection or grave consequences to the women or themselves.

Recent research on female prostitutes indicates that oral sex is requested more frequently than intercourse. The prostitutes studied also preferred performing oral sex to having intercourse with their clients because it is faster (it doesn't involve taking off clothes), less tiring, and doesn't necessarily involve the expense of renting a room.

Because of the high prevalence of sexually transmitted diseases, at least among street prostitutes, information about how many men in our society have availed themselves of their services is pertinent. A recent Kinsey Institute review of sex behavior related to spread of the AIDS virus estimated that approximately one in three American men have had sex with a prostitute at least once in their lives. In a study of men 50 and older, 7 percent reported at least one such contact since the age of 50 and 34 percent said they had paid for sex at least once in their lives.

What is prostitution like in cultures different from ours in the United States? Or is it all pretty much the same around the world?

Cultures have different values, making it difficult to come up with a universal definition for prostitution. The usual Western definition, that prostitution is the exchange of sex for money or trade, does not always apply because some cultures use the concept of "gifts" as opposed to payment of fees or valuables.

There are a few sexually liberal societies where the idea of prostitution is unknown. One such example is described in Margaret Mead's reports of Samoa.

Societies have implemented different types of control over prostitution and these laws are constantly changing. In ancient Greece, Rome, Palestine, and China, prostitutes were required to live in restricted areas or to wear distinctive dress. Government licensing and taxation of prostitution began in early Roman times and exists today in some countries.

Current laws differ greatly from country to country. In France, Britain, Italy, Japan, and some other countries, prostitution is not a crime. Although legal in West Germany, prostitutes are required to be registered and undergo mandatory health checks.

Many cities have local ordinances governing prostitution. Even though the Netherlands does not have laws against prostitution, Amsterdam has laws against soliciting that result in areas where prostitutes sit in picture windows waiting for customers to approach them.

In the United States, every state has regulations regarding prostitution. Laws not only vary from state to state, but from city to city. Only Nevada, for example, has a local option law under which some counties and cities can license "houses of ill repute," while soliciting customers in other areas is outlawed.

My husband seems obsessed with porn. He rents porno movies at least once a week, receives subscriptions monthly, and buys swinger magazines and other sex things and papers. I know he masturbates daily, but we only make love once a month and only after watching a porno movie.

We've been married nine years and every year he accumulates more and more of this stuff. I would not mind, but this porno is all he reads besides the newspaper and he never rents any other kind of movie. I'm so confused. He says there's nothing wrong with him, and he's normal, but I'm really concerned about him. Is this normal or is he oversexed?

If a man is masturbating daily and having intercourse with his wife once a month, they have a problem. The two of you need an outside referee to help you figure out what is going on and help you learn how to discuss disagreements and negotiate solutions that you're both comfortable with.

Some completely happy, well-adjusted men do look at explicit sexual items regularly, and some use these things to aid sexual arousal. Many men who are happily married and have sex regularly with their wives also masturbate, just as many happily married women masturbate and also have sex with their husbands.

These behaviors are not a problem unless they interfere with the relationship or intrude on other aspects of life. Locate a sex counselor or sex therapist *(see Appendix)*. Both of you should go to the first appointment, but go alone if your husband doesn't want to go. You need support to resolve these problems satisfactorily.

I am 24 and have been married for four months. Before getting married, I had known my husband for two years and we were engaged for one year.

I recently discovered something about my husband that has left me unable to look at him or be near him. When paying our phone bill, I discovered that he has been calling a telephone sex service. When I confronted him about this, he admitted he gets great sexual satisfaction by masturbating when making these calls. He has been doing this since he was in his teens.

I find it extremely repulsive and feel hurt, inadequate, and confused. Up until this point he and I had (what I thought was) a very satisfying sex life. I knew absolutely nothing of his telephone activities. These calls are more than just "dirty talk"; they are extremely crude and often describe unnatural sex acts.

I have told him that he has a serious problem and should get psychiatric help. He has told me he doesn't think it's a problem and has no intention of giving up this practice. Is this normal? What should I do?

Find a qualified sex therapist, psychologist, or psychiatrist who is knowledgeable about sexual behavior to help you sort out your feelings about your relationship and to help boost your self-esteem. This area is too complicated and emotionally charged for most people to resolve by themselves.

Many women who discover that their partner masturbates (or has sexual fantasies that do not include them) assume that this occurs because they are not good enough as lovers. Another common reaction is that the partner must not really love them or he would not be thinking about or talking to someone else.

It's important for you to accept the fact that you did not cause this behavior in your husband nor can you change it by yourself. You also should not be surprised if you learn that it does not change or diminish his love for you or his satisfaction with your sex life as a couple.

There isn't much research on telephone services, but they appear to play a role similar to that of erotic books, magazine stories, videotapes, or prostitutes. The customer pays to have a sexual conversation that matches a favorite sexual fantasy. Although arousal may indeed occur during the call, recalling these phone conversations may also provide arousal for later sexual encounters with you.

This type of behavior may be an example of a lovemap—the way in which people define what is sexually stimulating. Your husband may need to have sexually explicit conversations as a source of sexual stimulation. It is important to find out what role the telephone calls play: occasional recreation, a supplement to his sex life with you, or a repeated routine that is his sole sexual stimulation or essential to having sex with you.

A skilled therapist can help you determine what role these calls play in your relationship and can suggest appropriate options. Although it would be best if you and your husband went to the therapist together, you should go alone even if he won't go along.

Could you please write about fisting? I'm 15 and all my friends are talking about it. Some of them have done it but some of us are afraid to. My sister is 17 and she lets her boyfriend do it a lot. My boyfriend keeps asking me to do it and I want to but I have to know if it is OK first. I can't talk to my mom about it. She does not want us to do any sex until 18. My friend's boyfriend brought over a tape that showed couples fisting and they seemed to enjoy it a lot. It looks OK but I am afraid it would hurt a lot at first.

Fisting is one of the slang words for the insertion of the hand or fist into the rectum or vagina. There has not been much research, but one investigator estimates that 50,000 people in the United States have engaged in this activity, many of them homosexual males. Even less is known about vaginal fisting.

Though some people find it pleasurable to have their rectum or vagina penetrated this way, this activity can be harmful. Problems include rupture of the anal sphincter, perforation of the colon, various rectal infections, and tears in the mucous membranes of the anus and rectum. Few people who try this activity have any knowledge of anatomy, so that perforation occurs when force is used against the natural curves and broad muscle supports of the pelvis. Pressure on the vagus nerve, which has receptors in the colon, can produce heart arrhythmias that could be fatal. Damage to the vagina and cervix are also possible as a result of vaginal fisting.

For most people fisting would not only be painful but could lead to serious health problems. Remember that the people you see in videotapes, movies, or still photos are being paid to portray activities as arousing, but that doesn't mean the activities are arousing to all people or even enjoyable.

When I was a young girl my teenage brother was found hanged in the basement. It was called a suicide, but I know that wasn't it. I once found him hanging with a rope around his neck, looking at lingerie pictures he'd cut from catalogs.

He made me promise not to tell and said lots of his friends did it, too. Lately a few older kids in our town have committed "suicide" and I worry it's because kids are experimenting like my brother. Please warn kids that it's dangerous.

Autoerotic or *sexual asphyxia* is the deliberate reduction of oxygen to the brain— temporary suffocation. It is rumored to enhance orgasm, but no research has ever verified this effect. *Sexual asphyxia is dangerous*: It can cause brain damage or death by reducing blood flow to the brain. Unfortunately, it is one of those topics that many hesitate or refuse to discuss because it touches on so many sensitive issues: sexuality, masturbation, bondage. Although there are no data on couples who engage in this behavior, there is evidence that this also takes place and can lead to death.

We don't know how many people engage in sexual asphyxia, but one study estimated that between 500 and 1000 people die each year in the United States from this practice. This is a conservative estimate; experts believe many more such cases aren't reported or are mislabeled suicide. Dormitory counselors at several major universities have confirmed that this type of death is common enough to be mentioned during their training.

An FBI analysis of 132 cases of autoerotic asphyxia (asphyxia during solitary masturbation) established that most victims were men, with an average age of 26.5 years. The age of these individuals ranged from preadolescent boys to one victim in his 70s. The techniques included ropes and chains for hanging by the neck, devices for passing electrical current through the body, and hoses for inhaling toxic gases or chemicals. Some cases involved visually erotic materials, detailed diaries of previous incidents, elaborate bondage devices, and the wearing of women's clothing.

Even though most victims were found to have constructed what they *thought* were self-rescue devices (slip knots in ropes, keys to unlock padlocks) they died because the slip knots didn't work, or they miscalculated the timing, the pressure of bonds, intensity of the voltage or toxic effects. Also, people don't know that there is an automatic reflex involved: When a certain area on the neck is pressed sudden unconsciousness follows and the person then cannot protect himself or herself from strangulation. These victims were usually found by family members or friends who were not aware of the activities. Most victims were described as happy, well-adjusted, and nonsuicidal.

Warning signs that a person may be experimenting with sexual asphyxia include possession of ropes, chains, gags, or inhaler devices such as plastic bags; a rash or red area around the neck; and/or disoriented behavior after having been alone awhile. Even though parents or friends may ask the person if this is going on, it is not unusual for him or her to deny it.

But if you have reason to believe someone you know is experimenting with this behavior, try to convince him or her to talk with a counselor or sex therapist who can explain how dangerous sexual asphyxia is and suggest safer methods of achieving sexual satisfaction.

This behavior is *very dangerous*. There are *absolutely no* fail-safe rescue systems. Do *not* try this under any circumstances.

TRANSVESTISM

It can be difficult to understand why a person wears the clothes of the opposite sex (called *cross-dressing*). In this section we are discussing an individual who while cross-dressing clearly understands that he (most are male) is a man and likes having a penis to use for sexual activities. The sexual partners of these men also clearly view the individual as male and think of their sexual interactions as either heterosexual (in the case of a woman whose male partner needs to wear female clothing to have an erection) or homosexual (when a man has sex with another man who wears women's clothing).

This behavior is called *transvestism* and usually differs from transexualism, which is discussed in Chapter 14.

I'm engaged to marry a man who I'm completely in love with, but he has just told me something I can't understand. He says he loves me too (and acts like he

does, if you know what I mean) and wants to get married and have kids, but he wears ladies' panties!

I don't know what to think. He acts just like other men I've gotten serious with. Does this mean he's secretly a homosexual? He doesn't seem like anything but a real man. What should I do?

Talk to him about how confused you feel and ask him about his past partners, sexual thoughts, and fantasies. Chances are that he is completely heterosexual behaviorally (he only has or wants to have sex with women) and that he psychologically thinks of himself as a male. You will probably find that the only difference between him and other heterosexual men you've known is that he just happens to feel more sexually aroused if he wears (or imagines he's wearing) ladies' panties.

One survey of men who subscribed to a magazine for transvestites found that the majority were above average in intelligence and career attainment, and that more than 75 percent had been married and were parents. The vast majority were sexually attracted to women, not to other men. In another study, almost 90 percent of those surveyed identified themselves as heterosexual, and only 28 percent reported any homosexual experience (which is similar to the proportion of men in the general population who have participated in homosexual activity at least once since puberty). By the way, homosexual males are every bit as "real" as heterosexual males.

Although nearly one-half of transvestites surveyed did not wear opposite-sex clothing outside of their homes, some did. In these cases, there may be a risk of the transvestite's secret becoming known or the risk of arrest and public embarrassment.

You might wish to consult a sex therapist or counselor experienced in working with transvestites and their partners to help you decide what to do (see Appendix). Many women have quite happy marital and family lives with transvestite men; some even help their partner by buying the female garments he needs and cooperate in keeping his secret from family and friends. Other women find the behavior distressing and that it hinders their own ability to become sexually aroused.

Only you can decide how you feel about this, but talk with a therapist if you have doubts. Either go alone or ask your fiancé to go with you.

I am a young guy who prefers to wear women's panties rather than male underpants. I like the nice soft silk and lace and it makes me feel so good wearing them. Do you think there is any harm in this at all?

If doing this seems to limit the development of relationships with others, is required for sexual functioning, jeopardizes your work, or otherwise intrudes into other aspects of your life, then find a qualified counselor.

How do you get the panties? If you steal them, then you risk being caught and having your behavior made public. Although individual cases differ, fetishism of this type (discussed more fully later in this chapter) is not generally thought of as being inherently dangerous to the person or to others. Any "harm" is usually a result of being rejected by partners, friends, or family who discover the "secret," or not being able to interact with a partner as a whole person.

I'm a man who enjoys wearing women's clothing. (I'm not a homosexual.) I've never worn them in front of anyone I know and I've never told anyone about this before. How many other people do this? What causes it?

Do you do this because it is sexually arousing to you? Or do you wear women's clothes because it makes you feel more "natural?" The first question involves using the clothes as a fetish, which can be an aspect of transvestism. The second may involve a different kind of behavior called transexualism, discussed in Chapter 14.

We don't know how many people cross-dress (wear clothes of the opposite sex). We do know it's not rare for men, and that there are even organizations, magazines, and clothing stores that cater to male transvestites.

Researchers speculate that during adolescence these men developed an erotic response to women's clothes and then experienced a sexual response to the act of putting on and wearing those clothes. Often fantasizing later about the cross-dressing experience is necessary for sexual arousal with a partner. No one has yet determined why this happens to some men and not to others.

In other cases, men use clothing, make-up, hairstyles, and sometimes take hormones or have implants to enlarge the breasts to impersonate the opposite sex. This is most commonly seen among some homosexual men who use this behavior to attract males for sexual partners (one slang term used for these men is *drag queen*) or for theatrical performances.

I would like to learn more about transvestites. Where could I find the special organizations and magazines about this subject?

These organizations include: The Society for the Second Self, Box 194, Tulare, CA 93275 (publishes the magazine *Transvestia*); The Tiffany Club, Box 19, Wayland, MA 01778 (publishes *TV/TS Tapestry*); and *The Transsexual Voice*, P.O. Box 16314, Atlanta, GA 30321. They can supply you with names of other groups and publications. There is also a 24-hour telephone hotline: North American Transvestites-Transsexuals Contact Service (206-329-TVTS).

You can also find more information in books on sexual behavior. Check for these at public libraries or bookstores and look in the index for headings like Transvestism and Cross-dressing.

PARAPHILIAS

In everyday terms, the behaviors we discuss here are sometimes derogatorily called perversions. Scientists call these behaviors *paraphilias* (Greek *para* means "beyond" or "outside of the usual", and *philia* means "love").

Some paraphilias are similar to behaviors most of us do not find unusual or disruptive to satisfying interpersonal relationships and are perfectly normal, such as a husband's greater arousal when his wife wears black, lacy underwear. This kind of behavior only becomes a problem (and is then called a paraphilia) if it involves the *necessity* of a particular object or behavior for the person to achieve arousal and satisfaction, thus interfering with the development or maintenance of an intimate relationship between two whole, responsive, loving individuals.

Other paraphilias involve more dramatic behaviors that most people find incomprehensible and about which sexual partners are likely to object (such as a husband not being able to become aroused or have intercourse *unless* his wife ties him up and treats him like a slave). The most extreme of these behaviors include some that are truly physically and psychologically harmful to others, such as rape and lust murder. Paraphilias refer to behaviors, *not* fantasy. *Imagining* unusual sexual situations or behaviors to enhance stimulation or arousal is not uncommon.

Because these behaviors deviate from social norms, prohibitions against many are included in the laws of various countries, states, and localities. Interestingly, in some cases behaviors thought dangerous in one country or locale are treated differently elsewhere, in either the actual laws or in the enthusiasm with which laws are enforced. One example is exhibitionism; in some places in the United States a man urinating in a public area (even if no one except the policeman is nearby) will be arrested and charged with indecent exposure, while in other countries a man who deliberately shows his penis to a woman while masturbating is simply ignored, pitied, or sent to get psychological help. Obviously, laws and strict enforcement are necessary when behaviors include nonconsenting partners (involving either force, as in rape, or incapacity to give legal consent, as with children).

Scientists know very little about paraphilic behaviors. It is even difficult to estimate how *many* people engage in these specific behaviors, because only those who get into trouble legally or have marital difficulties are brought to the attention of researchers, therapists, or legal authorities. It is, however, generally agreed that many more males than females have a paraphilia as part of their sexual behavior pattern. Perhaps this is partly explained by the biological evidence that males depend more upon sight and smell for sexual arousal, while females rely more on touch.

We also do not know *why* some people have paraphilias, but the beginnings of these behavior patterns are thought to become a part of an individual's lovemap very early in childhood, and a few may be related to hormonal or developmental factors that influence brain development before birth. In some instances, paraphilic behavior does not emerge until later in life, perhaps due to physical changes in the brain such as an injury, tumor, or other disease.

There is a considerable difference between having a specific fantasy one uses for arousal and actually needing to act out the fantasy in order to perform sexually. Moreover, there are differences among individuals in how each uses the paraphilia. Some are aroused only while the paraphilic behavior is actually taking place, while others replay the act in their minds (like a videotape) in order to perform sexually later. But even when a person can use this recall mechanism to carry on what seems to the partner a normal sex life, eventually the paraphilic behavior must be repeated—it is as though the mental "videotape" wears out or gets stale and isn't arousing any more.

Regardless of whether the specific behavior itself or as viewed by others, is just rather mildly odd, objectionably "kinky," or violently dangerous, the crucial points are: The person did not voluntarily "choose" the behavior; punishment does not prevent recurrence of the behavior; nor can the person voluntarily control the behavior by willpower. Moreover, many of the same paraphilias can be present whether a person is heterosexual, homosexual, or bisexual—so acquiring a specific paraphilia is not necessarily related to a person's sexual-partner orientation.

Also it is important to understand that paraphilias are not "catching." They are *not* acquired from exposure to the content of books, movies, magazines— or from other people with the behavior. For example, a person who is not "turned on" by some specific behavior, such as coprophilia (arousal by watching a partner have a bowel movement or by being rubbed with feces), can watch hundreds of hours of movies showing this and still feel nothing except revulsion, boredom, or some other emotion—but the person will not feel sexual arousal or be turned into a coprophiliac.

Skilled treatment for paraphilias is not widely available. Individuals or couples who are experiencing concerns or difficulties related to such behaviors should try to locate a qualified therapist or psychologist who has experience in treating paraphilias. In most cases, this will mean contacting a university or medical school which operates a sex dysfunctions clinic, then asking to be referred to an appropriate specialist.

The most successful treatment found so far for severe paraphilias or those that endanger others is a combination of treatment with injections of medroxy-progesterone acetate (which reduces or eliminates sex drive and sexual fantasy, thus reducing the compulsive need to engage in the paraphilic behavior) and skilled counseling. Once the man is calmed by this specific hormonal drug, it is possible for him to begin to work on changing his sexual pattern. If the man has a partner, participation by the partner in counseling has also been found to be helpful.

When it is clear that the individual has learned to be sexually satisfied by behaviors that do not include the paraphilia, the injections can be stopped; this hormone has no known irreversible effects. The same cannot be said for castration, a treatment sometimes recommended by the uninformed. If after treatment it is clear that the behavior cannot be eliminated or controlled, then the individual can elect to continue the hormone treatment indefinitely.

Often just finding out that one's specific behavior is shared by others is helpful; many paraphiliacs fear that their problem is unique to them. Reassurance can be gained by finding a magazine or newsletter devoted to a particular paraphilia and then writing to the magazine. One way to do this is to go to an "adult" bookstore and ask to see magazines that include the particular behavior.

The work of Dr. John Money, Director of the Psychohormonal Research Unit at the Johns Hopkins Hospital in Baltimore, has contributed much of what is known about paraphilias, their relationship to an individual's personal lovemap *(see Chapter 5)*, and treatment for these problems. Many of the details in this section come from his books, two of which are listed at the end of this chapter. He has grouped various types of paraphilias into six general categories:

• **Sacrificial paraphilias** (when one or both partners must be "punished" for experiencing "lust"). These include sadism (arousal from inflicting humiliation, bondage, punishment, or pain); masochism (arousal from receiving the above); and symphorophilia (arousal by accidents or catastrophes). These can range in degree from mutually consenting playacting to the most horrible of lust murders of complete strangers (erotophonophilia).

* **Predatory paraphilias** (when feeling "lust" can be indulged in only when sex or an object is stolen or taken by force). A person with this type of paraphilia may imagine or play the role of either the predator or the prey. This group includes rape, breaking and entering to steal items, and kidnapping. Again, the actual behavior can range from stealing a nonvaluable object, mutual playacting between partners involving pretended force and resistance, to forcible rape of a terrified stranger (biastophilia).

* **Mercantile paraphilias** (when only "wicked" persons may feel sexual pleasure). These cases do not always involve actual prostitution, but can also involve pretending that one's partner is a prostitute or gigolo who is paid for sexual services. Another example is paying for telephone calls where the customer can talk to a person as though he or she were a prostitute or male hustler.

* **Fetish paraphilias** (when a token that symbolizes "wickedness" for that particular person is included in the sexual act). The token itself is called a fetish, and it is the fetish that is, in a way, "blamed" for sexual arousal and yet is necessary for arousal. The meaning of the word *fetish* is "an object with the powers of magic." These were widely used by traditional cultures as items associated with sorcery or as protective charms or amulets (similar to carrying a rabbit's foot or four-leaf clover for good luck).

Women's panties, bras, stockings and other garments are common fetishes, as are certain parts of females such as hair, breasts, or feet (or more often, pictures of these objects or body parts). Another type of common fetish involves arousal from the feel or texture of an item such as rubber, latex, or leather. Fetishes can also involve taboo smells or body excretions (such as soiled undergarments, feces, or urine as in coprophilia or urophilia). Some fetishes (such as being dependent upon diapers, rubber pants, or enemas [klismaphilia] for sexual arousal and/or orgasm) more obviously originate in early childhood than others.

The fetish object may be worn by the sexual partner, by the man himself, or simply looked at or touched while the man masturbates with no partner present. As you can imagine, a society which assumes that most males become aroused by looking at female breasts does not view this common, strong preference in the same way it views a male who needs to be urinated on to become aroused; but the relationship between a person's lovemap and his sexual behavior is the same. And remember, the fetish must be *necessary*, not just preferred, for it to be classified as a paraphilia.

* **Eligibility paraphilias** (when the sexual partner must be outside the group considered acceptable as sexual partners). In these paraphilias the partner selection is repetitive, so that once a partner changes to become "acceptable" by social norms, she/he must be discarded and a new one meeting the specialized criteria must again be found.

One example is needing partners from a different age group. In pedophilia, the partner must be much younger, often prepubertal; when the partner grows up and reaches puberty, a new one must be found. The opposite paraphilia, needing an older partner, is called gerontophilia. In ephebophilia

Illustration No. 17. For the fetishist, objects like feet or shoes can replace an individual as the focus of sexual desire and arousal. This photograph is one of many once available for purchase. Note the extreme height of the heel, which enhances their value to a shoe fetishist but is of little use to a woman as functional footwear.

Shoe fetish. Late 1950s. Black-and-white photograph, 8″ x 10″. The Kinsey Institute Collections.

(when an older person is compelled to seek adolescent partners) society may not condemn or notice the age difference, but there may be a series of divorces as the older person must seek a more youthful partner every few years.

Other types of eligibility paraphilias include zoophilia (animals), needing a partner from a different racial group; or needing fat, short, deformed, or other specific attributes in a partner. Sometimes other types of distancing are involved, such as differences of social class, or the most extreme—a dead partner (necrophilia).

• **Allurement paraphilias** (when some specific stage of behavior that usually precedes intercourse becomes the "main event"; this separates the "wicked" act of becoming aroused from intercourse itself, keeping intercourse "pure").

One example is exhibitionism (peodeiktophilia); a man displays his penis to a stranger, elicits a shocked or frightened response, and then returns home to his partner to have intercourse or to masturbate. The Peeping Tom derives his arousal only from looking at a forbidden sight, the narratophile only from erotic conversations, and the pictophile only from looking at erotic pictures. Whether the behavior is making obscene telephone calls, watching burlesque shows, or making erotic videotapes of themselves, there is a distancing between the man and the recipient of his actions— which does not include having intercourse with them.

In one type of allurement behavior (frotteurism), the man does make body contact by rubbing or pressing against a stranger in a crowded place, like a bus, but the encounter remains anonymous.

This is not a complete listing of all possible paraphilias. Some others are discussed below. For a full discussion, see the list of readings at the end of this chapter.

I enjoy spanking women! I feel that most women not only need, but in their deep subconscious mind WANT a man to spank them. The problem is that far too many females have been brainwashed by the feminists into thinking that if they meet a man's needs then something is wrong with them.

How can I help a woman understand that a little game playing can be a healthy expression of human emotion? The male drive is to dominate and the female drive is to be the object of attention. To spank the bottom of a woman, and then to caress her is such an exciting thing that I fail to see why the women I know are afraid to really let themselves go and find release of passion. I'd like any advice you can give me on dealing with women who want to be spanked but who do not want to admit they want and/or need a good spanking.

At the risk of sounding insensitive, let me say that unless you are *very* selective in choosing your female partners you may end up spending more time with police, lawyers, and the courts than in sexual encounters.

If spanking is necessary for sexual arousal it is categorized under the paraphilia called *sadism*. And if being spanked is required for sexual arousal it is called *masochism*. Some people enjoy spanking, wrestling, or other types of physical "horsing around" as part of sex, but are fully capable of functioning without it. It is not clear from your letter what role spanking serves in your sexual functioning, but your assumptions about women are not correct.

Researchers estimate that 5 percent to 10 percent of the U.S. population engages in sadomasochism for sexual pleasure on at least an occasional basis, with most incidents being either mild or staged activities involving no real pain or violence. It appears that many more individuals prefer to play the masochist's role than the sadist's. It also appears that males are more likely to prefer sadomasochistic activities than females. This means that male sadists may have difficulty in finding willing masochistic females to be sexual partners.

If partners are located, an agreement is reached about what will occur. The giving and receiving of actual or pretended physical pain or psychological humiliation occurs in most cases only within a carefully prearranged script. Any change from the expected scenario generally reduces sexual pleasure.

Most often it is the receiver (the masochist), not the giver (the sadist), who sets and controls the exact type and extent of the couple's activities. It might also interest you to know that in many such heterosexual relationships, the so-called traditional sex roles are reversed—with men playing the submissive or masochistic role. Sadomasochistic activities can also occur between homosexual couples.

As to your particular questions, the vast majority of women do *not* want to be spanked and do *not* associate being spanked with sexual pleasure. If any of your partners say they don't want to be spanked and you do it anyway, you can be charged with assault and battery. A lawyer would probably advise you that when a woman says no to any sexual activity, that is exactly what she means. If spanking is necessary for your sexual arousal or satisfaction, you will have to continue looking for the statistically few women for whom being spanked is a component of their sexual pleasure, or find a counselor or therapist who can help you learn to derive sexual pleasure without practicing this activity.

Yesterday a man exhibited himself to me on the bus. I was terrified and couldn't sleep because I was convinced he had followed me home and would break into my apartment. When I asked the landlady if anyone had been hanging around and told her why, she laughed about it and said I didn't have to worry about men who did that. I can't believe that a man who did what he did isn't dangerous.

Fortunately, your landlady is right. Being the unwilling observer of an exhibitionist, sometimes called a "flasher," can be frightening, but these men very rarely follow women or initiate any other type of contact. The man has a psychological need to witness your shock at seeing his penis; that both validates his "maleness" and is the source of his sexual arousal. Later he will recall the pleasure he felt from your reaction and either masturbate or have sex with a partner.

Depriving exhibitionists of a shocked reaction is about all you can do if it happens again. Calmly look away, move so you cannot see the man, or pretend nothing is happening. Most important, the clinical evidence shows that men who do this are rarely, if ever, dangerous, and they don't expand their behavior to include more violent aspects at some future time.

Recent studies have reported that some women are deeply disturbed by witnessing a flasher. If you find this is true for you, seek reassurance from a counselor.

It is very important that I learn about the sexual disorder called "Peeping Tom masturbation." Does it lead to other sexual disorders, such as child molestation or rape?

According to the current understanding of the voyeur or "Peeping Tom," it's extremely rare for a person with this paraphilia to also have other paraphilias like pedophilia (love of children) or a need to rape.

Many people will take advantage of peeking at nudity or sexual activity, especially if they rarely have such an opportunity. Erotic films and videotapes provide a safe opportunity to experience this for millions of men and women. But they don't *need* this stimulation to become sexually aroused or to have an orgasm, while voyeurs *must* peep to perform sexually later.

Some voyeurs masturbate while they are spying, with or without reaching an orgasm; others do not even have an erection. All of them, however, tend to "relive" their peeping later, alone or with a partner, replaying it in the imagination like a videotape. This is the only way they are able to get an erection and reach an orgasm.

If a rapist peers into windows looking for victims and is apprehended at that point, he is likely to be labeled a Peeping Tom instead of a rapist. In contrast, the true Peeping Tom does his peeping over and over again, without committing rape, and nearly always without ever entering a dwelling or interacting with the object of his interest.

Treatment for men in legal or marital trouble because of peeping can include combined hormonal and counseling therapy.

I had a phone call from a man who said he was a doctor doing research for The Kinsey Institute. He asked me very intimate questions and I told him things I have never even told my husband. I told a friend about the interview and she said I'd better check with you because he might be some kind of weirdo. Now I'm scared. Does this man work for you?

No, I can confidently say that he does not. The Kinsey Institute has never conducted telephone interviews. However, you are probably not in any personal danger because, for men who have the need to make obscene calls, the call alone provides sexual pleasure.

You have been the victim of a particular type of obscene telephone call in which the caller impersonates a "trustworthy" person such as a scientist, physician, or priest. We receive several reports each year from all over the country about so-called "Kinsey interviews." We believe many others go unreported; these impostors sound convincing, and no one likes to admit to being gullible.

Most other types of obscene calls involve the use of sexual language or other statements designed to shock the listener. Anyone receiving any type of obscene call should refrain from reacting in any way and hang up immediately. The objective is to deprive the caller of the pleasure of an audience or a shocked reaction.

In the unlikely event that you receive a second call, hang up immediately and call the telephone company. With the assistance of the police, they are often successful at catching the few men who do make repeat calls to the same person. New telephone equipment which should be available to a wider market in the near future permits the locking in of a trace on the telephone number of an unwanted caller by the person receiving the call. This should make it much easier to identify obscene callers.

Most people who make obscene phone calls dial numbers at random, do not make repeat calls, and do not engage in any other type of sexual offense. In other words, their behavior does not escalate from making phone calls to molesting the people they call.

For future reference, let me tell you how to distinguish a reputable scientist from an impersonator. A legitimate sex researcher always will notify police departments and other local agencies before contacting any subject. Even when initial contact is by telephone, the researcher will encourage you to call the police, a hospital, university, or other unit to verify their credentials. You will be told how the confidentiality of your answers and your privacy will be guaranteed. Any reputable scientist will not begin to ask you questions during the first call, but allow you time to decide if you wish to be interviewed. Then, you will be recontacted or asked to contact the researcher with your decision.

Remember that even if you do agree to participate in a research project, you have the right to decline to answer any question, and you can withdraw from a study at any time (these protections are included as part of the "informed consent" procedures that must be followed by reputable researchers).

Whenever I read about sexual fetishes, it's always about males. Are there any female fetishists?

Fetishism has mostly been studied in males. This is because most research studies are done on clinical populations; that is, on individuals who have sought therapy or have been arrested or imprisoned. The fact that males appear to derive sexual arousal more often from sight and smell than do females may explain why men are more likely to acquire a fetish that is integrated as a dominating feature of their lovemap. Thus, based on case histories and theory, most clinicians and researchers believe that fetishism is much rarer in women than men.

We don't know how many people are fetishists. This is one of the sexual behaviors that only comes to the attention of others when the fetishist gets into some sort of legal trouble or difficulty. Physicians or counselors generally become aware of sexual-fetishistic behavior in three ways: when the fetishist's partner refuses to cooperate and the marriage is in disarray, when the fetish object becomes so specialized it is difficult to obtain (so sexual functioning is impaired), or when the person becomes concerned about sexual identity or "normality."

Is it possible that fulfilling a sexual fetish could be more rewarding to a man than sexual intercourse with a woman?

Yes. There's clinical evidence that some people derive greater sexual pleasure from interacting with a specific object than from sexual activity with another individual. And for some, involvement with the fetish object is the person's *only* sexual activity; for others it is necessary for interaction with a partner.

Most of us find certain kinds of clothing, for instance, more sexually arousing than others or an important part of a favorite fantasy. The difference between that and fetishism depends on whether the clothes are absolutely necessary for sexual arousal. It would not be unusual, for example, for a man to be more sexually aroused if his wife came to bed wearing a sheer nightgown (which the two of them use as an unspoken signal that she would like to have sex) than if she appeared wearing her usual high-necked flannel nightwear.

But if the man is not interested in his wife *unless* she is wearing that particular nightgown, or if he prefers seeing the nightgown alone (without his wife in it), the man is said to have a sexual fetish. It doesn't appear to be unusual for this type of mild fetish behavior (such as becoming more aroused if one's partner wears a revealing nightgown rather than a more modest one) to exist throughout an individual's life, and should be viewed as a problem *only* if it causes personal, marital, social, or legal difficulties.

I've noticed that women with long hair attract a lot of attention from men. What makes men so attracted to long hair?

Several clinicians have speculated that in the United States men find long hair on women to be more "feminine" than short hair, but there have been no research studies on the subject.

Male preferences of women's hair styles vary from one culture to another and sometimes from one generation to the next, depending on how each group defines the "ideal woman." Of course there are always individual men who have their own personal preferences, regardless of what the culture is favoring at any particular time.

In some cultures it is believed that only husbands or close family should be permitted to see a woman's hair uncovered or falling loosely down her back. Such restrictions imply that women with hair in disarray or loosened from binding are less inhibited or more sexually available than other women, which is the implication behind the phrase "she let down her hair." In Oriental art, for example, women depicted with disordered hairdos are often meant to be viewed as having had a recent sexual encounter.

A few men have very strong sexual feelings about long hair on women, and need their partners to have long hair in order to function sexually. This is one type of sexual fetish.

I am a male of 34 years. This will be a strange one for you. Ever since I was six or older, a woman's hair has given me fascination and sexual arousments. I took hair styling for a few months. But quit because when the girls young or old came in and wanted their long hair cut short, it gave me an erection. I wanted to cut it, then didn't want to cut it, at different times, so I quit.

Just the thought of a girl sitting in the chair after I have the cape on, I pile the hair up and clip it, then let it down. It's beautiful hair, then she says cut if off short. It gives me an erection. What's going on here? Am I crazy or queer?

It sounds as though the image of a woman with long hair is your favorite, most dependable method of becoming sexually aroused in real life as well as fantasy. We don't know how many people rely on this particular fetish for sexual arousal.

This shouldn't be a problem unless long hair is your sole object of sexual interest or your sexual response to hair interferes with your daily life, as your letter suggests. If you are unable to form a loving relationship with a partner

Illustration No. 18. The sexual fetish is an object or part of the body, like hair, that is necessary for sexual arousal. This photograph is one of hundreds of such items marketed to individuals with specific fetishes donated to The Kinsey Institute's collection of materials.

Hair fetish. Late 1940s. Black-and-white photograph, 8½″ x 10″. The Kinsey Institute Collections.

who does not have long hair, or feel no sexual interest in a real person but do become aroused by a photograph of an unknown woman with long hair, then you might wish to consult a therapist to discuss ways of increasing the range of your ability to respond sexually. Having this fetish doesn't indicate that you are homosexual, if that's what you meant by using the derogatory word queer.

I am a young male nearing my mid-twenties. Since I was nine years old I have had a foot fetish and have been strongly attracted to women's feet and do not understand why and I also especially love the smell of them and also their socks and stockings and shoes that are soaked with sweat from their perspiring feet. I masturbate nightly thinking about strong foot odor and am starting to feel extremely guilty about this practice which to most people would be considered to be very perverted.

I also obtain an erection while in public places and am very ashamed of myself. I fantasize constantly of having my face smothered with a woman's feet while she is wearing soiled stockings she has worn for several days without changing them.

One type of fetishism occurs when a person focuses on one body part, or one inanimate object, as the repeatedly preferred or only method of achieving sexual excitement. Feet and the smell of feet are common fetishes.

You should seek help if your interest in women's feet dominates your life and relationships, or causes anxiety, guilt, shame, or stress. If it affects your social life, your schoolwork, or your relationships with friends, family, and lovers, therapy will be helpful.

I'm a 44-year-old man, and I've slept on a rubber sheet and in rubber baby pants for as long as I can remember. I'm ashamed to say that I am very much

attached to these things. Do many adults have this kind of attachment to childhood things?

It sounds like you are describing the paraphilia called infantilism. Are these items involved in either sexual arousal or orgasm for you? Other aspects of infantilism can be the desire to sleep in a crib, be fed from a bottle, and receive other attention usually associated with infant care, such as being diapered.

Therapists who have treated such clients speculate that infantilism occurs when a person feels that he or she was only truly loved when a baby. Other researchers suggest the explanation is that, for some people, their earliest awareness of sexual feelings and responses (such as erections) occurred while wearing rubber pants or diapers, and somehow these two events became connected.

Regardless of how such items become a part of a person's sexual life, this behavior is frequently concealed from family, friends, and often even from spouses. The Kinsey Institute collections include a magazine published by individuals who have this particular paraphilia. The publication includes editorials, letters to the editor, articles, and a classified section, so obviously you are not alone in your dependence on this behavior pattern.

If having this fetish intrudes on your ability to lead a happy, fulfilling life, or to form an intimate caring relationship, find a sex counselor or therapist experienced in helping individuals resolve paraphilias.

I lost my leg in an auto accident at age 16 and, until recently, had assumed that no man would ever find me attractive. I am now happily married, but uncertain about my husband's behavior. I know about other types of fetishes and wonder if that's what's going on.

My husband seems fascinated by my stump, as though it is sexually a plus. (In my eyes, my stump looks grotesque.) My husband cannot explain what is behind this, but a friend who is also an amputee told me her husband is that way, too.

We've been calling it our "fringe benefit" for losing legs, and it's a small consolation that helps make life a little more bearable. Still, we are very curious as to what is behind this attraction.

There is a *possibility* that you and your friend might be married to acrotomophiliacs (in Greek *acro* means "extremity," *tomo* means "cut," and *philia* means "love"). Data from one study of 183 persons who expressed a sexual interest in partners without limbs (admittedly a small, self-selected, nonrandom group of subjects) showed that most became aware of their attraction to amputees around the time of puberty. Fewer than half could identify any particular event that led to their interest.

Most had achieved higher-than-average educational and occupational status. Answers to questions about their childhood and parents showed that 80 percent got along well with their parents and most had no greater interest than the general population in other specialized erotic interests such as bondage or sadism.

There is some question as to whether these respondents should even be categorized as having a paraphilia, since most were also capable of satisfactory sexual interaction with partners who were *not* amputees. For many, this interest may not be very different from men who have a strong preference for women with large breasts, the difference being that one is acceptable and is seen as an asset by our culture at this time in history and the other is not.

Specialists who work with disabled women have noted that some have a poor body image and become particularly confused if a man becomes attracted to them. Your husband may be reacting to your doubts about your physical attractiveness by being overly reassuring about your missing leg and may not have a fetish reaction to the stump at all. Besides, even if he is attracted to amputees, you are not the only female amputee in the world—but he did *choose you* to be his wife.

Further Readings

Allgeier, A., and Allgeier, E. *Sexual Interactions.* 2nd ed. Lexington, MA: D. C. Heath and Company, 1988.
(A comprehensive book often used as a textbook but understandable to the general public.)

Bancroft, J. *Human Sexuality and Its Problems.* 2nd ed. Edinburgh: Churchill Livingstone, 1989.
(A scholarly book on a wide range of issues related to human sexuality, written from a medical perspective.)

Comfort, A. *The Joy of Sex.* New York: Simon and Schuster, 1972.
(A national bestselling book dealing with a wide range of human behaviors, written for the general public.)

————. *More Joy: A Lovemaking Companion to the joy of sex.* New York: Crown Publishers, Inc., 1987.
(An updated sequel to the 1972 book, also written for the general public.)

The Diagram Group. *Sex: A user's manual.* New York: The Putnam Publishing Group, 1981.
(A book written for the general public, which was intended as a straightforward visual guide to all aspects of human sexuality.)

Bass, E. *I Never Told Anyone.* New York: Harper & Row, 1983.
(A book about sexual victimization.)

Bass, E., and Davis, L. *The Courage to Heal.* New York: Harper & Row, 1988.
(Addresses the victims of incest but is also relevant to rape victims and anyone dealing with long-term healing as a result of sexual victimization.)

Kirkpatrick, M., ed. *Women's Sexual Experience: Explorations of the dark continent.* New York: Plenum Press, 1982.
(A collection of readings about different subgroups of women written by many different authors.)

Klein, F. and Wolf, T. J., eds. *Two Lives to Lead: Bisexuality in men and women.* New York: Harrington Park Press, 1985.
(Consists of scientific articles on bisexuality.)

Loulan, J. *Lesbian Sex.* San Francisco: Spinsters Ink., 1984.
(Written by a lesbian counselor for lesbians, this book addresses a wide range of topics related to lesbian sexuality in a non-technical, easy-to-read style.)

————. *Lesbian Passion: Loving ourselves and each other.* San Francisco: Spinsters/ Aunt Lute Book Company, 1987.

(Written by a lesbian counselor, this book addresses self-esteem, intimacy, and relationship issues faced by lesbians and includes data on the lives of 1600 lesbians.)

Masters, W. H.; Johnson, V. E.; and Kolodny, R. C. *Masters and Johnson on Sex and Human Loving*. Boston: Little, Brown and Company, 1982.
(A comprehensive coverage of human sexuality that is understandable and useful for the general public.)

McWhirter, D. P., and Mattison, A. M. *The Male Couple: How relationships develop*. Englewood Cliffs, NJ: Prentice-Hall, Inc., 1984.
(A description of research on gay male couples, which is easy to read and deals with relationship issues that are also relevant to heterosexuals.)

McWhirter, D. P.; Sanders, S. A.; and Reinisch, J. M., eds. *Homosexuality/ Heterosexuality: Concepts of sexual orientation*. New York: Oxford University Press, 1990.
(A collection of scholarly papers by leading researchers in the field of human sexuality.)

Money, J. *Gay, Straight, and In-Between: The sexology of erotic orientation*. New York: Oxford University Press, 1988.
(A scientifically-oriented book on the physiological, genetic, and social factors that influence sexual orientation.)

————. *Vandalized Lovemaps*. Buffalo, NY: Prometheus Books, 1990. (A book about how paraphilias develop.)

Weinrich, J. D. *Sexual Landscapes: Why we are what we are, why we love whom we love*. New York: Charles Scribner's Sons, 1987.
(A book written in everyday language about sexual orientation.)

Wolman, B. B., and Money, J. *Handbook of Human Sexuality*. Englewood Cliffs, NJ: Prentice-Hall, Inc., 1980.
(A collection of scientific papers by leading researchers in the field of human sexuality.)

Wyatt, G. E., and Powell, G. J. *Lasting Effects of Child Sexual Abuse*. Newbury Park: Sage Publications, 1988.
(A collection of scientific papers which evaluates the state of research on the effects of child sexual abuse.)

8

Problems With Sexual Functioning

Sex is often considered as instinctive and automatic as such other biological functions as breathing, but it is actually a complicated process involving many physical, psychological, and social factors.

In fact, each topic discussed in this book has a direct bearing on how we function in the sexual aspects of our lives. All of the following factors affect our ability to function sexually:

- The hormonal events taking place in utero (before we were born)
- Interactions with parents and others during childhood
- The encoding of "lovemaps" as we began to experience sexual arousal
- Interactions with peers during adolescence
- How we feel about ourselves and our bodies
- Whether our past sexual activities (either by ourselves or with others) are recalled as pleasant experiences
- Our physical and emotional health.

Moreover, when sex involves a partner, all of the same variables are involved for the other person as well. Further, sexual interaction will be influenced by the types of nonsexual interactions we have had with that person.

Thus each sexual interaction has been called a "sensory-motor-neuro-hormonal-vascular-psycho-social-cultural interpersonal event." In plain English this means that each partner's nervous system, muscles, brain, hormones, and blood system must be in good working order. Each partner must also be reasonably psychologically well-adjusted and have a positive view of sex; and both must agree they want to have sex together at a particular time and in some mutually agreeable fashion. Perhaps we should be more surprised when a sexual interaction is *satisfactory* than when it is not!

There have been attempts to estimate how many people in the general population have problems with sexual functioning, but the answer is not clear. One survey in Great Britain found that 59 percent of women and 49 percent of men reported experiencing a problem with sex at some point in their lives. However, many people who have sexual problems do not seek treatment.

It has also been suggested that admitting to having a sexual problem and seeking a solution has become more socially acceptable in the past decade because of more frequent discussions of sexual topics by the media. This coverage may be a double-edged sword, however, if couples are left with the impression that some new medication or treatment will magically cure all their sexual difficulties. Individuals may also begin to believe that everyone's sex life *always* can be (or everyone else's already is) like fireworks, bells, or earth tremors.

Much of this chapter will discuss sexual problems (sexual dysfunctions) in terms of heterosexual couples. Many homosexual and bisexual couples as well as single men and women also have similar difficulties; the same therapies are available to treat these couples and individuals. Much of what we know about both dysfunctions and successful treatments come from studies done with white, middle-class couples. Different problems and treatments may be relevant for other socioeconomic and cultural groups. The needs of these groups deserve further research.

Even so, the primary message of this chapter is that help *is* available for assessment and treatment of the vast majority of sexual problems. Furthermore, many of the current methods involve fewer treatment sessions (and hence lower costs) than was true with the therapies of the past.

SEXUAL DESIRE

In the 1970s, following Masters and Johnson's books about sexual functioning and dysfunctions, most sex therapists reported that clients came to them about problems with female orgasm or male erection. Now, nearly half of all clients are diagnosed as having problems with sexual desire. Patients still *state* that their problem has to do with orgasm or erection, but it is easier to admit that something is wrong with one's body than to admit that one feels little or no sexual desire or interest.

Dr. Harold Lief and Dr. Helen Kaplan, highly respected sex therapists and educators, were among the first to point out that low desire was a separate sexual problem, and perhaps one of the most important. This is because low desire often causes the more obvious physical symptoms associated with lack of arousal and orgasm.

Problems with low or inhibited desire are what many people used to refer to as "frigidity" or "impotence." These terms convey two common misconceptions: that women normally have little spontaneous interest in sex and that men are naturally always ready and able to have sex at any opportunity. These assumptions are false.

Desire itself is generally referred to as a person's sex drive, libido, sexual interest, or feelings of being horny. Contrary to earlier data, which showed that more women than men had low sexual desire, sex therapists now find that equal numbers of men and women have this problem.

What is involved in low or inhibited sexual desire? One of the major elements appears to be conflict within the relationship, often anger. Other factors include unrealistic ideas about what sex should be like; poor body image; low self-esteem; lack of intimacy and trust between partners; pressure to have sex more frequently from the partner with a higher sex drive; boredom; and inability to adjust to the more mundane feelings that accompany the day-to-day interactions in a long-term committed relationship after experiencing the ecstatic feelings associated with being "in love" and involved in courtship.

For some people, low desire means not initiating sexual activity; for others, it is not being responsive when the partner suggests having sex. In some cases, low desire affects all sexual interactions; in others, it is specific to one situation, activity, or partner.

Although most desire problems are not caused by physical problems, a few are. Some medications (such as those for high blood pressure), some chronic diseases (such as diabetes), hormone imbalances, and chromosome abnormalities can directly reduce sexual desire for some individuals. Some psychiatric illnesses (such as depression) can also reduce desire.

Once underlying medical or psychological problems are ruled out or treated, therapy consists of assessing each partner's feelings about the relationship and expectations about sex. Assessment is usually followed by homework assignments for the couple, which they must report on at the next meeting at the sex therapist's office. Depending on the specific case, assignments may be as basic as giving hugs more often. Often agreements are negotiated on how frequently the couple will have intercourse or which type of activities will be engaged in. Education about normal physical responses, foreplay techniques, intercourse positions, and how to communicate needs, hurt feelings, or wishes is sometimes all that is needed.

Various methods are being used to treat problems of desire. No single method has yet proved notably more effective than others, perhaps because the causes of low desire are so varied. Factors that do appear to increase the likelihood of success, however, include a high motivation by the male partner for improving the relationship, faithfully carrying out the homework assignments, a commitment by both partners to continue the relationship, and the quality of the relationship as a whole.

Some individuals have a more severely negative reaction to sex. Called "sexual aversion," this is often typified by an extreme aversion to and avoidance of any genital contact with a sexual partner. Sometimes accompanied by full-scale panic attacks, this problem may require the use of medications to reduce the extremely high anxiety level before other therapy methods can begin.

The goal of therapy, however, must be to clarify exactly what is taking place within the relationship, not simply to increase the level of sexual desire or expand the sexual repertoire of the partner labeled as "having the problem." This requires careful listening and questioning by the therapist. No one should be pressured to perform sexually when one's partner is domineering or manipulative about family finances or other nonsexual aspects of the relationship, or is insensitive to differences in personal or cultural values. For some people, just the fear that they will not meet society's expectations (let alone their partner's) lowers desire. If we continue to perpetuate the false message that good sex is always easy fun and that all one has to do is "let go," many people will simply stop having sex (or passively endure sex without enjoyment) and continue to view themselves as failures.

I've been married for 15 years; for the last 10 I've had no sexual feelings for my husband. I love him but he just doesn't "turn me on." This is putting a strain on my marriage. What can I do to correct the situation?

It is difficult to determine from your letter exactly what the problem is. Do you mean that you are no longer attracted to your husband, that you don't have orgasms during intercourse, or that you have stopped having intercourse altogether? Do you give and receive affection in other ways besides intercourse? Do you have negative feelings about your husband's physical appearance or sexual techniques? Has something changed about your general health, or are you taking prescription drugs? Do you drink alcohol and if so, how often? Did this change of feeling occur about the same time as a pregnancy or birth?

A sex therapist (see Appendix) could help you define the causes of your problem by asking these and other questions.

It is not unusual for couples who have been together several years to lose their former feelings of excitement and romance. Additionally, the stress of daily living can easily affect sexual functioning. Only a trained professional can help you determine whether a medical condition, physical problem, psychological difficulty or even just marital "staleness" is involved. Many of these difficulties can be overcome with only a few therapy sessions, so it is worth finding help if you feel your relationship is deteriorating.

I'm a 40-year-old woman who for two years now has lost my sexual desires. My husband and I never had this problem for six years; in fact we had sex every chance we could. I just can't figure it out; I love my husband. Now he is lucky to make love to me once a month.

It seems I'm always tired. I've been to doctors, but they don't know what my problem is and I found it embarrassing to talk about. I know deep down my husband can't be happy with this new me and he'll go to someone else.

Because you mention being tired, you should make an appointment with a sex dysfunctions clinic that has physicians on staff (see Appendix) or a specialist in gynecologic endocrinology for a complete checkup to rule out any underlying diseases or hormonal problems. When you call to make the appointment, tell the receptionist you've experienced a reduction in your previous level of sexual desire. Take along a list of all drugs you are taking, including vitamins, birth control pills, and nonprescription drugs such as tobacco and alcohol. Ask the doctor to review the list for possible sex-related side effects.

The most common health related causes of low sexual desire are depression, severe stress, side effects of drugs such as alcohol or high blood pressure medication, illnesses such as kidney disease, and changes in hormonal levels, especially testosterone. Any disruption of normal brain or nervous system activity can impair the physical mechanisms necessary for experiencing desire.

If no physical cause is found, you will then need an evaluation by a trained and experienced sex therapist or counselor. Your husband will probably be asked to attend at least the first appointment with you.

My sexual desire fluctuates with my menstrual cycle. For about a week each month I'm not very interested in sex. For the other 20 days, it also varies from

very strong to mild interest. My partner's sexual desire, however, is high every day, particularly every morning of his life.

During the two years of our relationship, it has become evident that he prefers having sex quickly every morning. To me this seems like a hygienic ritual or a habit. I prefer sex about twice a week and want it to be much more leisurely and satisfying.

When he was married his wife refused to have sex with him at all, and when I refuse I can see his hurt and feel guilty. What can I do? I'm willing to give him my body but am afraid that I will grow resentful at the loss of quality encounters.

You should start to talk together about your feelings, preferences, and concerns. Many couples complain about unequal levels of sexual desire or differ about when or how often to have sex, so you're not alone. Women frequently prefer more cuddling and foreplay than do men. For other couples, disagreements often involve the issue of satisfaction and not frequency.

For some women sexual desire does fluctuate during the menstrual cycle; some studies find it is highest at midcycle, others find it's highest just after menstruation, and still others find it's more related to the day of the week (for example, Saturday) and has nothing at all to do with hormonal cycles. Many men's desire is highest when they awaken in the morning.

In your case, negotiation and compromise may be in order. If the two of you cannot do that by yourselves, then a few visits to a sex counselor or therapist may be helpful. Let me stress that any solution must be seen as *mutually* satisfactory (meaning that neither individual gets his or her preference entirely). This is more easily achieved when other nonsexual aspects of the relationship are in balance and satisfying, and when the compromise is negotiated by an objective third party such as an experienced sex therapist or counselor.

I know that my situation must exist but I've never read anything about it. My husband has not had an erection in years. However, he has no trouble ejaculating. I've tried everything including oral sex to help him attain an erection. Nothing we've tried helps. Doctors say there is no medical reason for his failure to have an erection. He says that I "turn him on" more than any woman has in his past.

His favorite way is to snuggle, move as in intercourse and ejaculate on me. At first this method (four years now) was flattering to me. I thought that he was so aroused that he could not control himself. Wrong. He likes this. I think he has always done this, prefers and enjoys it. Maybe from a fear of getting a young lady "in trouble" when he was a young man.

Personally, it's so disgusting to me that I can not understand it. We have a wonderful life in every other way. But our sex life is horrible! I'm sure if he knew how I felt it would hurt him deeply. On the other hand, it is so selfish of him (or dumb) to expect me to enjoy this. How could I get him to see that I get nothing but a disgusting feeling? We have been married four years and we are in our 50s. He doesn't satisfy my sexual desires in any way. For the first time in my life, I've had to learn to masturbate. I just don't know what to do about this problem.

There is no reason for you to suffer silently; you have every right to a satisfying sex life. You should share with your husband how unsatisfactory you find your sexual relationship. It's possible he is acting in ways that were acceptable in a former relationship. He may have no idea what *you* need for sexual stimulation and enjoyment. This inability to talk about sex or the lack of basic information about sexual functioning may, in fact, be the major sexual problem for most couples. A counselor can help the two of you tell each other what you like and dislike, and provide the necessary information to put your sexual relationship on the right track.

The mechanisms governing erection, ejaculation, and orgasm are separate, so it is possible—and not uncommon—for a man to retain interest in sex and to ejaculate even though his penis is not erect. Your husband needs a medical examination from a physician who specializes in sexual dysfunctions to determine if the physical capacity for erection exists.

In the event your husband cannot achieve an erection, then training in mutually satisfying sexual alternatives which don't involve erection and penetration should be discussed. It is important to be honest about your own feelings, goals, and needs throughout this process of evaluation and treatment, telling your husband, the doctors, and counselors clearly what you like and dislike about your sex life and what you believe would make it better for you.

Unless your husband completely rejects a medical examination or therapy, all decisions are best made together. If he won't go for an evaluation, go by yourself to talk with a sex therapist. It will help you; and often the reluctant partner agrees to go once it's clear that the problem is being taken seriously.

I'm 62, physically active, and in good health. However, my appetite for sex has diminished from once a week to once every two weeks. I can still perform once a week, but the appetite is missing. And, like with a good meal, the appetite is an important ingredient. This drop in frequency doesn't seem to matter to my wife. What kind of doctor should I see?

Any number of factors can affect sexual desire, including psychological causes (depression or stress), physical causes (a change in hormone levels, the side effect of a medication, or alcohol consumption), or a combination of these.

A substantial number of physically healthy men engage in sexual activity once every two weeks or even less frequently. According to one survey of more than 4000 Americans age 50 or older, 75 percent of married men had sex once a week or less. However, some researchers suspect that the cultural expectation that older people should "slow down" may be as much of a factor as loss of actual desire or ability. Even though having sex every two weeks is neither unhealthy nor abnormal, if you're bothered by a decrease in sexual desire, it's time to seek expert help.

You say this change doesn't "seem" to matter to your wife. This suggests you haven't discussed it thoroughly with her. You may be surprised when you do. Communication is essential to a good sex life and a happy long-term marriage. Ask her to go along to your appointment and talk about each other's desires. By doing this your sex life may be improved even beyond its earlier level.

During the past few months my husband has developed a number of problems. He's been drinking what seems to be gallons of water every day. He

won't tell me how much he weighs, but I'm sure he's lost at least 10 pounds. On top of that, our sex life has, well, disappeared. He just seems to have lost interest in sex lately, but I'm afraid it's a cover-up for impotence.

Please don't suggest he see a doctor. I've tried to get him to make an appointment, but he won't listen to me. Can you tell me what's wrong?

All of the changes you mentioned—thirst, weight loss, and erection problems—can be signs of diabetes. In 50 percent to 60 percent of men found to be diabetic, the first signs of the illness are decreasing firmness of erections. If he has a sexual problem and if it is due to diabetes, he has a good chance of restoring his sexual functioning if he can bring the disease under control.

Your husband *must* have a medical examination to find out what's wrong. The longer diabetes remains untreated, the more severe the damage done to the vascular (blood vessel) system and other organs. Left untreated, it is life-threatening.

I'm confused about the exact meaning of impotence. Does it mean that a man can become sexually aroused without getting an erection or does it mean that a man doesn't become aroused enough to get an erection?

Also, if a man can become sexually aroused without getting an erection, doesn't that prove that his impotence is caused by a physical problem, not a psychological one?

There are several processes involved in male sexual response: sexual desire, erection, orgasm, and ejaculation. Any one or more of these processes can be disrupted by physical or psychological causes (or a combination of both) resulting in disorders or dysfunctions of sexual desire, erectile capacity, ejaculation, or orgasm.

Both of your examples describe sexual dysfunctions. Instead of the vague term impotence, experts now favor using more precise descriptive terms. Your first example is referred to as "erectile difficulty"; the second is called "low sexual desire."

Effects of Rape

I am a 23-year-old girl. I've had several boyfriends in the past but never succeeding in making love with any of them. My first experience of sex was not with a boy who I liked. When I was 20 years old I was raped by a middle-aged man (he was a boss, when I was working in a pub). It was so painful.

Since then, however, I have tried but never succeeded. When my boyfriend tries to do it, I always remember how painful it was. So I refuse violently. Nobody could get into me because of my behavior. Now I am irritated by myself. Why can't I do it, not even with my boyfriend who I really love? It is sad. I can't put in my finger or even a tampon.

I've been to see two doctors. One male doctor said the problem was really a mental thing and said maybe you'll never be able to do it forever. He also said "I suggest you don't think about sex." A female doctor said that lots of people can't do it because of pain, and she gave me tranquilizers to take before trying to have sex. What am I to do about these two different opinions?

Both of the doctors should have told you to find help from a rape crisis group or from a sex therapist experienced in treating women who have been raped. It is easy to believe you are the only one in the world living through this crisis, but when you speak to other women who have shared similar experiences you will discover that it is not unusual for women to be sexually dysfunctional after rape or sexual abuse.

Check to see if there is a rape crisis center in your area. In the United States, such organizations are listed in the telephone book under such headings as Rape, Rape Victim Assistance, or Rape Counseling. These agencies provide counseling to rape and abuse victims. Some also sponsor group meetings, during which women with similar problems can discuss how to cope with the emotional aspects of being a rape victim.

Some rape victims experience vaginismus, an involuntary tightening of vaginal muscles (discussed later in this chapter). Please contact someone who is familiar with treating rape victims: The advice you've gotten from the physicians you have seen is insensitive and ignorant, not at all in line with what is currently recommended as treatment for rape victims. Your experience underlines the importance of seeking help and support from individuals trained and experienced in treating women who have been sexually assaulted.

I am living common-law with a nice girl. We get along fine. We have a nice home, lots of food, and everything we need to be happy. Except that my girl is not very sexual. We have intercourse about three times a month. I am very hot blooded and I would like our sex life to improve to about three or four times a week. We have been together 2½ years.

She tells me a lot has to do with her past. She was raped by four guys when she was young and she also lived with a man that forced her to have sex without even getting her wet (foreplay). Now, I am very understanding that way, but the fact still remains that I need more sex with my friend. I truthfully have never cheated on her, but I get those visions of what it would be like with another woman. I do love her very much and I wouldn't leave her for sex. But I do not know how long I can go on masturbating by myself.

We have talked about it, but she always tells me that if what happened to her in the past had happened to me, I would feel the same towards sex. I am confused. Please let me know what I could do.

It's wonderful that you've talked to her about it and that you are understanding. Keep being supportive—but understand that you cannot change her attitudes about sex on your own. The best way you can help her is to find a therapist or counselor who has experience in working with women who have been raped or find a support group made up of women who share her experience.

Many women who have experienced rape or sexual abuse have difficulty with intimate relationships later in their lives. These problems can persist for many years and can seriously affect sexual functioning along with nonsexual behaviors—a woman may doubt her own self-worth, lose self-esteem, or fear emotional intimacy.

Researchers report that these women often have an inability to trust other people and shut down their feelings of affection. Many are afraid of men, avoid sex altogether, or have difficulty becoming sexually aroused.

Various kinds of therapy have successfully treated these and other related problems. Some research has found greater improvement when rape victims are treated in a group setting with other rape victims; these women often feel better about themselves after talking with others who have shared their experiences. Groups like this, which are often free, are available in many communities. Check in the telephone book or call the nearest community mental health center to locate such a self-help or therapist-led group.

I've heard that a woman can't be raped unless she wants to be. Is that true? How about men? Can men be raped by women?

It is absolutely *not* true that a woman must cooperate in order for a rape to be carried out. Even though many rapists claim that their victims did not resist, or even enjoyed it once the act had begun, the victims themselves attribute their reactions to fear, not sexual desire.

For years it was thought that a man could not be raped by a woman. But research on a very few rare cases of men who had been raped by women found that those men, when threatened with physical violence, were able to function sexually. Recent research has shown that some men, just like many women, have had sex under conditions that they felt were coercive. Even though physical violence was not involved, they experienced lasting negative psychological effects.

Male reactions after violent assault were similar to those of female rape victims. In addition to physical trauma, they experienced psychological trauma, including feeling a sense of violation and a loss of control over their own bodies and lives.

Some researchers view rape as an act of aggression and not primarily as a sexual act. Perhaps this view would make it easier to prosecute rape cases based on violation of consent instead of on the specifics of resistance by the victim or the degree of penetration involved.

Aphrodisiacs

The search for an herb, drug, or potion that enhances sexual desire has been underway for centuries and continues today. *NO* such substance has yet been proven effective, despite claims to the contrary made by companies that advertise such products (by direct mail, for example).

Buying these products is a waste of money better spent on visiting a qualified sex therapist or physician familiar with diagnosing sexual problems. Fortunately, a recent ruling by the U.S. Food and Drug Administration (FDA) prohibits interstate commerce and over-the-counter (OTC) sales after January 6, 1990, of "any product that bears labeling claims that it will arouse or increase sexual desire, or that it will improve sexual performance" because "there is a lack of adequate data to establish general recognition of the safety and effectiveness of any of these ingredients, or any other ingredient, for OTC use as an aphrodisiac. Labeling claims for OTC use as aphrodisiacs are either false, misleading, or unsupported by scientific data." The ingredients listed in this ruling include cantharides ("Spanish fly"), ginseng, mandrake, vitamins, and yohimbine among many others.

I've seen ads for pills called Corazine-dL, which say "doctor's answer for healthy erections." The ad also says: "Any man who wants sex regularly, who wants the joy of waking up daily with a stiff erection... who wants to know every morning that he is still living as a man can enjoy erections that will stand up tall and proud all night long... thanks to this help from medical science!"

The ad includes a lot of pictures of a man and woman in all kinds of romantic poses. It goes on to say that "you don't need a prescription to be cured of your problems with ejaculation because now medicine has found a way to give a man all the 'spunk and spurt' he needs, when he needs it, without treating him with dangerous drugs." Should I send these people a check, or what?

Don't waste your money! This isn't the first time a manufacturer has advertised a product that "protects" manhood, keeps sperm count healthy, increases ejaculate, promotes and maintains erections, revives interest in sex, provides greater sexual fulfillment, and guarantees morning erections every day—in essence, does it all.

Although the ad implies that researchers or doctors have proved the drug works, with careful reading you'll notice that the ad cites no scientific publication, which means that you can't go to a library and check out the study for yourself. There is also no listing of chemical ingredients, so you can't consult a pharmacologist to find out what the effects of the chemicals are on the body. And because there are no doctors' addresses, you can't call their hospitals or universities to request further information about their qualifications and reputations.

To date, no one has yet discovered a drug that "cures" any *one* male sexual dysfunction for most men, let alone all the separate steps involved in healthy sexual functioning: desire, arousal, erection, orgasm, ejaculation, plus sperm production. The day someone discovers a drug that reliably cures even one of these male dysfunctions for a majority of patients, not only will the inventor or drug company become fabulously wealthy (people already spend a fortune on bogus products), but every newspaper, radio program, television show, and magazine in the country will tell you about it and include information about the research that you or your physician can easily verify.

This much-anticipated event has not yet occurred. The FDA reports that "no drug on the market will produce the effects described in this ad."

I often receive ads in the mail for pills promising to restore vigor to older men. I usually just throw them out, but I got one today I would like you to check for me.
This one claims to be approved by the Kinsey Institute and by Masters and Johnson. Doesn't this one sound respectable?

It certainly sounds that way, but nearly everything in the ad is absolutely false. There is no Mexican Branch of either The Kinsey Institute or The Masters and Johnson Institute, and neither of our offices has endorsed, approved or is selling any such product—despite what this ad for "Orgatron-12" may say.

According to the ad, Orgatron-12 is "produced under strictest supervision of the Federal Pharmacia of Mexico." We can find no official government unit or registered private organization with that name in Mexico. The ad attributes research on this substance to a Dr. Leland Thomas, Nobel Prize-winning scientist. We could find no such physician listed in medical directories or listed as a recipient of a Nobel Prize. We are also absolutely certain that no Nobel Prize has yet been awarded for "advances in sexual research for older men," as the ad claims this Dr. Thomas has received.

Also, we cannot find documentation of any research project, in the United States or in Mexico, involving 900 impotent men, 884 of whom became potent while more than half "noted a measurable increase in the size of their sexual organs." Nor can we locate evidence that a jipuri plant (called Orgatron-12's main ingredient) "is known to have been used by the Aztecs as a powerful sexual stimulant." Also, a search of biology reference books found no reference to such a plant or any clues to the scientific name such a plant might be listed under.

Finally, the ad displayed an issue of something called the *American Journal of Human Sexuality*, which also doesn't appear to exist; it's not listed in any periodical directories and no one at The Kinsey Institute has ever seen or heard of this journal.

I have read that yohimbine is used to treat impotence. Does this drug replace the implant operation? A lot of us elderly men will be interested in your comments.

Much of the early research involving yohimbine was conducted on rats and other laboratory animals. To date there have been few research reports on the effects of yohimbine on humans, although there are studies currently under way aimed at clarifying this matter. This research uses the prescription drug yohimbine hydrochloride, *not* the various yohimbine products often listed as an ingredient in ads for aphrodisiacs or sold over the counter.

Until more carefully controlled comparative studies are completed, men should continue to seek an accurate diagnosis of exactly what is causing trouble with erections and use treatments demonstrated to effectively treat that particular problem. If you can't resist the ads for over-the-counter preparations that supposedly include yohimbine (which are filled with vague references to research and pictures of smiling men), at least consult your physician before taking these pills. It is impossible to know what is in products that have not been tested or approved by the FDA, and many of these yohimbine products tested by reliable laboratories also contain a form of strychnine (a deadly poison).

To date, the FDA has approved the prescription drug yohimbine hydrochloride only for treatment of blood pressure problems, and even this approval carries warnings about use of the drug and possible side effects such as elevation of blood pressure and increased heart rate.

I've read somewhere that taking vitamin E will increase sex drive. This is something I'd very much like to do for myself, as I've tried just about everything else. I know it would help my marriage if my sex drive got a boost. So, is it true that vitamin E helps your sex drive?

Not according to current evidence. If you eat properly, your body has all the vitamin E it needs for normal sexual functioning. The widespread erroneous idea that supplemental vitamin E boosts sex drive probably results from misinterpretation of studies that rats deprived of vitamin E developed atrophy of the testicles and ovaries; these abnormalities were reversed when the rats were then given vitamin E.

Careful scientific studies of humans given vitamin E found no increase in sex drive among individuals with normal levels of vitamin E. Individuals who are *deficient* in vitamin E do have lower sex drives, but so do individuals with many other problems, including such serious diseases as cystic fibrosis and prolonged malnutrition.

Regardless of the evidence, if you decide to take vitamin E, you need to know that it is fat-soluble, so it accumulates in the body. It has not been found to be toxic in the usual range of supplement doses, from 100 to 1000 IU per day, but cases of overdoses have resulted in headaches, nausea, and muscle weakness. Vitamin E is also an anticoagulant, so anyone taking it should stop two weeks before any elective surgery; it also can enhance the effects of anticoagulant drugs like Coumadin or Panwarfin, so ask your physician about taking vitamin E if you take these medications.

Besides, some experts believe that the natural vitamin E found in food is more active in the body than synthetic forms. Natural sources of vitamin E include soybeans, sweet potatoes, greens such as turnip leaves, whole-grain cereal, breads, and wheat germ.

I am almost 20 years old and I have never had an orgasm. I read in a magazine that niacin, vasopressin, phenylalanine, and vitamin B⁶ help in having orgasms. Is this true? I've been going out with my boyfriend for a little less than a year—I take sex very seriously. I don't sleep around and I'm getting concerned that something is wrong.

I found no research reporting any link between the vitamins niacin or B⁶, or the amino acid phenylalanine, and orgasm. If a person were deficient in these substances it might be difficult to have orgasms, but probably because you would be ill.

Most people who eat a balanced diet have adequate amounts of these substances. Sources of niacin include liver and milk, phenylalanine is also in milk as well as other foods, and vitamin B⁶ is also found in many foods, including cereals.

Vasopressin is a natural hormone made in the pituitary gland of humans and some animals, but synthetic vasopressin is prescribed to treat postsurgical swelling of the abdomen and some diabetic patients. Surely, the magazine was not suggesting that people having sexual difficulties obtain prescription vasopressin for self-medication. This is a strong medication with potentially serious side effects. Problems with orgasm are much more easily and safely solved by consulting a sex therapist. Anorgasmia is discussed later in this chapter.

I've read that alcohol can cause impotence, but I don't think that's true. I have better sex after I've had a few drinks. Why don't doctors just tell people with sex problems to drink?

Alcohol is a depressant drug and chemically acts to slow down, reduce, or stop the physical processes necessary for sexual arousal and orgasm. In men, alcohol can inhibit arousal, reduce erectile capacity, and slow or eliminate ejaculation and orgasm. In women, arousal, vaginal blood volume, and orgasm are all reduced with increased levels of alcohol.

Long-term alcohol use can lead to significant physical changes that can affect sexuality, some of which may be irreversible even if a person were to stop drinking. For example, alcohol consumption temporarily lowers testosterone levels and sperm counts in men. For men who drink regularly or on a prolonged basis, permanent sterility and testicular atrophy (shrinking) may result. Moreover, not only is testosterone lowered, but estrogen (a "female" hormone) is increased, which can lead to irreversible breast enlargement (gynecomastia).

The amount that is harmful differs from one man or woman to the next, but similar effects on women who drink heavily have been noted, including atrophy of the ovaries, menstrual irregularities, and infertility.

Depressant drugs such as alcohol also have psychological effects. For some people this includes reducing sexual inhibitions, which may help a few individuals who feel shy or guilty to more freely express or experience their sexual desire and arousal. Others may use alcohol to excuse behavior that would be unacceptable to them when sober.

Physical and psychological reactions to alcohol vary widely from person to person. For example, 45 percent of the male respondents to a survey done by *Psychology Today* magazine said that alcohol enhanced their sexual pleasure, but 42 percent reported that it decreased enjoyment.

Masters and Johnson describe a typical situation in which a man experienced an episode of high alcohol intoxication that resulted in erectile failure. The failure caused the man to become anxious about his sexual performance, which led to the use of more alcohol to lessen the anxiety, which led to further erection failures.

We also know alcohol can have a devastating effect on the fetus of a pregnant woman. For these and other reasons, anyone with sexual difficulties should consult a physician, therapist, or clinic rather than turning to beer, wine, or other liquors.

I heard that a lack of hormones could keep a man from performing. Can I get hormones from changing my diet or do I need a prescription to get some pills to take?

Do you suspect your hormone levels are too low? The only way to know whether this is the case is to have blood tests taken. If a blood test shows that you are deficient in testosterone, then taking supplemental testosterone *might* have some effect. But researchers have found that the effect is to increase sexual thoughts or fantasies rather than to increase erectile ability. Moreover, the physician would probably recommend injections, because testosterone in some pill forms is not as effective.

However, if your hormone levels are normal, taking testosterone in any form is not likely to help and may actually do serious harm. One risk is that any undetected cancer in the prostate might be stimulated to grow.

I know of no dietary source of testosterone. Both pills and injections require prescription by a physician because these are powerful drugs with potentially serious mental and physical side effects that require careful monitoring while you use them.

I've heard that the army puts saltpeter in food to stop men from wanting to have sex. Is this true?

No, although this is a widespread myth. Other variations of this myth are that saltpeter is put into food in prisons, at colleges, at summer camps, on military ships, or anywhere that men are isolated from women.

Saltpeter (potassium nitrate) is used in making fireworks and gunpowder, preserving meat, and tempering steel. There is absolutely no scientific evidence that it reduces the sex drive or prevents erection. No effect on sexual desire or functioning has been observed from its use as a food preservative. But if a man *thinks* that he has consumed something that will diminish his sexual interest or abilities, his sexual functioning may well be reduced.

Enclosed is an ad for a chemical attractant. It claims that the male wearer will induce emotional and physical attraction in women. What do you think?

There is no good scientific evidence to support this product's claims for "instant sex appeal." Many such products are advertised by mail or in magazines and most claim to contain pheromones (chemicals naturally secreted by the body that carry messages to other members of the same species) or some "secret" ingredient.

Experiments with animals have reported that contact with androstenone—the ingredient mentioned in the ad you sent—does cause female pigs in heat to assume the mating position, but I found no evidence of a similar effect on human females. So if you were to invest $24 in this product, you might find that the sows in your area will respond favorably, but I wouldn't count on women beating a path to your door.

Even if human sexual-attractant pheromones are ever discovered, it's unlikely that they could manipulate a woman's feelings to the point that she would overlook a man's other characteristics. Also human pheromones would probably work very slowly, over the course of several weeks or months, not during one date or a casual encounter.

AROUSAL

Among the thousands of letters received by The Kinsey Institute each year questions about erections are the number one category. Problems with "getting it up" and "keeping it hard" affect men of all ages.

It is not uncommon for a healthy man of any age to experience occasional erectile failure. This can be caused by a number of relatively minor psychological and physical factors, from stress and fatigue to short-term illness and alcohol consumption. When it happens to you, it's probably best to view it as an isolated incident. Don't become fixated on the idea that you've become "impotent," or the worry itself can produce more erection problems in the future. Understanding that an occasional incident of failing to obtain or maintain an erection is natural for most men may help you avoid misinterpreting these events.

Persistent erectile failure, on the other hand, should not be treated casually. Contrary to common belief, most chronic erection problems are not caused solely by psychological factors but are often indications of some physical or medical problem. That's why it's so important for men to see a physician, preferably a urologist trained to diagnose sexual problems, to pinpoint the cause of persistent erectile failure. A careful medical and sexual history, a complete physical evaluation, and a psychological evaluation are often needed to adequately diagnose and treat erectile difficulties. The important fact to know is that the vast majority of these difficulties *can* be successfully treated.

As discussed in Chapter 6, the crucial factor for physical sexual arousal in both men and women is vasocongestion of the genitals. In men, the most obvious result is erection of the penis; in women the signs of arousal include vaginal lubrication and swelling of the labia.

Erection Problems

Diagnosis of male arousal problems involves assessment of both physical and psychological factors. Obviously, all of the brain, hormones, nerves, muscles, veins, and genital structures must be intact and in good working order for erection to occur and be sustained. Most men with erection problems believe that they have a problem with one of these physical factors, and most have heard about various types of medical solutions (ranging from hormone injections to penile implants). There is no doubt that these medical solutions are effective.

Insisting on an "instant solution," however, may actually backfire and have negative, not positive, effects on a man's sexual life. Physical problems often lead to psychological problems (including problems with the relationship). Thus it should come as no surprise that just providing a man erections often doesn't make his sexual life any more pleasurable. Even after a physical problem is resolved, psychological factors can continue to cause problems. That's why sex therapy is often a necessary step in the full recovery of sexual functioning.

It is vitally important that psychological and relationship factors be assessed as part of a full evaluation, before going ahead with medical solutions— especially those that are irreversible, such as penile implants. Unfortunately, some physicians and surgeons proceed with treatment for erectile difficulties without first conducting a psychological assessment of the patient, and often without even speaking with his partner.

This is why reputable clinics and physicians insist on including a psychological assessment of the man *and* interviewing his partner. While it's wonderful that so many new medical solutions are available, having an erection doesn't do a man much good if his partner won't have sex with him.

I've always enjoyed sex with my wife, having fathered six children. Recently I've had trouble attaining an erection and maintaining it long enough to reach satisfaction. My wife is understanding, but this is really bothering me no end when I can't follow up lovemaking with total satisfaction. My doctor tells me this is "psychological" and that you have to work through it yourself. I don't seem to be making any progress.

For years, researchers felt that most erection problems were caused by purely psychological problems. But more recent studies have revealed that erectile difficulties can have many physical causes.

One study of men coming to a Veterans Administration health center found that 34 percent admitted having erectile difficulties. Of those who chose to be evaluated for this problem, the erection problems of only 14 percent were attributed to purely psychological causes. Twenty-eight percent were diagnosed as having various hormonal imbalances and 25 percent had erection problems caused by medications; other causes included diabetes, 9 percent; neurological (brain and nerves), 7 percent; urological (kidney, bladder, urethra), 6 percent; and various other problems (such as the after effects of surgery) totaled 4 percent. In only 7 percent of the cases was no specific cause found.

Couples rarely can work these problems out for themselves, even when a psychological or relationship problem is found to be the cause. You need to make an appointment at a clinic that specializes in diagnosis and treatment of sexual dysfunctions (see Appendix).

How can you tell if a man's erection problems are because of some medical condition or something that's all in his head?

When a man is able to become sexually excited and reports feeling intense desire but does not achieve penile erection sufficient for sexual intercourse, the cause can be either physical (organic), psychological (psychogenic), or a combination of both.

There are a number of tests available for distinguishing between organic and psychogenic causes of erectile problems. These include NPT (nocturnal penile tumescence) monitoring in a sleep laboratory, blood tests for levels of testosterone and prolactin hormones, and ultrasound assessment of blood flow in the penis.

But it's important not to overlook the possibility of a combination of factors. Erection problems caused by a particular medication, for instance, may not be resolved even after the man stops taking the drug. There are many examples of organic erectile failure that have led to performance anxiety (when the man becomes so fearful of failure or embarrassed that he cannot achieve or maintain erections) which persists even after the physical problems are solved.

I'm in my early 40s. During my sleeping hours I am awakened every couple of hours or so with an erection, but during daytime hours it seems nearly impossible to have a natural erection. What is happening?

I am not sure what you mean by a "natural erection." As men age, it is not unusual for them to need more direct stimulation of the penis to get an erection firm enough for intercourse (in comparison to their younger years, when firm erections were often spontaneous, or appeared immediately at the thought of sex or the sight of a desirable partner).

Nearly all males have erections during a particular stage of sleep (see Chapter 6). Evidence that a man has nighttime erections but not daytime erections has been interpreted by some to mean that his erectile problems are caused by psychological rather than physical factors. But other researchers question this idea, pointing out that some apparently healthy men don't have nighttime erections. It's not yet clear whether these men have physical problems caused by factors yet to be discovered, whether their lack of night erections is actually due to psychological factors, or a combination of factors is at work.

Frankly, we still know so little about all the hormonal, blood-system, brain, nervous-system, and psychological mechanisms involved in erection that it remains possible that nighttime and daytime erections are really different phenomena.

Based on what we currently know, however, there are several possible explanations for your situation that you'll need to explore with a specialist. He or she will conduct various tests. Be sure to tell the physician about all prescription and nonprescription drugs you take and the time of day you take them, including alcohol and any illegal drugs.

Possible psychological causes will also be discussed. One common cause of erectile dysfunction is "spectatoring"—when a person becomes focused on whether he or she will be "successful" at having sex. This close monitoring (Do I have an erection yet? Am I going to have an orgasm this time?) can block the natural pattern of the automatic physical responses required for effective functioning. This problem, among many others, can be successfully treated by a qualified sex therapist who will assign homework such as practicing relaxation and learning to focus on feeling pleasurable sensations.

I'm 23 and have erection difficulties. I am so introspective and analytical that I can't seem to get the thought of failure out of my head. This has deteriorated my once-strong libido and shaken my confidence in developing relationships. Women (even if patient and understanding) could easily look to greener pastures. I need help, but I'm low on cash. What can I do?

The fear of failure and the fear of being ridiculed were found in one study to be the most common types of performance anxiety. This kind of anxiety can directly interfere with the physical conditions required for arousal, erection, and orgasm. Fortunately, therapies based on the "sensate-focus" model designed by Masters and Johnson are effective treatment for many people with performance anxieties. In these treatments, a patient is taught to focus on the pleasurable feelings and sensations involved without the pressure to perform intercourse. Therapy consists of assignments you do at home and can be done by people who do not have partners.

Call your local mental health center and ask if they offer treatments for sexual performance anxiety. Most public agencies have a fee schedule based on a patient's ability to pay, and some offer group sessions which further reduce costs. If you are a veteran of the U.S. armed forces, check with the Veterans Administration; many VA centers offer such therapy.

And, by the way, you may be misinformed about the types of sexual stimulation women need for arousal and orgasm; thrusting by an erect penis does not produce orgasm for the vast majority of women.

I'm 72 years old, diabetic (controlled by diet and Glucotrol pills), and haven't been able to achieve an erection for nearly three years. Until my wife died earlier this year she helped me have orgasm even though my penis was not fully erect.

I would like to end my loneliness but hesitate to ask any woman to dinner or a social event because of my situation. Is my sex life over? Are there any medicines, pills, etc. to help my situation? I heard about operations on TV that might solve the problem, but I'm afraid I can't afford something like that.

As you already discovered with your wife, a man doesn't have to deprive himself of companionship, affection, or sexual activities simply because of erection problems. Not only can you achieve orgasm, but you can also help your partner to have orgasms even if you do not have erections.

You should consider beginning new social activities without worrying about erectile capacity, since in most circumstances a dinner invitation is not presumed to also include intercourse. Then, if you find a partner who cares for you and wants to have a sexual relationship, the ways of showing love without a complete erection are likely to work out as well with her as they did with your wife. There is more information about diabetes and sex in Chapter 18.

I'm 69 and in very good health, but impotent. Taking pills from a urologist did little good for erections. Now he wants me to go for injections into the penis to open up the blood flow to get erections. Is this advisable? Is it dangerous? Are there side effects? How long would this last?

Since I don't know which diagnostic tests you've had, what was found and what type of injections have been recommended, I can only give you a general answer. Insufficient blood flow to the penis and problems with blood vessels in the penis can cause erectile difficulties. Tests to determine whether these factors are involved include a Doppler analysis of penile arteries (using ultrasound to evaluate blood flow) and NPT monitoring in a sleep laboratory to measure erections during sleep.

If all other possible causes of erection problems have been ruled out and if these preliminary tests show that reduced blood flow is likely to be causing erection problems, then more complicated tests are done to pinpoint exactly where the problem is located. Using penile arteriography and/or corpus cavernosography (X-rays taken of the penis after a special dye has been injected), a physician can determine which of the many blood vessels are involved.

Without such tests, it can be difficult to locate a specific cause for erectile problems and even more difficult to recommend the best treatment. If you have had all of these tests and the urologist has shown you X-rays or other evidence of exactly where the blood vessels are blocked, then he or she will also be able to tell you the chances for success of the suggested treatment.

Ask how many men the physician has treated with this procedure, how many regained erectile functioning, and—most important—how long they've been followed up to see whether the problems returned. Some surgical attempts to correct or bypass penile blood vessels have looked successful immediately after surgery, but patients report a return of erection problems after a year or two.

Get a second opinion from another specialist before making a decision about the diagnosis and treatment options. Insist on being given full information and keep asking questions until you clearly understand what has been found and why a particular treatment is being recommended. And if you have a sexual partner, insist on adequate counseling for both of you before making any decisions about treatment.

I am 68, in good health and mentally alert, but have a problem maintaining an erection. Recently, I heard a TV report about injecting a liquid directly into the penis. This was not a penile implant and the only side effect was the possibility of not getting rid of an erection.
Are you familiar with this procedure?

To understand these injections, you should first understand how a natural erection comes about (*see Chapter 6).* Before considering any treatment you must first have an evaluation to determine whether all the necessary physical components are intact. If evaluation by a physician experienced in the use of this technique establishes that you may benefit from penile injections, then make sure that both you and your partner receive adequate training in how this is done and the warning signs of potential problems.

Research studies on penile injections have reported success rates ranging from 65 to 100 percent, negative-side-effects rates from 2 to 13 percent, and that about 50 percent of men (one out of two) drop out of such treatment programs.

In this procedure, a vasoactive drug (usually papaverine, or a combination of papaverine and phentolamine) is injected into the corpus cavernosum of the penis using a syringe and needle. Correct dosage varies and careful training on self-injection is required. An erection is obtained in a few minutes and may last for an hour or so. A man is given enough medication for one month and must be examined carefully when he goes to pick up the next month's supply. For a few men who used papavirine, natural erectile ability seems to have been restored after a series of these injections.

These drugs have not been approved for this use by the U.S. Food and Drug Administration, and the manufacturer has recently issued a statement packaged with the product that it is not indicated for use in the penis as treatment for impotence. Out of concern for legal liability, a patient will most likely be asked to sign a statement absolving the physician from legal responsibility. Ask how many men the physician has treated, the success rate, and rate of negative side effects before agreeing to any treatment.

These injections have only been in use for a few years, so long-term negative side effects are not yet known, but negative short-term effects include pain, irritation at the injection site, and changes in blood pressure. About 5 percent of users have experienced priapism (a persistent painful erection); if this continues for more than four hours, tissue damage to the penis can result, so emergency treatment to reverse the erection must be done.

New research is being done with other vasodilating drugs that produce erections but without the risk of priapism. Although some of these are injected into the penis, researchers are experimenting with new oral drugs as well.

You mentioned difficulty with "maintaining" an erection rather than with getting one—and this often involves a different problem. If, for example, you lose erections because a defect in the blood system allows the blood to drain out of the spongy cylinders of the penis before orgasm, microsurgery to repair that defect might be a more effective treatment for you. Or, perhaps you and your partner simply need to try positions and techniques to increase penile stimulation. This is why a full evaluation is necessary *before* trying something just because it was on television. Consult a specialist in diagnosing erection problems.

One quite effective erection tool is seldom mentioned: the vacuum device.

No doctor myself, I learned about this device from a foremost urologist. I had set up an appointment with him for a $4000 implant when he suggested that the vacuum device be tried first. To my delight there was no need for the implant. Obviously a doctor only interested in the big bucks would not have recommended a $50 alternative. I think you will find that the vacuum device in thousands of cases can be a thrifty alternative to an ancient vexation.

All kinds of vacuum pumps and other external devices claiming to produce or maintain erections have been around for decades. The Kinsey Institute has a brochure from 1904, for example, that extols the virtues of a vacuum pump as "a way to perfect manhood like a benediction after all else has failed and hope is dead."

There has been renewed interest in whether a safe and effective vacuum device could help some men but few scientific reports are available. A physician who reportedly has prescribed a vacuum device and studied results in more than 100 men declined to supply data on successes, failures, or problems. There is a published report from Great Britain on nine men who used one type of vacuum pump. The men placed the flaccid penis in an acrylic tube and used a pump to apply a specified vacuum pressure for seven to twenty minutes to force blood into the penile tissues. When the penis was rigid, rubber rings were placed around the base of the penis (to prevent the blood from draining out) and the cylinder removed. The erection was maintained until the rings were removed (not longer than thirty minutes later), but at orgasm the rings prevented ejaculation. There were complaints of pain and numbness, and after six months *all* the men were less enthusiastic about the device and three said they would not use it further.

Other recent studies of small groups of patients reported some success with a slightly different type of vacuum device that has a flexible tube for the penis; it looks somewhat like a thick condom. Unlike other vacuum pumps, this device is kept on the penis during intercourse.

We have also received literature from a U.S. manufacturer of a vacuum pump (available by prescription from physicians) reporting on a survey of 1517 men and their partners. Even though it is impossible to assess the validity of this survey, it was interesting to note that 40 percent reported discomfort or pain during use, that for 25 percent discomfort or pain lasted from one to more than seven weeks or had not stopped, and that 31 percent of the users' partners were unhappy with or had no particular reaction to the device.

Physicians and therapists who do not recommend such devices have told us of medical problems they've seen caused by vacuum pumps and penile rings— including external abrasion of the penile shaft, damage to internal penile tissue, and infection or irritation of the urinary tract. Various models advertise safety valves or other modifications that claim to reduce tissue damage, but until enough scientific data are available on a vacuum device establishing it as both effective and safe, men should be aware that permanent damage to their genitals and urinary tract is possible.

I assume you're using the device under a doctor's supervision and have been told what to do if you have the slightest irritation, pain, or other problem. No man should attempt to apply vacuum pumps or rings to his genitals unless he's under the close supervision of a competent physician who also provides counseling for both the patient and his partner.

I'm 63 years old. Is there anything to help the sex life of a man my age? What about the penile implant I've read about?

There are two basic types of penile implants in use today. Both have advantages and disadvantages.

The inflatable types of implant consist of two inflatable silicone cylinders inserted into the erectile areas of the penis; these are connected via tubing and a pump to a small balloon in the abdomen. Fluid in the reservoir balloon in the abdomen flows into the cylinders in the penis when the man activates a pump that hangs in his scrotum. When the man no longer needs the erection, he switches a valve on the pump; this deflates the penile cylinders and the fluid flows back into the abdominal reservoir (*see Illustration 19*). A newer type of inflatable implant has all these components in one cylinder in the penis.

The other type (semirigid implants) involves insertion of rodlike silicone forms into the penis. After surgery the penis is always erect but can be pushed down so that it is concealed by clothing.

The inflatable type of implant is closest to natural functioning. It involves however, a complicated mechanical system, longer and more extensive surgery, and can malfunction, requiring surgery to replace mechanical failures. These devices cost several thousands of dollars plus surgical fees and about five days of hospitalization. Operating this type of implant requires some training and manual dexterity on the part of the man or his partner.

Although less costly and less subject to mechanical failure, problems with semirigid implants include irritation of the penile tissue and difficulty in performing some urological tests or examinations.

Thousands of both types of penile implant have been used since their introduction in the 1970s, and 95 percent of all patients report they are generally pleased with the results, but one study found that 75 percent felt their penis was shortened by the surgery (which is often the case) and 65 percent reported decreased sensitivity of the penis. There have also been reports that there was greater pain with healing than expected and that choice of sexual positions was more limited after surgery. Because implant surgery destroys any existing natural erectile capacity, it's important that implant surgery be reserved for cases where all other treatment options have been tried, and that a man and his partner be told exactly what the procedure involves and what can be expected following surgery.

A friend who is diabetic has become impotent. Even though he no longer has erections, he still feels sexual desire and ejaculates. His urologist suggested a penile implant, but when he told his wife about the surgery she said, "If you're doing this for my benefit, forget it." Now she won't even talk about it.

He still thinks about having the operation, and wonders if implants are covered by insurance. He continues to need sexual release and I think they both need to go back to making love in order to open communication routes again.

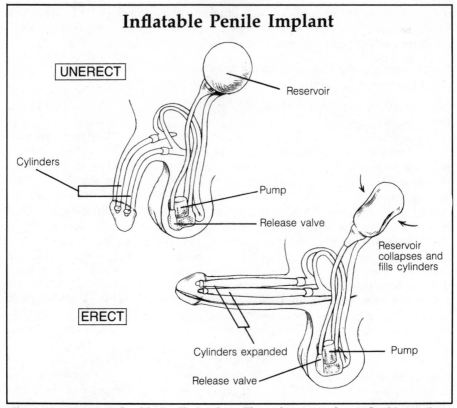

Inflatable Penile Implant

UNERECT

Reservoir

Cylinders

Pump

Release valve

Reservoir
collapses and
fills cylinders

ERECT

Cylinders expanded

Pump

Release valve

Illustration No. 19. **Inflatable Penile Implant.** These drawings of an inflatable penile implant show the various parts of this type of implant and where they are placed inside the body.

Most experts would suggest that the reverse is true: Communication should come *before* lovemaking. Sex itself doesn't open communication; sex provides only one route of expressing affection, love, and caring. If your friend does decide in favor of an implant, the sequence of treatments in a case like this should be medical and psychological evaluation of both partners, trying nonsurgical treatments, *then* deciding about penile-implant surgery.

Your friend should ask his physician to recommend a sex-dysfunctions clinic or a sex therapist skilled in working with couples. Counseling on communication and lovemaking techniques that don't require an erection should come first; this usually takes only a few appointments. If his wife will not accompany him, then he should go alone but continue to encourage her participation so that the counselor can hear her side of the story.

Your friend's wife has a valid point: Having penile-implant surgery should not be viewed as a gift to a sexual partner. Penile implants alone don't alter preexisting feelings about the relationship or sexual techniques. That's why reputable implant programs insist that *both* patients and their partners be evaluated before surgery. Perhaps your friend's wife feels that their lovemaking wasn't satisfying—that's why partners must participate in discussions about penile implants. It's the only way to ensure that *their* needs are met as well.

He should also ask his insurance carrier about coverage for penile-implant surgery and counseling. Many insurance policies cover these costs, especially if a medical evaluation establishes that the erection difficulties result from a chronic illness, such as diabetes.

Is it possible to get a penis transplant? If so, is there a way for a man to choose the penis he is to receive? Can he select the size?

There are no scientific reports of transplanting a penis from one man to another, and there are only a few reports of a man's *own* penis being reattached after being accidentally amputated or injured. In several such cases men regained the ability to urinate and slowly also reacquired sensitivity of the penis. Researchers are working on designing special penile implants for such men so that they can also have erections.

Specialists in transplanting other organs and body parts speculate that transplanting a penis would be more complicated than transplanting either a heart or kidneys, since it would be much more difficult to match up veins, nerves, muscles, and tissues. If a penis transplant is ever done successfully, I'm sure it will be widely covered by the media, because penis size and repair after injury to the genitals concern many men.

Vaginal Problems

As with males, adequate arousal in females relies on both psychological and physical factors. Not enough psychological or physical stimulation during foreplay, reduced vaginal lubrication due to a low level of estrogen, vaginal infections, and some diseases and medications can all result in reduced genital responses.

When arousal and vasocongestion do not occur properly in women penetration can be difficult, painful, or impossible; and even if intercourse is possible, the vagina can become irritated, thrusting may cause pain deep inside the pelvic area, and orgasm becomes unlikely.

I'm too embarrassed to ask this question of my doctor or anyone else. I'm the mother of four children. My husband constantly complains that when we make love I'm too large inside. What can I do?

You haven't said a word about your own sexual functioning and satisfaction. Do you become aroused, do you have orgasms, and how do you come to orgasm? When a woman is fully aroused, during the plateau phase of sexual response (*as explained in Chapter 6*) the outer third of the vagina narrows while the inner two-thirds balloons open. This is normal, even for women who have delivered several children. The narrowing of the outer end of the vagina should provide sufficient friction for an adequately erect penis.

Explain this to your husband and try increasing foreplay to help you reach that level of arousal which will increase the tightness of the outer end of the vagina. Increased foreplay may also help him to attain a full erection.

At your next annual pelvic exam, ask the gynecologist to see if you have had any damage to the pelvic muscles or vaginal opening from childbirth and to assess the tone of your pelvic muscles. Although these physical problems can exist, the actual existence of a "too large" vagina is very rare.

You and your husband should consider making an appointment with a sex therapist. Therapists point out that in many cases improvement comes with educating the couple about basic sexual responses. Satisfaction with intercourse can be increased by teaching a couple how to increase arousal, and *constructively* tell one another what type of activity, touching, or movement is most arousing. Learning how to communicate sexual preferences is as valuable in some cases as learning specific sexual techniques. If your husband will not go with you to a sex therapist, go alone. You need to get some help in understanding normal sexual responses and in learning techniques for increasing your own pleasure. Your vagina is probably just fine.

I was a virgin before my first marriage, which lasted 17 years before ending in divorce. I always hated sex with my husband. Now I've been seeing a man for about a year and sex has been wonderful with him, but there seems to be a problem with penetration. He seems to have trouble entering me.

I'm convinced something is wrong with my body. I am too embarrassed to see a doctor. Can you tell me what is wrong? I feel like I could never marry again without wondering if I have a problem.

Start by asking your partner if he thinks there's a problem with penetration. It may be that he doesn't perceive a problem or would welcome the opportunity to talk with you about any sexual concerns he might have.

Perhaps you're attempting intercourse before you are sexually aroused enough to be sufficiently lubricated or for your labia to swell. Or you may be one of the many women who do not produce much lubrication. Try increasing foreplay and using a water-based lubricant (such as K-Y jelly or Lubrin suppositories, which can be purchased without a prescription) before penetration to see if that changes the situation.

If this doesn't help, there are several other possible explanations. First, ask your physician to check your basic medical condition; one early sign of diabetes in women is decreased lubrication. Have you been having an annual gynecological pelvic examination? If not, you should. If so, has your gynecologist mentioned anything unusual about your vaginal opening? If she or he hasn't, there is probably nothing physically wrong. But, at your next annual gynecological exam, ask specifically about the condition of your vaginal lining, the opening into the vagina and your external genitals. You did not mention your age, but you could be experiencing changes related to lowered estrogen as you move toward menopause (*see Chapter 9*). Ask your physician to check your blood to see if hormone levels are adequate for maintaining genital health and sexual functioning.

If no explanation is found, ask to be referred to a sex therapist. It could be that having had painful intercourse with your husband, you are unable to relax enough to experience full arousal. You also haven't mentioned whether or how you have orgasms. An assessment by a sex therapist can determine if you and your friend might be able to try various techniques to increase your arousal and ability to have orgasms.

I'm 35 and was diagnosed several years ago as having vaginismus. I was told to go home and practice dilating myself. I couldn't manage even one finger because of the pain. I also have no lubrication; K-Y jelly doesn't help. I had my hymen removed at age 23, which made no difference.

All penetration is out: intercourse, pelvic examinations, tampons. In 15 years of marriage I've had intercourse once; it was worse than going to a dentist.

Anyone I've ever told about this, including doctors, is shocked—which confirms how rare it is. Do you know of any treatments? Or is this a problem I must be prepared to live with?

We don't know the exact frequency of vaginismus (an involuntary contraction of the muscles surrounding the opening to the vagina), since many women don't go for treatment, but Masters and Johnson estimate that 2 to 3 percent of all adult women have this problem.

Vaginismus usually has a physical basis, even though the actual condition itself is psychological. In other words, a vaginismus patient may have experienced vaginal pain, associated it with penetration, and then involuntarily tightens the vaginal muscles whenever penetration is likely. In other cases, the cause of vaginismus is a lack of information about her own body or sexual functioning, or an overall fear of or distaste for sex.

It is sad but not surprising that the physicians you have seen so far were shocked, because most have little or no training in sexual medicine and few women report this problem to their physicians.

Don't be discouraged: Vaginismus has one of the highest success rates for treatment (nearly 100 percent) of all sexual problems.

Find a qualified sex therapist with experience in treating vaginismus. Treatment combines education; counseling; and, when a woman is ready, gradual dilation (opening) of the vagina. After practicing relaxing the muscles in the thighs, the patient inserts a small dilator into her vagina, using a water-based lubricant, and holds it for a few minutes. The first size of dilator used is smaller than a finger; the patient slowly progresses to larger dilators. The woman may continue to use dilators for several months until she's confident that her vagina can easily accommodate an erect penis.

Discussions about sexual functioning and coital techniques also take place, although intercourse is usually forbidden until a later stage of therapy, when the woman is certain of her pain-free capacity. When a couple is involved, the sexual partner may be encouraged to be present for the therapy sessions. At the point intercourse is to be tried, the couple is given instructions to follow at home, including how the woman can control penetration when she's ready, and which positions (such as woman-on-top or side-by-side) permit her to control the rhythm and depth of thrusting.

It is not unusual for a woman's vaginismus to lead to functioning difficulties for her male partner as well. He may be understandably afraid of causing his partner pain, or he may doubt his abilities as a lover—two issues that must also be discussed in therapy. But your condition is not unique; it can be successfully treated, and you can indeed gain normal sexual functioning with proper therapy.

PAIN DURING INTERCOURSE

Both men and women can experience pain during intercourse. Called dyspareunia, it can occur at any point in the process of sexual arousal, intercourse, orgasm, or after orgasm.

It's important to seek a diagnosis at a center staffed by both physicians and sex therapists because both physical and psychological factors can be involved. It must be determined when the pain begins, where it is felt in the body, and how the couple reacts to the pain.

Physical causes for dyspareunia in women include vaginal infections, scar tissue from an improperly healed episiotomy, endometriosis, menopausal changes in vaginal tissues, and urinary-tract infections among many others. In men infections of the prostate, urinary tract, or seminal vesicles are some physical causes of dyspareunia. Some medications can also lead to pain during sex. Diagnostic tests for physical causes are conducted after a sex therapist pinpoints the timing, location, and duration of the pain.

Therapists estimate, however, that 50 percent of all cases of dyspareunia result from inadequate sexual information about foreplay and arousal techniques, anxieties or guilt about sex that block the physical process of arousal, or problems in the relationship that prevent the mutual giving and receiving of pleasure.

Is it normal to experience intense pain during intercourse when the penis is in deep? This has happened for years now. I have had a history of ovarian cysts. Could this be the problem?

Intense pain during intercourse is never normal even if you've had it for years. During sexual activity, just as in any other activity, pain should be interpreted as a warning sign to be reported to your doctor and diagnosed.

Dyspareunia during deep thrusting is common and can have many causes; pain from ovarian cysts is only one. Have your gynecologist check for all possible problems in the pelvic area, such as pelvic inflammatory disease, endometriosis, and a retroverted uterus. If you're using an IUD (intrauterine device), tell the doctor, because an IUD can sometimes be the source of pain with deep thrusting. Pain at other stages of intercourse, such as during penetration, usually has different causes.

If no physical problem is found, consult a sex therapist. Perhaps your level of arousal is not high enough to lift the cervix and uterus away from the upper end of the vagina before deep thrusting begins. Or, perhaps using a different position will solve the problem. Try those positions in which the woman can control the depth of thrusting, such as the woman-on-top or side-by-side facing each other. But do not delay seeking help. Just worrying about whether the pain will occur is enough to block the natural pattern of sexual responses and increase the likelihood of pain.

Is it possible for a wife's vaginal atrophy to cause her husband's impotence?

Yes. In fact, there are many cases in which one partner's physical changes cause sexual problems in the other partner. This has been documented in a number of studies of aging couples. As the woman's estrogen level decreases, she's more likely to have vaginal dryness, atrophy (shrinking) of the vagina and external genitals, thinning of the vaginal lining, and a tendency to vaginal and urinary infections. These changes often result in painful intercourse, bleeding after intercourse, and vaginismus.

In one study, husbands interpreted these normal biological changes associated with low estrogen as being rejection by their wives. As the women's physical responsiveness diminished, the husbands tried harder and became more intent on sexually arousing their wives. These men eventually became very anxious about the adequacy of their own sexual performance and developed problems with erections.

Some husbands reported that they had pain in the penis or groin area as they attempted to penetrate a severely atrophied or dry partner. These men stopped approaching their wives sexually at all, because they feared hurting the woman or themselves.

In the same study, wives with low estrogen levels reported that they had lost not just their genital responses, but also their sensitivity to touch. Many no longer wanted to be touched at all, and they described all body areas as feeling numb. Their male partners viewed this negative reaction to touching (especially of the breasts and genitals) as a rejection of their sexual advances and, in some cases, ultimately themselves. These men then developed erectile problems.

Therapists who have worked with older couples emphasize the importance of educating both partners about the physical changes that may appear with aging so that these changes are not interpreted as sexual rejection or loss of love.

Studies have also found that one of the most effective treatments is correcting the wife's hormonal balance by hormone-replacement therapy (HRT) and treating any vaginal or urinary infections (see Chapter 9). In these studies, once the woman's physical problems were treated, the effect of standard sex therapy was rapid and both partners regained satisfactory sexual responsiveness, functioning, and pleasure.

My husband and I are in our mid-50s. We've enjoyed sex for all our married life until about two years ago. My husband experiences severe head pain at climax. We've seen a general doctor, a specialist in internal medicine, and a neurologist. No one has found a cause for the headaches. They say they don't know what to do.

Our problem is that now I am apprehensive about sex because I don't like to see him experience the pain and he is apprehensive because, of course, he doesn't want to feel pain. Have you ever heard of this before? What can we do about it?

Although there are no data on how many people have headaches during, or as a result of, sexual activity, they are not usually related to a serious illness. There are several types of headaches associated with sex, and both men and women can be affected.

The most common and least frightening type is associated with the normally increased muscular tension of sexual excitement in the muscles of the neck, face, and jaw. This can create enough tension to cause severe pain or dull, aching headaches. Some people find relief by learning muscle relaxation techniques.

Ask your doctor to refer you to a therapist who is trained to teach muscle relaxation exercises.

A more frightening type of headache is one which occurs suddenly, immediately before or at orgasm. Often people who have this type of headache at orgasm also have had difficulty with migraine headaches when they're not having sex. It is thought that this type of headache is related to the rise in blood pressure at orgasm and can be treated by changing intercourse positions (having the partner with the headache lie down during intercourse rather than being on top, sitting, or standing). Sometimes high blood pressure or migraine headache medications are prescribed to be taken before intercourse begins.

Much more rarely a sudden, severe headache at orgasm can be a sign of a serious problem such as hemorrhage of a blood vessel. Whenever a headache is accompanied by nausea, vomiting, rigidity of the neck, or lack of full consciousness, a medical diagnosis must be sought immediately—even if it means going to a hospital emergency room.

All headaches during sex should be thoroughly investigated by a neurologist or a specialist in headaches. Testing may include a CT scan, checks of blood pressure, or taking samples of spinal fluid. Fortunately, few sex-related headaches indicate serious illness and most can be resolved by relaxation training or medication.

My husband has had painful erections for the past two and a half months. This is the only symptom he has. He says the pain is not unbearable, but it is uncomfortable. He is too embarrassed to see a doctor. Nothing else is noticeably wrong with either one of us, just a pain in his penis when it is erect. What could be wrong? I am very concerned about this.

The pain could be caused by a number of things. It's going to take a visit to a physician who specializes in diagnosing male sexual dysfunctions, and probably some tests, to determine if medical treatment is necessary. A number of infections and skin problems can affect the foreskin, glans (head of the penis) and other surfaces of the penis. Another source of penile pain during erection can be infections of the urethra or prostate. Problems like these won't disappear without medical treatment.

If no infections or obvious physical problems are found, the pain could be an allergic reaction to some chemical (for example, contraceptive foam, lubricants, laundry soap, or any other substance to which the penis is exposed). Or, pain during erection can be one early sign of Peyronie's disease (see Chapter 9). And certain sexual devices, like penile rings or vacuum pumps, can scratch or damage penile tissue. If your husband has used such devices, he needs to mention this to the physician for an accurate diagnosis and effective treatment.

Encourage your husband to consult a specialist. This physician will be more familiar with genital problems and, because he or she has dealt with many men with similar problems, will be better able to relieve your husband's embarrassment about being examined and discussing sexual topics.

My husband had a terrible thing happen to him. While making love, he seemed to have a hard time in getting it in. He pushed until it hurt him. Now it seems that when he gets an erection, a section near the end bends and will not

straighten out. It's quite impossible to make love. This happened a year and a half ago.

What is this? Did a muscle shrink? Can anything be done to correct it? We would appreciate any information you can give us.

It is possible, though not common, for a man to injure his penis during sex. The pain is usually so severe that the man goes immediately to a physician or a hospital. Even if your husband didn't experience that level of pain, a less extensive injury might be involved. He should consult a urologist who specializes in diagnosing male sexual dysfunctions to see why his penis is bent.

Some penile injuries involve the thin membranes that surround each of the three cylinders that run inside, from the base to the tip of the penis (see Chapter 3). These membranes must be unbroken to produce rigidity. A tear in one of the membranes can result in a curved or bent penis during erection. Tears in the membranes can be surgically repaired.

More frequently, a penis that develops a curve during erection is caused by growth of a fibrous area along the shaft of the penis, a condition known as Peyronie's disease. It's possible that an early stage of Peyronie's disease made penetration difficult in the first place, and it is this condition, rather than injury, that has caused the curve (see Chapter 9).

I am 47 and having problems with intercourse. During the early stage of intercourse I have pain in my groin on the left side. This pain causes, or helps cause, my erection to subside. This is frustrating for both me and my wife. My left testicle is tender after intercourse (completed or not).

My doctor could find nothing wrong but stated that I should have a yearly check of my genitals. Could he have missed something? I still have the pain.

You should consider seeing another doctor, such as a urologist who specializes in diagnosing male sexual dysfunctions. It is not unusual for a man to feel a dull ache in the testicles when he has been sexually aroused but doesn't reach orgasm; that kind of pain should gradually go away when the vasocongestion of the genitals subsides. Also, some men find touching or pressure on their genitals painful for a while after orgasm.

You did not mention what happens to the pain when you masturbate to orgasm; if there is no pain with that activity, this will be useful information to give to the urologist. The diagnosis will involve a close examination of your external genitals and internal organs to see whether anything is physically wrong and tests to see if an infection is involved.

Even if a physical cause for the pain is found and corrected, it is not unusual for a couple to have trouble regaining sexual functioning. Anything that interrupts the sequence of physical and psychological progress toward orgasm (even the memory of pain or fear it will occur at a certain point) can result in loss of erection. If this happens to you, ask to speak with a sex therapist.

Physicians who have not been specifically trained in sexual functioning (which is, unfortunately, not a part of standard medical education in the United States) or who are uncomfortable in dealing with sexual matters can indeed "miss" the cause of a sexual problem.

My husband and I have been married a year. Lately I realized we've been having sex about once a month, less often than when we were first married. When I asked him about it (thinking I was no longer attractive to him), he said it's because his testicles feel like they go up inside him when he ejaculates and it's quite painful.

I've never heard of this. Could it be caused by a hernia of some type? His work involves heavy lifting. He's in his 30s.

A number of different problems can cause pain at ejaculation, and diagnosing a cause can be complicated. The most common causes are infections of the prostate or urethra. Hernias can also sometimes be involved, as can the cremaster muscles, which pull the testicles close to the body at orgasm. It is also not unusual for pain to be referred (transferred) from some other location to the testicles, so that it seems the pain is in the testicles, but it actually originates in the prostate or some other nearby body part.

Your husband needs to be examined by a urologist, preferably one with special training in diagnosing and treating sexual problems (see Appendix).

Your letter is a good illustration of why it is important to talk about feelings and beliefs about sex with your partner. Asking your husband was the right thing to do before you came to believe that you were no longer attractive.

I'm having a problem with my girlfriend. It seems that every time my semen gets on her skin, she breaks out in a rash. The rash lasts about an hour or so.

She's become increasingly concerned that my semen is "toxic" and may be doing her internal damage as well. She also thinks this would give us trouble if we decided to get married and have children.

Does she have just cause to fear my semen? Can this be treated to make it more compatible with her? P.S.: She has sensitive skin and gets rashes for other reasons, like wearing wool.

There are a few reports documenting cases of allergic reactions to semen, ranging from vaginal irritation to life-threatening anaphylactic shock. Most of these women were also allergic to many other substances. Experimental treatments consisting of using the semen from the partner to prepare fluid for immunotherapy have been effective; then the couple has regular intercourse to keep the immune response working satisfactorily.

You don't say exactly where the rash appears, but you should know that a skin flush is one of the normal markers of sexual arousal or orgasm. This flush is often described as a rash or red splotches appearing on the neck, chest, or other body areas. It may last for only a few minutes or last until the body returns to its normal, unaroused resting state. (Not all people have this type of flush, and if the rash you describe is confined to areas exposed to semen, such as the thighs or genitals, this flush probably wouldn't apply in your case.)

Try using condoms for several weeks to see if the rash continues to appear; if not, then consult a dermatologist or an allergy specialist and report the outcome of your experiment. Questions about any fertility effects can only be answered after a physician determines whether an allergy exists and what treatments may be helpful.

Illustration No. 20. **Manual Stimulation During Intercourse.** Two positions showing how a man can provide clitoral stimulation to his partner during intercourse.

ORGASM

Females

Both females and males have concerns about female orgasm; many have the *mistaken* idea that the penile thrusting of intercourse is sufficient stimulation to produce orgasm for most women. This is not true. The only reason the issue of female orgasm during intercourse is discussed in this chapter is because so many people worry about it.

In fact, more than half of all women (some researchers say as many as 75 percent) require stimulation of the clitoris to have orgasm. This is done manually by the woman or by her partner, or orally by her partner, either before or after intercourse; or it is done during intercourse, by the woman or her partner touching her clitoris. All of these behaviors are "normal" and do not mean that either the woman or her partner is deficient in any way. Moreover, precisely these techniques are recommended when a couple has therapy to increase the likelihood of orgasm for the female partner (*see Illustration 20*).

If added stimulation does not help, the woman should have a physical evaluation including checks for diabetes, hormone levels, and strength of vaginal muscles. If no physical problem exists, a few brief visits to a qualified sex therapist can help the couple understand how female arousal and orgasm works and learn techniques, positions, and communication patterns that aid female orgasmic response. Single women can achieve similar success by either individual therapy or group counseling sessions.

I am 23 and have a problem concerning nonachievement of orgasm during intercourse. Since childhood I've been able to bring myself to climax by masturbation, but can only climax during intercourse if I touch myself at the same time.

I was also able to teach my husband how to do this for me, but I don't understand why I can't have a natural orgasm. I'm fit and eat only healthy natural foods. Could it be that I'm still sexually immature, have a mental block, or am frigid? We both hope we can naturally achieve mutual orgasm.

What you are currently doing to have orgasms during intercourse *is completely natural*. Sigmund Freud originated the erroneous concept that women can have two types of orgasm, immature (clitoral) and mature (vaginal, through intercourse.) His belief was based on theory alone with no scientific research. But sex researchers now understand that reaching orgasm using clitoral stimulation is as valid, or "mature," as any other kind of orgasm. The whole notion may have stemmed from the mistaken idea that a woman must have a man for complete sexual satisfaction. We now know that physiologically there is no difference between orgasms, regardless of the type of stimulation used to achieve the orgasm.

It is normal, and also "natural," to need clitoral touching to have an orgasm during intercourse. The fact that you've shown your husband how to help you achieve orgasm this way is probably the most important step in making intercourse more satisfying for you.

If by "mutual orgasm" you mean both partners having orgasm at the same time, this is a different issue and also is not common. In fact, most sex therapists discourage couples from setting simultaneous orgasms as a goal. Monitoring each other's progress toward orgasm may disrupt the sensations necessary for reaching your own orgasm. You also miss the enjoyment of experiencing your partner's pleasure at orgasm.

If both partners do happen to achieve orgasm at the same time, and they want to do this, that's fine. If the woman never achieves orgasm by means of penile thrusting alone, that's fine, too. What isn't fine is setting unrealistic goals or performance standards. Even though your sexual functioning sounds healthy and normal, if you or your husband continue to feel that something is missing, consult a sex therapist, who can reassure you about your sex life.

Is it true that some women are nonorgasmic? I've never had an orgasm during intercourse but have had many orgasms by other means. What does that make me—orgasmic or nonorgasmic?

It makes you orgasmic, but like most women, you just don't achieve orgasm by intercourse alone. Approximately 10 percent of all women have never had an orgasm by any means (this is called total anorgasmia). Between 50 and 75 percent of women who have orgasms by other types of stimulation do not have orgasms when the only form of stimulation is penile thrusting during intercourse. So it is "normal" for a woman not to achieve orgasm by intercourse alone.

Clinicians who use counseling and masturbation therapy to treat women for total anorgasmia report that nearly all can be taught to achieve orgasm. The treatment outcome for lack of orgasm during intercourse is that around half are eventually able to reach orgasm by penile thrusting alone.

In this therapy, the couple follows a series of homework assignments that begin with sensate-focus exercises (learning what types of touching give a partner pleasure), proceed to genital touching (learning what types of stimulation produce orgasm), and then intercourse (the man penetrates just when the woman is about to have an orgasm from manual stimulation of the clitoris).

The couple does these exercises in the privacy of their own home. The program usually consists of a weekly meeting with the therapist, during which the couple reports on what happened when they tried the assignment and receive instructions on what to try during the next week. Such treatment programs are considered highly successful at increasing a couple's capacity for feeling sexual pleasure. But many experts stress that simply understanding that manual stimulation during intercourse is really the norm may actually be a more satisfying solution.

One important aspect of the therapy is providing information about what can be realistically expected from the sexual partnership and debunking the expectations of "perfect" sexual performance, which are often based on myths and misinformation. This is especially important when the male partner feels that "no-hands" orgasms are necessary, or that if his partner needs clitoral stimulation he is a poor lover or there's something wrong with the size or shape of his penis.

I do not reach a climax during intercourse, but do when my husband massages my clitoris. I've read that this is normal, and I'm comfortable about it.
  But the problem is that I can only reach a climax if I am laying on my back with my legs tense. If I'm relaxed, I don't climax. Is this common?

Yes, because gradually increased muscular tension is part of the necessary buildup of sexual arousal that is released at orgasm.

But if you feel it is important to broaden your range of sexual activities, experiment with other positions to see if any of them can include tensing the legs; then gradually try positions in which your legs are spread more apart. You might also try increasing muscle tension in your abdomen and pelvic area while reducing it in your legs, but being totally relaxed every place in your body won't work.

If you and your husband are comfortable about and satisfied with your sexual functioning as a couple, there is no need to change what you do.

I read about a doctor who uses laser therapy to help frigid women have climaxes. How effective is this?

I've seen only one article describing this, and that appeared in a popular magazine. According to the story, a physician in Paris applied a laser instrument to the genitals of twenty women who had never had an orgasm. After these treatments, six women reported reaching orgasm during masturbation and seven women reported reduced pain in the genital area and thought they might eventually reach orgasm with masturbation. This reported 65 percent improvement rate is not as high as the rate reported by clinicians for other, more accepted types of treatments for anorgasmia, such as masturbation training.

Until findings on laser therapy are published in a reputable journal (one in which scientists carefully review the methods and measurements used by the author before an article is published), it is impossible to judge its validity as a safe and effective treatment for anorgasmia. Moreover, improper use of lasers could cause scarring or damage, so I would not recommend such a therapy technique until research conducted by other scientists verified its effectiveness and until more is known about any possible long-term side effects—especially since other very effective treatments which carry no health risks are readily available.

I'm a 20-year-old female who had a healthy sex life until about five months ago. Now when I have sex I feel as if I'm going to urinate. (I have a few times already, and this is very embarrassing to me.)

Other than during sex, my urination seems normal. Please tell me how to stop this from happening.

Have an examination by a urologist who has expertise in diagnosing women's problems in sexual functioning. You should be checked to see whether you have a urinary infection. The urethra and the bladder are located where they can receive direct penile pressure or irritation in some intercourse positions. Changing positions and emptying the bladder before sex can sometimes help.

In some cases, the wetness is caused by secretions from a vaginal infection, infected glands near the vaginal opening, or a heavier-than-usual production of vaginal lubrication. In older women, changes in supporting pelvic muscles or pelvic nerves can lead to urine release during sex.

Appropriate treatment depends on what is found by the examination, but for many women therapy involves strengthening of the pubococcygeal muscle (PC) that extends across the floor of the pelvis and runs on both sides of the vaginal opening. As far as anyone can tell, these exercises don't cause harm and they appear to help some, but not all, women. These are generally based on exercises developed in the 1940s by Dr. A. H. Kegel to improve the pelvic muscle tone of incontinent (unable-to-hold-urine) women.

A woman first locates the PC muscle during urination by starting and stopping urine flow while holding her legs wide apart. The muscle that is being contracted and released is the PC. Once a woman finds the PC muscle, she can do these exercises any time and any place. Exercises consist of contracting the PC muscle, holding it for five seconds, and then relaxing it. This exercise is usually done ten times and then repeated several times later in the day for a total of 100 contractions each day. Then a week or so later, a woman can add twenty-five to fifty rapid PC contractions (ten at a time) each day. Like any other exercise, start slowly and stop if the muscle becomes sore. You can check on your progress by inserting a finger into your vagina while you contract the PC muscle.

If the urologist is not able to make a definitive diagnosis or help you achieve satisfactory urinary control, ask to be referred to a sex therapist who can help you regain your previous satisfaction with your sex life.

Males

Orgasm and ejaculation are two separate processes for males, even though they usually happen only a second or so apart.

Problems with ejaculation are the fourth most common question asked by men who write to the institute; but, as you will see, women also ask about male ejaculation—especially once they've heard the term *premature ejaculation.*

Therapists estimate that early ejaculation ("coming" before the man wishes to do so) is the most common sexual problem among younger men. Therapy that teaches a man how to gain control of his ejaculatory process is successful in more than 95 percent of all cases, taking an average of only fourteen visits to a therapist.

Even though many of these successful techniques can be tried at home without a therapist, it's important first to see a physician to rule out prostate and urinary infections, diabetes, and other physical conditions. The older folklore about trying to slow ejaculation by distracting yourself (biting your tongue, doing multiplication tables in your head, or using anesthetic creams) does *not* work, and in fact increases the problem by increasing a man's anxiety or decreasing his enjoyment.

Because therapy is so likely to be successful, don't postpone getting help. Left untreated, early ejaculation can eventually lead to erection problems as a man becomes more and more stressed about his "failure to perform" intercourse the "right" way.

I've always heard about premature ejaculation but never understood it completely. Assuming there's no physical reason for being so speedy, what would cause someone to ejaculate prematurely? Why would someone start doing it that way?

There are a number of ways early ejaculation is thought to begin. In many cases, men have trained themselves to ejaculate quickly. For example, during adolescence many boys masturbate to ejaculation very quickly to avoid being caught or because extended periods of privacy were rare. Moreover, young men who participated in ejaculation contests ("circle jerks") are rewarded by being the first to ejaculate, as this erroneously is seen as being more "manly."

Men who practiced withdrawal as a type of birth control may establish a pattern of sexual activity that leaves them unaccustomed to the feelings of extended contact with the vagina. Then, when they stop practicing withdrawal, they still have a pattern of brief coital contact, ejaculating soon after penetration.

A partner's insistence upon longer duration of intercourse can contribute to anxiety—which only worsens the problem.

It is thought that men who do not have problems with early ejaculation grew up following a different type of pattern. For example, during masturbation they focused on enjoying it as a slower, more sensuous, whole-body experience. As they began to interact with partners they learned to enjoy both giving and receiving pleasurable touching for itself, so that foreplay was not simply something a man "did" to his partner, with his pleasurable sensations coming only from intercourse. These men also seem to prefer a slower rhythm of thrusting, try different intercourse positions, and feel secure in their partner relationships.

As a result, these men learn to recognize the level of arousal that precedes the moment of "ejaculatory inevitability"—the point at which a man cannot stop his ejaculation and orgasm. Whenever they sense they are close to this point, they reduce thrusting, slow down, change positions, or focus on their partner or enjoying pleasurable feelings in other parts of their body. The result is that ejaculation is consciously delayed until they choose to ejaculate.

Even men who usually have good control occasionally ejaculate very quickly, as for example after a long period of abstinence or if they are particularly highly aroused.

Is it true that if a man cannot perform at least 100 strokes during intercourse he is suffering from premature ejaculation? If so, how is this cured?

Before 1970, premature ejaculation was sometimes defined by specific durations of intercourse (for example, less than two minutes) or the number of thrusts before ejaculation. However, beginning with the work of Masters and Johnson, the definitions of early ejaculation have changed to include a focus on the interaction between the sexual partners and whether the male can consciously control his ejaculation until he wishes to ejaculate.

If you and your partner are satisfied with the sexual activities and pleasure you share, you shouldn't be watching a clock or counting strokes. No particular length of time is "too quick" or "too long" unless a couple finds it is a problem for them. Partners who are highly aroused before insertion, for instance, may find one minute of intercourse mutually satisfying while another couple prefers to have more intercourse time.

In any case, counting the number of strokes distracts from feeling the sensations involved in sexual arousal and activity and may itself contribute to problems controlling ejaculation.

A few physical problems can contribute to premature ejaculation, so if therapy isn't successful, a physical examination should be done to rule out spinal cord disorders, neurologic problems, or diseases such as multiple sclerosis.

Therapy for early ejaculation consists of a series of assignments to be done at home. First, a man learns to recognize when his arousal has reached the level just before ejaculatory inevitability. Without thinking about holding back, a man or his partner strokes his penis while he relaxes and enjoys the pleasurable sensations. As he nears ejaculation, he stops stimulation (or signals his partner to stop) for a few seconds— just long enough for the level of arousal to subside slightly, but not long enough to lose his erection. Then stimulation resumes, and this "stop-start" pattern is repeated three times; then stimulation proceeds to ejaculation, which he is told to fully enjoy.

From dry hand stimulation, homework assignments progress to masturbation with Vaseline or in the shower with soap. Once the man has successfully gained control with these more erotic sensations, the couple has intercourse in the woman-on-top position. (If a couple depends on condoms or a diaphragm for contraception, the Vaseline or any other oil-based lubricant must be washed off before the man enters the woman's vagina; these products can weaken latex in less than a minute.) She does the thrusting, starting and stopping at his signal. As he gains recognition and control of his point of ejaculatory inevitability, he is permitted to move and thrust, stopping or slowing if he nears ejaculation.

Throughout all exercises, the man is to focus on enjoying all the separate sensations and pleasures, including orgasm when he finally chooses to ejaculate. These exercises must be done on a regular schedule, two or three times each week, and if at any point a man finds he is getting tense or consciously trying to hold back, the exercise is stopped.

As Kaplan explains in her book *PE: How to Overcome Premature Ejaculation* (listed at the end of this chapter), the idea is to think of arousal as a scale running from 1 to 10. Learn the sensations of being aroused at about the 8 level. The goal is to enjoy the feelings of staying at a level of around 5 to 7 for five minutes or so by adjusting the speed of thrusting.

Other therapists use the squeeze technique designed by Masters and Johnson (*see Illustration 21*). All these therapy methods focus on learning to broaden the sensations experienced during arousal, enjoying them, and reducing the anxiety felt about not having control of ejaculation.

I ejaculate very quickly, in less than a minute. Is it because I'm uncircumcised?

Uncircumcised men who ejaculate sooner than they would like often blame the problem on having a foreskin, while many circumcised men who ejaculate too soon blame it on *not* having a foreskin. Neither assessment is valid, since each man's reactions to stimulation are not solely dependent on the presence or absence of a foreskin. Researchers have not found significant differences in sexual responses between these two groups of men, and therapy works equally well for both circumcised and uncircumcised men.

I have a man who pre-ejaculates constantly and in the past two years there was only one time he was able to keep his erection long enough to make me reach orgasm. I call him Jack Rabbit because all he needs is an embrace or a few kisses and then is unable to even get near my vagina. He ejaculates and I am left love-starved and he is relieved. We have even tried several hours later or in the morning, but the same thing happens.

What causes this? Is there any help for him? One psychiatrist put him on Thioridazine, which didn't work. One told him to get another woman. I think it's me that needs another man, who can perform before ejaculating. After two years I'm ready to climb the walls as I do not want to cheat on him.

Squeeze Technique

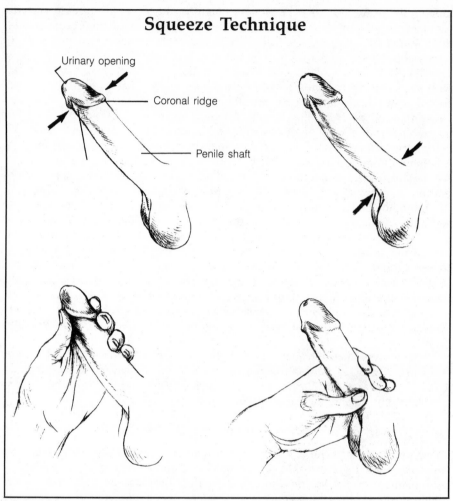

Urinary opening

Coronal ridge

Penile shaft

Illustration No. 21. **Squeeze Technique.** The steps in squeeze technique therapy are similar to those in the "stop-start" method except that the man or his partner briefly squeezes the penis for about four seconds when he feels close to ejaculatory inevitability, which helps delay ejaculation. Then manual stimulation continues. When the couple begins to try intercourse, the partner moves off the penis and uses the squeeze at the head of the penis as was done in earlier manual exercises (bottom left). Once the man has better control, the squeeze technique is done at the base of the penis without having the partner dismount and with the penis still inside (right). The squeeze always is applied on the bottom and top surfaces of the penis, never on the sides.

Since the man does not "give" a woman an orgasm or "make" her have one, a couple has to learn how each partner can contribute to the other's sexual pleasure. Even if your partner could not achieve an erection, there are many ways that he could help you reach orgasm or that you could touch yourself to have an orgasm.

Because more than half of all women do not reach orgasm through penile thrusting alone, you and your partner might investigate techniques that focus on the other ways women use to reach orgasm during lovemaking and men use to increase the time between penetration and orgasm. Each of you needs to accept responsibility for your own orgasms.

It is important to know that most therapists consider early ejaculation a problem of the *couple's* sexual functioning, not just the man's or the woman's problem. I understand your frustration, but I urge you to channel that feeling productively: find a sex therapist. The success rate for treatment is nearly 100 percent.

The drug you mentioned is a tranquilizer; some doctors do prescribe sedatives or depressants for premature ejaculation. However, these drugs are not usually as successful as other treatments; they can also disrupt other aspects of sexual functioning, such as achieving erection. The success rate of nondrug therapies is so high that it's not worth risking potential drug side effects.

My husband and I are having a problem. Before our marriage, my husband masturbated for sexual satisfaction. Now, during intercourse, he easily gets and maintains an erection, but has difficulty in having an orgasm. He says this is because he feels a different sensation than he does with masturbation.

What can be done to increase his sexual fulfillment during intercourse? Currently, we only reach orgasm by touching each other. Is this unusual?

Your husband's problem is fairly common, and can range from an occasional inability to ejaculate during intercourse to the inability to ejaculate at all in the presence of a partner. If it happens occasionally, there's generally no need for concern. But if it becomes the usual pattern, it makes sense to see a sex therapist.

Traditionally this has been called "retarded ejaculation" and was thought to be caused by physical factors (a disease such as diabetes or a drug such as a sedative can reduce the sensations needed for orgasm), psychological factors (an unconscious fear such as worry about hurting the woman or causing a pregnancy, or guilt about sexual pleasure) or a combination of both. Many men report feeling exactly what your husband describes: a difference between the friction available from masturbation and that from vaginal intercourse.

In some cases, the man tries so hard to give his partner pleasure that he loses track of his own sensations, never reaching the high level of arousal necessary to have an orgasm and ejaculate. This can occur even though he is aroused enough to get and maintain an erection, sometimes for very long periods of time.

The first step in traditional treatment programs is to rule out any disease- or drug-related causes, and then use counseling to help the couple gain the level and type of functioning they wish to have. This requires an experienced sex therapist or counselor who works with a physician or medical clinic. In treatment, it's common for the couple to receive specific homework assignments, the results of which are discussed with the therapist at the next meeting. For example, assignments may be aimed at helping the man learn to focus on his own sensations instead of only trying to please his partner (if that is found to be a problem).

As you mentioned, the man's problem may involve his need for a more vigorous direct touch for orgasm (instead of the softer vaginal touch). In this case, assignments may involve having him come very close to orgasm with touching before beginning intercourse and then gradually shortening the time spent touching.

A newer therapy method differs in that it treats males with this problem in the same way as females who don't have orgasms. Rather than having intercourse simply because the man has an erection, the couple instead does exercises that increase the man's level of arousal. Intercourse is not attempted until the *man* feels he is ready to have an orgasm that way and has learned to enjoy the sensations of nondemanding touching and arousal.

Having both partners involved is crucial in some cases and helpful in most others. A woman often needs help to overcome misunderstandings about the reason for the man's problem; many women erroneously believe that they aren't really attractive to their partner, and that this somehow causes the problem.

Delayed orgasm or an inability to achieve orgasm during intercourse doesn't often improve by itself. Don't be hesitant about seeking help.

Further Readings

Barbach, L. G. *For Yourself: The fulfillment of female sexuality.* Garden City, NY: Doubleday & Co., Inc., 1975.
(A program of self-therapy for women who have difficulty with orgasm.)

Heiman, J., LoPiccolo, J., & LoPiccolo, L. *Becoming Orgasmic: A sexual growth program for women.* Englewood Cliffs, NJ: Prentice-Hall, Inc., 1976.
(An easy to read self-help book for women.)

Kaplan, H. S. *PE: How to Overcome Premature Ejaculation.* New York: Brunner/Mazel, Inc., 1989.
(Describes the causes of and the treatments for premature ejaculation. An easy-to-read book.)

Leiblum, S. R., and Rosen, R. C., eds. *Sexual Desire Disorders.* New York: The Guilford Press, 1988.
(A collection of highly technical writings by clinicians and scientists addressing all aspects of sexual desire difficulties. Includes actual case studies to highlight particular problems of desire.)

————. *Principles and Practice of Sex Therapy: Update for the 1990's.* 2nd ed. New York: The Guilford Press, 1989.
(A collection of writings by experts in the field of sex therapy. Addresses the most common sexual problems and the latest treatment approaches.)

Norback, J., and Weitz, P. *Sourcebook of Sex Therapy, Counseling, and Family Planning.* New York: Van Nostrand Reinhold Company, 1983.
(Provides extensive information on issues related to family planning and sex therapy including listings of accredited counselors, clinics, and facilities.)

Pearsall, P. *Super Marital Sex: Loving for life.* New York: Doubleday, 1987.
(Based on a study of 1000 couples, this book addresses sexual satisfaction in committed relationships and provides numerous self-help suggestions.)

Wagner, G. & Green, R. *Impotence: Physiological, psychological, surgical diagnosis and treatment.* NY: Plenum Press, 1981.
(Overview of several different causes of and treatments for erection problems.)

9

Sex and Aging

Just as hormonal events shaped our brains and bodies before birth and set the stage for puberty and reproductive functioning, hormones continue to play an important role in our later years, determining many of the ways we physically change as we age.

As we grow older, men have less significant hormonal changes than do women. As men age, their hormone levels remain relatively steady and their testicles continue to produce sperm as they have since puberty. Most men do have a gradual decline in testosterone production, and some organs such as the prostate and testicles may show a reduced ability to respond to testosterone, resulting in fewer sperm in the ejaculate and less semen. But unless they're affected by serious disease or illness, most men will continue to produce testosterone, sperm, and semen until the end of life.

The changes for women are much more dramatic. The brain, sex hormones, and regularity of ovulation frequently begin to change once a woman reaches her forties, and some women begin these changes as early as their thirties. By the average age of 51 in the United States, a woman has her last menstrual flow—called the menopause.

Chapter 2 explored the major role estrogen plays in the female reproductive cycle. The reduced level of estrogen causes many of the physical changes older women experience. Although estrogen levels may drop gradually over fifteen years or so, for quite a few women the decrease takes place during a relatively brief span of three or four years.

Low levels of sex hormones, particularly estrogen, have many physical and health implications for older women. As one example, the development of osteoporosis (the depletion of calcium stored in the bones) is directly related to the level of estrogen. This explains why women are at greater risk than men for this potentially crippling, and in some cases life-threatening, disease.

Another health problem that increases with age more significantly for women than for men is the risk of coronary artery disease. Although the incidence of heart disease is three times greater for men than for women between ages 45 to

64, by age 65 women have caught up and both sexes are at equal risk for these problems. This is presumably because the levels of female sex hormones have some type of protective effect which diminishes during menopausal changes.

The health of women's genital and urinary systems is also dependent on estrogen. When estrogen drops, the tissues, nerves, muscles, veins, and organs of the pelvic area gradually change, increasing the likelihood of vaginal and urinary infections, as well as hernias of the uterus, bladder, or bowel which protrude into the vagina.

We discuss the effects of aging on sexuality later in this chapter. But whether or not a man or women is sexually active, it is vitally important to monitor changes in hormone levels, of the genitals, and in the reproductive system. One's health, perhaps even one's life, depends on it.

Annual examinations are absolutely required even if a person has never had sex in his or her life. For men, this means a yearly medical check of the genitals and the prostate gland beginning at age 40 supplemented by monthly self-examinations of the genitals and the testicles *(see Chapter 17)*. For women, it means yearly gynecological examinations, Pap tests, and breast exams (supplemented by monthly self-examinations of the breasts and genitals). Every woman also should have annual mammograms (breast X-rays) beginning at age 50 for the rest of her life *(see Chapter 17)*.

As average life expectancy continues to increase, our society will have a greater percentage of people who are age 60 and older. In past decades, many men and women assumed that illness, restricted activity, or death was imminent at retirement. Today they can expect to continue many years of active and fulfilling work and/or play after age 65. Yes, physical changes are associated with getting older. But these can be countered by a sensible diet, exercise, annual checkups, a positive attitude, and for the many women who will live nearly one-third of their lives after menopause, by taking hormones.

Finding adequate supportive health care is not easy for many older men and women; few physicians have had specialized training in gerontology and most physicians do not have the time to keep up with new research findings in this field. If your family physician, gynecologist, or urologist does not appear to be knowledgeable about or sensitive to your questions about aging, there are several organizations that can help you locate an appropriately trained and experienced physician. Write and ask for a list of physicians in your area:

American Geriatrics Society
770 Lexington Avenue
New York, NY 10021

Gerontological Society
Clinical Medicine Section
1411 K Street, N.W., Suite 300
Washington, DC 20005

National Institute on Aging (NIH)
Office of Information
Bethesda, MD 20205

WOMEN, HORMONES, AGING, AND HEALTH

There is no doubt that for many women taking estrogen reduces the incidence of hot flashes and night sweats, prevents negative changes in the genitals and urinary tract, preserves existing bone structure (reducing the risk of bone fractures due to osteoporosis), and lowers the risk of coronary artery disease. Taking estrogen may also provide protection against other cardiovascular diseases.

Taking Estrogen

How does a woman decide whether or not to take estrogen? First, not all women experience hot flashes or night sweats, deterioration of the genitals or urinary tract; and not all women are at high risk for osteoporosis or coronary artery disease. A thorough physical examination around the age of 45, including measurement of bone density and blood cholesterol levels, can help you assess your individual risk factors for osteoporosis and coronary artery disease. The decision should be made by each woman in consultation with her physician.

Osteoporosis: The Risk Factors

You're at higher risk for developing osteoporosis if you:
• Have a mother or sister with severe osteoporosis
• Are white or oriental
• Are small-boned
• Are thin
• Smoke cigarettes
• Drink alcohol regularly
• Do little weight-bearing exercise and lead a sedentary lifestyle
• Consumed less than 1000 mg of calcium per day in your younger years
• Use cortisone drugs on a long-term basis
• Had an endocrine disease that resulted in low estrogen levels earlier in life

---

If tests such as an ultrasound (of the kneecap) or DPA (dual photon absorptiometry) establish that your bones are thick and dense, a good exercise program (such as walking or biking), in combination with a diet or mineral supplements that includes at least 1500 mg of calcium a day (equivalent to five eight-ounce glasses of skim milk) may provide adequate protection against osteoporosis without taking estrogen.

If the blood tests also show your blood cholesterol level to be in the low risk range, and that the HDL level (the "healthy" type of cholesterol) is high as compared to LDL (the "unhealthy" type), you may be able to maintain your low risk of cardiovascular disease without taking estrogen. One important way to lower risk is by following a diet that carefully limits high-cholesterol foods, especially those with fats high in LDL, and by participating in an exercise program that enhances cardiovascular fitness.

If a woman also has no difficulties with hot flashes or night sweats, her annual pelvic exam continues to show that her genitals and vaginal lining are healthy, and she does not have recurring vaginal or urinary-tract infections, she may not need to take estrogen.

That still leaves millions of women who are indeed negatively affected by low estrogen. Twenty to 25 percent of women are at high risk of developing osteoporosis (200,000 postmenopausal women suffer hip fractures in the United States every year, and by age 60, 25 percent have spinal compression fractures). Fifty percent are at risk for cardiovascular disease; 75 percent experience hot flashes and night sweats (which can be debilitating for at least one out of four postmenopausal women); and unknown millions of older women suffer with vaginal, urinary, and other pelvic problems.

Long-term studies of estrogen use show a 50 percent reduction in the overall death rate for women (including those from osteoporosis and cardiovascular problems), reduction or complete elimination of hot flashes and night sweats, and preservation of the healthy condition of the genital area. The data available at this point demonstrate that the benefits of taking estrogen outweigh the risks for many women.

There are, however, some women who should not take estrogen or should take it only under close medical supervision. These include women who have breast cancer or uterine cancer, liver or gall bladder disease, high blood pressure, a history of deep vein thrombosis (blood clots), and those who smoke cigarettes or who have had a stroke.

Women who have menopausal symptoms and who can consider using estrogen must then decide what type of estrogen to take. Estrogen's beneficial effects on health must be balanced against its potentially negative side effects, which at this point revolve mainly around whether it increases a woman's risk of developing breast cancer. It appears from the research available that the type of conjugated estrogens which are usually prescribed in the United States (one brand name is Premarin) have a lower risk of being associated with breast cancer than other types of estrogen. Women who do not have a uterus (it is estimated that 30 to 40 percent of U.S. adult women have had a hysterectomy) need concern themselves only with making a decision about estrogen.

Taking Both Estrogen and Progestin (HRT)

In the 1960s and 1970s researchers found that women who had been taking estrogen to treat menopausal symptoms had a four to seven times greater risk of developing endometrial cancer (cancer of the lining of the uterus). Researchers theorized that this was due to the fact that the uterine lining remained built up (the "proliferative" stage), without the monthly shedding characteristic of the menstrual flow (the "secretory" phase). *(See Illustration 4 in Chapter 2.)*

That in mind, researchers suggested taking a progestin with the estrogen to mimic the hormone patterns of the reproductive cycle of a woman's younger years to lower the risk of endometrial cancer. This addition of a progestin, and taking estrogen and progestin in a monthly pattern (twenty-five days of estrogen coupled with seven to ten days of progestin taken with the final days of estrogen, and no hormones at all for the last five to six days of each month) is called cyclic hormone replacement therapy (HRT).

In use only since the early 1980s, this type of cyclic HRT does indeed appear to reduce the risk of developing endometrial cancer—dropping it to the same level as women who do not take estrogen. Obviously, any long-term effects of this new way of taking hormones cannot be fully assessed for many years.

Therefore, women who still have their uterus must decide whether to also take a progestin in the HRT cyclic pattern. Even though taking progestin with estrogen is clearly protective of the uterus, researchers are already looking at the possible risks of using progestin in two specific areas: breast cancer and cardiovascular disease (because of the possibility that progestin alters blood cholesterol levels). So far the results are contradictory, with some studies reporting decreased risks and others reporting increased risks. These studies are difficult to compare in terms of the types of estrogen and progestin prescribed, their dosages, and their duration of use. Therefore, each woman will need medical testing to determine whether her risks for cardiovascular disease are high (two examples of high risk are high cholesterol levels and having a family history of early heart attack). If she's at high risk, she might consider avoiding use of progestin until more research is available on cyclic HRT or other ways of taking progestin.

For 1987 (the last year for which data are available) there were an estimated 300,000 new cases of endometrial cancer in the U.S., but because it is usually diagnosed early, the prognosis for survival is good (92 percent) and could be improved if all women had annual pelvic exams and Pap tests.

In looking for safer ways to take estrogen and progestin, recent studies have reported that changing from the cyclic HRT pattern to an even newer pattern of taking both estrogen and progestin every day (instead of in the monthly cyclic pattern usually now prescribed) may provide protection for the uterus and may also keep blood cholesterol levels low. This type of steady HRT pattern also appears to eliminate the monthly menstrual flow produced by the cyclic HRT pattern—something many women object to.

All women taking HRT in any form must have annual (and in some cases more frequent) gynecological exams, Pap tests, cholesterol tests, and mammograms. If a woman has a uterus and her bleeding patterns change, she should also have an endometrial biopsy to determine the health of her uterine lining. Take only the smallest dosages of estrogen and progestin necessary to control menopausal symptoms. And keep up-to-date on HRT research by asking your physician "What's new?" at every visit. Ask if recommendations on dosage, types of hormones, and the number of days to take them each month have changed in any way and if you are following the safest pattern.

I'm 45 and I'm having a very hard time with my menstruations. Heavy bleeding and heat waves that keep me awake at night. Swelling and bad temper follow. Needless to say, I face one hellish week a month. My gynecologist prescribed Provera, to be taken for 10 days beginning on the 15th day of my cycle. He refuses to admit that I'm entering menopause because my periods are still very regular. I'd like to know what's going on with my body.

Abnormal uterine bleeding can be difficult to diagnose. But when abnormal bleeding is combined with hot flashes, it is important to consider menopause as a possible cause—regardless of your age and the regularity of your flow. Ask your doctor for a full hormonal evaluation. If he doesn't do these blood tests, ask to be referred to a gynecological endocrinologist who has a special interest in menopausal women.

Once uterine tumors and other major problems have been ruled out, the goal of treatment for abnormal bleeding is to stabilize hormone levels, particularly estrogen. Since you are already taking Provera (a progestin), ask the specialist about adding an estrogen drug and taking both in a monthly pattern that mimics the body's natural reproductive cycle.

I have a question I am too ashamed to ask my family doctor. I am a woman, 54 years old, and haven't had a menstrual period for three and a half years. I want to know if I can assume that I can no longer get pregnant.

It sounds as if you've passed menopause, the last menstrual flow. The average age for a woman in the United States to reach menopause is 51. But there can also be other reasons to explain why you've stopped menstruating, so you must see a physician *now*—preferably a gynecologist. You need to have a pelvic exam and Pap test.

As for the possibility of becoming pregnant, the general rule is that a woman should consider herself able to become pregnant until one full year after her last menstrual period. Since you're almost four years beyond your last menstruation, it's highly unlikely that your ovaries continue to release eggs. Without an egg available for the sperm to fertilize, you can't get pregnant.

If you want to be certain, have your physician check the hormone levels in your blood and urine. If the levels of estrogen and FSH (a brain hormone) are high, it's another sign that the ovaries are not producing hormones or eggs.

Don't be too embarrassed to discuss these issues with a physician. He or she has certainly heard the same question from many women your age.

I'd like to know when a woman is through with menopause. I'm 60 and had my last period at age 56. I've asked my doctor this question and his answer is always "When you stop thinking about it."

Technically speaking, you've already completed your menopause. Menopause means, literally, the last menstrual flow. Since it's more than one year since you've had any menstrual bleeding, you are now considered postmenopausal.

These labels, however, aren't nearly as important as how the hormonal changes affect you as an individual.

Although some women report few or no physical symptoms as the hormonal levels change, the majority of women experience measurable physical effects as the level of estrogen production drops. These commonly include hot flashes, decreased vaginal lubrication, thinning of the vaginal walls, and changes in the entire genital area, including the urinary tract.

Regardless of what your physician has told you, these menopausal symptoms are not in your head and you can't stop them by mentally tuning them out.

Consider consulting a physician who specializes in endocrinology or aging to discuss whether HRT is appropriate in your case.

I want to know how long a woman has to keep going for those gynecology exams and Pap smears. My doctor wants me to be checked every six months instead of once a year. I thought that after five children and all these years I could just skip it. I'm now 70, and so many women I know don't go anymore.

Then the payoff: This doctor was so rough I was all black and blue the next morning! I told him about it on the next trip and he said he wanted to be thorough! (I noticed he was gentler.)

I feel that after five children and one miscarriage, I've had enough of these exams. If these friends don't go, I thought maybe I could skip it too. What do you think?

You would be taking an unnecessary and foolish risk to stop having regular pelvic and breast exams and Pap tests. The incidence of cancer of the cervix, the endometrium, and the breast increases significantly as a woman gets older. Go for regular examinations and encourage your friends to do the same. These cancers, detected at an early stage, can now almost always be successfully treated.

Although annual breast and pelvic examinations as well as Pap tests and mammograms are generally recommended, some physicians suggest more frequent exams if a woman is known to be at higher risk for certain diseases. For example, women who've had many pregnancies may be at greater risk for cervical cancer, which may be why your doctor has put you on a six-month schedule. Ask him for the reason at your next visit.

Good for you for complaining about rough treatment! All women should insist on having the gentlest examination possible. You should not be left bruised or black and blue from a routine exam! *(For more information on making these exams more comfortable see Chapter 17).*

I'm over 50 and I wonder if there is any way of ensuring that a Pap test is not a painful experience. I know that medical books say it's painless but I (and a surprising number of my friends) find it painful, dread having it done and some of us postpone it. My doctor always acts irritated when I complain and says "Can't you relax?" But how can I when it hurts?

And is it true that using a lubricant on the instrument can spoil the test results?

A pelvic examination, including a Pap test, should *not* be painful and having them regularly can literally save your life.

Menopause can cause changes in the genitals and the vagina that can increase discomfort. Postmenopausal women also have a higher risk of vaginal infections and irritation of the vaginal lining, which can also be a source of pain during an exam. Ask if your discomfort is due to vaginal atrophy. If it is, ask whether you should be using HRT to improve the health of your vaginal area. A physician sensitive to the health problems of older patients should have already raised these issues.

There are a number of ways to reduce the discomfort, but the list doesn't include using a lubricant on the speculum, since it can indeed distort or invalidate test results. But you can ask that the speculum be heated in warm water; the water will help lubricate the speculum and the warmth will make it more comfortable. The actual Pap test shouldn't be painful once the speculum has been inserted and opened.

It's unfortunate that your doctor expresses irritation when you tell him how you feel. His irritation may, in fact, make it even more difficult for you to feel comfortable and relaxed. But he is correct when he advises you to relax, since the more relaxed the vaginal and abdominal muscles are, the more comfortable the exam. The problem for many women is that, once they've had a painful examination, they *involuntarily* tense up. The solution is to experience a comfortable examination so that future ones aren't a source of anxiety.

Frankly, some doctors are more "painless" than others, and it's up to each woman to find the one who gives the most gentle as well as thorough pelvic examinations.

Is it normal for a healthy woman's pubic hair to thin as she reaches middle age? If not, would a hysterectomy cause that to happen? My wife is 53 and still has her ovaries.

Yes, some women do report thinning of pubic hair, as well as head hair, as they approach menopause. Even though your wife doesn't have a uterus, she will still technically go through menopause because her ovaries will continue to follow their natural pattern, eventually ceasing production of estrogen and progestin.

It is likely that her thinning pubic hair is related to this natural process of aging rather than to having had her uterus removed by hysterectomy.

I'm 76 years old. Since 1952 or 1953 I've had hot flashes. Because my boys were in the service I thought it was my nerves. It started from my toes to my head like a flash and then from a hot sweat I got a chill and since then it never stopped.

Twenty years ago I had a complete hysterectomy, so I thought the flashes would stop but they didn't. The doctor told me I was one out of a million to still have them. I'm always in a hot sweat or a chill and my husband and I argue constantly about the heat and air conditioning. What's happening to me? Is there a cure?

A hot flash is a set of involuntary reflexes triggered by the brain. Though researchers are still trying to determine what causes hot flashes, we do know that they're related to fluctuations in the levels of hormones and other substances circulating in the blood.

Here's what happens in a hot flash, which typically lasts three and a half minutes: Skin temperature suddenly rises one to four degrees Fahrenheit. Blood vessels near the surface of the skin open so blood can move to the skin to radiate the heat outward. This causes perspiration, which then evaporates and causes the chilly feeling. Heartbeat and blood pressure fluctuate. The levels of blood chemicals and other body substances surge and fall.

Researchers estimate that 85 percent of women will experience hot flashes as they reach the time they have their last menstrual period or immediately after having their ovaries surgically removed. What's more, between 25 percent and 50 percent of the women who have hot flashes will continue to have them for many years. A few women even have hot flashes during their reproductive years, around the time of menstrual flow; two-thirds of women begin to have hot flashes as their first menopausal symptom, long before they have their last menstrual flow; and other women don't begin having hot flashes until many years after menopause is over. Your doctor was mistaken when he said you were "one in a million."

I suggest you get a second medical opinion, preferably from a gynecologist who also has training in endocrinology or gerontology. The most effective treatment for hot flashes is taking estrogen. You should start with the lowest dosage. If after three or four months you still have the hot flashes, ask about increasing the dosage or changing brands. Keep experimenting with your physician's monitoring until the hot flashes disappear or are reduced.

Several studies show that nearly 100 percent of women receiving estrogen in appropriate individualized doses report reduction of hot flashes and approximately 80 percent report complete relief.

Nonhormonal treatments for easing hot flashes include reducing stress, wearing cotton bras, using cotton sheets, and avoiding alcohol and hot drinks such as tea and coffee. Fanning and taking lukewarm showers may help. Try wearing several layers of lightweight cotton clothing so that items can be removed or added as your body temperature changes.

I would like to know how you get a yeast infection and what you do to keep it from coming back. I am 70 and have had no sex for 20 years since my husband passed away. I had three children with no infections of any kind. I do not understand how this happened to me.

You don't have to have sex to develop a vaginal infection. The vaginal infection commonly called yeast is also called candidiasis or moniliasis. This infection occurs when an organism (Candida albicans) which can be normally present inside the vagina multiplies much more quickly than usual.

Taking antibiotics is one common cause of this type of vaginal infection; this reaction to antibiotics can occur at any age (even in young girls), whether a woman is having sex or not.

Among older women, yeast infections can also be encouraged by lowered levels of estrogen following menopause. Genital tissues gradually become thinner and more easily infected. If that's true in your case, preventing future vaginal infections may involve taking estrogen or HRT to help make your genital tissues less vulnerable.

No older woman should feel embarrassed about seeking help for these problems, nor should she worry that having a vaginal infection will be misunderstood to mean that she is having sex.

I have a very personal problem of the vagina. I'm 69 years old, a widow for six years. I have this terrible vaginal odor, which I try to cure by douching and cleanliness. Now this summer, I got this terrible vaginal itching and irritation. I bathe each day and wash after every toilet trip. What is the problem?

It could be a number of things. But only a doctor can distinguish among them and prescribe a treatment, so make an appointment with your gynecologist.

Vaginal discharge that has a bad odor is usually associated with bacterial vaginosis caused primarily by Gardnerella vaginalis and other bacteria, or more rarely by infections of Trichomonas vaginalis (a protozoan). Vaginal infections are also associated with diabetes in some women. The gynecologist must check for all possible infectious organisms in order to prescribe the correct treatment.

A healthy vagina needs no douching. Douching can, in fact, create an environment more vulnerable to infection and it also makes accurate diagnosis difficult. For these reasons it's important to stop douching until you see a doctor; then follow his or her recommendations about whether to douche or not. Thorough, gentle daily washing of the external folds of the genitals is usually sufficient to prevent odors unless an infection is present.

I'm a woman approaching 40. Last year I had an attack of kidney stones and I've been trying to stay away from high-calcium foods such as milk, cheese, and yogurt to prevent more stones.

But I've read about osteoporosis, the weakening of bones, and now I'm worried that my low calcium intake will cause this condition.

This is a complicated question and you're right to be concerned about your diet. Osteoporosis (literally "bones with holes") accounts for more than one million bone fractures each year. These fractures are mostly of the hip, back vertebrae, and the wrist and occur primarily in older women.

Contrary to popular misconception, bones are living parts of your body, continuously losing old tissue, and adding new tissue. When there's not enough calcium in the diet, this mineral is withdrawn from the bones to keep the calcium level in the blood constant. This prolonged withdrawal of calcium leaves bones looking like Swiss cheese or honeycombs, brittle and easily broken.

Drinking alcoholic beverages, smoking cigarettes, consuming too much salt, eating a diet too high in proteins and too low in vitamin D are all factors thought to increase bone loss. The natural decrease in estrogen a woman experiences with aging as she nears menopause also contributes to bone loss.

The National Institutes of Health (NIH) recommend two key dietary approaches for preventing and treating osteoporosis: increasing the amount of calcium in the food you eat or using calcium supplements. But the institutes warn that people with a history of kidney stones should not take calcium supplements except on the advice of a physician.

Fortunately, there are other measures you can take to halt or reverse bone loss. Regular exercise, especially weight-bearing exercises such as walking (as opposed to swimming), appears to actually increase bone mass even in elderly patients. And for women who have a low level of estrogen, taking replacement estrogen also appears to dramatically reduce the rate of bone loss.

New techniques for measuring bone mass are becoming more widely available. Together with blood tests to measure estrogen, a physician can use these techniques to help you design a diet and exercise program to keep your bones as healthy as possible as you approach menopause.

I'm 76 and I still have my uterus. Eighteen months ago, with very little provocation, I received a fracture to my back. X-rays showed severe osteoporosis. A reliable orthopedist who is a professor at one of the largest schools of medicine prescribed estrogen. After taking this for nine months, I went to an endocrinologist (who is also a professor in another equally reliable medical school). He told me to stop taking the medicine because hormone-replacement therapy is not helpful for osteoporosis 10 years beyond menopause. Which doctor is right?

As you have discovered, experts sometimes disagree about taking estrogen to prevent or to treat osteoporosis. That's because research studies report differing results. It's not possible for every physician to keep up with all the research findings in every field. That's why finding a doctor who specializes in treating your particular problem is necessary to get the most up-to-date diagnosis and treatment.

Nevertheless, it *is* clear that estrogen guards against the bone loss of osteoporosis and that, for many women, taking calcium without having an adequate estrogen level is not enough to protect the bones (women with a uterus should consider HRT).

Perhaps the endocrinologist was reacting to data showing that bone loss begins as soon as estrogen levels drop and is fastest in the two or three years just after menopause. But research also shows that taking estrogen even many years after menopause, and even *after* a fracture has occurred, can prevent further bone loss.

The last physician you saw may have overlooked the fact that people are living longer and expect to remain active for more years. Preserving the bone mass of an otherwise healthy 76-year-old woman would not have seemed as important a generation ago as it is today.

Because there is a disagreement about your care, see if you can find a gerontologist (see p. 212) to review your records and help you decide what to do. If you begin taking estrogen again, maintain the treatment consistently, since stopping and starting is not good for your bones.

I am 76 years old now and when I was 41 I had a complete hysterectomy. My doctor, who operated on me, never believed in giving me any hormones. Is it too late now to take hormones? What happens to a woman's body when her ovaries are removed and those hormones aren't replaced?

The effects of oophorectomy (surgical removal of the ovaries) vary greatly and are similar to those of natural menopause but are much more abrupt. Find a physician who specializes in treating postmenopausal women. Have a complete examination, including a pelvic exam and a measurement of your bone mass or strength.

If these tests reveal conditions that could be treated by taking estrogen, then it's certainly not too late. Not all women develop these problems, however, so there would be no reason to begin taking hormones unless the examination of your genitals and bone mass and blood tests show they are necessary.

I'm a 55-year-old woman who started going through menopause several years ago. At first I was taking only Premarin. Now my doctor has added Provera. With the Premarin alone, my menstrual periods had stopped completely. But since also taking Provera, I'm on a regular, normal menstrual cycle.

I still have mixed emotions about taking these hormones and I certainly dislike the idea of having regular periods for the rest of my life. But I am primarily concerned as to whether or not I might become pregnant, since I'm menstruating again. Must I also use some type of birth control for the rest of my days? When I ask my doctor he just waggles his hand and says "Don't worry about it."

It is very unlikely that you'll become pregnant, since pregnancy can only occur when an egg has been released from the ovaries (ovulation). If you're several years past menopause, it's doubtful that you're continuing to ovulate, and HRT does not induce ovulation in postmenopausal women. Your physician could do a blood test for FSH hormone level to double-check if this truly bothers you.

As for menstrual flow, that can happen with cyclic HRT whether or not you're releasing an egg. Menstruation (the shedding of the endometrium, the lining of the uterus) is a result of fluctuations in the level of certain hormones, primarily estrogen and progesterone. (Premarin is an estrogen, Provera a synthetic progesterone or progestin.) Taking these drugs on a cyclic basis mimics the levels you produced naturally earlier in life, so the uterus responds by first thickening its lining under the influence of the estrogen and then shedding the lining under the influence of the progestin (see Illustration 4 in Chapter 2).

I know you're not pleased with the idea of having periods forever, but please understand why your doctor added the progestin to your regimen: Taking estrogen alone has been linked by researchers to a slightly increased risk of endometrial cancer. With the addition of progestin you're menstruating again, and it is this process of regularly shedding your endometrium that is thought to reduce the risk of endometrial cancer.

Do low doses of estrogen for three weeks, accompanied by progestin the last week, then no hormones at all for a week always cause a menstrual period?

Isn't there a way to take these hormones but avoid having periods? I understand how important it is to my health to take them, but is there a way to get the benefits without the bother?

Researchers are now looking at a type of HRT that uses these hormones on a steady, rather than cyclic, basis. This steady pattern does not appear to result in menstrual flow. But until there is more information, using HRT in the cyclic pattern you describe is thought to be the safest method of providing these hormones after menopause or surgical removal of the ovaries for women who still have a uterus.

Ask your physician to follow the progress of research on the steady type of HRT and let you know when there is enough data to use this safely.

I am taking HRT to control menopausal problems and reduce the risk of osteoporosis. However, when my doctor explained it he stressed that I might begin to have menstrual bleeding again on the days I take no hormones.

This has not happened. Is there something wrong with me if I menstruate on other days?

Probably not, but report this to your physician. Researchers are still trying to determine which bleeding patterns signal problems and which can be considered "normal" for women on cyclic HRT.

Every woman on HRT should keep accurate monthly records of the days each hormone is taken and the days bleeding or spotting occur. The record should also note days of any other possible hormonal side effects, such as breast tenderness. Take these records to your regular gynecological exam.

Until a woman and her physician determine the best dosage and timing for that woman's health, regular checkups and a review of her cycle records are important. If you are concerned about your bleeding pattern, especially if it changes from one month to the next or if you have bleeding or spotting in the first weeks of each cycle, tell your physician immediately and ask about having an endometrial biopsy (to check the condition of the lining of the uterus) or adjusting your hormone dosages.

I'm taking hormone pills to help me get through menopause. They work OK, but I've heard about a new skin patch that may work even better. Is the skin patch the same as the pills? Which one is best?

Women who take estrogen pills might want to talk with a physician about the relatively new estrogen skin patches, called the estradiol transdermal system or Estraderm.

Estrogen pills and estrogen patches appear to be equally effective in reducing *some* of the physical problems associated with menopause or surgical removal of the ovaries (including hot flashes, disrupted sleep, vaginal atrophy, and painful urination), but the effectiveness of the patches with regard to osteoporosis has not yet been established.

The pills and the skin patches are thought to be equally safe, especially when used in a cyclic pattern. For women who still have a uterus, this means HRT, which also includes taking a progestin pill for several days each month and using no hormones at all for the last several days each month.

The primary difference between estrogen pills and estrogen skin patches is the way the estrogen enters the bloodstream. Pills are processed in the liver before entering the bloodstream; with the skin patch, the estrogen flows directly through the skin into the bloodstream. This bypassing of the liver is thought to avoid negative side effects for at least some women.

The skin patches, which look like small round Band-Aids, are applied to the abdominal skin and changed twice a week. They cost about twice as much as estrogen pills.

To date, the most common negative side effect of the estrogen skin patches reported has been that about 17 percent of women experience redness and irritation of the skin where the patch is applied.

The patches are available in two different dosages. As with the estrogen pills, it may take several months before a woman and her physician decide which dosage is most effective in eliminating her menopausal symptoms.

Is it possible to be allergic to the drugs used for HRT? I get sick to my stomach each month when I start taking the Provera.

Yes, it is possible that you are reacting to the Provera, a brand name for medroxyprogesterone acetate, one type of progestin drug. Whether it's an allergy or just a sensitive stomach is a question for your physician.

Although Provera is the most widely prescribed progestin used for HRT, ask your physician if you can try a different type of progestin. Several forms and dosages of progestin are available, such as Norethindrone (Norlutin is one brand name), norethindrone acetate (Norlutate and Aygestin), and norgestrel (Ovrette). All four are also used in some formulas of birth control pills. The first three types may have more androgenic (male-like) side effects for some women, such as growth of facial hair. They also may be more likely to maintain or increase sex drive.

You and your physician may have to experiment with several types to determine which progestin and at what dosage is best for you.

MEN, HORMONES, AGING, AND HEALTH

One of the most significant health problems associated with aging for men is enlargement of the prostate gland. This benign enlargement is discussed along with prostate infections and cancer of the prostate in Chapter 17.

Do men go through menopause? If so, what are the signs? I'm divorced now, but looking back on it all it seems to me that the trouble with my marriage started with financial problems and then one thing led to another. The affairs, his not wanting to get old, not wanting to be a grandfather, etc., etc.

It is too late for me, but maybe there are other women who would like to know more about male menopause (fact or fiction). Was it male menopause or was my husband just tired of our marriage and wanted out?

As far as we know now, men don't experience anything comparable to the female menopause or climacteric. Men have no specific alteration or change in their physical condition similar to the significant physical and hormonal changes in women around and after menopause (the final menstrual flow).

Some men do experience a gradual decline in hormone levels beginning in their twenties, and by age 50 most men have a lower level of testosterone, but the change is gradual and relatively small in comparison to women. Women experience a more abrupt change in hormone levels around the time menstruation stops in their forties or fifties.

As for a middle-aged man's extramarital affairs and his aversion to aging, clinicians generally attribute the cause to psychological factors in the man, not hormones. Regardless of age, financial or economic difficulties are cited as the leading cause of marital discord and divorce.

Is testosterone-replacement therapy something a man should consider as he grows older?

Not as a matter of course. Testosterone, a hormone produced in higher amounts by men than by women, has been shown to decline with age for some men. But current medical thinking is that unless a man's testosterone level is tested and found to be exceptionally low, there's no benefit in adding more and there may be negative mental and physical health-related side effects.

Research on men who took testosterone reported that there was some increase in the amount of sexual thoughts and fantasies, but there was no increase in erectile ability.

If you suspect a hormonal imbalance, ask your physician or an endocrinologist for a complete physical examination, including a screening for levels of testosterone and prolactin (a pituitary hormone). If you do need to take testosterone, make sure you follow the recommended schedule for prostate examinations. Changes in the prostate can be one side effect of taking testosterone.

Do men get hairier as they age?

As millions of men with male-pattern baldness will tell you, men don't necessarily get hairier as they age. If you're asking whether men develop more facial hair, head hair, pubic hair, or other body hair as they grow older, the answer is generally no. This hair becomes less dense with aging.

During adulthood, density of hair varies greatly from one man to the next and includes variation not only in head hair but also in beard growth and growth of hairs in the eyebrows, ears, and nostrils.

The amount and pattern of body hair is primarily determined by heredity, although hormonal factors may be involved in some cases. Aging generally decreases the density of hair and is accompanied by loss of pigment from the hair itself, which is why both men and women also have more white hair as they get older.

My husband is 66. Within the last six months, he has developed a severe bend at the end of his penis, making sex painful for both of us. He's worried but won't see a doctor because he's too embarrassed and insists he's too old anyway. Is there surgery to correct this? And how common is it?

A person is never too old to seek help with gaining sexual satisfaction. Your husband must see a physician, preferably a urologist, for an accurate diagnosis. If he has Peyronie's disease, surgery to remove the fibrous plaque has been successful in severe cases, but often other treatments are tried first.

Peyronie's disease usually has three symptoms: a curve that appears in adulthood in the erect penis, possible pain with erection, and a mass or a hardened area on a section of the penis. This tough area or band is made up of fibrous tissues which build up in the penis. Intercourse can become difficult, painful, or impossible, depending on the extent of the curve.

Many treatments have been proposed over the years, including taking POTABA, vitamin E, cortisone injections into the plaque, radiation treatments to dissolve the plaque, and surgery. But none of these treatments has proved successful in a high percentage of cases and some, such as radiation, are no longer recommended.

Another approach is simply to wait and see what happens. In some cases—the actual percentage isn't clear—Peyronie's disease disappears without any treatment. That potential for spontaneous recovery makes it difficult for researchers to determine whether a man has gotten better because of a specific treatment or if he would have improved anyway, without any treatment at all.

Experts on Peyronie's disease often advise first trying the lowest-risk treatment, such as taking POTABA for several months. If improvement does not occur and if having intercourse is difficult or painful, then surgery is usually recommended.

There are several different surgical techniques to remove the fibrous area, but so far none are reported to yield uniformly good results with all patients. About 20 percent have some problem after surgery, including lack of erection, loss of sensitivity at the tip of the penis, and shortening of the penis. There also may be variations in surgical success rates, depending on the expertise and experience of the surgeon and the size and location of the fibrous area. Sex counseling both before and after surgery is recommended for the man and his partner.

To date, the surgery with the most reliable success rate is implantation of a penile prosthesis. This surgery includes removal of the fibrous area to ensure that erections will be straight enough for intercourse. In one review of 93 men who had penile implants to correct Peyronie's disease, only two reported poor results.

We don't know how many men have Peyronie's disease because many older men react as your husband does and don't seek treatment. Although we think this disease usually begins in men between the ages of 40 to 60, it has been known to occur in men as young as 18.

Regardless of age, any man who notices a sudden change in his sexual anatomy or functioning should go to a urologist and overcome any embarrassment long enough to clearly describe his symptoms. Take along a Polaroid picture of your erect penis or draw a picture and hand it to the doctor if that makes it easier. Older people have the right to healthy sexuality and a satisfying sex life. They may need to insist that physicians take this right seriously—otherwise they should find a physician who respects this desire.

I've read some things about Peyronie's disease lately. I'm 59 and my penis does seem to curve a bit but I think it's been that way all my life. How do I know if I have Peyronie's?

It is not unusual for a man to have a slight curvature of the erect penis, and, if it has been that way throughout his life, it is probably not Peyronie's disease. Curves resulting from Peyronie's disease usually appear relatively suddenly and are an obvious change from the way a man's penis has been for years.

I'm a 60-year-old man who's been diagnosed as having Peyronie's disease. What causes Peyronie's? And can a woman give it to a man?

Science doesn't yet have many answers about Peyronie's disease. We know that the curve in the erect penis is caused when a plaque of fibrous tissue builds up in one area of the penis, but researchers still don't know what causes the fibrous areas to begin to appear.

Until recently, Peyronie's disease was thought to be related only to aging and to be rare. Now it appears that other factors may be involved in some cases, and many more men are affected. For example, Peyronie's is now listed as a possible but rare side effect for certain classes of drugs such as beta blockers (prescribed for high blood pressure and heart disease). One researcher has found a surprisingly high incidence of Peyronie's in a group of adolescent boys with sickle-cell anemia, a genetic blood disease.

To date, no one has reported that Peyronie's disease can be transmitted by sexual or any other type of contact, so it is not thought possible to catch it from a woman or from someone else with Peyronie's.

SEXUALITY AND AGING

The very title of this section may seem a contradiction in terms to some readers, particularly younger ones. Sexuality and aging? In the same way children—even adult children—have trouble imagining their parents having sex, some people are flabbergasted by the idea of older people being sexually active. If one believes that sex is only for procreation, instead of being one pleasurable aspect of life, then it is also easy to think that people beyond their reproductive years are (or should be) finished with sexuality.

Tragically, older people who express sexual interests are sometimes labeled perverted; men are dubbed "dirty old men," while women may be perceived as senile. In a culture imbued with Norman Rockwell images of grandmothers baking cookies and grandfathers whittling on the front porch, many find it difficult to imagine older people having sex just like everyone else.

But most do.

A person does, however, experience specific changes in sexual response as he or she ages. When, or even *if*, these changes occur varies widely—there is no age at which men or women in general are "over the hill" sexually. And many changes may be due more to medications, chronic illness, or the psychological expectation that older people should not have sex, than they are to the aging process itself.

Compared to the sexual responses of early adulthood as described in Chapter 6, older women may notice the following changes during the arousal phase: less muscle tension, less vaginal lubrication, reduced elasticity of the vaginal walls, and little increase in breast size. The intensity of muscle spasms at orgasm may also decrease.

Changes in male arousal may include: needing more time and more direct stimulation of the penis for getting an erection and reaching orgasm, erections that may be less firm, and testicles that may not elevate as high up in the scrotum during arousal. At ejaculation, there may be less semen, and orgasmic muscle spasms may be less intense. It is also common for men to feel less of a need to ejaculate during each sex act, and the refractory period (the time between one ejaculation and the next time a man can ejaculate again) may increase.

People who don't realize that these changes are normal, and that they don't have to decrease sexual pleasure, often panic at the first sign of change, despair that their sex lives are over, stop having sex altogether, or cease being physically affectionate with their partners.

Those who understand that these changes are normal may welcome them, viewing this new stage in their lives as a chance to be more leisurely in their sexual encounters and less pressured by performance standards and the urgency for release. In fact, some couples enjoy these changes and use them to improve their sex lives. For example, men who had problems with premature ejaculation in their youth may find that the decreased urgency to ejaculate permits them to have intercourse for longer periods of time. And couples where the man now needs direct stimulation of the penis to get erections can use this as a reason to try new stimulation techniques which may bring increased enjoyment for both partners.

Many couples who are not able to have intercourse continue to express affection and physical intimacy in ways other than intercourse, such as mutual touching or oral-genital activities. Healthy and satisfying sexuality can include many different ways of physically expressing love and caring; sex is more than just intercourse.

Older people who have trouble with specific aspects of sexual functioning

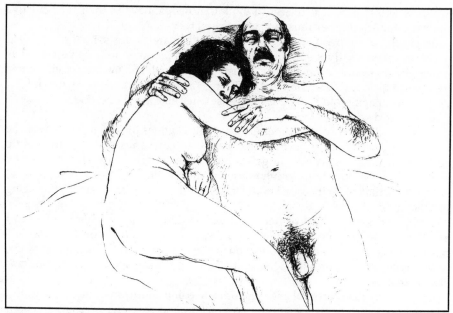

Illustration No. 22. **Sharing Physical Closeness is Important at Any Age.**

should seek evaluation and treatment, just as younger people should *(see Appendix)*. The same treatments and therapies can be just as successful and are especially rewarding when the solution can be as simple as replacing lost hormones or receiving information from a therapist about different techniques for increasing stimulation.

Some sexual patterns established early in life may continue as we age. Those who had lower frequencies of sexual activity in their youth may continue to have sex less frequently, while those who were more active are likely to continue being so in later years.

Individual Sexual Behaviors

I am a 74-year-old widow and have this problem of touching myself, especially my breasts and nipples. I do this until I have an orgasm. I'm too ashamed to speak of this to anyone. Is there any way to stop doing this?

Sexual feelings are usually seen as a sign that a person is in good mental and physical health, and are not considered to be a problem unless these feelings are distressing. Regardless of age, many single people satisfy their sexual needs through self-touching or masturbation.

During the 1940s, Kinsey found that approximately 50 percent of widowed, separated, or divorced women in their fifties masturbated to orgasm an average of about once every three weeks; and among women of all ages, more than 11 percent touched their breasts during masturbation. Some women are able to reach orgasm by stimulating only their nipples and breasts. This is perfectly normal too.

In a more recent study of Americans age 50 and older, 33 percent of women age 70 and older reported masturbation. Among men age 70 and older, 43 percent reported they masturbated.

Masturbation can actually have health benefits for older women. Research on postmenopausal women has shown that those who experience orgasm regularly (through intercourse, masturbation, oral stimulation, or other means) have less vaginal atrophy and fewer genital problems than do women who have no sexual activity.

After reading about an older lady who masturbated I got the courage to write for help. I'm too embarrassed to talk to my doctor about this.

I'm in my late 70s and have been masturbating since my husband died nine years ago. Just lately, my body feels sore and there's a pressure there that feels as though I must urinate. After two days without masturbating, I feel fine. Am I hurting my body?

It's very unlikely that masturbation is harming you. In fact, having regular sexual activity (whether with a partner or by self-touching) has been shown to be physically beneficial for older women.

Because aging can cause changes in a woman's urinary tract as well as in her genitals, you should have your gynecologist conduct tests to see if you have a urinary or vaginal infection. You need only say that you feel urgency to urinate and need to be tested; there's no need to tell anything about masturbating if you feel uncomfortable about discussing it.

Low estrogen can cause older women to be more susceptible to such infections. Taking estrogen or cyclic HRT is not just for women with partners, so ask about trying hormones if your level of estrogen is low or if a pelvic exam shows that your genitals are atrophied or the tissues thinned and more susceptible to infection.

I am a widower, 76 years old. My wife died three months ago after 50 years of marriage, a normal sexual life, and six children.

I never had any sexual contacts other than with my wife all these years, and don't want this now, but I get sexual thoughts. I have sought appeasement in masturbation (about once every 10 to 14 days).

Is this the best way to satisfy my sexual feelings, or do I have to take other measures for this problem?

First of all, don't think that having sexual feelings is a problem. Experiencing sexual desire and being able to achieve erection and orgasm are signs of your physical and mental well-being.

The physical effects of stimulation, orgasm, and ejaculation are basically the same as far as your body is concerned—whether they result from masturbation or from sexual activity with someone else.

You are the best judge as to whether masturbation also satisfies any psychological needs you may have, such as for intimacy with another person. Many people find masturbation physically and psychologically satisfying, while others find adequate pleasure only when a partner is involved.

I'm in my 60s and in pretty good health. The frequency and quality of my erections have decreased in recent years but my real concern involves another matter. I was wondering why I no longer have nocturnal emissions (wet dreams). I still have erections during my sleep, but have not had a wet dream for many years.

Is this part of the aging process or am I unusual? At what age do wet dreams usually cease?

The incidence of nocturnal emissions (ejaculation during sleep) does seem to decrease with age. But the frequency of this type of orgasm, like all other types of sexual outlets, varies tremendously from one man to the next. It is, therefore, impossible to say whether nocturnal emissions stop at any particular age. In fact, Kinsey's data on more than 5000 men found that about 20 percent had never had a nocturnal emission at any age.

Involuntary erections during the REM (Rapid Eye Movement) stage of sleep also appear to decline with age. In one study of males age 3 to 79, the average total erection time each night declined from a high of more than three hours at age 20 to about an hour and a half at age 50, then stayed at about this level until age 80. No men older than 80 were studied.

Studies of healthy men older than 70 have shown that these sleep erections continue throughout life, although as a man ages they may become less firm.

Several of us older gentlemen in the neighborhood have been receiving mail-order literature about pills which cure impotence. Is there such a thing?

No pill or liquid sold by mail will produce erections; and in fact, such advertising has finally been prohibited.

Erection problems can only be successfully treated by first having a medical diagnosis of the cause and then following the treatment which is recommended according to each man's individual situation (see Chapter 8).

I grew up when sex was not a subject to think about, much less talk about. I have passed middle age, been married to the same man for 40 years, and am still in the dark when it comes to sex.

I'm concerned because sometimes when I sleep I am awakened by a very deep and satisfying orgasm. What causes this? They are more real and wonderful than anything I ever experience with my husband. They don't happen often, and I do nothing to bring them on. I must say I enjoy this unasked-for pleasure.

In my waking hours, sex never enters my mind, but I am unable to control these sleep orgasms. Is it normal to be this way?

Yes. It is estimated that about 40 percent of women have had orgasms during sleep, and they seem to become more common as a woman gets older.

These orgasms in women are similar to men's nocturnal emissions (wet dreams), which also are not under voluntary or conscious control. Researchers do not yet know why some people have orgasms during sleep while others do not, but either situation appears to be quite normal.

Sex With Partners

I am 60 and in good health. My wife has been very sick for over a year, with no hope of getting well. I would not think of going out with another woman. This means I have not had any sex of any kind now for the past year. I talked this over with my doctor and really got no answer.

I don't want to seem dumb, but is there some way to ejaculate without intercourse with a woman? For weeks now my penis has not gotten stiff. I worry that the longer I go without sex, I may not be able to have sex later on in life.

Who do I talk to?

You don't seem dumb, and your distress is understandable. Theoretically, a man doesn't jeopardize his health by refraining from ejaculation. But many clinicians report that some older men do have difficulty regaining sexual functioning if they have gone a long period of time without any sexual activity.

There are ways to ejaculate without having intercourse. These include wet dreams during sleep and masturbation. In one recent survey of Americans age 50 and older, 52 percent of the married men questioned reported that they masturbated, as did 36 percent of the married women. Some of their situations were much like your own, involving sick or disabled spouses. Many couples for whom intercourse was impossible reported mutual satisfaction from holding each other or being close during masturbation.

This survey also showed that couples with good sexual communication experiment to find ways in which the healthy partner can achieve orgasm while both partners feel the comfort and pleasure of being physically close and expressing affection. If you are comfortable talking about sex with your wife, it's time to discuss this. You may discover that she is missing physical closeness as much as you are. If you are not comfortable discussing sex with her, find a reputable sex therapist or counselor if you wish to talk with someone about this (see Appendix).

If you continue to lack erections, especially during sleep or upon first awakening, you may want to have a medical checkup to determine if there is a physical explanation. For example, erectile difficulties can be one of the earliest symptoms of diabetes; most men regain erectile capacity when the diabetes is diagnosed and treated and can maintain sexual functioning for many years.

My wife and I are in our late 70s. I have just realized that for the last 12 years, our sex life was more like a rape than pleasure for my wife. Before, it was excellent.

My wife becomes aroused only after stimulation of an area deep in her vagina. This requires deep penetration before her excitement lubricates the vaginal walls.

We have tried lubricating jelly, but this does not lubricate deep enough. She also says that she has had few orgasms in the last 12 years, and that makes me sad. What can be done?

The information in your letter sounds like the symptoms of vaginal atrophy, which is often associated with the reduced hormone levels that accompany menopause. Treatment with appropriate hormones may help. So your wife should make an appointment with a gynecologist who can assess her hormone levels.

Until she's seen a physician, you can try putting lubricating jelly or saliva on your penis; or use an applicator to insert the jelly deep into your wife's vagina or try vaginal lubricating suppositories. These nonprescription, water-based suppositories, called Lubrin inserts, are placed into the vagina several minutes before penetration begins. They melt with body heat and provide lubrication that is similar to natural lubrication. Lubrin can be found in many drugstores in the feminine hygiene section.

I applaud you and your wife for talking openly about sex. Your ability to communicate will make it easier for you both to experiment with any new techniques a physician or sex therapist may recommend to heighten your wife's capacity for arousal.

My wife and I are in our 50s and having a problem. My wife used to be slick down there but has gotten so dry that it hurt both of us. A doctor gave her estrogen to put inside, which helped only a little. He told her not to use too much, because it could cause problems in the long run. She also is losing all the hair down there. Surely that means something is wrong. She has not had a period for about 14 years, is a heavy smoker, takes no drugs, and has hot flashes. How can our problem be solved?

It sounds as though your wife has three common symptoms of low estrogen: hot flashes, lack of vaginal lubrication, and changes in the vagina. Thinning pubic hair also is not unusual for women or men as they age.

Although some women find that use of an estrogen cream applied to the vagina relieves the genital discomfort and dryness, many others do much better with estrogen pills or HRT. However, women who smoke are often advised to stop smoking before using replacement hormones.

You could try using a water-based lubricant (not the estrogen cream) during intercourse. There have been reports that male partners of women who use vaginal creams with estrogen have developed gynecomastia (breast enlargement). These creams should not be used as a lubricant during intercourse; instead they should be used at some other time of day when you do not expect to have intercourse soon. This will avoid exposing the penis to estrogen which can be absorbed through penile skin.

Your wife really needs a second opinion about her condition, preferably from a physician who is familiar with prescribing and monitoring HRT. If her friends can't recommend someone, contact the groups listed on page 212.

I'm a 60-year-old female with a problem even my gynecologist couldn't solve. My vagina secretes so much mucus that it causes problems with intercourse. I thought that when you got older the vagina was supposed to get dry; the opposite has happened in my case. What can I do to stop the excess?

The amount of vaginal lubrication varies greatly from one woman to another. Not all women have reduced lubrication after menopause, especially if their estrogen level remains high. But there are some physical problems your gynecologist should check for. Various types of infectious organisms can grow out of control in the vagina or infect the cervix (the area of the uterus at the inside end of the vagina), causing high amounts of mucus. It may take many different tests to find out exactly which organism is involved.

If it is absolutely clear that there is no infection and blood tests show adequate estrogen, ask whether occasional douching or wearing a tampon for an hour or so before intercourse might help in your case.

I haven't wanted to talk to my doctor about this so I decided to write to you. For the past six to eight months, I just don't have any sexual desire at all. I just don't have any feelings, even during foreplay. An orgasm is nearly impossible.

I'm 54, in good health, have taken estrogen for several years, and now take Provera as well. My husband is beginning to wonder about me. I am in good health otherwise.

It is not unusual for sexual responsiveness to gradually slow down as a person gets older, even for women taking HRT. Each step in the process of arousal may take longer and require more stimulation.

Women who once were aroused by the mere thought of sex, for instance, now may need much more kissing, body caressing, and touching of the clitoris or genital area before they feel fully aroused and ready for intercourse.

But when loss of sexual desire occurs suddenly (over just a few months) at any age, a medical and psychological evaluation is necessary. Because this can be an early sign of physical illness or psychological distress, try to locate a specialist in assessing sex dysfunctions in women *(see Appendix)*. Be sure to tell the physician about all the medications you take, including the names and dosages prescribed for the hormones. The specialist may suggest adding a little androgen (a hormone produced in higher amounts by men and thought to be important for sexual desire in both sexes).

If no medical or psychological conditions requiring treatment are found, that specialist can recommend a sex counselor or therapist. Getting information about trying various sexual techniques to increase arousal has helped many older couples regain sexual interest and functioning.

I am a 65-year-old male, in good health, and have an active sex life. When I was 25 I had mumps, which affected my right testicle. It reduced the testicle to about one-third the size of the other one. This seemed to cause me no trouble as I fathered two children.

I still have sex about twice a week. My penis gets hard, but I have very little semen when I climax. This reduces the pleasure for me, and I suspect it reduces pleasure for my partner. We haven't discussed it, but our sex life—and life in general—is suffering as a result. Is there anything I can do to improve this situation?

Your reduced semen probably has more to do with aging than with having had mumps at 25, especially since you fathered two children. Most men find that they ejaculate less semen as they get older and many men also need more time and more direct stimulation of the penis for full arousal, an erection, and orgasm.

Have a medical evaluation *(see Appendix)* to see whether the lowered semen volume is simply part of the aging process or whether there is a medical problem such as prostate enlargement or an infection. If no physical problems are diagnosed, speak with a sex therapist. If you're spending too much time thinking about ejaculation, you can miss feeling the overall pleasurable sensations of the total sexual experience—that will certainly diminish sexual satisfaction.

If you can't talk to your wife about your concerns and her possible reaction, you both should go to a sex therapist to correct any erroneous assumptions either of you may have. For example, most women do not feel a man ejaculate inside of them but can feel the spasms of his penis at his orgasm.

However, your wife may sense your anxiety about sex and wrongly assume that you're no longer attracted to her. As women age, some are especially vulnerable to anxiety about their changing appearance and often fear that they are no longer sexually attractive. This may be a more likely explanation if she seems less interested in having sex, but only a therapist can help you sort out what is going on and suggest how to regain satisfaction for both of you.

I've read about REM erections and I'm trying to relate that information back to myself. I'm 70 years old and have these erections in the morning about four mornings a week. But I can only get a semi-erection at bedtime, which is the time I prefer. What can I do about my bedtime performance?

If you notice erections in the morning, it is likely that your erectile capacity is still intact, which would rule out most of the major physical causes of complete erectile failure, such as a disease.

Do you take any medication or drink alcohol? It's possible that erection difficulties only at certain times of the day are due to the time a drug is taken. Or it may be that you're simply tired at the end of the day. If that's the case, many clinicians recommend taking a midday nap so you feel more energetic in the evening. Also, consider changing the time of sexual activity to the time of day when you feel best or when you have the least difficulty getting erections; in your case, perhaps that means sex in the morning.

A different explanation may be that you expect erections to be as automatic as they were in your youth. But many older men can have erections only after they or their partner strokes and/or stimulates the penis in other ways. You might also try having intercourse in positions other than man-on-top; sometimes it's more difficult to maintain erections in this position. One suggestion is lying side by side with you behind your partner *(see Illustration 33 in Chapter 18)*.

If these suggestions don't help, consult a qualified sex therapist. *(See Appendix.)*

Further Readings

Brecher, E. M. *Love, Sex and Aging: A Consumers Union report.* Boston, MA: Little, Brown and Company, 1984.
    (An easy-to-read report on 4,426 women and men aged 50-93 who responded to a questionnaire on love and sex.)
Burnett, R. G. *Menopause: All your questions answered.* Chicago, IL: Contemporary Books, Inc., 1987.

(A book about menopause written in a popular style using a question-and-answer format.)

Butler, R. N., and Lewis, M. I. *Love and Sex After 60*. Rev. ed. New York: Harper & Row, Publishers, 1988.

(Addresses some of the most common problems faced by people age 60 or older in a popular style.)

Cutler, W. B.; Garcia, C-R.; and Edwards, D. A. *Menopause: A guide for women and the men who love them*. New York: W.W. Norton and Company, 1983.

(A comprehensive book on menopause based on a large scientific study but written in an easy-to-read style.)

Doress, P. B., et al. *Ourselves, Growing Older: Women aging with knowledge and power*. New York: Simon and Schuster, 1987.

(An informative book written by women which examines the health concerns of middle-aged and older women.)

Schover, L. R. *Prime Time: Sexual health for men over fifty*. New York: Holt, Rinehart and Winston, 1984.

(A helpful book which provides common-sense information about men's sexual health.)

10

Sexuality Before Birth

Even before you began reading this book, you already had some important notions about sexuality. Among the most basic of these ideas is that human beings are divided into males and females from the beginning of life to the end, that males always have a penis and scrotum and females always have a clitoris and labia. But sexuality is far more complicated than that. There are so many levels of basic maleness and femaleness that scientists have found it necessary to formulate a set of categories to describe human sex, gender, and reproductive capacity fully and accurately. These are the stages by which sexuality develops from conception to adulthood. Each stage provides the foundation for the next in male or female development.

- **Chromosomal sex** (Do a person's cells have the XX-female or XY-male chromosome pattern?)
- **Gonadal sex** (Does the person have testicles or ovaries?)
- **Hormonal sex** (Does the person have more of the so-called male or androgenic hormones, or more estrogens and progestins, the so-called female hormones?)
- **Sex of internal organs** (Does the person have a prostate gland, for example, or is there a uterus?)
- **Sex of external organs** (Is there a penis or a clitoris, a scrotum or labia?)
- **Brain sex** (Does the brain have male or female structures and levels of chemicals?)
- **Sex assigned at birth** (What was said when the doctor looked at the newborn: "It's a boy" or "It's a girl"?)
- **Gender identity/role** (Does the person think "I'm a girl" or "I'm a boy," and what does the person say or do to make others think "That's a girl" or "That's a boy"?)
- **Sexual orientation identity** (Is the person attracted to and does he or she fall in love with same-sex or opposite-sex partners?)

Keeping these nine different stages in mind, I want to begin with a brief description of the ways we acquire or develop these basic elements of our sex, gender, and reproductive capacity, and then discuss how they affect our lives.

Sexual and psychosexual development is one of the areas on which my research efforts have concentrated over the past 20 years.

CHROMOSOMAL SEX

At the moment of conception, when a sperm enters an egg, one aspect of a person's sexual development—chromosomal sex—is immediately fixed. Each cell of our bodies contains 46 chromosomes (a chromosome is a threadlike structure in the nucleus, or center, of each cell on which our millions of genes are located). Two of these chromosomes are called the sex chromosomes.

The egg from the mother always carries an X sex chromosome. Each sperm from the father can carry either an X or Y sex chromosome; a typical ejaculate probably carries equal numbers of both kinds of sperm. Because the mother always contributes an X, it is the father's sperm that determines the sex of the offspring. When the sperm and egg join, the result is a single cell (called a zygote) containing 46 chromosomes, two of which are either an XX (female chromosome pattern) or an XY (male chromosome pattern). The effects of having an XY (male) pattern or the XX (female) pattern will not become important for another five or six weeks, when the message "Make a male" (which is on the Y chromosome) begins to affect development of the embryo. By the way, the other 44 chromosomes carry various other genetic messages, such as "Make blue eyes" or "Make curly hair."

GONADAL SEX

The two embryonic gonads (which will become either ovaries or testicles) are important because they will produce either female or male hormones and either eggs or sperm at puberty.

The single-celled zygote divides into more cells and grows as it moves toward the uterus (see Illustration 28 in Chapter 15). By the fourth week after fertilization the collection of cells is called an embryo, and by the sixth week of development the areas that will become gonads appear.

Except for the sex chromosomes within the cells, for almost the first month and a half of development there are no obvious differences between males and females. If the cells carry a Y chromosome, the process of turning the gonads into testicles begins around the sixth week, and by the eighth week the gonads have begun to produce the so-called male hormone testosterone.

If the cells do not carry a Y chromosome, the same gonads continue growth and eventually develop into ovaries. Between this point and the birth of the newborn seven months later, the gonads continue to develop and gradually move away from their original location high in the abdomen. If they are ovaries, they move down into the lower abdomen or pelvic area. If the gonads become testicles they move completely down out of the abdomen and into the scrotum.

HORMONAL SEX

The types and amounts of hormones in our bodies play crucial roles at various points in our lives. Before birth all embryos are exposed to estrogens (the so-called female hormones) through the mother's blood. When the embryo

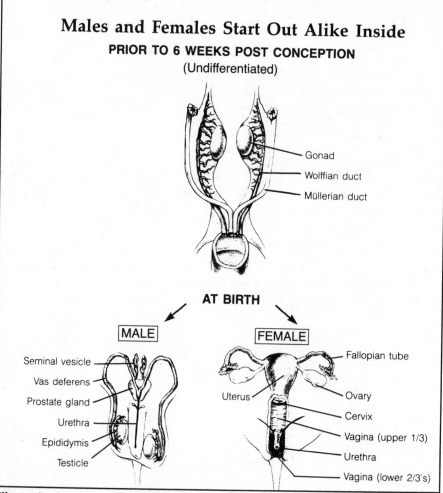

Males and Females Start Out Alike Inside

PRIOR TO 6 WEEKS POST CONCEPTION
(Undifferentiated)

Gonad
Wolffian duct
Müllerian duct

AT BIRTH

MALE

Seminal vesicle
Vas deferens
Prostate gland
Urethra
Epididymis
Testicle

FEMALE

Fallopian tube
Uterus
Ovary
Cervix
Vagina (upper 1/3)
Urethra
Vagina (lower 2/3's)

Illustration No. 23. **Males and Females Start Out Alike Inside.** The top drawing has been greatly enlarged to show details of the existing structure; in reality, six weeks after fertilization the entire embryo measures little more than half an inch. The bottom drawings show the fully developed male and female internal organs.

has an XX (female) sex chromosome pattern, these estrogens may stimulate development of female internal and external sex organs. It has been said that nature's basic pattern is to make females; in other words, if nothing is added to the embryonic environment, all embryos would develop internal and external female genitalia.

However, for those embryos with an XY (male) chromosome pattern, something *is* added: the so-called male hormones, particularly testosterone. Production of these hormones begins about eight weeks after conception and (among many other changes) turns potential labia into a scrotum and the potential clitoris into the head of a penis.

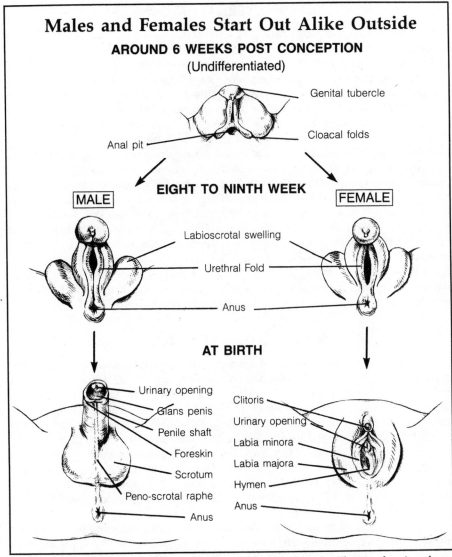

Males and Females Start Out Alike Outside

AROUND 6 WEEKS POST CONCEPTION
(Undifferentiated)

Genital tubercle

Anal pit

Cloacal folds

EIGHT TO NINTH WEEK

MALE

FEMALE

Labioscrotal swelling

Urethral Fold

Anus

AT BIRTH

Urinary opening

Glans penis

Penile shaft

Foreskin

Scrotum

Peno-scrotal raphe

Anus

Clitoris

Urinary opening

Labia minora

Labia majora

Hymen

Anus

Illustration No. 24. **Males and Females Start Out Alike Outside.** The top drawing shows in detail that male and female embryos look alike six weeks after fertilization. The center drawings, show that few differences are noticeable even at nine weeks of development, when the entire embryo measures less than two inches. The bottom drawings show the fully developed male and female genitals at birth.

At puberty, male and female hormonal patterns influence whether a person will develop breasts or a facial beard, for example. Hormones also regulate whether a person with testicles will continuously produce sperm, or a person with ovaries will release eggs on a regular cyclic basis and have menstrual flows. Adult hormones also affect sexual desire and sexual functioning.

SEX OF INTERNAL ORGANS

All embryos begin with two sets of internal sex and reproductive duct systems, called the Mullerian ducts and the Wolffian ducts (*see Illustration 23*), which may develop into either female (from the Mullerian) or male (from the Wolffian) internal organs. If the embryo has XX (female) chromosomes and is exposed only to the mother's hormones, the Mullerian duct system develops into two Fallopian tubes, the uterus, the cervix, and the upper (inner) one-third of the vagina. Because the embryo has no "male" hormonal stimulation, the Wolffian system does not develop and shrinks to almost nothing.

Embryos with XY (male) chromosomes follow a different developmental path. Around the eighth week after conception, the gonads, now testicles, begin to produce a special substance that blocks development of the Mullerian (female) duct system and it shrinks to almost nothing. A second hormone called testosterone (a "male" hormone) is also produced and it stimulates the Wolffian duct system to develop into a set of tubes leading from each of the two testicles to the base of what will become the penis. These tubes or ducts include the epididymis, seminal vesicles, and vas deferens. The same "male" hormones stimulate development of a prostate gland that becomes part of the genital duct system. By the fourteenth week after conception, there finally are clear differences between the structures of male and female internal sex organs.

SEX OF EXTERNAL ORGANS

As shown in Illustration 24, all embryos begin exactly alike, with identical structures on the outside. These include a genital tubercle and the cloacal folds that will form urinary and anal openings and either female or male genitals. Changes in the external appearance of male and female embryos begin about eight weeks after conception. In XX (female) embryos, by birth the genital structures have developed into a clitoris, the outer and inner lips (labia majora and labia minora) of the vulva surrounding the vaginal opening, the outer two-thirds of the vagina (which grows to meet the other one-third developing from the internal duct structure), and the anus. The opening of the vagina remains sealed by a thin layer of tissue called the hymen, which usually begins to disappear shortly after birth.

Under the influence of "male" hormones from the testicles in XY (male) embryos, the tissues that would have become the inner lips of the vulva begin to fuse together and form the underside of the penile shaft. The tissues that become a clitoris in a female form the glans penis (the tip or head of the penis) and the top two-thirds of the penile shaft, and the tissues of what would have become labia majora (the outer lips) grow together and become a scrotum. The fusing together of these tissues produces a ridge of skin on the bottom of the penis shaft and the scrotum; this is called the raphe. These male genitals take several months to develop. During this time the urethra (the tube through which males urinate and ejaculate) must also form and lengthen so that it is contained inside of the penis and opens at the tip of the penis. Shortly before birth, the testicles move down from the abdomen into the scrotum.

BRAIN SEX

Although scientists have much to learn about the differences between male and female brains, there is clear evidence that some differences in structure do exist and that these differences appear to be produced by hormones, just as they produce the external genitals. What is not clear is what specific roles these brain differences play in either sexual behavior or reproduction.

As one example, it is thought that the hormonal environment of the embryo and fetus affects the development of the hypothalamus (a part of the brain which plays a role in hormone production later in life). In animals, at puberty those who were exposed to male hormones before birth establish a fairly even pattern of sex hormone production (characteristic of males), while those who were not exposed to male hormones show a cyclic fluctuating pattern of sex hormone production resulting in reproductive cycles (characteristic of females). It is not yet clear how important the prenatal hormone environment is to the establishment of these patterns in humans.

SEX ASSIGNED AT BIRTH

During the nine months prior to birth, an extremely complex and fragile biological process involving chromosomes, hormones, tissue structures, and growth has occurred. As you can well imagine, many steps in this process (called sexual differentiation) are subject to difficulties. One possible result is that a baby's external genitals may not "match" its internal sex organs. Or, all the aspects of sex may in fact appear to "match" at birth but at puberty an apparently normal boy develops breasts and his penis does not grow. *(These types of problems are discussed in Chapter 14.)*

It is actually quite miraculous that for the vast majority of pregnancies this complicated, interlocking series of biological events culminates in the birth of a perfectly formed (inside and out, top to bottom) healthy baby boy or baby girl. It is at this point that psychological and social factors, culture, upbringing, and other environmental influences begin to play the major role in a person's sexual development.

Based usually on only a quick look at the baby's genitals, the doctor announces "It's a girl!" or "It's a boy!" This seemingly simple statement will have a profound effect on a person's life. Identifying our children by sex seems to be an ongoing mission for most parents, whether through color-coding clothing, hairstyles, toys, or room motifs.

Identifying a child by sex is not merely a mission for its parents; everyone else needs the information too. When a baby is born, in fact, most people ask about its sex even before they ask whether or not the child is healthy. The answer to that question—boy or girl?—then helps determine how we respond to a baby: the way we handle it, the way we play with it, the way we talk to it. Many people who might toss a baby boy into the air, for instance, would refrain from doing so with a baby girl.

Misidentifying a child is considered a major social blunder. We've all had the experience of meeting a baby who is not easily identifiable. If we decide to guess the baby's sex, mistakenly calling a baby boy "pretty" or a baby girl "handsome," we risk offending the parents who have, in the spirit of equality, dressed their infant in green or yellow.

The behavior of the sexes, especially during infancy, is much more similar than it is different. Infant boys don't exhibit some kind of special masculine behavior that invites a toss into the air, and baby girls don't behave in a special feminine way that would encourage adults to coo at them or cuddle them more gently. A Kinsey Institute study of 5000 full-term male and female babies does show some small differences between the sexes, but they are very subtle and are not likely to be noticed by most observers.

GENDER IDENTITY/ROLE

An individual's gender *identity* ("I am a boy" or "I am a girl") becomes established between 18 months and three years of age. However, this doesn't mean that children fully understand what it means to be female or male, and it is not unusual for a boy to say he wants to be a "mommy" when he grows up, particularly in a society that doesn't explain that females have uteruses and males don't.

A person's enactment of gender *role* includes everything he or she says or does which suggests to others that he or she is a male or a female. This includes the outward expression of what society expects as maleness or femaleness of clothing, hair styles, interests, careers, and so forth. I do not believe that little girls or boys should be restricted or encouraged in a particular direction *simply* on the basis of their sex. Girls should know that they can grow up to be doctors or firefighters, and boys should know that they can be dancers or nurses.

But in terms of gender identity, I strongly believe that children should know from the very beginning that there are differences between the sexes and that these differences are important. If you ask a child to explain why a particular person is a boy, you're likely to hear "Because he has short hair." It's a common response but also a confusing one. Children should know that there are some real, unalterable differences between the sexes that clearly distinguish males from females, unlike hair length, make-up, or clothing style, which are a matter of choice.

For example, they should know that females have a vulva and vagina and will have breasts, and that males have a penis and scrotum. Each should take pride in her or his own genitalia. They should know that boys grow up to be men who ejaculate and impregnate and that girls grow up to be women who menstruate, gestate, and lactate. We want our children—both boys and girls—to know that when they grow up they will have the ability to reproduce and must act responsibly when they become sexually active.

The aspects of how and when a person develops his or her **SEXUAL ORIENTATION IDENTITY** (whether he or she is attracted to and falls in love with opposite-sex or same-sex partners) are discussed in Chapter 7.

Genetic make-up, hormones, brain development, anatomy, social and family influences—all these factors comprise the elements that mold each person into an adult woman or man; we then carry these influences with us into our relationships with others, particularly sexual relationships.

Further Readings

England, M. A. *Color Atlas of Life Before Birth: Normal fetal development*. Chicago: Year Book Medical Publishers Inc., 1983.
(Photographs of fetal development before birth.)

Money, J., and Ehrhardt, A. A. *Man & Woman, Boy & Girl: Differentiation and dimorphism of gender identity*. Baltimore, MD: The Johns Hopkins University Press, 1972.
(Among many topics includes detailed discussion of the stages of sexual development and gender/identity role.)

Nilsson, L. *A Child is Born*. New York: Delacorte Press/Seymour Lawrence, 1976.
(Photographs of fetal development before birth.)

11

Infant and Childhood Sexuality

Human sexuality and the sexual feelings associated with it do not begin in adolescence and end when one reaches retirement age. Sexuality begins long before birth and continues to the end of life.

Immediately after birth all babies experience major hormonal changes. Within a day or two of delivery the levels of both testosterone and estrogen drop dramatically. In boys, testosterone rises about a month later, stays high for about a month, and then drops again to the low level that both girls and boys maintain until the hormonal changes of puberty begin from about age eight to 12.

Physical sexual development during infancy and childhood seems minor in comparison to the dramatic psychological, intellectual, and social changes children experience during puberty. However, a number of important processes essential to sexual development do take place during the childhood years.

Between birth and age three, a child forms his or her **gender identity**. The concept of "I am a boy" or "I am a girl" becomes fixed during this stage and rarely changes later in life. This internal psychological concept is shaped by both biological and environmental factors. It is based on how a child is treated and how she or he reacts to the responses of others.

Gender role enactment (what a person does or says that suggests that one is a male or female) also emerges during this developmental period and is built on the basic understanding of sexual identity. Gender role continues to evolve somewhat throughout a person's life as he or she selects a career or becomes a parent, for example. A child learns his or her gender role primarily in two ways. First, a child learns what it means to be one sex or the other by copying the actions of others of the same sex; boys, for instance, imitate their fathers or other male role models. Secondly, a boy also learns how the opposite sex is expected to act by observing his mother and other women. This further defines how one's own gender is expected to act—"I'm also a boy because I don't do girl things."

While children are refining their gender roles, they are often rigid in their ideas about what males and females must or must not do. In general, individuals who are more confident about their gender identity/role are also more

Illustration No. 25 Probably once used as a house support, this large African wood sculpture of a mother and her two children was carved between 1900 and 1920. The theme of the nursing mother appears frequently in art throughout history.

Carved house post. Yoruba people, Nigeria. Early 20th century. Wood, height 6'. The Kinsey Institute Collections; donated by Dr. John Money.

flexible in their ideas about masculinity and femininity and less rigid in their notions about what is appropriate behavior for themselves and others.

Gender role also includes a person's sexual arousal and responses. Researchers theorize that during childhood we acquire elements of the patterns of sexuality which become more obvious in adolescence and then will be prominent features of our adult sexual lives. For example, gaining the ability to give and receive affection in childhood may determine whether a person can bond with another person in a loving relationship later as an adult.

There is still little research on the sexual aspects of childhood, but what does exist clearly refutes the Freudian concept of a "latency period." Freud believed children were not interested in and did not think about sex or have any sexual feelings. In fact, some researchers now refer to that psychological theory as "the myth of latency."

SEXUAL RESPONSE AND SEXUAL BEHAVIOR

We know from ultrasound pictures that male fetuses experience penile erections in the womb. Thus involuntary genital responses begin even before birth. Newborn baby boys have erections and baby girls experience genital swelling and vaginal lubrication, biological responses similar to those of adults. If you don't notice physical changes during a baby's waking hours, they are probably happening during the rapid eye movement (REM) phase of sleep, again similar to what happens in adults.

It would be a mistake, however, to apply adult perceptions of sexuality to infants and children. In early infancy, for example, erection or genital swelling are involuntary responses. Perhaps this is the brain's way of checking all the "circuits" to make sure that the brain, nerves, blood system, muscles, and organs are in working order.

Infants also may exhibit genital responses in other situations, such as when they are nursing, being cuddled, or bathed. These normal responses to being held and loved are an important aspect of the bond between parents and child and may be one way of showing genuine pleasure. These pleasurable experiences are thought to be important later in life, preparing adolescents and young adults to exchange affection and establish intimate bonds with others. Certainly, infant animals raised without physical affection do not develop the usual pattern of mating or parental behavior as adults.

As infants gain control of hand movements they explore their bodies and eventually discover that touching their genitals feels good, even better than sucking their fingers and playing with their toes. They also may touch themselves this way during periods of anxiety or emotional excitement, perhaps as a way of reassuring themselves. Although infants are capable of having orgasms, deliberate masturbation to orgasm rarely begins before a child is between one and two years old, but some never do this and many start later. This kind of behavior is normal. It, however, does not include feelings and emotions like those experienced during puberty and throughout adulthood.

By the age of two, the child is curious about the world and other people and is ready to investigate. Children often hug, cuddle, kiss, climb on top of one another, and look at each others' genitals. Though this is perfectly normal behavior for children at this age, many parents attempt to inhibit this kind of activity. Some children heed their parents' admonitions and stop; others secretly continue the activity but feel guilty about it.

By four or five, children are even more sexually curious. They may engage in more frequent masturbation, begin sex play with other children ("playing doctor"), and are intrigued with parents' bathroom activities. The highest rate of sex play among children occurs between the ages of six and ten.

This is also the time when children spend most of their time playing in sex-segregated groups. So it should come as no surprise that the sex play that goes on at this age is often sex-segregated. It is not unusual for children to exhibit their genitals to one another, touch each other's genitals, and masturbate together. Boys, more often than girls, masturbate in groups.

I frequently hear from concerned parents who wonder whether this kind of behavior indicates their child's future sexual orientation. If a boy engages in sex play with other boys, will he become a homosexual as an adult? Will a girl turn out to be a lesbian? I also hear from adults who are plagued by memories of their own childhood sex play—happily married men who wonder whether masturbating with other boys during childhood or adolescence indicates hidden homosexual desires. Sexual exploration among same-sex peers during childhood and early adolescence is completely normal, and sexual orientation *cannot* be predicted from these behaviors.

A recent study of parents of six- and seven-year-olds reported that 52 percent of their sons had engaged in sex play with other boys and 34 percent had sex play with girls; 37 percent of their daughters had activities with other girls and 35 percent with boys. (Remember that this was only the sex play parents *knew* about.) Activities at this age include simply looking at each other's bodies and "playing doctor" but may also involve attempts at intercourse or insertion of objects.

The progression from reacting to the sensual elements of parental bonding to self-masturbation and sex play with peers is thought to be an important learning process in humans. It is a part of healthy psychosexual adjustment in that it develops self-esteem and the ability to interact with others.

By the age of eight or nine, children have become aware that sexual arousal is a specific type of erotic sensation and will seek these pleasurable experiences. The erotic element of various sights, self-touches, and ideas begins to form. As we will see in the next chapter, the hormonal changes of puberty often begin by the age of eight or nine, so this shift from generalized sex play to more deliberate arousal occurs around the same time that many children are also experiencing physical growth and changes.

PARENTAL REACTION TO CHILDHOOD SEX BEHAVIOR

During the nineteenth century—as recently as a hundred years ago— parents attempted to discourage masturbation by forcing their children to wear strait-jackets or metal mittens to bed. They buckled them into elaborate "genital cages" that resembled medieval chastity belts, and inserted boys' penises into spike-lined tubes designed to inhibit erections. Doctors advised parents to wrap their children in cold, wet sheets; tie their hands to the bedposts or tie their legs together; or eliminate from children's diets a wide range of foods, from cheese to asparagus, believed to cause nocturnal erections. If that didn't do the trick, more permanent methods were prescribed: Leeches were applied to the genitals; genital tissue was burned away by electric current or a hot iron; and, when even more extreme measures were sought, castration and clitoridectomy (surgical removal of the clitoris) were prescribed. This actually happened in the United States, not in some far-off land.

Happily, such dire "remedies" are no longer recommended, but two products invented as antimasturbation remedies are still around. In the 1830s the Reverend Sylvester Graham developed a special flour as part of a program to combat lust. Graham crackers still carry his name. In 1898, one of his followers, John Harvey Kellogg, produced a breakfast cereal to help maintain health by reducing sexual desire—corn flakes! Needless to say, neither product reduced sexual desire or masturbation.

How should parents respond to children's sexuality? Parents who scowl, scold, or punish in response to a child's exploring his or her genitals may be teaching the child that this kind of pleasure is wrong and that the *child* is "bad" for engaging in this kind of behavior. This message may hinder the ability to give and receive erotic pleasure as an adult and ultimately interfere with the ability to establish a loving and intimate relationship.

Acknowledging sexuality instead of discouraging it can strengthen a child's self-esteem, build a positive body image, and encourage competency and assertiveness. This does not mean that expressions of sexuality must go unguided. When children reach the ages of two or three, parents can begin to teach them that self-touching is appropriate in private. At this time parents can also begin to talk about their personal values, such as that sex and privacy go together.

Using the Right Words

Another way parents send out negative messages about sexuality is by using silly words (or no words at all) to describe sexual anatomy. Whether they call genitals "pee-pee" or "privates" or nothing at all, parents are telling children that these body parts are significantly different, embarrassing, mysterious, or taboo compared to such other body parts as the eyes, nose, and knees, which have names openly used in conversation.

Even parents who pride themselves on more open communication about sexuality may find themselves classifying all female genitals together as vagina, instead of using the more accurate vulva, or differentiating the vagina from the clitoris, labia, urethra, and anus.

If this seems too medical or unnecessary, consider how confusion about genitalia can lead to serious misconceptions. A little boy has no trouble distinguishing his penis from his anus, but because of the closer proximity of the anus to the female genitals a little girl who hasn't been taught otherwise may incorrectly associate her genitals with defecation and may consider her entire vulval area as "dirty" or unhygienic. Each little girl should know that she has a vaginal opening between the urinary and anal openings. This is very important because during toilet training she must learn to wipe from front to back after using the toilet so that fecal material is wiped away from the vaginal opening. Even very young girls can, and do, get vaginal infections from improper hygienic practices.

Talking with Children about Sex

From the moment a child is born, and in many subtle ways, you tell your child about sexuality, whether intentionally or not. Parents tell their children about sexuality by conveying their personal feelings about sexuality and the "goodness" or "badness" of body parts and behaviors. The way parents express physical affection in front of their children, the language they use to describe sexual anatomy, the way they wash their child's genitals, their responses to an infant's genital exploration, their explanation of such bodily functions as menstruation or nocturnal emissions—all these things, and the facial expressions and body language that accompany them, tell the child how *you* feel and, therefore, how you expect *them* to feel about sexuality and about themselves.

Parents convey ideas about sexuality from the very start, even though they usually don't begin actively to teach about sexuality, if they do it at all, until a child is much older. Often parents wait for a child to ask questions or express worries. For example, I believe that many young boys begin worrying about penis size when they first see their fathers naked and compare their genitals to those of an adult. Many men might not have anxiety about being "too small" if all fathers said something like "Look at our feet. Mine are much bigger than yours. As you grow your feet will get bigger and so will the rest of you. When you grow up your feet will be big like mine and so will your penis."

As our letters from adolescents and adults prove, too many parents do not give their children accurate or sufficient information about issues such as sexual functioning, reproduction, contraception, and sexually transmitted diseases.

Children most often get their information, or misinformation, about sexuality from friends, television, sisters, brothers, cousins, and their own inventive imaginations—sometimes based on their parents' reactions to their behavior. It is a good idea to give your children accurate information about sex as they grow up, before misinformation is absorbed or invented. In fact, you should encourage your child to check with you about things they've heard or think they know about sex so you can correct any misconceptions. "Facts" picked up "on the street" are nearly always inaccurate and much more frightening than the truth.

Parents should take the initiative and raise topics related to reproduction and sexuality in ways appropriate to each individual child's age, interest, and level of understanding. A relative's or friend's pregnancy, for example, presents a fine opportunity to talk about how babies grow inside their mothers. Use the correct terminology. For instance, say that a baby grows inside the woman's uterus— and describe it correctly as a special nestlike place just for growing babies—not the belly or stomach.

By four, most children are curious about how babies are made and have either asked about this or invented some story for themselves that "explains" how this occurs. By five, children are fascinated by various words for sexual parts and may repeat sexual jokes. Although they usually do not yet understand what's "funny" about the joke, they clearly know it is somehow taboo, a "dirty" joke. By age six or seven, children have collected enough "data" to know that males and females have distinctly different anatomies, especially genitals.

Given all this, parents who wish to make sure that their children have correct, reassuring information about their own bodies, sex, and reproduction must begin talking about these topics early. Don't be afraid that you're "putting ideas into their heads"; chances are they've already wondered about it. And realize that children don't really "hear" what they are not ready to understand. Tell boys about girls (for example, talk about menstruation) and tell girls about boys (for example, talk about erections). Be sure to answer any questions your child asks, and then check to make sure the answer was understood.

You do not have to be an expert to discuss sexuality with your children. There are books you can turn to for information or that are written for parents to read to children (some are listed at the end of this chapter). If you don't know the answer to a question, say "I'm not sure about that, but I'll find out and tell you." Children respect adults who are willing to reveal they don't know something when they don't. It means that the child doesn't get the idea that he or she has to know everything or to be perfect. Although you may not be an expert on the facts you *are* an expert on *your own values*. It's a good idea to combine giving information about sex with sharing statements that tell how you feel about the role of sex in a person's life.

At what age do infants discover that their genitals are a pleasure source? My niece's son is 18 months old and has discovered that putting his hand in his diaper and touching his penis is the way to go. Unfortunately, while this is pleasant for the little fellow, it is acutely embarrassing to his mother and other adults.

Is it possible to modify his behavior by discipline without risking later emotional or sexual problems?

It is normal for little boys to touch their penises, and it is not unusual for most adults from our culture who observe this to feel awkward or embarrassed. During their first year, babies spend a great deal of time exploring their own bodies—and most discover that touching the genitals or putting pressure on them feels better than touching other parts of their bodies. Many little boys spend significant time throughout the day holding or touching their penises while little girls sometimes rock back and forth, rubbing their vulvas. Some children may even masturbate to orgasm. A few demonstrate great pride in having learned this new skill. The problem is that many adults are not comfortable with this behavior.

As you suggested, there is evidence that when a child is punished for this behavior, there can be serious repercussions later. Sex therapists say that many of the adults they treat for problems in sexual functioning were warned as children never to touch themselves "down there" or were punished for touching themselves.

Based on what researchers and clinicians currently understand, the best advice for parents is to attempt to convey, calmly and reassuringly, that even though masturbation is normal, it is something to be done in private. Even young children can understand this message if it is repeated calmly and simply.

Parents of a child under two might quietly take the child to his own crib, away from any adults who are upset by this behavior. But at bedtime or nap time when the child is usually alone, parents should not attempt to interfere with this normal investigative self-touching, which some children use as a part of relaxation and getting ready for sleep.

It is difficult for adults to remember that young children have not yet acquired the concept that certain kinds of touch are "sexual" and do not have sexual feelings that are equivalent to those of adults. In other words, when children touch their genitals, it is simply because it feels pleasant or offers comfort or relaxation; in some ways, this behavior is similar to thumb-sucking.

Sometime after the age of two, parents can explain that touching the genitals is something done privately. Going to the bathroom is an example of another private activity. The child will gradually begin to recognize the difference between private and public activities.

Our 4-year-old daughter has a habit we've never seen in other children. Since she was two, her favorite position when watching TV or playing is to lie on her belly with a cushion between her legs and sway back and forth.

What does this signify and how should we parents react?

Since you've written to The Kinsey Institute, I assume you interpret her swaying on the pillow to be sexual. Masturbation by providing friction against the genitals with a pillow, toy, hand, or foot is *not* uncommon at age two and has been documented in even younger children.

This is not unusual behavior and calls for no special response by a parent unless it becomes distressing to others. In that event, explain that it must be done in the privacy of her room.

I have read about early puberty in a 7-year-old girl and think something like that may be wrong with my 3-year-old boy.

He touches himself and his body responds. This happens a lot and a babysitter has quit because she says it makes her uncomfortable. Other people have noticed it too. I called a child psychiatrist who said not to "overreact." But now a few people have hinted that maybe I'm exposing him to pornographic books or movies. I would never do such a thing!

He's normal in physical appearance (doesn't have pubic hair or genital enlargement) but this behavior is unlike any other three-year-old I've ever seen.

What can I do? What is an "overreaction" anyway? A relative said if I overreacted it would cause him to hate sex or women later in life.

A boy's ability to have erections does not mean that he's entering early puberty, nor is it an indication of any other type of hormonal problem. Erections begin even before birth; they are normal and a sign of health. The problem appears to be his behavior in front of others, not his physical responses. He is old enough for you to help him understand that, even though touching his penis and having an erection may feel good, other people don't want to see it. He can learn that this is a type of "personal" activity that is best done in privacy.

Clinical reports of children evaluated and treated for frequent public masturbation often stress how important it is for parents, teachers, and other adults to continue to show affection toward the child. For example, a parent's hugs aren't sexual and withdrawing physical affection may make a child feel like a "bad" person, unworthy of love. Instead, praise your son when he doesn't touch himself in public, or agree on a treat he'd like as a reward for not masturbating in front of others for some set period of time. Make it clear that genital touching is fine when done privately, in his room.

I have an 8-year-old son who loves girls. While he was at day camp for a month the supervisor phoned me and told me that he had kissed a girl counselor. He also was caught kissing the babysitter's daughter, and when he was 5, I caught him playing doctor with his older sister.

The day camp says he has sexual problems and I should seek psychological help for him. Do you think that an 8-year-old who likes girls and sneaks a kiss here and there requires help? I don't want to make a federal case out of this if it's a passing phase that boys go through, but I do want to get him help if he needs it.

It is common for both boys and girls to be curious about other people's bodies and to mimic adult behavior, such as kissing.

In one survey, kindergarten teachers reported that children often sought body contact with them. The children wanted to be held close, sit on the teacher's lap, and be kissed. The teachers interpreted these behaviors as the children wanting to experience security, closeness to an adult, and affection. And 20 percent reported that in some instances the child attempted to explore the teacher's body.

It also is not unusual for a child to test adult limits to find out how people will react. This testing often involves sex, since children are quick to discover that this topic is highly taboo for many adults. But your son's behavior has generated difficulty for him and for you—regardless of whether he is engaging in common sexual curiosity, play, or testing. A children's counselor could help determine why he continues this behavior when he has found out that it upsets others. Seeing a professional counselor may help sort out which of many possible issues are involved and help you deal with it. Because the therapist is objective, he or she is likely to be more successful in discovering from your son why he is doing these things that are getting him into trouble.

Sometimes parents withhold physical affection (hugging and kissing) from sons because they fear it is not appropriate, will stimulate them sexually, or will cause them to become "effeminate." However, all children need physical affection for healthy psychosocial development, and if it is not available from parents may seek it elsewhere. It is also important to determine whether your son touches adults because he is curious about their bodies, is looking for answers to questions he's afraid to ask, wants the attention he gets from others' reactions, or is deliberately seeking arousal.

A skilled counselor can help explain to your son that certain behaviors are not appropriate and suggest better ways for him to express affection, curiosity, or sexual feelings. Moreover, because mimicking adult sexual behavior may in some cases be one sign of sexual abuse, the counselor may also be able to determine whether your son has been approached by an adult and help you decide what steps to take if that has happened.

One further point: Sometimes parents give their sons double messages. They tell them not to do sexual things but are also unintentionally applauding their son's early sexual activities, reacting as if "boys will be boys." (They usually are not amused at all by the same behavior in their daughters!) It is important for your son to understand that he may not force his affections or sexual touching on others—adult or child. If he is asked to stop touching but continues to touch, he may need some help in dealing with aggressive feelings.

Ask if the day camp can recommend a qualified therapist. Or call the nearest university, medical school, community mental health center, or large hospital and ask for an appointment with a child psychologist, psychiatrist, or a counselor who specializes in children's psychosexual development.

I'm very upset. I just caught my 10-year-old son and four of his best friends (all boys the same age) masturbating in our garage. Does that mean he's a homosexual? Or is one of the other boys a homosexual?

Neither is a valid assumption. Studies, including one conducted by The Kinsey Institute, have found that same-sex genital activity in childhood and adolescence does not predict adult homosexual behavior.

The behavior you witnessed is typical of children your son's age. When Kinsey interviewed thousands of adult males during the 1940s, 57 percent remembered engaging in such sex play and 70 percent of the preadolescent boys he interviewed reported this type of play among their friends. The term sex play meant actual genital touching and did not include less specifically sexual behavior such as wrestling or "playing doctor" while clothed.

Kinsey estimated that nearly all boys and about 20 percent of girls engaged in sex play with other children about their own age before they reached puberty. More recent research has reported similar or higher percentages.

This behavior, which occurs during childhood, usually decreases in frequency around puberty, when youngsters begin to view themselves as adults and want others to do likewise. This usually coincides with the beginning of interest in relational sex. The bottom line is: You needn't worry.

Does seeing parents naked harm a child? My 8-year-old boy and 6-year-old girl always walk in and out of the bathroom while my husband and I are bathing. So far they have not seemed shocked or upset. Now my sister-in-law says we've raised them wrong and they won't be normal.

First, let's remember that exposure to nudity is the norm for many cultures and among families who must share crowded living quarters. In some families in the United States adult nudity is considered completely acceptable, while others find it totally unacceptable. Most people have a more middle-of-the-road attitude, feeling that adult nudity is acceptable in limited settings, such as private areas of the home (bedroom and bathroom) or in a few public places, such as locker rooms.

Many psychiatrists suggest that seeing parents nude in appropriate settings like the bathroom is not harmful for children up to the age of 10 or 11, the age at which many adolescents begin to display an increased need for privacy and begin to shut doors regardless of the parents' behavior.

Generally in the United States, most parents follow the same rules with their older children that they follow with unrelated adults. In some families these rules are that daughters continue to see their mothers but not their fathers. In other, more modest families, children do not see their parents in the nude and parents don't see their children naked either. In still other families, the bathroom door remains open.

Research on female college students faced with dormitory bathrooms without doors showed that girls exposed to bathroom nudity at home viewed the situation as routine; girls from more modest backgrounds felt self-conscious at first, then came to view the nudity as nonsexual and routine.

So each family makes its own rules; yours do not have to match your sister-in-law's or anyone else's to be "normal" or appropriate. It is whatever is comfortable for you and your husband that counts, and as your children become adolescents their feelings must also be respected.

My husband and I are always very careful to lock the door when we make love so our young son doesn't "catch us in the act." I've heard that it could traumatize him for life. Is that true?

The way a child responds to witnessing his parents having sex (often called the "primal scene" by psychoanalysts) probably relates more to the parents' reactions and the family atmosphere regarding openness and affection than to anything else.

If the child hears noises that sound like violent behavior, if parents appear alarmed or ashamed, or if they order the child back to bed without explanation, then the child may well believe that what he or she has seen was wrong or threatening.

On the other hand, if they treat the child calmly and attend to his or her needs (a hug, a glass of water, whatever) seeing parents having sex will probably have little or no effect. If your son should happen to walk in while you and your husband are having sex, he may ask you to explain your activity. When you compose yourself, you might want to tell him that you were physically expressing your love for each other in a way that married people do, then give him a hug and send him back to bed. The underlying rationale is that having sex is one way adults express their love and that it's appropriate and it's private. Having a lock on your bedroom door is a good way to assure your privacy. You can always get up to open the door if he needs something.

When my son was born, and for a few weeks afterward, his breasts seemed pretty swollen and his testicles also looked very big to me. His body eventually looked normal, but I still wonder what caused that. As a new mother, I was terribly concerned at the time.

What you describe is normal for newborns. During pregnancy, the mother secretes many hormones that the fetus absorbs. The effects of these hormones, particularly estrogens, cause newborns to exhibit several physical signs that are characteristic of reproductive maturity. Both girls and boys may have prominent breasts and genitals, and girls may also have slight bleeding from the vagina, suggestive of menstruation.

These hormone-stimulated features disappear within a few weeks after birth.

I'm worried about my 2½-year-old son and am too embarrassed to see a pediatrician. His penis is so small that when he stands sideways he looks like a girl. It's usually retracted into the fleshy part of his pubic area, so that even from the front it looks like another belly button. The only time it protrudes even slightly is when he urinates.

When he was born I didn't think he was unusual, but since then I've seen other baby boys and their genitals are much larger. He's circumcised, but it's a problem to keep his penis clean, and it's often red and irritated.

Does this mean he won't be able to have sexual relations when he grows up? Should something be done about it? Or am I worrying needlessly?

The likelihood is that your son's genital formation and development are fine, but to be sure you must check with your pediatrician or a pediatric endocrinologist (see Appendix) who is an expert on sexual development. Physicians have been asked this and other questions about genitals many times, so don't feel embarrassed.

Genital problems are not uncommon in infants and children of either sex; these problems are usually easily and successfully corrected. Various surgical and hormonal treatments are available, but it will take a medical examination to determine whether treatment is needed.

Remember that children are expert at perceiving when adults are worried. Therefore get a professional opinion soon, so that your concerns won't cause him to become self-conscious about his body. Like most other boys, he may at some point go through a period of thinking his genitals are smaller than those of other males. You should be prepared to handle his concerns with accurate information.

Parents are often worried about the effect of a genital problem on a young boy's self-esteem, particularly if the child observes that his penis is different from his friends', or if other children notice and tease. Don't wait for your son to tell you he is concerned about his penis size or that the other children have commented on it. After you've seen the specialist, talk with your son. Perhaps you could raise the topic while you're bathing him.

We are concerned about the small penis size of our 3-year-old. He's smaller than any other same age boy we've seen. Even his grandmother, who has knowledge of me when I was that age, has expressed concern. Even though we find it embarrassing when someone points this out to us, we're even more concerned about him ending up with some sort of inferiority complex.

We know that as far as reproductive capabilities are concerned, penis size is not very important. We would surely like to see him normal in every way possible, so that he does not have to live his life under any kind of complex. Is there anything we can do to correct the situation? He's medically normal in every other respect.

Normal boys differ greatly in development of the genitals, so that making comparisons by age is not very useful. In general, each boy has some growth in penis size between birth and around age 5, then there is little further growth until age 10 or 11 when growth toward adult size begins in response to pubertal hormones. However, full size is not reached for some until they reach their twenties. Because you are concerned, have your son evaluated by a pediatric endocrinologist *(see Appendix)*. Chances are that your son's penis size is within the normal range for boys his age and no medical treatment will be necessary.

However, you are right to be concerned about his psychological development and self-esteem. Specialists can refer you to a qualified source for counseling necessary to help both you and your son handle any future comments or problems. Your son may need to be repeatedly told that his penis is just fine and it will grow to be like his father's when he grows up. Sometimes it helps to rehearse what he might say if a playmate teases him: "I'm normal and my penis is just right for me. It will grow when I'm older. Not all penises look alike."

In the unlikely event that a problem is found, a specialist can design and monitor a treatment program in cooperation with your family physician, so that frequent travel to a distant medical facility may not be necessary.

My six-year-old daughter cannot control her urine, and neither antibiotics or psychologists have helped her. Her vagina is slightly swollen and red, and when she urinates it hurts. What could be wrong with her?

Urinary incontinence (the inability to control urine flow, during the day or at night) can have many different causes. One of the most likely is a urinary and/or vaginal infection. It is not unusual for young girls to have such infections, which is why it is important to teach girls to always wipe from front to back after using the toilet.

Make an appointment for your daughter with the department of urology at the nearest major medical center, with a pediatric urologist if possible. If a simple urinary infection is not found, she will need to be carefully checked for vaginal infection and congenital abnormalities (anatomical problems she may have been born with) of the bladder and urinary tract. A complete urinalysis and evaluation of kidney function should also be done, including a check for diabetes.

The first pelvic examination can be a frightening experience, especially for younger girls, so stay with your daughter during the examination and reassure her. The exam can be done gently and painlessly by a pediatric urologist with much experience in evaluating children.

Treatment will depend on what, if anything, is found by the various tests. Don't hesitate to get medical attention. This should not wait.

PRECOCIOUS PUBERTY

What exactly is precocious puberty? I think my niece may be experiencing this, but I'm not sure.

True precocious puberty is defined as beginning to develop physical adult sexual characteristics too early. In girls developing breasts before age eight, and in boys enlargement of the testicles and changes in scrotal skin before age nine, can be signs of precocious puberty.

Although early puberty is rare (affecting one in 10,000 children), consult a specialist if it is suspected. The hormones involved in puberty also affect bone growth. Left untreated, precocious puberty may severely limit a child's adult height.

Various types of hormonal treatments have been tried in the past, with varying degrees of success. One new drug currently involved in clinical trials (Lupron) appears promising and is awaiting FDA approval. This drug literally stops the pituitary from sending hormonal messages to all the other organs involved in pubertal development. Unlike earlier treatments, this one has resulted in patients reaching full adult height. It must, however, be carefully prescribed, the effects monitored closely, and dosages adjusted to each individual child's situation. The same drug appears to be effective for both boys and girls, and so far no negative side effects have been found (it has been used for five years). Because only those researchers specializing in the study and treatment of precocious puberty have access to the newest drugs and the sophisticated tests necessary for assessment, finding a specialist is worth the effort.

There is evidence that children who are obviously faster or slower than their peers in terms of the physical changes of puberty are more likely to have psychological and social problems as well. Specialists in pediatric endocrinology (*see Appendix*) understand how important counseling is for both the children and their parents in order to promote normal psychological development.

My youngest daughter is 7, almost 8. She started developing breasts almost a year ago and, at this point, is nearly ready for her first bra. At first I couldn't believe this was happening. She's very thin, so it's not fat, and she's never had any other medical problems.

Her two older sisters didn't do this until they were 11 or 12, and I'm very small myself, so I don't understand this. I realize this is not normal, but is this something I should be concerned about? Should she be seen by a doctor? I never say a word around her, but other kids are already making fun of her. It just breaks my heart. I want to make sure she's healthy.

Breast development starting before age eight can be a sign of a problem. You should consult a pediatric endocrinologist as soon as possible *(see Appendix)*.

Even though you have not mentioned your concerns to your daughter, children are acutely aware of their own body changes and constantly compare their own development with that of their friends. You should talk with your daughter about her body and any concerns she may have, especially since the changes are so obvious that other children have noticed and commented.

[NOTE: This letter is an example of how some parents may refuse to talk to their children about sex under any circumstances. In this case, the situation was obvious. The mother was clearly concerned and other children were reacting to it, yet there had still been no discussion with her daughter. The idea that a child won't notice these developments is not realistic.]

I'm afraid my daughter has some kind of hormonal imbalance. She is 8 years old and in second grade. She's had a complete personality change this year: fighting with friends, explosive outbursts of temper at home, and crying for no apparent reason.

I commented several months ago that if I didn't know better I'd say she was going through puberty. Two months ago while getting her out of the bath I noticed she had pubic hair, and her breasts looked more rounded.

What should I do? What kind of doctor do I call so that I'm not treated like a neurotic mother? Should I look for any other signs or is there even any reason to be concerned?

The likelihood is that your daughter is beginning an early, but completely normal, puberty. However, a thorough physical evaluation, including a neurologic examination and other tests, is the only way to rule out any possible physical problems. And if there is a problem, the earlier she is diagnosed the better the outcome and the smaller the effect on her adult stature. Have her examined by a pediatric endocrinologist *(see Appendix)*.

Premature adrenarche (the development of pubic hair before age nine in girls) can simply be the first sign of the series of steps of normal puberty, or it can be a signal of an adrenal (a hormone-producing gland) problem. Similarly, premature thelarche (breast development before age eight) can be due to a too-early high level of estrogen or simply be the beginning of a normal puberty.

Regardless of the outcome of the evaluation of your daughter's physical status, the physician who does the diagnosis should be able to recommend a qualified person to assess her psychological status and provide counseling if necessary. And yes, if she has started puberty, she might be experiencing the beginning of hormonal cycles and have some of the emotional symptoms associated with puberty for some girls.

I think my youngest son is starting to go through puberty, but he's only 8. His penis is getting bigger, he's starting to grow pubic hair, and he has told me that he has had a nocturnal emission. My oldest son went through puberty at 13 and my other son, who is 12, still has not gone through puberty.

I want to know if going through puberty at such an early age could be harmful to my son.

It may be that your son is fine and is simply entering puberty early, but it's also important to check whether there are any medical problems causing this. If problems are found, appropriate treatments can be prescribed. Locate a pediatric endocrinologist to do the evaluation (*see Appendix*). Left untreated, if these are signs of precocious puberty, there are potential negative consequences.

Many people think of puberty as occurring over a short period of time or even as a single event (first ejaculation in boys and first menstruation in girls). In fact, development of adult sexual and reproductive characteristics is only one aspect of a long and complex maturation process which begins before birth and continues during childhood, throughout adolescence, and into early adulthood.

The age at which various hormonal and other processes start and end varies greatly from one person to the next; even the timing of specific events among brothers is often not the same.

However, the appearance of physical changes such as pubic hair and testicle enlargement before age nine in boys is considered early and calls for diagnosis. Don't delay; make an appointment now so if treatment is indicated it can be started in time to regulate growth in height.

Further Readings

Calderone, M. S., and Ramey, J. W. *Talking With Your Child About Sex: Questions and answers from birth to puberty.* New York: Ballantine Books, Division of Random House, 1982.
(Presents an overview of each stage of development from birth through puberty and provides parents with answers for the questions children are likely to ask.)

Gordon, S., and Gordon, J. *Raising a Child Conservatively in a Sexually Permissive World.* New York: Simon and Schuster, 1983.
(A book for parents who want to provide sex education for their children within the context of their own values.)

Intons-Peterson, M. J. *Children's Concept of Gender.* Norwood, N.J.: Ablex Publishing Corporation, 1988.
(A research-based but easily read book addressing how children acquire knowledge about gender and which factors determine the expression of gender-stereotypic behavior.)

Leight, L. *Raising Sexually Healthy Children.* New York: Rawson Associates, 1988.
(A very readable book for parents interested in answering their children's questions about sex with factual answers and in keeping with their own sexual values.)

Mayle, P. *Where Did I Come From?* Secaucus, NJ: Lyle Stuart Inc., 1973.
(An illustrated book for children explaining the facts of life in a simple and straightforward way. Good for parents and children to read together.)
_____. *"What's Happening to Me?": The answers to some of the world's most embarrassing questions.* Secaucus, NJ: Lyle Stuart Inc., 1975.
(A book for children approaching or entering puberty. Provides answers to some of the most common questions in an easy-to-understand format. Good for parents and children to read together.)
Miller, J., and Pelham, D. *The Facts of Life.* New York: Viking Penguin Inc., 1984.
(Three-dimensional, movable illustrations show the development of a fetus from conception to birth.)
Reinisch, J. M.; Rosenblum, L. A.; and Sanders, S. A., eds. *Masculinity/ Femininity: Basic perspectives.* New York: Oxford University Press, 1987.
(A collection of writings by scientists and researchers concerned with the meaning, development, and implications of masculinity and femininity.)
Sanchez, G. J. *Let's Talk about Sex and Loving.* Burlingame, CA: Yes Press, 1983.
(A book with simple, straightforward information about sex and love to be read by parents to their children. Encourages parents to give children the facts within the context of their own values.)

12

Puberty

Each girl or boy has a highly individualized schedule for moving from childhood to adulthood. Puberty—gaining the physical ability to reproduce— is marked by various physical, psychological, and social changes. Puberty is part of a process that started before birth and continued to unfold through childhood as a result of the effects of various hormones on the brain and body.

Many young people fear that they are developing too slowly, too quickly, or differently from their peers, a fear fueled by a lack of information about pubertal development. It may help to know that puberty can normally begin as early as age eight, or as late as age 15; these early changes are inside and can't be seen. Sexual development to adult status may be completed in only a year or so or may take six years or longer. The timing of adolescent changes can be affected by a variety of factors: the age at which your parents began puberty (heredity), nutrition, climate, percentage of body fat, and many other factors.

You also need to know that the same hormonal changes that stimulate the physical development from child to adult also bring other normal changes: intensified sexual feelings and fantasies; more frequent spontaneous erections; increased vaginal lubrication; and a higher incidence of masturbation.

The period of adolescence encompasses not only the physical changes of puberty but also the psychological, social, and environmental aspects of gaining full adulthood. The psychosexual maturation begun in childhood continues; this is a time when a young person's interactions with others set the stage for adulthood. In adolescence young people fall in love, rehearse pair-bonding, further define those attributes they find most desirable in themselves and their partners, and clarify which sights, sounds, smells, and other factors trigger sexual arousal and sexual satisfaction.

Dr. James M. Tanner, a British physician, first grouped many of the physical changes of puberty into developmental stages for each sex. Young people should find these descriptions of each age group reassuring because each stage covers a wide age range. For example, among a group of 14-year-old boys you can see some who as yet have no visible physical signs of pubertal change, others who look like adults, and the rest at various stages in between—*all completely normal* *(see Illustration 26 and 27)*. (Descriptions of the stages of female and male puberty appear later in this chapter.)

A SPECIAL NOTE FOR PARENTS

As any parent can attest, the time between the onset of puberty and the late teenage years is a period of tremendous physical transformation. Some young people pass through this era smoothly while others experience various degrees of emotional upheaval. It is a time when young women and men continue to define what it means to be masculine or feminine, anguish over their appearance, and rehearse the dance of courtship. It is also a time when the hormones that trigger the second main phase of sexual development become influential. Not coincidentally, this is when young people expand their sexual activities, which may include kissing, petting, experiencing orgasm, and, for many older teenagers, sexual intercourse. It is when a person's patterns of adult sexuality become more defined. And it is often a time of strong emotions.

It is impossible to read many of the letters from young people and not be moved by their desperation, urgency, fear, shame, embarrassment, and need for information. Some are worried that they're developing too slowly: "This is a very embarrassing problem and it's beginning to depress me that I'll be lonely when I'm older" writes one boy who fears that his penis is too small. We often hear from parents who are concerned about the same issues. "My son is very depressed, threatening to take his life" writes a woman whose son believes his testicles are smaller than average.

Boys aren't alone in expressing body-image anxiety. Girls worry about breasts that are too big, too small, or don't match.

Quite a few are too scared or embarrassed to talk to parents, and parents themselves are often just as uneasy about discussing these issues. "I have a problem and I'm too embarrassed to approach anyone else" begins a letter from a girl who worries about an irregular menstrual flow and wonders whether this is a result of masturbation. "I'm concerned and embarrassed" writes the mother of a 14-year-old boy whose chest hair has begun to grow. "I'm too embarrassed to ask anybody about this" says a girl who believes her breasts are unusually shaped. A 14-year-old boy who is scheduled to be circumcised writes "I couldn't ask the doctor these questions because my father was there"—he wants to know whether circumcised boys masturbate. (Both circumcised and uncircumcised boys masturbate.)

And sometimes when these young people do try to talk with an adult, the ensuing conversation apparently only strengthens their resolve to stay silent. "I tried to tell my mom about it once, but she thinks I must be too young to have PMS (Premenstrual Syndrome)" writes a 15-year-old-girl.

On the positive side, there are parents who do not seem threatened by their children's approach to adulthood. One letter, from a divorced father with joint custody of his daughter, wanted to know how best to mark (or even celebrate) her first period. "I realize she's beginning to go through puberty," he wrote, "and would like to talk to her about menstruation and tell her how proud I am that she's becoming a young woman."

Parents would do well to follow this father's lead. Too many parents avoid

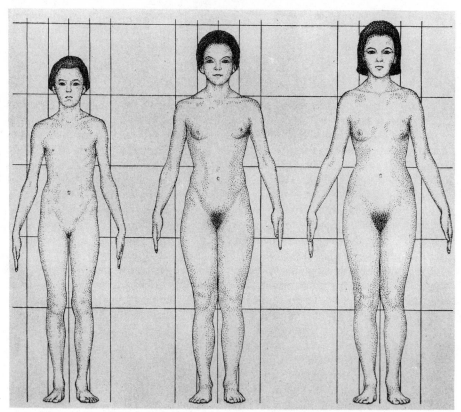

Illustrations 26 and 27 (facing page). **Individuals Often Look Different Even at the Same Age.** All three of these girls are 12.75 years old and all three of the boys are 14.75 years old. Even though they look different, all are normal. The physical changes of puberty don't begin at the same age or progress at the same rate for everyone. From "Growing Up," by J. M. Tanner. Copyright © 1973 by Scientific American, Inc. All rights reserved.

discussing sexuality with their children and teenagers because they worry that discussion will seem like giving permission. This is not true. Providing sexual information has been shown to *delay* the age of first intercourse and *prevent* unwanted pregnancy. Often parents believe that their children are too young to talk about these issues. Some are too embarrassed to talk about sex with their own spouses, let alone with their children.

Whatever your apprehensions, you need to overcome them and start talking with your children about sex or at least providing them accurate written information. Physical changes can normally begin as young as eight. Although that may seem very young to most parents, by that age boys should know that their testicles will begin to grow and should be taught how to look for symptoms of testicular cancer. If children know what to expect *in advance*, they won't be frightened or confused by the changes they will experience in their bodies and in their feelings. And they are less likely to believe the myths and incorrect information they will hear from friends.

Adolescents have sexual feelings. Nothing you do or don't do is going to

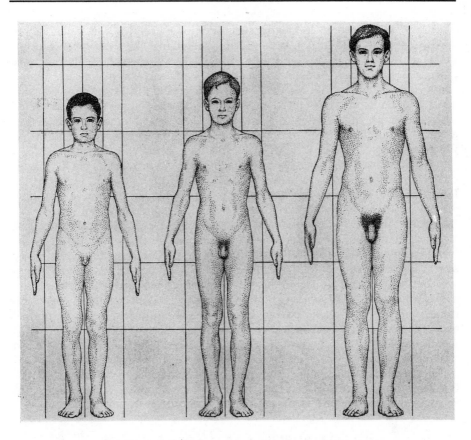

change that. It is clear from research that they fall in love, engage in sexual activity such as kissing or petting, and more than half have had intercourse by age 17. It is important that they receive the basic information they desperately need to keep them healthy.

Adolescents need to know whether the physical changes in their bodies are normal, how reproduction takes place, how to prevent an unwanted pregnancy, and how to protect themselves from sexually transmitted diseases. If you don't tell them these facts, your children will ask their friends and risk getting information that is not only inaccurate (and thus may lead to disease or pregnancy) but may also cause needless worry or alarm. If you need help in talking about sex, look at some of the books listed at the end of this chapter and either read them with your children or give one to your child to read.

If your son or daughter asks a question you cannot answer, say "I'm not sure about that but I'll find out," and then ask your family physician or go to the library and find the answer. Young people respect adults who admit they don't know all the answers and are willing to find them.

This is also the time to clearly state your own feelings and values about sexuality and its role in one's life. Saying something like "Whatever you do, don't get pregnant" is not adequate. You might tell them that the emotions associated with falling in love can be strong at any age and that sexual arousal can be overwhelming. But also teach that each person can learn to set personal goals and limits and avoid the risks of pregnancies or sexually transmitted diseases while still savoring the emotions of love and enjoying feelings of arousal. Young people need to learn effective ways of saying no and standing up for their values in a way that doesn't lower their status with friends.

Even though most of us believe that parents should be responsible for the sex education of their children, many of us don't feel comfortable in this role. Dr. John Bancroft, a respected sex researcher, has speculated that there may be a special problem involved when parents attempt to discuss sexual issues with their children. Sex is one of our culture's most taboo topics. Moreover, the incest taboo against sexual interactions between family members is even stronger. For many people, talking can feel close to doing, especially for those who notice sexual arousal whenever they talk about sex. This can be frightening to a parent who fears that sexual arousal in this context is a sign of incestuous feelings for a son or daughter. What happens next? Many times, unfortunately, all communication about sex stops, and parents may even restrain themselves from normal expressions of affection toward their children.

Given all this, our society may in fact be asking many parents to do something that is very difficult for them to do well. It is natural to feel awkward about discussing sexual behavior, feelings, and values with your own children. But keep trying. If it is just too uncomfortable, find another adult you trust to speak to them or provide written materials appropriate to their ages.

FEMALE PUBERTY AND ADOLESCENCE

The most common questions we receive from girls and young women ages ten to 19 years old are on the following topics: pubertal development (too fast or slow), problems with menstruation, curiosity about female sexual responses, vaginal problems (such as infections), breast size, and contraceptive methods.

The general physical changes for girls during puberty follow. These five stages are meant to be guidelines only. Not all young women follow the same developmental pattern, nor do they all proceed through these changes at the same speed. It is also completely normal for some physical changes to appear in a different order.

The Stages of Female Pubertal Development

- **Beginning sometime between ages 8 and 11.** Changes are mostly internal, as hormones from the brain signal the ovaries and other internal reproductive organs to begin growing. This increases the amount of estrogen produced, which will cause many of the more noticeable physical markers that will appear later.
- **Beginning sometime between ages 9 and 15.** First the areola (the darker area around the nipple) and then the breasts increase in size and develop a more rounded shape. Although pubic hair is still sparse, it becomes darker and coarser. Growth in height continues, and body fat continues to round

body contours. Normal vaginal discharge becomes noticeable. Sweat and oil glands become more active, and acne may appear. The internal and external reproductive organs and genitals grow, making the vagina longer and the labia more pronounced.

- **Beginning sometime between ages 10 and 16.** The areola and nipples grow, often forming a second mound sticking out from the rounded breast mound. Pubic hair begins to take a triangular shape and grows to cover the center of the mons (the fatty mound over the pubic bone). Underarm hair appears. Menarche (the first menstrual flow) occurs. Internal organs continue to develop and the ovaries may begin to release mature eggs capable of being fertilized. Growth in height slows.
- **Beginning sometime between ages 12 and 19.** Breast development nears adult size and shape, pubic hair fully covers the mons and spreads to the top of the thighs, the voice may deepen slightly (not as much as in males), and menstrual cycles gradually become more regular. Some further changes in body shape may occur into the early twenties.

Basic Health Care Steps

There are several basic health care steps young women should begin during puberty.

Do you thoroughly examine your breasts each month after your menstrual period? Do you keep records of your menstrual flow and any symptoms, such as cramps? Do you look at your genitals regularly? This involves using a hand mirror to look closely at all the external surfaces (see the women's section of Chapter 17 for how to do these things).

Have you ever had a gynecological examination and Pap test? Beginning at age 18 (or earlier if sexually active) every woman should have an annual examination. Doing this regularly is the best way to spot problems with internal and external organs, such as a vaginal infection, enlargement of an ovary, or changes in the cells of the cervix (the opening between the vagina and the uterus). *(For information on what to expect during a pelvic examination, see Chapter 17).*

Every woman must do these things, whether she is sexually active or not. Vaginal infections can occur in girls and women who have never had sex, have not yet even reached puberty, or are past menopause. Being a virgin does not protect a woman against serious diseases of the reproductive organs.

If you cannot bring yourself to follow these necessary and simple health routines, you need to talk with someone who can help you gain a healthier, prouder, and more responsible attitude toward your own body.

Perhaps you would feel most comfortable talking with a female physician or counselor. If you don't know of someone, consider calling a family-planning clinic like Planned Parenthood. Most offer basic health care and information to women in a sensitive and caring way.

This isn't really a question, but other women should know this. When I was a teenager, my mom set up an appointment for me to have an exam for menstrual problems. She said the doctor would explain what happens during a pelvic when I got there.

My first embarrassing moment was when I was told to undress and I only took off my outer clothes. How was I to know what they meant? The second

was being positioned by the nurse without knowing why *that* position was required. And the third was my screaming and scrambling to get off the table, unaware that this intimate touch was a pelvic exam.

To their credit, the doctor and nurse seemed ashamed that they assumed that because I was in my teens, I'd already either had an exam or some intimate contact with a boyfriend. I was angry at everyone, my mom for her lack of details, the nurse and doctor for assuming I was sexually active.

I've yet to see anyone tell parents to tell daughters what to expect during an exam so basic to a woman's life. There should be no reason for a girl's first exam to produce shock, anger, embarrassment, or shame.

Thank you for your letter. I hope that all parents who read this will follow your excellent suggestion.

All nurses and physicians who do pelvic exams should ask each woman if it is her first exam. They should then take the time to explain the procedure before beginning. But if they don't ask, tell them it's your first exam and that you need information about what to expect. *(For a complete description of a pelvic exam see Chapter 17.)*

Breast Concerns

Many young women write to us with questions about the size and appearance of their breasts, issues that continue to be of concern in adulthood as well.

Try to accept your breasts as they are. Don't judge yourself against the bodies you see in magazines. Many of them have been altered by cosmetic surgery; moreover, breasts are important aspects of sexual attractiveness only to *some* partners, certainly not to all. Women's breasts, like all body parts, come in a wide variety of shapes and sizes *(see Chapter 4)*.

My daughter is worried about the size of her breasts and would like to be reassured. Are a girl's breasts fully developed at the time she first menstruates? If not, until what age do they continue to grow?

Adult breast size is not usually attained until sometime after the first menstruation occurs, but pubertal growth patterns vary from one young woman to the next. Breast development can continue into the early twenties. Moreover, a woman's breast size often fluctuates throughout her life due to changes in hormone levels, pregnancy, weight gain, or weight loss. Because of these normal changes, most women do not have a "permanent" breast size. Some women, for example, find that their breasts are always much larger the week before menstruation than they are during the other three weeks of each reproductive cycle.

If your daughter is truly upset about her breast size, see if your family physician can recommend a specialist in adolescent development for her to talk with. Unless she has a hormonal deficiency (in which case she probably would not menstruate and would also lack other signs of development), she may need help with her emotional concerns rather than a specific medical treatment.

I'm a 14-year-old and have not sexually matured. But I am beginning to. Two months ago on my right breast I started developing a round lump, then it got bigger and it's hard. When I press it, it hurts a bit. My left breast hasn't got a

lump. The lump is near my right nipple. My mum tells me she had this when she was young. I don't know what to do. Please help, for it's urgent!!!

It is not unusual for "nodules" or lumps to appear in one or both breasts as a young woman's hormones begin changing to adult levels, but it can be reassuring to have the lump checked by a gynecologist if it remains for two or three months. Any serious breast disease is very rare at your age.

Congratulations on beginning self-examinations of your breasts early and on being able to talk with your mother about your concerns—both are important for physical and emotional health as you progress through your teenage years.

I have a very serious problem I hope you can help me with. As I first developed breasts everything was "normal," but as they got bigger one breast became larger than the other.

I've been living with this problem for three years now. I've been doing breast exercises on just the smaller one but it doesn't seem to be getting any bigger. I'm too embarrassed to ask anybody about this in person.

Medical professionals have been saying for years that no woman has equal breasts; one is always slightly larger than the other. Some researchers now estimate that more than half of all American women have visible size differences between their two breasts, and nearly one-fourth have one breast that is 20 percent larger than the other.

Exercise will not increase the amount of breast tissue in the smaller breast, although it could increase the underlying chest muscles so that the breast might appear a little larger. The best option is to overcome your embarrassment; it may help to remind yourself that millions of women have breasts like yours. A therapist or counselor can help you feel more comfortable about the appearance of your body (see Chapter 4).

Concerns About Menstruation

It is normal for young women to have an irregular pattern of menstrual cycles when they first begin menstruation, meaning that it is not always the same number of days between periods and that not all periods last the same number of days. Information about what happens inside a woman's body during each reproductive cycle is in Chapter 2. It is important that you fully understand the connection between having menstrual periods and being fertile (capable of becoming pregnant) which is explained in Chapter 15.

I'm a divorced father with joint custody of my daughter (age 11) and son (age 9). My daughter and I have a great, honest relationship and have been able to talk about just about everything. I realize she's beginning to go through puberty and would like to talk to her about menstruation and tell her how proud I am that she's becoming a young woman, but am not sure what to do or say.

Congratulations on having such an open and loving relationship with your daughter. I wish more parents felt and acted as you do. You are right, the first menstruation (menarche) is indeed a significant life event and is generally seen as the major sign that a girl is becoming a woman. Research on adolescent girls has shown that it is important to them that they be prepared for menarche *before* it happens. The girls studied wanted to know about menstrual physiology (what exactly is going on inside the body) and menstrual hygiene (how to deal with the blood flow). They emphasized that they also wanted to be told that menstruation was normal and healthy, since the appearance of blood in other circumstances is usually a sign of disease or injury. They also wanted reassurance that menstrual flow could be managed without disrupting other aspects of one's life, such as school athletics and social events.

In many cultures, menarche is celebrated by entire families, and even whole villages, with special feasts or ritual dances. Among some groups, young women change their style of clothing or hair arrangement to signal to everyone that they are now adults and available for marriage. Most Western cultures no longer provide a formal ritual to acknowledge a girl's passage into reproductive adulthood, so many parents and friends, like you, aren't sure what to say or do.

Researchers asked some young women between the ages of eight and 17 what types of ceremony or social acknowledgment they thought would be appropriate. The most frequently selected response was to be told "Congratulations, you're growing up." Some parents report having a special meal or taking their daughter out to dinner—a symbolic gesture appreciated by some young women. Other young women prefer a less public show of support, such as a gift of flowers or some other token of their new womanly status.

You and your daughter will have to design a ritual, or "rite of passage," special to the two of you. You might tell your daughter that you're aware she's going through puberty and ask her how she would prefer to mark this important transition. Tell her you'd like to know when she has her first period so you'll know when to carry out whatever plan you've agreed to.

If she acts uncomfortable about the idea of a public celebration (for example, she might like to go to dinner with you but does not want her brother to know what the fuss is about), then take her out alone or agree on a more private gesture. Set up a simple signal (for example, a call from her saying "It's finally happened") and assure her that her new adult status will not be the focus of conversation unless she brings it up.

Offer now, or at any time in the future, to answer any questions she may have and to give her your view of how males feel about such womanly functions. Many girls worry that boys will tease them about menstruating, and instead you can help her feel confident and proud of this important step into womanhood. Incidentally, it's also important to talk about menstruation with your son. Male ignorance about female reproductive cycles can lead to confusion, misunderstanding, and a lack of sensitivity to sisters, mothers, and future wives and daughters—as well as to unplanned pregnancies.

I am 13 and impatient. I have been watching my friends' physical development with envy. Until recently, so was my best friend, but then she got her period too. Now I stand alone. I'm not like most 13-year-old cases (worried I'm not normal) because I know my body has its own unique timetable, but what I need is encouragement. How long do I have to wait? I show all other forms of puberty except menstruation and extreme breast development. I am really looking forward to becoming a woman but I lack the patience. Please tell me what to do!!!

Wait just a little longer. The average age of menarche in the United States is just before age 13 (meaning that some girls menstruate before then, and some menstruate after), so you're certainly well within the normal age range for not starting yet. Actually, most girls have their first period anytime between age 10 and age 16. Since the other pubertal changes (breast development, appearance of pubic hair, growth spurt in height) have taken place, it sounds as if you will get your first menstrual period within the next year.

Worrying about being "late" is a problem in itself. If the information here doesn't make you feel better, you might talk to your parents, a school counselor, school nurse, favorite teacher, or an adult you trust.

If you still have not had a period by age 16, then you might want to consult a pediatric endocrinologist (see Appendix). The physician will first ask you some questions, measure your height, and look closely at the outside of your body. A blood sample may be taken in order to check your hormone levels, and other tests (such as X-rays) may be ordered. A pelvic examination is not usually necessary.

I am 14 and very worried. All of my friends already have menstruated and I haven't. I am also very thin, and I am beginning to wonder if I am normal and if I will ever have my period.

Your thinness could be a factor. A certain amount of body fat is needed for menstruation to occur. For example, ballet dancers and gymnasts who have very low amounts of body fat often have delayed menarche.

If you haven't noticed *any* signs of early pubertal changes and if your rate of development is not similar to other women in your family (ask your mother, sisters, and grandmothers when they started to menstruate), it is time for you to see a physician.

But if you've already noticed some pubertal changes such as pubic hair growth and your rate of development is like that of some of the other women in your family, you can probably wait until you're 16 to see a physician. If you're too worried to wait, however, go now so you can be reassured and stop worrying.

I'm 13 and had my first period three months ago. First I want to know how I can tell when it will come again and if my next one will last as long as my first one, because it lasted eight days.

There is no way to predict when you will have your next period or how many days it will last. It can take as long as seven years for young women to establish their regular, more predictable menstrual cycles.

So far, you seem to be following a common pattern. In the United States, the length of time between menstrual flows for young women is often longer than for older women, because the ovaries take longer to produce a mature egg for release.

Also, some young women have periods lasting longer than five days (the average for older women) and/or have a heavier flow. During menstrual flow, the uterus sheds its lining, which is composed of endometrial tissue. The lining builds up again between periods. If the uterus has a longer time to rebuild this lining, as it often does for young women, it may take more days to shed it, simply because more lining was produced.

As long as you are in good general health, skipping three or four months between periods at your age is not a sign of trouble. Meanwhile, you will simply have to wait and see what your body does next and be prepared. That means keeping a supply of sanitary napkins and/or tampons readily available.

I have a big problem, and I'm too embarrassed to approach anyone else. About two or three years ago I started getting my period. Then a very funny thing happened: I never got it once a month. I get it maybe every two or three months, and sometimes every four months.

I'm too scared to go to the family doctor. Also, I'm wondering if self-stimulation by rubbing your clitoris would have anything to do with my problem about my menstrual cycle?

There is no evidence to suggest that masturbation can affect the menstrual cycle, with the possible exception that orgasm reportedly eases menstrual cramps for some women.

Since you only started menstruating two or three years ago, chances are that you are maturing normally and your periods will gradually become more regular and move closer together. In a few cases, long cycles can be a sign of a problem, so if your cycles don't become more regular over the next few years, or if you continue to worry, go to a gynecologist. You don't need to tell the doctor about your masturbating.

I'm 15 years old and I got my first menstrual period three years ago. I wondered what causes menstrual cramps and will I have them all my life? Also, I've heard that the pain could just be in my head. Is this true? It seems very real to me.

Menstrual pain (dysmenorrhea) can come from the uterus, lower abdomen, lower back, or upper thighs. Some women report accompanying nausea, dizziness, and headaches. These symptoms are medically verifiable and are *not* imaginary.

Regular exercise and a healthy diet are sufficient to reduce menstrual discomfort for many women, but others must take ibuprofen or some other antiprostaglandin medications. If you can't reduce your discomfort by yourself, see a gynecologist. *(There is more information about cramps in Chapter 17.)*

I'm 14 years old and every month for about a week before my period I can't control myself. I'm a grouch toward my family. I sleep for about 10 or 11 hours a day. I also cry *very* easily about unimportant things. I personally think it's PMS. I tried to tell my mom about it once, but she thinks I must be too young to have PMS. Am I too young?

No, you're definitely not too young. Interestingly, not only can PMS appear in adolescent women, but it's possible that it may in rare instances begin in younger girls who haven't even begun menstruating. This is because their hormone levels are already cycling, even though their menstrual periods have not yet appeared.

PMS is related to hormonal changes the week or so before menstrual flow begins in each cycle. Symptoms can be either physical or emotional. Starting today, get a calendar or diary and keep an accurate daily record of your menstrual cycles, your general health, and your emotions. Make a note on days when anything increases stress for you, such as school exams or arguments with your friends and family. Mark the day you begin to flow and when you have any discomfort. If you keep good records, you can help a physician determine what may be involved.

Also eat a healthy diet, try to keep salt intake as low as possible to reduce fluid retention, and begin a mild to moderate exercise program if you don't already exercise regularly. These steps have reportedly helped many women reduce PMS symptoms. *(There is more information about PMS in Chapter 17.)*

Because PMS is treatable, and because it is a physical (not solely mental) problem for many women, it is worth consulting a gynecologist for an evaluation if your symptoms continue. Take your records to the appointment.

I want to start using tampons. But I'm very confused about using them. Will it fit the vagina or damage the vagina or hymen (I'm still a virgin)? Can you feel the tampon inside you?

A woman is a virgin until she has had sexual intercourse, whether or not she has a hymen (the thin layer of tissue that covers the vaginal opening). Although the hymen completely covers the vaginal opening at birth, it then mostly disappears; if it didn't, young women would not be able to have periods. So tampon use does not harm the hymen, even if a young woman still has some pieces of the hymen left in her vagina. It doesn't damage the vagina either, but should always be inserted *gently*.

If you can feel the tampon after it is inserted, it is not inserted correctly; it is probably not in far enough and is too close to the vaginal opening. Take it out and try again with another tampon. It may take several tries before you learn how to place a tampon properly. *(For more information on tampons, see Chapter 17.)*

Vaginal Discharge and Infections

It is normal for women to have a slight vaginal discharge during their reproductive years. But, for at least 20 percent of women, a vaginal infection (vaginitis) occurs that may increase the discharge; change its color, texture, or smell; and cause swelling or irritation. It is not uncommon for even very young girls to have vaginal infections or irritation of the vulva accompanied by pain, burning, and itching. The only way to diagnose and treat a vaginal infection is by having a pelvic examination. *(For more information on vaginal discharges see Chapter 17.)*

I'm 14 and have not started menstruating yet. A couple of months ago I started having a much heavier discharge and sometimes irritation and soreness in that area. I'm uncomfortable talking about this with anyone.
    What is causing this? Is it normal? What can I do about it?

There are two types of vaginal discharge. One is a normal marker of pubertal change; this can often be heavy and alarms some young women who don't know what to expect. Increased hormone levels account for the appearance of this discharge at puberty, which may leave a slight stain on underwear. The second type of discharge can also be caused by hormonal fluctuations, which encourage the naturally occurring vaginal bacteria or yeast to grow out of balance.

Try wearing only cotton underwear and drying gently and carefully after bathing to see if the irritation is caused by moisture. Always wipe from front to back after using the toilet. If the vaginal discharge persists or you have itching or burning, see a physician (preferably a gynecologist), who can check for a vaginal infection.

MALE PUBERTY AND ADOLESCENCE

Young men up to age 19 most commonly ask about sexual development (too fast or too slow), penis size, whether masturbation is harmful to their health, testicle size, and orgasm and ejaculation—particularly nocturnal emissions (ejaculations while sleeping).

Most boys don't notice the first changes that begin puberty because they take place inside the body. A boy's testicles begin to mature and produce increased amounts of testosterone—which, in turn, cause the growth of the prostate gland and other internal organs related to adult male reproduction. During this time, spontaneous (involuntary) erections begin to occur more frequently.

What follows is a description of the stages of puberty for boys. As for girls, these should be used only as a guideline, not a rigid checklist to be applied to all boys. It is completely normal for certain physical changes to appear on a slower or faster schedule and not always to appear in the following sequence.

The Stages of Male Pubertal Development

- **Beginning sometime between ages 9 and 15.** The first external physical change noticed is when the testicles begin to grow, the skin of the scrotum becomes redder and coarser, and a few straight pubic hairs appear at the base of the penis. Testosterone also gradually changes the shape of the body as muscle mass develops and the boy begins to grow taller. The areola (circle of darker skin around the nipple) also grows larger and darker.
- **Beginning sometime between ages 11 and 16.** The penis begins to grow longer; the testicles and scrotum continue to grow. Pubic hair becomes coarser, more curled, and spreads to cover the area between the legs. The body gains in height, the shoulders broaden, and the hips narrow. As the larynx (voice box) enlarges, a boy's voice begins to deepen. Sparse facial and underarm hair appears.
- **Beginning sometime between ages 11 and 17.** The penis begins to increase in circumference as well as in length (though more slowly), and the testicles continue to increase in size. The texture of the pubic hair looks more like an adult's, and growth of facial and underarm hair increases. Shaving may begin. The internal reproductive organs have matured enough to produce the first ejaculation of semen (and sperm). Nearly half of all boys have gynecomastia (breast enlargement), which will decrease in a year or two. Increased skin oils may produce acne.

- **Beginning sometime between ages 14 and 18.** The body nears final adult height and the genitals achieve adult shape and size, with pubic hair spreading to the thighs and slightly upward toward the belly. Chest hair appears, facial hair reaches full growth, and shaving becomes more frequent. For some young men, further increases in height, body hair, and muscle growth and strength continue into their early twenties.

My son, age 14 years 4 months, has already developed a heavy growth of hair on his chest, stomach, and navel. This began growing about six months ago and I'm concerned about the overly rapid rate he's developing. He began shaving at 11-and-a-half and now this.

His classmates are teasing him and calling him names. What should we do? I'm concerned and embarrassed.

Try to control your embarrassment. Your son needs your understanding and support; if he senses that you feel anxious or ashamed, it may intensify his own worries about being "different" and damage his self-esteem.

Psychological counseling is frequently recommended when a boy looks different from his peers in order to help him cope with remarks about his appearance. This can help him feel proud and not embarrassed about his beginning manhood.

If he had other signs of puberty before age 10, such as full growth of the penis and testicles or a deepening of his voice, it would be appropriate to ask your pediatrician or a pediatric endocrinologist to check his hormone levels. *(See Appendix.)*

Genital Concerns

Worries about penis size are not restricted to young men; these concerns carry over into adulthood. There are many more questions about penis size in Chapter 4.

I'm a 14-year-old boy and think something is wrong with me. My body doesn't seem to be developing as fast as my friends', if you know what I mean.

Assuming you mean your genitals aren't as big as those of some of your friends, or you don't have as much pubic hair, it is not time to worry. Puberty is a widely variable process, with the growth of the penis often not beginning until age 16. If, however, you've noticed no growth in your testicles and have no signs of pubic hair near your penis, check with a physician.

I'm a 15-year-old male and I have a problem. I have some pubic hair but no growth of my penis or testicles. I also have no facial hair. I am beginning to be concerned that something is wrong. I always hear that a penis works just as well smaller as it would bigger, but I am too self-conscious to even think of that. I would refuse to have sexual relations with anyone if it ever came to that. This is a very embarrassing problem and it is beginning to depress me that I will be lonely when older. Please help. This is a very serious problem for me.

Having pubic hair is a good sign that you've started to develop, but if you're still worried even after reading the guidelines on male puberty and adolescence, check with your family doctor. She or he can test to make sure your hormones are functioning properly. Or make an appointment with a pediatric endocrinologist *(see Appendix)*. In the unlikely event some hormonal imbalance is found, this is a good age to begin treatment.

Most likely you'll find out that you're just fine, but be frank and tell the doctor that your situation is depressing you. Ask that he or she help you get counseling to handle your feelings. Research has shown that young men and women whose pubertal changes are different from their friends' are somewhat more likely to have problems with self-esteem that can affect both their adolescent and adult lives.

I am 17. These past four to five months I have become a little curious because my penis is not growing at all. It has been the same size for the past year, approximately. I shave regularly, hair is starting to grow on my chest and I have a lot of hair under my arms and around my penis. Masturbation on the average of two times a week doesn't seem to help either.

The fact that you haven't noticed growth in the past year isn't necessarily a cause for concern. It is normal for the genital growth rate to slow down as a young man approaches the end of puberty.

Masturbation can not make the penis grow nor can it slow or stop its growth. Masturbation has nothing to do with the development of either a boy's or girl's genitals.

My 17-year-old son came to me the other day and told me he has been embarrassed for several years at school in physical education class when the boys have to take showers together. My son finally pulled down his shorts and showed me why. His penis is smaller than his five-year-old brother's! He is too embarrassed to let me take him to a doctor. What is wrong that his penis hasn't grown all these years? What can be done? Aren't his growing years about up?

Not necessarily. He may still be going through the various stages of puberty. Or he may turn out to be an adult whose penis is small when flaccid but average in size when it is erect. This is explained in Chapter 3.

There are other indicators of development that are more important than penis size. Have his testicles and scrotum enlarged? Does he have pubic hair? Has he ejaculated? If these markers are not present, then it is time for him to see a doctor, preferably a pediatric endocrinologist. *(See Appendix.)*

If the only problem involved is the size of his penis, arrange for him to visit a urologist to be checked for any structural problems such as a short urethra (the tube that leads from the bladder to the opening in the head of the penis). This condition is called chordee and pulls the penis closer to the body, making it appear shorter. These types of congenital (present-from-birth) problems can be resolved with surgery, preserving full urinary and sexual functioning.

Regardless of what medical examinations find, he may need counseling to help him cope with his feelings.

I am 17. When I was 15, I masturbated heavily, about five times a week. After about one year of this, I noticed four brown spots on the head of my penis. I have quit masturbating for five months, but these spots still remain.

I learned in school that one way of telling if you have AIDS is brown spots. I have no other symptoms of AIDS except for diarrhea. My question is, is this AIDS? Please answer my letter—it's a matter of life or death.

P.S. I have never had any type of sex with anyone. I have never used drugs.

The physical changes during puberty include some changes in the texture and color of the skin of the genitals. A physician can tell you if your spots are part of this normal process—they probably are.

Did you have a blood transfusion between 1981 and 1986? Were you prescribed a medication made from blood (such as those used to treat hemophilia)? If your answer to these questions is no, then it is nearly impossible that you have been infected by the AIDS virus or any other sexually transmitted disease.

For peace of mind, ask your physician about the brown spots. You need not mention masturbation unless you want to. By age 15, nearly 90 percent of boys have masturbated.

I'm a young teen facing a problem which concerns my parents' crazy theory about male testes. My parents think that my testes have greatly expanded, and think that this is the result of my playing a wind instrument, the tenor saxophone. They insist I must stop playing. By their constant talking and persuasion, I've been almost convinced. I don't want to go without the thing I love.

I am not aware of any research that links testicular enlargement with playing a wind instrument, and it is very unlikly that your musicianship has anything to do with the growth of your testicles. The likelihood is that you are just having the normal increase in genital size that occurs with puberty. However, to reassure your parents and rule out any health problems, have a urologist check your testicles to see if they are healthy. Only a medical examination can determine whether there is some problem with your testicles and what caused the change.

Is there a way to relieve pain in the testicles due to the lack of opportunity to have intercourse? My girlfriend said she'd never heard of it. Do only some guys get it?

I assume your question refers to testicular aching or discomfort caused by prolonged sexual arousal without ejaculation or orgasm, commonly called "blue balls." (In some areas of the United States, this slang term was also used to mean gonorrhea.) A similar condition can occur in women's vulvas.

For both sexes, the cause is the accumulation of blood (vasocongestion) in the pelvic and genital area, and it is a normal part of the phase of sexual response called arousal.

The symptoms of vasocongestion for both sexes are quickly relieved by orgasm (from sexual activity with a partner, masturbation, or involuntarily during sleep). They are also relieved when arousal is simply allowed to subside, by stopping further sexual stimulation.

There is no evidence that this temporary condition does any physical harm.

Erection and Ejaculation

Erections, even in nonsexual situations, are normal and one sign of good health; many young men nevertheless have questions and concerns about erections. Nocturnal emissions, or "wet dreams," are also normal and an indication that your body is functioning well. Though they may be a bit alarming to someone who isn't prepared for them and doesn't realize this is a natural part of growing up, nocturnal emissions are healthy, cannot be controlled, and should not be a cause for concern.

I'm a 15-year-old male and I am still in my puberty stage. I often have erections any time of the day. Sometimes it happens in the shower after gym and I find this very embarrassing. Is there anything I can do to stop them?

Some males experience an increase in the rate of spontaneous erections beginning around age eight. These involuntary erections often occur without sexual thoughts or sexual stimulation. You can get an erection when genitals rub against clothing, when you become chilled, or while taking a shower. It is normal to have erections in such situations but just as normal not to have them. Each young man reacts in his own way to the physical, hormonal, and psychological changes of puberty.

Some young men feel guilty or anxious about spontaneous erections, especially when they occur in nonsexual situations. Attempts to control spontaneous erections may cause problems with later sexual functioning. It is impossible for most young men to control these spontaneous erections anyway. Those who try will probably fail, causing even more guilt, fear, and anxiety.

You should also know that they are more noticeable to you than they are to others. They usually will go away within a few minutes if you can stop worrying about them. The erection may last longer if you become anxious when it appears; the penis will not get soft until the muscles at the base of the penis relax and the extra blood flows back into the bloodstream.

You can be certain that some of your friends are going through the same experience, although boys usually don't talk about this. Unfortunately, many young men fear that having an erection around other males, such as when showering after a gym class, is a sign of homosexuality. This is not the case.

What is a "wet dream"? Some of my friends claim they have had them. I'm 14 and haven't yet. Does that mean something is wrong with me?

No. By age 14, only about 25 percent of young men report having had an ejaculation, or "wet dream" during sleep (a "nocturnal emission" in scientific terms). Most, but not all, males have at least one such experience, usually during the period of pubertal changes. Some young men have them regularly.

Internal changes during puberty include growth of the prostate gland (which makes the fluid in the ejaculate) and development of the seminal vesicles and other organs through which the semen and sperm will travel. Sperm production in the testicles also begins.

Nocturnal emissions are completely normal and cannot be consciously controlled. They may occur either with or without explicitly sexual dreams in the same way adult males, and even fetuses and babies, experience erections during dream states, regardless of the dream content.

I'm glad you asked about "wet dreams." It is just as important for young men to be informed in advance about this body fluid as it is for young women to be informed before their first menstrual flow. There have been reports of boys who were terrified by the appearance of this unknown nonurine fluid and wrongly assumed it was a sign of illness or injury.

I am a male, will be 14 in a month, have never ejaculated, and I think there is a problem. Whenever I have a wet dream the substance that comes out is not like the milky-white semen I have heard about. It is a jellylike clear substance usually accompanied by urine. Should I tell my parents? See a doctor? Or just wait? I am worried.

Also, is it true you cannot urinate while having an erection? If not, is there something wrong with me if I do?

What you've probably experienced is an involuntary nocturnal emission. The color and appearance of the ejaculate can vary. It may be yellowish (although it is not urine) or more white. Some of the ejaculate may be clear, and that may be fluid from the Cowper's glands. The semen you describe sounds normal.

Despite what you have heard, it *is* possible to urinate with a partial erection. Only when an erection is at its fullest and just before ejaculation does the internal bladder sphincter (it's like a valve) close to prevent urine from flowing through the urethra. Once a man has awakened, walked to the bathroom, and thought about urinating, his arousal and erection have usually diminished enough for urination.

But by all means talk to your parents about this if you are comfortable doing so. They may have already guessed that you have reached this stage of development and feel awkward about being the first to raise the topic. It is also quite appropriate to ask your physician about this the next time you have an appointment. It is not likely that anything is wrong, but checking your progress through the various pubertal stages is considered an important aspect of health. Doctors are used to being asked about this.

SEXUAL RESPONSES IN
YOUNG WOMEN AND MEN

The genital touching that often begins in infancy and progresses for many children to masturbation and orgasm long before puberty becomes even more common during adolescence. And although many young boys and girls have engaged in childhood sex play, now they become more aware of (and concerned about) sexual feelings for specific individuals.

Sexual responses such as erections and vaginal lubrication become more obvious as adolescents reach adult hormonal levels. As young people move toward adulthood, their sexual interactions may bring new concerns, such as their attractiveness to others, responsibilities of unwanted parenthood, and fear of sexually transmitted diseases. They may also begin questioning their own sexual response patterns and their ability to have orgasms.

I am a 15-year-old girl and I started with my period last year and ever since then I have been having sex urges and I don't know what to do about them. They have been very strong at times and I even get a discharge when I dream about sex or while I'm having sex urges. How can I control these urges? And what do they have to do with periods? And why do I get a discharge during sexy dreams and sex urges?

Your "sex urges" are normal. You cannot control your sexual feelings (they're healthy and a sign you are growing up), but you are in charge of your own behavior. Unfortunately, many adolescents are not told that puberty involves psychological changes as well as physical changes. Along with menstruation, it is common to experience increased sexual desires, dreams, fantasies, and arousal. Learning how to manage these feelings and making decisions about your sexual behavior are part of the transition to adulthood.

The level of estrogen in young women increases dramatically during puberty, reaching an amount that is eight to ten times the level found in the body during childhood. This causes the normal discharge that gradually flows from the vagina as you describe. In fact, it's part of the natural cleansing process of the vagina. The increased estrogen, combined with other hormonal changes, also causes menstruation to begin. Sometimes lubrication results from a thought or fantasy that is related to sex, but at other times it is spontaneous and doesn't have any connection to sex.

For many young people, sexual feelings or urges can be quite strong. Some young men and women who do not understand that sexual feelings are a normal part of biological growth feel shame or fear. Each individual's unique set of personal values and circumstances will help determine how reproductive biology mixes with sexual feelings and behavior. With time and experience, most people become more comfortable with their sexual feelings and learn how to incorporate them into other aspects of their lives. Unfortunately, scientists know very little about how humans do this, so there are no data from which to offer you guidelines. Just be patient with yourself.

I am a 17-year-old girl who has sexual fantasies, often *very* sexy, but: 1) I don't have a boyfriend, and 2) I'm not sexually active and don't plan to be for a long time. Are there ways to satisfy my hunger? (I don't mean to sound sex-hungry.) Would masturbation help, or would you think I'm too young? Please tell me if this will make me sexually incompetent or if it will hurt me in any other way. I'm nervous.

Masturbation is common among young women, although not as many young women masturbate as do young men. A recent study of women ages 18 to 36 showed that 37 percent had masturbated during childhood and another study reported that more than 75 percent had masturbated during adolescence.

There is no scientific evidence that masturbation has any negative physical effects. In fact, there is some evidence that women who masturbate have fewer sexual problems later in life than women who do not. Many of the therapy programs that treat women who do not have orgasms are based on teaching them how to masturbate to orgasm.

Experts on adolescent behavior suggest that sexual fantasies may serve several purposes for young adults, including being a safe substitute for having sex with others. They also may provide an important type of mental "rehearsal" that makes later sexual encounters more comfortable or pleasurable.

It could be normal for a 15-year-old boy to masturbate, but is it normal to reach ejaculation? My brother is 15, and since last year or so he masturbates to ejaculate. He does this every day—twice a day many times. I am concerned about this and do not know if this is abnormal. Please explain this behavior.

You can stop worrying about your brother. The first ejaculation usually occurs between the ages of 11 and 17, but it can occur as young as eight, or not until the early twenties. The ability to ejaculate at your brother's age is well within the normal range.

Ejaculation is not a sign of illness. It normally accompanies orgasm (the spasmodic release of muscular tension) when a boy reaches the pubertal stage at which his hormones have caused the prostate gland and other internal organs to mature to the point when they produce semen. Boys who haven't yet reached that stage of puberty do not produce ejaculate when they masturbate to orgasm.

Research on boys 15 and younger who masturbate to orgasm report an average frequency of around three times a week—with some doing it less often, some more often, and some not at all. To masturbate once, or even twice, a day is not unusual.

I'm a 16-year-old male who has been masturbating an average of three times a week since I was 13 years old. Will this decrease my ability to maintain an erection or father children in future years?

There is no evidence that sexuality can be "used up" during youth, leaving a person unable to have erections or to produce sperm later in life. In fact, the opposite appears to be true. Studies of sexually active older people show that they were also likely to have been sexually active early in their lives.

My 18-year-old son has dated girls for several years. He is now in love and having sex with a beautiful girl. But recently he told me he had two homosexual experiences as a pre-teen and has been bothered by them ever since.

He is afraid of being gay because he enjoys looking at other men and has disturbing thoughts. I've told him I didn't think that what he experiences is unusual for heterosexuals, and he has had some counseling. Can you shed some light on this?

It is not unusual for men whose adult behavior is completely heterosexual to have had some same-sex experiences in their youth and/or to have erotic feelings and fantasies about other men throughout their lives. Experiencing this does not necessarily mean that a man is homosexual, nor does it predict his future behavior.

Continue your open and supportive communication with your son. It may be that he is seeking reassurance that you will still love him even if his attraction to other males continues. Encourage your son to continue counseling. Let him select a different counselor if he doesn't care for the current one.

FERTILITY AND ADOLESCENCE

At what age are adolescents fertile? Is it true that once a boy is able to ejaculate he can get a girl pregnant, and that when a girl gets her first period, she can become pregnant?

You are correct about some boys. Ejaculation of semen is a signal that the internal reproductive organs are reaching maturity, and sperm may be present in even the first ejaculation. For girls, however, the onset of fertility can be more difficult to establish. The thing that is important is not whether she's menstruating but whether she is releasing eggs. This is difficult to determine without sophisticated testing. Moreover, there are also cases of young women becoming pregnant *before* they have even had their first period. That's because in each cycle the egg is released (ovulation) before the uterus sheds its lining (menstrual flow). *(See Illustration 4 in Chapter 2.)*

Although many young women are not fully fertile in the first few years of menstruation (because they are not yet releasing eggs regularly), some are highly fertile quite early in life. The youngest mother on record is a girl aged five years six months who delivered a 6½-pound baby boy by caesarean section. This Peruvian girl had begun menstruating at age three and is one of the most well known examples of early puberty in females.

Contraception

The most effective method of preventing unwanted pregnancy is to abstain from any sexual activity in which semen is deposited inside the vagina or near the vaginal opening. Various types of sexual activities that do not include intercourse are discussed in Chapter 7. If you decide to have intercourse and you do not want a pregnancy, you must use an effective method of birth control each time you have intercourse. If you are not ready to learn about contraception and be responsible about using it *every time* you have intercourse you are *not* mature enough to be having sex. *(For a complete discussion of these issues, see Chapter 16.)*

Sexually active teenagers should also be concerned about sexually transmitted diseases and informed about how to prevent them. Read Chapter 19.

My daughter is 15 and has asked to be put on the Pill. She does not have a steady boyfriend, basically does group things with the girls. I feel I would be "damned if I do and damned if I don't" if I approve the Pill. Maybe you can answer some of my questions.

Am I right to assume that if she does not have a steady boyfriend then she will give herself to anyone anytime and get a bad reputation? If she starts on the Pill at 15, will she have problems later in life when she wants children?

You seem to believe that being on the Pill would encourage your daughter to begin having sex. This idea is based on the belief that the only reason teens don't have sex is fear of becoming pregnant and that once this constraint is removed they would be sexually indiscriminate. I found no research supporting this theory, though there is one study which evaluated the effect of making contraceptives (along with sex education) readily available to adolescents. This study indicated that teenage girls who had such access were more likely to *delay* first intercourse.

Has your daughter told you *why* she wants to take the Pill? Some young women have heard that taking oral contraceptives will reduce menstrual pain and the symptoms of premenstrual syndrome (PMS). This does work in some cases, but not in all. If your daughter's reasons are medical, consult a gynecologist. In general, there is not thought to be any reduction in future fertility for women who start taking oral contraceptives in their teens. However, experts do suggest that young women should be menstruating regularly for at least six months or a year before beginning the Pill.

Be grateful that your daughter feels comfortable talking to you about the Pill. The next step is to find out why she wants it. If it's for birth control, you need to clearly communicate your own attitudes and values on the issue. It would also be a good idea to describe other forms of contraception available, and discuss how well each prevents unwanted pregnancy and exposure to sexually transmitted disease *(see Chapter 16)*. So far, she's apparently acting very responsibly about these matters and you might want to compliment her for that since many adolescents and even some adult women are not so responsible.

During your discussion, you might want to point out that research has shown that the experience of first intercourse is likely to be more positive when it is in a mutually caring and loving relationship.

I am a 17-year-old girl who has not yet experienced sexual intercourse, but my boyfriend and I have discussed it. When, and if, we do make love, he has condoms. How reliable are they, and what special instructions should we know? If I were to use a spermicide with them, does it go inside me or on the condom?

I have also contemplated getting birth-control pills. Do I have to have an exam first? Do I have to get parental permission? If I lie and say I'm 18, is there any way they could check?

I'm pleased to hear that you and your boyfriend are giving serious and responsible thought to this important decision. Unfortunately, most young people begin having intercourse without first having thoughtful discussions and without using a contraceptive method.

Although I will briefly answer your specific questions, you should think about going to a family planning clinic. Call before you go and ask whether they require parental consent or parental notification before issuing prescription contraceptives. In some states parental involvement is required until age 18, and it is best to know this before you go. Even if a clinic can't legally prescribe the Pill to you in your state, go anyway. The clinic can provide information you need about other contraceptive methods and preventing sexually transmitted diseases. There are various forms of the contraceptive pill and it may be necessary to try several different types before finding the one that best suits your personal chemistry. This would be true whether you went to a clinic or a private physician. The staff can also help you make informed decisions that are best for you and your future.

Condoms can be very effective (as low as one pregnancy per 100 couples using them properly for a year) *if* they are used every time and according to the information in Chapter 16.

Using a spermicidal foam does increase the effectiveness of condoms. Moreover, using latex condoms and spermicides with an ingredient called nonoxynol-9 reduces the risk of many sexually transmitted diseases. *(See Chapter 19 for more information.)*

Getting a prescription for oral contraceptives does require a medical examination, but it is a good idea to have a pelvic exam before beginning intercourse anyway. It is important not to falsify or conceal information (such as your age), since recommendations about the safety of contraceptive methods depend on an accurate picture of your health and personal situation.

You and your boyfriend should seriously consider your long-term goals (both individually and as a couple) before having intercourse, because no contraceptive is 100 percent effective. In addition, the emotional implications of dealing with a relationship that includes intercourse can be even more difficult for adolescents than it is for adults. Perhaps you could think of waiting for intercourse in terms of "not yet" rather than "no." At some point in your lives intercourse will indeed occur when you and the relationship are really ready for it.

You should also consider trying to discuss this matter with your parents or other concerned adults if possible. The guilt of acting against parental values or wishes can turn out to be very stressful.

Further Readings

Bancroft, J., and Reinisch, J. M., eds. *Adolescence and Puberty.* New York: Oxford University Press, in press.
(A collection of academic and scientific papers on the biological, psychological, and social aspects of puberty.)

Bell, R., et al. *Changing Bodies, Changing Lives: A book for teens on sex and relationships.* New York: Vintage Books, 1988.
(Provides accurate and thorough information about sex for teenagers.)

Brooks-Gunn, J., and Peterson, A. C., eds. *Girls at Puberty: Biological and psychosocial perspectives.* New York: Plenum Press, 1983.
(A collection of scholarly writings addressing the biological, psychological, and social aspects of female puberty.)

Madaras, L. *The What's Happening to My Body? Book for Girls: A growing up guide for parents and daughters.* New York: Newmarket Press, 1983.
(An easy-to-read book with answers for parents dealing with the changes of adolescence.)

_____. *The What's Happening to My Body? Book for Boys: A growing up guide for parents and sons.* New York: Newmarket Press, 1984.
(An easy-to-read book with answers for parents dealing with the changes of adolescence.)

McCoy, K., and Wibblesman, C. *The New Teenage Body Book.* Los Angeles, CA: The Body Press, A Division of Price Stern Sloan, Inc., 1987.
(A book for teenagers with up-to-date information about the physical and emotional changes of puberty.)

13

Sex and the Disabled

The institute receives many letters from individuals who have a disability of some type, or from their family or friends. We have room for only a few examples, but hopefully they will convey the idea that even though these individuals may be "special" or "different" in some way, their concerns about sex and reproduction are much like everyone else's.

A mentally retarded boy who lives on our block seems to be getting closer to manhood. He's a nice enough kid but I worry about the obvious things. There are other children on this block and he plays very nicely with them. But shouldn't this boy be sent to a home now so he doesn't sexually molest other children?

No. Both evidence and common sense suggest that he should not be exiled to an institution or special home. For the moderately mentally handicapped, remaining at home and interacting with family and peers is best. (I assume the boy is only moderately handicapped because your letter mentioned he lived at home and played well with other children.)

The mentally handicapped are more likely to be *victims* than perpetrators of sexual exploitation. That's because many are trusting, readily affectionate, follow orders ("don't tell anyone"), and cannot evaluate the motivations of others. All these characteristics make the mentally handicapped more vulnerable to sexual molestation than their nonhandicapped peers.

Three percent of the population of the United States is classified as mentally handicapped, most only moderately so. Research on their sexual development and behavior has shown that they are similar to the nonhandicapped. It may be difficult for them, however, to handle the physical and emotional changes of puberty. Without special educational programs to help them learn about physical changes and our society's rules for handling sexual feelings, some *inadvertently* behave in socially unacceptable ways.

There are *no* scientific data to support the myth that the mentally handicapped have no control over their sexuality or have higher sex drives. These individuals sometimes do get into trouble because they have not been taught basic social rules, such as not touching their genitalia in public. If they do get into legal trouble, 95 percent of the time it is for nonviolent offenses, such as "indecent exposure."

It is difficult enough for parents to deal with the emerging sexuality of their normally intelligent children, but the parents of some handicapped children feel even more protective. If your neighbors have not yet done so, you could encourage them to enroll their child in a sex education program especially designed for the moderately mentally handicapped. Check with local social service agencies to see who provides services for the mentally handicapped in your area. It is routine for such centers to provide basic sex education to all of their clients, especially those approaching puberty. But you do not have to worry any more than you would with a nonhandicapped adolescent that this boy will be sexually aggressive.

I'm a college student. There is a blind girl who lives in my dorm and she keeps asking me questions about sex. I don't really mind discussing this with her except that I'm afraid I'll say the wrong thing and she'll get into trouble. For the life of me I can't figure out what to do.

The most important thing to remember is not that she's blind, but that she's a young woman with questions about sex. You should treat her questions as you would any other young woman in your dorm who is curious about sexuality.

Some research on the sexual behavior of visually impaired people has established that their feelings, attitudes, and behavior are similar to those of sighted people, with the exception of those whose blindness is caused by an illness that may also affect sexuality (such as diabetes).

Scientists once thought that children who were born visually impaired would have a higher level of gender confusion and, therefore, problems with sexual development. But studies have shown that by age three, visually impaired boys and girls are concentrating on activities typical of their sighted age and same-sex peers. They are also clear about their gender identity.

If problems are going to occur, it's most likely to be during adolescence. If they have difficulty learning to meet people and initiate friendships, most or all can be overcome by special education programs. In our culture, men are expected to initiate dating and sexual behavior. Some of the visually impaired men studied have said that they have ignored their sexual feelings and needs because of the extra effort involved in learning correct social skills and because they feared rejection. Some visually impaired women report that men hesitate to approach them because of their handicap, so they are faced with both the task of learning social skills and the risk of violating social conventions by initiating contact.

One way you can help your dormmate is to suggest she call the American Foundation for the Blind (1-800-232-5463, or in New York City 212-620-2000). They will send her a list of books about sex in Braille and on audiotape. If they list items she would like, they will send them to her.

Although many schools for the visually impaired also offer sex education, getting basic information about reproductive parts and functions is often not enough—as illustrated by one adolescent boy's comment after a limited sex education program: "I think I now know *what* a girl's breasts are, but I still don't know *where* they are." Therefore basic sex education should be augmented by being able to explore life-size dolls and to participate in discussions of sexual responsibilities and personal values.

I'm 18 years old and disabled from a car accident. It's very hard for me to have a relationship with a girl. As a result, I masturbate a lot. It relieves tension, makes me feel like a man, and takes some of the frustration out of life.

The thing I have to know is, is this bad for me? Even before the accident I masturbated some and was pretty sure that other boys my age did, too. Just give me the facts about this. I don't want to see a sex therapist.

You're absolutely correct in thinking that other boys and men—even those who are not disabled and are married and regularly active with a partner— masturbate. In fact, research shows that nearly all men masturbate to orgasm, and that no physical harm results from this behavior.

Most physical disabilities don't reduce interest in sex or the capacity for sexual functioning, even though a few disabilities may make intercourse difficult or impossible. Many other handicapped people also report problems with finding sexual partners. For these reasons, masturbation to orgasm is frequently the most common sexual activity for disabled individuals. Remember, it's normal for your sex life to continue, even if some adjustments must be made.

You may be surprised to learn that your physician, physical therapist, or other health care professionals wouldn't mind discussing this topic with you. In fact, many professionals who work with the physically disabled have had special training in this area. You might also wish to ask another male patient how he copes with his disability and his sexuality. Many hospitals and clinics have sex education classes for physically disabled patients. Ask your physician if these classes are offered near you.

Another source of information in the United States includes regional Independent Living Centers. For the one nearest you, write Research and Training Center in Independent Living, University of Kansas, 3111 Haworth Hall, Lawrence, KS 60045. Some cities and states also have special services. For example, the Information Center for Individuals with Disabilities (20 Park Plaza, Room 330, Boston, MA 02116) offers a pen-pal program so that disabled persons can make friends with other disabled persons.

My 12-year-old granddaughter has cerebral palsy. She cannot walk or talk, plus she is getting somewhat spastic. She requires almost total care. However, she is a bright little girl and very much aware of the world around her.

We're concerned about what to do when she starts her period. We are afraid she will not understand what it is about and have a hard time coping with the discharge and discomfort. We worry about her personal hygiene, especially at school. Plus, she still wets the bed at night and that would add to the problem.

For some time we have discussed her having a hysterectomy, but this is not

an easy solution to even think about. What are the alternatives to solve this problem?

Write to the United Cerebral Palsy Association, Program Department, Suite 1112, 1522 K Street N.W., Washington, DC 20005, Attention: Fran Smith, Assistant to the Director. They will be happy to send you pamphlets about sexual or personal hygiene concerns. If you have specific questions not answered by the pamphlets, call their public relations office at 1-800-USA-5UCP.

The effects of cerebral palsy vary so enormously from one person to the next that it is difficult to make statements about what might be best for your granddaughter. However, hysterectomy (surgical removal of the uterus), is *not* usually recommended as the best way of handling a girl's pubertal maturation. Moreover, the disabled person herself must be actively involved in any irreversible decision about her own body.

There are training programs designed to teach her how to manage menstrual flow. Which type of training is most appropriate depends more on what your granddaughter can do than on what she cannot. You've said she's bright and that she goes to school, so it should not be any more difficult for her to understand the concept of menstruation than it is for a nondisabled girl. Even if she also has a degree of mental handicap or learning disability—and most people with cerebral palsy do not—much can be done to prepare her for adolescent changes. But the key, as for all girls, is for her to know about menstruation, what to expect, and what to do *before* her first flow appears.

She needs to know that she is not sick and has not injured herself. She should understand that menstrual flow is one normal part of any woman's life, that all young women do this at puberty, and that it continues on a regular basis. She also needs to know there will be other changes in her body, such as breast development and pubic hair growth.

It may be that she's already aware of much of this information from observing her mother or other women or from overhearing comments among other girls at school. This is usually a hot topic among adolescents, whether or not they are disabled.

How to cope with menstrual flow may depend on her degree of motor control, but there are several training programs designed for professionals and/or parents to teach their students or children how to do this. It is, however, crucial that she be taught about menstrual flow *before* it appears and frightens her.

A study of one menstrual-hygiene education program for developmentally disabled adolescent girls reported a high success rate. In this study the girls had IQs ranging from 23 to 70, so if your granddaughter's IQ is at the high end of this range or higher, she should have no difficulty learning how to cope with menstruation. This program taught that when you grow up, "red stuff" will come out of the body between your legs. A doll filled with red food coloring was used to illustrate this, and the girls were taught that the "red stuff" should go on a sanitary napkin, not on their panties. Then the young women practiced wearing, changing, and properly disposing of sanitary napkins (the kind held inside the panties by adhesive strips). This program was begun well before first menstruation and the girls practiced once a month or so until they had their first menstrual flows. The mothers of these young women reported that about half remembered what to do as soon as the first menstrual flow appeared, and that nearly all of the rest needed only a few reminders of what to do. The mothers reportedly were delighted by the training program and said it reduced their fears of how to manage menstruation. They were as proud of their daughters' responsible behavior as were the young women themselves.

My son has some cerebral palsy and speech and hearing problems, but still is normal in so many ways. He needs some release from his sexual desires, and I do not know how to handle this.

Call or write the United Cerebral Palsy Association (see preceding answer), or write the Sex Information and Education Council of the United States (SIECUS, 33 Washington Place, Fifth Floor, New York, NY 10003). Both groups supply information and educational material about cerebral palsy and sexuality. Also write the Coalition on Sexuality and Disability (122 E. 23rd Street, New York, NY 10010); they sponsor training programs in sexuality for professionals who work with the disabled and could refer you to someone near your home with whom you can talk.

Here is another suggestion: Do you know any adult males with cerebral palsy who might be willing to talk to your son about how they manage sexually? Many communities sponsor group discussions in which people with disabilities can meet and talk with one another about how to deal with sexuality and other areas of daily living.

The effects of cerebral palsy vary enormously from one person to the next, so it is impossible for me to guess the extent of your son's disabilities. In general, however, cerebral palsy does not impair sexual interest, orgasm, or fertility. However, the type or degree of muscle spasticity or involuntary body movement may limit some sexual activities or rule out some positions.

You do not mention your son's age, but if he is going through puberty, it is especially important that you seek ways to provide him with information on sex. Talking about sex is difficult for most parents, not just for those with disabled children, so don't be embarrassed to seek help and advice—other parents do, and that's what these groups are used to doing. It will be easy to ask them for help.

Disabled children do need special attention in getting sexual information, especially if they are excluded from the usual sources of such learning, such as playing with peers. Moreover, as adolescents, they may not get the opportunities others do to learn and practice the social skills involved in meeting and dating potential partners.

14

Unfinished Development and Sexual Mismatches

The process of establishing a clear chromosomal, gonadal, or hormonal human sex pattern is sometimes not completed. External genitals may not look either completely male or female, and what is inside the body may not match what is outside. Some of these problems of biological development are obvious at birth; others are not noticeable until puberty or even later (as when an individual tries to become a parent but cannot).

There are other completely different types of mismatches, biological and psychological. Sometimes a person is completely male or female in all biological and physical respects but psychologically *feels* that he or she is of the other sex. Among the most common types of unfinished biological development are problems with the genitals. Especially in the male, the complex process which causes the testicles to move down from the abdomen into the scrotum and the penis shaft to fuse around the urethra *(see Illustration 24 in Chapter 10)* may not be finished by birth. Similar processes that develop the male or female internal reproductive organs can also go wrong, leading to either missing or duplicated tubes, ducts, and organs.

PROBLEMS WITH EXTERNAL SEX ORGANS

Problems with external genitals are usually noticed at birth or shortly thereafter. The exact cause and incidence of these congenital problems (present from birth) are not yet known.

Our 15-month-old son was diagnosed as having cryptorchidism (an undescended testis). Our pediatrician referred us to a urologist, who after two visits suggested an operation to bring down the left testis.
Is surgery necessary? What are the chances of it descending on its own?

Around 3 percent of full-term baby boys and 30 percent of premature boys are born with at least one testicle that has not completed its descent from the abdomen (where the testes are formed during fetal development) to the scrotum *(see Illustration 23 in Chapter 10).*

Medical thinking about proper treatment for undescended testicles has changed over the years. It used to be thought that treatment should be delayed until after puberty in the hope that the increased hormones at puberty would cause the undescended testicle (or testicles) to move down into the scrotum without medical intervention.

Research has now established, however, that changes in the tissue of undescended testicles can be seen through powerful new microscopes by the age of one year and that in only a very few cases does a testicle descend on its own after the first year of life. These changes can later lead to problems with sperm production and greatly increase a male's risk of testicular cancer.

Current recommendations are that diagnosis and plans for treatment of cryptorchidism begin soon after birth so undescended testicles are exposed to the higher heat of the abdomen for the shortest possible time. Choosing among available treatment plans depends to a large extent on the exact location of the testicle. Pinpointing this requires careful diagnosis and may require repeated skilled examinations. Treatment involves use of hormonal drugs to stimulate the testicle to complete the process of descending into the scrotum by itself, surgery to lower it into the scrotum, or a combination of both.

Surgery for your son has already been recommended, so it's time to seek a second opinion. Because several of the newest treatment plans involve use of hormones and careful monitoring of dose-related responses, find a pediatric endocrinologist *(see Appendix).* This professional will know about experienced surgeons if hormone therapy is not effective or appropriate.

Another reason for seeing a specialist is that most emphasize the crucial need for education and counseling of both parents and child. You need to be adequately informed about the risks involved in each proposed treatment and the necessity of long-term follow-up. Your child has probably noticed your concerns already, and his genitals have been the object of close scrutiny; therefore he needs to be reassured about the status of his body. Your son will also need to be taught how to examine his testicles carefully (as all adolescent boys and adult males should) and how to respond to any future problems.

Start seeking a qualified physician now. The process can be time-consuming but should not be delayed. Having normal-looking genitals appears to be an important factor in a boy's early development of a good self-image. Also,the risks of later infertility and testicular cancer may be increased the longer a testicle is exposed to the higher temperature of the body rather than that of the cooler scrotum.

My year-old son was born with a torsioned (twisted) testicle which has slowly disappeared. I wasn't too concerned because the doctors assured me that his remaining testicle would produce sufficient hormones for him to be a normal male.

Now his one normal testicle has suddenly disappeared. The doctors are perplexed; they don't know what happened to it. When he reaches 20 months of age they're going to operate to see if they can find the normal testicle and remove any of the undissolved torsioned testicle.

Have you ever heard of testicles disappearing? Is there any hope of him being a normal male? Will he have to take hormones all his life?

Consult a pediatric endocrinologist right now for a second opinion on your son's condition—this problem calls for a specialist. With expert care and timely surgery, treatment will most likely preserve his ability to make enough testosterone and sperm for him to develop normally and father children. It is not unusual between birth and puberty for a testicle to move out of the scrotum, back up into the abdomen, and be difficult for a physician to detect. In fact, a genital examination itself can cause the testicle to retract.

Experts recommend that the child be completely relaxed and warm (even placed in a warm bath if necessary) when the physician tries to find the testicle. If the tissue of the scrotum appears normal and if a testicle can be felt and then pushed into the scrotum, surgery is sometimes not necessary. For some boys, it is normal for the testicle to periodically move into and out of the scrotum until puberty. If, however, a testicle cannot be found, tests or surgery may be needed to locate it. Surgery and/or hormonal treatments may also be required if the testicle cannot be pushed into the scrotum.

Your son will most likely need surgery to remove any tissue that might be remaining from the first testicle that disappeared (the torsioned testicle), since that tissue is at high risk for developing disease. You should also ask the doctors about putting a testicle-shaped implant into the scrotum to replace the torsioned testicle. These implants come in several sizes and are replaced when necessary to match the growth of the rest of his body. Thus he can look like other boys now and later like other men, which is important to his feelings of self-esteem.

When I was 5 years old, I had an operation for an undescended testicle. Now I'm 16 and the only thing the operation did was to leave me with a scar. I would like to know three things:
   1. Am I going to be just as much of a man as my friends? (I still don't shave.)
   2. Is this going to injure my ability to have sex?
   3. Will it be hard for me to become a father?

It is hard to tell from your letter whether the operation was successful (the testicle was lowered into your scrotum) or if it remains inside your abdomen or was removed. You only need one testicle in your scrotum for your pubertal development, sexual functioning, and ability to father children to be normal. But why worry when you can allay your fears by being checked by a specialist?

If the testicle is still up inside your body, it is very important to see a specialist as soon as possible. The risk of testicular cancer and possible fertility problems are increased the longer the testicle remains in the abdomen. For this reason, some specialists recommend removal of the undescended testicle as a protective measure.

Be assured that, done properly, examination or even surgical removal of the undescended testicle will not harm the other testicle, the penis, or any other part of the reproductive or hormonal system. Consider having an artificial testicle-shaped implant inserted into your scrotum so you look just like other men.

One healthy testicle can produce sufficient male hormones to trigger normal pubertal development and result in all the usual male characteristics such as facial hair and normal sexual functioning. Sperm production from one testicle is also sufficient to become a father. *(See Chapter 12 for normal differences in the timing of pubertal development.)*

From what I've been told, I have a mild form of hypospadias. There's an opening below the head of my penis, out of which the fluids flow. So far, this has not been a problem, but I'm curious about how this will affect my sexual performance and whether I can inseminate a woman. Is surgery required?

Hypospadias is a condition in which the urethra (the tube that carries urine and semen through the penis) does not fuse together completely during fetal development *(see Illustration 24 in Chapter 10)*. This opening then occurs somewhere along the penile shaft rather than at the tip. Some degree of hypospadias is found in as many as one out of every 125 live male births in some population samples studied, and may also involve a condition called chordee (curvature of the penis, caused by the urethra being shorter than the other penile structures). No one is yet certain why these conditions occur.

Hypospadias does not necessarily mean that there are problems with any of the other genital or reproductive organs, so having hypospadias does not necessarily mean that there are also problems with your sperm or your testicles or other reproductive organs. A semen analysis can quickly determine whether your sperm are healthy.

In some cases surgical repairs when performed by a surgeon trained and experienced in this procedure may be successful at creating an opening at the tip of the penis that functions normally for urination, sex, and reproduction. One study of 34 men who had such surgery in childhood found no differences in sexual adjustment or fertility between those men and men born with the opening at the tip. The researchers did note, however, that the hypospadiac men began sexual activity at a later age and had fewer sexual partners than the other group of men. Speculation was that these men were concerned about how potential partners might react to the appearance of their genitals.

In your case, surgery would not be necessary for full fertility since semen will be deposited deep enough in a vagina. In fact, unless the appearance of your penis bothers you greatly, some experts recommend against surgery because of an increased risk of later urinary-tract infections.

During a trivia game I had the question "What is wrong with a man who has diphallasparatus?" The correct answer was given as "He was born with two penises." Is that possible? What would cause it?

Diphallia or penis duplication is extremely rare. The earliest medical description of such a case occurred in 1609 and fewer than 80 cases have been reported since then. No one knows why such physical abnormalities occur, but it's likely that between eight and 12 weeks of fetal life (when the external genitals of male babies develop) some type of disruption occurs in the normal fusing of the structures that will become the penis *(see Illustration 24 in Chapter 10)*.

Fortunately, the prognosis is now excellent for most types of genital defects. Many can be surgically corrected early in the baby's life. Each such defect, however, requires individualized assessment and treatment by a physician who specializes in reconstructive genital surgery. It is also important to evaluate whether there are problems with the structure of the internal reproductive organs.

PROBLEMS WITH INTERNAL SEX ORGANS

Internal sex organs can be incompletely developed or incorrectly formed even when everything else about a person is fine. It's usually a case of the normal process of development being unfinished—for some reason, normal development stopped somewhere along the way.

Recently my 19-year-old daughter was diagnosed as having a septum in her vagina. Our gynecologist found a double vagina and a double cervix. He doesn't know if there are any other problems in her reproductive system.

So far, her only problem is that she can't use tampons because it's painful and the flow comes out of the unblocked side anyway.

We have consulted two gynecologists and both feel she should wait to correct this problem until she's married and ready to have children. Both also assure us this is not uncommon, that many women have it, and it's not abnormal.

How common is this? Why do they want to wait so long for surgery? My daughter hopes to marry after college and is already worried about getting pregnant, carrying a baby, and having a normal delivery. The doctors assure her this is all possible even without surgery.

Technically, the doctors appear to have given you and your daughter accurate information. Having a septate vagina (a vagina divided lengthwise by a membrane) with a cervix at the end of each vagina is not rare. Articles about how to manage this problem state that there often are no problems with pregnancy and delivery even without corrective surgery.

No research on the psychological aspects of this particular condition or on how psychosocial development might be affected appears to have been done. People who believe that their bodies are different or abnormal, however, can have severe difficulty developing a healthy body image and in forming intimate relationships.

For that reason it may be important for you to help your daughter find a professional who can give her both accurate medical information and psychological support. Even though surgery may not actually be required for your daughter to conceive and give birth, there may be good reasons for considering corrective surgery now. In some cases, the vagina is too small for comfortable intercourse until the membrane is removed. She should be sure to tell the specialist that she finds wearing tampons painful.

Surgery will also depend on the severity of any additional internal problems found (such as the shape of her uterus). If surgery is necessary or desirable, discuss the best timing. Any postoperative complications or worries about surgery could add to the usual stresses of sexual functioning and marital adjustment during the difficult first year after the wedding.

Locate a fertility expert *(see Chapter 15)* who is familiar with diagnostic examination to assess the status of her reproductive tract. This professional will also be able to recommend the most highly trained and skillful surgeon in your area who is experienced with this particular type of reconstructive surgery.

CHROMOSOMAL DISORDERS

Most humans have forty-six chromosomes, two of which are the sex chromosomes (46XX is the normal female pattern and 46XY is the normal male pattern). Sometimes, however, individuals are born with extra or missing sex chromosomes, and these variations can affect that person's sexual and reproductive life. Researchers have identified more than seventy types of abnormalities of the sex chromosomes, but examples of only the most common ones appear here.

We just found out that our 24-year-old son was born with 47 chromosomes and that this is called Klinefelter's syndrome. How does something like this occur? Do you know of any organization for people afflicted with this problem?

No one yet knows exactly what causes a person's cells to carry more than the ordinary number of chromosomes. The only current explanation is that something happens shortly after conception, when the fertilized egg (zygote) begins the complex process of dividing and an extra chromosome is somehow added to the basic make-up of the developing embryo. In the case of Klinefelter's syndrome, there is an extra X sex chromosome, so the man has a 47XXY pattern instead of the usual 46XY. Klinefelter's syndrome is not thought to be caused by a defect in either the mother or the father, nor does it appear to run in families.

Researchers estimate that one in every 400 to 700 males has some degree of Klinefelter's syndrome—an amazingly high incidence of a potentially serious problem about which few people have ever heard. One explanation may be that Klinefelter's syndrome is not usually suspected unless a boy's testicles do not enlarge during puberty or until an adult male undergoes a detailed fertility evaluation (including chromosome studies) to find out why he has been unable to father a child. Accurate diagnosis of Klinefelter's syndrome is done by reading a buccal smear (a scraping of a few cells from the mouth, inside the cheek) or by karyotyping done from a blood sample (staining and photographing the chromosome patterns inside several cells).

Many of these men appear normal in all respects, although they may produce less testosterone than other men, and most do not produce sperm. In cases where Klinefelter's has a pronounced effect on appearance (small testicles, growth of breast tissue, and sparse beard growth), there can be problems with psychosexual development at puberty as the young man realizes he no longer looks like his friends. Testosterone injections can help masculinize appearance, increase sexual interest, and improve erection problems but will not change the fact that the testicles do not produce sperm. So if your son wants to have a family, it will most likely be by donor insemination, adoption, or by marrying a woman who already has children.

Most medical schools have a department of endocrinology. Call the one nearest you and ask for an appointment to speak with someone about Klinefelter's syndrome. That person will have names of counselors or therapists with experience in working with families who have had to deal with similar problems.

We have read about Klinefelter's syndrome, a chromosomal problem in boys. Our 15-year-old daughter is undergoing tests for Turner's syndrome. We've found little written about it. Could you give us more information?

Turner's syndrome was first described in 1938, but its underlying chromosomal basis was not understood until 1959, when modern techniques of observing and counting human chromosomes became available.

The genetically normal human female has the 46XX chromosomal pattern; the Turner's-syndrome female has only 45 chromosomes. The missing chromosome is one of the X sex chromosomes (and is written as 45X or 46XO); in some cases, a second sex chromosome exists, but it is not complete or is altered in some way.

Turner's syndrome occurs in one out of every 2500 females. No one knows why this happens in the early stages of embryonic development, but (like Klinefelter's syndrome, discussed above) it is not thought to be linked to anything transmitted by or done by the parents. Many females born with Turner's syndrome look fine at birth but lack ovaries (or have only streaks of ovarian tissue) and therefore rarely produce eggs or female hormones. Some have defects of the heart, kidneys, or ears that bring them to medical attention at birth or during early childhood, but most cases are not detected until these girls fail to show breast development and do not begin to menstruate at puberty. Many, but not all, are short-statured.

Women with Turner's syndrome must take hormones to develop breasts and to menstruate. With appropriate medical and psychological support, most will appear normal physically, can enjoy a normal sex life, and have a family by adoption or marrying a man who already has children.

When informed that a lack of female hormones is involved, many parents conclude that their Turner's-syndrome daughter will be decidedly unfeminine. The opposite is true. These women demonstrate high levels of traditionally feminine behavior and maternal interest from early childhood. Nor is a conflict of gender identity or role involved— these women are certain in their minds that they are females and act feminine. Most are even more interested than genetically normal girls in appearance factors such as concern with hair styles and less interested in physical or outdoor activities, roughhousing, or other tomboyish behavior.

You didn't mention where your daughter is being examined. Even though treatment of the condition can be carried out by most general physicians, it is important to first have an evaluation at a medical center that includes pediatric endocrinologists and psychologists or psychiatrists experienced in helping and supporting women with Turner's syndrome and their families.

There may be some difficult decisions to make. For example, some clinicians recommend waiting until a young woman has reached her maximum height before starting female hormone therapy (estrogen and progestin taken cyclically). This waiting period, however, occurs when a girl faces the greatest peer pressure for being "different" (because she has no breast development or pubic hair and doesn't menstruate), so she may need counseling from a professional experienced in working with such concerns.

For more information write to Turner's Syndrome Society, York University, Administrative Studies Building #006, 4700 Keele Street, Downsview, Ontario M3J 1P3, Canada. They also have branches in ten states in the U.S.

A number of years ago, when I was working on my master's degree, I attended a class on human sexuality. One topic I found interesting was about chromosome patterns found in the Speck syndrome.

Would you explain the Speck syndrome? It was named for the man who murdered a number of nurses and had the XYY pattern. I've tried to find out more about this but have been unable to find any information.

Perhaps the reason you had trouble finding information about the "Speck syndrome" is that Richard Speck (who was convicted of murdering eight nurses) was tested and found to have a normal XY chromosome pattern. The accepted label in textbooks or scientific publications of the condition you're interested in is the XYY syndrome or 47XYY pattern.

As you may recall, interest in this chromosomal pattern was based on the idea that certain chromosome patterns are linked to particular behaviors, especially behaviors dangerous to society. The speculation was that having an extra Y chromosome indicated a greater tendency toward aggressive, even violent, behavior. Because the Y chromosome is the one that only males have, it therefore was misunderstood to be the genetic material that accounts for *all* masculine traits. Thus, having two Y chromosomes was wrongly suspected to make a man extra-masculine, but in some type of negative way.

Later research has found more similarities than differences between men with the 46XY (normal) pattern and the 47XYY pattern and did not find XYY men more physically aggressive or violent. The only tentative conclusion about behavior that could be drawn related to the extra Y chromosome was that perhaps some of these individuals might have difficulty with impulse control.

The 47XYY pattern occurs in approximately one out of every 500 to 1000 males. They have fewer sexual and reproductive problems than men with Klinefelter's syndrome, so they are probably rarely brought to the attention of the medical community. Although some have malformation of the testicles and low sperm production, many are fertile and their children have normal chromosome patterns. The only other physical finding is that they may be taller than average.

GONADAL AND HORMONAL DISORDERS

One important role of the gonads is to produce the hormones that govern physical appearance. Testicles make testosterone, which stimulates facial hair and a deep voice, for example, and ovaries produce the estrogen that stimulates breast development.

Instead of having two testicles (males) or two ovaries (females), some extremely rare individuals are born with one testicle and one ovary or have two matching gonads with both including a mixture of testicular and ovarian tissue.

There may be both Fallopian tubes (females) and vas deferens (males), or one of each on opposite sides of the reproductive tract, but there is usually a uterus. The chromosomal pattern is most often 46XX (the normal female pattern); the external genitals may look either male or female, but most often are not clearly one or the other.

This condition is called *true hermaphroditism* and is very rare. Most of these few individuals are not fertile (producing neither eggs nor sperm), although there has been one documented case of a child being born to a true hermaphrodite.

More common gonadal disorders do occur and these are grouped together under the term *pseudohermaphroditism*. A pseudohermaphrodite can be either a chromosomal 46XX female with ovaries, Fallopian tubes, and a uterus but who has male-appearing genitals, or a chromosomal 46XY male with testicles, vas deferens, and other ducts of the male reproductive tract but who has genitals that look female.

Although we don't know exactly why such disorders occur, remember that we all start out with gonads that have the potential to become either testicles or ovaries and two sets of ducts that can develop into either the male or female reproductive tract, depending on the hormones present during fetal development. It is the hormones produced by the gonads that determine the way in which the internal reproductive organs and external genitals will develop. In male and female pseudohermaphrodites, mixed hormonal messages sent or received before birth result in mixtures of male and female organs and genitals.

Unless the genitals of a newborn are noticeably unusual, physicians often simply declare the baby to be "boy" or "girl" without further investigation or tests. The result is that biological discrepancies between the gonads and genitals often aren't noticed until puberty, when a girl's menstruation fails to occur or her clitoris enlarges to look more like a penis, or when the body of a boy fails to masculinize or begins to develop feminine characteristics like breasts.

However, if physicians or parents suspect something is wrong with a newborn's genitals in the first few months, thorough testing followed by a combination of reconstructive surgery and later treatment with appropriate hormones permits the child to be assigned or reassigned to whichever sex promises the best chance for normal psychological and reproductive development.

The most common type of female pseudohermaphroditism is the adrenogenital syndrome, in which the chromosomal pattern is normal (46XX) and all internal structures are female but the genitals look more or less male. Early surgery and hormonal treatment to stop the production of male hormones from the adrenal glands (located atop the kidneys) result in a girl who appears normal in all respects and can have children.

The most common type of male pseudohermaphrodites have the normal (46XY) chromosomal pattern and have testicles, but their genitals often look completely female (unless one or both testicles have descended into the labia, a characteristic an observant physician would notice). In this condition, called androgen insensitivity syndrome, or testicular feminization syndrome, the testicles produce testosterone but the cells of the body cannot respond. These individuals have a clitoris, labia, and the lower portion of a vagina but have no upper vagina or uterus. They also lack the male reproductive ducts. When this condition is diagnosed, the testicles are removed and at puberty estrogen treatment will result in the development of breasts and a feminine contour. These women are very feminine in both behavior and interests and often choose to have children through adoption.

In these and most other types of sexual physical-development problems, the treatment goal is to use surgery and/or hormones at the appropriate stages of life to make the body look like one sex or the other. If the problem is not diagnosed until the child is older, treatment is designed to match the person's physical appearance with his or her already-established male or female gender identity/role.

Some of these disorders are genetic and can be inherited, although the vast majority of genital or hormonal abnormalities are the result of causes other than heredity. One example of a nongenetic cause occurs when the developing fetus is exposed to hormones or other drugs taken by the mother during pregnancy. The result can be changes in the external genitals, or more often just subtle behavioral changes such as increased assertive behavior.

None of these conditions is common, even though we do not know exactly how many occur—and individuals born with unusual chromosome patterns, gonadal disorders, or ambiguous genitalia can develop appropriately as masculine or feminine with proper psychological support and hormonal and surgical treatment. They can also fall in love and become responsible spouses and parents.

I am a farm girl. I'm 20 years old, now living in a big city and working in a restaurant. There are lots of nice girls working there. I am sort of bewildered about sexes. A girl working at this restaurant would always drive me home. I asked her to my apartment when the weather was bad. She is nice and after that evening she said she would stay and share the rent and so on.

We have shared the apartment a month now. I'm not much of a run around nor is she. About two Sundays ago in the afternoon she told me she was a hermaphrodite. I didn't know what she meant so she showed me her pubic area. I was quite surprised. I never knew such a thing could happen to a girl. I promised her I would never tell on her to other girls that work at the restaurant.

Can a hermaphrodite get a girl pregnant? I'm asking because I saw she had testicles inside those lip rolls we girls have. The penis is very small. She only gets a faint erection. And she has a large phallus, or head of the glans. She feels bad that she's in this condition. But I told her she was healthy otherwise. How could such a thing happen? Is it heredity?

The idea that only two clearly distinctive sexes exist doesn't hold for a significant number of people. Your roommate is apparently among them, although she's probably not a true hermaphrodite. It is more likely that she has either "adrenogenital syndrome" or the condition called "androgen insensitivity syndrome."

Encourage your friend to call the department of endocrinology or genetics at the nearest medical school and ask for an appointment with someone familiar with diagnosing developmental sexual disorders. Once her chromosomal pattern, gonadal sex, hormone levels, and the status of internal organs are established, hormonal treatment and reconstructive surgery can help make her external appearance match her female psychological gender identity and feminine role. If adrenogenital syndrome is found, she may be fertile as a female and able to become pregnant and bear children.

Whatever her physical status is found to be, the most important aspect of her life now is how she feels about herself (from what you describe she clearly thinks of herself as female) and how others react to her (you refer to her as a female). This concept of gender identity/role is more important and permanent than what a person's genitals look like. It is for this reason that after twelve to eighteen months of age (the age at which a person's gender identity as either male or female is thought to be set for life) corrective surgery and hormone treatments are used to "match" physical appearance with a person's psychological sense of self and not with their chromosomes or gonads.

It sounds as if you've been a supportive friend. Keep up the good work by encouraging your roommate to get appropriate medical attention. She should not view herself as so different that she is condemned to a life of secrecy. Her situation should be seen as a physical condition that can be successfully treated.

TRANSEXUALISM

For most people the psychological concept of being either a male or a female is permanently fixed by the age of twelve to eighteen months. The person's gender identity and, as they mature, their masculine or feminine gender role and behavior matches their biological sex. For some, however, the sex they identify with psychologically (*feel* that they are) does not match their chromosome pattern, gonads, hormone levels, internal sex organs, or genitals—even when all of these biological characteristics are perfectly matched.

True transexuals honestly feel that they are trapped in the wrong body, so when they wear clothing or hair styles of the opposite sex it is an expression of what they feel is their true gender. Unlike the vast majority of transvestites discussed in Chapter 7, transexuals are usually no more aroused by wearing feminine clothing than are biological females who wear a dress or biological males who put on three-piece suits.

Another difference between transexuals and transvestites is that transexuals are literally offended by their existing bodies and want them changed, no matter the pain or expense. Transvestites are not interested in getting rid of their penises.

Is it possible for a person to go through life thinking he or she is of one sex but, in fact, being another? Where can such a person go to be tested without going through a family doctor?

Since a person's sex is usually "assigned" at birth based on how the external genitals look, this situation can occasionally occur. When a baby's genitalia do not clearly resemble those of either sex, chromosomal tests and investigation of internal organs, such as the uterus or vas deferens, are done to determine the biological sex and to see if there are any problems such as those discussed above. If you think something is wrong physically with your body, consult an endocrinologist or other specialist (*see Appendix*).

There are individuals with completely normal bodies who are totally convinced they are the opposite sex. If you think this is what is going on, consult a specialist in gender identity. Call the nearest medical school, ask for the department of endocrinology, and say that you need to have an appointment with the staff member most familiar with problems of sex assignment and gender identity.

If I wanted a sex change operation, would I have to speak with a psychiatrist first? Couldn't I just go ahead and do it? I don't want to spend the money or time on a shrink.

You most definitely will have to be evaluated by one or more psychiatrists, plus several other types of specialists, before being accepted by a reputable center for changing from one sex to the other. An initial evaluation will also include thorough medical tests to determine your chromosomal and hormonal status as well as your general health. Many clinics also want to interview family members, sexual partners, and friends if they are willing.

If you are accepted into a transexual program, the first step is usually to live and work successfully as a member of the opposite sex for one year, then to continue a successful life style while being on hormone therapy for another year—all before ever beginning the more irreversible surgical alterations of the reproductive organs and body. The full procedure varies, depending on the clinic, and takes several years, but has been found to produce the best overall results.

Changing one's physical sex is a complicated process. If you decide to pursue this, you must be prepared to spend a great deal of time (and perhaps money) working with specialists.

Most transexual programs are located at medical schools or large hospitals. Call the department of endocrinology and ask if they treat transexuals or if they can tell you the nearest place that does.

If I have a sex change operation from woman to man, can they make my face look like anyone I want? And, if I didn't get face surgery, how long would I be in the hospital?

Facial surgery is not a standard step in transexual treatment. The primary alteration in facial appearance for a female-to-male transexual is the growth of male-pattern facial hair, which results from being treated with testosterone for several months.

Depending upon which surgical steps you qualify for and elect to have, you will be in and out of the hospital several times. For example, the first surgical step is to flatten the breasts and reposition the nipples. The patient is in the hospital about three days, but must avoid lifting or doing manual labor for two to three months. This usually is not done until after the female has successfully lived as a man for at least one full year and has taken male hormones, which change body contours, grow facial hair, lower the voice, and enlarge the clitoris.

A second surgery is done weeks or months later to remove the uterus, ovaries, and Fallopian tubes; this requires another stay of several days, plus weeks of healing. No one has yet devised a fully adequate way of creating a functional penis, but some patients choose to have a series of operations that create a penislike flap of skin from an area of the lower abdomen, fuse the labia into a simulated scrotum, and insert artificial testicles. This procedure has a high rate of complications from infection, and there is little or no feeling in the penis. But after surgery, you can usually stand up to urinate like a man.

Clinical studies have shown that many female-to-male transexuals have little difficulty finding a woman partner, successfully marrying, and raising an adopted or donor-inseminated family without any genital surgery.

I'm a man trapped in a woman's body. Even though I've never had a regular period, usually only three a year, I'd like to stop having any at all. A friend of mine says this can be done by psychological means, that if a person doesn't feel like a real woman, it's possible to not have any periods. Is this true?

It is possible for psychological factors to delay or disrupt menstrual cycles, but this is generally true only in the case of strong feelings, such as extreme anxiety or fear, or if severe stress is prolonged over a period of time (one example is imprisonment in a concentration camp).

Because I assume you do have a uterus, ovaries, and a female hormonal system, it is unlikely that your occasional menstrual flows will stop without medical treatment until you reach natural menopause, regardless of how strongly you feel about being a male or how often you wish that you didn't have periods.

You should not believe that being able to psychologically suppress menstrual flow is some sort of valid test for being a true female-to-male transexual; it is not, because your hormones and organs are not under your conscious control. Questions of gender identity are much more complicated and call for help that is much more complex than a simple belief in "mind over matter."

If you want to pursue transexual treatment, you must locate a specialist who can inform you about this lengthy process. Then either hormone treatment (with testosterone) or surgery to remove your uterus will stop your menstrual periods.

Is it possible for a male who had a sex-change operation to have a period? Could he have a baby? Someone told me they transplant vaginas and ovaries for this purpose.

No, a biological male—even after surgical and hormonal treatment to achieve the external appearance of a female—will not have menstrual bleeding. There is no possibility of pregnancy either, since the surgery doesn't involve either constructing or transplanting internal organs of the female reproductive tract. Functioning ovaries and a uterus (or womb, where a baby grows) cannot be transplanted.

Even though a vagina that looks like a natural vagina and can respond to sexual stimulation is created surgically from the person's *own* tissues, it doesn't lead to a uterus or other female organs, so reproduction isn't possible.

Surgical steps in male-to-female transexual treatment include removing the testicles, using part of the penis to construct a clitoris, and the skin from the scrotum and penis to create labia and to line the newly created vagina. In many cases nerve endings, and thus feeling, in the genital area can be preserved so that sexual arousal and orgasm are possible.

I'm 16 and, although physically male, have been living as a female for several years. My parents died and now I live with a relative in a small town and the doctor won't refill my prescription for hormones. What will happen to me?

Assuming you had been receiving the hormones for gender dysphoria (unhappiness with the sex of your body) or transexualism, I suggest you contact the nearest teaching hospital or medical school and ask for an appointment with a physician who specializes in endocrinology and has experience with transexual therapy.

Being treated with hormones at your age is unusual. Before 18, psychological therapy is usually offered, but parents and doctors rarely agree to begin use of hormones until a person is older and more certain about his or her sexual identity.

Men who had been taking estrogens for approximately six months and then stopped showed a gradual return to male hormonal levels in about one month. Within three to four weeks the testicles increased to normal size and erection and ejaculation reappeared, but any increase in breast tissue and nipple size remained. If a decrease in beard growth was noticed after beginning the estrogen, beard growth began again once the patients stopped taking the hormones. In your case, if your voice had not deepened or facial hair developed before beginning estrogen, both these effects will probably occur in response to your testosterone (which will no longer be suppressed by taking estrogen).

Because of your age, it's essential for you to share these concerns with your legal guardian and ask for help in finding adequate psychological and medical treatment.

Who pays for a sex change operation and how much does it cost?

Because the full evaluation, testing, and various treatment steps (including plastic and reconstructive surgery) take several years, the costs can be quite high. A few insurance companies have been known to cover some of the drug and/or surgical expenses, but it is usually up to each client either to pay expenses, to arrange payment by an insurance company or government agency, or to find a clinic that sets fees on a sliding scale based on the patient's income.

I'm a woman who wants a man's body and doesn't know how to get it. I've phoned and talked with several different doctors, nurses, and specialists all across Canada, and none have given me satisfying information as to how to go about having a sex change operation. How do I get ahold of gender-dysphoria specialists?

This process cannot be conducted by telephone or mail, so do not be disappointed that the specialists you call give little information over the phone. Each case is so different that specific answers to your questions cannot be given until after a complete evaluation has been done.

For referrals to specialists in either female-to-male or male-to-female procedures in Canada, write to FACT (Box 291, Station A, Hamilton, Ontario, Canada L8N-3C8) or to Gender Identity Clinic (Clarke Institute of Psychiatry, Toronto, Ontario, Canada M5T-IR8).

In the United States, write to J2CP Information Services (P.O. Box 184, San Juan Capistrano, CA 92693).

Further Readings

Money, J. *Sex Errors of the Body: Dilemmas, education, counseling.* Baltimore: The
Johns Hopkins Press, 1968.
(A scholarly text describing specific aspects of unfinished biological development with a special emphasis on the educational and counseling needs of
affected individuals.)

15

From Sex to Parenthood

REPRODUCTION

Reproduction is the process by which animals and plants produce new individuals. But judging from the letters received by The Kinsey Institute, many people aren't clear about how reproduction takes place. In humans, reproduction technically begins when one of the male's sperm penetrates the female's egg. This initial event in the process of reproduction is referred to as fertilization or conception and produces a single cell called a zygote.

Although most people understand this basic idea, many remain confused about the specific details. When is an egg available for sperm to fertilize it? Where do the sperm and egg meet? How long does it take for sperm to get from the vagina to the egg? How do offspring end up with or without certain characteristics of the parents? The answers to such questions provide practical information that can help a person either reproduce (become pregnant) or avoid reproducing (use contraceptive methods more effectively).

When is an egg available for fertilization?

A woman is born with two ovaries, each containing approximately 200,000 immature eggs. Before birth, her brain, hormone-releasing organs, and reproductive tract were "programmed" to mature and begin releasing eggs at puberty. Approximately once a month between puberty and menopause the brain sends a chemical message to the pituitary gland (located at the base of the brain), signaling it to produce a special hormone (FSH) that causes the ovaries to begin the process of maturing an egg. This maturation process triggers an increase in another hormone (estrogen), which signals the brain to have the pituitary gland produce a different hormone (LH). The rise in LH causes the **ovary** to release the mature **egg** *(for an illustration of a woman's reproductive cycles see Chapter 2)*.

The release of an egg from an ovary—called ovulation—occurs about halfway between the first day of one menstrual flow and the first day of the next menstrual flow.

The egg (which is smaller than the period at the end of this sentence) floats out of the ovary. The egg is surrounded by a cloudlike covering of other cells and fluid from the **ovarian follicle**, inside which it developed. Also in response to these hormone levels, the **fimbriae** of the **Fallopian tube** near that ovary (*see Illustration 28)* move closer to and surround the ovary, and the entire Fallopian tube begins to contract rhythmically. It is thought that the waving motions of the fimbriae sweep the egg into the opening of the Fallopian tube.

Just inside the fimbriae is the widest part of the Fallopian tube, called the **ampulla**, and here the egg and sperm meet. Scientists are still not sure how long after ovulation each egg remains viable (in a condition suitable for fertilization by a sperm), but it is estimated to be a very brief time, between six and twenty-four hours. This means that out of each reproductive cycle of about one month, an egg is available for fertilization for one day or less.

Once an egg is fertilized, the contractions and the motion of the cilia (little hairlike projections) on the lining of the tube begin to move the egg toward the uterus.

How long does it take for sperm to reach the egg?

Before a **sperm** appears in a man's semen it has already spent approximately seventy days developing into its mature state while moving from the Sertoli cell in the testicles (where it was produced) through various tubes to the ducts near the base of the penis (*see Illustration 5 and Chapter 3).* Here it is held with millions of other sperm until the man ejaculates.

After ejaculation of the semen into the vagina, the sperm must travel through the **cervical os** (the tiny opening in the **cervix** between the inner end of the **vagina** and the **uterus**), through the uterus, into the end of one of the Fallopian tubes where it connects to the uterus, and down the length of the Fallopian tube to the ampulla to meet the newly released egg.

In humans, this trip of approximately six inches can take as little as five minutes since sperm are fast swimmers, but it's not likely that fertilization will take place that quickly. Fertilization cannot occur until the sperm have undergone a complicated process called capacitation (removal of a special coating or substance from the surface of the sperm). Capacitation occurs inside the uterus and Fallopian tubes and is estimated to take seven hours.

Theoretically, this means that having sex seven hours before an egg was released could result in fertilization. It is also reasonable to assume that having sex any time up to about seventeen hours after ovulation might also result in fertilization. But because sperm can live in the female reproductive tract for several days, having sex at times even days before ovulation can also result in fertilization. In fact, live sperm have been found in the cervix 205 hours (or eight-and-a-half days) after ejaculation. This means that intercourse any time from eight days before ovulation up to and including the day of ovulation itself could result in fertilization of an egg.

What happens when sperm reach the egg?

Those sperm which have already undergone capacitation undergo a second change as they near the cloud of cells surrounding the egg. Of the 200 to 300 million sperm deposited in the vagina, only several hundred arrive in the

Reproduction

FERTILIZATION

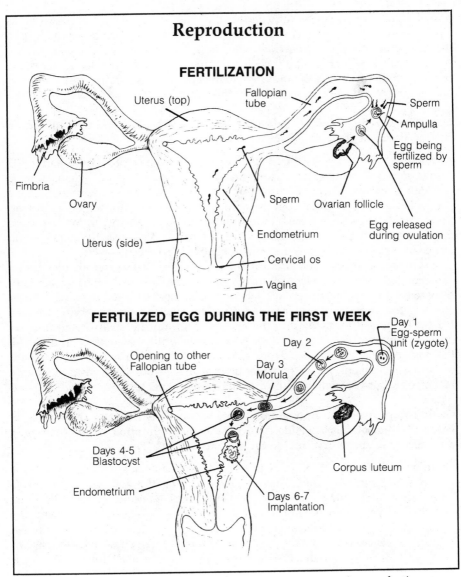

FERTILIZED EGG DURING THE FIRST WEEK

Illustration No. 28. **Reproduction.** These drawings show a woman's reproductive organs, the right side drawn as though the front half of the organs have been removed so you can see inside. Many elements are shown much larger than they actually are. For example, a human egg is smaller than the period at the end of this sentence; human sperm cannot be seen at all without a microscope; and the inside of a woman's Fallopian tube is about the size of a hairbrush bristle.

ampulla. Many sperm bump into the egg, releasing several substances. These substances break up the cloud of cells surrounding the egg and produce further changes in the nearby sperm; this is called the acrosome reaction. This reaction makes it possible for sperm to penetrate the outer layers of the egg. As soon as one sperm has fully penetrated the outer layer, the surface of the egg changes so that no other sperm can penetrate.

Any failure in the complex chemical process of capacitation or acrosome reaction of sperm during their journey to the egg may make it impossible for any of the sperm to penetrate and fertilize the egg.

How does heredity work? In other words, how do children end up with certain characteristics of their parents?

As the egg and sperm fuse, the 23 chromosomes from the mother's egg and the 23 chromosomes from the father's sperm line up as 23 matched pairs, making a single cell with 46 chromosomes. Each pair of chromosomes carries "messages" (called genes) from the father and from the mother that will program cell development. These genes include every piece of basic information necessary for this one cell to make a particular person, including male or female (*see Chapter 10*), short or tall, eye color, light or dark skin, and susceptibility to certain diseases.

About thirty hours after fertilization, the single-celled zygote divides into a two-celled zygote (with each cell carrying the same hereditary messages). After three days the zygote has divided into 16 cells and is called a **morula**. After reaching the uterus and undergoing further cell divisions the embryo is called a **blastocyst**, which implants into the endometrium on the sixth or seventh day after fertilization. The division of cells continues until the embryo produces all the types of cells that will be needed to make one individual. Even in adulthood, each of the millions of cells in our bodies carries the same basic hereditary messages originally contained in the single-celled zygote.

Could you please settle an ongoing debate between my husband and me? What is the lifespan of sperm inside the woman's body? In other words, how long does the male sperm live inside the woman's body?

Sperm may survive for around eight days inside a woman's body because some sperm enter crypts, or folds, in the cervix. During the middle of a woman's reproductive cycle, the mucus of the cervix changes to encourage sperm to swim into these crypts. Just before ovulation, the cervical os opens wider and the texture of the mucus changes, enabling sperm to swim forward into the uterus.

Tests of cervical mucus forty-eight hours after intercourse have shown as many live, healthy sperm as there were immediately after intercourse. It is thought that sperm leave the cervical area gradually, with some entering the uterus immediately after ejaculation while others wait in the crypts for various lengths of time. Having the sperm travel up into the uterus in smaller groups over a number of days probably makes it more likely that some sperm will be in the right place when an egg arrives.

The area where each Fallopian tube attaches to the uterus also appears to act as a type of holding area for sperm, perhaps permitting only a few sperm at a time to pass into a Fallopian tube. Again, this means that there are healthy sperm entering the Fallopian tubes over an extended period, thus increasing the likelihood of at least one meeting an egg.

Once in the Fallopian tube, sperm can live for as long as 85 hours. The

Fallopian tube is filled with a fluid rich in sugars and other chemicals necessary for sperm survival.

These lengthy survival times are all dependent upon the composition of cervical mucus and the fluids in the Fallopian tubes, which vary throughout each reproductive cycle. These optimum conditions occur only around the time of ovulation. At other times in the reproductive cycle, few sperm even pass through the cervix because the consistency of the mucus blocks entry. Since the vagina is highly acidic, sperm that do not enter the cervix become inactive in two to six hours.

Therefore sperm can live inside a woman's body for anywhere from two hours to eight days or so, depending on the stage of the woman's reproductive cycle when ejaculation occurs.

It seems that women have more trouble getting pregnant these days, and I think it's because they wait too long to start families. Isn't it true that the older a woman gets, the harder it is to get pregnant because your organs get harder to operate?

There are no data from which to say whether there are generally more fertility problems today or not; but if there are, one factor may be the rising incidence of certain sexually transmitted diseases (STDs) that damage the reproductive tract.

A woman's fertility is thought to be greatest between ages 18 and 28, when ovulation occurs most regularly. During the pubertal years, menstrual cycles may be irregular and an egg is not always released during each cycle. Irregular and anovulatory cycles (cycles in which an egg is *not* released midway between two menstrual flows) gradually begin to reappear in some women as they near the age of 30. For example, in a study of women inseminated with donor sperm, 54 percent of those older than 35 became pregnant as compared to 74 percent of those between ages 26 and 30.

This reduction in fertility is usually very gradual, however, so that a woman is capable of becoming pregnant until her ovaries stop releasing eggs altogether at menopause. Even after the last menstrual flow (menopause), women are still advised to use contraception for one full year to provide protection *if* an egg should happen to be released.

Some researchers have noted, incidentally, that delaying childbearing until a couple is in their thirties or early forties increases the likelihood that the parental relationship is stable and that the couple has made progress toward personal or career goals. For these reasons, delaying childbearing until later in life may actually have some benefits for the family.

Are younger men more fertile than older men?

Men begin to produce sperm during puberty and, if healthy, continue to produce sperm until they die. Theoretically, a man can impregnate a woman at any age after he reaches puberty. In general, the number of sperm in each ejaculation is thought to be highest between ages 21 and 30.

However, many factors can temporarily reduce an individual male's sperm count. These include the length of time since the previous ejaculation, stress, fever, the temperature of the testicles, and infections of the reproductive organs.

Why do humans usually have only one baby at a time while dogs and cats have lots of babies at once?

Animals like dogs and cats have multiple births because they release several eggs in one reproductive cycle. Human females, on the other hand, usually release only one egg during each cycle.

Most multiple births in humans are due to the release of more than one egg at a time (fraternal twins, triplets, quadruplets, etc.). These siblings are no more or less alike than brothers and sisters born at different times. More rarely, two or more babies are born as a result of one fertilized egg dividing and separating very shortly after conception (identical twins or triplets).

My wife is distraught at the idea we might have twins, because she heard that twins skip a generation. My father was a twin. My two sisters have not had any twins in four pregnancies. What is the likelihood we'll have twins?

There is a heredity factor in twinning, but it's greater for women than for men. The average rate of twinning in the United States is around one set in 100 births. If a woman is herself a fraternal twin, her chances of twinning increase to one set per fifty-eight pregnancies. The twin rate is not significantly increased, however, if it is the man who is a fraternal twin. I found no research that suggests that twinning skips a generation.

Two years ago I became the great-grandmother of identical triplet girls. What are the odds of this happening?

The predicted rate of triplet births is approximately one in 10,000 births, which is about 100 times more rare than twin births, and identical triplets would be even more rare.

Multiple-birth rates are known to vary somewhat by a woman's age. For example, mothers aged 35 to 39 are about four times more likely to have triplets than are mothers aged 15 to 19. The use of fertility drugs also greatly increases the possibility of multiple births, with the rate as high as 40 percent following use of some fertility drugs.

I can't imagine what would cause Siamese twins. How do they get joined together?

Siamese twins (more properly called conjoined twins) result from an incomplete separation of identical twins: a single fertilized egg has divided into two zygotes but for some reason did not fully complete the process of separation. As a result, the twins are born joined together at some part of their bodies. Siamese twins do not result from two zygotes growing together somehow.

The name itself comes from the early 1800s, when a pair of conjoined twins, Chang and Eng, born in Siam (hence, the term Siamese), were brought to the U.S. and received widespread publicity. They married two women who were not Siamese twins; one couple had twelve children and the other ten. All the children were normal and none were twins. Chang and Eng lived to the age of 63.

What kind of doctor should we go to to find out if my husband and I have any undesirable genes that could be passed on to our children if we decide to have

any in the future? Also, what kind of tests would be done and is the procedure expensive? We both know little about our family histories.

Currently, there is no one general test to screen for all 2000 known genetic diseases and not all of the diseases have individualized tests. For example, Tay-Sachs disease, (caused by the lack of an important enzyme) results in death by the age of 3 or 4 and occurs in approximately one in every 360,000 births in the general population. However, its occurrence is about one in 2500 births among Ashkenazi Jews (the name refers to those who originally settled in middle and northern Europe many centuries ago). In order for the child to inherit this disease, both parents must be carriers, and the egg and the sperm must both have this disease-producing gene. In the case of Tay-Sachs disease, the carrier status of a person can be easily checked by a simple blood test.

If you are concerned about the possibility of passing on a genetic problem, begin compiling as much information as you can about your families. Gather the dates of birth and death and the medical histories of each partner's parents, grandparents, aunts, uncles, brothers, and sisters. Genetic counseling is generally recommended for anyone who is aware of a family history of inherited disorders; who knows he or she has a genetic disorder; who already has had a child with a congenital (existing at birth) disorder; or who is a member of a group known to be at high risk for a particular disorder (such as blacks for sickle-cell anemia).

Genetic counseling can be costly. If you intend to pursue this matter but have limited funds, ask your local March of Dimes chapter if any financial support is available. Some individual organizations provide financial aid for testing for specific diseases; for example, The National Tay-Sachs and Allied Diseases Association (92 Washington Ave., Cedarhurst, NY 11516) will suggest a screening center for that disorder. You can write to the National Society of Genetic Counselors, 233 Canterbury Drive, Wallingford, PA 19086, for referral to a counselor in your area.

PLANNING A FAMILY

Planning for a healthy baby should begin months before conception. Once you decide to start your family, have a thorough medical evaluation of your general and reproductive health. To identify her most fertile time, a woman should keep accurate records of her reproductive cycles, especially Basal Body Temperature (BBT) and observations of cervical mucus *(see Illustration 4 in Chapter 2).*

Other things you may need to consider with your physician include whether or not to continue prescription and nonprescription medications (both the mother and the father), the mother's weight, and any preexisting medical conditions in either the father or the mother.

The couple may also need to evaluate their current method of contraception, especially if the woman is using a hormonal substance such as the Pill.

Once you and your partner are as healthy as you can be and are ready to start your family, stop using contraception and enjoy yourselves. Both of you should review the woman's BBT and cervical mucus records and have intercourse every other day during the most fertile time of each cycle (beginning approximately eight days before ovulation is expected to occur and continuing up to the day after ovulation has occurred). Of course, you can also have intercourse whenever you like during the rest of the cycle. When you have intercourse, mark it down on your charts.

If your temperature records are hard to interpret (as many are), take them to your gynecologist and ask for a professional opinion regarding which days are likely to be the most fertile for you.

Keep recording your cycle information, especially your BBT, because you'll both want to know as soon as possible when you've conceived. Seeing your temperature remain elevated beyond its usual number of days is one clue that you may be pregnant, even before you realize that your menstrual flow is later than usual. You can also use a home pregnancy test kit to see if you're pregnant, but at the point that your period is two weeks late, go to your obstetrician (or whomever you have selected to monitor the pregnancy) for an examination. Early prenatal care is important.

Don't worry if you don't get pregnant right away. A couple should not worry about being infertile until they have had unprotected intercourse during the woman's most fertile time for a year without pregnancy. In one study of more than 5000 couples, more than half were pregnant within the first three months, 15 percent took four to six months, 13 percent took seven to twelve months, 8 percent required one to two years, and 6 percent tried for more than two years; but all these couples did eventually become pregnant.

There is only about a 20 percent chance of getting pregnant in each monthly reproductive cycle, so taking several months to get pregnant doesn't necessarily mean that there is something wrong with you.

There are many excellent, comprehensive books about pregnancy and childbirth available in libraries and bookstores today including those listed at the end of this chapter. This chapter is not intended to replace these books but to provide a sampling of the questions received by The Kinsey Institute.

Would a baby be affected if it was conceived only a short time after the mother stopped using birth control pills?

It depends on what you mean by a short time and, to some degree, on your age. Most studies report that women who stop taking oral contraceptives in order to become pregnant suffer no higher rate of miscarriage, birth defects, or infant deaths than do other women.

There are studies, however, that report a slightly increased risk of birth defects when the mother continues to take oral contraceptives *after* conception or when she takes them in the menstrual cycle in which conception occurred. In other words, there seems to be a small increased risk when women do not have one complete, Pill-free menstrual cycle between the time they stop taking the Pill and the time of conception. There is also a slightly higher risk for mothers over 30 who take the Pill.

Because we know that other hormones can affect fetal development, in order to be as safe as possible women who are using oral contraceptives should stop taking the Pill and use another method of contraception (such as condoms or a diaphragm used with a spermicidal foam or jelly) for two or three menstrual cycles before attempting to conceive. Then stop using any contraception.

I use a spermicidal foam for contraception. I know it's not the best method, but it suits my life right now. Can foam hurt the baby if you use it between the time you conceive and when you find out you're pregnant?

This is an excellent question because it highlights the lack of an accurate early pregnancy test. As it stands now, most women do not know they're pregnant for several weeks after conception and many are surprised. It's likely, therefore, that many women who are not trying to get pregnant will inadvertently use contraceptive foams and jellies during the early stages of pregnancy.

Even though one study did report a greater incidence of birth defects among women using spermicides, other experts have questioned those findings and now believe there are few or no risks.

Increasing Your Chances of Becoming Pregnant

My husband and I have been married for almost two years and I have begun to think of starting a family. Because I am a teacher and would like to return to work after having the baby with as little disruption to my schedule as possible, we would like to have the baby in June so that I could stay at home with the baby for three months before I had to return to the classroom in September. (I would like to stay home longer, but because of our finances that is not possible.)

Should we start trying to get pregnant in September? I'm sure it's difficult to give us an exact answer, but we could use some guidelines. I'm using a diaphragm for contraception now, if that makes a difference.

If you are committed to planning the birth around the school schedule, you should begin now to keep accurate records of your menstrual cycles, Basal Body Temperature (BBT), and cervical mucus changes. You could also try the home test kits that measure the LH surge before ovulation. These are the only ways to try to predict the days you are most likely to be fertile 266 days before you wish to have a baby (the average time between conception and birth).

BBT charts and cervical mucus changes can be difficult to interpret; the changes are slight and can be influenced by other factors that can mask the change at ovulation. When you have a gynecological exam to establish your general reproductive health, ask the doctor to look at your records to make sure you are following the procedures correctly.

Even if you and your husband are in perfect health, and even if you have absolutely regular and predictable ovulation cycles, the chance of conception on a first try is about 20 percent. Although science can provide you some information on ways to try to plan the timing of the birth of a child, your chances of actually carrying out an exact plan are not guaranteed.

You might want to think now about how you'll react if your plan doesn't work out. Becoming tense as "the big day" approaches may put a great deal of pressure on your husband and make intercourse impossible. Or, having your menstrual flow appear when you assumed you'd be pregnant could make you feel like a "failure." Try to build in more flexibility or you risk feeling frustrated and unhappy.

My husband and I have tried unsuccessfully for eight months to become pregnant. Our doctor suggested my husband and I have intercourse every three days, plus at the time I ovulate.

I use the temperature and the mucus methods to check for ovulation. The problem is that the mucus becomes stringy three or four days before my temperature reaches its peak. Therefore I'm confused about when I'm most fertile.

Mucus is best suited for assisting sperm through the cervix when it resembles raw egg white, is clear, and can be stretched into a string between your thumb and index finger. The length of time during each monthly cycle that mucus is clear and stringy varies from woman to woman. Some women have this type of mucus for nearly a week, others for only one day, and some never do. If it does appear, it is usually before ovulation. Your temperature rise of about one-half a degree does not occur until *after* ovulation.

Based on the information in your letter, having intercourse every other day beginning when your mucus changes should mean that sperm will be available on the day the egg is released. Some sperm will wait in the cervix and others will wait in the Fallopian tubes, so there should be sperm available whenever the egg is released.

Unless your physician has established that your ovulation pattern is too irregular to use these methods effectively, don't worry about when you should have intercourse in the rest of your cycle.

I want to get pregnant very badly and my doctor says there's nothing wrong with me or my husband. Could different lovemaking positions help?

It is thought that some intercourse positions may help place the sperm near the cervix and keep them there. According to some clinicians, the best positions for depositing sperm near the cervix are rear-entry positions (both kneeling with the man facing the woman's back, or both lying on your sides with the man curled around the woman's back [spoon position]—*see Illustrations 29 and 33*).

As for retaining sperm near the cervix, it may help if your husband removes his penis immediately after ejaculation while it's still erect. This may help keep semen from flowing out of the vagina as quickly. It may also be helpful to remain lying on your back with your hips on a pillow for twenty minutes or so after ejaculation. Most important, make sure you're having intercourse during your most fertile days.

If after twelve months you're still not pregnant, go back to the doctor and ask to be referred to a fertility specialist. Until the proper tests are done, no one—not even a physician—can be certain whether or not a person is fertile.

Please tell me if it's possible, if I'm not having an orgasm when we make love, for me to become pregnant. Or do you have to orgasm for the pregnancy process to begin?

No, you don't need to have an orgasm to get pregnant. Sperm are powerful swimmers on their own, and if conditions are right will journey through the cervix, uterus, and Fallopian tubes whether or not a woman has an orgasm.

My wife and I are trying for our second child and I need to know if something is fact or fiction. A friend told us that three other couples got pregnant because

the husband took cold showers or baths, and that this increases the sperm count. Is this true?

Several things can create the kind of heat that can reduce sperm count. One is taking regular long soaks in a hot bath. Another is wearing tight underwear that holds the testicles against the body. When low sperm count is due to these factors, a man can usually reverse the problem simply by changing his habits. Increasing sperm count can take several months, however, because it takes about seventy days from the time a testicle produces a sperm cell until it appears in the ejaculate.

So cold showers are not the solution. In fact, there is speculation that prolonged exposure to cold (such as working in a cold storage area) may be as detrimental to the sperm count as is prolonged exposure to heat.

I'm planning to marry a man who has been married before and has also had several long-term affairs. Having children is very important to me.

I'm worried he may be infertile. None of the women in his past got pregnant by him, although they eventually had children with other men. My gynecologist says I'm OK, although I've never tried to get pregnant and currently use birth control.

My fiancé has never had a sperm count and sees no reason to get one now. How can I stop worrying about whether he can father children?

Talk to him about how you feel and what you are worried about. It could be that he was simply behaving very responsibly in his earlier relationships and used contraception effectively. In any case, past evidence of either fertility or absence of fertility in either men or women isn't a reliable predictor of future reproductive ability, especially if a person changes partners.

The best way to find out if you can become pregnant is by trying, which means having frequent unprotected intercourse on your fertile days for a full year. Unless your gynecologist did extensive testing to establish that you are currently ovulating and everything is fine with your internal organs and hormone levels, you can't be sure that you are fertile either.

If worry about this is causing a problem in your relationship or you have difficulty talking to your fiancé about your concerns, you might want to consult a marriage counselor or therapist who could help the two of you sort out goals and priorities that are mutually agreeable *before* you marry.

My wife and I will be trying to conceive a baby this fall. We would both prefer a girl. I remember hearing about a new product being tested that would give an 80 percent chance of having a girl. Is this available yet?

My husband and I have two beautiful daughters and we would like to have a third child; however, we would like to heighten our chances of having a male child. On television we saw a program about how to increase the likelihood of having boys.

My own doctor doesn't know anything about this procedure. Do you know which hospital is experimenting with impregnating women with only male sperm?

In spite of reports and many books that claim success for various sex-selection methods that can be safely done at home, your odds of having a boy or a girl are fifty-fifty.

One example of methods suggested by some authors is altering the chemical balance of the vagina by using either vinegar- or baking soda-based douches. Although scientists disagree about the effectiveness of these methods, most agree they are unlikely to harm either the couple or the baby. Recent studies of methods that attempt to alter vaginal chemistry by extreme diets, however, found that they can be dangerous to the women's general health and should be carried out only if she is under the close supervision of a physician.

Another method you may have heard about is the gender-selection kits that were widely available in drugstores in the United States, packed in pink and blue boxes. These kits, which sold for around $50, received a great deal of media attention several years ago. Soon after their debut, the U.S. Food and Drug Administration issued a Notice of Deceptive Products and Misleading Claims against the manufacturer, stating that the kits were a "gross deception of the consumer." Many scientists refute the theory on which the method was based, that having intercourse at certain times in a woman's cycle could determine the sex of a baby.

To date, the various sperm-separation methods are the only methods that have been shown to alter the birth ratio, and even those are not guaranteed. One technique was patented by Dr. Ronald J. Ericsson and is available at licensed centers. So far, clinics using this procedure to produce boys claim a 75 to 80 percent success rate and a 65 to 70 percent success rate for conceiving girls.

Another researcher, Dr. Nancy Alexander, who is affiliated with the Jones Institute in Norfolk, Virginia, reportedly has a different process that has resulted in eight girls out of ten (80 percent) tries to conceive a girl. Other methods are reportedly available at the Philadelphia Fertility Institute and at Keio University in Tokyo, but I could find no reports on success rates of these methods.

You should also be aware that to date no major medical association or other disinterested group has evaluated or endorsed any of these methods of sex selection. More important, you should ask yourself what you will do if you conceive. Will you have tests to determine if you've conceived the sex you wanted? If it's the "wrong" sex, then what?

Much more research is needed on the basic make-up of sperm and vaginal fluids and about what happens during conception before couples can rely on selecting the sex of their children. Until then, Aristotle's ancient advice to the Greeks, based on myth, is probably as valid as current advice (and is free and does no physical harm): If you want a boy, have intercourse in a north wind; if you want a girl, do it in a south wind. In other words, there is not much you can do except leave it to nature and love whatever you get.

How many days should a woman wait after her period is late before going to the doctor for a pregnancy test? How accurate are the tests you do by yourself at home? How soon can I be absolutely sure I'm pregnant?

If it's been ten or more days since your menstrual flow was due, now would be the time for a pregnancy test. Other early symptoms of pregnancy can include changes in the size and tenderness of your breasts, nausea or vomiting, frequent urination, and fatigue. However, some pregnant women have no symptoms while other women who are not pregnant have similar symptoms every month during the week before menstrual flow.

All pregnancy tests are based on measuring the presence of hCG (human chorionic gonadotropin, a hormone secreted only during pregnancy) in urine or blood. The earliest tests you can have are highly specialized radioimmunoassays of a blood sample; they are highly accurate as early as one week after conception—even before your menstrual flow is late. But the equipment to do these tests is located only at larger hospitals, fertility clinics, and research centers.

As soon as your menstrual flow is a day late, you can ask your obstetrician to do a sensitive test for monoclonal antibodies to hCG in either urine or blood. This evaluation costs around $20 and can be highly accurate *if* it shows a positive result. However, if the result is negative, you may need a repeat test in one to two weeks because you could actually be pregnant but not have had enough hCG to detect on the first test.

When your menstrual flow is one to three days late (in other words, two weeks or more after conception), you could try one of the pregnancy home test kits. These cost less than $20 and claim accuracy rates around 95 percent, but you must follow instructions carefully. In one study of women using these tests, nearly half had inaccurate results around the time flow was expected, so repeat the test a week later to see if the results are the same.

By the time your menstrual flow is two weeks late (about a month after conception), a two-minute slide test for hCG in your urine can detect pregnancy with 98 percent accuracy. These are inexpensive (about $5), or even free at some clinics.

Regardless of which test is used, you need to be examined by your obstetrician or other health care professional as soon as possible to either verify the pregnancy (by looking at your cervix) or to find out why your menstrual flow is late. Take along your BBT charts and other records so an accurate conception date can be established.

Concerns About Getting Pregnant

Is there any research on the effects of jogging on the female reproductive system? I now jog about 15 to 20 miles per week. My gynecologist has advised me that if I ever want to conceive, I will have to cut my jogging in half or, preferably, cease jogging altogether.

One study of married women who participated in the Olympics between 1952 and 1972 showed that all of those women who desired children were able to conceive. But it is also true that about 20 percent of women who are engaged in rigorous athletic conditioning experience irregular menstruation or fail to ovulate. This is probably due to a number of factors, including weight loss, a low percentage of body fat, a restricted diet, and the physical or emotional stress related to training.

If you've been having irregular cycles or there is a suspicion that you are not ovulating, then you may indeed need to increase your percentage of body fat.

I'm 30 and have had a very bad yeast infection for approximately nine years. Many physicians and gynecologists have prescribed different medications, but nothing seems to help.

Now I want to have a family. Does a yeast infection have any effect on getting pregnant or childbearing?

Vaginal infections can make it more difficult for some women to get pregnant; more important, you need to find out exactly which organism is causing the infection. Many organisms that cause vaginal infections can also result in reduced fertility by scarring the reproductive organs. *(For more information, see Chapter 19.)*

It is worth taking the time now to get an accurate diagnosis of exactly which organism is causing your vaginal infection. Getting it cleared up before becoming pregnant is also important. Recent research has found that some organisms involved in vaginal infections are related to an increased risk of premature birth. Many women have trouble with vaginal infections during pregnancy due to changes in hormone levels.

Try going to a sexually transmitted disease (STD) clinic or specialist for diagnosis and treatment of the vaginal infection. Your husband should be tested and if necessary treated at the same time, to avoid passing the infectious organism back to you.

Most medications for vaginal infections are safe when used during pregnancy, but not all. For example, Flagyl, used to treat trichomoniasis, should not be used during the first three months of pregnancy.

I have been trying unsuccessfully for six months to get pregnant with our third child. During an examination, the doctor said my uterus is tilted towards the back. Is that causing the delay?

The position of the uterus differs among women. In most women it tilts forward, but in about 20 percent of women the uterus is tilted to the back. This is often called a tipped (or retroverted) uterus.

The position of the uterus does not affect the ability to conceive, carry, or deliver a baby. Before this was known, many women were advised to have surgery to "correct" the position of the uterus. This often did more damage than good because it created scar tissue that actually reduced fertility. As you have seen, your uterus worked well for your two previous pregnancies, so keep trying. Six months is not a long time to try, but if you're not pregnant in another six months, consult a fertility expert.

I am 30 and have just been told that I have a didelphys uterus and a duplicated cervix. What are my chances of having children? What special care will I need?

Uterus didelphys is also called a double uterus. This congenital (present at birth) condition may be found alone or in combination with a double cervix and/or a double vagina.

No one knows why these abnormalities occur *(see Chapter 14)*. Further evaluations will be needed to assess how your body might respond to a pregnancy. Both the uterus and the cervix must be able to expand during pregnancy and labor. If a pregnancy is advised, you will need careful monitoring, including ultrasound evaluations, as the uterus containing the pregnancy enlarges.

Women with uterine abnormalities have a risk of uterine rupture plus an increased risk of miscarriage or premature birth. Caesarean delivery is frequently necessary. But many women like you can and do carry and deliver healthy, full-term babies. In fact, many women and their physicians are not aware of the existence of these malformations until they are discovered after a pregnancy problem.

Because these malformations are not common and few physicians are experienced in handling such pregnancies, find a fertility specialist with experience managing problem pregnancies. Find out exactly what kind of specialized monitoring will be required. In some cases at least part of the care can be managed by a local physician.

I'm 30 years old and had surgery two years ago to remove fibroid tumors from my uterus. The tumors were not cancerous. My doctor said that my uterus was filled with lots of little tumors and not all of them could be removed.

I've been told that there is nothing preventing me from becoming pregnant, but I have a 50-50 chance of miscarriage if a tumor grows while the baby grows. What are the chances of this happening?

The outlook is not as bleak as the word *tumor* would indicate. Uterine myomas (noncancerous tumors commonly called fibroids) are thought to exist in about 25 percent of all women over age 35, although many women have few symptoms or problems. Uterine myomas frequently do increase in size during pregnancy, but this does not usually cause spontaneous abortion (miscarriage).

The actual risk is not known, but researchers estimate that as many as 7 percent of all pregnant women have uterine myomas. And even though these women have a slightly higher risk of miscarriage, the overall risk is not nearly as great as 50 percent.

Although most women have no difficulty, a woman who knows she has uterine myomas and wants to have children should consult an obstetrician experienced in managing such pregnancies. In some cases, surgery to remove fibroids (myomectomy) before becoming pregnant may be recommended, but be sure to get a second opinion from a specialist in fertility before proceeding with surgery.

I am 23 and was on birth-control pills for four years. I stopped the Pill in February and didn't see my period until June. I've had two pregnancy tests; both came out negative. Shouldn't I be getting my periods back by now?

Both my husband and I want a baby. But my doctor said that I'm unable to get pregnant now because I was on the Pill for so long. I don't think my husband needs a sperm check, reason being there might be something wrong with me. Please let me know what to do.

Four years is *not* considered a long time to take oral contraceptives, and research shows that overall fertility rates of women who took the Pill are the same as those of women who did not, regardless of how long the Pill was taken. In one study of pregnancy rates among women who had taken the Pill, 25 percent took at least 12 months to conceive, and 10 percent took 24 months to conceive. Therefore your delay of eight or nine months is not unusual.

Ninety percent of women who stop taking the Pill do begin regular ovulation (release of a mature egg) within three months, but women who had irregular cycles or who did not ovulate before taking the Pill are likely to have the same problems after stopping the Pill. Only a handful of women have been found to have fertility problems directly related to use of the Pill.

You need to see a gynecologist or a fertility specialist to find out what is really going on. Amenorrhea (absence of menstruation) can be associated with such a wide range of possible causes that accurate diagnosis requires a thorough medical history, physical examination, and probably several blood tests to evaluate your hormone levels. It is standard procedure for your husband to have a semen analysis, since in nearly half of all couples with delayed fertility a male problem is involved.

I think I may have taken one or two DES pills in the mid-1950s to prevent miscarriage when I was pregnant with my daughter. My daughter has had a miscarriage and is having trouble getting pregnant again. Does DES cause reduced fertility or problems with pregnancy?

Thousands of pregnant women in the United States were treated with DES (diethylstilbestrol, one type of synthetic estrogen) from 1945 through 1971 because it was believed that it would prevent miscarriage. In the 1960s, however, an alarming number of young women were diagnosed as having a rare type of vaginal cancer. By 1971, it was discovered that the only thing these women had in common was that their mothers had taken DES during pregnancy.

More recent research has determined that this type of cancer occurs in about one of every 10,000 women exposed to DES before birth. Other possible problems, such as malformations of the cervix and uterus, may also be associated with DES exposure. It is not yet clear to what extent DES exposure lowers fertility or affects carrying a normal pregnancy.

If your daughter continues to have difficulty with pregnancy, she should consult a fertility clinic or specialist. It's important that she tell each of her physicians that she may have been exposed to DES so that this can be taken into consideration when she is evaluated.

I'd like to ask about the problem of not being able to have my sperm pump out or squirt out when I have orgasms. I am concerned because I want to have children and I want to know if this will prevent me. I have one son 10 years old, so I can't recall when this began. All I know is it's been like this since I can remember. My sex life is wonderful. I'm 32 years old and married.

Having semen pump or squirt forcefully from the penis is not necessary for conception. Because sperm can swim on their own into a woman's reproductive tract, women can even become pregnant from semen deposited on the vulva near the outer opening of the vagina.

Many different problems can lead to a loss of ejaculatory response. For example, diabetes can change ejaculatory patterns. Other possible causes include back injuries and surgery, prostate problems, and damage to the spinal cord. Several antipsychotic and antidepressant drugs are also known to reduce ejaculatory volume or response for some men.

Researchers suspect this problem may be more frequent than we realize, but clinicians speculate that many men with ejaculatory problems are too embarrassed to mention it to a physician unless they become concerned about fertility.

Because the problem can be corrected in some instances (for example, by bringing diabetes under control or by changing drug prescriptions), it's worthwhile to have a complete physical. Consider going to a specialist in male sexual dysfunctions *(see Appendix)*.

My fiancé, 24, is paralyzed from a lacrosse game in college (C-5 quadriplegic). We plan to get married and would like information about techniques available to extract sperm. Are there clinics that do this work in our area?

Call the nearest fertility clinic or medical school and ask if they work with paralyzed men. If not, ask for the name of the nearest specialist or clinic that does. You didn't mention how long your fiancé has been paralyzed, but he should consider seeking a fertility evaluation as soon as possible rather than waiting until the time you decide to try to start a family.

In some cases the quality of sperm in paralyzed men seems to deteriorate over time so that even when sperm can be recovered, they are not capable of producing a pregnancy. Speculation is that this could be due to higher temperatures in the testicles of paralyzed males, perhaps caused by long periods sitting in wheelchairs with their thighs held closely together.

Although not successful in all cases, electrical stimulation of the nerves inside the rectum sometimes produces ejaculation, and the sperm can be used for insemination. When external ejaculation does not occur, sometimes the bladder can be catheterized and sperm appearing there collected, frozen, and held for later attempts at insemination, if the couple so chooses.

I know that you and your fiancé are hopeful about starting a family, but please try to think of these techniques as experimental only. They don't yet have a high rate of success, but this does not mean you can't explore other options, such as donor insemination or adoption.

I am a 30-year-old woman wno has been smoking marijuana on a regular basis since I was 21. I am married and planning on getting pregnant.

Is there any truth to stories that using marijuana can make you sterile? I do not intend to smoke or drink once I become pregnant.

There is some evidence that smoking marijuana can disrupt ovulation in women and reduce the number of healthy sperm produced by men. Alcohol has been shown to have similar effects on fertility. Continuing to smoke marijuana or drink alcohol might indeed make it more difficult for you to get pregnant.

There are two problems with waiting to stop smoking and drinking until *after* you become pregnant. First, by the time most women discover they are pregnant, development has been underway for several weeks and the embryo may already have been affected.

Second, since it is not always easy to stop using marijuana, tobacco, or alcohol, it's best to make this adjustment in your life style three months or more before becoming pregnant. There is some evidence that the process of stopping drug use is itself stressful, and maternal stress is not good for the fetus.

Are there any scientific facts to back up doctors who tell pregnant women to stop drinking alcohol? It seems most medical advice centers around telling

women they can't do something. Since most doctors are men, I wonder if they're just biased.

Although some people maintain that an occasional drink shouldn't hurt, alcohol does cross the placenta to the fetus. Many researchers, myself included, feel strongly that pregnant women should avoid alcohol entirely. Because we now suspect that fetal damage from alcohol can occur before the woman even suspects she might be pregnant, women who are trying to get pregnant or who are not using effective contraception shouldn't drink at all.

We've known for many years now that babies born to female alcoholics often have Fetal Alcohol Syndrome (FAS). FAS is characterized by mental retardation, poor motor development, short bodies, and facial and eye abnormalities. It is now clear that some women who have drunk very little during pregnancy also have babies with FAS.

Traditionally most doctors and researchers have been men. However, women who study pregnancy issues—myself included—have found similar results in their own research.

My husband and I would like to start a family this fall but we have one concern. This summer we have both been spraying pest-control products. We follow directions carefully, but one still breathes the vapors. Our concern is that the sperm may be affected, or perhaps that chemicals may still be in our bodies, therefore affecting a fetus. We would like to know if these fears are justified and should we postpone any conception, or can we go ahead with our plans?

No studies have been done with home insecticides that show whether they affect either human fertility rates or birth defects, and usually the amount of chemicals used by a conscientious gardener would be small.

Common sense, however, suggests avoiding *any* unnecessary contact with these chemicals when trying to conceive or during pregnancy. To be as safe as possible, both you and your husband should avoid exposure to insecticides or herbicides for three months before attempting conception.

Can a woman in her late 30s safely have a normal baby (her first) if she has endometriosis?

Reproduction problems related to endometriosis are primarily related to problems of *getting* pregnant, not to having a safe pregnancy or delivering a healthy baby. The lining of the uterus is called the endometrium; endometriosis is a condition in which endometrial tissue becomes implanted on other internal organs, such as the ovaries or Fallopian tubes. Researchers estimate that between 31 to 75 percent of women with endometriosis can become pregnant without special treatments.

But accurate diagnosis is important. If you haven't yet had a laparoscopy, consider having this done by a gynecologist skilled in this technique. A thin scope is inserted into the abdomen so the doctor can see your reproductive organs. This is the *only* way to accurately diagnose endometriosis and to find out the extent of any problems. For example, the physician can see whether the ends of your Fallopian tubes are open and able to receive an egg. Moreover, during the laparoscopy itself, some endometrial deposits can often be removed by using a laser or other surgical instruments.

Other options include abdominal surgery to remove extensive endometrial deposits (which can increase the pregnancy rate by about 35 percent), use of hormonal drugs, or a combination of surgery and drugs.

The symptoms of endometriosis generally subside during pregnancy, probably because of reduced hormonal fluctuations. However, pregnant women with endometriosis need careful prenatal monitoring, since there are a few recorded cases in which the endometriosis spread during pregnancy.

If hormonal treatment is recommended, it is important to make sure you are not pregnant before you take hormones. Then use an effective method of birth control so that you don't accidentally become pregnant until after the treatment ends.

I am 31 and began having seizures (grand mal and petit mal) five years ago. For the past four years I have taken Dilantin and still have a few seizures each year.

My husband and I are talking about starting a family. What should I know about taking this drug and its effect on pregnancy? What effect would a seizure have on a fetus?

According to the Epilepsy Foundation of America, the majority (at least 90 percent) of mothers who take antiepileptic medications, including Dilantin, have normal babies. They also state that there is a two to three times greater-than-average risk of birth defects in children born to epileptic mothers; it is not clear whether this increased risk is due to the medications or to the epileptic condition itself.

Discuss the issue of pregnancy with your physician. Seizures can become more frequent during pregnancy and drug dosages may require close monitoring and readjustments. Dosage may also need to be changed again after childbirth. Babies born to epileptic mothers may also require special testing and treatment in the first few hours after birth. Find an obstetrician who is experienced in handling pregnancies in epileptic women so you'll get the most skilled care possible.

If you still have unanswered questions about your condition or pregnancy, write to the Epilepsy Foundation of America, 4351 Garden City Drive, Landover, MD 20785.

Problems Getting Pregnant

An estimated 20 percent of couples in the United States who want to have children have difficulty becoming pregnant. Only within the last decade have treatments involving hormonal drugs and new technologies become both highly successful and more widely available. The majority of couples experiencing fertility problems can now be helped.

Any couple that has not conceived after having unprotected intercourse during the woman's most fertile time in each cycle for a full year should seek an evaluation of their fertility.

Although some gynecologists and urologists are competent at basic testing and interpretation of results, most physicians have not received special training in fertility problems and do not have access to or familiarity with the specialized equipment and laboratories necessary to diagnose and treat more complicated problems. Because of this, to save time for couples whose "biological clock" is ticking away, and to save money by avoiding repeated testing, I recommend consulting a fertility specialist or clinic after twelve months of trying, or after six months if the woman is age 30 or older, or if a health problem known to affect fertility exists.

Contrary to popular belief that fertility problems are usually due to a problem with the woman, testing actually finds that in 40 percent of cases it is a problem with the male partner. In another 40 percent it is a problem with the female, and in 10 percent of cases both partners have a problem. A specific cause is not found in only 10 percent of cases. This is why reputable clinics insist that *both* partners be evaluated before discussing treatment options. Since testing of sperm is the easiest and least expensive, having an evaluation of the man's semen is a logical first step.

Write to the American Fertility Society, 2140 11th Avenue South, Suite 200, Birmingham, AL 35205-2800 for referral to a specialist in your area.

The disappointment involved in being unable to conceive (combined with the stress, discomfort, expense, and tension of testing, diagnosis, and treatment) often leads to marital and sexual problems. Many clinics now offer counseling to couples, or you can write to RESOLVE, 5 Water Street, Arlington, MA 02174. They will refer you to the nearest support group.

I am a 25-year-old female. I have never been pregnant and have fairly regular menstrual cycles. I took birth control pills for four years and used contraceptive foam for a year.

About a year ago I quit using contraceptives, hoping to become pregnant. In June, I put forth a conscious effort to try to get pregnant by counting days and using ovulation prediction tests. I've talked to several doctors, and they tell me I have signs of ovulation, to keep trying, and that I shouldn't consider expensive fertility work-ups yet.

I am at a loss. I feel so depressed toward the middle of each month's cycle that I spend a lot of time alone crying about this situation. I'm uncomfortable around my friends who have babies, maybe even envious more than uncomfortable. No one knows I'm having this problem. They just think I'm not ready to start my family yet. I am.

I believe the problem is me and not my husband, who has a child from a previous marriage. What can I do?

The feelings you describe are common among women who are having difficulty getting pregnant as fast as they expected to. Even though your physicians have given you accurate information (it does take many fertile couples a full year or more of consciously timing intercourse to become pregnant), it may be time for you and your husband to locate a fertility specialist.

Make an appointment for both you and your husband. Tell the specialist or fertility clinic that you may wish to delay beginning testing until you've received basic information and some counseling. The first tests, such as a semen analysis, are not particularly costly. (Just because your husband fathered one child does not mean that he is still fertile). Take your menstrual cycle and temperature records to the meeting.

I urge you to seriously consider doing this before your marriage suffers. It is not unusual for couples worried about fertility to secretly blame one another, withdraw from interactions with friends who have children, or develop stress-related sexual problems due to the need to schedule intercourse during fertile days.

I'm 25 and can't seem to have children. I have been involved in sexual intercourse without birth control since I was 15 years old and I've had four male companions, one of them I'm married to right now and none of them have gotten me pregnant.

I've gone to a few doctors about this and all they tell me is to take my basal temperature. When I take the record back, they tell me nothing's wrong, I'm ovulating properly, and I should have no problem getting pregnant. They've also said I could have some test, but I can't afford a lot of tests.

What could be the problem and where can I get some help that won't cost a bundle of money? We don't make a lot of money but we still want kids.

Don't give up hope. Keeping BBT records is usually just the first step in diagnosing fertility problems. Did any of the physicians you saw explain how to read the temperature charts to predict your most fertile days and when to have intercourse? *(See Illustration 4 in Chapter 2.)* Did any explain how to check your cervical mucus? Did any recommend trying home test kits, which predict ovulation so you'd know when to have sex? These cost around $30 to $40 at drugstores and don't require a prescription (one brand name is Ovukit). Follow directions carefully.

If having intercourse during your most fertile time for a year doesn't produce a pregnancy, the next step would be to have your husband's semen analyzed. A simple, basic analysis costs around $30. Family planning clinics often provide such basic tests at minimal costs.

If both you and your husband seem fine based on BBT records and semen analysis, then it's time to see a fertility specialist for a more detailed evaluation.

Fertility testing and treatments are expensive, and not all health insurance policies cover such costs. If you have insurance, check to see whether it will pay for any tests or treatments related to fertility problems. Get a list of fertility clinics *(see page 322)*; call or write and ask about fees, especially the cost of the first appointment. Units that accept federal funds usually must offer services on a sliding scale based on income.

It's worth finding a specialist if you need to—most specialists will do only those tests necessary at each step and will be better equipped to accurately interpret laboratory results than physicians who don't deal with these types of problems on a daily basis. As a result, you might end up spending less time and money because you won't be going back and forth among general physicians, gynecologists, and urologists, each of whom may want to repeat tests.

Take your BBT records (marked to show when you had intercourse) and copies of all records and test results from other physicians to the first appointment. After the first meeting you should have a better idea of what to expect in terms of costs. You can then decide whether to proceed and at what pace. You don't have to have all the tests and treatments done at once.

What percentage of males are infertile, specifically from not producing any sperm or having it blocked from leaving the body?

In one study of 1294 men classified as having fertility problems, specialists could not establish a cause in approximately 5 percent of the men. Among the remaining 95 percent, 14 percent had testicular failure (no sperm production), 7 percent had some type of obstruction of the ducts or tubes leading from the testes to the penis, and 4 percent did not produce sperm because of cryptorchidism (undescended testicle). The most frequently diagnosed problem, however, was varicocele (a collection of large veins in the scrotum), which reduced the sperm counts of nearly 40 percent of these subjects.

For many men, varicocele can be surgically repaired, resulting in a pregnancy rate of 50 percent or higher. Seek out the best, most experienced, most successful surgeon you can find. Start with a fertility specialist or clinic, because sometimes surgery is followed by use of hormonal drugs to further increase sperm count and viability.

My wife and I have been unable to conceive for over a year. After several examinations and tests on her, our doctor has suggested a sperm count for me. What sort of procedure should I expect?

You will probably be told not to have intercourse or masturbate for forty-eight to seventy-two hours before the test. You will then collect the semen sample by masturbating and ejaculating into a sterile glass container. The physician will provide a private area for you to collect your sample in the office.

Most fertility specialists recommend the masturbation method to collect sperm. Trying to withdraw during intercourse in time to ejaculate into the container is not thought to be a good way to collect the semen since the first few drops which contain the highest number of sperm are often lost.

Collecting the semen by ejaculating into a condom is also not recommended, because many condoms contain a spermicide, a lubricant, or ingredients for preservation of the latex, all of which can immobilize sperm or interfere with the test results. However, if a man's religion forbids masturbation, fertility clinics can provide a special type of condom made especially for this purpose.

The laboratory report on a basic analysis will contain several different types of information, including the volume of the semen, the number of viable (live) sperm, the consistency of the semen, the shape and health of the sperm, their ability to swim, and the presence of white blood cells that signify an infection someplace in the male reproductive tract.

A single semen evaluation, however, is not usually an adequate evaluation of male fertility, since many factors can temporarily increase or decrease the number of sperm. A high fever, for example, can reduce the number of healthy sperm in an ejaculation many weeks after the fever has occurred. So don't be surprised if the specialist asks for a second sample to be done a week or so later.

My husband has been told he has a low sperm count. Doctors told me they didn't see why I can't have children on my part. The sperm count is the only thing wrong with my husband. Is there anything we can buy or do to build it up? Is there a fertility drug or vitamin he can buy? We want children very much.

If he's eating a well-balanced diet, no vitamin or nonprescription drug will be effective in increasing the amount or health of sperm. There's no single recommended treatment for a low sperm count because it can be caused by several factors, each requiring a different treatment.

Because the number of sperm can vary considerably from temporary causes such as a fever or a virus, most infertility specialists recommend at least two or three evaluations several weeks apart before finalizing the dianosis of "low sperm count."

Any treatment depends on the exact diagnosis. For example, problems of the male reproductive tract such as infections are treated with drugs, and some blockages require microsurgery. If the testicles are producing sperm, even in small numbers, the semen from several ejaculations can be collected, frozen, and the sperm pooled together and used for insemination.

If you and your husband want to try some things on your own before consulting a doctor, you might reduce body heat on the testicles by switching from jockey shorts to boxer shorts and avoiding very hot baths, have intercourse every other day beginning a week before ovulation is expected, and remain lying down on your back for twenty minutes or so after intercourse to keep the ejaculate close to your cervix. If these steps don't help, consult a specialist in male fertility.

My wife and I have been married for 10 years. We have been trying to have a baby for the last five years. I went to my M.D. and he did a sperm test five times. They all came out zero sperm. I asked what can be done about this and he said there is nothing he can do, just learn to live with it.

What can I do now? My wife and I are almost at the end. She has been determined fertile so we know it's me. Please help.

Find a fertility expert who specializes in male fertility problems or a fertility clinic. A total lack of sperm in the ejaculate (called azoospermia) can mean a number of different things. It could be, for instance, that you're making sperm in your testicles but have a blockage in the long series of tubes or ducts through which sperm must travel to the penis. *(See Illustration 5 in Chapter 3.)* Many of these blockages can be surgically corrected.

One of the key things to determine is whether you are making sperm. This often requires a testicular biopsy in which a small sample of tissue is taken from the testicles and examined. The full and accurate interpretation of this tissue requires a great deal of expertise, another reason why you must locate a specialist.

You also may need tests to determine various hormonal levels or to see if some correctable condition is involved. In any event, ask your physician for copies of your previous semen-analysis reports. There are many other pieces of information that may be useful to the specialist in addition to the zero sperm count (such as the level of a sugar called fructose in the ejaculate, which can indicate a blockage in the reproductive system).

One important option you do not mention is the use of insemination. For example, some men actually make sperm, but they end up in their urine instead of in their semen. In cases like this, specialists may be able to recover the sperm and use them to successfully impregnate the woman.

My fiancé had been married before, tried to have a baby for four years, and was told by three doctors he could never father a child because of a low sperm count. Because of this, I stopped taking the Pill. Two months later (before we were married) I became pregnant. I was upset. His family didn't believe it because they knew about his sperm count.

I had a pregnancy with no problems and we're very happy now, but maybe other couples should know about this.

Your letter highlights one of the many gaps in our knowledge of fertility. Until the last few years, men who were found to have fewer than 60 million sperm per milliliter of ejaculate were often told they had a "low sperm count." Any difficulty with the couple conceiving was thought to be due to the man's reduced sperm count.

Studies of men who had already fathered children showed that 20 percent of them had fewer than 20 million sperm per milliliter of ejaculate. Now many fertility specialists have revised their definition so that a man with at least 10 million sperm per milliliter of ejaculate should be considered potentially fertile.

It is also possible that your husband's first wife played a role in that couple's inability to conceive, because in about half of all infertility cases the female is found to be the source of the problem. Perhaps these points will help your new in-laws to understand how this could happen.

You are right to tell people who can't get pregnant that they should not give up until they've been to a fertility specialist. My husband and I wasted three years and went through severe emotional problems because we were loyal to his urologist and my family doctor, both of whom claimed to be doing as much for us as could be done anywhere. My family doctor finally reached the point of telling me that he didn't want to hear about my personal problems.

I finally got the nerve to call a medical school two hours away and made an appointment. We were tested in ways that had not been done in our home town. We also were told about several new methods of insemination. We elected to try something called "sperm washing." After two tries I became pregnant, and we have a beautiful baby.

People need to know that going to a specialist is worth the extra trouble to get off work and make a trip whenever it's time to ovulate. We had been afraid that in a big clinic we would feel lost or like cattle. The opposite was true: The clinic staff was even more supportive than our local doctors, because they were more familiar with the emotions involved.

Fertility specialists and centers are quick to learn about new findings, since they hear of them informally (such as at scientific meetings), often many months before they are published in journals read by other physicians. (It often takes a year or more between the time a report is submitted to a journal and the day it appears in print.) Any physician can call himself or herself a fertility specialist, but to be really expert takes much additional study, training, and experience beyond regular specialization in gynecology, urology, or endocrinology. Taking the time to find a qualified specialist often saves time in the long run.

Fertility Testing and Treatments

How can a couple choose a good fertility clinic or specialist? My best suggestion is to write the American Fertility Society and ask them to recommend a specialist or clinic. Once you have received the list, call and ask:

- If the clinic has access to a group of specialists, including an endocrinologist, gynecologist, urologist, and reproductive biologist, for example.
- What kinds of problems were treated the previous year and what were the success rates for various procedures. If you have some idea about your problem (low sperm count or lack of ovulation, for example) ask specifically about it.
- How long does a complete evaluation take? Most try to compress the process into two or three months, but it can be extended over a longer time if the couple chooses to go more slowly.
- What is the cost of the initial visit and which tests are usually conducted during the first visit?

What can a couple expect when they go to a fertility clinic or specialist? Most clinics structure their evaluation in a series of phases. At the first visit a complete medical history is compiled and a thorough physical examination is conducted on each partner; the man also has a semen analysis. If there are questions about the man's semen, his blood may be sampled to test for levels of various hormones. The results of any tests the couple has already completed elsewhere, the couple's BBT charts, and any other records are reviewed. This initial visit may cost several hundred dollars, depending on which tests are done.

If the man's semen seems adequate, the woman becomes the focus of the next phase. Tests are conducted over the course of a single reproductive cycle, including blood tests to determine the levels of various hormones (to see if they rise and fall as they should); an endometrial biopsy just before the menstrual flow is expected (to see if the lining of the uterus is being properly built up to support a fertilized egg); and a postcoital test to determine whether sperm are able to swim into and through the cervix. This phase may also cost several hundred dollars, depending on how many tests and analyses need to be done.

At this point, the specialists may present the couple with a description of what they suspect may be involved and propose treatments, such as taking special drugs to alter hormone levels for several months, a change in intercourse positions, or changes in the timing of intercourse during the cycle. Half of all couples may find that their problems are solved at this stage of testing and that only hormonal treatments are needed to be able to conceive.

However, if it is clear that hormone levels are normal or the couple does not respond to a trial of hormone therapy, the next stage is to check inside the body to see if the internal reproductive organs are healthy and functioning as they should. For the woman this usually includes an ultrasound picture of her uterus, a hysteroscopy to look at the inside surface of the uterus, a hysterosalpingogram to see if the Fallopian tubes are open, and a laparoscopy to look inside her abdomen to see the outside surfaces of the ovaries, Fallopian tubes, and uterus. The cost of this full stage of testing is around $2000.

For the man who is suspected of having a problem in his internal reproductive system, this stage of tests involves a vasogram (X-ray of the reproductive tract to look for blockages along the route sperm must travel) and/or a testicular biopsy (a tiny section of one testicle is removed for close examination). These tests also involve anesthesia and a brief hospital stay, all of which cost approximately $1500 to $2000.

Once couples have completed the tests needed at this stage, specialists should have a very clear picture of what the problems are, what treatments are recommended, what each costs, and the likelihood of success for each option.

I've been taking the fertility drug Clomid for three months. What are the chances of conceiving with this drug? Also, please tell me if there are any side effects?

Clomiphene citrate (sold under various brand names, one of which is Clomid) is a drug widely prescribed for women who are having difficulty getting pregnant. Clomiphene has one very specific action: it increases the hormones that stimulate the follicles of the ovaries to mature eggs. Many other possible causes of infertility (such as blocked Fallopian tubes) won't be remedied by clomiphene.

Before prescribing this drug, a physician must *first* determine that there are no disorders of the pituitary, adrenal, or thyroid glands, any of which can also disrupt the hormone cycle required to stimulate egg release. A physician must also establish that a woman has a functional ovary from which to release an egg; if the ovary is not capable of potential ovulation, clomiphene won't help.

If irregularity or lack of ovulation is proved to be the *only* cause of the infertility, then a couple using clomiphene can expect to almost match the conception rate of the general population—80 percent to 90 percent. It's an encouraging figure until one learns that only about 50 percent of women using clomiphene become pregnant. This is often because problems other than the lack of ovulation are involved and then other treatments must be explored.

Clomiphene treatment is typically started on the fifth day after menstrual flow begins in a given cycle; 50 milligrams is taken daily for five days. The woman must also take her BBT each morning and keep careful records. The couple is advised to have intercourse every other day for one week beginning five days after the last day on which medicine was taken. The woman usually has a pelvic exam at the end of that cycle.

If evidence of ovulation is not noted from temperature records or hormone tests, the dosage is increased during the next cycle. This sequence can continue up to a maximum dosage of 250 milligrams a day, but most specialists recommend only a three-cycle test, with an ultrasound examination during the third cycle to check the ovaries for egg development. Depending on what is found, other hormonal drugs such as hCG (human chorionic gonadotropin) are tried or other tests are done.

There are some side effects to clomiphene, such as acne, hot flashes, and breast tenderness. The drug is considered generally safe for the woman and, if conception occurs, the fetus, when used with careful monitoring. There is an increased rate of having twins (about 8 percent versus the usual 1 percent) but no increased risk of abnormalities.

This drug and others recently developed to treat specific fertility problems have proved to be a blessing for some infertile couples, but not for all. If you haven't conceived after 3 months (especially if you and your husband haven't had other standard tests), consult a fertility expert.

My husband was found to have a low sperm count and for three months has taken Clomid. Is this drug known to be successful? Is it too early to seek a fertility specialist?

No, it's not too early to seek the advice of a specialist. The usual procedure *before* using this drug is to rule out other possible causes of infertility for both partners, then to establish the male's capacity to respond to the drug. This is determined by a testicular biopsy and tests of various hormone levels.

Experiments using clomiphene citrate (Clomid is a brand name) to treat male infertility have noted an increase in testosterone levels and the number and motility (ability to swim strongly in a forward direction) of sperm. But some men using the drug at first showed an increase, and then a decrease, in sperm count.

You didn't mention how low your husband's sperm count was, but you should know that there's a 25 percent pregnancy rate, even without treatments, among men found to have so-called "low sperm counts."

Because you have already become involved with one infertility treatment based on a relatively powerful drug, it's time for both of you to be evaluated by a specialist to determine whether taking that drug is the most appropriate treatment or whether other steps will be more helpful.

My husband and I have been trying to have a child for nearly two years now. So far, no luck. My husband had a sperm count done; I had a hysterosalpingo-gram, a dye test, a postcoital test, and a laparoscopy. All these tests have found nothing wrong with either of us.

My doctor isn't a fertility specialist but he's an excellent doctor with whom I feel comfortable. He's had me on Clomid, APL injections, and estrogen for approximately one year on and off. Now he wants me to try Pergonal. I want more information before I take this drug.

What are the side effects? What are the chances I'll get pregnant if I take it?

Pergonal is a purified mixture of gonadotropins (hormones made in the pituitary gland at the base of the brain) extracted from the urine of postmenopausal women who have high levels of these hormones because their ovaries have stopped making estrogen. When injected, these hormones carry the message "Make more estrogen" to the ovaries, which stimulates growth of the ovarian follicles holding the eggs.

The woman has daily blood tests of estrogen levels, and the follicles are monitored by ultrasound until they reach a specific size. Then a second hormo-nal drug—hCG—is given to trigger actual release of the matured egg or eggs. In one study of Pergonal therapy, 87 percent of the women ovulated and more than half eventually became pregnant.

There are two primary risks involved. Between 1 percent and 3 percent of women using Pergonal experience overstimulation of the ovary (a painful and potentially damaging enlargement) requiring immediate hospitalization. Also, there is about a 20 percent chance of multiple births, which have a lower rate of full-term survival than do single births. Most of the recent, well-publicized multiple births were related to Pergonal treatment.

Pergonal is effective *only* if a woman's infertility is caused by the failure to ovulate. Effective and safe use also requires constant monitoring using sophisticated tests, with results available on a daily basis, to determne the condition of the ovaries and the exact day the second drug (hCG) should be given.

Furthermore, the manufacturer of Pergonal cautions, "It should become obvious that, unless a physician is willing to devote considerable time to these patients and be familiar with and conduct the necessary laboratory studies, he should not use Pergonal."

You're lucky to have found an excellent and sensitive personal physician, but unless you are being closely monitored by daily laboratory tests and ultrasound, go to a fertility specialist who has special equipment, round-the-clock laboratory support, and the experience required to use these drugs safely.

I am 28 and have been trying to get pregnant for five years. I've had an infertility work-up. My doctor has diagnosed me as having Stein-Leventhal syndrome. My doctor put me on Clomid, Parlodel, and prednisone. I take my temperature every morning but so far no luck. Isn't there some drug to thin out the hard shell surrounding the ovary so an egg has no problem getting out and I could get pregnant? If I do get pregnant, what are my chances of having a normal baby?

The various drugs you're taking are often used to treat infertility due to Stein-Leventhal syndrome (more commonly called Polycystic Ovarian Disease or PCOD) when it co-exists with other hormonal problems.

You did not say how you take these drugs, what tests you've had, or what else the physician may have found. So I can only outline the complex PCOD situation and briefly describe some general treatments.

In PCOD, the ovaries do not release an egg every month or do not release eggs at all. The egg follicles swell and change into a cyst, and the membranes around the ovaries thicken (perhaps this was the "shell" you referred to, but human eggs are not like bird eggs and have no hard shell). Women with PCOD have constant levels of various hormones, unlike the normally fluctuating monthly hormone patterns of women without PCOD.

Diagnosing PCOD can be difficult and includes extensive blood testing for the levels of many hormones. Depending on the hormone levels found, proper treatment can include several different drugs such as prednisone, bromocriptine (Parlodel), or pure FSH.

These types of hormonal manipulations are done to stabilize a woman's menstrual cycles before a pregnancy is attempted. It is not unusual for this testing, retesting, and stabilizing stage of treatment to take several months.

If the drugs you're taking don't result in ovulation, the next step may be to try even stronger drugs such as hMG (human menopausal gonadotropin, Pergonal). This fertility drug is expensive (often more than $1000 per monthly cycle) and requires even more careful monitoring to ensure that the ovaries are not damaged. Monitoring, preferably with vaginal ultrasound, is also essential to determine how many eggs are developing to avoid the high risk of multiple pregnancies.

As you can see, treating infertility related to PCOD takes a great deal of testing, monitoring, and time. Because the drugs used are extremely powerful, it is important that a pregnancy be detected quickly and the drugs stopped immediately. If done correctly, the chances of having a healthy, normal baby are equal to those of women who do not have PCOD.

If you are being cared for by an experienced fertility specialist, your chances of becoming pregnant without high risks are good. However, if you and your husband have not been thoroughly tested for other possible problems or are not being carefully monitored by blood tests and ultrasound, you should consult a fertility clinic.

Is it true that a male who has had a vasectomy can have it reversed in order to have children?

It is true that he can try, but reversal is not always successful. Using microsurgical techniques, a surgeon can attempt to reconnect the vas deferens (the tubes that carry sperm from the testicles), which were cut during vasectomy. Chances for success vary, depending on the condition of the remaining tubes, how much of the tubes were removed, how long ago the vasectomy was done, and the skill of the surgeon.

The highest success rates are reported among men whose vasectomies are reversed within ten years, who had only a small section of vas deferens removed, and for whom the section removed was not near the end of the vas that connects to the epididymis, another section of the tube system (see Illustration 5 in Chapter 3).

However, researchers point out that the most crucial predictor of successful reversal is the skill, technique, and experience of the microsurgeon who performs the reversal surgery.

When operated on by the most skillful microsurgeons, 90 percent of vasectomized men accepted for surgery (and not all applicants are accepted) produced a normal, healthy sperm count from three to twelve months after surgery. Of these, 75 percent of the couples reported a pregnancy.

If you're interested in finding out more about this procedure, locate a fertility clinic or fertility expert. A fertility clinic can recommend other options, such as donor insemination, if surgery is not possible or is not successful in your case.

Reversing a vasectomy is much more complicated (and more expensive) than getting a vasectomy. Most studies place the total cost for vasectomy reversal at around $10,000. This is one reason why men are counseled to use other methods of contraception until they are *absolutely* certain that they want no more children.

I had my tubes tied and now I want to have a baby. My doctor says he doesn't have the right tools. Where can I get them untied? How much will it cost?

Although not always successful, it's possible in some cases to reverse tubal sterilization so that a woman can naturally conceive a baby. However, it's complicated, costly, and involves major surgery.

Although tubal sterilization is commonly referred to as "tying the tubes," a great deal more is involved than tying a knot. It involves removing, burning, clamping, or blocking an entire section of each Fallopian tube. Repair of the tubes requires an incision into the abdomen and tedious reconstruction of the tubes using microsurgery.

The success rate for tubal reanastomosis (reconstruction of the tubes) currently is reported to be between 20 and 90 percent, depending on what section of the tubes is involved (the closer to the uterus the better), how much of the tubes are damaged, and what type of procedure was used (some clamps or stitches reverse better than does burning). If you've ever had an infection in your tubes, the resulting swelling and scarring might further reduce your chances.

Success can be improved by selecting a physician who is highly experienced and specializes in this reconstructive procedure. The technical skill required is very high since the tubes themselves are tiny, the repair thread is so thin it is nearly invisible, and any stitch that leaves a rough spot on the inside of the tubes increases the risk of an ectopic pregnancy (when the fertilized egg implants and grows in a tube rather than in the uterus). Contact a fertility specialist who can also tell you whether other options, such as in vitro fertilization, might be more appropriate in your case.

Although surgical fees and hospital costs vary across the country, the total bill could be approximately $12,000.

I seem to be sterile because of scarring in the Fallopian tubes—the result of an infection caused by an IUD many years ago. Is there any way of successfully reversing this type of infertility? How about using lasers or microsurgery?

Both lasers and microsurgery have been used successfully to open or repair scarred Fallopian tubes damaged by infection. A newer technique called TBT (transcervical balloon tuboplasty) is also available in a few centers. The rate of pregnancy following these procedures varies greatly, depending on the type of damage found, its location, and the skill of the surgeon.

A single blockage in the middle of a Fallopian tube or at the end nearest the uterus, for example, is more successfully repaired than a blockage at the ends of the tubes near the ovaries, where the fimbriae must be in motion to sweep the egg into the Fallopian tube. In some cases of tubal infection, the entire tubal structure of muscles and tiny hairlike cilia are so badly damaged that surgery won't help.

A number of diagnostic steps may be required to determine exactly where your tubes are blocked or damaged and which procedure might correct the problem. These include examination by hysteroscope (a thin instrument inserted through the vagina and cervix), which permits a close look at the inside of the uterus and the openings into the Fallopian tubes. Examination by laparoscope (an instrument inserted through a small incision in the abdomen) provides a look at the outside surface of the ovaries, tubes, uterus, and other pelvic organs.

The equipment and experienced personnel to do the tests and any corrective treatments are not yet widely available, so locate a fertility clinic or specialist highly experienced in tubal repair.

I've heard doctors talk about getting eggs for in vitro fertilization. I thought only one egg matured per month. I can't imagine them finding a tiny egg without major surgery.

Many of the new infertility treatments including in vitro fertilization, GIFT (gamete intrafallopian transfer), ZIFT (zygote intrafallopian transfer), PROST (transfer of a pronucleus), and TEST (transfer of an embryo), involve collecting eggs just before they are ready to be released from the ovaries. This used to be done by inserting a laparoscope (a thin microscope-like instrument) through a small incision near the navel. Now most fertility specialists use a procedure involving vaginal ultrasound to guide a needle inserted through the wall of the vagina. There are usually several mature eggs available because the woman is given fertility drugs to stimulate her ovaries before this step.

The specialist uses the ultrasound or the laparoscope to find the eggs. Then a small suction device draws them from the ovarian follicles into a sterile tube and out of the woman's body. The newest procedures are carried out in an operating room but the patient does not necessarily require general anesthesia. Discomfort is minimal and incisions are small.

Then the eggs and sperm from the father's semen are mixed in a special solution in a glass laboratory dish. If sperm fertilize one or more eggs, they are allowed to develop for a few hours or days (depending on the procedure) and then are placed in the woman's uterus or a Fallopian tube through a small tube inserted through the cervix (which does not require any surgery at all).

Two months ago I attempted in vitro fertilization. The doctor retrieved five eggs, all were fertilized, the transfer went perfectly, but implantation did not occur. I've heard that only one of three in vitro attempts is successful. Why is this?

Successful implantation of a pre-embryo in the uterus is the least understood step in the process of in vitro fertilization. When implantation occurs, it is usually two to three days after the fertilized egg is deposited in the woman's uterus which must be in the cycle stage most able to support implantation. Often hormonal drugs are used to obtain the best possible uterine environment.

Slightly different procedures such as GIFT, ZIFT, PROST, and TEST are being used to overcome problems with implantation. For example, in GIFT, the eggs are mixed with sperm and then placed into a Fallopian tube rather than the uterus. It is thought that this more closely mimics the natural fertilization and implantation process (see Illustration 28).

Estimates of the overall success rate for in vitro fertilization for 1988 were that 12 percent of couples had a full-term pregnancy. The rate for GIFT was 21 percent, but there are not yet data on the newer methods. Success rates for different clinics vary, so it's important for any couple considering these procedures to ask a number of questions: for example, How many couples did you treat last year? How many egg retrievals per couple were done and how many clinical pregnancies resulted? Established clinics may be able to cite what is called a "take home baby" rate. Make sure the data reflect a full 12 months and not just selected months in which many births occurred. Ask if the same experts still work at the clinic that worked there when the data were compiled.

Also ask about screening criteria. Clinics that accept only younger women (age 35 or younger) will have higher success rates, but that may not accurately reflect their status as compared to clinics that also accept older women (the success rate in that case may be a little lower); if you're 35 or older you will want to consider the clinic most experienced in dealing with older couples. If a clinic you contact won't provide this information, find another clinic willing to do so.

It is important to try to keep the failure rates of these new procedures in perspective. It is estimated that about 50 percent of eggs fertilized by sexual intercourse do not implant or they miscarry in the first two or three weeks after conception—without a woman even realizing that conception had occurred (these are called "missed abortions"). Moreover, between four to twenty weeks after conception, spontaneous abortion (miscarriage) occurs in around 20 percent of diagnosed pregnancies.

The first in vitro baby was born in 1978. Actually, remarkable progress has been made in only a short time. If one considers that couples without fertility problems have only a 20 percent chance of success in each reproductive cycle, even a 10 percent success rate for in vitro fertilization sounds wonderful since these couples would not have been able to have children at all only a decade ago.

My doctor found that I am infertile, and my wife and I have decided to consider artificial insemination. Frozen sperm is the choice of the clinic we visited. How are donors chosen for the procedure? What are the risks involved? Can a good match be made for us?

Donor insemination is the term most often used to describe the use of sperm from a donor not known to the couple. This method accounts for the birth of 20,000 to 60,000 healthy babies each year in the United States alone.

Donor insemination is an excellent option for couples in which the husband is either infertile or carries a high risk of passing on a genetic disease. Many couples prefer donor insemination to adoption because, among other reasons, they have the opportunity to experience the pregnancy and the baby inherits the mother's genetic makeup.

Ask the clinic how it screens donors, because policies do vary. It's important that this screening include a careful family medical history of each donor, a thorough screening for all sexually transmitted diseases (including AIDS), and a list of each donor's physical characteristics so that a donor who physically resembles the father can be selected.

With careful donor screening, the chances of having a healthy baby are high, comparable to those in the general population. Donors to frozen-sperm banks usually are more thoroughly screened than are donors of fresh semen and there's time to do follow-up tests on the donor. Moreover, the American Fertility Society and the Centers for Disease Control agree that use of fresh semen is no longer recommended. Since frozen sperm banks can store the sperm, there are more donors to choose from. You should also be given a copy of the donor's family medical history so that your child's physicians can refer to it for any future medical evaluations. You will not, however, be given the name of the donor, nor will he be given yours.

Laws covering donor insemination vary from state to state, so ask the clinic about your legal status regarding the offspring. In most cases, you will be asked to sign a document that establishes you as the legal father of any child conceived following insemination.

From 70 to 80 percent of women who use donor insemination become pregnant, but only about 15 percent conceive in the first attempt. It often takes several tries (with insemination being done at the time of highest fertility each cycle) before conception occurs.

The pregnancy rate for frozen sperm is a little lower than the rate for fresh sperm. This may be because the timing of insemination must be more precisely matched to the woman's release of an egg, since frozen sperm appear to live for a shorter time than do fresh sperm. However, frozen sperm carry no increased risk of genetic damage or birth defects compared to fresh sperm.

There is also a comparable program for women who do not release eggs or who carry a genetic disease. In these "egg donor" programs a woman is hired to undergo the hormonal stimulation and retrieval steps used for in vitro fertilization or other procedures, but after the donor eggs and the father's sperm are mixed, they are placed inside the wife, who then carries the pregnancy to term. The child has genetic material from the father and the egg donor. The pregnancy rate for these procedures is around 20 percent. Hormonal drugs must be used so that the environment of the mother's uterus and the time of the donor's egg release coincide.

My wife and I would like to have a child, but it's not possible for her to conceive. We're interested in finding a surrogate mother, but don't know where to start.

Because all types of surrogate procedures involve complicated legal issues, you might first want to consult a lawyer to see what laws are involved in your state. Locate a fertility clinic near you or write to the American Fertility Society to ask for information about surrogate programs.

PREGNANCY AND BIRTH

I've heard that even if a woman is pregnant she can still have her menstrual flow. Is this true?

No, a pregnant woman does not continue to have her "true" menstrual flow. About 30 percent of women do have bleeding at some point during a pregnancy, but that bleeding is not menstruation. Even when bleeding occurs on exactly those days a woman would have expected to have her menstrual flow if she were not pregnant (which does happen to some women), it is considered to be different from menstruation. The amount of blood is usually less than the usual menstrual flow and lighter in color (pinkish rather than dark red).

One of the most common causes of bleeding in the early weeks of pregnancy results from implantation of the embryo in the lining of the uterus (a normal process). In some women, however, bleeding can be a sign that the placenta is not producing enough progesterone or that there's an irritation or infection of the cervix or vagina. Sometimes, strenuous activity or a fall can jar the uterus enough to cause bleeding from the placenta. Or bleeding can be the first signal of a serious medical emergency—for example, an ectopic pregnancy (when the embryo implants and begins to grow in a Fallopian tube or location other than the uterus).

For these reasons, *all* bleeding during pregnancy must be reported to your physician immediately. If the bleeding is accompanied by pain or cramping and you cannot reach your physician, go to a hospital emergency room.

A friend is pregnant and has a yeast infection. I thought I read someplace that this could harm a baby, but my friend says she's not worried.

Your friend should insist that her obstetrician does careful testing for all possible organisms known to cause vaginal infections. Many infectious organisms can cause symptoms that appear to be simple vaginal infections, but some organisms can cause serious problems for a fetus and may result in premature birth or infection of the newborn during the birth process.

Could you tell me if it is possible for a woman to ever have a normal baby, if the woman has herpes?

Yes. Many thousands of healthy babies are born to women with herpes each year. With an estimated 20 million or more infected Americans, there are only about 700 babies born with herpes every year (one out of every 7,500 live births). And most of those cases occurred because the mothers had their first herpes outbreak during pregnancy. Primary genital herpes infections during pregnancy are related to increased miscarriage and prematurity (a good reason to use condoms when you are pregnant). Recurrent herpes outbreaks are not associated with prematurity or miscarriage.

But herpes does require special management and attention in a pregnant woman. If there are active herpes sores in the mother's vagina or genital area at the time of birth, there's a chance the baby can be infected. (Some researchers put this risk at 50 percent.) Since a newborn's immune system is weak, herpes can be a serious health problem.

With careful monitoring, and the understanding that *if* a herpes sore is present near the end of the pregnancy a caesarean delivery will be performed, there's no reason for a woman who already has herpes to fear passing the virus to her newborn.

I'm 20 years old and three months pregnant. I'm afraid that I won't produce enough lubrication or get wide enough for a baby to come out.

I've never had an orgasm and never produce enough lubrication or get wide enough to have good sex, so I don't see how I will be able to have a baby. I've talked to other girls about this and no one knows what to say.

Call your doctor or your local hospital and sign up for childbirth classes. Getting basic information about how a baby is born and how to prepare for labor and delivery should help reduce your concerns. You'll learn that a woman's vagina expands naturally during childbirth, allowing the baby to pass through.

The response of your body during intercourse (*see Chapter 6*) is different from your body's responses during delivery of a baby. The physical mechanisms that dilate (open) the cervix and push the baby out of the uterus are not known to be related to either orgasmic capacity or lubrication during sexual arousal.

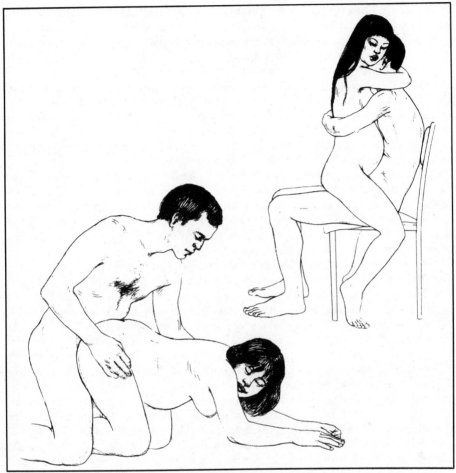

Illustration No. 29. **Two Intercourse Positions Recommended During Pregnancy.** The kneeling position may be most comfortable when the woman has a backache or is in the final stages of pregnancy. The man should avoid deep thrusting. In the sitting position, the woman can control the depth of penetration. Sitting or propped-up positions may be preferred when the woman is experiencing indigestion or heartburn even in early pregnancy.

It is also important that you receive good prenatal care. I urge you to find a physician or clinic with whom you can talk openly about these concerns.

Does making love during pregnancy hurt the baby or the mother?

There is no scientific evidence that sexual intercourse at any stage of pregnancy harms the vast majority of mothers or babies. Those couples whose pregnancy ended in miscarriage should understand that it is extremely unlikely that sexual activity was a direct cause of the loss.

There are, however, a few exceptions to this general rule. For example, if the woman has vaginal bleeding, pain, or leakage of amniotic fluid, sexual intercourse should be discontinued until a physician advises otherwise. Women who have a history of premature labor and delivery or miscarriages, or whose cervix has already dilated, may be cautioned against having intercourse or told to use a condom. The uterine contractions associated with an orgasm may induce labor, which can be a problem if the fetus is not fully developed. On the other hand, orgasm is one nonchemical way to initiate the uterine contractions needed for delivery at the end of the full gestation period.

Moreover the prostaglandins in semen may induce uterine contractions in some women—another reason for using a condom.

Studies have compared babies born to women who continued sexual intercourse throughout pregnancy with those of women who stopped having intercourse at some point in the pregnancy. Research also has compared babies born to mothers who reported having orgasms with babies whose mothers didn't have orgasms. In both studies, researchers found no significant differences among these babies on any measures of infant health.

However, for complete safety, there are two sexual practices that women must avoid during pregnancy: (1) Forcefully blowing air into the vagina (which should never be done) can cause an embolism (an air bubble), which can lead to death of the mother and the fetus, and (2) having sex with someone who carries a sexually transmitted disease, which can lead to fetal defects, disease, and in some cases death, depending on which STD organism is involved.

Not all pregnant women are interested in having sex, and some are interested in sex during some points of the pregnancy but not at others. Research by Masters and Johnson on pregnant women revealed a decreased desire for sex in the first trimester (months one to three), a rise in sexual interest in the second trimester (months four to six), and a gradual decline in the third trimester (month seven to birth). Other researchers report different patterns of sexual activity or interest in sex. Many books on pregnancy simply state that sexual desire and activity during pregnancy varies widely from one woman to the next.

Are some sex positions better during pregnancy? I'm afraid that having my husband be on top is not going to be pleasant very much longer.

Yes, positions that don't press on the woman's rounded abdomen are usually more comfortable.

Examples include two rear-entry positions (having both partners on their knees, with the male behind the female, or lying together on your sides with the male curled around the female's back—see Illustration 33 in Chapter 18). If you want to have intercourse facing each other, try having your husband sit on a chair while you straddle his lap; since your feet will be on the floor, you can also control the depth of penetration by shifting your weight and position.

Another option is for you to lie with your buttocks at the edge of the bed and your feet supported on a chair, with your husband between your legs, facing you.

We have a question we find a little difficult to ask our doctor. We're trying to have children and wonder if saliva on the penis before entering the vagina could cause miscarriage in early pregnancy?

No, the small amount of human saliva involved is not known to affect pregnancy in any adverse way. There is no reported connection between saliva and miscarriages.

I am three months pregnant. I enjoy oral sex with my husband and sometimes swallow his semen. What effect will the semen have on my baby?

None, as long as your husband is free of any STD organisms *(see Chapter 19).*

Are men affected physically by their wife's pregnancy? This sounds crazy, but it seems as if one of my friends gets fat and sick to his stomach every time his wife is pregnant—and then gets well as soon as she has the baby.

Yes, some men experience various physical ailments while their wives are pregnant. Some of these complaints resemble symptoms frequently associated with pregnancy—nausea, vomiting, loss of appetite, food cravings, headaches, backaches, insomnia, and temporary weight gains. Ailments may appear at any point during the wife's pregnancy and last only a short time, or continue until she has delivered the baby. In some cases, the father experiences abdominal cramps and chest pain during the wife's labor. (Keep in mind that we are discussing ordinary men who are *not* under the delusion that they themselves are pregnant—an extremely rare mental disorder.)

Some experts claim that these men feel so sympathetic with the mothers' physical problems they actually begin to experience the same physical discomfort. Others point out that the symptoms also resemble those of common anxiety, which may increase as the expectant father worries about supporting a larger family, loss of the woman's income, changes in the relationship, or other issues related to parenthood.

In some other cultures, fathers are expected to exhibit certain behaviors during the mother's pregnancy and childbirth. Anthropologists have studied the practice called couvade (French "to hatch"), since Marco Polo observed this custom in the Far East during the fourteenth century. Also documented in African, South American, American Indian, and Southern Pacific cultures, couvade is a ritual where the father acts out labor and childbirth. This custom has been explained as either a way for the father to prove his paternity or a courageous act of drawing bad luck to himself so that the mother can safely deliver a healthy baby.

CONCERNS AFTER THE BABY ARRIVES

I am expecting our first child and recently saw a film of a circumcision. I was surprised to learn that no anesthesia is used.

Is circumcision advisable for baby boys? And if we decide to have a son circumcised, can we request that anesthesia be used?

In 1989 the American Academy of Pediatrics (AAP) released a statement concerning circumcision of male newborns that outlined the potential medical benefits, as well as the risks, associated with this procedure.

Circumcision reduces a male's risk of penile cancer and prevents phimosis, paraphimosis, and balanopothitis (all infections of the foreskin). It may also reduce an infant's risk of urinary tract infection. Studies of the relationship between various STDs and circumcision yield conflicting findings. However, the risk of some STDs (especially those due to the various strains of human papillomavirus) may be reduced for both the man and his sexual partners. In a study of military personnel, a higher rate of gonorrhea was associated with uncircumcised white men. A relationship with higher rates of genital ulcers, AIDS, viral infections, syphilis, and genital herpes may also exist but requires further careful research to be confirmed. The incidence of cervical cancer also appears to be higher for women whose uncircumcised partners are infected with human papillomavirus.

Whether or not to use an anesthetic during circumcision remains unclear because there are still little data on this question. There is no doubt that most newborn males exhibit behavioral and physical signs of pain, both during the procedure and for a few hours after circumcision. Although using a small amount of lidocaine (a local anesthetic) will reduce pain, any risks of using this drug on newborns are not yet known.

The AAP points out that the decision to circumcise one's son will be influenced by the parents' beliefs, religion, cultural attitudes, and traditions. They recommend that each physician fully explain to the parents both the benefits and risks—such as penile damage, although this is very rare.

If you decide not to circumcise your son, it is extremely important for you to understand how to keep the penis clean. Unlike earlier recommendations that the foreskin be forced back to clean under it, it is now known that this is possible in only 4 percent of newborns. At birth the foreskin is usually still developing and may not become separated from the head of the penis for many months. By the age of three, the foreskin can be fully retracted in 80 to 90 percent of uncircumcised boys. So gentle washing of the surface should be done until the foreskin is easily retractable. Each boy should be taught how to carry out this important hygienic step.

One further point: If your son's penis looks different from his father's and perhaps his friends', you will need to explain that even though this is the case, both circumcised and uncircumcised penises are just fine. These conversations should begin at a young age, before he begins to ask questions.

My husband and I are expecting a baby and wonder whether, if it is a boy, he should be circumcised at birth or later. Is there any physical or psychological harm in having a boy circumcised later?

Although I am not aware of any research on circumcisions done after infancy for nonmedical reasons, I suspect that it would not be a good idea to wait. A few traditional cultures do practice circumcision or other cutting of the foreskin or genitals as part of a ritual transition from puberty into adulthood. One assumes that boys in these cultures view the experience as welcome, even if it is uncomfortable, since it means they are then regarded as men and treated as adults.

Since this type of ritual is not part of our culture, circumcision at puberty would not likely be so positive an experience. There could be real psychological problems, and there certainly is discomfort involved. Most males discover the pleasurable sensations in their genitals at a very young age and understandably fear that genital surgery might spoil their pleasure or interfere with erections.

If you and your husband decide not to have your son circumcised right after birth, any decision about later circumcision should be left completely to your son to decide.

I'm considering breast-feeding and know the advantages for the baby. But what are the advantages or disadvantages for myself? Also, what exactly is the change in appearance of the breasts if you breast-feed?

Changes in appearance of the breasts, such as droopiness or stretch marks in the skin, are related to the changes your body undergoes during pregnancy and not to breast-feeding. Postpregnancy appearance of the breasts differs greatly among women and cannot be predicted. Most physicians do recommend wearing a bra with good support during pregnancy and as long as you breast-feed.

There are both physiological and psychological benefits for the mother who breast-feeds. Nursing helps stimulate the uterus to contract back to its original size; this is why many physicians recommend beginning breast-feeding immediately after delivery. Other benefits for many women include the easy feeding (especially at night or away from home), closer emotional bonding with the baby, and pleasurable sensations.

Would you be kind enough to tell me why I have a squeezing feeling in my vagina which began when I started nursing my second child.

It was not clear from your letter if your vaginal squeezing occurs all the time, during sex, or only when you nurse. I ask this because it is not unusual for nursing mothers to have uterine and vaginal contractions when the baby is nursing. These contractions occur because the baby's sucking can release a specific substance (oxytocin) from the mother's brain, which in high amounts causes involuntary contractions of the mother's uterus and vagina. Some women become concerned about having these contractions, thinking that such feelings should only be associated with having sex or being sexually aroused. These contractions are normal during nursing.

I'm nursing my first baby and do not want to get pregnant again for several years. What type of birth control is safe to use while I'm nursing?

Anything a nursing mother ingests can show up in her milk and may affect her baby. Even some vegetables have been shown to cause problems; for example, asparagus may cause gas. That is why you must be especially careful in choosing your birth control method right now.

Several contraceptive methods can be used soon after childbirth and appear to be safe for both the nursing mother and her baby. These include condoms and spermicides such as foams, creams, and jellies. Although diaphragms also do not affect breast-feeding, most doctors suggest women wait until their six-week checkup before having a diaphragm fitted because of changes in the uterus and vagina.

Although more research is needed on the use of birth control while breast-feeding, the Pill (especially any containing estrogen) has been shown to decrease milk supply in some women. In addition, we do not yet know the long-term effects on the baby of consuming hormones in the Pill that appear in the milk.

I'm 26 and had my first child 15 months ago. I breast-fed her for two months. I still have not started having my periods again. I read that your period should start again 12 to 18 months after you stop breast-feeding. Is this true?

The length of time between childbirth and reappearance of menstrual flow varies greatly, whether or not a woman nurses her baby. In one study, 91 percent of non-nursing mothers and 33 percent of nursing mothers had menstruated by three months after childbirth. It's time to ask your family physician or gynecologist about your lack of menstrual flow.

I am a 37-year-old mother still nursing my 19-month-old son. I began getting periods again about three months ago, although one of them was three weeks late. I'm wondering how much nursing my son will protect me from getting pregnant.

It is true that while a woman is breast-feeding she may not release eggs as regularly as usual (thereby somewhat reducing her risk of pregnancy), but breast-feeding is not a reliable method of contraception. Moreover, any contraceptive effect would end immediately when she stopped nursing or even if she missed a feeding. Until you see the doctor, use a reliable method of contraception (such as condoms and foam) that will not appear in your breast milk.

I experienced painful intercourse for months after each of my two children were born. After the first baby, I tried to chalk it up to a bungled delivery of a very large baby, but before my second childbirth I had the good fortune to read about how the nursing mother's reduced estrogen levels can cause atrophy of the vaginal tissues. I then had confidence that my hormones would normalize and the pain would stop when I quit nursing, and it did.

Doctors either seem to be unaware of this or don't want to reveal this information. Please discuss this so other women don't have to go through this problem or worry. Also, are there any other physical effects of altered hormonal levels while nursing?

All new mothers, not just those who breast-feed their babies, need information about sex after childbirth. Both partners should know, for example, how to cope with the woman's vaginal changes and be encouraged to use other sexual activities to express love until intercourse becomes comfortable again.

There are several reasons intercourse might be uncomfortable. It may take several months for an episiotomy (a surgical enlargement of the vaginal opening) or a repaired vaginal tear to heal completely. The vagina may lack natural lubrication and vaginal tissues may become thin and easily irritated from the low level of estrogen following childbirth. Estrogen levels also remain low when a woman breast-feeds.

There is some evidence that the hormonal changes following pregnancy and/or breast-feeding affect a woman's interest in sex, but factors such as fatigue from child care or focusing on the new role of motherhood may have a more direct impact than do hormone levels.

Techniques to help couples cope with changes after childbirth include using mutual touching and/or oral-genital activities until the vagina is healed. Nonprescription water-soluble lubricating products (such as K-Y jelly or Lubrin inserts) can be used if the vagina isn't producing enough natural lubrication when intercourse is attempted. Some experts also suggest that couples use intercourse positions (such as side-by-side; *see Illustration 33 in Chapter 18*) that permit the woman more control over insertion and depth of thrusting, which should be gentle.

It is important that both partners know what to expect and that a couple talk together about any physical changes and their feelings. It is not unusual for the man to fear inadvertently hurting the woman or for the woman to fear vaginal damage to the point that she experiences vaginismus (involuntary contraction of the muscles around the opening of the vagina), discussed in Chapter 8.

Couples who have difficulty regaining pleasurable sexual functioning within several months following childbirth should talk with a sex therapist or marriage counselor. Even a single visit may be enough to end unfounded fears or misunderstandings and to return to the pleasure enjoyed prior to delivery.

How soon after having a baby can I have sex? My husband is hinting that "it's time," and I'd like to begin again too.

You can resume intercourse when your vagina and cervix are fully healed. For some women this may take only two weeks, but other women take longer. If you had a caesarean delivery you may have to wait longer before having intercourse. Intercourse before healing is complete increases the risks of infecting any small tears in the vagina or the episiotomy (if you had one). In some cases it can take the episiotomy one or two months to heal fully enough to feel comfortable during intercourse. Check with your obstetrician to see how your healing is coming along.

In the meantime, consider expressing your love in ways that don't include intercourse. Helping your husband masturbate or engaging in oral-genital activities are two ways of doing this.

I'm 21 and had a baby boy five months ago. A couple of weeks before he was born, I lost all interest in sex with my husband. As of now, I still have no interest.

My husband is a very good-looking man but I can't bring myself to do anything more than cuddle with him. Any other sexual activities seem to turn me off. This is really worrying me; I know it upsets my husband. What's wrong with me?

It is not unusual for women to lose interest in sex after childbirth. This can be due to physical problems, including damage to vaginal tissues or changes in muscle support of the pelvic organs, that can result in discomfort or pain during intercourse. If you are breast-feeding your son, the lowered level of estrogen may reduce vaginal lubrication, which is another possible cause of discomfort during sex.

Other common factors include the effects of the dramatic change in life style associated with raising a child plus physical exhaustion from child care and disrupted sleep. Any person who doesn't feel well is likely to experience reduced sexual desire.

Even when desire is there, sex can be affected by the experience of being a new parent. Couples are often too distracted to fully enjoy sex—focusing on listening for the baby's cries, for example. They may feel sex must now be scheduled or restricted to times when they are sure the baby won't need their attention. Trying to repress any lovemaking sounds or vocalizations so that the baby is not awakened can also interfere with pleasure.

Psychological factors can also be involved. For example, you mentioned that your husband is "good-looking." If you feel you are less attractive after having a pregnancy, you may need reassurance about your appearance.

Remember you both have acquired new roles. You are now a mother and your husband is now a father. Sometimes the notion that "good" mothers and fathers do not have sex (or should not act like lovers) becomes difficult to overcome.

If the lack of desire continues but your general health is good and any gynecological discomfort from childbirth is gone, you should both consult a marriage counselor or sex therapist familiar with these concerns.

My husband acts like he resents our son. He says I spend all my time with the baby and don't love him any more. I do love him, but is this a normal change when a couple starts a family?

It depends on the couple. Some studies report that having a baby improved the marital relationship while other studies point to the birth of the first child as a major marital crisis. One survey reported that for more than one-half of couples, their sex life had not recovered even a full year after birth of the first child.

It's also not unusual for either partner to feel jealous of the new baby or feel pressured into competition for affection and attention. If your husband continues to feel this way after several months, it's important that you talk with a marriage counselor.

Further Readings

Behrman, S. J.; Kistner, R. W.; and Patton, G. W., Jr. *Progress in Infertility*. 3rd ed. Boston, MA: Little, Brown and Company, 1988.
(This is a highly technical book but anyone with a specific fertility problem will find extensive information on tests and treatments.)

Bellina, J. H., and Wilson, J. *You Can Have a Baby: Everything you need to know about fertility*. Toronto: Bantam Books, 1984.
(An overview of how to overcome fertility problems written in a popular style.)

The Columbia University College of Physicians and Surgeons. *Complete Guide to Pregnancy*. New York: Crown Publishers, Inc., 1988.
(A helpful guide to all aspects of pregnancy.)

Wisot, A., and Meldrum, D. *New Options for Fertility*. New York: Pharos Books, 1990.
(One of the most current, easily readable, overviews of treatments for fertility problems and success rates for various techniques.)

16

Contraception

From the preceding chapter you know that reproduction involves a woman's egg being fertilized by a man's sperm, which is called conception. Here we explore the ways of preventing conception: *contraception*.

The most statistically perfect method of contraception is abstinence, which is defined as "denial of the appetites"—in this case, sexual appetite. Abstinence is not a realistic method of contraception for most adults. Contraceptive potions and devices are mentioned in historical records from thousands of years ago—interest in and use of contraception did not begin with the Pill, the diaphragm, or the condom.

Even though we now have several effective methods of contraception, modern couples often don't have a much clearer idea of how to have sex and not become pregnant than did the Egyptians or other ancient cultures. In the last five years letters to The Kinsey Institute have asked:

Can you get pregnant the first time you have sex?
Yes.
Can you get pregnant if you have sex during your menstrual flow?
Yes.
Can a girl get pregnant before she has her first menstrual flow?
Yes.
Can you get pregnant if you have sex standing up?
Yes.
Can you get pregnant if you have sex for only a few seconds?
Yes.
Can you get pregnant if the penis is withdrawn just before ejaculation?
Yes.
Can you get pregnant while you are breast-feeding?
Yes.
Can you get pregnant if ejaculation occurs on, but not inside, the female genitals?
Yes.

Can you get pregnant if you have sex in a bathtub, pool, or lake?
Yes.
Can you get pregnant if you douche immediately after sex?
Yes.
Can you get pregnant by swallowing semen?
No.

Although the presence of sperm in semen was not discovered until 1677, we know that most civilizations understood the connection between pregnancy and intercourse. Since ancient times, people have attempted to neutralize the fertilizing effects of intercourse.

An Egyptian papyrus from 1850 B.C. lists such contraceptive methods as crocodile dung mixed with a paste to form a pessary (a substance or device placed in the vagina to prevent sperm from entering the uterus). The effectiveness of this method was not reported, but based on what we now know about hygiene, putting dung in the vagina is clearly not a good idea. A 1550 B.C. papyrus describes a tamponlike pessary made from lint and then coated with ground acacia (a type of tree), colocynth (a fruit-bearing plant), dates, and honey. This device might have been somewhat effective, because acacia breaks down into lactic acid, an ingredient in modern spermicides. Records from Greek, Roman, Islamic, Persian, and other ancient cultures all include recipes for potions to be swallowed or inserted into the body to prevent pregnancy.

The Bible, the Talmud, and writings from other religions also mention various methods, including coitus interruptus (withdrawal), the use of vaginal sponges, and the preparation of contraceptive concoctions. According to some historians, the biblical story of Onan in the book of Genesis (33:9) verifies that those ancient peoples understood the connection between intercourse and pregnancy; it serves as one illustration that they knew about coitus interruptus at that time. (The story is *not* about masturbation, as many people believe).

The first description of a condom appeared in 1564. Made of linen, it was initially promoted as a protection against syphilis (it didn't work). In the 1700s condoms began to be made from animal intestines and were widely used for contraception. By that time, shops specializing in contraceptive products had appeared in Europe.

The history of contraception in the United States began in the mid-1700s with the importing of Hooper's Female Pills from England. A principal ingredient in the pill was aloes, an abortifacient (a drug that induces miscarriage).

Publications dating from 1830 recommended coitus interruptus, vaginal sponges, condoms, and douching (which doesn't work) to prevent pregnancy. Charles Goodyear discovered how to vulcanize rubber in 1843, and shortly thereafter rubber condoms were manufactured in large numbers. By 1880, one author noted that "probably more than one half of the adult population in the U.S. . . . is resorting to birth control."

Around the time of the Civil War, chemical abortifacients were widely advertised in newspapers and even available by mail, as were condoms and pessaries. Douche syringes, douche chemicals (some of which used opium, prussic acid, and strychnine—which we now know are very dangerous), vaginal sponges, and cervical caps made of beeswax were also easily obtained.

The widespread availability of birth control devices was not without controversy. In 1867 a doctor wrote: "There is scarcely a young woman ... whose marriage can be announced in the paper without her being insulted within a week by receiving through the mail a printed circular offering information and instrumentalities, and all needed facilities by which ... the increase of the family may be thwarted."

Then, in 1873, Congress passed the Comstock Law, which labeled birth control information obscene, and raids on producers and distributors began. In one raid in 1880, 64,000 "articles for immoral use of rubber" were confiscated. Yet condoms, cervical caps, vaginal sponges, and other devices continued to be available from some physicians and pharmacists.

Around 1880, the diaphragm was invented in Germany, followed in 1909 by an intrauterine device (IUD). The idea that there is a "safe" time in a woman's cycle to have sex also became popular in the nineteenth century. Unfortunately, abstinence from sex was recommended from the time of menstrual bleeding until midcycle—a schedule which makes conception *more*, not less, likely. Not until the 1930s did researchers in Japan and Austria discover that women release an egg at midcycle—not immediately after menstruation, as had been believed.

Until the Food and Drug Administration approved the first birth control pill in 1960, the diaphragm used with spermicidal jellies was the method recommended most frequently by physicians and women's clinics in the United States.

CONTRACEPTIVE METHODS

Every person—or, preferably, each couple through mutual discussion— should choose a contraceptive method based on accurate information about failure rates, reversibility (for the time when they do decide to start a family), safety, and their personal health status.

Age, life style, and personal values also play an important role in choosing a contraceptive method. We now also know that a person's health and later fertility can be affected by sexually transmitted diseases (STDs) such as chlamydia and the viruses that cause genital warts and AIDS. Therefore, people must also consider those methods which offer effective protection against STDs. It is also true that the "best" choice for contraception at one point in a person's life may not be the "best" at another time—as general health, circumstances, or relationships change.

There are three basic concepts to keep in mind as you evaluate various contraceptive methods: Not using any method for one year (leaving it to chance) will result in pregnancy for 90 out of 100 couples; no contraceptive method is 100 percent effective; and the risk of dying from *any* approved contraceptive method is far smaller than the risk of dying from pregnancy and childbirth for the vast majority of women.

Approximate costs for each method of contraception are provided later in this chapter, but these vary widely. If cost is a major consideration, go to a family planning clinic. Most clinics have a sliding scale for fees and people with low incomes can receive health care services and products at little or no cost.

The rest of this chapter is devoted to questions and answers about specific contraceptive methods, arranged from the *most* to the *least* effective when used consistently and according to instructions. The table that follows summarizes information about these methods, which are explained more fully in the text.

Contraceptive method	Lowest observed failure rate in 100 users who used method correctly for one year	Failure rate in 100 typical users who used method for one year	Reversibility	Protection against STDs
Vasectomy	0.4	0.4	Not Usually	No
Tubal sterilization	0.4	0.4	Not Usually	No
Combined oral contraceptive pills	0.5	2.0	Yes	No, but associated with reduced risk and severity of PID+
Progestin-only pills	1.0	2.5	Yes	No, but may reduce risk of PID+
IUD	1.5**	5.0**	Yes (except if fertility is impaired by infection)	No, and *may* increase risk of PID +
Condom	2.0	10	Yes	Yes, but better if used with spermicide*
Condom and spermicide	+ +	2-3	Yes	Yes*
Diaphragm with spermicide	2.0	19	Yes	Some*
Cervical cap	2.0	13	Yes	Some*
Spermicidal foams, creams, jellies, and vaginal suppositories	3-5	18	Yes	Some*

Contraceptive method (cont.)	Lowest observed failure rate in 100 users who used method correctly for one year	Failure rate in 100 typical users who used method for one year	Reversibility	Protection against STDs
Sponge with spermicide	9-11	10-20	Yes	Some*
Coitus interruptus (withdrawal)	16	23	Yes	No
Fertility awareness (basal body temperature, mucus method, calendar, and "rhythm")	2-20	24	Yes	No
Douching	+ +	40	Yes	No, and may increase the risk of PID+, subsequent infertility, or ectopic pregnancy
Chance—no contraception used	90	90	Yes (unless fertility has been impaired by exposure to STDs)	No

Note: The majority of the failure rate data in columns 1 and 2 are from *Contraceptive Technology,* 13th revised edition. Different failure rates found in other studies are discussed for each method in the chapter.

*Also provide some protection against STDs if they contain nonoxynol-9 or octoxynol.

**These data are for brands of IUDs no longer available in the U.S.

+PID—Pelvic Inflammatory Disease *(see Chapter 19)*

+ +Data not available

Vasectomy and Tubal Sterilization

Surgical sterilization, whether vasectomy for men or tubal sterilization for women, is considered the most effective form of contraception available to date. It is also the most popular among married couples age 30 and older in the United States, with nearly 17 million U.S. men and women having chosen sterilization and many millions more in other countries.

Vasectomy means cutting a man's vas deferens (see Illustration 5 in Chapter 3), the two tubes that carry sperm from where they are produced in each testicle up into his body on their journey toward the penis. These tubes can be easily reached through a small opening made in the scrotum. The result is that no sperm can reach the area inside the body where semen is pooled for ejaculation.

Tubal ligation literally means "tying" a woman's Fallopian tubes (see Illustration 3 in Chapter 2), the two tubes through which eggs from the ovaries travel to the uterus and inside which sperm meet the egg for fertilization. There are different ways of performing a tubal sterilization, all of which involve surgery to go inside a woman's body (either through the abdomen or vagina) to cut, burn, tie, clip, or otherwise block the tubes.

The failure rate (when pregnancy occurs, or when sperm still appear in the ejaculate) following vasectomy is 160 for every 100,000 men on a lifetime basis. Lifetime failure rates following tubal sterilization vary from 276 to 326 per 100,000 women, depending on the specific surgical technique used. If pregnancy does occur women who have had a tubal ligation have a higher risk of ectopic pregnancy (when a fertilized egg implants in the tube rather than in the uterus), a life-threatening situation.

Risk of death from these procedures is zero for vasectomy, compared with 4.72 per 100,000 women for tubal sterilization by laparoscopy and 2.29 per 100,000 women by abdominal incision (most of these deaths are associated with risks related to anesthesia rather than the surgery itself).

Clearly, vasectomy for the man is a more effective and far safer choice for a couple than is tubal sterilization for the woman. It is also less expensive and carries a lower risk of complications following the procedure (6170 complications following abdominal tubals and 2100 after laparoscopic tubals as compared to 43 after vasectomy per 100,000).

Unfortunately, there are widespread myths that vasectomy reduces a man's sex drive, makes him unable to ejaculate, or carries long-term health risks—none of which are true.

Both vasectomy and tubal sterilization must be considered permanent and *irreversible*, despite claims to the contrary. Another disadvantage is that neither procedure provides protection against STDs; some researchers, however, speculate that in the case of those STDs carried by sperm, vasectomy may reduce risks for a man's sexual partner.

My husband and I are considering sterilization to avoid future pregnancies. We're both in our 30s. Which is safest, tubal ligation or vasectomy? We are mainly concerned with health.

Vasectomy is the much safer procedure, taking into account a variety of health measures. According to major studies over a 15-year period, there were no deaths in the United States attributed to vasectomy, but there were an average of more than four deaths per 100,000 for laparoscopies and more than two deaths per 100,000 for abdominal incision (two different methods for doing tubal sterilizations). Vasectomies also have a lower failure rate.

If a man decides to have a vasectomy, he faces few negative long-term side effects. Even though about 50 to 75 percent of vasectomized men develop antibodies to their sperm, this doesn't seem to be a health problem. One study of monkeys indicated that these antibodies increased atherosclerotic problems in blood vessels (hardening of the arteries), but no such evidence has been found in many studies of humans. Moreover, one large study of more than 10,000 vasectomized men (most of whom had had their vasectomies at least eight to 10 years before the study) reported *lower* rates of heart attacks, diabetes, and deaths due to cancer or cardiovascular disease as compared to 10,000 men who had not had vasectomies.

Complications following the traditional type of vasectomy (cutting a one-half inch incision in the scrotum) include occasional temporary discomfort or swelling and formation of a blood clot at the surgical site; more serious, but rare, side effects are infections of the epididymis *(see Illustration 5 in Chapter 3)* or other male tubes or ducts. Some four or five of each 100 men who have a vasectomy will experience a complication, but most are temporary and easily treated by using ice packs, wearing a jock strap for a short time for support, or taking aspirin or antibiotics. A newer method of vasectomy developed in China involves using a special needle to make a tiny opening into the scrotum to reach the vas deferens tubes; research in the U.S. on this "no scalpel" method reports a greatly reduced incidence of complications. This method does not even require stitches to close the scrotum.

After a vasectomy, a couple should use condoms or some other method of contraception until the man has had two semen analyses showing no sperm in the ejaculate. It takes several weeks (10 to 20 ejaculations) for sperm already in the tubes and ducts inside a man's body to finish their maturation and journey through the reproductive tract.

The risk of complications following tubal sterilization varies from around 2 percent to 11 percent, depending on the type of surgery and anesthesia used. They include various types of abdominal infections, postoperative bleeding, punctures of other organs, and postsurgical scarring. It is important to be aware that tubal ligation is major surgery; it involves general anesthesia and sometimes opening of the abdominal cavity. Also, infection in the abdomen is much more serious than infection in the scrotum. The rate of postsurgical complications also varies with the skill of the surgeon; those who perform more procedures each year have lower postsurgical complication rates.

What's the typical cost of a vasectomy compared with having one's tubes tied? My husband and I are thinking about sterilization but we're concerned about the cost.

The average cost of a vasectomy ranges from less than $200 to around $1000, depending on whether it is done in a clinic or a hospital. This is much lower than for a tubal sterilization, which ranges from around $1500 to more than

$2000 depending on the type of surgery and anesthesia used. Some insurance companies cover the cost of either procedure, and many family planning clinics will adjust their fees to a person's income.

My husband is considering having a vasectomy. Can it be reversed and, if so, what is the reversal success rate?

Thinking about reversibility of a contraceptive method is important; but if you're thinking about having a family, vasectomy isn't the contraceptive method for you right now. Surgically reconnecting the vas deferens is possible in some cases, but is certainly not guaranteed to be successful. The conception rate following microsurgery to repair the vas deferens after a vasectomy depends on a number of variables and ranges between 18 and 60 percent. *(See Chapter 15 for more information.)*

If you're not ready to make a permanent decision, talk to your physician or family planning clinic about using other, more completely reversible, methods of contraception. In addition, if your husband decides to have a vasectomy, ask about the possibility of having some of his semen frozen and stored in a sperm bank. Then, if he wanted to father a child after the vasectomy, the semen could be thawed and used for insemination.

My husband had a vasectomy a year ago. He had his sperm count checked at six weeks and at nine weeks and still had sperm in the ejaculate.

He's decided not to go back for any more sperm counts. He says he must be sterile by now, so we're not using any birth control. I'm not sure about this, and feel great relief every time I start my period. Are the sperm usually gone by now?

Any man who is found to have live sperm in his ejaculate in the post-vasectomy tests should be reexamined. In fewer than one out of 100 vasectomies, a nerve or blood vessel is mistakenly cut instead of the vas deferens; to check for this error, most physicians send the cut pieces from the vas deferens to a laboratory to confirm that they have cut the correct structure. More rarely, in one of 100,000 cases, a man is found to have a third vas deferens that was not noticed during the vasectomy.

Some physicians also recommend having a final "safety check" sperm count one year after the vasectomy. This is to determine whether the cut ends of the vas deferens have recanalized (spontaneously grown back together in such a way that sperm can again move from the testicles to the reproductive tract). Recanalization occurs in about 1 percent of all vasectomies.

You should use some other form of contraception until he goes back to the physician to have the situation checked out.

What happens to a man's sperm after he's had a vasectomy? What happens to a woman's eggs after she's had a tubal ligation? Do they just accumulate somewhere inside the body?

Neither sperm nor eggs accumulate in the body. They quickly disintegrate and are absorbed by the body. The volume absorbed is very small, and absorption is a common process for the human body. Millions of red blood cells, for instance, die, are absorbed, and then replaced in the circulatory system each day.

Both before and after a vasectomy men produce seminal fluid in the prostate and sperm in the testicles. A vasectomy cuts only the tubes that carried sperm from the testicles to where they mixed with the seminal fluid, so men continue to ejaculate semen (minus only the sperm) after a vasectomy. Men do not notice a difference in the quantity of semen ejaculated, because the amount of sperm missing from the ejaculate is equivalent to only a tiny drop.

Women's bodies also continue to carry out their reproductive cycles after a tubal sterilization. The ovaries still release eggs and the woman menstruates in her usual cycle. The only change is that sperm can no longer travel through a Fallopian tube to meet an egg. The egg that is absorbed each month is also tiny, smaller than the period at the end of this sentence.

Does having your tubes tied change your sex drive? Is it dangerous to have this done in your 40s? How long do you have to stay in the hospital?

There are two common false myths about tubal sterilization: that it changes your sex life and that it causes menopause. It does neither. Cutting or blocking the Fallopian tubes is a mechanical procedure which does not change your hormonal levels or anything else related to your reproductive cycles. You will still menstruate, and there is no physical reason why your sex drive should change.

There are a few medical reasons, however, why some women should *not* have tubal ligations. Tubal sterilization involves abdominal surgery and use of an anesthetic. Both carry a small statistical risk, even for healthy people. Those with certain types of health problems—heart disease, obesity, diabetes, infection of the Fallopian tubes—face a higher risk from the surgery, anesthesia, and postoperative infection. Finally, a woman shouldn't have a tubal ligation if there's a chance she might already be pregnant.

Although there are several methods for cutting or blocking the tubes, one of the most widely used is the laparoscopy (commonly referred to as "Band-Aid" or "belly-button" surgery). Using special equipment inserted through a small incision just below the navel, gas is pumped into the abdomen. This enables the doctor to clearly see the Fallopian tubes to cut, burn, or clamp a small section of each tube. A similar method, called a "mini-lap," uses a small incision just above the pubic hairline. Both methods are sometimes performed with only a local anesthetic.

The woman can usually go home the same day, although she should arrange a ride home from the clinic or hospital. There may be pain in the shoulders or chest for a day or two, should any bubbles remain from the gas used in the surgery. A woman should arrange to take it easy for several days after surgery, but some can return to regular activity the next day.

Shortly after having a tubal sterilization five years ago, I suffered from excessive menstrual bleeding and blood clotting, which led to anemia. I finally ended up having a partial hysterectomy at the age of 28.

Two friends have also experienced severe side effects and had to have hysterectomies at a young age. Have any studies been done on the side effects of tubal sterilization?

One large study of 2456 women before tubal ligation and two years after reported that most women had no increase in menstrual problems. Although some women did have increased menstrual pain and bleeding, many other women reported having less pain and bleeding than they did before the operation.

The effects of tubal sterilization probably vary as much from one woman to the next as do the effects of other surgeries and medications; in addition, other factors, not yet clear, probably determine whether a particular woman has negative or positive effects. Choosing a trained and highly experienced physician who does many tubal ligations each year may also be important.

Scientists continue to publish contradictory findings about whether some sort of "poststerilization syndrome" (side effects after surgery) exists, and if so, what causes are involved. One recent study found that 10 to 16 percent of women reported painful menstruation after surgery and speculated that tubal ligation may alter prostaglandin production or contractibility of the uterus in some women. More research is needed. Until then, vasectomy is probably the best choice for most couples.

I am a 34-year-old woman expecting my second child at the end of the month. This will be a repeat C-section and my doctor will perform the sterilization right after the baby is born. What I would like to know is if there are any mental side effects? My doctor did mention PMS as a possible side effect of sterilization.

If you've had no problems with PMS (premenstrual syndrome) before tubal sterilization, no data support the idea that it would generate this kind of problem afterward.

Research on psychological side effects report that only about 10 percent of women are dissatisfied with sterilization, and in most of these cases it was because they changed their minds about wanting more children.

Some researchers recommend that a woman wait for a few months after she's had a child before deciding on sterilization. There is a small chance that this baby will not be healthy and she may want another one. Also, making the decision while she is tired of being pregnant may not accurately reflect how she will feel about another pregnancy later.

I had my tubes tied through my navel. Now it seems that whenever I do anything unusually strenuous, I bleed and can feel a pull from my navel area. Do I have to quit lifting anything? I'm only 43.

Make an appointment with a gynecologist for a pelvic examination. This should not be happening after a tubal sterilization. You didn't say whether you bleed from the incision or from the vagina, but *any* unusual bleeding must be investigated whether a woman has had surgical sterilization or not.

I had a tubal sterilization but was told afterward there's a 2 percent chance I could still get pregnant. Is this true?

Approximately four of every 1000 women who undergo a tubal sterilization subsequently become pregnant. When pregnancy occurs, the most common explanation is that the woman was already pregnant before the surgery. Many physicans insist that a woman use another contraceptive method (such as condoms and spermicide) the month before the surgery. They prefer to perform the surgery right at the end of a menstrual period, reducing the risk that a fertilized egg is already on its way to the uterus.

Three other possibilities are recanalization (the tubes spontaneously grow back together), an incomplete closure of one or both tubes during the surgery, or that some other structure (such as a ligament) was cut or blocked instead of a Fallopian tube.

I had my tubes tied a year ago, after our fourth child was born. From the moment I had the operation done I have been miserable. Every time I look at the scar I hate myself for what I did because I was being pressured by everyone about having enough children already. I kept telling myself in my mind that it was the right thing to do.

I'm only 28 years old, love children and some of my happiest times were when I was pregnant. Is it possible to have the procedure reversed? How expensive is it?

It is sometimes possible to reverse tubal sterilization, but the chance varies for a successful tubal reanastomosis, or reconstruction of the Fallopian tubes. *(See Chapter 15 for more information).* Moreover, reanastomosis involves major abdominal surgery and extremely careful and skilled microsurgery, plus several days' hospital stay. This is quite costly.

You might want to talk with a fertility specialist. Perhaps in vitro fertilization or some other reproductive procedure that bypasses the Fallopian tubes (while still using your eggs and your partner's sperm) might be safer and more likely to be successful.

Also, think about talking with a counselor who can help you come to terms with your decision to have tubal ligation. Taking care of yourself and those you care about requires too much energy and love for you to spend time being angry at yourself.

Oral Hormonal Contraceptives (The Pill)

The next most effective method of contraception after sterilization is taking oral hormonal pills (the Pill), containing a combination of an estrogen and a progestin or a progestin alone. The failure rate is 2 to 3 women out of every 100 women who take them for one year.

The risk of death from using the Pill is lower than the risk of death from pregnancy and childbirth, except for women older than 40 or women who smoke cigarettes. It is estimated that in the United States there are about 500 deaths each year among the millions of Pill users. Researchers believe, however, that that low figure could be reduced even further—42 deaths per year—if all women using the Pill stopped at age 40, did not smoke, and used only newer, lower-dose formulations. A disturbing survey recently found that 30 percent of women continue to use the older, higher-dose formulations, and that many of these are older women.

One risk of using a progestin-only pill is that if pregnancy results, there is a greater chance of ectopic (tubal) pregnancy.

Approximately six million women in the U.S. currently use one of the more than sixty types of the Pill now available. This is fewer than the more than 10 million women who used the Pill during the mid-1970s. Presumably the decrease is due to a great deal of misunderstanding about potential negative side effects, nearly all of which have been refuted by larger and more recent studies. In addition, the amounts of hormones in the Pill, particularly estrogen, have been significantly reduced from the amounts used between 1960 and 1975.

The Pill works by tricking the body into altering the amounts and the pattern of natural hormones released by the ovaries. The result is that eggs are not usually released, the cervical mucus remains impenetrable to sperm, and the uterine lining does not permit implantation of a zygote even if an egg and sperm were to meet. This reduced build-up of the lining of the uterus is also why many women have lighter menstrual flow while they take the Pill.

Some women should not take the Pill. These include women with previous blood clots, those who have suffered a stroke, coronary artery disease, or breast cancer—and women who smoke. Others who may be at increased risk of serious side effects are women with high blood pressure, diabetes, gall bladder disease, or irregular menstrual cycles.

Every woman taking the Pill should memorize the following danger signals and report them to her physician or clinic immediately: severe abdominal pain, severe chest pain, or shortness of breath; severe headache, dizziness, weakness, or numbness; loss or blurring of vision; speech problems; or severe pain in the calf or thigh. If women taking the Pill reported these warning signs promptly so that their physicians could carefully evaluate the cause, the annual U.S. death rate from Pill use would drop to fewer than 15 women out of the more than six million taking the Pill.

Some studies find that using the Pill decreases or does not change a woman's risk for breast cancer; other studies suggest there is increased risk of breast cancer. However, the Pill clearly appears to reduce a woman's risk of ovarian and endometrial cancer, with this protection continuing for several years after she stops taking the Pill. Whether there is any increased risk for cervical cancer is not clear, because women who use the Pill may also begin intercourse at a younger age and have more sexual partners during their lifetime—two factors known to increase the risk of cervical cancer.

Other health benefits of taking the Pill for some women include reduced menstrual cramps, lower incidence of ovarian cysts, reduced PMS symptoms, more regular cycles, and a decreased incidence of fibrocystic breast problems. The Pill seems to have a dramatic effect in lowering the risk of PID (pelvic inflammatory disease). Studies in Europe and the United States report a 50 to 70 percent reduction in hospitalization for PID if a woman is taking the Pill, particularly if she has taken it for more than twelve months.

Another beneficial reason for choosing the Pill is that it is highly reversible. When a woman decides to get pregnant, all she need do is switch to a barrier method for at least one full cycle. This enables her body to resume its natural hormonal cycling; then she stops using any form of contraception.

One of the drawbacks of choosing the Pill for contraception is that it does not provide protection against STDs. The Pill may also reduce the effectiveness of antibiotics used to treat STDs—and taking antibiotics for any infection can also reduce the effectiveness of the Pill.

I have been taking birth control pills for 10 years. Last year I was told I should have been taking six-month breaks (use some other birth control, but no pills) every once in a while. I was unaware that I was supposed to take a break until last year. Is it true that I was supposed to be taking six-month breaks?

Whoever told you that needs to be updated. When oral hormonal contraceptives were first introduced, they were usually prescribed for only a year or two at a time; back then, women were advised to take frequent rests or "breaks." Now we know that starting and stopping the Pill over and over may make it more difficult to become pregnant when a woman wants to have a child.

Many women now begin using the Pill in their teens and use it continuously until they decide to have children. Using the Pill this way is considered safe, with no impact on future fertility, as long as a woman had six months to a year of regular menstrual flows before going on the Pill; is carefully screened for any existing medical problems before taking the Pill; and is examined each year during the entire time in which she takes the Pill.

If her physician or clinic detects signs of possible trouble at her annual examination and Pap test, she may be advised to use some other form of contraception until the health condition improves or is corrected. For example, an increase in blood pressure would be one reason that a woman might be advised to stop taking the Pill for several months or longer.

I take birth-control pills in a pattern of 21 days on, seven days off. Am I safe from getting pregnant from the first day I take the pills or do I have to wait a few days? The instructions don't say.

I asked my doctor and he said, "They're supposed to be effective right away, but who knows?" His answer made me nervous. Now I'm afraid to have intercourse the first week of taking the pills.

I asked five other women who also take these pills and they don't know either. I wonder how many women are a wreck over this. My husband is ready to strangle me. And should I be concerned if I forget to take a pill now and then?

For the very first month—and *only* that first month—that you begin taking the Pill, don't consider yourself safe until you've taken the Pill for ten days, starting no later than seven days after the start of your last period. During this waiting time (which starts the first day of your period), use some other method for those seventeen days, such as condoms and spermicidal foam.

But after that initial month, the protection is in effect *every* day, whether it's one of the twenty-one days you take a pill or one of the seven you don't.

You *should*, however, be concerned if you miss taking a pill. If you miss more than one pill—or if you vomit up a pill due to illness—you should use a back-up method of birth control (such as condoms and contraceptive foam) for the rest of that cycle. Whenever an unscheduled gap in the hormone dose occurs, there is a chance that an egg will be released and available for conception.

Because it takes longer for the "minipill" (containing only progestin) to regulate the body's hormones, most physicians recommend using another method of contraception for the first several months while taking that type of pill.

If you don't know what kind of oral contraceptive you're using, call your doctor and ask. If you have further questions about how to take the Pill or about its effectiveness, ask your pharmacist. And always read the manufacturer's package insert information.

Do some medications become less effective if taken with birth control pills? Do some drugs interfere with the effectiveness of the Pill?

Yes, interactions with certain drugs can reduce the effectiveness of oral contraceptives. Among these are such commonly prescribed antibiotics as ampicillin and tetracycline. Other types of drugs that also appear to decrease contraceptive effectiveness include barbiturates (sedatives), carbamazepine (an anticonvulsant and painkiller), and phenytoin and primidone (anticonvulsants).

The reverse is also true: Oral contraceptives can reduce the effectiveness of other drugs such as anticoagulants, antidepressants, and some antibiotics.

The list of possible drug interactions is extensive. Whenever you get a prescription, tell your physician that you take oral contraceptives and ask if you should use some other type of contraceptive method (such as condoms and spermicidal foam) as a back-up method.

Make a list of all your medications and ask a pharmacist whether they reduce your contraceptive protection and what you should do about it. Most pharmacists keep on top of current information about drug interactions and are willing to help you get the information you need.

I've read that it's not advisable for women over 35 to take birth-control pills, especially women who smoke. What about nonsmokers? I've had adverse reactions to IUDs and contraceptive foams.

I'm 39, have never smoked, have one child, normal blood pressure, and have no health problems I'm aware of. Is it advisable for women over 35 in good health and nonsmokers to avoid the pill?

Death related to Pill use does appear to increase significantly with age. Since you've had difficulty with some other methods in the past, consult a gynecologist about the best birth-control method for you. It is important to use some type of method if you don't wish to bear more children.

When you see your physician, ask him or her about the so-called minipill. This contains no estrogen and a smaller amount of progestin than other pills. "Minipills" are fairly new, so there are no long-term studies of side effects, but many clinicians think they may be safer than estrogen-containing pills for use by women over 35.

However, one of the common side effects of progestin-only pills is irregular bleeding. Any woman who takes these pills must be committed to having annual gynecological exams and Pap tests to make sure that any irregular bleeding is not a symptom of a serious problem. There is also some concern that progestin may change blood lipid levels, so also have an annual cholesterol check.

I have not had a period for two years. I have told several doctors about this and they have all said that this is common among women who take the Pill (I've taken oral contraceptives for four years with no other side effects).

Is this true or is this dangerous to my health?

It is true that the newer, low-dose type of Pill can result in either very scanty bleeding or a total absence of bleeding (amenorrhea) for some women. However, you should be evaluated to check that the absence of menstrual flow is indeed related to the Pill.

In general, the first step in testing is to determine whether a woman has become pregnant. If she has not, the next step is often to try a different type of pill to see if menstrual bleeding returns. Other tests are to check hormonal levels and for chronic disorders, such as diabetes. Depending on test results, the next stage may be an evaluation of the ovaries, hypothalamus, and pituitary.

Some women worry needlessly that if they don't menstruate the flow is somehow staying inside of them and is dangerous. However, with many oral contraceptives, no uterine lining is built up at all. You may simply need to be reassured that you are not having a menstrual flow because your uterus is not building up the endometrium each month.

If the idea of not menstruating bothers you, consider changing to a different method.

I am 16 and would like to get on the Pill. My friend told me about a girl who went blind in one eye because of the Pill. Is that really possible?

There are a very few reports of vision and eye problems associated with taking hormonal contraceptive pills, but permanent blindness is extremely rare. Some women on the Pill do find it difficult to wear contact lenses.

Any woman taking the Pill needs to know, however, that blurred vision is one of the danger signals that must be reported to a physician *immediately*.

I am sort of alarmed whenever someone gives high recommendations to some methods of birth control. I took the Pill for years and was never warned not to, even though I smoked and my mother died from embolisms from her heart or lungs, I don't know which.

My 19-year-old daughter took the Pill and developed high blood pressure. My half-sister (age 34) suffered a major brain aneurysm, and I have since learned that a number of women in her age group have them.

A young women I know was being treated for PID for months, had been bleeding internally, nearly died, and is now recovering from a total hysterectomy. Now my spa attendant says that four or five of the regulars are out with PID. All these women used IUDs or the sponge.

What is going on? I don't think women are getting all the facts about the Pill and IUDs. Why aren't women told the truth about the possible side effects?

The guidelines for prescribing contraceptive methods and monitoring for possible side effects are based on long-term studies of hundreds of thousands of women. In actuality, negative side effects are not widespread even though they may seem common when they affect women you know personally. It's also tempting to attribute problems solely to one cause (such as use of oral contraceptives or an IUD) when other factors may have been involved, such as smoking, diet, or exposure to a sexually transmitted organism.

It is generally safe for women *with no risk factors* to use the Pill as long as they follow their physician's instructions about reporting danger signals promptly and having checkups on a regular schedule.

There are other causes of uterine and Fallopian tube PID infections, including the organisms that cause gonorrhea and chlamydial vaginal infections. There is evidence that taking oral contraceptives may reduce a woman's risk of having some types of PID and may also lessen the severity of a pelvic infection.

You imply that the medical community is actively engaged in concealing widespread negative side effects of the Pill and IUD. I don't agree. Even if some physicians are not as thorough or well-informed as others, it is also clear that some women do not listen carefully to instructions, report danger signals promptly, or schedule and keep appointments for checkups.

Whatever happened to the "morning-after pill"? Is such a pill available?

For sexually active individuals, the best protection against unplanned pregnancy is the careful use of contraceptives before or at the time of intercourse, not the morning after. However, medical emergencies such as rape do occur and sometimes condoms do break, necessitating use of a "morning after" method.

Treatments vary (depending on what methods are approved for each country) but usually involve taking extremely high doses of one or more synthetic hormones within seventy-two hours of unprotected intercourse. All have side effects including nausea and vomiting.

This should be used only as an emergency measure and not as a primary method of birth control. In addition to the unpleasant side effects and health risks, some women become pregnant anyway and risk exposing the fetus to high levels of hormones which may cause abnormalities.

Intrauterine Device (IUD)

An IUD is a device inserted into the uterus and left there to prevent conception. Legend has it that the first IUD was used in Arabia, where camel drivers put stones into their camels' uteri before leaving on long journeys so they would not become pregnant during the trip. Over the centuries hundreds of such devices have been tried with various materials (silver, gold, copper, and plastic) and shapes (loops, spirals, Ts, and 7s.) It appears that IUDs work by chemically altering the uterine environment thus interfering with the sperm as they travel through the uterus, before they meet the egg.

Only two types of IUDs are currently available in the United States: Paraguard (a copper-bearing device) and Progestasert (a progestin-releasing device). Due to the high incidence of pelvic infections, infertility, and some deaths associated with the Dalkon Shield (and the resulting legal cases), manufacturers of other IUDs removed their products from the U.S. market. Further investigation suggests that problems with the Dalkon Shield may have been related to its multifilament string and not to the device itself.

It is estimated that fewer than two million women in the United States currently choose an IUD for contraception, although many millions more still have IUDs in place that were inserted before many of these products were withdrawn from the market. Because IUDs must be removed on a regular basis (for example, Copper-7s and Copper-Ts are to be removed three years after insertion), many women must now decide which of the two available types of IUDs to use—or change to a different method of contraception.

The failure rate of the Progestasert for 100 women using it for one year is 2.6 for women who have not had a previous pregnancy and 1.8 for women who have. (This means that around 2 women out of 100 will become pregnant.) Women who have not had a previous pregnancy also have a higher rate (7.4 percent) of spontaneous expulsions (when the IUD pops out) than women who have (3.1 percent); more of these women (15.1 percent) also have to have the IUD removed for medical reasons. In addition, this particular IUD must be removed and a new one inserted each year.

Paraguard has been in use for a little over one year, so not much data are available, but its failure rate appears to be low (0.5 percent—5 out of 1000). It can be left in place for four years—an advantage because the highest rate of infection with IUDs occurs in the first few months after insertion. This is thought to be because the IUD has the opportunity to pick up infectious organisms from the vagina or cervix during insertion.

Currently most clinics suggest certain women should not use an IUD due to the somewhat increased risk of PID (Pelvic Inflammatory Disease), a condition that can reduce fertility by causing scarring of the Fallopian tubes. Women are at higher risk of developing PID if they are not in a sexual relationship that is mutually exclusive; they are at high risk for catching STDs or have symptoms of an STD; or they have a history of ectopic (tubal) pregnancy. The manufacturer of Paraguard also states that women who have *not* had a previous pregnancy should not use an IUD.

It is recommended that women in low-risk groups who do decide to use an IUD have it inserted by a physician or at a clinic experienced in doing the procedure. There have been reports that clinics less experienced with IUD insertions accidentally cut the cervix three times more often than those experienced in IUD insertion.

Costs of an IUD plus insertion range from $115 to $290, depending on the clinic or physician's fees.

After the birth of our second child three years ago, we decided not to have any more children. My doctor suggested we use an IUD for birth control.

Guess what? Three months ago I found out I was pregnant. Did the doctor make a mistake? Could the device be defective?

Overall data (most based on IUDs no longer available) are that of 100 women who use an IUD for one year, 4 or 5 will become pregnant. This compares with 2 out of 100 women per year who use oral contraceptives. Still, for some women IUDs are considered one of the more effective choices of birth control.

You should see a doctor for an examination. He or she needs to determine whether or not you expelled the IUD (about 10 percent of women do so during the first year) and then became pregnant or whether both the IUD and the fetus are inside your uterus. Even though the frequency of fetal defects or fetal death is not increased by the presence of some IUDs during pregnancy (scientists are not yet sure about any fetal risks from progestin-bearing IUDs), the rate of spontaneous abortion (miscarriage) is much higher, about 50 percent compared to 15 percent for all other pregnancies.

If the string from the IUD can be seen, the IUD may be removed to reduce the risk of miscarriage and infection. If the string is not visible and you continue the pregnancy with the IUD in place, your physician will tell you how to watch for symptoms of uterine infection (headaches, fever, chills, etc.) that require an *immediate* trip to the doctor or to a hospital. Even though many women have delivered healthy babies while an IUD is still inside, such a pregnancy requires careful monitoring by a competent obstetrician.

After my daughter was born four years ago, I used an IUD but had trouble finding the string. I went to my gynecologist and he said they were going to give my body a rest. Since they have taken it out (three years ago) I haven't been using anything for protection. But I haven't gotten pregnant. I was wondering, could the IUD have made me sterile? I'm worried because I hear so much about sterility and causes of it. I have a four-year-old daughter and would eventually like to have more.

Fertility involves a number of complicated factors best evaluated by a competent physician after a thorough examination and interpretation of tests *(see Chapter 15)*. Many things could have changed in either your fertility or your partner's since you became pregnant with your daughter.

There are research findings that suggest that using an IUD can reduce fertility somewhat for some women because of an increased rate of PID. However, women who have had a pregnancy before using an IUD (as you have) appear to have a lower rate of PID.

Because so much controversy remains about these issues, you might want to have a complete checkup by a fertility expert when you decide you're ready to have more children.

Barrier Methods

So far we have explored contraceptive methods that work by disrupting the travel of sperm through the male reproductive tract (vasectomy), disrupting the travel of eggs and sperm through the female reproductive tract (tubal sterilization), reducing the release of eggs (the Pill), or interfering with the travel of sperm (IUD).

Barrier methods work differently. In these methods, sperm are trapped at the point of ejaculation (condoms), retained in the vagina so they cannot swim through the woman's cervix (diaphragms, sponges, and cervical caps), or inactivated with a chemical (spermicides—foams, creams, jellies, and suppositories).

Another major difference between barrier methods and those discussed earlier is that the use of barrier methods is directly linked to the time intercourse occurs and therefore involves conscious planning and preparation. You have to acknowledge that intercourse may occur and have the condom or other barrier device ready for use.

Unfortunately, many couples avoid accepting the responsibilities associated with having sex, not wanting to think about sex until it "just happens." Many younger women fear that being prepared with contraceptives conveys the idea that they are promiscuous. The dangers known to be associated with pregnancy and infection with sexually transmitted diseases, however, must be recognized as far more serious than such concerns.

Barrier methods must also be used *each and every time* intercourse occurs. Used consistently and correctly, some barrier methods can have failure rates nearly as low as the Pill. In addition, they can provide good protection against many STDs and are highly reversible. When a couple desires a pregnancy they simply stop using the method. With the exception of the diaphragm and cervical cap, which must be properly fitted and therefore prescribed by a health clinic or physician, barrier devices do not require a prescription, are widely available, and are modestly priced. Negative side effects or health risks with barrier methods are very rare; very few people report allergic reactions to spermicides or latex rubber, but changing brands often eliminates the reaction.

In fact, barrier methods, especially when used in combinations (such as condoms or diaphragms with spermicides that have nonoxynol-9 or octoxynol as an ingredient) can provide one of the safest and most effective methods of contraception available *if* used correctly and used each time.

WARNING

Oil or petroleum-based lubricants destroy latex rubber condoms, diaphragms, and cervical caps. You may not be able to see the damage but microscopic holes through which sperm and infectious organisms can escape are likely to occur. Within 60 seconds, holes appear which are big enough for some STD organisms to pass through, and soon after these devices deteriorate enough for sperm to get through. Therefore, products like Vaseline, baby oil, Crisco, butter, Nivea, Vaseline Intensive Care, or other lotions should *not* be used with these contraceptive methods. When more vaginal lubrication is desired, use only *water-based* products like K-Y jelly or Lubrin inserts.

Condoms

A condom is a sheath made of latex rubber or animal intestine (sometimes called "skins") that is rolled onto an erect penis. Only latex condoms have been shown to protect against the smaller-size STD viruses such as HIV (the AIDS virus) and hepatitis-B. Latex condoms come in various sizes, shapes, thicknesses, colors, and textures and are widely available. The cost for one dozen good-quality latex condoms is less than $10.

I'm a male, 18, and a high-school senior. A current trend at our school is for males to carry one or two condoms in the wallet just in case they're needed. My question is: Will the friction and heat from being carried in a wallet affect the condition of the condom?

Yes! Prolonged exposure to body heat can indeed cause condoms to deteriorate. Any condom that has become brittle or sticky is likely to break or develop small holes through which sperm and the organisms that cause STDs can escape during intercourse. Don't use a condom that appears to have lost its original flexibility, and *never* use a condom more than once.

Condoms should be stored in a dark, cool, dry place. It is not a good idea to carry them in a wallet, your pocket, or the glove compartment of your car for

How to Use a Condom

Open package carefully, taking care not to damage condom with fingernails. Do not unroll or stretch out the condom. Put a drop of spermicide in the tip of the condom. Be sure none of the spermicide gets on the penis shaft so condom doesn't slip off. If uncircumcised, pull back foreskin before putting on condom.

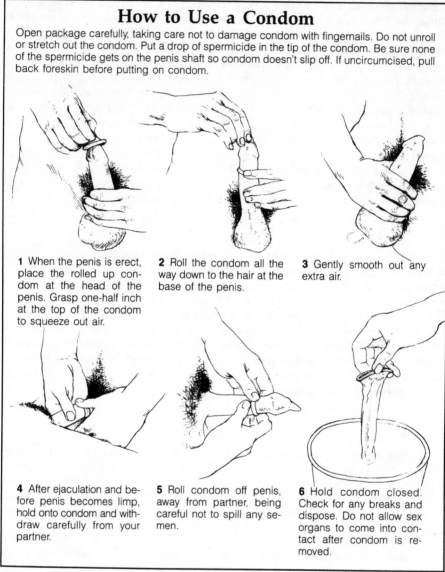

1 When the penis is erect, place the rolled up condom at the head of the penis. Grasp one-half inch at the top of the condom to squeeze out air.

2 Roll the condom all the way down to the hair at the base of the penis.

3 Gently smooth out any extra air.

4 After ejaculation and before penis becomes limp, hold onto condom and withdraw carefully from your partner.

5 Roll condom off penis, away from partner, being careful not to spill any semen.

6 Hold condom closed. Check for any breaks and dispose. Do not allow sex organs to come into contact after condom is removed.

Illustration No. 30. **How To Use a Condom**

any length of time. Many of the better quality condoms have an expiration date on the packet and should be discarded if not used before that date. Stored correctly, good-quality condoms can remain in good condition for several years.

A condom should be put on the erect penis during foreplay, before any pre-ejaculatory fluid appears. (Don't wait to put it on just before ejaculation). Either partner can put the condom on the erect penis, making it a part of your lovemaking. Until the condom is in place, keep the penis away from the partner's genitals. Leave about one-half inch at the tip of the condom to allow space for the ejaculate or use a condom with a reservoir tip *(see Illustration 30.)*

After ejaculation, the penis should be withdrawn while it's still erect, or semen may seep out—hold on to the base of the condom as you withdraw your penis from your partner. Always check the condom before throwing it away to see if there are any tears in it. If so, the partner should immediately add an application of spermicide.

I am 20 and have never gone to see a doctor about birth control. My boyfriend and I have been going together for a couple of years and have been using condoms. So far, everything is fine.

Are condoms alone safe enough, or is something else safe besides the Pill? I do not want to go on the Pill.

In general, for every 100 women who use only condoms for one year, 10 will get pregnant during that year. But when condoms are used together with a spermicide, only 2 or 3 pregnancies occur, *if* both are used correctly and every time the couple has sex. Condoms and a spermicide will also provide protection against STDs, especially if the spermicide has nonoxynol-9 or octoxynol as an ingredient.

Condoms do break. Two British studies found a pregnancy rate due to broken condoms of 1.4 per 100 couples using condoms for one year. Estimates of condom failures range from one in 1000 to one in 100, depending on the quality of the condom. Spermicides provide additional protection if a condom breaks.

This rate compares favorably with the use of the Pill: two to three women out of 100 will become pregnant during a year using only the Pill, but the Pill provides little or no protection against STDs.

You should use spermicides according to the instructions—most must be inserted deep in the vagina and close to the time you have intercourse. Use more spermicide and a *new* condom if you have sex again. Also, do not douche after sex; this will wash the protective spermicide away from the cervix where it needs to stay until all the sperm are immobilized. Putting a dab of spermicide into the tip of the condom before putting it on also may increase effectiveness. *(See Illustration 30.)*

My penis is relatively small, but that has never diminished my enjoyment of sex or my wife's. But now there's a problem. She had to stop taking birth-control pills, and we have to use condoms. They seem too wide for me and slip off. Do they make condoms in different sizes?

Yes. Condoms are manufactured in different sizes, but the smaller sizes have not been marketed as widely in the United States as they have in Europe and Asia. Some speculate that manufacturers fear American men would not want to buy a condom labeled "small."

Within the last couple of years, however, condoms with a narrower circumference have been offered in the United States by a few companies and are reportedly selling very well. These are usually described as fitting "more snugly for extra sensitivity" or in some other way that doesn't directly relate to the sensitive issue of penis size.

Ask your local dealer to stock this type, which measures approximately 49 mm across the flat width (one half the measurement around the total condom). The usual flat-width measurement in the United States is about 52 mm. If you cannot locate a narrower condom, you might try the models labeled "contoured." Some of these are narrow where the head of the penis fits and stay more snugly in place.

Research on couples who use condoms regularly report that about 20 percent of both men and women cite the worry that the condom will slip off as a significant disadvantage of condoms. Many couples also report that this concern alters their sexual techniques so that they move less vigorously during sex. Clearly many other men would also be interested in a greater selection of condom sizes.

I am 18 and have pain during intercourse. My fiancé and I have never had intercourse without a condom. Is it possible that I have developed an allergy to condoms? I have many allergies, including skin reactions to make-up and clothes sizing. If this is the cause of my pain, would using natural-membrane condoms help?

Some people are indeed allergic to latex-rubber condoms. Some are also allergic to the chemicals in the spermicides often used with condoms or to the coating on spermicidal or lubricated condoms. One way to test whether you are allergic to condoms is to switch to a condom made of natural animal membranes or to stop using them with a chemical spermicide. However, only *latex* condoms provide protection against many STDs.

There are many other, more likely reasons for pain during intercourse *(see Chapter 8)*. Make an appointment to see a gynecologist or go to family planning clinic. Describe when your pain occurs—for example, during penetration or during deep thrusting. The physician can determine what causes are involved by doing a pelvic examination, which may include taking samples of vaginal secretions. You should be having annual pelvic exams now anyway, both because you are sexually active and because you are 18.

It's important to understand that you increase your risk of conception and STDs if you experiment with having sex without condoms. If the gynecologist decides that there are no physical causes for your pain, ask about other contraceptive methods appropriate for you.

Diaphragms

A diaphragm is a flexible metal ring covered by a dome-shaped piece of latex rubber. A tablespoon of spermicidal cream or jelly is placed inside the dome and then spread into a thin film around the rim. The diaphragm is then placed high inside the woman's vagina, covering and completely surrounding her cervix *(see Illustration 31)*. It must be inserted shortly before intercourse (spermicide gradually loses effectiveness) and must remain in place for six hours after intercourse. If a second intercourse occurs before the six hours are up, place more spermicide into the vagina without removing the diaphragm. A diaphragm must be fitted and prescribed by a physician or health clinic, lasts about two years with proper care, and costs around $15 at a clinic and more from a private physician; enough spermicidal cream and jelly for about ten uses costs $12 or less.

How to Use a Diaphragm

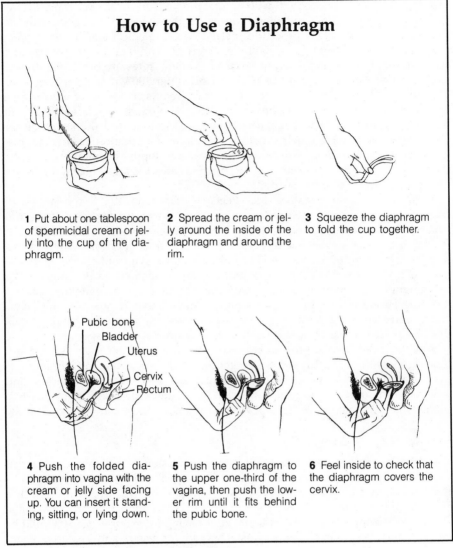

1 Put about one tablespoon of spermicidal cream or jelly into the cup of the diaphragm.

2 Spread the cream or jelly around the inside of the diaphragm and around the rim.

3 Squeeze the diaphragm to fold the cup together.

Pubic bone
Bladder
Uterus
Cervix
Rectum

4 Push the folded diaphragm into vagina with the cream or jelly side facing up. You can insert it standing, sitting, or lying down.

5 Push the diaphragm to the upper one-third of the vagina, then push the lower rim until it fits behind the pubic bone.

6 Feel inside to check that the diaphragm covers the cervix.

Illustration No. 31. **How to Use a Diaphragm**

I decided to try to use a diaphragm for birth control because my doctor said they are fairly reliable and have no side effects. However, I'm not sure I'm getting it in right. How can I be sure the diaphragm is correctly in place?

Selection of the proper-size diaphragm and training in insertion are important factors in the effectiveness of a diaphragm in preventing pregnancy. Go back to your gynecologist, put in the diaphragm before the appointment, and have him or her check to see whether you've placed it correctly.

In one study conducted by the Sanger Bureau in New York City, diaphragms were 98 percent successful (only 2 pregnancies per 100 users per year) when each woman was first fitted with a diaphragm, practiced insertion of the diaphragm in the office, and then returned to the office a week later with the diaphragm in place. This procedure permitted the medical staff to verify that each woman was inserting the diaphragm correctly and that the proper size and style of diaphragm had been prescribed. Failure rates in other diaphragm studies range from around 10 to 19 pregnancies per 100 women per year.

Diaphragms come in three styles and in a range of sizes, some of which come with a plastic inserter to aid in getting the diaphragm in place. Proper fit depends on an individual woman's vaginal muscle tone and the shape of her pubic-bone arch (which helps hold it in place) in addition to her vaginal diameter. Because sexual arousal increases vaginal depth and moves the cervix away from the end of the vagina, a diaphragm that is too small may fail to cover the cervix when it is most needed.

There can be some negative side effects. A diaphragm that is too large may cause pain for either the woman or her partner during intercourse. If the rim irritates the vaginal walls or thrusting pushes it against the nearby urethra, a woman may be at greater risk of vaginal or urinary tract infections. There is also a slight risk (about one in two million) of toxic shock syndrome (TSS) so do not use the diaphragm during menstruation. Allergic reactions to the latex of the diaphragm or the spermicide used with the diaphragm also sometimes occur.

Until you are certain that you have the proper size and type of diaphragm, that you are inserting it correctly, and that it is staying in place over the cervix during sex, use some other method, such as condoms and a spermicide.

You also need to take proper care of the diaphragm. After each use, wash it thoroughly with mild soap and water, gently dry it on a towel, and store it in its case away from heat and light. Check it regularly for cracks, small holes, and any puckering of the latex around the rim. Get refitted for a new one every two years, whenever you notice signs of wear, or if your weight changes significantly.

Cervical cap

A cervical cap is a small latex, thimble-shaped version of a diaphragm that fits over only the cervix (rather than against the vaginal walls like a diaphragm). It must be fitted and prescribed by a physician or clinic. It, too, is used with a spermicide that is placed inside the cap. It is inserted shortly before intercourse and must be kept in place for six hours after having intercourse. Caps should be cleaned and stored like diaphragms, checked for wear, and replaced every twelve to eighteen months. The cost of a cervical cap is similar to a diaphragm. Enough spermicide for about ten uses costs $12 or less.

I've heard of a contraceptive device for women called a cervical cap. It's quite popular in Europe but little known in the United States. I've heard it's similar to a diaphragm, only smaller. Can you tell me why they aren't more available here? How can I obtain one?

Even though cervical caps have been widely available in Europe for decades, they have only been approved by the FDA for sale in the United States since 1988. Until twenty or thirty years ago, caps were made of silver or copper but now are made of soft latex rubber or plastic.

You are correct that cervical caps are similar to diaphragms in many ways. Caps, too, must be fitted by trained medical personnel, used with a spermicide, and require a woman to learn and practice correct insertion and removal techniques. Failure rates are higher than with diaphragms—as high as 23 pregnancies per 100 women using the method for a year in one study.

There appears to be nearly a 30 percent chance that the cap will be dislodged during sex. Moreover, scientists now realize that a woman's cervix not only moves during arousal but changes size and shape during her reproductive cycle. Some estimate that 10 percent of women should have at least two different sizes of cap, to be used at different times of the month to allow for these changes.

In one study, 70 percent of women stopped using the cap because of difficulty with insertion, proper placement and removal, and it loosened during sex.

One of the reasons interest in the cervical cap was so high was because it could theoretically be worn for longer lengths of time (several days). But in some studies, women complained of bad odors if it was left in place for two or more days, and in one study researchers noted that prolonged use caused changes in the cells of the cervix. There are no data as yet on TSS risks, but a woman using the cap should probably follow the guidelines for the diaphragm and not use it during her period.

The idea behind the cervical cap has been around for centuries. Caps made of beeswax were used by Hungarian and German women, each individually molded to fit that woman's cervix. By 1838, a German gynecologist used beeswax molds to shape an individually fitted rubber cap. Little has changed in the concept since then.

Spermicides

Spermicides are available in various forms: foam, creams, jellies, dissolvable tablets, and suppositories. Spermicides do not require a prescription, but directions for use must be carefully followed. Enough foam for twenty uses costs around $9. Enough cream or jelly for about ten uses costs $12 or less.

Used correctly, spermicides work in two ways. The active chemical in a spermicide literally disables sperm, and the base—the foam, cream, or jelly—covers the cervix, acting as a mechanical barrier. An important additional advantage is that if the spermicide contains nonoxynol-9 or octoxynol, it also apparently provides protection against many STDs: Nisseria gonorrhoeae (gonorrhea), trichomonas vaginalis, herpes virus, AIDS virus, Treponema pallidum (syphilis), Ureaplasma urealyticum, and perhaps chlamydia.

Creams, jellies, and foams should be used according to instructions on the container and begin to lose effectiveness after thirty minutes. Tablets and suppositories require ten to fifteen minutes to dissolve before they become protective. All should be inserted high in the vagina, as close as possible to the cervical opening. Foam appears to provide the best covering of the cervix, tablets and suppositories the least. Used alone, spermicides have a typical failure rate of about 18 to 21 per 100 women per year. They are more effective when used with another form of contraception, such as a diaphragm or condom.

Spermicides are widely available, do not require a prescription, are relatively inexpensive, and generally considered safe.

I'm apparently allergic to nonoxynol, the spermicide used in every foam I can find. Are there any other effective foams that use some other chemical?

Allergic reactions to nonoxynol-9 are fairly unusual. Most estimates place these reactions at about 5 percent of all users. It could be you're allergic to one of the other ingredients in the product, not the active ingredient nonoxynol-9. Because base ingredients vary from one brand-name product to another, you might want to try another brand that uses different filler ingredients.

You might also consider spermicides that use a slightly different chemical, such as octoxynol, which has also been found to be effective against some STDs.

Consider other sources of vaginal irritation and itching. Other causes of problems include yeast or other infectious organisms and an allergy to latex or to ingredients used to package condoms. (*For other causes of vaginal irritation see Chapters 17 and 19.*) Ask a physician to diagnose the cause of irritation.

Are contraceptive creams with nonoxynol toxic? If a person has oral sex after a woman inserts her diaphragm and cream, is the cream safe to ingest?

Most spermicidal creams, foams, jellies, and other similar contraceptive products sold in the United States use either nonoxynol-9 or octoxynol as the active ingredient. There appear to be no reports of danger from ingesting small amounts of these chemicals during oral-genital contact.

A few contraceptive products use phenylmercuric acetate or phenylmercuric nitrate as the active ingredient. Because some research has questioned the safety of mercurials, you might want to be cautious about using or ingesting these products. The active ingredient will be stated on the label.

Contraceptive sponge

This is a small, round polyurethane sponge with one dimpled side that fits at the end of the vagina over the cervix. The other side has a loop for removal. Each soft sponge has a spermicide that is activated by moistening it in water before insertion. It must be left in place for eight hours after having sex, then removed and discarded. If you have sex again before it's time to remove the sponge, add an application of spermicide into the vagina without removing the sponge. The failure rate for the contraceptive sponge is around 18 percent (10 to 20 of 100 women per year). The sponge is sold without a prescription in packages of three or twelve at drugstores. Three sponges cost about $5.

I used the contraceptive sponge for about half a year and then stopped. Later I heard something about the sponge on television, but missed what the problem was. Does the sponge have bad side effects? Could it cause infertility?

The only media reports we know of involving the contraceptive sponge concerned a handful of cases of TSS. The manufacturer agreed to revise the package insert to include information about TSS symptoms. (*See Chapter 17 for more on TSS.*) The risk of TSS associated with the sponge is estimated to be 1 in every 2 million women (the same as for the diaphragm). One way to reduce the risk of TSS is to remove the sponge no later than eight hours after having sex, and never use it during menstruation or for three to six weeks after having a baby.

I have seen no reports linking the contraceptive sponge to infertility, but its protective effects against various STD organisms (due to the spermicide) should reduce a woman's risk of PID and later problems of infertility.

Withdrawal (Coitus Interruptus)

Our religion forbids the use of birth control so my husband sometimes pulls out during intercourse. How effective is it? Can this do any harm?

With a failure rate of 23 percent, withdrawal is clearly *not* considered one of the more effective methods of contraception. However, for those with strong religious convictions, it remains one of the few options that has at least some effect.

Your husband doesn't have to actually ejaculate inside of you in order for you to become pregnant. Sperm have been found in the clear pre-ejaculatory fluid which can appear at the tip of the penis during arousal long before ejaculation occurs.

You can also become pregnant if your husband withdraws after he has begun to ejaculate. There are more sperm in the first one or two spurts than in the later ejaculatory spasms; and sometimes the male isn't able to withdraw until ejaculation has already begun.

You can also become pregnant if your partner withdraws, then ejaculates near, though not inside, the vaginal opening (on the labia or other parts of the vulva). Sperm are strong swimmers (faster for their size than the greatest Olympic champions) and can swim relatively long distances and around many obstacles to reach their goal.

Withdrawal doesn't physically harm either one of you, but it can pose other problems. It can affect the natural sequence of intercourse if both partners are only thinking "Will he stop in time?" There is the chance that withdrawal can lead to sexual difficulties because both partners are focusing on only this one aspect of the male sexual response. Suddenly stopping intercourse can leave the woman dissatisfied unless other means are used for her to achieve orgasm, either before or after intercourse.

Some researchers have stressed that failure rates for coitus interruptus can be lower for those men who are aware of and can control their point of ejaculatory inevitability. Unfortunately, younger men who attempt this method have rarely gained this kind of control because their experience is limited to masturbation, which is often done quickly. But couples who care for each other, help each other enjoy sex and orgasms, and know each other well enough to help the man gain control may do better than the statistics imply. Although far from perfect, this method is better than using nothing at all.

I'm in high school and have been going out with this kid for about a year now. We've been having sex for about two months. We have no birth control whatsoever. He says that he doesn't want to use a condom because "it doesn't feel the same." So he just removes his penis before he releases sperm. I know my friend's boyfriend says the same thing also.

If my mom would find out that I was on the Pill already she would kill me, so I have to use this option instead. Should I worry about becoming pregnant? This is a giant worry in my life.

Yes, you should worry about getting pregnant. For every 100 women who rely on withdrawal for one year, 23 will become pregnant—that's about one out of four. And the pregnancy risk for teenagers may be even higher. *(See the preceding answer for information on the various reasons why withdrawal doesn't work effectively.)*

Please talk with a counselor at a family-planning clinic who can help you understand the risks involved in continuing to have sex this way, which also exposes you to STDs. You *do* have other options, regardless of what your boyfriend says, and one of them is to say "No more intercourse until we find and use an effective method of protection for me." I suspect your mother would be even more upset if you become pregnant as a result of not using contraception.

Unfortunately, your boyfriend's attitude toward condoms is not unusual. Since the middle of this century, Americans have been reluctant to use condoms, often on the grounds that men complain that they diminish sensation and interfere with pleasure. This attitude is not necessarily shared by the rest of the world. Fifty percent of Japanese, 32 percent of Finnish, 25 percent of Danish, and 18 percent of British married couples report using condoms. In the United States only 15 percent of married couples report condom use, although the rate has recently increased from 9 percent to 16 percent among *unmarried* couples—perhaps because information that condoms can help prevent STDs and thus later fertility problems has finally reached the public.

Fertility Awareness Methods

A woman's egg is only available for fertilization for a day or less in each cycle, but sperm can reach the egg from semen deposited in the vagina anytime from approximately eight days before ovulation plus the day of ovulation. *(For more information see Chapter 15.)*

The goal of fertility awareness (also called "natural family planning" or the "rhythm method") is to predict when ovulation will occur in a given cycle so that a couple who does not want to conceive does not have sex anytime near the woman's fertile time.

The basic varieties of fertility awareness are the calendar, basal body temperature, and cervical mucus methods. The typical failure rate for fertility awareness methods is high—24 pregnancies out of 100 couples who use the method for one year. To achieve a better rate couples must have good training; *both* partners must be committed to abstaining from intercourse during the entire fertile time; multiple fertility awareness methods should be used; and instructions must be closely followed every day. When all this is done *and* the woman also has fairly regular cycles, the failure rate can sometimes be reduced to around 2 to 10 pregnancies per 100 couples.

All these methods require a woman to pay close attention to her body and to keep accurate records of her reproductive cycles. All women should be keeping such records anyway, because this information is invaluable for noticing if cycle irregularities or changes appear— symptoms that require a medical examination regardless of the type of contraception used.

The **calendar** method is based on the assumption that ovulation will occur about fourteen days *before* the next menstrual flow begins. Ovulation occurs at approximately the middle of a reproductive cycle, which begins with the first day of menstrual flow of one period and ends on the first day of flow in the next *(see Illustration 4 in Chapter 2)*. A woman keeps records of her first day of menstrual flow for six full cycles (not all cycles will last the same number of days). She identifies the shortest cycle, takes that number of days, and subtracts 18—this is considered the *first* "unsafe" day after each menstrual flow begins. She then identifies her longest cycle, takes that number of days, and subtracts 11—this is thought to be her *last* "unsafe" day in a cycle.

Then the couple does not have intercourse on any "unsafe" days. For most couples, this means no intercourse for at least ten consecutive days in the middle of every cycle. This method, however, does not take into account the fact that many women have such irregular cycles that future "unsafe" days cannot be accurately predicted from records of past cycles.

The **basal body temperature** (BBT)—*basal* means "resting"—method helps some couples because it can show when ovulation has actually occurred in a cycle. In many women basal temperature rises by 0.4 to 0.8 degrees Fahrenheit within twenty-four hours *after* ovulation and stays higher until her next menstrual flow. This rise is due to an increase in progesterone produced by the corpus luteum *(see Illustration 4 in Chapter 2)*. Using a special thermometer (one that shows a range only from 96° F to 100° F, making it easier to see fractions of degrees) a woman takes her basal temperature each morning before she gets out of bed, drinks or eats anything, or smokes. Then she records the temperature on a chart. After keeping such charts for six months, the couple should theoretically be able to see the day ovulation occurred in past cycles. To prevent pregnancy, no intercourse is permitted for at least seven days before the temperature is *expected* to rise in future cycles, plus the three days after it actually has risen in each cycle.

Although slightly better than the calendar method, the BBT failure rate is still around 20 per 100 couples per year, except for those couples who follow the so-called "strict" BBT method; no intercourse is permitted from the first day of menstrual flow until four days after the BBT has risen. Having sex only on those few remaining days (for many couples this would mean only ten or eleven days in each cycle) does yield a lower failure rate—6 pregnancies per 100 couples per year.

A third awareness technique—checking for the consistency of **cervical mucus**— is also recommended by some groups. This method is based on the theory that the estrogen level peaks just before ovulation. As a woman's level of estrogen rises in the first part of her cycle *(see Illustration 4 in Chapter 2)*, it not only stimulates growth of an egg but also affects her cervix, producing more mucus and of a different type. The color and texture differ from cervical mucus at other stages of the cycle. At the highest estrogen levels the mucus looks like raw egg white, can be slowly stretched between the fingertips to a strand the length of four inches, and makes a woman feel wet, slippery, or oily around the vaginal opening. At other times, the woman's vulval area feels drier, the mucus looks more yellow or milky and will not stretch between the fingertips.

Although most women using the mucus method monitor their cervical mucus at the vaginal opening, some use a speculum (the instrument used by a gynecologist to open the vagina so the cervix can be seen) and a mirror to look at the cervix itself. These women can also look for changes in the os (the opening in the cervix). The os is closed during most of the cycle, but begins to open around the same time that mucus production increases. This permits sperm to enter more easily around the time of ovulation. The cervix also opens at menstruation.

As with other awareness methods, mucus observations are recorded on a chart, and a couple wishing to avoid pregnancy has intercourse only on those days after ovulation is over in one cycle up to the first day of menstrual flow in the next cycle. Then they may also have intercourse on alternate days after menstrual flow stops, so long as the "egg white" type of mucus has not appeared. In one study of couples using only the mucus method, the failure rate was nearly 40 per 100 couples.

The major problem with all these fertility awareness methods is that many women do not have temperature changes or mucus changes that match the patterns these methods are based on. Also, a wide array of common events can change temperature (having a cold or the flu, sleeping late, stress) or change mucus secretions (vaginal infections, taking medications, being sexually aroused) for even those women who are usually regular and who are conscientious about monitoring and recording observations.

Within the past few years, a fourth method of fertility awareness has become available—**home test kits** that look for the presence of LH (leutinizing hormone) in a woman's urine. It is the sudden rise in LH that stimulates release of an egg from the ovaries (*see Illustration 4 in Chapter 2*). After the rise in LH, ovulation usually occurs within twenty-four to thirty-eight hours, although some women also have variable patterns of LH secretion. Even though these kits are marketed for couples who are trying to *get* pregnant, they might also be useful for couples trying to avoid pregnancy when used in conjunction with the other awareness methods. The more methods used, the better.

Although highly accurate (from 95 to 100 percent when done according to instructions) these LH home test kits are expensive—about $40 for enough materials to do around ten samples. Of course, a couple wishing to avoid pregnancy would still need to record the LH pattern for several months, then stop having intercourse several days before the LH surge was expected in each cycle so that no sperm were waiting in the woman's reproductive tract (*see Chapter 15*).

All of the fertility awareness methods are highly reversible when a couple decides to start a family and most cost nothing or are inexpensive, but none offer any protection against STDs.

Which days are safe? In other words, which days can I have sex and not worry about getting pregnant?

The answer is that *no* days can be absolutely guaranteed to be "safe" from conception. Furthermore, there is no way to give easy rules that apply to all women. Any time sperm are present when an egg is released (and sperm can live for as many as eight days in the woman's reproductive tract), pregnancy is possible. This means that for those women who have regular menstrual cycles of twenty-eight days, the greatest likelihood of conception is when intercourse occurs during a ten-to-fourteen-day span in the middle of the reproductive cycle, halfway between the first day of one menstrual flow and the first day of the next expected menstrual flow. (*See Illustration 4 in Chapter 2.*)

Monitoring your body's signals related to ovulation requires special training and daily accurate record keeping. Help is often needed to interpret these records because changes in cervical mucus and daily temperature can be subtle. These methods also demand lengthy periods of abstinence from intercourse.

If you want to try fertility awareness methods, ask your gynecologist or family-planning center for information or for recommendations about groups in your community that offer such training.

I've read studies in which the failure rates of natural birth control methods were either very high or very low. What do I believe?

The failure rates cited for the basal body temperature and cervical mucus methods come from various studies, including a World Health Organization multinational study conducted at five different research centers. That study reported 19.4 pregnancies per 100 women per year. Other comparable large studies in the United States, Colombia, and England have reported pregnancy rates ranging from 16 to 30 women for every 100 women using these methods for one year.

There are studies reporting lower failure rates for these methods. In fact, one study in West Germany reported a pregnancy rate of 0.3 percent (fewer than one in 100). These low rates, however, appear to result from including only those couples who are highly committed to the method and willing to have intercourse only on days following ovulation, about eleven days out of each cycle. For some couples, especially those completely committed to the record-keeping and abstinence requirements for reasons of religious doctrine or health, failure rates can be quite low.

Regardless of commitment, however, failure can and does occur due to many factors, such as irregular cycles induced by illness or stress, slight temperature increases from mild infections or even the use of electric blankets, changes in daily schedules, or vaginal discharges from infections or medication.

Because most women don't have highly predictable menstrual cycles and most couples don't have intercourse in patterns that include abstinence for twelve or more consecutive days out of each cycle, it's not surprising that these methods have much higher pregnancy rates when tested on large, diverse populations.

However, several aspects of the "natural" methods of birth control do deserve special consideration for some women. None introduce chemicals or hormones into a woman's body, all are based on a woman being extremely aware of her body and its changes during her reproductive cycle and on keeping accurate records of those changes (which is beneficial for all women), and they can provide extremely useful information for couples who are trying to *get* pregnant.

Douching

Douching is forcing a liquid into the vagina and letting it drain back out. The failure rate for douching is 40 percent (out of 100 women using this method for one year, 40 will become pregnant). Moreover, most douching liquids offer no protection against STDs, as do some other methods of contraception, and new data have revealed that douching may increase the risk of developing PID and its consequences—infertility and ectopic pregnancy.

I've heard that a good contraceptive douche after quickie sex is a shaken-up Coke or 7-Up or other similar pop, even ginger ale. True?

No! Douching with a carbonated liquid can also be deadly. It is possible for bubbles from carbonated beverages to enter the bloodstream by rising from the vagina into the uterus, leading to a potentially deadly embolism (an air bubble in a blood vessel). Don't try it.

Although some soft drinks have been shown to kill some sperm in laboratory test tubes, they have little contraceptive value in real-life situations because sperm move too quickly to be destroyed by douching with *any* solution. By the time you begin douching, enough sperm are likely to have already found their way into the cervix, and once sperm have entered the cervical mucus they are beyond the reach of a douching liquid.

Abortion

Except for sexual abstinence, none of the various contraceptive surgeries, products, devices, and other methods currently available are 100 percent effective. Statistically, even among the most conscientious, careful couples using the most effective methods in exactly the prescribed way, a few will experience a contraceptive failure.

The question of what options are available for coping with contraceptive failures to couples who live in the United States will be decided by the American legal system. If abortion remains a legal option, each couple's decision will be based on their personal values and circumstances.

Abortion should *not* be viewed as simply another contraceptive method, nor should it be used as the primary or only way of preventing pregnancy.

For those couples who truly do want a family at some point but worry that an abortion may damage their future ability to conceive, data available indicate that having a safe, early, medically approved abortion does not reduce future fertility. Moreover, a review of more than 250 studies of possible psychological effects of abortion by the U.S. Surgeon General and the American Psychological Association found that abortion does not cause short-term or long-term negative effects for the majority of women undergoing an abortion.

CONTRACEPTION IN THE FUTURE

Researchers are continually investigating more effective, safe, and convenient methods of birth control. Some of these are currently being used in other countries and are undergoing tests in the United States. None have yet been approved for sale in the U.S. but some may be available within a few years. Others have negative side effects (such as reduced sex drive) that may deter people from using them, even if they are found to be safe and are made available. We have room to discuss only a few.

I have heard about a new contraceptive pill that you take only once a month. I'm very sorry to say I can't remember the name. The purpose of the pill is to

make you start getting your period automatically. You need not take any other kind of birth control. If you happen to be pregnant when you take the pill it somehow removes the embryo from the uterus. Hope I told that right. I myself believe it would be very useful.

The drug you heard about was probably RU486 (mifepristone), developed by Dr. Etienne-Emile Baulieu. It is not yet available in the U.S. In one study by a team of French researchers, RU486 was given to 100 women who had missed their periods and intended to have abortions. The drug reinstated menstrual flow in eighty-five of these women.

RU486 acts by blocking the effect of progesterone, a hormone necessary to thicken the lining of the uterus. This blocking results in changes which decrease the likelihood that a fertilized egg can implant in the uterine lining. Whether it will ever be available for use in the United States is the subject of political debate as well as scientific study. Some U.S. researchers are investigating the contraceptive effects of this method. To date, studies involve only small numbers of women using it for short periods of time.

Even though RU486 may eventually be shown to be an effective method of contraception, a great deal more research is needed to establish the appropriate dosage and when the pill should be taken each month.

There appear to be no serious short-term side effects, but studies will also be necessary to evaluate long-term side effects.

Recently I heard about a new birth control device popular in Europe (somewhere in Sweden, I think) where an operation on the female's left arm is done and a small paper-thin something is inserted. I would like to know anything you know about it.

You probably heard about Norplant, which is manufactured in Finland. Developed by the Population Council (an international nonprofit organization) and tested in fourteen countries, this revolutionary approach to long-term contraception is expected eventually to be approved for use in the United States. Norplant works by inhibiting ovulation and by making the cervical mucus thicker. This stops the sperm from swimming through the cervix into the uterus.

Six small, flexible tubes—each about the size of a paper match—are inserted under the skin on the inside of a woman's upper left or right arm just above the crease of the elbow. The procedure requires only a local anesthetic for the tiny slit through which a hollow needle is maneuvered to place the implants. The insertion takes about fifteen minutes. The projected cost in the United States is about $60. Contraceptive protection becomes effective within twenty-four hours after insertion and lasts for five years. For continued contraceptive protection after five years, the first set of implants is removed and another set inserted.

The drug sealed into the tubes is levonorgestrel, a synthetic progestin (a laboratory-produced hormone similar to one manufactured in higher amounts by women than by men) that has been used for years in oral contraceptives. The amount of hormone steadily released into the bloodstream is much lower than the amount found in most birth-control pills, and the implants don't include estrogen (another hormone produced naturally by women and used in most oral contraceptives, but which some researchers suspect of having negative side effects). Because both the drug and the material used to make the tubes have been in use for many years, researchers predict that side effects will be minimal, even with long-term use (although this particular method has been studied for only ten years).

The level of effectiveness (between 0.2 and 1.3 pregnancies per 100 women per year) is as high as for surgical methods of birth control, but this new method is immediately and inexpensively reversible by simply opening the skin and sliding the implants out. So far, pregnancy rates following removal are comparable to normal pregnancy rates and the babies born have been normal.

The most common side effect is disturbance of a woman's menstrual patterns, with a majority of users reporting more days of flow, even though the volume is usually lighter. These menstrual changes tend to diminish after a few months.

Women with breast cancer, liver disease, or abnormal uterine bleeding are advised not to use Norplant and no woman who is already pregnant should have the implants inserted into her arm. Until more research is available on the effect of these implants on babies, women who are breast-feeding should also not use this type of hormonal product.

Even though they disliked the side effect of menstrual changes, 80 percent of women who used the implants recommended them to friends and neighbors and 78 percent said they would use the implants again if they were available.

I heard someone was making a female condom. What does this look like?

A "female condom" is being tested but has not yet been approved for sale in the United States. Called Femshield, it consists of a polyurethane condom-shaped sheath with two flexible rings. The ring on the inner (closed) end of the condom helps with insertion and with keeping the condom in place inside the vagina. The ring on the outer (open) end keeps the condom from being pushed inside the vagina and also covers part of the vulva. This should provide protection against STDs to a larger genital area than does the male condom. As yet there are no data on the effectiveness of this new type of condom.

My husband (age 39) and I (age 37) have five children. We would like to have one more child, then do something permanent about birth control. Neither of us likes the idea of surgical procedures, such as vasectomy or tubal sterilization. Some time ago I read about research on using silicone injections in the Fallopian tubes. Is there more information on this? Where can I get this done?

The concept of using silicone to plug the Fallopian tubes rather than cutting, burning, or clamping them is still under investigation. The original idea was to develop a contraceptive method that would be more easily reversed than traditional tubal sterilization. Unfortunately, the silicone plugs do not appear to enhance reversibility. There is also still a need for a long-term evaluation of whether silicone plugs might increase the risk of ectopic (tubal) pregnancies.

What is the progress on an oral contraceptive for men?

A safe oral contraceptive for men is still a long way off. Researchers are testing several drugs. One that looks promising is a synthetic hormone that decreases development of sperm by preventing the brain's naturally produced hormones from signaling the man's testicles to produce mature sperm.

Interestingly, these drugs (called LH-RH analogs and LH-RH antagonists) are destroyed by gastric acids, so they are currently being tested as a nasal inhalant (like a spray for a stuffy nose) rather than as a pill or as injections.

Results so far show that, although the testicles do stop sperm production, they also stop producing testosterone, thereby lowering the sex drive. It is doubtful that many men would prefer this to using condoms or having vasectomies.

A different hormonal substance, called inhibin, is also being tested. It appears also to lower sperm counts but without lowering testosterone. However, it will be many years before this has been tested thoroughly enough for approval.

INEFFECTIVE CONTRACEPTION

The following letters are included in this chapter only to illustrate some of the widespread myths and misinformation about contraception. None of these are effective methods.

In discussions of barrier-type contraceptives I don't find mention of the teenager's favorite, namely, Saran Wrap, which is readily available, generally effective, and inexpensive. It can also be used, in sheet form, as a barrier to prevent the spread of herpes from one body to the other.

Effective? Absolutely not, neither as contraception nor as protection against herpes and other STDs! No plastic wrap, brand-name or not, works. If Saran Wrap is, in fact, the "teenagers' favorite," this might help explain the high rate of unplanned pregnancies and STDs among young people.

Plastic wrap is not designed to fit like a condom and is far too easy to tear or dislodge. It can also contain small holes that are impossible to see without a microscope but are large enough for sperm to swim through. Disease organisms, particularly tiny viruses (like those which cause herpes, AIDS, and genital warts) can pass through even smaller spaces.

I've heard a good method of birth control for men is to masturbate before having intercourse. Is it true that you use up your sperm the first time and then are safe for a couple of hours?

No. Healthy, fertile men have a tremendous store of sperm and there are always enough sperm available to cause a pregnancy in every ejaculation. Any man who tried to use multiple ejaculations as a form of birth control would collapse from exhaustion before he ran out of sperm. Even though the volume of semen is reduced when a man has several ejaculations close together and there are fewer sperm in the semen, there can still be several million sperm in even a single drop!

Men produce nearly 50,000 sperm every minute, and even though this process of sperm production, or spermatogenesis, takes more than seventy days to complete, from their growth in the testicles to their appearance in semen, it is continuous—starting at puberty.

Further Readings

Consumer Reports Magazine. March 1989, Vol. 54, no. 3, pp. 135-141. *Can You Rely on Condoms?*
(Has rankings of condom durability and other factors by brand name. Most public libraries have copies of this magazine.)

Goldstein, M., and Feldberg, M. *The Vasectomy Book: A complete guide to decision making.* Los Angeles, CA: J.P. Tarcher, Inc., 1982.
(A helpful book for anyone interested in weighing the benefits and risks of vasectomy.)

Hatcher, R. A.; Guest, F.; Stewart, F.; Stewart, G. K.; Trussell, J.; Cerel, S.; and Cates, W. *Contraceptive Technology.* New York: Irvington Publishers, Inc. (a new edition is issued every other year).
(A data-based book on contraceptive methods and issues. A helpful and up-to-date resource for anyone with a specific question about contraception.)

Shapiro, H. I. *The New Birth Control Book: A complete guide for women and men.* New York: Prentice Hall Press, 1988.
(An easy-to-read book which discusses birth control in a question-and-answer format.)

17

Personal Sexual Health

This chapter is about how to take care of your sexual and reproductive-related health and contains important information for everyone, whether or not you are sexually active. Each person must take responsibility for monitoring his or her own body by doing self-examinations regularly and noticing any changes or symptoms. Also included is information about what to expect when you go to a doctor for standard examinations and a discussion of the fears and concerns we all have that keep many people from going to a doctor (especially if a problem involves sexuality).

FEMALE SEXUAL HEALTH

Women who understand the basics of their own external anatomy and the internal changes during each reproductive cycle can recognize signs of problems or illness earlier than women who do not. These women are also better prepared to make decisions about their bodies' "care and maintenance." Every woman must take responsibility for maintaining her own health. This includes conducting regular self-examinations and scheduling medical examinations on an annual basis and whenever changes or symptoms of a problem are noticed.

Menstruation

Keeping Menstrual Records

Every woman between puberty and menopause should keep records of her reproductive cycles. These records will provide a detailed, accurate history which is invaluable for diagnosing many different types of problems. Actual records are much more useful to a physician than the usually vague recollections a woman has about her cycle pattern or when any changes or symptoms first appeared.

Look at Illustration 4 in Chapter 2 to see what a reproductive cycle looks like. This drawing shows a cycle length of 28 days between one menstrual flow and the next, but cycle length varies from one woman to another and can even vary from one cycle to the next for the same woman. Having anywhere from 25 to 34 days between the start of one menstrual flow and the start of the next is considered quite normal.

On a calendar or in a diary, note exactly which day menstrual flow appears, marking it "Day 1." Day 1 isn't likely to be the first day of a calendar month but is simply called that, even though it's really March 12, June 16, October 25, or whenever. Each day after that, mark whether there is any menstrual flow, plus any other information important to you, such as cramps, extra-heavy bleeding, mood changes, or breast tenderness.

If you are concerned about PMS (Premenstrual Syndrome), you will want to write on your calendar (especially during the week or so *before* your flow) whenever you notice special symptoms, such as headaches or irritability. Other items to record are discussed later in this chapter.

If you're interested in finding your most fertile time, there is additional information you will want to record on your calendar, especially around the middle of your cycle. These include taking your basal body temperature (BBT) and checking your cervical mucus *(see Chapter 16).*

Look at your own records every few months or so just to make sure your pattern hasn't changed in a way that's new for you. If it has, consult your physician.

When I visit the gynecologist the nurse always asks me the date of my last period, but I never know how to precisely define the very first day of the flow. Often when I'm expecting my period I'll notice the faintest, tiniest, palest brown or pink spot in my discharge. Then there's nothing for two days. Then comes the blood for four or five days. So when does my period begin? At the first sign of that pale tiny pink spot? Or is it two days later, when it's obviously blood?

A short, light flow of blood is called spotting. On the menstrual records you keep, mark down "spotting" on each day this happens. On days when the flow is more steady and/or more heavy, write "flow."

Take your records the next time you go to the gynecologist and ask which type of bleeding (spotting or flow) you should use as your Day 1.

I'm a 14-year-old girl who doesn't know if she has a serious problem or not. It all started two months ago during my period. (I've had my period for about two years now.) The first couple of days it was normal, but the last was a brown color. The month before that, I had two periods, both a brownish-red color. I haven't told my mother yet and don't think I could. Is this normal or do I have a serious problem?

There is a wide range of "normal" menstrual patterns, and women rarely compare their menstrual flows so they don't have a clear idea of what's "normal" for women in general.

The color and consistency of flow depends on how fast you're shedding the uterine lining. Faster shedding gives a redder color; slower shedding produces a brownish color. Brown is simply the color of older, drier blood. Pale pink, bright, or dark red (or nearly black in some cases) is normal for some women.

You are still in the process of maturing and during the next few years your periods may vary a lot in color, amount, and timing.

I'm 17 and often go as many as 60 days between periods. Is this a problem?

In young women it is not unusual for the number of days between periods to vary. It takes an average of seven years for most girls to reach the more regular cycle pattern they will maintain during adulthood.

It is a myth that each menstrual cycle is one month long. The range of cycle lengths considered normal for adult women is 25 to 34 days, but research has shown that young women between the ages of 15 and 19 often have longer periods of time between menstrual flows than do women of other age groups.

Other causes of long cycles or skipped menstrual flow include stress, weight loss, inadequate nutrition, and regular strenuous exercise—all of which can alter hormone levels.

Long cycles or missed periods are usually associated with the lack of the release of an egg from an ovary (called anovulation). This also is not unusual for younger women. However, you might want to consult a gynecologist just to check. Certainly, older women who have cycle lengths between 35 and 90 days (called oligomenorrhea) should see a physician.

Long cycles or skipped periods are usually not a problem for younger women unless a woman wishes to become pregnant or is having menstrual periods that are more than ninety days apart (called amenorrhea), in which case she *must* consult a gynecologist. Hormonal medications can be used to stimulate ovulation or to trigger the uterus to shed its lining on a more regular basis if that is medically necessary.

Do women who live together have their menstrual periods at the same time? This has begun to happen to me and my new roommate—and some of my other friends have mentioned it, too.

Researchers have documented that women who spend a lot of time together—roommates, best friends, mothers and daughters, sisters, and women who work together—tend to begin their menstrual periods on or about the same day. This phenomenon is called "menstrual synchrony."

When new groups are formed, or when a new woman enters an established group, it seems to take about four months for menstrual cycles to synchronize. One study of seven lifeguards who worked together found that even though their menstrual periods were far apart at the beginning of the summer, after three months they all began their flows within four days of each other.

We don't yet know exactly how menstrual synchrony develops. Researchers have ruled out simple explanations such as similar diets or mutual times of stress, because entire college dormitories and women's prisons do not cycle together. It is also not related to lunar or seasonal cycles, nor is it due to verbal influence (women telling one another when menstruation occurs).

Most of the research has shown that menstrual synchrony is somehow related to the amount of time spent together, and some fascinating laboratory tests suggest an underlying physiological cause. In tests researchers rubbed underarm sweat from some women with very regular cycles (the "donors") combined with alcohol under the noses of some research subjects and plain alcohol alone under the noses of other women. After four months, the women exposed to the donors' sweat menstruated within three days of the donors' cycle. Cycles of the women rubbed with only alcohol did not change.

Because of these results, scientists now speculate that women emit different chemicals from their bodies during the various stages of their monthly cycles and that those chemicals can trigger changes in the menstrual cycles of other women.

The existence of such pheromones (chemical substances made by the body that stimulate responses from other members of the same species) have been found in many animals and are associated with specific behaviors, including mating. It will be interesting to see if researchers can find similar "chemical communicators" in humans and measure their effects on the reproductive behavior of both women and men.

Why do women have menstruation? Why does the body have to hemorrhage? Is it excess blood that we must get rid of?

Menstrual flow is a sign of good health. It indicates that the complicated sequence of female reproductive events is functioning well.

The flow consists of various fluids from the uterus, pieces of the endometrium (the lining of the uterus), and blood from the endometrial tissue—not directly from veins or arteries. Although it may seem like a lot of blood, in the vast majority of women it is far from being a hemorrhage: The average total amount of blood in each menstrual flow is only about two fluid ounces (the same as four to five tablespoons) spread over four or five days. A few women do have exceptionally heavy menstruation; a flow that is greater than three fluid ounces requires medical attention and monitoring for anemia.

Although menstrual flow may look like regular blood, it is not and does not come directly from the blood vessels. Menstrual flow therefore cannot be thought of as "excess blood."

One of my friends told me that she had sex while she was flowing and *nothing happened*. Is that true?

You do not say what you think might happen if a woman has sex during menstruation. Although some women object to doing this because it seems messier, other women say that sexual activity or orgasm during menstruation is beneficial because it reduces menstrual cramps. Some partners also prefer to avoid having sex during the menstrual flow, while others either don't care or actually prefer it.

The only caution is that the AIDS virus may be transmitted more easily during menstrual flow and that in general, because menstruation is a time when the cervix is open, there may be a greater likelihood of sexually transmitted disease (STD) organisms entering the uterus (*see Chapter 19*).

Menstrual Problems

Women are out en masse in the workforce. Why must they be forced to pretend they are men? Once a month, at least on the first day, many women suffer with cramps. I did, and needed to lie down and stay off my feet for most of the first

day. In Japan, I understand, this womanly function is accepted, and women are excused from work once a month. Not in this enlightened country.

Researchers estimate that between 30 and 50 percent of women have at least some symptoms during some menstrual cycles, but only about 10 percent of women occasionally have menstrual symptoms severe enough to interfere with their daily lives.

Recently, scientists have begun to understand that most distress or pain during the menstrual flow is related to the level of prostaglandins (substances made in many parts of the body, including the uterus), which is highest just as the flow begins and usually stays high for two or three days. Prostaglandins trigger uterine contractions that can be the cause of menstrual cramps. Women with dysmenorrhea (pain during menstruation) have much higher prostaglandin levels in their menstrual flow than do women who have no menstrual discomfort.

Drugs that have an antiprostaglandin effect produce relief for approximately 80 percent of dysmenorrheic women. Aspirin appears to relieve minor discomfort, but newer drugs such as ibuprofen, mefenamic acid, naproxen, and indomethacin produce dramatic improvements.

Your information about Japan is only partially correct. The labor laws of that country do specify that "menstrual leave" should be available to women workers. But according to an expert on the study of Japanese women, they rarely claim this leave, fearful that they'll be fired for being "lazy workers."

I'm 35 and I have allergies to pain relievers. I've read that regular exercise and a healthy diet are sufficient to reduce menstrual discomfort for many women without the use of drugs.

I am interested in knowing what kind of exercises I can do plus the type of diet to follow.

Physicians who treat women with dysmenorrhea recommend a healthy, balanced diet and regular exercise. But be prepared for a lifelong commitment to the program; it won't work if you only eat properly and exercise during your period.

This dietary approach includes increasing potassium-rich foods, which help prevent fluid retention (if that's part of your problem), and reducing sodium (salt) consumption. Foods high in natural potassium include bananas, oranges, broccoli, wheat germ, and potatoes.

The types of exercise recommended are general aerobic exercises that measurably increase heart rate, not those that focus on muscle development or body toning in a specific area. I recommend low-impact aerobics, since there is less risk of damage to joints and the spine. These activities release endorphins, frequently referred to as the body's natural opiate. This natural painkiller appears to reduce menstrual pain for some women.

Ask your doctor if your allergy to pain relievers includes the antiprostaglandins. If it doesn't, you might want to consider trying one of these (*see preceding answer*).

What can you tell me about PMS? I have reason to believe I have this and would like to know more about it before I bring my symptoms to the attention of my doctor.

What makes premenstrual syndrome (PMS) unique is not necessarily its symptoms. Whether male, female, menstruating or not, anyone with any number of health disorders can experience the symptoms often listed for PMS, from headaches to a stuffy nose, fluid retention to fatigue, depression to irritability.

What *is* unique about PMS is its timing and regularity. While the symptoms may differ from woman to woman, they appear during the week or two before menstrual flow begins and then disappear at menstruation. This pattern may be repeated in each reproductive cycle.

Many physicians will not attempt to diagnose PMS until a woman has kept detailed records of at least three cycles, so keep good records. If you suspect you have PMS, record such symptoms as headaches, breast tenderness, bloatedness, depression, irritability, lethargy, skin lesions, stuffy nose, anxiety, trouble sleeping, emotionality (including crying more easily than usual), or anything else you feel are noteworthy changes during each cycle.

Take these records with you when you see your physician. If he or she is not familiar with diagnosing and treating PMS, ask to be referred to a physician who is. Because a great deal of research is being done now on PMS, information about treatments is changing rapidly.

It is difficult to study the emotional problems associated with the menstrual cycle because one woman's stress may be another's stimulation. Some researchers feel that treatments for physical symptoms also reduce psychological symptoms, such as feeling tired, depressed, or irritable.

In Great Britain, several women accused of violent crimes have attempted to use PMS as a legal defense similar to insanity. I'm not yet convinced that PMS or other menstrual disorders should be included in laws or social policies that could affect all women. The majority of women have no symptoms, or only mild problems that do not interfere with their ability to perform on the job or to lead productive lives.

The majority of my menstruation days are accompanied by a runny nose and/or pressure and pain in my sinuses. Have you any evidence to support this phenomenon? My gynecologist and medical G.P. do not know of any correlation. Nor do they even believe me. One did prescribe an antihistamine, which didn't help.

Researchers who have investigated PMS (premenstrual syndrome) do list sinusitis and rhinitis (runny nose) as two of the symptoms that occur in a regular, cyclic pattern for some women. In one study of PMS symptoms, 7 percent of the women reported having rhinitis. Asthma may also worsen premenstrually.

It is not yet clear exactly what is involved, but these symptoms may be related to water retention by specific nasal or sinus tissues. Or there may be an increased allergic sensitivity due to a lowered level of circulating progesterone.

In other words, you may be allergic to something every day of the month but only notice symptoms on those days your progesterone drops (a normal part of the monthly cycle). All this still may not explain what happens in your case, since PMS symptoms usually decrease when the menstrual flow begins.

If the problems are so severe they interfere with your life, you may want to consult an allergy specialist. There may be something in your environment you should be avoiding altogether or during certain days of your cycle.

I've heard that progesterone can alleviate premenstrual syndrome. If so, why don't all women take progesterone?

There is evidence that taking progesterone reduces premenstrual symptoms for *some*, not all, women. And this has been shown to be effective only for those symptoms occurring between ovulation (about fourteen days before menstrual flow begins) and the beginning of the menstrual flow.

As for your suggestion, prescribing progesterone to all women isn't a good idea. First of all, not all women have premenstrual difficulties, and others have problems only once or twice a year. Second, even though women naturally produce progesterone during their reproductive years, we still don't know the effects of taking supplemental progesterone over a long period of time. At this point, most experts caution that progesterone be given only in severe cases of PMS.

My 19-year-old daughter suffers cramping, pain, and general malaise in the four to six days in advance of her period and during her period. This condition has gone on for years, and in my opinion has gotten worse.

Her gynecologist has tried diuretics and Motrin with no success and now he's moving toward narcotic drugs, which I oppose since she's a college student and needs her wits about her. Any advice you might render would be greatly appreciated.

The drugs your daughter has tried are often effective at relieving cramps and pain during menstruation. Pain during the flow is a common menstrual problem for some women. In contrast, pain *preceding* the flow is one of the signs of endometriosis (when pieces of the lining of the uterus—the endometrium—implant on internal organs such as the ovaries). In these cases experts recommend a complete medical evaluation, including a diagnostic laparoscopy by a gynecologist who specializes in reproductive endocrinology or endometriosis.

There are other stronger types of antiprostaglandin drugs than Motrin that your daughter may try *if* she is found to have no internal disorders. Narcotic drugs do reduce pain (and may be necessary in some cases) but first it is important to find out exactly what is causing your daughter's menstrual difficulties. Moreover, you're right to be concerned about narcotics; they can be addictive and affect mental and physical abilities.

For a number of years I have suffered severe cramping during ovulation. At times the pain is so bad that it wakes me from a sound sleep. It also seems that steady cramping occurs at night or early in the morning. When I approached my doctor about this he informed me I must be releasing a chemical while I released an egg. He seemed to be nonconcerned.

Could you explain why this happens? Is this normal, or does this indicate a problem with my ovaries or Fallopian tubes? How is it treated?

Pain or cramps in the lower abdomen or back during ovulation bears the German name *Mittelschmertz*, "middle pain," because the pain occurs approximately halfway between menstrual cycles. Painful ovulation is normal for many women and its existence is well known, but research has not yet determined what causes the pain.

To date, Mittelschmertz has not been linked to any particular problems with the ovaries or other reproductive organs. Some women experience only a twinge of pain, while others report several hours of cramping so severe that it has occasionally been confused with appendicitis or ectopic (tubal) pregnancy.

Some experts have suggested using oral contraceptives to stop the process of ovulation and hence the ovulation pain. Those experts who consider Mittelschmertz a symptom of premenstrual syndrome or pelvic congestion syndrome suggest that progesterone (suppositories or injections) be used a couple of days before ovulation is expected. I found no reports evaluating either the short- or long-term effectiveness of either treatment. Get a second opinion from a gynecologic endocrinologist *(see Appendix)* who would be familiar with hormonal evaluations and treatments.

Menstrual Hygiene

I've always been curious about what women used in past centuries for "feminine protection" during their periods. You are the only person I could think of who would answer this question.

Based on the earliest recorded descriptions, the materials used to collect menstrual flow were disposable and actually similar to products used today. Women generally used whatever absorbent materials were readily available and shaped them into either a type of external pad or an internal tampon. In some traditional societies, however, women simply ignored the flow and just regularly disposed of their floor coverings or clothing.

Material used for pads included all types of grass and fibrous materials. Tampons were rolled from papyrus (in Egypt), wool (in Rome), paper (in Japan), and vegetable fiber (in Indonesia). In some cultures, women buried or simply discarded the used materials.

In those cultures where menstrual blood was thought to have dangerous or mysterious powers, women carefully burned their pads or tampons to protect themselves and their group from whatever assorted evils or witchcraft were part of their beliefs.

Where cloth was available and affordable, it was folded to form pads, which most women laundered and reused each month. This method of menstrual hygiene was the one used by most women in the United States until fairly recently.

The first factory in the United States to produce disposable pads introduced them in 1896. Called Lister's Towels, they were not a commercial success—possibly because the Comstock Law prohibited dissemination of any information or product related to birth control, and Lister's Towels may have somehow fallen under that ban.

The first successful disposable pad or sanitary napkin, Kotex, was introduced in 1921 and the first disposable tampon, Tampax, in 1933. Interestingly, the "new" tampon idea generated a flood of public opposition based on the fear that its use was a secret method of contraception or, even worse, of masturbation. Neither assumption was true. Today most women in the U.S. use disposable pads and/or tampons.

I am writing about the trouble some women have at night with leaking at the edges of sanitary napkins. What works for me is to wear two napkins, one

toward the front and one toward the back, and overlapping in the middle. Do you have any other suggestions?

Based on our mail, you're correct in thinking that many women might use a special extra-absorbent and protective napkin for night use, but other women have mentioned that they need extra width along with a longer length. Individual problems with napkins may be related to sleeping positions, or even sleepwear; snug-fitting cotton underwear or pajama bottoms may help keep the napkin in place.

Some manufacturers have in fact introduced sanitary napkins for nighttime use, designed to have the effect of two overlapping napkins. Brands designed with little "wings" at the sides to reduce the chance of leaking might also be worth trying. Other women have suggested using "hospital size" napkins if you can find them—try a medical supply store. Another recommendation was to buy "adult diapers" used for incontinence; these are sold under many different brand names, are inexpensive, and are available in most drugstores.

I've started having my periods. What is a douche? Should I douche after my period?

Douche means a flow of water or other fluid into a body part or cavity. It can also mean the liquid itself and/or the instrument or container used to introduce the fluid into the body.

Women of many different cultures have been putting fluids into the vagina for centuries. One early reference from 1450 B.C. involves a douche fluid of wine and garlic. Some cultures believed that douching the vagina was important for general health, some believed that douching was contraceptive (it is **not**), and others believed that it helped one's love life.

Our own mothers and grandmothers were often told that douching was an essential part of women's cleanliness, and women have passed down instructions and recipes for douche mixtures from one generation to the next. It has been estimated that half of American women douche occasionally.

We now know that the vagina cleans itself naturally, even during menstruation. Therefore, douching is not really necessary. The tissue that lines the vagina consists of mucous membranes (just like the mouth, throat, or nose) and produces secretions that act as natural cleaners, moving any internal surface matter out of the vagina. When these secretions reach the outside folds of the genitals, careful daily washing is, of course, necessary to prevent odors.

Douching can interfere with the vagina's ability to fight infectious organisms and with diagnosis of vaginal problems, so do not douche for 24 hours before a pelvic exam. Moreover, recent research has shown that douching increases a woman's risk of pelvic inflammatory disease (PID)—see Chapter 19.

Tampons and TSS

Every woman who uses tampons should read the package-insert information, which changes as new research findings become available. Too often women assume that they know what the package insert says and discard it without reading it.

While tampons have been blamed in most cases of Toxic Shock Syndrome

(TSS), the risk of developing it is quite low: from one to seventeen cases per 100,000 menstruating girls and women per year in the United States.

Researchers now agree that Staphylococcus aureus is probably the specific organism that causes Toxic Shock Syndrome (TSS), but it is not yet clear exactly what other factors might help to predict which women will get the disease. Staphylococcus aureus can exist normally in the body without causing difficulty unless it grows out of control; one way that happens is by having a highly absorbent tampon in the vagina or wearing a tampon for a long period of time. The organism does not come on the tampons themselves.

One way to lower your risk of developing TSS is by wearing external sanitary napkins instead of tampons, using a napkin at night, and changing your tampons frequently (every four to six hours during the day).

Any woman who develops a high fever, vomiting, dizziness, diarrhea, muscle pain, or a skin rash that looks like a sunburn (some TSS symptoms) should see a physician or go to a hospital emergency room *immediately*. If using a tampon at the time, remove it immediately and wear a sanitary napkin to the medical office.

The majority of TSS cases occur among women under age 30, but it is now clear that the TSS organism can infect people who are not menstruating, at any age, and can also infect men, though rarely.

I'm a little confused about choosing the right tampon for my needs. It seems that there are so many out there, from slender to super, but I still don't know which is best in terms of lowest absorbency and reducing the risk of TSS.

As of March 1990 the U.S. Food and Drug Administration required that tampons sold in the United States (except those sold in vending machines) must carry a prominent label on the package stating the absorbency rating of that particular brand and type of tampon. This is so that women may select the lowest absorbency that manages their flow. Some days you will need a higher absorbency tampon; other days a less absorbent one will do just fine. Use the lowest absorbency you need and this will reduce your risk of developing TSS.

Starting with the lowest absorbency rating, these official labels read Junior Absorbency, Regular Absorbency, Super Absorbency, and Super Plus Absorbency. *All* brands of tampons are required to use these same labels so that women can make direct comparisons about absorbency among different brands. Do not confuse these newer, standardized labels with the older form of brand names, which were not standardized, comparable, or regulated.

I've worn tampons for about two years. I change every four hours and wear a sanitary napkin at night. Still, I'd like to know if using tampons can cause any complications other than TSS.

Some women will forget to remove a tampon when they should, especially at the end of their period when menstrual flow is light. Bacteria can form, changing the delicate balance of vaginal environment and encouraging vaginal infection to begin. The forgotten tampon is usually discovered when a woman goes to a gynecologist to find out why she has an offensive vaginal odor.

There is some evidence that using tampons at times other than during menstruation is not a good idea. Some women, for example, wear tampons throughout the month to absorb normal vaginal secretions. This can dry the vaginal lining and may cause changes in the vaginal tissues. These women should use pantiliners instead, if they wish to avoid getting vaginal discharge on their underwear.

My 16-year-old daughter has been using tampons for her monthly period for some time now, knowing I told her to use mini- or maxi-pads instead.

She says that tampons are more comfortable. But I once read that they form blood clots because they stop the flow of blood, and that they are cancerous. My sister had one stuck up inside of her for a while and never knew it until she developed bad pains and the doctor had to pull it out. These are the reasons I don't want my daughter using tampons, but she won't listen to me.

I found no research linking tampons to cancer or to blood clots. And although there doesn't appear to be any research on how many women neglect to remove tampons, reports on individual cases imply that the worst thing about it is the embarrassment a woman may feel when her doctor discovers the tampon or when the odor becomes noticeable. Her life, however, is usually not threatened.

The next time you and your daughter discuss tampon use, however, you might want to talk about TSS. This is a valid health concern for young women who use tampons.

Self-examination of the External Genitals

Most women have at least heard that they should check their breasts once a month for lumps and changes, but fewer women know that they should also regularly self-examine their external genitalia.

All women, whether they are sexually active or not, should carefully examine themselves every few months between their annual appointments with a gynecologist. Women who are sexually active with more than one partner or with a partner who has sex with other people should do self-examinations *each* month because obvious symptoms of various sexually transmitted diseases (STDs) can come and go, or appear many months after exposure to a disease organism.

To examine yourself, get into a comfortable position (such as lying down on the bed) so that you can direct a good light onto your vulva. You can see more of the area by using a hand mirror. *(An illustration and description of the external genitals are in Chapter 2.)*

Starting at your mons, spread the pubic hair apart and look for any bumps, blisters, sores, or warts and feel for any lumps or growths. Continuing downward, look carefully at the outside of the outer lips and other areas covered by pubic hair. Spreading the outer lips open, gently pull up the fold of skin covering the clitoral glans and look closely for these same signs of problems. Next look at the inside of the outer lips and both sides of the inner lips. With the inner lips held open, look at the area around the urinary opening and the opening to the vagina.

As you examine your genitals, take note of your vaginal discharge. One sign of vaginal infections and some STDs is a change in the texture, color, or smell of the discharge.

If you notice any bumps, blisters, sores, warts, lumps, or any changes in your genitals or your vaginal discharge, make an appointment to see a physician, preferably a gynecologist.

Not too long ago my sister and I heard a lecture on knowing your own body. Following the suggestion to look at your personal place in a mirror, my sister did so. She said she saw little pink tabs of skin with something else and pink flesh.

Not long after that she developed an intensely painful itch in her personal place despite the fact that we are meticulously clean people with perfect hygiene. It has lasted and lasted and she uses anti-itch creams to no avail.

She decided to look again, and the area is now red. The part where those tiny pink tabs of skin were now looks like a whitish thing, which is the main itching place.

It would be obscene for ladies of our age to seek professional help and be examined there. Nothing in the world could make us do so. Even writing this is embarrassing and awful as can be.

Please state how we can treat this embarrassing problem.

There is nothing "obscene" about seeking professional help for problems with any area of the body, including the genitals.

Don't get the idea that your sister somehow caused the problem by looking at her genitals with a mirror. She didn't. And it's unlikely the itching is because her personal hygiene isn't good enough. Itching can be a result of taking antibiotics or other prescription drugs or having low estrogen levels.

Nonprescription treatments are not effective in curing vaginal infections, so she shouldn't try treating this herself. *Only* an examination by a physician, preferably a gynecologist, can determine the cause and the best treatment of your sister's discomfort. The white spots you describe could indicate a serious skin condition, or even be an early warning sign of cancer of the genital area.

Ask your friends to recommend a gynecologist they trust, or call your local medical society or the nearest medical school and ask for the names of gynecologists who specialize in treating older women. If your sister thinks she would be more comfortable seeing a female physician or one from a particular age group, have her say so when she calls. *Both* of you should have a pelvic exam, Pap test, breast exam, and mammogram *every year*!

I've been told I have a condition known as "lichen sclerosus vulva." Can you inform me as to: At what age does this occur? Can it be prevented? Does it only occur in reproductive areas?

Although lichen sclerosus can occur on any skin area at any age in both sexes, it is most commonly seen on the vulva in postmenopausal women. This disease looks like eruptions of small, whitish, round pimples followed by wrinkling or depression of the skin area. A biopsy is usually done to distinguish this problem from other skin diseases.

Researchers do not yet know what causes this disorder and, consequently, do not know how to prevent it. There are also no completely effective treatments yet, but a great deal of new research is under way.

The area should be checked regularly for tissue changes. Progression to cancer is rare (only 2 to 3 percent), but relief from discomfort is important and physicians usually prescribe creams to apply to the area. Testosterone cream appears to be more effective than creams containing estrogen. In some cases, the affected areas must be surgically removed. Because it is important to have a biopsy and careful monitoring, you might want to locate a physician who specializes in gynecological problems of postmenopausal women.

I am a 38-year-old who has gone through menopause. I have been told I have leukoplakia of the labia and clitoris. I had a biopsy done and it was negative. I was wondering, can this turn into cancer? Was this caused by menopause?

Leukoplakia refers to one type of change in mucous membranes such as those of the mouth, vagina, and labia. It usually looks like a patchy white area. The likelihood of leukoplakia increases with age and can be associated with the hormonal changes of menopause due to the thinning of the skin of the genitals.

Although not considered a serious disease itself, leukoplakia sometimes, but not always, precedes a cancerous change in the area. That's why a biopsy is done as soon as a leukoplakia patch is found. The progression to cancer is not inevitable and doesn't occur in many cases, but regular checkups are needed to spot any further changes as soon as possible.

I had a vaginal infection that lasted a year. My gynecologist gave me every cream available for yeast infections, because that is what showed up on the tests.

When I decided to change doctors to find the answer to my problem, I had no idea what I was in for. After two doctors' opinions and a biopsy, I was sent to a women's cancer center. Even though I am relatively young for this disease (40), I was diagnosed as having Paget's, a type of skin cancer which required two skin grafts and finally the new laser to remove the diseased cells.

With frequent checkups, I hope to keep on top of the problem before it spreads as it did in that first year. Why do I never hear or read about anyone else having this Paget's disease?

Paget's disease is a type of skin cancer that can appear on the nipples, in the groin area, or on the vulva. Although not common, any woman age 50 or older who has chronic vaginal itching that doesn't respond to treatment for vaginal infections should consider having a biopsy for cancer of the vulva.

Perhaps we don't hear more about Paget's disease because many women don't have any idea that such problems exist. Doctors have found that in many cases of cancer of the female genitalia, patients should have been able to see and feel changes for months, even years, before they sought medical help.

Don't be confused; there are several diseases with the name Paget. Sir James Paget (1814-1899) was a brilliant surgeon who identified many different disorders and served Queen Victoria of Great Britain and the Prince of Wales. The most common Paget's disease is "Paget's disease of bone" (also called osteitis deformans).

What causes inflammation of the Bartholin's glands and how is it treated?

Women have several glands near the opening of the vagina. One pair is the Bartholin's glands (named for the anatomist who first described them) located on the back side of the vagina toward the anus. These glands secrete a fluid, unless the opening or duct becomes closed. Blockage causes the gland to enlarge and feel like a lump.

The causes of problems with Bartholin's glands can range from general irritation of the genital skin to gonorrhea, which is why a test for various STD organisms is usually standard procedure for an enlarged Bartholin's gland.

If the gland simply closes for some reason and fills with fluid, the condition is called a cyst and is not usually painful. No treatment is required unless the enlargement is annoying, in which case the gland can be surgically opened or removed.

If, however, a duct closes and an infection begins, it is called an abscess. The gland fills with pus and becomes painful. Treatment usually includes antibiotics and warm baths to control and drain the infection. If the duct does not open, the gland can be surgically opened and drained.

Although scientists are not sure why, problems with the Bartholin's glands tend to recur in some women. One long-term solution is marsupialization (in which the gland is surgically altered so that fluid or pus cannot accumulate).

Breasts

Self-Examination of the Breasts

Female breasts are related to the reproductive system. They are affected by the changes that occur in each reproductive cycle, whether or not a pregnancy begins.

Each breast consists of fifteen to twenty glandular lobes (arranged something like a cluster of grapes) that produce milk after childbirth. Each lobe is connected by a duct (or tube) to the nipple. Fatty tissue and fiber tissue surround the lobes and make the breast feel soft.

The nipple at the tip of each breast and the surrounding areola are covered with darker skin. Muscles in this area cause the nipple to stiffen in response to touch, sexual arousal, or temperature change. Breast size has no relationship to the volume of milk a woman can produce if she chooses to breast-feed.

Every woman, beginning at puberty and for the rest of her life, must examine her breasts each month. The best time to do this is two or three days after menstrual flow stops, the time when most women's breasts are least likely to be tender.

The goal is to become familiar with how your own breasts look and feel so that any change is noticed right away. During the self-exam you're looking for any changes such as a lump, discharge from a nipple, or puckering or dimpling of the skin.

If something suspicious is found, report it to your physician. The vast majority (80 percent) of lumps that can be felt are *not* cancerous.

Ask your gynecologist for a brochure describing how to do a breast self-examination with easy-to-follow illustrations. Or call the National Cancer Institute Hotline (1-800-422-6237) and they will send you one.

About eight days before my period, my breasts start to get tender. Three to four days before my period they're so sore I'm in tears until my period. Is this normal for them to get that sore? What is the actual soreness? Fluids? Is there a way to alleviate the pain?

About half of women during their reproductive years have some degree of breast tenderness during the week before the menstrual flow. Other women have lumps, and some have both tenderness and lumps during that week. The lumps are from the accumulation of fluids in the glands and ducts of the breast. These changes are caused by the hormonal fluctuations of the reproductive cycle. The lumps and tenderness should disappear during or right after the menstrual flow.

Discuss your problem with a gynecologist. Some women say the condition improves when they take hormones (such as a synthetic progesterone). Others report improvement using oral contraceptives, presumably because they stabilize hormone levels.

Many physicians treat breast tenderness with aspirin or other mild analgesics (painkillers) rather than by hormone medications unless the pain is severe. Make sure you eat a well-balanced, low-salt diet, which many doctors feel will reduce the discomfort.

I've been told I have fibrocystic disease. Does that mean I'll have breast cancer?

Until recently, the tendency to collect fluid in the breast ducts and/or to develop benign (noncancerous) lumps was labeled "fibrocystic disease" of the breast. Some researchers now argue that any condition that can be found in at least 50 percent of all women should not be labeled a disease and that the name of this problem should be changed to "lumpy breasts" or "fibrocystic condition" so that women are not unduly alarmed.

It has also been established that having this condition does not increase a woman's risk of having breast cancer. In fact, pain or tenderness is not usually present in the early stages of breast cancer.

All women should have an annual breast exam, examine their own breasts each month, and keep records of any lumps or changes. Any lump or soreness that does not disappear when menstruation begins should be reported to a physician immediately. A mammogram (breast X-ray) or biopsy (withdrawing fluid through a needle or removing the lump surgically) may be recommended.

I have read taking vitamin E can cure breast lumps. True?

Recent research suggests that taking 400 to 600 IUs of vitamin E daily may reduce the symptoms of one specific type of breast lump, the type involved in fibrocystic condition.

Is it possible for a woman who is not a mother to secrete a milky liquid from her nipples?

Yes, but she should consult her physician, because this could be a symptom of a problem such as a tumor of the pituitary gland.

Galactorrhea (secretion of a clear or milky discharge from the breasts) appears frequently during puberty and pregnancy and sometimes for as long as two years after a pregnancy. It is related to high levels of a hormone called prolactin but may also appear when a person takes high blood pressure medications, antidepressants, tranquilizers, or hormonal contraceptive pills. (But do *not* stop taking any of these medications without first talking to your physician.)

Mammograms

All women must be concerned about breast cancer because the risk is very high— in the United States one in every ten women will have breast cancer. Although monthly self-examinations and yearly examinations by a physician are important, experts believe that some breast cancers may be present for six to eight years before reaching a size that is large enough to be felt by manual examination. But many of those cancers can be detected by mammography (breast X-ray).

Studies have also shown that the rate of death from breast cancer is 30 percent lower among women over 50 who get an annual mammogram. Finding breast cancer early increases a woman's chance of survival and usually requires less extensive surgery and/or other treatment.

The American Cancer Society, the National Cancer Institute, and other medical associations recommend that every woman have a mammogram between the ages of 35 and 40. This will be used to compare with later mammograms to spot changes more easily; it is often called a baseline mammogram. Then women between 40 and 49 should have mammograms every other year, and women 50 and older should have a mammogram every year. More frequent or less frequent mammograms may be recommended by a physician, depending on a woman's individual risk factors or what is found during an examination.

If you've heard that radiation from mammograms is dangerous, stop worrying. The use of more sensitive film and the dosages from the newer X-ray equipment are so low that any risk from radiation is far outweighed by the value of early detection of a cancer. With all its benefits of early cancer detection, the mammogram is still not the perfect diagnostic tool. Approximately 10 percent to 15 percent of breast cancers do not show up on these X-rays. For this reason, women must also do monthly self-examinations and have a yearly examination by a physician to check for lumps and other changes in the breast.

Because of my age, my gynecologist has ordered a mammogram twice. In the first instance, the procedure was completely painless and my visit to the clinic uneventful. The second time, during which I was given to understand that new mammogram equipment was used, the pain was excruciating.

Was this second experience due to the newer equipment that was utilized or the lack of expertise (and compassion!) of that particular technician? Would it be permissible to ask my doctor to order that the older mammogram equipment be used—since it was virtually pain-free? If it is essential to utilize the newer equipment, would you have any suggestions to make my next visit for this important diagnostic test more anxiety-free?

First, a mammogram should not be excruciating, although it may sometimes be uncomfortable. Aside from producing a better X-ray picture, the new mammogram equipment emits a radiation dosage that is ten times lower than that of the older machines. That lowered radiation dosage should be reason enough to prefer the new equipment to the old.

Women whose breasts become more tender at certain points of their menstrual cycle (often during the week before menstrual flow starts) should schedule mammograms when their breasts are least sensitive (usually right after menstruation stops).

The new machines do require that the breasts be compressed enough to get a clear image, but the compression should last only as long as it takes the technician to take the X-ray.

Any woman who experiences pain during a mammogram should ask the technician if there can be less compression and that compression last for the shortest time possible. If that doesn't help, report your experience to the hospital or clinic, or ask your physician to report it for you.

No concerned physician wants a patient to avoid a lifesaving procedure out of fear or dread. Ask him or her to check that mammograms are being done both properly and with sensitivity to the patient's physical and psychological feelings. Some women's clinics emphasize being more supportive, including reducing anxiety, providing test results immediately, and showing videotapes about self-examination.

Vaginal Infections

The vagina is a little world all its own—an environment which includes a host of friendly and helpful organisms that are necessary to the health of the reproductive system. Under normal circumstances these organisms can counteract any unusual organisms that may stray into the vaginal environment from the rectum or the skin. They also help control other organisms that normally live in the vagina in small numbers but cause trouble if they are allowed to increase in number.

Some common causes of vaginal infections are taking antibiotics; keeping the genitals too moist by wearing panties made from nonabsorbent synthetic materials; wearing tight clothing; hormonal changes during pregnancy; stress; contamination by fecal material (always wipe from front to back after using the toilet), or infection by a sexually transmitted disease (STD) organism (*see Chapter 19*).

If you and your partner have been tested for all the various organisms that can cause vaginal infections and no specific organism is found, talk with your physician about the possibility of allergies. Allergic reactions to chemicals, soaps, perfumes, laundry detergents, scented panty-liners, and other products can mimic the symptoms of vaginal infections.

You need to go to a doctor to diagnose each separate occurrence of vaginal infection so that appropriate medication is prescribed. Automatically using a medication that cleared up one infection is often unsuccessful, even when symptoms seem the same. It is also not unusual for a woman to have infections caused by two or more microorganisms at the same time. When only one is diagnosed and treated, the other continues to grow and often requires a different medication.

Postmenopausal women often experience vaginal irritation and infection because of low estrogen levels. For some women, the level of estrogen begins dropping many years before the actual menopause. If you've had trouble with recurring vaginal infections, you may want to have your gynecologist check your estrogen level.

If you're sexually active and are being treated for a vaginal infection, your partner(s) should be treated simultaneously to avoid reinfection. The organisms that cause vaginal infections can also infect men *(see Chapter 19).*

In mid-1990 new research suggested that spermicides with nonoxynol-9 may increase yeast and bacteria in the vagina and urinary tract, especially when used with a diaphragm. This new finding appears to be relevant only to those women with a history of recurrent and severe yeast and E. coli infections of the vagina and urinary tract.

I have been married two years and have suffered several vaginal infections— all traceable to sexual activity. My dear husband is terrific about abstinence while they clear up, but I'm getting fed up with this cycle. About 85 percent of the time I have intercourse I get an infection.

I've been to my GP and my gynecologist. Both say my husband doesn't need to be treated and vaginal infections are to be expected. In fact, my gynecologist said "It's the price we pay for intercourse."

So we have sex, I get an infection and an expensive shot, the infection clears up, we abstain for a while, try sex again and bang (pardon the pun) another infection.

I wear cotton underwear, keep clean (my husband and I both wash before and after sex, even tried not washing), use lubricants or don't use lubricants— nothing seems to prevent the infection. I've been tested for diabetes, chlamydia, and other conditions.

My husband says if this was a male problem it would've been cured by now. Is there a solution?

Your physicians are wrong. It is important that *both* you and your husband be thoroughly examined. Even the common "yeast" vaginal infections can be harbored by male partners without any symptoms at all. Your current pattern sounds like the ping-pong effect (when an infectious organism is passed back and forth between partners) because only one partner is being treated. You and your husband need to be treated at the same time to avoid reinfection.

There is also the possibility that your current treatment is not completely eliminating the organism(s) causing your infections, leaving a few that regrow after treatment. If you use a diaphragm or cervical cap for contraception or use a douche, it's possible to reinfect yourself (many organisms can live on the surfaces of a diaphragm, cervical cap, or douche nozzle if they are not thoroughly cleaned).

Many different organisms can cause symptoms of vaginal infection, nearly all have also been found in men, and testing can be complicated. Try to find a specialist in STDs; they are often more familiar than other physicians with the latest diagnostic tests and have experience with more sophisticated laboratory procedures and interpretation of test results.

Follow instructions carefully. For example, you must take the full amount of any medication prescribed for the full duration prescribed (do not stop just because your symptoms disappear). You both should schedule a follow-up test to check whether a treatment has been completely successful. Also ask the STD specialist what to do about sexual activity during treatment. It may be that using condoms will permit you to continue having intercourse during treatment.

I was under the impression that when you had a hysterectomy vaginal infections and discharge would no longer be a problem. Apparently this isn't the case. I am living proof. What causes this?

A hysterectomy (surgical removal of the uterus) does not make a woman immune from vaginal infections although uterine infections are impossible. The causes of vaginal infections are as varied for you as they are for women who haven't had hysterectomies. Testing to diagnose the exact cause and proper treatments is as necessary for women who have had hysterectomies as for those who have not.

Self-help Suggestions and When Not to Use Them

Over the years we have received hundreds of letters from women who have itching or other symptoms of vaginal infection and who do not want to go to a physician. Many hundreds of other women have written to describe various ways they believe reduced the frequency or severity of vaginal infections for them.

What follows are some of their suggestions. Before trying any of these home remedies you must know that *no* self-treatment should be attempted for longer than two or three days—after that you *must* see a physician. Vaginal infections can be an early warning sign of serious diseases such as diabetes, which should not be ignored and, left untreated, vaginal infections can lead to scarring of the internal organs and permanent infertility *(see Chapter 19)*.

- Letter writers' suggestions for which there is some research or clinical support:

  Avoid scented soap and don't use bubble bath
  Avoid scented sanitary napkins and tampons
  Wear only white cotton underwear
  Wear only pantyhose with cotton crotches
  Always urinate after having sex
  Use only plain white unscented toilet paper
  Always wipe from front to back after using the toilet
  Use an unscented, pre-moistened towelette (such as Tucks) to wipe after using the toilet).

- Letter writers' suggestions that might be helpful and at least probably would not be harmful:

  Don't take antibiotics unless you absolutely must
  Get a prescription for Aci•jel and use it while taking antibiotics
  Eat yogurt, acidophilus milk or tablets, vitamin B, brewer's yeast, and herbal tea
  Avoid eating pizza, doughnuts, chocolate, coffee, yeast, cheese, and mushrooms
  Change towels and washcloths every time you shower or bathe

Wear only stockings, never pantyhose
Take pantyhose off as soon as you get home from work
Avoid underwear altogether or wear skirts instead of pants
Use some other type of contraception besides the Pill
[*NOTE:* Obviously, these unsolicited suggestions contradict one another in some cases.]

● Writers' suggestions for which there is *no* evidence for helpfulness and, in some cases, may even encourage or mask an infection. These suggestions are presented *only* because many women have heard about them and believe them to be completely safe, which is not necessarily the case:

Douche with two to three tablespoons of yogurt in a quart of warm water
Use three to four tablespoons of baking soda in douche water
Put a glob of yogurt into the vagina
Use damp toilet paper because it cleans better than dry

Let me emphasize once again that vaginal infections must be diagnosed and treated by a physician, especially if they tend to recur and whenever symptoms persist for two or three days after trying *any* self-help suggestion.

Cystitis

Cystitis is an inflammation or infection of the urinary tract.

I'm female and recently had a urinary infection. My doctor laughed and said it looked like some "honeymoon" disease to him. I took some pills that cleared it up, but now I wonder about the real name of what I had. (I was not on a honeymoon when this started.)

"Honeymoon cystitis" is a dated, and not very respectful, expression which implied that many women had urinary infections after their honeymoons, presumably due to having sexual activity. But you certainly don't have to be on a honeymoon—or even sexually active—to get cystitis (the correct name for this problem).

The symptoms can occur at any point in a woman's life and include: burning during urination, frequent urination, an urgent need to urinate (even when the bladder is empty), bloody urine, and pain. The condition can appear suddenly and the symptoms can be quite severe.

These infections are related to sexual activity for some women. Urinary infections are thought to occur more frequently in women than in men because the urethra (the tube that carries urine from the bladder to the outside) is only about an inch long (compared to approximately six inches in men). And, because a woman's urinary opening is located very near her vaginal opening, sexual activity can transfer normal organisms from the genital skin, vagina, or anus into the urethra or bladder.

Cystitis can also be caused by many different STD organisms (*see Chapter 19*) so a sexual partner should be treated at the same time.

Some preventative measures include urinating, even if just a few drops, soon after sexual activity and keeping the urine more acidic (which is thought to help kill bacteria) by drinking cranberry juice. Certain sexual positions—penetration from behind, for instance—can increase the chance of bacterial transfer, so try other positions. Also those who have anal sex should make absolutely sure their partner's penis is washed thoroughly before having vaginal intercourse.

It is important that a physician determine the exact cause (or multiple causes) of a urinary tract infection so that the most effective medication is prescribed. And, have a retest to make sure that all the infectious organisms are gone.

Is it possible for there to be a connection between cystitis and sexual intercourse? I am 70 years old and recently recovered from my fifth attack of cystitis. These attacks have increased as I have aged. My doctor says I have atrophic vaginitis, so I am using Premarin. Can there be a relationship between these problems?

Yes. The rubbing of sexual activity can move normal skin bacteria into the opening of the urethra, which is very near the vagina. Plus the rate of urinary tract infections increases for older women whether they are having sex or not, probably because their vulval area is more easily irritated. One effect of the decrease in estrogen associated with the menopause is thinning of the vaginal tissues (called atrophic vaginitis). Similar changes take place in other genital areas so that the urethra becomes less protected and more easily irritated.

Replacing lost estrogen can restore the condition of the vagina and urinary tract. Premarin is one brand name of estrogen, but you did not say whether you're using it in pill form or as a vaginal cream. If you're using it in cream form, it is possible that not enough estrogen is being absorbed into your bloodstream. Talk to your physician about taking an estrogen in pill form along with a progestin drug if needed. (*For more information on treating menopausal symptoms, see Chapter 9*).

Cystitis is treated with antibiotics. To kill all the bacteria and prevent a recurrence, you need to take *all* the medicine prescribed, regardless of whether obvious symptoms disappear before all the medication is used. And, be retested to make sure that all the infectious organisms are gone. (*See Chapter 19 for a discussion of the various organisms that can cause cystitis.*)

Gynecological Examinations and Pap Tests

A gynecological examination includes a breast examination, evaluation of the external genitals, a pelvic examination of the vagina and internal organs of the reproductive system, and a Pap test (a sample taken of tissues of the cervix to check for abnormal cells). It has been said that if each woman had a Pap test once a year, the rate of death from cervical cancer would be *zero*. In 1988, it was estimated that 12,900 women in the United States would develop cancer of the cervix and 7000 would die from this disease.

Pick an easy-to-remember date (like your birthday) and on that date call and make an appointment for a gynecological examination and Pap test. *Do this every year!*

Some important things to keep in mind: Do not douche before a pelvic exam because it can alter test results and mask symptoms, and try to schedule the exam during the middle of a reproductive cycle (*see Illustration 4 in Chapter 2*). Pap test results can also be altered if taken during your menstrual flow.

All women age 18 and older must have a gynecological examination and a Pap test once every year *whether they are sexually active or not.* This includes women who are not menstruating, who have passed menopause, and who have had hysterectomies. There are only two exceptions: Women even younger than 18 must have annual exams if they are sexually active, and women whose mothers took DES (diethylstilbestrol) during pregnancy must begin having gynecological exams by age 14.

Sexually active women should insist on being checked for the most common STDs such as chlamydia at each annual examination. Even without producing symptoms, many STD organisms can damage the reproductive organs and lead to infertility if not diagnosed and treated early.

I am 20 and will be seeing a gynecologist for the first time. I am nervous, scared, and embarrassed since this is a personal matter. I would appreciate advice to help me prepare for my visit.

In one study of women age 18 to 50, 85 percent reported feeling uncomfortable, frightened, exposed, self-conscious, undignified, like "part of a production line," and "like a child" about pelvic examinations. These women also complained that examinations were "painful" and "rushed."

Three key steps you can take to make your first gynecological examination a good experience: Choose your gynecologist carefully, arrange the circumstances so that you feel comfortable, and speak up immediately if you become at all concerned.

Begin by asking your female friends or relatives to recommend a gynecologist who makes them feel comfortable. If you prefer a female gynecologist (some women do), call the local medical society and ask if there is a female gynecologist nearby. Or call a women's clinic or an organization like Planned Parenthood and ask for their recommendation. There are also nurse-practitioners available who are often highly skilled, gentle, and work under the supervision of a physician.

Ask a friend or relative to accompany you if it would make you more comfortable. Some gynecologists routinely have a female nurse or assistant present during the examination.

When you arrive tell the staff and the physician that this is your first pelvic exam; it will make everyone more helpful and, hopefully, more informative. First, you will be shown to the bathroom and asked to collect a urine sample; emptying your bladder also makes the exam more comfortable. You may have your blood pressure checked and a blood sample taken by an assistant or nurse. Then you'll be led to an examining room, asked to undress completely and to put on a gown and a lap drape; these ensure that your body is covered during the exam.

After the physician enters the room, you will be asked to sit on the examining table. Usually the breasts are examined first; most physicians also do a general check of the throat, lungs, and general health.

At some point the physician will ask you to lie on your back, with your buttocks at the edge of the table and your feet in the stirrups, which are metal holders for the feet. Most women report feeling very vulnerable and exposed when lying on their back with their knees spread apart, but this position is truly the best for an exam. A physician should explain this, and then explain each step of the exam as he or she proceeds and what is being found. If this information is not offered, ask. Some women do report they would rather not talk with the physician during the exam, preferring to wait until it's over. Tell the physician which you prefer.

First the external genitals are examined; then a speculum (an instrument designed to hold the sides of the vagina open) is inserted so the physician can more clearly inspect the inside of the vagina and the cervix. Speculums come in smaller and larger sizes, so that little or no discomfort should be involved. A physician cannot tell by looking at the outside of your body what size of speculum will be best. Warming the speculum with warm water also helps, as does very slow insertion. It's OK to ask your physician to do these things, but using a lubricant on the speculum cannot be done because it alters test results. If insertion is uncomfortable, ask the gynecologist to try a smaller or shorter speculum, or to go more slowly so that you can relax your muscles.

Then a small sample of tissue from the cervix is collected; this is the Pap test; samples of any vaginal discharge may also be collected. Done properly, these steps are usually painless, but they can feel strange.

Then the speculum is slowly removed and the physician inserts one or two fingers of one hand in the vagina while using the other hand to press on the outside of the abdomen. This allows the physician to feel the uterus and the ovaries. There may be some discomfort or tenderness as these internal organs are gently moved around to check for enlargement, cysts, or other problems. Finally, the physician will insert a finger into the rectum to check it and to feel the outline of the uterus more clearly. Pushing out with your muscles gently will often make insertion in the anus more comfortable.

The more you can relax your abdominal muscles, the less discomfort there will be during the examination. It may help to exhale slowly as the physician inserts the speculum. A woman who has been hurt during exams in the past may have trouble controlling her muscle responses in order to relax. In some cases, a woman will unconsciously constrict her vaginal muscles to the point that an examination is not possible; this condition is called vaginismus. *(See Chapter 8.)*

If you feel pain or become uncomfortable or distressed during the examination, say so. If the physician does not slow the procedure or become more gentle, ask him or her to stop. Then get up from the table, get dressed, leave, and find another physician who will promise to be gentle. Remember, it is your responsibility to represent your best interests.

After your examination you will be asked to get dressed (again, in private). Once you are ready, the physician may come back into the room or you may go to a different office to discuss what was found and have any additional questions answered. You should know that any information about you will remain confidential. It is also your right to expect that information you provide will be received in a nonjudgmental manner. For example, if you mention that you are sexually active it would be inappropriate for the physician to scold you. It would be appropriate, however, for him or her to then ask about your use of contraception and protection against STDs.

Bring a list of any questions you want to ask and a paper and pen with which to write information down. It is hard for most people to remember information given by a physician during the stress of an examination. You should expect that your questions will be answered fully. Keep asking until you understand the answers. Change physicians if you're not satisfied with his or her ability to educate and inform you fully.

As a final step, ask how you will find out about the results of your Pap test and any other tests. Will they call you, should you call them, or will they send them in the mail—and when? If you haven't heard from them by the date they set, you should call them and keep calling until you are told the results.

Even after 20 pelvic examinations since age 19 (I am now 33), there is always some anxiety prior to and during the exam. I have had pelvics sometimes with, but generally without, office attendants and once with my older sister present, as well. Once my boyfriend (now my husband) asked to be present. My physician, with my consent, honored this request.

There was a different, improved attitude of respect in the examination room. The gynecologist took more time to explain things and the examination seemed more thorough. It also allayed my husband's concerns about what transpires in such circumstances. My husband has occasionally raised questions and inquiries for my benefit that I would have overlooked or been too intimidated to ask while lying on my back with heels in the stirrups. Please recommend that women consider having husbands or male companions present for gynecological examinations. I expect that most women would find the experience rewarding.

This is an excellent suggestion for women who, like you, have an open, supportive relationship with a male partner. Mothers, sisters, or friends also make good companions. However, there may be some occasions when, even in the best of relationships, a woman might prefer a private meeting with her physician. By the way, do you accompany your husband to his physical examinations as well?

During a pelvic exam the physician inserted her finger into my rectum, looked at me disgustedly and said, scornfully, "Didn't anyone ever tell you to have an enema before you go for a pelvic exam?!"

I was so ashamed I wanted to cry. Is it true that you have to give yourself an enema before a pelvic?

This physician behaved *very* inappropriately. Sometimes if a woman is constipated, the mass in the bowel may make it difficult to clearly feel the internal organs, such as the ovaries. In that case, the appropriate response is to ask the woman to go home, reschedule a second visit, and have an enema before that visit. But *always* giving yourself an enema before going for a pelvic exam is *not* part of standard medical advice.

Recently a doctor in our town was arrested for sexually abusing 25 women patients. Apparently he assaulted more ladies, but they wouldn't testify. What gets me is that he continued to practice medicine while he appealed to the state medical board, which wanted to take his license away.

How often does this happen and how could something like this go on for so

many years with so many people? It would also be of interest to know why state medical boards seem to avoid taking any action against reported sexual abuse by doctors.

Surveys of U.S. doctors reveal that between 5 percent and 10 percent report having had at least one incident of sex with their patients. This is professionally, ethically, and legally *unacceptable behavior*. Based on the cases that have been brought to the courts, and what we already know about rape victims, we can draw some conclusions about how such behavior can continue for many years.

Rape victims are more likely to report the crime if the rapist is a stranger and the act inflicts visible injuries. But victims who know their attackers or who think they have no evidence to prove assault are less likely to report the crime, which often is the case in so-called "acquaintance" or "date" rape.

Cases like these generally don't involve the use of a knife or gun, or result in physical injuries requiring medical attention. In your example, not only did the victims know their attacker, but the man occupied a high social, economic, and educational status within the community—all making it more difficult for the women to report the crime.

Many abused patients report feeling that somehow they are to blame for the incident. Even after a victim has decided to tell a family member or friend, the reaction often is "How could you let that happen?" Women victims also report a sense of powerlessness. ("What good is my word against a doctor's? They all cover up each other's mistakes.")

Some doctors escape detection for many years by carefully selecting victims they think are passive and afraid to question authority figures. Some victims say nothing to the doctor or office staff because they "don't want to cause a scene." If a doctor abuses only a few patients (while providing acceptable care to the majority), this only perpetuates the idea that if anything did happen, it must have been the patient's fault, not the doctor's, and usually means that many members of the community will support the physician based on their personal experience with him.

Typically, the victims change doctors, tell their friends not to use the doctor, or insist that a relative or friend accompany them to future appointments. In the past, the few patients who went to the police or to medical review boards were often told that since they had no "proof," nothing could be done. Hopefully, this reaction is changing as more authorities become aware that such behavior takes place and that the public deserves protection.

Anyone who is touched or treated in a way that seems to violate medical ethics should make a record of exactly what happened and call a local crisis center so that a report is logged. Ask for information about how to file a formal complaint, or consult a lawyer for advice on how to proceed.

I should emphasize that sexual abuse of patients includes behaviors other than intercourse, such as rubbing or manipulating the genitals or breasts or caressing other areas of the body. Doctors who prolong internal examinations of the vagina beyond two or three minutes without explaining what they are doing and why it is necessary, or who insist on vaginal or breast exams for conditions having nothing to do with these parts of the body, may also be suspected of misconduct.

Even though sexual abuse of patients is not thought to be common, there are some things a patient should do to avoid being victimized. If a physician refuses to permit you to have a nurse or friend present during any physical examination, he is suspect; leave and change doctors. If at any point in an examination you feel uncomfortable and the doctor does not give you an adequate and fully satisfying explanation of what he is doing and why he is doing it, get up, get dressed, leave, and find another professional.

Results of Pap tests

Named for Dr. George Papanicolaou, who developed it in 1942, the Pap test, or Pap smear, is a painless procedure. While the speculum is in the vagina, the physician takes a few cells from the cervix with a cotton swab or special spatula. The cells are placed on a slide, sprayed with a fixative, and sent to a laboratory to be examined under a microscope.

Recently there has been some controversy over the accuracy of Pap test readings, particularly false negatives (when abnormal cells are actually present but the report says that no abnormal cells were found).

There are several steps you or your physician can take to improve the accuracy of the reading: Don't have the test done when you're having your menstrual flow; make sure the physician does not use a lubricant on the speculum; have the physician wipe away any excessive vaginal discharge before the sample is taken; and make sure that the slide is immediately sprayed with fixative after the sample is taken. There are also differences among laboratories— some have a higher accuracy rating than others. Ask your physician whether he or she is aware of the laboratory's reputation for accuracy.

Even with all these precautions, the Pap test has a false-negative rate of at least 15 percent. This makes it even more important that a woman have a Pap test **every year**, just in case her last Pap test missed evidence of precancerous changes in the cervix.

I had a Pap done and it came back a "one." Does that indicate a precancerous condition, and if so, what is the treatment?

Although laboratories differ as to how they classify Pap test results, in most cases a rating of I (Roman numeral one) means that the laboratory technician saw no abnormal cells. You should follow the same procedure as all other women: Have another Pap test and pelvic examination in twelve months. If you have any questions, call your physician and ask for an explanation of the laboratory results. In the past, laboratories and doctors used the following categories or labels to report results:

- Class I usually means no abnormal cells were found.
- Class II means some unusual cells were seen but were probably from a vaginal infection.
- Class III designates a finding of atypical cells, indicating that further testing should be done.
- Classes IV and V report the finding of actual cancer cells.

Women on certain types of medication such as hormones for birth control or menopause, or those who've had a Class II or higher Pap test result, will usually be instructed by their doctor to have more frequent exams, perhaps every six months or even more often.

Recently, many laboratories have changed their reporting of Pap tests to consist of more specific and descriptive information rather than just classification numbers. For example, now if an infectious organism is found, an attempt is also made to identify it so the physician can recommend the appropriate treatment medication.

I finished my menopause when I was 49. I had a Pap smear and it showed atypical cells and it said a report was being sent to my doctor. OK. He never said anything, so last year I had some slight bleeding after intercourse. I came to the doctor, he took a smear for a Pap test. Again, atypical cells.

My doctor sent me to a gynecologist who did a "cholosectory" (or something that sounded like that). Then he did cryosurgery. At my six-month checkup the same thing: atypical cells.

His nurse called with a rundown of possible procedures, from a simple biopsy to laser surgery. When I saw the gynecologist again and asked about atypical cells, he looked nervous but said I shouldn't worry. Now I'm worried. I trust the gynecologist, but what are "atypical" cells and why are all these things necessary?

In Pap smear results, *atypical* means there was something irregular or abnormal about some of the cells collected from your vagina or cervix. This word may be used either with a class label of II or III, or used by itself.

Approximately forty-five of every 1000 Pap smears show abnormal cells of one sort or another, usually due to an infection. Repeated results of abnormality require further tests to determine what is causing the abnormality in the cervical or vaginal cells.

The American Medical Association recommends the following diagnostic and treatment options: a colposcopy (use of a telescope-like instrument to magnify the cervix and vaginal walls to get a good look at the surfaces) and cryosurgery (freezing to destroy abnormal tissue, which then promotes healing with new, healthy tissue). If atypical or abnormal cells are still present, the next steps involve various types of biopsy or surgery. A frequent finding of these tests is dysplasia, a type of abnormal cell thought to precede the appearance of cancer cells.

It may be that your gynecologist was afraid you would panic if he used the word *cancer*. You should not panic. Only about 25 percent (one out of four) cases of dysplasia later become cancer, while 50 percent never change at all and another 25 percent disappear with no treatment. Even if further testing finds carcinoma in situ (cancer cells localized in the surface layer of the cervix) or invasive cancer (cancer cells in deeper layers of tissue), appropriate treatment now cures nearly 100 percent of carcinoma in situ and 95 percent of invasive cancers, especially when found and treated early.

Laser surgery, although relatively new and not yet available everywhere, appears to be an excellent treatment for many women found to have carcinoma in situ.

The traditional treatment—hysterectomy—is now controversial and not as widely used as a decade ago. But, as with any major surgery, if a hysterectomy is suggested you should get a second opinion. Meanwhile, have the rest of the tests listed above or get a second opinion soon.

My Pap smear came back showing cervical dysplasia. The doctor did a freezing, then after my next smear she said I had another spot that was a step worse. At first she said she'd do another freezing, then changed her mind and said she'd just leave it alone.

Because she seemed hesitant, I decided to get another opinion. The second doctor also said I had dysplasia and did a freezing.

Why was the first doctor hesitant to do a second freezing? Are there after-effects from having two freezings? I've been trying to conceive for six months now with no success. (I told both doctors I wanted to have more children.)

Physicians differ somewhat in how they treat cervical dysplasia, or neoplasia, a term for the existence of atypical cells on the cervix. Cryosurgery (freezing the area of abnormal cells) is one treatment and is effective in many cases. Another treatment is called a cone biopsy (or conization), which removes a cone-shaped piece of cervical tissue. Cone biopsy both removes the dysplasia cells from the surface of the cervix and permits analysis of cells deeper inside the cervix.

Whether a physician decides to do cryosurgery, a cone biopsy, or some other treatment such as laser surgery depends on the type and extent of abnormal cells found. In some cases, physicians recommend careful monitoring with frequent Pap tests until it can be determined whether the dysplasia will resolve itself.

It is possible for cervical infections and treatments (including cryosurgery and cone biopsy) to interfere with mucus secretion and/or produce scarring sufficient to block the os (the tiny opening in the center of the cervix), although surgical scarring is only rarely the sole cause of infertility. *(For more on fertility see Chapter 15).*

There is no single "best way" to manage dysplasia, but it is important that you follow recommendations for follow-up Pap tests. Dysplasia can progress to cancer of the cervix, which is why each case of dysplasia warrants careful monitoring and/or treatment.

After Diagnosis

I have very heavy menstrual bleeding and my doctor says I must have a hysterectomy. Isn't there anything else that could be done so I don't have to lose my uterus?

Many women report having excessively heavy or long menstrual flow; others experience heavy bleeding at different times during the cycle. Most physicians just accept a woman's statements about her flow. One study which measured the menstrual flow of women who said it was excessive found that only 40 percent had losses that met the definition of excessive flow (menorrhagia): loss of 3 or more ounces.

The first step, therefore, is to decide whether menstrual flow is really abnormally high. If it is, then other steps need to be taken. If the woman uses an IUD, she should switch to some other type of contraception. A thorough examination of the cervix and the lining of the uterus should be done to check for polyps and uterine tumors; this also involves collecting a sample of endometrial tissue via a suction instrument or D & C (dilation and curettage). All women who have these conditions must also be checked for anemia.

Treatments vary. Some women found to have high levels of prostaglandins improve by taking mefenamic acid and, if fibrinolytic levels are abnormal, taking tranexamic acid or aminocaproic acid may help. These medications are taken during menstruation. Taking oral contraceptives also helps some women. If polyps or uterine tumors are found, they can usually be removed while still preserving the uterus and fertility.

Removing the endometrium by using a laser (called endometrial ablation) should be considered before having the entire uterus removed (hysterectomy). This procedure is less costly, involves less hospitalization, and has a lower rate of complications. Like hysterectomy, laser ablation ends the possibility of future pregnancy, but it appears to preserve much more of the organs responsible for sexual function. It is estimated that use of laser ablation would result in nearly 200,000 fewer hysterectomies in the U.S. each year. *(Hysterectomy is discussed in Chapter 18.)* However, not all surgeons are skilled in use of the laser and equipment is not yet widely available. Call the gynecology department at the nearest medical school and ask where this treatment is offered.

If my uterus hangs, do I need surgery? I'm afraid and will never have it done. Is there anything else doctors can do besides a hysterectomy? A friend mentioned a pessary. I feel good and have no bleeding. I'm scared.

I assume you've been told that you have a uterine prolapse, a condition in which the uterus or womb begins to slide down into the vagina, caused by weakening of the pelvic muscles. These conditions vary greatly from one woman to another, so it is impossible to answer your specific question without knowing more about your situation.

There are a few alternatives to surgery if the condition is not severe. Some women have been able to reduce their symptoms by doing pelvic exercises and practicing certain yoga positions.

In some cases, symptoms also can be relieved by wearing a pessary, a rubber device similar to a diaphragm that is fitted into the vagina to support the uterus. A woman wearing a pessary can usually continue having intercourse, though in some cases deep thrusting can hit the pessary, causing pain for both partners. Changing positions should help.

But a pessary doesn't permanently reverse the condition, and it must be removed, cleaned, and reinserted every month or so by qualified medical personnel.

Uterine prolapse is the most frequent reason given for performing a hysterectomy (surgical removal of the uterus), but consider other options first. If your condition is not an emergency, you have time to seek different medical opinions. But don't limit your questions to asking about hysterectomy. Ask also about trying a newer type of surgery that resuspends the uterus and repairs any damage found in the muscles of the pelvic area.

Last year I had a miscarriage. Afterwards, during the D and C, I heard the doctor say my uterus felt grainy. What does this mean?

What your doctor meant was that your uterine walls felt normal. The walls of a healthy uterus do feel gritty or grainy. A dilation and curettage (D and C) involves the dilation of the cervix so that a curette—a loop or spoon-shaped instrument—can be inserted to scrape the walls clean. When the uterus is clean, there's even a particular sound that can be heard as the curette is drawn along the surface of the uterus. This telltale sound differs markedly from that heard at the beginning of the procedure.

In the future, if you hear your doctor use a word or phrase that you don't understand or that worries you, ask for an explanation in plain English. If it is a medical term, patients should ask to have the word written down so they can look it up later in a medical reference book for more information.

I have a mild case of endometriosis. Two doctors have told me I should take Danazol. After reviewing the literature on Danazol about possible side effects (deepening voice, muscular development, enlargement of clitoris, and possible liver damage) I decided not to take the risks of that drug.

I'm more than willing to try other hormone therapies, but both doctors are only offering Danazol or nothing. Are my only options to take Danazol or just live with endometriosis? I belong to an HMO, so I can't go to a different doctor.

The pain of endometriosis varies greatly from one woman to another, and symptoms also vary, depending on where the endometrial-tissue deposits are located.

For some women, analgesics (painkillers) are an effective treatment for easing the pain. For others, hormonal birth-control pills alleviate the pain because they can induce a "pseudopregnancy" state in the body. This helps many women for whom endometriosis pain fluctuates with hormonal levels. The problems of endometriosis usually decrease during pregnancy and after menopause and are at their worst right before and during menstrual flow.

Some women with endometriosis have difficulty becoming pregnant because the disease can interfere with ovulation or eventually block the Fallopian tubes, which carry the egg from an ovary to the uterus. Some women with endometriosis also find intercourse painful, in itself reducing the chances for conception because they don't have intercourse regularly. Danazol, a synthetic hormone, has been useful in increasing the likelihood of conception for some women. It also reduces discomfort for women who have severe pain, but the pain often returns when the drug is discontinued. Many women do not like Danazol's androgenic (malelike) side effects—facial hair growth and weight gain, for example.

There is only one way to determine conclusively whether you have endometriosis: through a diagnostic laparoscopy, a way of looking inside the abdomen. Many of the endometrial deposits can be removed during laparoscopy itself or later by a second surgery, so that pain is reduced and fertility preserved.

Ask the staff at your HMO to refer you to a laparoscopy specialist. That specialist could also suggest other treatment options that your HMO physicians would then follow.

I was recently diagnosed as having polycystic ovary disease. Could you please tell me more about this disease and its treatment?

Also, is there any drug available to treat increased facial hair? If not, what is the best way to correct this embarrassing condition?

Because hirsutism (excessive facial and body hair) is one of the most common symptoms of polycystic ovarian disease (PCOD), effective control of your PCOD should also control future hair growth. The only way to remove the hair that grew before PCOD treatment is through depilation, electrolysis, bleaching, waxing, tweezing, or shaving.

Other symptoms of PCOD (also called Stein-Leventhal syndrome) include obesity, difficulty getting pregnant, and irregular menstruation after having normal puberty at the expected time. Women with PCOD often cannot predict how long menstrual flow will last, or when they will menstruate (some go several months between periods). Some have heavy menstrual flow.

The surface of the ovaries of women with PCOD becomes thickened, and although the ovarian follicles begin the process of maturing eggs, these are rarely released—hence the fertility problems, which often send PCOD women to their physicians.

The hormonal levels of women with PCOD do not fluctuate in the usual cyclic monthly pattern *(See Illustration 4 in Chapter 2)*. The problem seems to result when the pituitary gland and hypothalamus (parts of the brain involved in reproductive functioning) receive inappropriate signals about existing hormone levels. The woman is steadily exposed to high levels of some hormones such as androgens (which stimulate facial hair growth) and does not produce enough of some other hormones such as FSH (which chemically signals release of eggs from the ovaries).

Accurate diagnosis of PCOD involves blood tests to determine various hormonal levels. These tests may need to be repeated every few days to determine whether levels remain steady or fluctuate. It may take several months (and repeated testing) to determine whether a woman is receiving adequate treatment.

Because close and frequent interactions with the physician are usually necessary, women with PCOD should consider finding a physician who will take the time to explain this complex condition.

I once read in a book that women can get ovarian cysts at any age. Does that include teens? What are the symptoms?

All women, including teens and younger girls, can have ovarian enlargement. Between puberty and menopause, the reproductive years in which a woman produces cyclic hormones, the majority of ovarian enlargements are caused by cysts. These are thin-walled sacs filled with fluid.

Before puberty and after menopause, ovarian enlargement is more likely to be due to a tumor, which can be benign (noncancerous) or malignant (cancerous).

Not all ovarian problems are accompanied by symptoms. Most enlargements are found during an annual pelvic examination. Finding ovarian enlargement at an early stage is another reason that, starting no later than at age 18, women of all ages need annual examinations. This is especially important after age 35, when the risk of ovarian cancer increases.

A 35-year-old friend has just had surgery for ovarian cancer. I would like to be supportive to her and her family, but I know very little about this disease. I'm afraid I'll inadvertently say something upsetting to her, rather than being helpful.

Could you give me some basic information about ovarian cancer, treatments, and outcome?

Approximately 20,000 cases of ovarian cancer are estimated to be diagnosed in the United States each year. The average age at diagnosis is 62; it is rare before age 30. The outcome of each case depends on how early it is diagnosed and treated, the extent of the disease's spread found during surgery, and the type of cancer involved.

Unfortunately, early stages of ovarian cancer have few symptoms or early warning signals. By the time common symptoms occur (such as abdominal swelling, abdominal discomfort, or vague digestive complaints), the cancer has usually spread beyond the ovaries.

This is one reason yearly pelvic exams are essential and any enlargement of an ovary discovered during an annual pelvic examination must be followed closely. The vast majority of these ovarian enlargements are ovarian cysts or other noncancerous conditions, but even the few cancers that are detected make these yearly visits to a gynecologist worthwhile.

Treatment consists of surgical removal of the affected organs, which often include the ovaries, uterus, Fallopian tubes, and nearby tissues. In a few cases of younger women with an early stage of cancer in one ovary, only the affected ovary is removed. And the earlier the diagnosis the less extensive the surgery.

Radiation therapy (treatment with X-rays) and/or chemotherapy usually follow surgery. Several chemotherapy drugs have had good results, and combination therapy using three or more chemotherapy agents appears even more promising in terms of long-term survival rates. These treatments may be needed for many months, and some physicians then do a second abdominal surgery to ensure that the cancer has been eradicated.

Long-term survival depends on the stage of disease spread and the type of cancer involved, with an average five-year survival rate of 15 percent to 60 percent for the most common type of cancer. However, even some more advanced cancers, if treated with combination chemotherapy after extensive surgery, now show a five-year survival rate of more than 60 percent in some studies. The earlier the cancer is diagnosed, the better a woman's chances of long-term survival.

Encourage your friend to consult the best gynecological oncologist (women's cancer specialist) she can find. She might also consider volunteering to participate in a research project using experimental chemotherapy drugs or experimental combinations.

I am 39 and have been diagnosed by means of a sonogram to have two submucous fibroids in my uterus, each about an inch in diameter. At present, I have none of the problems associated with fibroids and enjoy wonderful health otherwise.

I have done much research on my own in medical books and have discovered that fibroids occur in about one in five women over age 30. The consensus

seems to be to ignore them until they become a problem and then have a hysterectomy or possibly myomectomy.

I am disturbed by the lack of information on any type of self-care or ways of retarding the growth of fibroids in order to avoid surgery. Are there any medications, nutritional guidelines, or other things I could be doing?

None that I have heard about, except the usual recommendation that women with fibroids should have pelvic examinations every six months (instead of once a year) just to check whether the fibroid tumors have begun to enlarge.

Most fibroid tumors grow very slowly or not at all, and few (one out of 200 women) become cancerous. Sometimes high levels of estrogen (from hormonal contraceptive pills or pregnancy) will cause fibroids to grow, and fibroids often become smaller after menopause, when the level of estrogen is low.

If a woman with uterine fibroids begins to have heavy menstrual bleeding, pain or pressure on the bladder or other internal organs, surgery may be recommended—either myomectomy (removal of the fibroids from the wall of the uterus) or hysterectomy. Sometimes fibroids can reduce a woman's ability to become pregnant and a myomectomy can improve her chances of pregnancy.

Any woman told she should have a hysterectomy should get at least one other medical opinion; go to a gynecologist or other specialist, not to a surgeon.

The medical community is gradually changing its view of the necessity for hysterectomy, so fewer are being recommended. Some specialists advocate a trial period of taking progestin hormones to reduce symptoms of uterine fibroids before recommending hysterectomy.

Recently I had a vaginal hysterectomy. The doctor left both ovaries. Is it possible to still get cysts on your ovaries and why do I still need Pap smears?

Yes, it is still possible to have ovarian cysts after removal of the uterus. Even after hysterectomy having Pap tests during your annual checkups is valuable in diagnosing other problems.

MALE SEXUAL HEALTH

Men are even less aware than women that they should perform regular self-examinations and that after age 40 they need to have an annual examination that includes a manual check of the prostate gland. Some men are not aware that the type of medical specialist called a urologist is the counterpart to a gynecologist. Early detection of changes in the testicles and the prostate gland can literally save your life.

Beginning with enlargement of the testicles at puberty (this can be as early as age 8) each boy and man should examine his testicles once a month for the rest of his life.

Self-examination of the External Genitals

Males should regularly examine their genitals. Using a good light and a hand mirror will make this easier to do. (*An illustration and description of the external genitals is in Chapter 3.*)

Begin by looking closely at the head of the penis and the urinary opening (if you're uncircumcised, pull back the foreskin). You're looking for any bumps, blisters, sores, warts, or changes in the color (such as redness or irritation) or texture of skin covering the entire glans penis area. Also note whether there is any discharge from the urinary opening.

Next examine the shaft of the penis, looking for the same types of changes. When you reach the base of the penis, spread apart the pubic hair and check the skin covered by the pubic hair. Using the mirror will help you see the underneath side of the penis and the back of the scrotum.

If you notice any discharge, blisters, irritation, or any other changes, report them to your physician or a urologist immediately. Symptoms of many STDs can disappear, so just because a sore heals does not mean that you are not infected with an STD or cannot spread it to others.

The best time to examine the testicles is right after a hot bath or shower. This makes the scrotum more relaxed and the testicles are farther away from the body. Standing up and using both hands, put your index and middle fingers on the bottom side of one testicle and your thumbs on the top side. Gently roll the testicle between the fingertips, feeling for lumps, firm areas, or changes in texture or size. A healthy testicle feels smooth, is rather firm, and is egg-shaped. Then do the same for the other testicle.

Inside the scrotum on the back of each testicle is the epididymis *(see Illustration 5 in Chapter 3)*. Sometimes this tube is confused with a testicular lump during self-examination. Even though most cancerous lumps are on the front or side of a testicle, check with a physician if you're not sure that what you're feeling is normal or if something has changed from your last self-examination.

For an illustrated brochure on how to do testicular self-exams, see your urologist or call the National Cancer Institute Hotline, 1-800-422-6237.

Having larger-than-normal testicles is not a sign of "manhood" (it does not increase fertility or sex drive) but could be a sign of disease. If you notice any change in your testicles, or if you feel any discomfort or pain, make an appointment with a physician—preferably a urologist—at once.

Testicles, Scrotum, and Penis

You hear so much about breast self-examinations for women. Why don't doctors show men (and teenage boys) how to examine themselves for testicular cancer? Most people seem to think that only elderly men need to worry about this.

I don't know why all boys aren't told about the importance of self-examination of the testicles. It could be because some physicians are embarrassed about discussing sex, or they don't take the threat of testicular cancer in younger men seriously enough.

The fact is that in the United States testicular cancer is found in about four of every 100,000 white men each year. The rate is lower among men of other races. This cancer is most common between the ages of 20 and 34 but also occurs among younger and older men. Males who have an undescended testicle or who have a testicle that descended into the scrotum several years after birth are at a greatly increased risk, because constant exposure to the body's higher temperature causes negative changes in the testicle.

If detected at an early stage, testicular cancer can be treated effectively, preserving the capacity to function sexually and to father children. Symptoms can include enlargement of a testicle or a feeling of heaviness in a testicle, but the most common symptom is a small hard lump (similar to a pea) on a testicle. Pain often does not occur until later stages of the disease.

The vast majority of lumps or changes felt in the scrotum and around the testicles are various cysts or accumulations of fluids and usually are not a sign of a serious disease. But because a lump or change can be cancer, it is very important to have *every* lump or change checked by a physician as soon as possible.

Do not wait to see if it goes away, and don't be shy about telling a physician's receptionist or secretary why you need the earliest available appointment. Say "I think I've found a change in one of my testicles" (or whatever informal words are easier for you).

My left testicle seems to have gotten bigger. What could cause that?

Many different problems can cause changes in the testicles or scrotum and must be checked by a physician immediately. The most sudden type of change is testicular torsion (when the testicle twists on its cord). This is usually accompanied by severe pain and must be treated immediately. In some cases the doctor can manually untwist the cord, but most cases require emergency surgery to open the scrotum and look at the testicle so the cord can be untwisted. Also, actually looking at the testicle is usually necessary to assess its condition since the twist in the cord cuts off the blood supply to the testicle and cell destruction—starting with the cells that produce sperm—begins very quickly.

A less serious cause of scrotal swelling is epididymoorchitis (infection and swelling of the epididymis and testicle, which usually is caused by a urinary infection, gonorrhea, or other STD organism (*see Chapter 19*). Antibiotics are an effective treatment and surgery isn't usually required, although it may be recommended if the diagnosis isn't clear, just to be absolutely certain there is no testicular damage involved.

Other problems that can cause enlargement of the scrotal area include hydrocele (an accumulation of normal fluid), hematocele (accumulation of blood from an injury or blow), inguinal hernia (a portion of the intestines extends into the scrotum), spermatocele (a cystlike accumulation of sperm), varicocele (enlargement of the veins of the scrotum), and various types of both benign and cancerous tumors. Although not all of these problems require surgery, all require careful diagnosis and regular checkups to watch for any changes.

Now that you know how serious some changes in the scrotum or testicles can be, please go immediately for medical evaluation.

It wasn't discovered until my 20s that my left testicle was undescended, and when I finally did know it, I was able to bring it down with my hand and found that it was about three-quarters the size of my right one.

Even though I have fathered two children, is it possible that at my age, 35, I would benefit by having the testicle brought down surgically to maintain proper sperm count? Or should I leave it alone and just bring it down

whenever it does go undescended? Also, is there a danger of the left testicle becoming cancerous?

There is a greater risk of testicular cancer among men with testicles that are undescended or whose testicles were not brought down into the scrotum within a few years after birth.

However, the risk appears to vary, depending on the location of the testicle inside the body. The higher the testicle, the greater the risk. For example, a testicle residing in the abdomen would be at greater risk of developing cancer than would a testicle in the inguinal canal (the path between the abdomen and the scrotum that a testicle normally follows during fetal development).

About 3 percent of full-term baby boys and 30 percent of premature baby boys are born with an undescended testicle. We don't know how many males have a retractile testicle (one that from time to time draws back up out of the scrotum). Because you can now bring the testicle down into the scrotum for a period of time, theoretically your risks would be somewhat reduced but would still be greater than for a man who did not have this problem at all.

As you've discovered, it is common for a man with only one testicle to produce sperm adequate to father children. Even so, there are good reasons to consider having the retractile testicle permanently brought down into the scrotum surgically. The best reason is that this will make it easier to self-examine the testicle on a monthly basis in order to note any changes that might be an early symptom of testicular cancer.

Another consideration is that if something should happen to your one normal testicle, you would lessen the cancer risk and be more likely to always have use of the surgically lowered testicle to produce testosterone. In addition, a testicle residing in the scrotum is less likely to be injured than one located near pelvic bones or hard abdominal muscles.

You should consult a urologist who is familiar with assessing undescended testicles. If you decide on surgery, ask to be referred to a surgeon experienced in orchiopexy (the surgical procedure that lowers a testicle into the scrotum) in adults.

Do you have any information on fluid in the scrotum?

The scrotum is the protective pouch inside which the testicles hang. It consists of several thick layers of elastic and muscular tissue beneath the layer of outer skin.

One layer of the scrotum is very close to the covering of the testicles. Usually there is a small space between the inner layer of the scrotum and the outer covering of the testicles. However, in some men the space is larger (it is not always clear what causes this) and becomes filled with fluid. This condition is called hydrocele.

Treatment varies from having the scrotum examined regularly to having surgery to correct the problem, depending on what is involved for a particular patient. A thorough examination by a urologist is needed to determine exactly what is involved and how it should be treated.

I have a problem with my left testicle. The cord seems to be twice as large and the testicle is quite large. It also gets irritated when I walk on hot days. Could this be a rupture or a hernia or something else?

Go to a urologist as soon as possible. If you can't get an appointment immediately (tell the receptionist when you call that you have an enlarged testicle), go to a hospital emergency room. There are many different reasons why the scrotum and/or its contents enlarge; some of those reasons can be quite serious.

I wonder if you can help me with my very male problem. I am a middle-aged man, uncircumcised, married. Neither my wife nor I have ever had another sexual partner.
　　The problem: From time to time I develop a kind of itching, scalded type of condition on my genitals. Sometimes this is so intense that the area "weeps."
　　I've had this problem since puberty. It is most uncomfortable. I shower a minimum of once a day, and am careful in washing that area—and in rinsing myself off. I am also careful to leave myself dry after urinating. Also, I change my underwear every time I bathe.
　　What am I doing or not doing? What can I do?

The next time this itching condition appears, see a urologist or dermatologist. Tests can be done to determine what is causing this and how best to treat it.
　　Many different conditions can cause itching, redness, and weeping of the skin of the male genitals. One common diagnosis is so-called jock itch, and hot weather seems to increase the problem.
　　Among the specific causes of jock itch are tinea cruris (a type of fungus), chafing from clothing that is too tight, allergic reactions to chemicals in detergents, soaps, and other products, and exposure to moistness, which can easily occur with sweating during hot weather.
　　Another common cause of itching of male genital skin is an organism called Candida albicans (yeast). This is the same organism that often causes vaginal infections in women, and it is not unusual for couples to pass this infection back and forth for long periods of time. The organism itself can be present in small numbers all the time; it doesn't pose a problem until it multiplies to levels high enough to cause discomfort.
　　Your wife, for example, could develop higher than normal levels of Candida albicans from taking an antibiotic, which would then infect your genital skin during intercourse, and you would later reinfect her as your condition worsened. To avoid this ping-pong effect, a man should receive treatment at the same time whenever a female partner is diagnosed as having a vaginal infection.
　　Treatments for jock itch can include cool wet dressings, using corticosteroid creams on the skin, and keeping the area dry and exposed to the air as much as possible. When scratching has caused a secondary infection of the skin, antibiotics may be needed as well. But these treatments may not be effective if the condition is caused by a fungus or an infectious organism other than bacteria. This is why a visit to a physician is necessary for an accurate diagnosis. It takes different medications (usually prescribed in lotion or cream form) to control problems caused by each specific organism.

I am over 60 and like so many old people was never circumcised, because they didn't do that much in the old days. I have a problem that the skin grows over the head of my penis and the head is unable to come out any more. Also, it started itching any time of the day, and scratching it makes it worse.

My doctor told me that there is nothing that can be done about it. I worry about infection.

Locate a urologist. Several conditions can make it difficult for an uncircumcised man to retract the foreskin. The most common is phimosis (having a foreskin too tight to pull back from the penis), which often involves an infection under the foreskin.

It is important that a physician determine what is going on and treat it, because irritation of many years' duration may be related to later cancerous changes in the penile skin. Treatment usually involves antibiotics and sometimes minor surgery to enlarge the opening in the foreskin.

My husband and I had a very satisfying sex life up until two years ago, at which time he had a penis infection and went to the hospital. They treated him quite some time and diagnosed his ailment as Balanitis xerotica obliterans. His condition cleared up but he has not been able to keep an erection since this time. Could you please explain this ailment and could it possibly be what is now causing his erection problems?

The doctors at the hospital did not explain to us anything about this disease and now my husband is too embarrassed to see a doctor. We certainly would like to enjoy sex again.

Your husband's former disease and his current erection difficulty could be related. Balanitis xerotica obliterans is the atrophy or shrinking of the glans (the tip of the penis). Causes range from nonsexual skin problems such as psoriasis to complications of diseases such as gonorrhea. In many cases physicians cannot identify a specific cause.

Despite his embarrassment, your husband should see a doctor, preferably a urologist. Although the infection may have cleared up, the penis tissue may have been scarred by the infection, which could lead to painful erections or painful intercourse.

A complete physical examination is in order since both balanitis and erectile difficulties are associated with diabetes. Your husband should also tell the physician about any medications he is taking, as some can reduce erectile functioning.

I had epidymitis in both balls. I lost one to TB and still fight to keep the other one. What I want to know is, can one or both balls be transplanted from another person? If not, would you know of someone to try this kind of research? I would be a test person. I am 48 years old.

On the back side of each testicle is a structure called the epididymis, a thin tube so tightly coiled that, if straightened out, it would measure about 20 feet long. After sperm leave the testicle, they pass through the epididymis, where they mature and become capable of forward motion.

Epididymitis, a common problem among men, is the infection of one or both epididymis tubes. It can be caused by various sexually transmitted organisms, abnormalities in the structure of the urinary tract, urinary tract infections, and prostate infections, among other factors. Tuberculosis can also be a cause of epididymis infection.

Treatment of epididymitis involves use of an antibiotic effective against the particular organism causing the infection, and bed rest with the scrotum elevated on a towel placed between the legs. A man may need to take antibiotics for a long period of time or until tests show the infection is completely gone.

Successful treatment depends on finding out which of many possible organisms is causing the epididymitis so that the correct antibiotic and dosage can be prescribed. This evaluation involves complicated laboratory tests and specialized analysis. If the organism can be sexually transmitted, then sexual partners must also be tested and treated at the same time as the patient.

Although there apparently have been some experiments with transplanting human testicles, this is not usually done and the long-term results are not clear. Besides, there are artificial testicle implants available that will result in a normal appearance. In addition, a man can take testosterone if his level of this important hormone is low.

In any case, these infections should not keep recurring, and you must get a second medical opinion to see why you're still having trouble. Much of the newest research and the best testing on epididymitis is being done by specialists in sexually transmitted diseases.

Not too long ago I had a rectal infection. I felt severe pain in my rectum and scrotum for two weeks, and finally took medicine for ten days.

Since my recovery I have noticed a light brown color in my ejaculate, which I suppose is blood. I no longer feel pain and I do not notice any unusual lumps in my testes.

Is this a sign of a serious illness? Do I need to see a specialist? I am 50, jog daily, and am in good physical condition.

Many different conditions can cause hematospermia, a condition in which blood appears in the ejaculate. The color of the blood can range from light red to dark brown.

It's important to rule out the existence of a serious disease, such as an infection or cancer of the prostate; however, in most cases, no cause is ever found. Even when hematospermia occurs on a prolonged basis, no damage to general physical health has been found, since only a tiny amount of blood is usually involved.

Blood in the semen can come from the prostate, seminal vesicles, urethra, vas deferens, or testicles. Hematospermia has been linked to a number of factors, such as infections, prolonged sexual activity, vasectomy, tuberculosis, various STD organisms, the use of anticoagulant drugs, and urological examinations as well as many other conditions and events.

See your personal physician or a urologist for an examination and any necessary tests. You may be asked for a sample of your ejaculate for analysis.

Even when all medical problems are ruled out, some men require psychological counseling in order to be reassured that their sexuality, fertility, and health are not being impaired by hematospermia.

Do not postpone making an appointment, however, since, in some cases, hematospermia is a sign of a disease that should be treated.

Breasts

A lecturer on alcohol consumption stated that alcohol causes breasts (both male and female) to increase in size. He said that the reason for this is unknown. Does alcohol, in fact, do this?

Alcohol consumption most definitely can cause breast enlargement in males, but I haven't seen any documentation of this occurring in females. In men, it has been established that alcohol decreases sperm production, decreases the rate of production of testosterone, and changes the make-up of existing testosterone so that it is less available for use by various body tissues.

What's more, excessive alcohol destroys liver cells, and it is the liver that deactivates the estrogen that all males normally produce. Estrogen is necessary for healthy sperm. When the liver stops deactivating estrogen, a man's breast tissue is stimulated to grow—just as estrogen increases female breast tissue at puberty.

In addition to the other serious health effects of prolonged alcohol consumption, specific sexual side effects can include loss of desire, loss of erectile ability, ejaculatory problems, and reduction of testicular size.

Self-examination of the Breasts

All men, whether or not they have gynecomastia (enlarged breasts), are subject to many of the same breast diseases—including breast cancer—that affect women. Approximately 900 cases of breast cancer occur in men each year in the United States, approximately one for every 100 cases of breast cancer in women. Thus each man should examine his breasts regularly. Any man who notices a lump, thickening, or change in his breast tissue; a discharge from the nipple; or lumps in the armpit should immediately consult a physician.

The Prostate Gland

During his lifetime a man's prostate gland may be subject to various infections and may change as a result of fluctuating hormone levels. Symptoms of a prostate problem include blood in the urine, trouble ejaculating, back pain, painful urination, changes in urinary flow, and an inability to urinate. If any of these symptoms occur at any age, a man should be examined by a urologist.

Benign prostatic hypertrophy (BPH; noncancerous enlargement of the prostate) is estimated to occur in more than 50 percent of American men over age 50 and nearly 75 percent of men 70 or older. The causes are still unclear.

Because the prostate gland surrounds the urethra, which carries urine from the bladder, enlargement of the prostate narrows this tube, and may cause urinary difficulties, bladder problems, and eventually damage to the kidneys. Treatments vary depending on the location and size of the prostate enlargement and include taking medications, insertion of a balloon-type device into the urethra, and surgery.

Cancer of the prostate is a different condition and is the third most common cause of cancer death in men (after lung and colorectal cancer). About one in eleven American men will develop prostate cancer during his lifetime. Black men in the United States have the highest rate of prostate cancer in the world. It appears that socioeconomic and life-style factors, such as diet, have more to do with this increased rate than do genetic racial factors. Prostate cancer is common in Western Europe and North America but rare in the Near East, some parts of Africa, and Central and South America. One factor scientists believe may contribute to these differences around the world is a diet rich in animal fats. For example, Japanese who live in Japan have a low rate of prostate cancer; the amount of animal fat in their diet is quite low compared to North Americans. Japanese living in Hawaii, however, have a much higher rate of prostate cancer; their diet is like that of most other Americans.

Besides diet, the important element in combating prostate cancer is early detection. This is why the National Cancer Institute says it is imperative for every man to have a manual examination of the prostate every year, beginning at age 40.

Before beginning the check of the prostate during a medical examination, the physician should explain that this involves inserting a finger into the rectum and that you may feel as though you have to urinate or defecate and that you may also experience an erection.

You will be asked to position your body in such a way that the physician can feel the prostate through the wall of the rectum. This may be standing on the floor, bent forward over the examination table. Two other positions are lying on your side on the examination table with the upper leg bent toward your chest and lying on the table on your side with both legs bent, your knees touching your chest.

It helps to relax as much as you can and to push down as the physician inserts a gloved, lubricated finger into your anus. The physician will feel the size, shape, and texture of the prostate gland; a healthy prostate feels smooth, somewhat rubbery, and two distinct parts can be felt. The physician should explain what he or she is finding, including a check of the walls of the rectum. If the seminal vesicles are infected, they may also be felt during the rectal exam (see Illustration 32).

If the prostate is infected and tender, touching it during the examination may be painful. If pain occurs, ask the physician to stop and to begin again when you are relaxed, or ask to try a different position.

After the examination, the physician will look at the tip of the penis to see whether examination of the prostate gland has produced any discharge from the urinary opening; a sample to test for infectious organisms is taken if a discharge has appeared.

My problem is that I am very sensitive around the anal area so when the doctor is giving me a prostate exam, I receive a full erection. I don't know why it happens because I am 100 percent heterosexual and it is very embarrassing to myself and probably to my doctor. I maintain this erection through the remainder of the physical, so there's no hiding it from the doctor.

Is this normal? Does this happen to many other heterosexual men? Is this

Prostate Examination

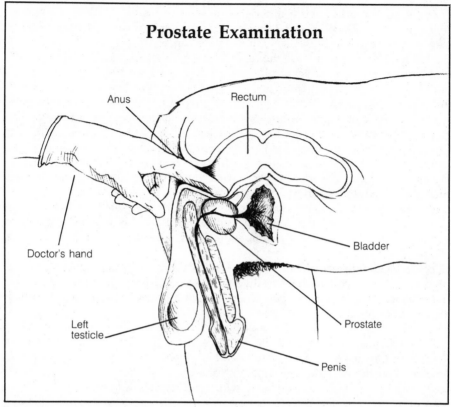

Illustration No. 32. **Prostate Examination.** This cutaway drawing is of a man bent over an examination table having a manual examination of the prostate gland. It depicts the man sideways and as though he were cut in half so you can see the organs inside the body and where the physician puts a finger to feel the prostate gland.

something that isn't embarrassing to the doctor because he is used to this occurrence? I have another physical coming up soon and dread going back.

Your erection is a normal physical response. Your comment about being "100 percent heterosexual" implies that you think that only homosexual men would get erections from this type of stimulation. This is not true—all men have nerves receptive to touch in that area. Men may also get erections during other stages of a physical, such as when their penis and scrotum are touched.

Your physician has seen this reaction many times and would not interpret it as sexual. It is unlikely that he finds it embarrassing. But your own embarrassment only helps to prolong the erection; once triggered by your physician's examination, the erection can remain for the duration of the exam because of the stress of embarrassment.

A regular prostate examination is an important part of a man's health care. Do not let your feelings about this normal reaction keep you from continuing your annual physicals.

What is the respective reliability of the two (that I know of) types of prostate exams? I had one recently which was based on a small blood sample taken from a finger. The results were negative. My age is 65.

I had always supposed that there must be a thorough physical examination of the prostate itself and whatever else is involved.

How often should the prostate be examined, in whatever form, and how can cancer of the prostate be avoided?

I assume that the blood test you had was for acid phosphatase, an enzyme found primarily in the prostate gland. The level of acid phosphatase is raised if cancer of the prostate is present but can also be raised by other conditions. This type of blood test can indeed detect prostate cancer, but only after it has spread beyond the prostate gland.

A newer blood test which measures prostate specific antigen (PSA) is considered to be more accurate, but again usually indicates that cancer has spread beyond the prostate gland itself. This test is also used to monitor a man after he has had surgery to remove the prostate to make sure that the cancer has been completely eliminated.

Most doctors still advise a man to have regular rectal examinations of the prostate for two reasons: first, because no existing blood tests can detect cancer that is still confined within the prostate gland itself and, second, because blood testing does not detect noncancerous problems with the prostate.

Maybe I'm just overly concerned, but I am afraid of developing prostate cancer. I've already had a prostate infection. How common is it? What causes it? And how is it treated?

As a man grows older, the risk of cancer of the prostate increases. Medical science does not yet know what causes cancer of the prostate. Autopsies on men who have died for other reasons show that nearly half of all older men have some degree of cancer of the prostate, but in two-thirds it doesn't cause symptoms, let alone death. Precisely because prostate cancer doesn't usually cause significant symptoms until the disease has spread to other areas clinicians urge all men, beginning at age 40, to have an annual examination of the prostate.

The gland can be felt by the doctor inserting a finger into the rectum. If a hardened area, nodule, or irregularity is noticed, X-ray, biopsy, or other tests are done to determine whether cancer is present. The sooner the cancer is diagnosed the better, because it makes prevention of the cancer spreading beyond the prostate gland more likely.

Treatment of prostate cancer includes removal of the prostate gland along with the use of various hormones or radiation, depending on whether the cancer has spread to other areas of the body. (For more information on prostate surgery see Chapter 18.)

Survival rates are becoming higher as scientists experiment with procedures and drugs that reduce the level of male hormones or block their effects.

Men of all ages need to know that most enlargements of the prostate are *not* cancerous but a sign of some less serious condition such as BPH. Fear of cancer should not cause a man to avoid annual prostate exams.

Further Readings

Black, J. *Body Talk: An A-Z guide to women's health.* Australia: Angus & Robertson Publishers, 1988.
(A helpful book written in encyclopedia-style—provides basic information about women's bodies and health.)

Boston Women's Health Book Collective. *The New Our Bodies, Ourselves: A book by and for women.* New York: Simon & Schuster, Inc., 1984.
(An easy-to-read and informative book about women's bodies and health care.)

Harrison, M. *Self-help for Premenstrual Syndrome.* New York: Random House, 1982.
(A slightly dated but still helpful book for women dealing with PMS.)

Lauersen, N. H., and deSwaan, C. *The Endometriosis Answer Book: New hope, new help.* New York: Rawson Associates, 1988.
(An easy-to-read book which provides informative answers to some of the most commonly asked questions about endometriosis.)

Rous, S. N. *The Prostate Book: Sound advice on symptoms and treatment.* New York: W. W. Norton & Company, 1988.
(A layman's guide to healthy prostate function, the typical diseases, and the most current treatment choices.)

Swanson, J. M., and Forrest, K. A. *Men's Reproductive Health.* New York: Springer Publishing Company, 1984.
(A scholarly but readable text on male physiology, anatomy, pathology, treatments, and sexuality with an emphasis on preventative health care and the importance of the individual making informed choices about his body.)

18

Sex and Disease, Surgery, and Drugs

The focus of this chapter is the sexual side effects of disease, surgery, and drugs rather than the conditions or treatments themselves. Books that deal in depth with medical problems are widely available at libraries and bookstores; some are listed in the Appendix.

With few exceptions, the letters in this chapter represent a determination to triumph over difficult circumstances. The institute has received letters about mastectomies, hysterectomies, orchiectomies, prostate cancer, and heart attack. But the discussion is not as grim as you might expect. In fact, it is often uplifting. These letters reflect an unwillingness to surrender sexuality to illness, medication, or surgery—even in the face of advancing age.

If there is anything at all discouraging in these letters it is the evidence that many clinicians are not preparing their patients, or their patients' sexual partners, for the possible impact of illness, surgery, or medication on sexual functioning. Patients are often not informed about potential changes in sexual response, whether lack of erections, difficulty in achieving orgasm, or a diminished sex drive. Many older patients complain of doctors who told them that striving for sexual functioning, at their age, was a fruitless or silly pursuit, a waste of money. Others write of doctors who seem embarrassed about discussing sex or refuse to discuss it at all.

Sometimes, as with surgery for noncancerous enlargement of the prostate, patients *believe* there should be a negative effect on erections even though most surgical techniques do not affect the ability to have erections. This belief itself can cause erectile problems. Or, these men will often misinterpret one change in sexual functioning (such as the absence of ejaculation at orgasm) to mean that *all* other functions, such as getting erections, are also lost. Again, this is often not true. This is why receiving accurate information on sexual functioning is essential whenever a physician diagnoses a disease, suggests surgery, or prescribes medication.

You may have to insist on a thorough explanation of how your sex life may be affected and change physicians if you don't get answers to your questions.

Surgery patients in particular should try to find a surgeon who is committed to giving sexual information before and after the operation, and who selects those surgical techniques most likely to preserve sexual responsiveness whenever possible. If you cannot find a sympathetic physician, find a sex therapist, psychologist, or psychiatrist with training and experience in dealing with the sexual effects of surgery, disease, and medications and seek information and support from this person. *(See Appendix.)*

There are many possible causes of sexual dysfunction. Don't assume that surgery, medication, or illness always cause sexual problems, or that if problems appear that they are permanent. The only way to find out what is causing a sexual problem and which treatment options can be considered is by having a thorough sexual evaluation, which usually includes both medical and psychological aspects. Most sex therapists routinely include the patient's sexual partner in all discussions because this greatly assists in the treatment process. If this is not offered, ask if your partner may accompany you to appointments. If your partner refuses to come along, go by yourself; individual counseling can also be effective.

Do not accept anyone's opinion that you're too old or too sick to be concerned about sex. Our increasing understanding of the immune system indicates that showing love and caring through touching and physical closeness is an important component of physical health and recovery from illness or surgery. The road to sexual recovery isn't always easy or smooth, but those with the patience and perseverance to explore treatment options will have success in regaining sexual enjoyment.

DISEASE AND SEXUAL FUNCTIONING

There can be either a direct or an indirect connection between a particular disease or medical condition and sexual functioning. A condition can affect sexuality directly, by damaging genital or other sexual responses, or indirectly, by causing pain or fatigue. For example, atherosclerosis (hardening of the arteries) may affect sexual functioning directly, by constricting blood flow to the penis, which then impairs erection. Arthritis, on the other hand, can affect sexual functioning indirectly, by making sexual activity so painful that the person avoids having sex.

In addition to the effects of the disease itself, treatments can disrupt or interfere with sexual responses. The psychological effects of being sick or injured can also affect sexual functioning; for example, if you believe your condition or treatment has made you unattractive or less desirable, this can reduce your desire or willingness to engage in sexual activity. Your partner's reactions to your illness can also impair his or her sexual feelings. And both partners may worry that sexual activity may make the patient's health worse.

It can be difficult to even think about sex, let alone engage in it, when you're not feeling well. Yet nongenital physical expressions of caring and closeness may be beneficial to a full and speedy recovery. Many people conquer the problems associated with a particular disease or treatment and go on to have satisfying sex lives. The help of a supportive physician (and in some cases a sex therapist), patience, perseverance, and a willingness to explore treatment options will often lead to a solution that is satisfying to both partners.

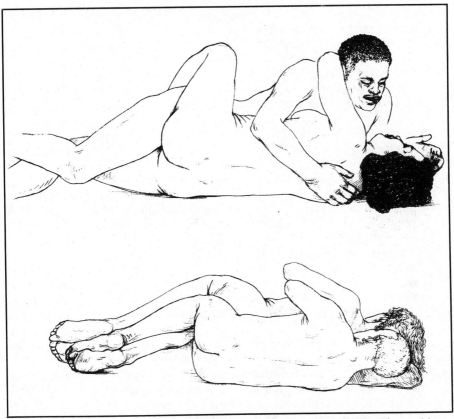

Illustration No. 33. **Two Intercourse Positions for People with Arthritis.** The position in which the man faces the woman's back (the "spoon position") may be most comfortable for women with hip pain. It may also be helpful for men with less rigid erections. The position with the couple facing each other is particularly beneficial for men with hip pain, and also for individuals who are ill, elderly, or tired. It is also comfortable for couples with extreme differences in height.

Arthritis

Are there any studies on the effects of arthritis on sexual behavior?

Arthritis, the general term for the many problems of rheumatoid disease, usually involves inflammation, pain, and stiffness in the joints and connective tissues. Twice as many women as men suffer from arthritis.

There have been no large studies of this question, but several small clinical studies have shown that approximately half of arthritic men and women experienced sexual problems—fatigue, weakness, pain, and limited movement in joints being the most common complaints. About 70 percent of arthritics with hip joint problems reported sexual problems, and women had more problems than men. Pain and stiffness of the hip joints were the main causes of sexual difficulty, and 18 percent reported a loss of libido or sex drive.

Some drugs used to treat arthritis, especially corticosteroids, have been shown to reduce the sex drive. However, one study that compared injection of the drug into the joints with taking it orally demonstrated no loss of libido with injections. There are no studies yet of the effect on sexual behavior of the newer and quite effective treatment using antiprostaglandins.

Patients who had surgery to replace the hip joints or improve their mobility reported a decrease of pain and stiffness, but not all their sexual difficulties were resolved, suggesting that a psychological component may also be involved. A person who perceives changes in his or her body or skin may feel unattractive and therefore inhibited from initiating or enjoying sexual activity.

Sex counseling of arthritis patients suggests several techniques that may improve sexual functioning: having sex at the time of day when the patient is in the least pain, preceding sex with a warm bath and massage, timing the taking of pain medication so that its best effects occur at the same time as sexual interaction, and using positions for intercourse that put the least stress on hips and other joints (*see Illustration 33*). Also, mild exercise and keeping limber is reported to be helpful.

The positions for intercourse that are most beneficial and comfortable for arthritics first take into account hip pain, then discomfort or inflexibility in other joints, and finally the pain of putting pressure or weight on the joint. Some positions are considered better than others, depending on the problem, but you may want to try them all until you find the ones that are the most comfortable for you.

For women with hip problems, the most highly recommended position is the one sometimes called the "spoon." Here, the man and the woman both lie on their sides with the man behind the woman. The penis enters the vagina from the back. For some couples, insertion of the penis is easily accomplished with the man curled around the woman's body, but insertion of the penis into the vagina can be made easier if the woman bends at the waist in the form of a modified V. The man can also place his upper leg between the legs of his partner.

For men with hip problems, the first recommendation is the position in which the couple lies side by side facing each other. The woman can then wrap just her upper leg around the upper hip of her partner or both legs around his hips. If the woman's legs are reasonably limber, another position is to have the man lying on his back and the woman sitting astride his hips with her knees, lower legs and feet on either side of his body; she can put her hands on the bed to control the amount of her weight on his pelvis. (*See Illustration 20 in Chapter 8.*)

I encourage the use of pillows all around to support weight and to cushion painful joints. A warm waterbed may enhance comfort and decrease strain. Using a heating pad on a particularly painful area, an electric blanket over you, or a bed warmer under the sheets can also ease pain and stiffness.

There is encouraging news here: Frequent sexual activity reduces the pain of arthritis by stimulating the adrenal glands to increase production of the body's own natural anti-inflammatory and pain-reducing corticosteroids.

I think I'm beginning menopause and am in quite a dilemma to know what to do. For nine years I have had rheumatoid arthritis, which has been controlled by anti-inflammatory drugs. It seems I've had more pain the last two years and

the last thing I want is to develop osteoporosis. I think that taking hormones would help me there as well as keeping me sexually active.

Also, I have fibrocystic breasts and my doctor has been telling me this will improve after menopause, which makes me suspect he will not prescribe hormones. Will taking hormones increase my arthritis or breast problems? And, if I begin taking hormones, how long should I continue to take them?

Hormone replacement therapy (HRT) should not increase either your arthritis or your problems with fibrocystic breasts. Like any other woman, you should have a thorough breast examination, including a mammogram, before beginning to take hormones, with repeat exams every six months.

The current medical thinking is that if a woman starts to take HRT at the beginning of menopause, it should continue for fifteen years and perhaps for the rest of her life to achieve full protection against osteoporosis. *(For further information on HRT, see Chapter 9.)*

High Blood Pressure

Here's one you won't believe. My new husband and I have found a new lease on life. He's 53 and I'm 41. He has high blood pressure, controlled by medication. His checkups every three months are great.

Here's my question: We have sex 12 to 15 times per week and it's getting better. The past eight months have been fantastic. But with his high blood pressure, is all this lovemaking hazardous to his health? We hope not.

Even though blood pressure does increase during sexual activity, reaching a peak at orgasm, sex is not hazardous to the health of people with high blood pressure when the condition is under control. One study demonstrated that the increased blood pressure at orgasm with one's spouse was somewhat lower than the response to moderate nonsexual physical activity.

In addition, cerebral hemorrhage, one type of medical emergency associated with high blood pressure, occurs as frequently during resting states, such as sleep, as it does during strenuous physical activity.

My question involves masturbation, which I have practiced for many years. I'm a 60-year-old man, single now, and I have no ethical qualms about this method of relieving sexual tension. But I do worry about the cardiovascular effect of masturbation, since I have borderline hypertension, but I suspect that the increase in heart rate, like other exercise, may not be harmful.

I'm reluctant to ask my doctor because it would embarrass me. And because of his reaction to earlier questions about sex, I suspect he doesn't feel comfortable with such questions.

There is no reason for you to worry about orgasm if, as you say, you have only a mild case of high blood pressure. Hypertension sometimes is at least partly due to stress or tension, and any activity that helps you relax, such as masturbation to orgasm, may actually have a beneficial effect. Masturbation is also generally less physically strenuous than intercourse.

Anyone with serious heart disease or uncontrolled high blood pressure should consult a physician about the advisability of sexual activity. Doctors rarely prohibit sexual activity except in acute cases. It is very important that you feel comfortable discussing sexual functioning with your physician. If your current doctor won't answer your questions about sex, or if he responds in a way that makes you feel uncomfortable or foolish for bringing up the topic, consider finding someone else.

Heart Conditions

For years (being a widow), I practiced masturbation. Each time I also reached a climax, and you know how this makes your heart pump harder. Last year I had congestive heart failure and was in the hospital. Now I'm feeling fine but haven't yet masturbated, even though I have the urge. Do you think it will be all right to start again or would having an orgasm be too much for my heart?

If your physician has told you that your condition has stabilized and if you are not prohibited from moderate physical activity, masturbation to orgasm should not exceed your physical capacity.

Also, many physicians point out that heart patients can monitor their physiological condition during sex just as they monitor their physical condition during other activities. For example, if extreme breathlessness, pain, or disturbing heart rhythms appear, you should stop activity at that point and rest. Then consult your physician about when you can try the activity again.

My husband is recovering from a heart attack. His doctor said he could resume sexual relations when he felt up to it. When is it safe for us to have sex again?

It is difficult to answer this without knowing specific information about your husband's case. And, unfortunately, there is not much research available on this subject.

However, this is what is known: A man should begin gradually, particularly if he is apprehensive about resuming sexual activity. One suggestion is that he first try masturbating alone, since he'll have complete control over the pace and timing of orgasm. Slow, nonathletic sexual intercourse is no harder on the heart than climbing two flights of stairs. So, if a man can manage a brisk walk or climbing stairs without difficulty, then intercourse should not cause a problem. In a study of American men over 50 years old, 86 percent of men who had suffered a heart attack resumed sexual activity.

Chest pain during intercourse should be treated like pain during exercise. If you take coronary dilators like nitroglycerine, use it 15 minutes to half an hour before having sex. Overeating or alcohol should be avoided before sexual intercourse, and just taking a short rest or slowing down if discomfort occurs can help in some cases.

Some researchers now think that risk exists only for certain types of heart attacks—those triggered by increased adrenal levels causing arrhythmia (uneven heartbeat), a condition that occurs during sexual activity but not with other forms of exercise or stress.

It may be reassuring to know that a Japanese study suggested men were more likely to suffer sudden death during extramarital sex than during sex with their wives. Perhaps this is the case because such encounters were likely to include a heavy meal, alcohol, and higher levels of stress or excitement.

Until more research is done, it is best to follow the recommendations of your physician. Most medical experts still agree, however, that careful exercise, a balanced diet, and other basics contribute to a good physical recovery and the safe resumption of sexual activity. By the way, even if you must refrain from intercourse for a short time on doctor's orders, there is no reason not to hug, kiss, and cuddle. Nongenital expressions of affection can reassure, comfort, and perhaps even speed recovery.

I am a woman, age 23, with mitral valve prolapse. Is it dangerous for me to have sex?

This is a question you must ask your physician because recommendations vary, depending on the seriousness of each patient's condition. Experts estimate that about 7 percent of all women between ages 14 and 30 have mitral valve prolapse, an abnormality of one of the heart valves. More women than men have this valve defect.

There are usually no symptoms, although a few patients have chest pain and some have tachycardia (rapid beating of the heart). Activities, including sexual activity, are usually not restricted unless symptoms of a more serious condition are present.

Blood Vessel Problems

I am 71, and I cannot get a proper erection or sustain it when I do. A urologist told me this was caused by hardening of the arteries and the penis not getting enough blood. Is this true? Are there any known treatments?

Atherosclerosis ("hardening of the arteries") is among the more common causes of erection problems related to reduction of the blood supply to the penis. In fact, erection problems have been recognized as one early symptom of this disease.

Various treatment procedures have been successful, depending on the extent and location of the blood-flow problems. Most treatments involve surgery to graft or bypass sections of the major blood vessels, as is done in heart bypass surgery. One new approach improves blood flow by inflating balloonlike objects where the veins are narrowed to widen the blood vessels. This procedure is called percutaneous transluminal angioplasty.

Did the urologist order tests such as an NPT (nocturnal penile tumescence monitoring during sleep), angiography (X-rays of the blood vessels after dye is injected), or a measurement of pressure in various arteries, including the penile arteries, using a Doppler signal? Such tests are useful in diagnosing the exact cause and location of erection problems.

Ask your urologist to arrange for complete testing for erectile dysfunction or to refer you to someone who specializes in such testing. That way, you can find out exactly what's not working properly and what treatment options are appropriate for you.

I am a 76-year-old male and two years ago I had phlebitis, first in one leg and the following year in the other. The phlebitis settled in the groin each time, leaving black and blue blotches.

Could this have any affect on the sex organs? Since the phlebitis, I am unable to get an erection and I was wondering if there is a way to solve this problem?

Thrombophlebitis, the inflammation of a blood vessel and formation of a blood clot, is a common problem, especially among older people. To have an erection, the blood vessels must deliver an adequate supply of blood to the penis, which may not be happening in your case. You did not mention how your phlebitis was treated, but many medications can also have sexual side effects.

It will take an expert with complete information on your condition to figure out whether your present erectile difficulty is due to problems with blood vessels, medication, some other condition, or a mixture of factors (*see Appendix*).

Diabetes

I'm a diabetic and in my late 50s. I have been taking one 250 mg. Diabinese pill daily since 1975. I stay on my diet, exercise and keep my blood sugar or diabetes under control. My sex drive has declined, which I know is normal to a certain extent. But I'm also experiencing difficulty in getting and maintaining an erection.

Is there anything you could suggest or recommend that would help me to improve the problems I am confronted with as well as other male diabetics? Is there any medication to cause blood to pass into the erectile tissues?

About half of all men with adult-onset diabetes (diabetes that begins in adulthood as opposed to diabetes that begins in childhood) report difficulty or the inability to attain or maintain an erection. About 2 percent report retrograde ejaculation, in which the seminal fluid flows into the bladder at orgasm rather than through the urethra and out the penis.

Although getting and keeping the diabetes under control restores erection capacity for some men, there is no known medication that will reverse erection difficulties that persist after the disease is properly controlled. However, there are other treatment options available including papaverine injections and penile implants. These are discussed in Chapter 8.

In the meantime, don't assume your lack of erections means you can have no sexual pleasure. Many men report that with sufficient stimulation (manual or oral) they can experience orgasm, including ejaculation, without erections.

I understand that oral sex is a possible form of lovemaking for people who can't perform sexual intercourse due to disabilities such as spinal cord injuries or severe diseases such as diabetes. I'm a woman with diabetes and would like to know how this applies to diabetics.

Diabetic women can have sexual difficulties similar to those of diabetic men. Although some studies have reported that diabetic women can experience orgasmic dysfunction even though many were orgasmic before the onset of the disease, four other scientifically controlled studies revealed no association between diabetes and lack of orgasm in women.

In women the equivalent situation of male erectile problems would be decreased lubrication and vaginal or vulvar swelling. One study did find some evidence for deficient vaginal lubrication in a group of diabetic women. There is also a higher rate of chronic vaginal infections among diabetic women that may cause discomfort during intercourse. Some diabetic women may also experience lowered sexual desire, but orgasmic problems may be more related to whether a woman is close to or past menopause than it is to diabetes.

Diabetics experiencing sexual difficulties have several options. Many report that their sex lives improve after psychological counseling. Others are helped when they learn to broaden their range of sexual techniques. Diabetic women should have regular testing for vaginal infections (and treatment if infection is found) to reduce vaginal irritation. Some women report improved functioning when they use water-based lubricants to increase lubrication.

Both sexes should pay close attention to control of the diabetes, since the incidence of sexual dysfunction increases when the disease is not adequately stabilized.

Other Health Problems

I am a 75-year-old man and I have emphysema—which, because of the physical exertion during intercourse, creates difficulty in breathing and causes a certain amount of panic. What can I do to improve my sex life?

Unfortunately, little research has been done on the sexual aspects of emphysema and other chronic obstructive pulmonary diseases (COPD). Research has found that COPD can affect sexual functioning in several different ways.

There can be physical, psychological, and even pharmacological factors involved; some medications prescribed for COPD can affect sexual functioning. Some men with COPD have problems with sex because they fear their partners are repelled by their coughing, shortness of breath, or other symptoms. Some partners withdraw affectionate touching or do not encourage sex because they fear the patient will die if breathing during sex becomes too strained. You will need a full medical examination to determine what is involved for you and how best to overcome the problems. Until then, you might want to try some of these techniques, which have reportedly helped some men with COPD:

1. Have sex at whatever time of day you feel best. If you take a medication to improve your breathing, have sex when the effects of that drug provide the most improvement.

2. Reduce your physical exertion during sex by experimenting with positions in which your partner moves more while you move as little as possible. *(See Illustration 20 in Chapter 8.)*

3. Talk with your partner about your sexual concerns, or arrange for both of you to speak with your physician about whether sexual exertion is dangerous.

Is there any connection between low thyroid and low sex drive? I thought I once read that there was a connection. I'm 45 and have been taking Synthroid for 12 years. I am much too embarrassed to ask my own doctor about this, but can anything be done to correct a lack of sex drive?

Hypothyroid patients, male and female, often have problems with sexual functioning and decreased sexual desire is a common complaint. It has been estimated that 80 percent of men with hypothyroidism have decreased sexual desire and 40 to

50 percent have erectile difficulties. Among women with hypothyroidism, approximately 80 percent have difficulty with sexual desire and becoming aroused. Your physician probably would not be surprised to hear of your problem because it is so common.

If sexual problems are due solely to a low level of thyroid hormone, taking thyroid replacement medication, such as the brand you use, should correct the problem, but it may take several months of increasing dosage and retesting before you know which dosage is just right for you. Or, if conditions in your life have changed since your current dosage was stabilized, you may need a new evaluation to identify the proper dose for this period of your life. It is possible that your sex problems are related to the approach of menopause rather than your thyroid condition (*see Chapter 9*).

If you get an unsympathetic or insensitive reaction when you try to talk about your sexual situation, find a different physician. Don't give up!

I've been seeing a really nice guy off and on for the past few years. Lately our relationship has become much more intimate. He seems to enjoy all kinds of foreplay but refuses to have sexual intercourse. The guy is 31 years old and he is still a virgin. He's an epileptic, and I think that's why he's avoided intercourse. What could happen during intercourse or orgasm? Could it cause an epileptic seizure?

In the past, epilepsy was erroneously regarded as being caused by masturbation. This was a foolish idea, but old notions don't disappear easily. It is yet another example of the idea that a person could be physically punished for self-stimulation. I can tell you that it is *rare* for sexual activity or orgasm to trigger an epileptic attack. Though just as rare, the reverse can occur: A few individuals experience sexual arousal during an epileptic seizure.

The most common association between epilepsy and sexuality, however, appears to be the possibility of a low level of interest in sex leading to a low rate of sexual activity and difficulty achieving arousal, establishing erection, and experiencing orgasm. In addition to low sexual interest, women with epilepsy may have difficulty experiencing increased arousal in response to stimulation. Further complicating the prognosis for each epileptic is the type of epilepsy, the exact area of the brain affected, and the age at which the epilepsy began.

It is now believed that drugs used to control epilepsy can also affect sexual functioning and may create erection problems, and there may be psychological and social factors involved as well. Because epilepsy often carries a social stigma (and parents tend to overprotect a child with epilepsy), social adjustment as an adult can be difficult.

Some researchers report that only half of all epileptic patients have any such sexual problems, and other researchers suggest that the percentage is even lower. Your friend may not be aware how rarely seizures are caused by orgasm. Encourage him to talk with an epilepsy specialist about any concerns he may have regarding sexual activity.

I recently suffered a slight stroke wherein my peripheral vision in my right eye was affected and my speech more so. After the stroke I no longer had nocturnal erections as I had always had before, and I'm impotent. Is this from the stroke?

I'm 68 but I had always had a very active sex life prior to the stroke. Will I have one again?

Being 68 is no reason to accept that your sex life is over unless you want it to be.

Loss of erectile capacity could be due to your stroke, medications, depression about having the stroke, psychological difficulties adjusting to the stroke, or any combination of these factors. It is possible for a stroke to damage areas of the brain that generate messages for sexual responses or to damage the pathways that carry these messages. But this is thought to be rare.

There has been almost no research on sexual functioning after a stroke, but one study of 105 stroke patients reported that most had no decrease in sexual desire, although 43 percent had decreased sexual frequency. Another more recent study of 50 men (average age 49) who had experienced a stroke reported that sexual interest and erectile ability usually returned within six to seven weeks, although recovery time varied. Sexual problems related to weakness or limited movement could usually be resolved by changes in sexual positions or using activities other than intercourse.

Emotional factors also can be involved. After a stroke, the fear of rejection or the perception of oneself as physically undesirable can reduce sexual arousal or interest. Fear of bringing on another stroke, depression over loss of a job, worry about medical costs, or a sense of hopelessness can also negatively affect sexual functioning.

Make an appointment for a full medical and psychological evaluation at a sex dysfunctions clinic. There is a good chance you'll be able to resume a satisfying sexual life.

I am a 39-year-old male and I have had trouble with my sex life for about 10 years. Ten years ago I was in a car accident. I had brain damage (aphasia) and was in a coma for 2½ months and my right side was paralyzed. I can still feel a big difference between my right and left sides.

Now I have trouble getting an erection. Even if my penis gets hard enough for penetration, the longer I have intercourse, the softer it gets. I can't even masturbate. I can only have intercourse when my partner and I are in bed and she either touches my penis or we have oral sex.

I have been to four urologists, two psychologists and now am seeing a psychiatrist. They say it is a result of the accident, but I disagree. I took Valium and Inderal for 2½ years, and then Librium and Inderal for another 2½ years. Could the drugs have caused my trouble?

First, it's not unusual for any man to require direct stimulation of the genitals to achieve an erection. Many 39-year-old males who've never been injured and take no medications need more direct touching or oral stimulation to obtain and keep erections than they needed when they were younger.

Don't automatically reject the idea that your sexual difficulties are related to your accident. Experts in the field of head injuries report that a loss of libido (a lack of interest in sex) is not unusual, especially for those who are in a coma for six or more hours. The brain is the most crucial sexual organ. If the sexual signals are disrupted or scrambled, desire and genital functioning can be altered.

Both Librium and Valium are benzodiazepine tranquilizers prescribed to relieve nervousness, encourage sleep, or relax muscles. They have been linked to decreased ejaculatory ability in some cases. Inderal (propranolol), a drug used to treat hypertension and heart disease, has been linked to decreased desire in a few cases and to decreased erectile ability, which may affect as many as 28 percent of patients taking this drug. But any sexual side effects are thought to be reversible by reducing the amount or by changing to some other medication; they are not thought to cause permanent dysfunctions.

Because many physical and psychological factors could be involved, ask your psychiatrist to recommend a clinic that specializes in assessing male sexual dysfunctions where a treatment program can be designed to suit your needs.

Can My Partner Catch My Disease?

If a man gets prostate infections continually, is there a chance he could infect his wife? Should he use condoms?

The causes of prostate infections continue to puzzle medical scientists, but it is thought that most infections arise from factors other than sexual activity. Some sexually transmitted diseases (STDs) may be involved in prostate infections, so the presence of any and all STDs should be ruled out by very thorough testing *(see Chapter 19)*. If testing finds an infectious organism, both partners should be treated simultaneously and you should use a condom during intercourse until retesting shows that you're both free of the organism. If testing reveals no infectious organisms, it is highly unlikely that you can infect your wife.

Can you tell me if it's safe for a woman to have sex with her husband after the doctors have said he has terminal cancer and only six months to live? Can I catch it? I'm afraid.

Among couples where one partner is terminally ill or has cancer, there are three common fears involved in dealing with sexual matters: The partner's fear that sex will hurt the patient, the patient's fear that he or she has become undesirable or unattractive, and the basic common fear that cancer is contagious—which is a myth. Your husband's doctor can put your fears to rest on all three counts.

The only exception to the "cancer is not catching" rule is if the man's cancer is related to the human papillomavirus (the one involved in genital warts). In this case, there is a risk that the woman could contract the virus and later develop cervical cancer. If human papillomavirus is involved, ask your doctor about using condoms and a spermicide.

Because continuing physical intimacy is very important for many cancer patients, you may want to find a counselor who can help you and your husband find ways to achieve the most enjoyable and satisfying six months possible. Most hospitals and mental health clinics now offer such counseling support services to the terminally ill and their families. It's important that you get help, if needed, during this very difficult period so that you are not left with both grief about your husband and feelings of fear or guilt about your sexual relationship.

I'm 49 and I have cancer. My doctor gives me another four to five years before my demise. Although I am afflicted I am very vigorous amorously. I detest condoms. My question is, can my sex fluids (sperm, etc.) transmit cancer cells into my wife and be absorbed through her vagina lining into her bloodstream causing her (of course) to also become afflicted with this awful disease?

According to the National Cancer Institute, there is no evidence that cancer can be transmitted by sex or other forms of contact. It is not considered a communicable disease. Your wife should continue to have her yearly pelvic and breast examinations and Pap smears, just as she should if you did not have cancer.

THE EFFECTS OF SURGERY ON SEX

Any kind of surgery can affect sexual functioning, particularly that which involves the genitals or reproductive system, or surgery that damages blood vessels or nerves that control the genitals. Surgery can also result in psychological effects that may influence sexual functioning. In the case of prostate surgery, for example, some changes (such as loss of ejaculate) are directly related to the surgery while erection problems may be caused solely by the expectation that sex will be changed by surgery. With some other surgeries, such as mastectomy, any later sexual dysfunction is usually (but not always) psychological. In still other cases, there is a combination of both factors.

Every surgery, especially when it will involve the genitals or reproductive organs, should be preceded by a discussion about sex. The sexual partner should be included in this discussion as well. If the physician doesn't raise the topic first, you should. Discuss the role of sexuality in your life so that your physician has a clear picture of your presurgical functioning and the importance of remaining sexually active. Insist on being told exactly what to expect in terms of future sexual functioning. You have a right to this information, especially since there appears to be a direct relationship between not getting the information and later problems with sexual response.

Surgery and Sexual Functioning in Men

Prostate Surgery

Surgery to correct problems with the prostate (the gland that produces semen located just below the bladder in men, *see Illustration 5 in Chapter 3)* is generally done to treat one of two different diseases: benign prostatic hypertrophy (BPH) or cancer of the prostate. The types of surgeries vary according to what is wrong and the effects of surgery on sexual functioning also vary. There are several different types of prostate surgery including transurethral resection and retropubic, suprapubic, and perineal incisions.

Until recently, surgery was the only treatment option for BPH. Now researchers are experimenting with several drugs that appear to improve the flow of urine for some men and avoid, or at least delay, surgery. Another alternative to surgery for BPH is balloon dilation of the prostate through the urethra. This involves inserting a tiny balloon up the urethra and inflating it for ten minutes at the segment which passes through the prostate and at the bladder neck. Only sedation and local anesthesia are necessary to prevent discomfort. In one study on the success of this procedure, symptoms of prostate enlargement were alleviated in a little more than half the patients. If surgery is recommended to treat BPH, ask if it is possible to try other treatments first.

Transurethral resection (called TUR or TURP) is one of the most common surgeries used to treat BPH and involves inserting a special instrument through the urethra. TURP interferes with erection in only about 5 percent of cases. The retropubic and suprapubic surgical approaches (incision in the lower abdomen) remove just the enlarged section of the prostate if the problem is BPH, or the entire prostate if the problem is cancer. When done correctly these two types of surgery usually do not affect the ability to achieve erections in 80 percent to 90 percent of cases.

The fourth type of surgical approach—incision in the perineum—has a much higher rate of postsurgical erection problems: When done to treat BPH, 40 percent to 50 percent of men have erection problems, depending on the amount of tissue removed; in radical perineal surgery for prostate cancer, the rate of erection problems is 98 percent. Nearly all men whose prostate cancer requires further control by taking hormone therapy experience erectile problems while taking the hormones.

Even though most men should continue to be able to have erections after prostate surgery, many men will no longer ejaculate as they did before surgery. One step in the normal ejaculation process is the closing of the neck of the bladder, which directs the semen into the urethra so it will exit through the penis. If surgery involves the bladder neck, it can no longer close properly and semen flows into the bladder instead of out through the penis (retrograde ejaculation).

Retrograde ejaculation is usually not correctable, but it also does not cause any health problems. Although semen no longer comes out of the penis at ejaculation, all the other sensations of orgasm should remain intact and be pleasurable.

Research on prostate surgery patients has shown that men who were clearly told *before* surgery exactly what to expect after surgery had far fewer sexual problems than did men who received no sexual information. In one study half the men scheduled for prostate surgery received a special explanation about the sexual effects of the operation, while the other half did not. This presurgery discussion included reassurance about the maintenance of sexual arousal and erections after surgery; the men were told that retrograde ejaculation might occur but that orgasm would continue. It was emphasized that retrograde ejaculation was the *only* change in sexual function that might occur. None of the men who were provided with this explanation *before* their prostate operation suffered erectile dysfunction after surgery. Of the patients who did not receive this kind of information, more than 60 percent (six out of ten) had sexual difficulties.

Can you tell me what was done to me in a prostate operation that left me impotent with no ejaculation and loss of erection? It wasn't cancer. I can't get the erection I once had that was hard as steel. When I do have intercourse with my wife, which is once in a month or longer, it is with half an erection. My wife is depressed and nervous as neither she or I get any satisfaction as before.

The doctors told me only that I wouldn't have any more children after the operation; they didn't tell me I would be a sterile man without my masculinity. I don't drink or smoke or use drugs of any kind. All I know is that I was ruined by this operation and both my wife and I lost our sex lives. Is there any way now for us to have a good, healthy sex life?

Yes, but it may take some time and persistence. First, you need to find a physician who is experienced in diagnosing and treating sexual dysfunctions *(see Appendix)*. Because the conditions requiring surgery on the prostate and the types of techniques used vary so much, it's impossible to answer your questions specifically.

Impairment of erection does not occur in most patients following surgery for BPH. However, changes in ejaculation (retrograde ejaculation) do often occur. It is estimated that between 30 to 90 percent of patients experience retrograde ejaculation. Although retrograde ejaculation is psychologically upsetting to many men, it does not harm you physically or affect any other phase of sexual functioning.

Take a copy of the records of your prostate surgery with you to the specialist. Even if the evaluation shows that your current physical capacity cannot be changed, the physician will discuss techniques to restore sexual satisfaction for both you and your wife.

Three years ago I had a prostate operation. Everything was fine with my sex life until about a year ago. I just couldn't get an erection any more. I called the doctor, and his answer was that no one could do anything for me and not to waste my money trying. I am 75. Is there anything I can do?

Yes. First, find a different physician for a second opinion. If your overall health is good, there is no reason why your age should be a barrier to treatment.

You may have to make some difficult decisions. After a complete evaluation by a urologist who specializes in treating sexual dysfunctions, you may be offered several options for treatment. Some of these options include self-injecting a chemical solution (such as papaverine) into the penis to produce an erection or having penile-implant surgery *(see Chapter 8)*.

Treatment for erectile dysfunctions requires highly individualized decisions made cooperatively between an informed patient (and his sexual partner if he has one) and an experienced, supportive physician who is sensitive to the patient's values and capabilities, regardless of age.

I am a 91-year-old male who had his testicles removed four years ago because of a malignant tumor on my prostate. The tumor has now disappeared.

I was very much sexually active until they were removed, and I still have a strong sexual urge but no erection. Can you help me, in any way, to have erections again?

I'm glad to hear that your cancer is under good control. For many men, prostate cancer can be treated effectively by depriving the cancer of the hormone testosterone either by removing the testicles or by taking estrogen (a hormone produced in higher amounts by women than men during the reproductive years).

Once a longer, healthier life is ensured, it is then common for men to seek help to regain their sexual functioning. Many specialists recommend that a penile implant be considered *(see Chapter 8)* and often suggest this even before surgery to remove the testicles. If the appearance of your scrotum bothers you, also ask about having artificial testicles placed in the scrotum.

If you are healthy, age should not be a barrier to having these surgeries to restore your erections and your former appearance. Research has shown that healthy older men can tolerate penile implant surgery just as well as younger men.

However, if there is a medical reason why you are not a good candidate for a penile implant, ask the physician to arrange for you to meet with a sex therapist. This person can describe and explain which sexual activities you can try so you can regain sexual satisfaction without having erections.

I have been unable to get any information about a married man's sexual life after he has had an orchiectomy operation (castration) to control cancer of the prostate gland. I don't think a medical doctor would completely understand what it is to be a eunuch under these circumstances unless he is one himself. I would appreciate any information you can provide.

Before I answer your question, readers should know that not all men with prostate cancer require surgical removal of the testicles, but many do. Cancer of the prostate is treated in many different ways, depending on the type of cancer involved and whether it has spread beyond the prostate.

Despite the positive effect of controlling the cancer, treatments can have negative physical and psychological effects, especially on sexual functioning. You do not mention whether you still feel sexual desire or whether you have retained any erectile capacity—some men do but many do not. Thinking of oneself as a eunuch or as "less than a man" can itself interfere with desire and erections.

A clinic that assesses sexual dysfunctions can evaluate what physical capacities you have. Moreover, they can assess whether penile implant surgery or surgery to implant artificial testicles into your scrotum would be beneficial. These implants can be very important to a man's sense of self-esteem.

I encourage you to pursue this matter, because giving and receiving love and physical closeness is valuable to everyone. Moreover, it may be one of the most important components in successfully fighting a serious illness, regardless of age.

I need information about men who have had a prostatectomy. I've been to doctors and to urologists but none has been able to assure me that having a penile implant or other device will work for me. Also, none of these doctors will arrange for me to talk to their other patients.

I had a radical prostatectomy 10 years ago because of cancer. Had I known about the consequent physical, mental, and family anguish I'm not sure I would've had the surgery.

Oh yes, I still have sexual desire, and mechanical stimulation of my penis gives some satisfaction, but I'm unable to achieve erection. I'd like to collect more information on this condition and talk to other men who have had the same problem.

Write to Recovery of Male Potency (ROMP), 27211 Lahser Road, Suite 208, Southfield, MI 48034 (1-800-835-7667). This is the main office for a self-help organization that can put you in touch with people in your area who have faced similar problems. Either this group or groups listed in the Appendix can help you locate a physician with whom you can explore options such as penile implant surgery.

Two years ago I was faced with prostate cancer and a surgeon at the clinic I went to took the time to explain about treatments. He told me that few men are good candidates for the new surgery that reduces the loss of potency (I was not) and that radiation treatment is almost the same as far as curing the cancer and keeping potency.

I opted for radiation treatment, and so far everything is still working and I feel great. I know this is not for everyone, but men should be informed about the option of radiation treatments.

You're absolutely right. Men with prostate cancer should be told about *all* treatment options appropriate to the stage of their condition and what the potential effects on their sex life would be for each option. You were fortunate to have found a physician who follows this philosophy and takes time for the necessary discussions.

The suitability of treatment options does vary from one patient to the next. Treatment for prostate cancer can include various surgical techniques, radiation therapy, removal of the testicles, hormonal therapy, chemotherapy, or combinations of these options.

Discussions should include the man's sexual partner, so that the couple has a clear idea of what to expect after treatment. There are reports of couples who stopped having sex after a man's treatment for prostate cancer, even though the man remained capable of becoming aroused and having erections and orgasms. In some of these cases, the partner became unwilling to have sex because of fears about catching the cancer, harming the patient, or other worries caused by not receiving accurate information. In others, the patient himself was concerned about his functioning and, mistakenly expecting to lose it, he did; or, retrograde ejaculation was misinterpreted to mean that erections were also not possible.

Not all men with prostate cancer will be able to preserve both their lives and the capacity for sexual arousal, erection, and orgasm as you have done, but each has the right to participate in making a fully informed decision about treatment. These decisions should be based on accurate information about future sexual functioning and how to retain or regain as much sexual functioning as is possible after surgery.

My husband of 49 years has recently completed 36 days of radiation treatment for prostate cancer. We knew about the problem of impotency, but after five months it has become more than a reality. What options should we consider as we begin a search for help?

What did you think of the physicians who diagnosed and treated your husband's prostate cancer? Did one stand out as being more aware of sexual concerns, offer sexual information without being asked, meet with you as a couple to discuss sexual effects of the treatment, and take the time to discuss sex in a forthright and supportive manner? If so, contact that physician and ask him or her to refer you to a qualified sex therapist or clinic; if not, see the Appendix.

If his radiation treatment is found to have reduced his erectile capacity permanently, then you may be asked to consider the option of having a penile prosthesis implanted surgically. It's important for you to be involved in all discussions of treatment or therapy options.

Many people don't realize that an erection is not necessary for male orgasm. Many men can have fulfilling orgasms without having an erection or ejaculation. Other sexual activities besides intercourse can produce satisfaction and permit a couple to have a loving, satisfying sexual relationship without being dependent on an erect penis.

Other Surgeries

Please discuss testicular mass, the surgery, convalescence, activity after surgery and complications. Will blood be needed for this operation? My husband is 68 years old, 6'9" and very active. He has been diagnosed as having a testicular mass. It has been confirmed by a second urologist. He does not want to have the surgery. I am hoping that once he reads your reply he will change his mind.

It is extremely important to find out what the mass is and to do so as quickly as possible!

If your husband is concerned about losing sexual capacity, he should know that erection and orgasm can often be retained or restored after treatment. And, if appearance after the possible removal of a testicle is a concern, natural-looking artificial implants are available.

Masses in or near the testicles can be related to a number of different conditions, some of which are correctable without surgery on the testicle itself. Surgery is also often necessary to determine what is going on elsewhere in the groin. If a tumor is found, it will be necessary to examine the cells to determine whether it is benign (noncancerous) or malignant (cancerous).

I realize that the idea of cancer is frightening and that many people delay any type of surgery because they don't want to have their worst fears verified. However, delay is the worst course of action; first, because if a mass is benign, the person and his family suffer needless prolonged worry; and, second, if it is a form of cancer, every day of delay reduces the treatment options available and the chances for a complete cure.

There is no way to speculate about what is wrong with your husband or what will be involved in either the surgery or the treatment. You both need to know that even if cancer is found, recent advances in radiation therapy and chemotherapy have produced extremely high cure rates for many types of testicular cancers.

When the cancer has not spread to the lungs, liver, or lymph system, nearly 100 percent of men with several types of cancer recover fully after surgery and do not have cancer in other sites later in life.

Please don't hesitate because of fears about contaminated blood, either. All blood is now screened for the AIDS virus and other serious communicable diseases, and some hospitals now have facilities that permit the banking and use of a patient's own blood before surgery whenever possible. Call and ask if the hospital provides "predeposit autologous donation."

How about some help for men who have lost a testicle? I had to have one of mine removed several years ago, and can attest to the fact that it is a real emotional blow to a man to lose this important part of his sexuality. Probably as much so as for a woman to lose a breast. Yet I have never heard of any available support system. And, while the cosmetic problem is obviously not as significant, is there nothing available to make us feel less lopsided?

Yes, there are artificial testicles similar to the silicone implants used for breast reconstruction. An artificial testicle is a chemically inert, silicone form shaped like a testicle and filled with silicone gel. The scrotum is surgically opened and the implant is attached to structures inside the scrotum by a small tag. Visually, the results look very natural.

Earlier implants made of silicone rubber, Lucite, or vitallium were solid and some patients complained they felt unnaturally hard. The newer silicone gel prosthesis has a more natural consistency and comes in four sizes, so the artificial testicle matches the remaining one or is appropriate to body size.

The availability of different sizes is important, since young boys who are born without a testicle or who lose one or both from disease or accident have been shown to be particularly affected by the lack of a normal male appearance. In some cases, boys as young as three have become concerned about their bodies, even though parents deliberately delayed explaining the condition to the child. Now, with graduated sizes of implants, a boy can look normal throughout his life by having surgery to replace the original implant with a larger one as he grows.

There are no national data to show how many men have had testicular implants, but it appears to be a safe procedure when done by a surgeon who is experienced with the implants. We also don't know how many boys or men could benefit from such surgery, but one limited study of nongovernmental hospitals indicated that 18,000 bilateral orchiectomies (removal of both testicles) and 27,000 unilateral orchiectomies (removal of one testicle) occurred in just these hospitals in 1970 alone.

Any local medical society should have the names of plastic surgeons or urologists specializing in this surgery. It's widely done now and at least one specialist should be available at most large hospitals.

Eight months ago my 58-year-old husband had bypass surgery on the aorta artery in the area of his breast bone all the way down his abdomen and both sides of his groin.

Our sex life was normal before, but now he's unable to ejaculate. Everything else is like it was. The surgeon told him some nerves may have been affected. Is there any hope that this will correct itself?

Some, but not all, men experience lack of ejaculation or loss of erectile capacity after aortal surgery. We don't yet have all the answers, but research suggests that a specific set of abdominal nerves is involved. Some of these nerves may be damaged during bypass surgery, which can result in retrograde ejaculation (when semen flows into the bladder instead of out the end of the penis at orgasm).

If your husband's surgery involved nerves responsible for ejaculation, then it's unlikely he will regain the ability to ejaculate through his penis. Retrograde ejaculation, however, is not harmful to his health, and it sounds as though he has retained the capacity to have erections and orgasms. If he is concerned about sterility, consult a fertility specialist *(see Chapter 15)*; viable sperm can often be recovered from the bladder and used for insemination.

My problem is the relationship with my husband of 30 years. We are in our middle 50s and have NO sex life. Two years ago he had a aorto-femoral bypass graft, and afterwards said it is impossible for him to have an erection. Is this true? Or is there someone else?

Aorto-femoral bypass surgery (one type of surgery to correct coronary artery disease) reportedly does reduce erectile functioning in some—but not all—cases, depending on which nerves remain intact after the surgery. The cardiovascular disease itself and medications prescribed for the disease can also cause problems with erections. Approximately half of coronary surgery patients had already reduced their rate of intercourse or had stopped having intercourse before surgery, and many feared resuming sex after surgery. This was generally due to a combination of physical and psychological factors.

Your letter implies that now the two of you engage in little or no intimate behavior, whether intercourse or cuddling. When there is no physical expression of love and affection in a relationship, it's not unusual for one partner to feel unattractive, or assume that the other person is having an affair. Some heart specialists insist that sexual partners be included in pre- and postsurgical discussions about sex, so that both partners are informed about the impact of treatment on current and future sexual activity—unfortunately, others do not provide this valuable service.

Both you and your husband need to be told about the importance of exchanging physical affection and about activities that do not require intercourse but do provide satisfaction for both partners. He may still be perfectly capable of orgasm and ejaculation even without erection, and he can certainly provide you with sexual pleasure. Make an appointment to see a person qualified to diagnose causes of erectile problems *(see Appendix)*.

You need help in restoring your own self-confidence, so if your husband is unwilling to be examined, go to counseling yourself. Even if you must begin counseling alone, you can share the information you receive with your husband.

A year ago my lover, age 56, had surgery to implant steel rods in his lower back. For several months he was forbidden to perform any strenuous physical activity and was only recently permitted to resume sexual relations. We find that he can become aroused enough to obtain an erection, but he is unable to maintain it to ejaculation. He was fine prior to surgery.

Could the surgery have caused the problem? Is the problem permanent? Would some new positions or medications help?

You will have to ask these questions of the surgeon. Back surgeries vary so greatly that it is impossible to generalize from one case to the next. I could find no specific studies reporting the sexual effects of various types of back surgery. However, any surgery that affects the nerves or the blood vessels that stimulate or nourish the genitals can interfere with sexual functioning. If the surgeon can't help you, find a physician who specializes in diagnosing and treating male sexual dysfunctions. Also, it may take more than one year for your partner to know how much of his former capacity will be recovered after surgery.

In the meantime, you might try having sex in positions other than those you've been using, but don't try any position that would flex or stress your friend's back beyond any limits set by his physician for other types of physical exertion. The woman-on-top position is one option. This works for some men who lose erections when they stop stimulation in order to insert the penis. Another position that has been suggested for weak erections is the "spoon" position (see illustration 33).

Surgery and Sexual Functioning in Women

Hysterectomy

Any woman who is told she needs a hysterectomy *must* get a second opinion. The rate of hysterectomy in the United States is currently under investigation and suspected of being much higher than necessary. It is noteworthy that hysterectomy rates are higher in some geographic regions of the country than in others. This difference does not appear to be due to differences in rates of disease. This has led to speculation that the decision to perform a hysterectomy may be related to factors other than the need to actually treat a disease.

The most common conditions leading to hysterectomy are cancer of the uterus, ovaries, or Fallopian tubes; uncontrollable uterine bleeding; noncancerous fibroid tumors; and endometriosis (often-painful deposits of uterine tissue that implant and grow on internal pelvic organs).

Hysterectomies are often referred to as total or partial, but it is important to find out exactly what is being removed (see Illustration 34).

Sexual problems following hysterectomy occur in a minority of women, but when they do they can have a debilitating effect on both the woman and her partner. There are a number of possible physical causes for the development of sexual dysfunctions. Loss of the uterus may negatively affect some women for whom uterine contractions were an important aspect of orgasm. Decreased hormone levels due to removal of the ovaries can result in shrinking of the vaginal tissues, loss of sexual desire and arousal, decreased vaginal lubrication, and diminished or lost orgasmic capability. If the cervix is removed, shortening of the vagina may make intercourse difficult until the vaginal tissues have been dilated or have stretched again. Internal scarring or damage to the nerves that connected the genital organs to the brain may cause pain or interfere with feeling sexual pleasure.

Psychological factors can also negatively affect sexual functioning after a hysterectomy. The uterus is a symbol of femininity for some women. Loss of the uterus means the end of fertility; and for some women fertility is an essential aspect of being a woman. Women with these feelings may experience both lowered self-esteem and depression—either of which can cause sexual dysfunction. If cancer was the reason for surgery, fear of the cancer returning can interfere with sexual feelings. In addition, both the woman and her partner may fear that sexual activity will injure her in some way.

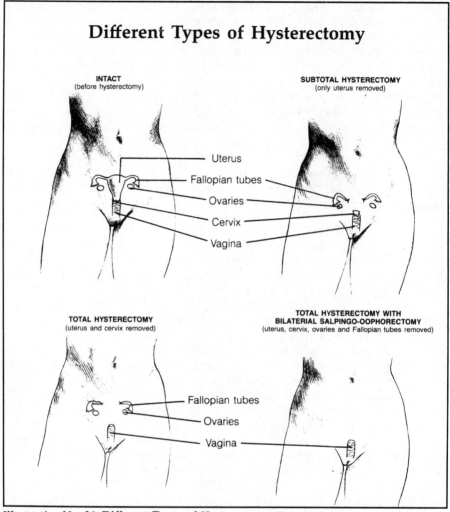

Different Types of Hysterectomy

INTACT
(before hysterectomy)

SUBTOTAL HYSTERECTOMY
(only uterus removed)

Uterus
Fallopian tubes
Ovaries
Cervix
Vagina

TOTAL HYSTERECTOMY
(uterus and cervix removed)

**TOTAL HYSTERECTOMY WITH
BILATERIAL SALPINGO-OOPHORECTOMY**
(uterus, cervix, ovaries and Fallopian tubes removed)

Fallopian tubes
Ovaries
Vagina

Illustration No. 34. **Different Types of Hysterectomy.** The top-left drawing shows the inside of a woman with all organs in place. The other three illustrate different types of hysterectomies and which internal organs remain after surgery.

A New Zealand study of sexuality and hysterectomy emphasizes both the importance of information prior to surgery and the low incidence of sexual dysfunction after surgery. A group of women who had been provided with an informational booklet by their physician before their hysterectomies were questioned about their sexual satisfaction approximately one year later. Similar to the men who were informed in advance about the possible sexual side effects of prostate surgery, these women also appeared to benefit from being told exactly what was going to be done and what the effects on sex might be. Forty-two percent reported *improvement* in their sexual lives following hysterectomy and 52 percent said that there was no change in their sexual enjoyment. The few women who experienced negative sexual effects were also those whose surgery involved the vagina to a greater extent.

After 25 years of a satisfying sex life, I just have undergone a complete hysterectomy (removal of uterus, ovaries, tubes) because of a severe infection. What, if anything, will take the place of these organs?

If you're asking whether artificial organs can be implanted to replace the uterus, ovaries and Fallopian tubes, there is no such procedure. Perhaps you imagine that you have a large void or empty space inside your body, or you worry that other organs will shift out of place. If that's the case, ask your doctor to show you a model or drawing of the inside of a woman's body. The nonpregnant uterus is about the size and shape of a small flat pear and the ovaries are each about the size of a grape. Removal of these relatively small organs does not leave an empty space or cause displacement of other organs.

If you're asking about replacing the hormonal role these organs played, hormones are often prescribed to women who have had hysterectomies which included removal of the ovaries. Taking estrogen may be necessary if you have hot flashes or other symptoms of menopause or are at high risk of osteoporosis *(see Chapter 9)*.

I'm scheduled to have my uterus and ovaries removed but still don't understand how my husband and I will have sex afterward. Where will the penis go?

The penis will still go where it always did (in the vagina). The penis never enters the uterus during intercourse anyway, even for women who have not had a hysterectomy. Regardless of the type of hysterectomy, most of a woman's vagina remains after the operation. In those cases where the cervix is also removed, the vagina may be shortened, but should remain able to accommodate a penis.

Women usually are told not to have sex until healing is complete, about six to eight weeks after the hysterectomy, and after they have been back to the physician to be checked to make sure everything is OK.

A few months ago my wife had a complete hysterectomy, including her ovaries and cervix. Now when we engage in intercourse (which has been very infrequent since the hysterectomy), it feels as though her vagina has been shortened. I have not mentioned this to my wife and am reluctant to discuss it with our doctor. Is what I described possible? Is it my imagination?

It's possible—and likely—that your wife's vagina is shorter. In some hysterectomies, about one-third of the upper vagina is removed along with the cervix, the area surrounding the tiny opening between the vagina and the uterus.

Sometimes the vagina retains its elasticity, in which case a woman does not have much difficulty resuming intercourse with full penetration. However, when the vagina does not easily stretch to regain its former capacity, intercourse can be difficult, painful, or even impossible.

Moreover, if your wife's estrogen level is low as a result of the bilateral oophorectomy (removal of both ovaries) or because of natural menopause, she also may have thinning and shrinking of vaginal tissue and loss of vaginal lubrication.

It is also not unusual for women to have negative feelings after a hysterectomy. For example, some women fear that intercourse will injure the surgical site, so they involuntarily tighten the vaginal muscles, preventing penetration. Some women also say that their sexual desire is reduced.

To resolve the problem, your wife should be examined by a physician who is understanding about sexual issues. He or she can diagnose exactly which physical problems may be involved and can help the two of you to regain satisfactory sexual functioning. You could ask your regular doctor to recommend a physician who specializes in sex therapy or in treating postmenopausal women.

Treatment options include gradual stretching of the vagina, use of a water-based lubricant during sex, taking replacement hormones, and trying sexual positions (such as woman-on-top) that allow the woman to control the depth of penetration.

Eleven years ago I had a complete hysterectomy. About six years ago I had an internal exam, at which point the doctor told me that I had an excessive amount of scar tissue and I should consider surgery.

Sorry to say that I have not had an internal exam since then. About one year ago, having intercourse became extremely painful and for the last six months, I experience bleeding for approximately an hour after intercourse. What should I do?

Make an appointment for a pelvic examination as soon as possible. The pain and bleeding might be related to your hysterectomy, or they might be signs of a different but serious problem.

Although you'll need a medical evaluation to find out for sure, the problem may be due to growth of scar tissue in the vagina. This condition sometimes occurs following gynecological surgery and often can be treated by using a vaginal dilator to increase the size of the vagina gradually. When the scar tissue is stretched, some bleeding can occur. Sometimes the pain can be reduced by using a cream or ointment with a local anesthetic. In some cases surgery may be necessary to remove the scar tissue. This should be done by a surgeon highly experienced in this procedure.

If you do not already have a gynecologist or a physician familiar with your gynecological history, try to find one who also will assess your hormonal status. Since you have been without ovaries for some time, a low level of estrogen may have contributed to your vaginal discomfort and bleeding.

Hysterectomy or not, with or without problems, whether or not they have ovaries, *all* women must have regular (at least yearly) pelvic and breast examinations. Unfortunately, some physicians tell their hysterectomy patients that they'll never have to worry about "female problems" again, but this does not mean that they will never need another pelvic examination.

My wife and I are in our mid-30s and have been married for four years. Up until a year ago, we had a beautiful relationship and enjoyed sex very much.

Then she had an operation in which her womb was removed. Now she just

doesn't care if she has sex or not. I can't touch or make love to her. It's driving me crazy. I have asked her to talk to her doctor, but she won't. She says that if I'm so worried about it, I can talk to the doctor myself. I love my wife very much and know she loves me. Everything else is fine as long as I don't try to have sex or talk about it. What can I do?

You didn't mention whether your wife's ovaries were also removed (oophorectomy) during the hysterectomy (surgical removal of the uterus) or why her uterus had to be removed.

It is important for you to know about the ovaries, because they are one of the main sources of hormones thought to affect a woman's sexual desire and functioning. Researchers have found that for many women taking replacement hormones (estrogen, and sometimes an androgen) increases vaginal lubrication, sexual feelings, and desire.

After hysterectomy, some women feel less feminine and desirable, fear that intercourse could cause internal damage, or mourn the lost capacity to bear children, all of which can reduce sexual desire.

It is also important to consider the reason for the surgery. If, for example, she was found to have cancer, she may be going through an understandable psychological depression.

A reasonable first step would be for her to see a gynecologist trained in endocrinology for a thorough examination (see Appendix). The physician needs to evaluate the current condition of her vagina, her hormone levels, and her general health. Ask that her medical records be sent from the doctor who did the surgery. Go with your wife to see the doctor. Ask questions and tell the physician about her reduced sexual desire if she won't.

If your wife refuses to see a physician, go by yourself to consult a sex counselor or therapist. You need to have a better understanding of what fears and concerns your wife has and how to reassure her. You should, of course, continue sharing nonsexual affection. Your wife may need to be shown that she is still loved and that you're as committed to the marriage as you were before the surgery.

Following a hysterectomy eight years ago at the age of 34, I experienced, along with standard menopausal symptoms, a dramatic loss of libido (loss of desire and arousal and lubrication response but not orgasm—that's still OK). The loss of libido has not responded to estrogen treatment, which I've only used off and on.

Now I've read a newspaper article that pinpoints testosterone as the hormone responsible for libido. Can women take this?

It is important to get a complete picture of which hormones your body is still producing, and in what amounts, before you consider hormone replacement. You and your physician might have to experiment with varying dosages, combinations, and treatment-cycle patterns before you notice any changes in your sexual functioning. Also these drugs will not work if you skip treatment days, decide to change dosages on your own, or ignore warning signs for known side effects. The use of replacement hormones also involves a commitment to thorough medical follow-ups.

For those women for whom estrogen does not improve sexual interest, enjoyment, and orgasmic capacity, adding a small dose of androgen (testosterone is one kind) *may* help. Some amount of androgen is thought to be required for female sexual functioning, but studies have not yet established what amount is necessary or its effect on libido.

One study of oophorectomized women who took testosterone in addition to estrogen and a progestin reported that they "felt better," but many did not report increased sexual activity. However, a Canadian study of women given various hormone regimens demonstrated a positive effect on sexual desire, fantasy, and arousal resulting from estrogen-androgen combinations. Additional research on a group of women studied at least two years after surgery also noted the enhancing effects on sexual motivation of treatment with estrogen and androgen; frequency of intercourse also appeared to increase.

You need to know, however, that androgen can have masculinizing side effects including increased facial hair and lowering of the voice, especially if the dose is too high. These effects might lower a woman's confidence in her sexual appeal and, in doing so, reduce her libido.

Mastectomy

It is estimated that approximately one out of every ten women in the United States will develop breast cancer during her life. Breast cancer is uncommon in women under the age of 35 and rare in those younger than 20. The majority of women with breast cancer are older than 50. Men can also develop breast cancer, but only 1 percent of all breast cancers are found in men.

Cancer surgery of the breast can be as limited as removal of the lump (lumpectomy) or as extensive as removal of the whole breast, the chest muscles, and the surrounding lymph nodes (including all those under the arm). This type of surgery is often referred to as radical mastectomy. Although radical mastectomy was the most common form of breast cancer surgery in the past, it is only used occasionally today. Other names for varying degrees of breast surgery are modified radical mastectomy, total or simple mastectomy, and partial or segmented mastectomy. Chemotherapy, which uses drugs to stop the growth of cancer cells, radiation therapy, or hormonal therapy may also be necessary when it is known or suspected that the cancer has spread beyond the breast.

If mastectomy is advised, it is *essential* to get at least one other medical opinion to determine which course of treatment is most appropriate. This decision will depend on the stage of the disease, your feelings, and life style. When cancer is identified early, many treatments can be equally beneficial, so the decision depends on how you think you will feel after the treatment is completed. For some women, living with a breast that once had cancer provokes too much anxiety to be worth saving the breast. For others, retaining as much of the breast as possible is very important aesthetically, sexually, or for self-esteem. Each woman should be active in making decisions about her treatment.

In addition to deciding on the type of surgery, you should also consider *when* to have the surgery done. A recent study found that women who had breast surgery near the middle of their reproductive cycles (*see Illustration 4*) at the time of ovulation were 4 to 5 times *less* likely to suffer a relapse or death than women who had surgery nearer menstruation. Researchers theorize that a woman's immune system is strongest near ovulation.

One of the best sources of information about breast cancer, the latest treatments, and recommendations for physicians is the Cancer Information Service of the National Cancer Institute (1-800-4-CANCER in the continental U.S.; 1-800-638-6070 in Alaska; 524-1234 in Oahu, Hawaii and collect from other islands).

A woman may experience a traumatic reaction to the results of breast surgery, particularly if she views her breasts as an important symbol of femininity. If losing her breasts causes depression, this obviously may affect her sexual functioning. Women who need nipple stimulation to become aroused or have orgasms may also have sexual problems after surgery. Still others experience no loss of self-esteem, no feelings of unattractiveness, and no loss of sexual response, pleasure, or satisfaction.

A woman can choose different ways to respond to the changes in her body shape that may result from surgery. Each woman must decide what is right for her by weighing the advantages and disadvantages of each possibility. Wearing a breast form (prosthesis) inside a bra is one alternative. Another is to have a new breast reconstructed surgically. Reconstruction of the breast by plastic or reconstructive surgery at the time of the mastectomy (or at any time afterward) is possible for almost every woman. However, when breast reconstruction is being considered as an option, planning *before* the mastectomy can greatly facilitate breast reconstruction and, in many cases, save the nipple. Finding both an experienced oncologist (cancer specialist) and a reconstructive surgeon who will work together will greatly enhance the final result.

My doctor tells me I must have a mastectomy. Will this ruin my sex life?

It doesn't have to. With good preoperative and postoperative information and counseling, a mastectomy need not ruin your sex life. Speaking only of physiology, your physical capacity to respond to stimulation and to experience orgasm should not be altered by breast surgery, unless you normally rely heavily on breast or nipple stimulation for sexual arousal or orgasm. Psychological reactions to mastectomy can also affect sexual behavior.

Research on women who have had their breasts removed shows that at least one-third report a negative effect on sexual functioning and that, for many women, the problems persisted for nearly a year after the operation. Many women changed their sexual behavior after mastectomy. They had sex less often, they rarely initiated intercourse, and they avoided positions where their breasts would be visible.

It's clear from one American Cancer Society poll that most women believed that having a mastectomy would impair their womanhood, and 9 percent even said they would rather die than have a mastectomy.

Any preexisting problems with self-esteem or sexual functioning can be aggravated by the surgery. One common pattern is for a woman to see herself as unattractive, so she withdraws from her sexual partner, who in turn feels rejected and then doesn't approach her. This cycle of misunderstanding can only be broken by talking to one another; counselors can help couples initiate such discussions. Counseling can also help single women who worry about when and how to tell a new sexual partner about the mastectomy; single women sometimes withdraw from relationships to avoid that "confession" point.

Despite women's fears, data show that the vast majority of men do not abandon a woman after a mastectomy. For some couples, in fact, such surgery has a positive effect—the woman values her partner for being there for her during a period of vulnerability, and the partner feels more protective and needed than before the surgical experience.

It is often up to the individual woman to insist on receiving adequate psychological support for herself and her partner. In one study, only 6 percent of mastectomy patients were offered preoperative information and counseling about sex. Many of the rest reported they wanted such counseling but felt they could not ask about sex until a health professional raised the topic first. Any spouse or partner should be involved in all pre- and postsurgical discussions with the oncologist, the plastic surgeon, and the sex therapist or counselor.

In most cases, sexual activity can be resumed as soon as the woman is released from the hospital. Surgeons suggest using specific positions and techniques that reduce pressure on, or contact with, the healing area, such as the woman sitting astride her partner *(see Illustration 20 in Chapter 8)*.

At age 60 I had a double mastectomy. Since then I've had not too much success at intercourse. It seems I need my breasts to reach an orgasm. Our sex life is very important to my husband and me. Is there any hope to get back my ability to achieve orgasm?

There is evidence that a physiological problem can be involved for those women for whom breast or nipple stimulation was an important source of sexual arousal or orgasm. One solution may be counseling to help retrain yourself to become sexually aroused by stimulation of other areas of your body. If your husband is willing to join you, go together to a sex therapist who has experience working with couples following mastectomy. Go alone if he does not wish to participate.

Sensate-focus exercises, one of the standard therapies used by most trained counselors, might be useful. These techniques teach a person to heighten their perception of different kinds of touching on various areas of the body and to use that stimulation to build sexual arousal and achieve orgasm.

I've just been told I have breast cancer and will need a mastectomy. My breasts are very important to my husband and me. I feel they are the symbol of my femininity. I know I have to have the surgery, but isn't there any way I could have a new breast made right away so I'd never have to live without one? Just thinking about it makes me depressed.

Breast reconstruction either at the time of the mastectomy, or several months or even years later, has increased over the last decade. Advance planning among the woman, her cancer surgeon, and her plastic/reconstructive surgeon assures the best results. While health considerations must come first, surgical decisions like saving the areolae and nipples must be made prior to the mastectomy. If not done at the same time as the mastectomy, reconstruction surgery usually takes place three to nine months later.

Evaluations of women after surgery have shown that reconstruction does not reduce the effectiveness of successfully treating the cancer, nor does it increase the likelihood of a recurrence. In fact, the survival rates for women with reconstructed and nonreconstructed breasts were the same in several studies.

Recent follow-up studies of hundreds of women in France, England, Israel, the Netherlands, Germany, Japan, and the United States demonstrate the success of breast reconstruction following mastectomy. For example, one study compared 100 German women who had reconstruction following mastectomy with 100 women who had not undergone reconstruction; no difference was found in either recurrences or overall survival rate between these two groups. A study of 120 French women reported that immediate reconstruction did not increase the hospital stay. Studies of women choosing reconstruction revealed reduced negative emotional responses following surgery; these women reported satisfaction with appearance in clothing, participation in sports, no change in self-esteem, and dramatic reduction in the psychological trauma. In a German study of 87 women, the surgeons noted that "many patients will accept mastectomy almost with a sense of relief when immediate reconstruction can be offered."

One technique for breast reconstruction involves implanting a silicon gel-filled envelope against the chest muscles. The resulting breast looks and feels much like the natural one to both the woman and her sexual partner.

Since cancer involves the nipple in only one out of 10 cases, many women have the option of saving the nipple and areola (dark area around the nipple) by temporarily grafting them to another part of the body. They are later restored to the reconstructed breast. If for some reason the nipple was not or could not be saved, a replacement can be constructed from other tissues if a woman wants this done. If additional color is needed, tattooing can be applied. In any case, whether the original nipple is used or a new one constructed, there will not be feeling in that nipple. (If tissue from the vulva has been used to form a nipple, the genital area may be sore for a week or so.)

PRESCRIPTION DRUGS AND SEXUAL FUNCTIONING

Every year The Kinsey Institute receives hundreds of questions about the sexual side effects of medications. A wide range of prescription drugs may affect sexual functioning. There is as yet only a limited number of scientific studies evaluating these effects, mostly on men. Much of the existing data comes from reports on just one or two men; there is even less information about women.

It is possible that any drug you are taking for the treatment of hypertension (high blood pressure), heart disease, anxiety or stress, depression, psychiatric illness, sleeplessness, convulsions, gastrointestinal disorders, or arthritis *may* affect your sexual functioning. Sometimes it can take several years before a medication causes sexual side effects. Therefore, if you develop a sexual dysfunction while being treated with a medication, go to your physician and tell him or her about your symptoms. Together you can work to discover whether it is the medication, some aspect of your illness, or something else in your life that is causing the dysfunction. Once the cause is identified, help is available to resolve the sexual difficulty.

Common sense would suggest that a physician would tell patients in advance about potential sex-related side effects, but often they don't. Some physicians do not because they believe that it will lead to anxiety about sexual functioning, which itself can result in dysfunction. However, a patient who does not know in advance about the possibility of such side effects may assume that any sexual problem is an inevitable sign of aging or an unavoidable consequence of the disease. As a result the patient doesn't seek a solution.

If you suspect that a medication has affected your sex life, talk to your physician. Ask if you can try a different dosage or another drug. No one should be embarrassed to mention sexual difficulties to a doctor or to ask for a solution. If your physician seems unwilling to help you, find one who will.

Unfortunately, solving problems with the sexual side effects of drugs is a trial-and-error process. One difficulty is that the same medication can affect individuals differently. Therefore, finding out whether a problem is due to a medication or some other physical or psychological factor is difficult and requires cooperation and patience on the part of both physician and patient. Once you have found a physician who is willing to work with you, stick with him or her until the problem has been solved regardless of how long it takes.

But do not experiment on your own; reducing or stopping medication can jeopardize your health.

Even if sexual problems appear and if it takes some time to diagnose and resolve them, do not assume your sex life is over. While you are working on finding a solution, there are sexual activities which can provide satisfaction. For example, even if a man does not have erections, often he can still have pleasurable ejaculation and orgasm. There are many sexual activities that can provide satisfying orgasms for both partners. Above all, continue to exchange affection with your partner.

Specific Drugs and Their Negative Sexual Effects

The list provided below represents more than 100 medications that *may* have an effect on sexual functioning. The same drug is often called by a different name by different manufacturers. Just because the name of your drug isn't listed does not mean that it is not capable of producing negative sexual side effects. Look to see if other drugs of the same type as the one you take are listed; if that drug lists symptoms similar to your own, suspect that your drug may be causing your problem. Another point: If your drug is listed but your symptoms are not, your suspicions are not necessarily wrong—that drug may still be the source of your problems.

When in doubt, speak directly to your physician about adjusting dosage or changing to a different drug. If your physician is not helpful, or if the problem persists despite trying several different medications, consult a sex dysfunctions clinic *(see Appendix)*.

Table 5. SPECIFIC DRUGS AND SYMPTOMS OF NEGATIVE SIDE EFFECTS

Condition/ Drug*	Reduced Desire	Erection Problems	Ejaculation Problems	Impaired Orgasm	Testicle Atrophy	Testicle Swelling	Peyronie's Disease	Priapism	Gynecomastia	Menstrual Changes
ALCOHOLISM										
Antabuse		X								
ANGINA										
Inderal	X	X								
ANTICONVULSANTS AND ANTIEPILEPTICS										
Carbamazepine		X								
Phenytoin	X	X								
ANTI-INFLAMMATORIES										
Naproxen		X	X							
TRANQUILIZERS										
Barbiturates	X	X								
Diazepam	X		X	X						
Librax	X									
Librium	X									
Serentil	X	X	X							
Tranxene	X									

Table 5. SPECIFIC DRUGS AND SYMPTOMS OF NEGATIVE SIDE EFFECTS (cont.)

Condition/ Drug*	Reduced Desire	Erection Problems	Ejaculation Problems	Impaired Orgasm	Testicle Atrophy	Testicle Swelling	Peyronie's Disease	Priapism	Gynecomastia	Menstrual Changes
Valium	X		X	X						
Xanax	X		X	X						
APPETITE SUPPRESSANTS										
Pondimin	X	X	X							
CANCER										
Alkeran	X	X			X				X	X
Cytosar	X									
Cytoxan	X	X							X	
Leukeran	X	X							X	X
Matulane	X	X								
Myleran	X	X			X				X	X
Oncovin	X								X	
Velban	X	X								
DEPRESSION										
Asendin	X	X	X	X						
Clomipramine	X	X	X	X						
Desipramine	X	X	X	X					X	
Desyrel		X						X		

Doxepin	X	X						
Elavil	X	X	X		X	X		
Etrafon	X	X	X			X		X
Imipramine	X	X	X	X				
Janimine	X	X	X	X				
Limbitrol	X	X			X	X		
Lithium	X	X						
Ludiomil	X	X						
Marplan		X	X	X				
Nardil	X	X	X	X				
Norpramin	X	X	X	X		X		
Parnate		X	X					
Pertofrane	X	X	X	X		X		
Tofranil	X	X	X	X				
Vivactil	X	X	X		X	X		

FLUID RETENTION (For example, Edema, Glaucoma)

Cardrase	X							
Chlorthalidone	X		X					
Daranide	X		X					
Diamox	X		X					

Table 5. SPECIFIC DRUGS AND SYMPTOMS OF NEGATIVE SIDE EFFECTS (cont.)

Condition/Drug*	Reduced Desire	Erection Problems	Ejaculation Problems	Impaired Orgasm	Testicle Atrophy	Testicle Swelling	Peyronie's Disease	Priapism	Gynecomastia	Menstrual Changes
Edecrin		X								
Furosemide		X								
Lasix		X								
Neptazane	X	X								
FUNGUS										
Nizoral	X	X							X	
GASTROINTESTINAL PROBLEMS/ANTIEMETIC										
Metoclopramide	X	X							X	X
Reglan	X	X							X	X
HEART ARRHYTHMIA										
Disopyramide		X								
Inderal	X	X								
HEART FAILURE										
Digoxin	X	X							X	
Lanoxin	X								X	
HIGH BLOOD LIPIDS										
Atromid-S	X	X								

HIGH BLOOD PRESSURE (Antihypertensives; Hypotensives)

Aldactazide	X	X				X	X
Aldomet	X	X	X		X	X	
Apresoline	X			X			
Blocadren	X	X					
Catapres	X	X					
Clonidine	X	X	X				
Corgard	X	X					
Corzide	X	X					
Dibenzyline			X				
Diulo	X	X					
Diuril	X	X					
Esidrix	X	X					
Esimil	X		X				
Eutonyl	X	X	X				
Guanfacine	X	X					
Hydro-Diuril	X	X					
Hydronol	X	X					
Hygroton	X	X					
Hylorel	X	X	X				

Table 5. SPECIFIC DRUGS AND SYMPTOMS OF NEGATIVE SIDE EFFECTS (cont.)

Condition/ Drug*	Reduced Desire	Erection Problems	Ejaculation Problems	Impaired Orgasm	Testicle Atrophy	Testicle Swelling	Peyronie's Disease	Priapism	Gynecomastia	Menstrual Changes
Inderal	X	X								
Inversine	X	X								
Ismelin	X	X	X							
Lopressor	X						X			
Methyldopa	X	X	X	X						
Midamor	X	X								
Minipress	X	X						X		
Minizide	X	X								
Normozide		X(?)	X	X						
Oretic	X	X								
Propranolol	X	X								
Raudixin	X	X							X	
Rauzide	X	X							X	
Serpasil (Reserpine)	X	X	X						X	
Spironolactone	X	X							X	X
Thalitone	X	X								
Thiuretic	X	X								
Trandate	X	X	X	X				X		
Zaroxolyn		X								

MUSCLE RELAXANTS

	1	2	3	4	5
Baclofen	X	X			

PSYCHOSIS

	1	2	3	4	5
Clorpromazine	X	X			
Haloperidol	X	X		X	X
Mellaril	X	X	X	X	X
Navane	X				
Permitil	X	X			
Prolixin	X	X			
Serentil	X	X	X		
Stelazine		X	X	X	X
Taractan		X	X		X
Thioridazine	X	X	X	X	X
Thiothixene	X		X		
Thorazine	X	X	X		X
Trilafon	X	X	X		X

ULCERS

	1	2	3	4	5
Tagamet	X		X		
Zantac	X				

*This list includes a mixture of brand names and generic names depending on which we thought would be most helpful.

Further Readings

Cutler, W. B. *Hysterectomy: Before and after*. New York: Harper & Row, Publishers, 1988.

(A guide to preventing and coping with hysterectomy written in an easy-to-read style. Includes discussions of the roles of Hormone Replacement Therapy, exercise, and nutrition in maintaining health after hysterectomy.)

Schover, R., and Jensen, S. B. *Sexuality and Chronic Illness: A comprehensive approach*. New York: The Guilford Press, 1988.

(A medical guide to the causes, assessment, and treatment of sexual problems among the chronically ill.)

19

Sexually Transmitted Diseases (STDs)

Most sexually transmitted diseases can be uncomfortable or even painful, terribly inconvenient, embarrassing, and anxiety-producing. Some kill. They can be passed on to those we care most about—our wives, husbands, and lovers by having sex and to our offspring before they are born.

Infection with the AIDS virus (Human Immunodeficiency Virus—HIV) leads to devastating illness and death in a large percentage of those infected. Human papillomavirus (HPV), which causes genital warts, appears to provide the first step in the development of genital cancers. Syphilis (now a curable disease *if* diagnosed and treated in its early stages) can lead after many years to paralysis, severe mental illness, and ultimately death if untreated.

Other STDs either never disappear or leave behind damage that is difficult or impossible to erase. Although not the scourge it was first thought to be, once the herpes virus enters the body it remains for the rest of a person's life and causes painful sores that can appear over and over again for many years. If not treated early enough, other STD organisms (like chlamydia and gonorrhea), often lead to scarring of the reproductive tract. This can result in infertility and the risk of pregnancy in the Fallopian tubes (ectopic pregnancy), which results in internal bleeding and sometimes death. Finally, many STDs can be transmitted from the mother to the fetus during pregnancy or delivery, often resulting in much more devastating and life-threatening illnesses in newborns than in adults.

I hope it is abundantly clear that any symptoms of genital infection must be immediately diagnosed and treated to protect both the infected individuals and their sexual partners. One of the problems in diagnosing STDs is that many different organisms cause nearly identical symptoms. Much more detailed information about all the diseases discussed in this chapter can be found in Dr. King Holmes' latest book which is listed at the end of this chapter. Holmes is one of the world's most eminent authorities on this topic.

A Special Note to Readers

For many, this chapter may be the most difficult to read in this entire book. One reason is that the topic itself is both serious with regard to health and sensitive because it can cause conflicts within relationships. The primary reason for difficulty, however, is that it is filled with long, complicated words and phrases.

I have used the full scientific and medical terms for diseases and infectious organisms. It is these words you need to know to figure out what your physician has diagnosed, which organisms were found by tests, and what needs to be done next in terms of treatment and further testing.

As you read this chapter for general information about STDs, don't let the big words slow you down—just skim over them and read the sections on how to protect yourself and the types of symptoms to watch for.

Then, if at some point you are told you have one of the conditions described in the section "If Your Doctor Says You Have..." or one of the specific organisms discussed later in the chapter, you will be able to read more slowly and carefully the information that directly applies to you.

Always ask your doctor to write down or to spell out the correct name of any disease or infectious organism so you can look it up in this book or in books at the public library. That basic information will help you decide whether there are other tests you might need, if other treatment options are available, and if there are special problems to watch out for such as risk of recurrence.

SOME IMPORTANT FACTS ABOUT STDs

- A large number of individuals who are infected with STDs experience *no* symptoms (this is called being asymptomatic). This is especially true for women who develop PID (Pelvic Inflammatory Disease) which can result in infertility without symptoms.
- Even if no symptoms are present, sexually active men and women should be tested for possible infection with the common (often asymptomatic) STDs during annual medical examinations. This is especially important for those individuals who are not in mutual sexually exclusive relationships and those who have changed partners since their last doctor's appointment.
- With respect to a number of STDs, women are at higher risk of becoming infected from *one* act of intercourse than are men.
- In general, women are more likely to be "receivers" and men are more likely to be "infectors." That is, women are more likely to catch STDs from men than men are from women.
- Some people are at increased risk of catching an STD *only* because of the behavior of their sexual partner outside the relationship.
- Douching to prevent STD infection is *not* effective and may increase the risk that a genital infection moves into the reproductive organs (PID) and leads to infertility.

- All STDs are treatable and most are curable *if* they are diagnosed and treated early.
- If you think you have been exposed to an STD and are uncomfortable about going to your family doctor (many people feel this way), go to a clinic that specializes in diagnosing and treating STDs. These are easily located by calling your local public health office.
- Women should *not* douche before any pelvic examination as this can hide symptoms and alter test results, making diagnosis of STDs difficult or impossible.
- When an STD is diagnosed, sexual partners should always be treated at the same time to avoid the ping-pong effect (passing the infection back and forth between partners).
- After STD treatment, have a follow-up test to make sure that the infection is gone.
- Any pregnant woman who suspects she has been exposed to an STD should tell her physician. The sooner treatments begin on her or on the baby following birth, the less the danger of serious consequences.

THINGS YOU CAN DO TO LOWER YOUR RISKS

"Safer sex" guidelines were developed in response to the AIDS epidemic. However, these guidelines for protecting oneself from the AIDS virus (HIV) are just as effective at protecting you from other STD organisms. The reason these are called "safer" rather than "safe" is because they are not 100 percent guaranteed, but they clearly do reduce your risks *if* used properly and every time.

"Safer Sex" Guidelines

1. **Delay sexual intercourse as long as possible.** Abstinence is the only completely safe behavior.
2. **Restrict the number of sexual partners you have.** The fewer sexual partners you have in your lifetime, the smaller your chance of being exposed to an STD.
3. **You are at lower risk for catching STDs when you are in a *mutual sexually exclusive relationship.*** This means that you *and* your partner have sex only with each other. If neither you nor your partner is infected with an STD, then you can safely engage in *any* sexual activity with each other that you choose.
4. **Learn as much as possible about any *new* potential sexual partner, but don't accept answers at face value.** Unfortunately, research shows that people lie about things such as how many partners they have had. In one study, 47 percent of men and 42 percent of women admitted telling dates that they had had fewer partners than was really the case. Researchers suspect people are even more likely to lie about homosexual activity, sex with prostitutes, or the use of illegal drugs.
5. **Don't assume that what people call themselves (heterosexual or homo-sexual) tells you anything about their actual sexual behavior.** Studies of men from the general population show that more than 30 percent (1 out

of 3) have had at least one sexual experience with another male since puberty. Three studies of homosexual men reported that between 62 and 79 percent had engaged in heterosexual intercourse. Four other studies found that 15 to 26 percent of homosexual men had been married. A recent Kinsey Institute study of lesbian women found that 74 percent had engaged in heterosexual intercourse at least once since age 18. So don't assume that a female partner is automatically in a low-risk group for STDs or that a male partner has never had sex with other men.

Furthermore, do not fool yourself into thinking that you can "guess" the sexual orientation of a person by gestures or other behaviors. As the survey in Chapter 1 shows, nearly 1 out of 3 American adults *think* they can always tell, but this is not true.

6. **Avoid high-risk sexual behaviors until you are *certain* your partner is not infected with an STD.** The most risky behaviors are unprotected anal intercourse and unprotected vaginal intercourse. By "unprotected" we mean engaging in these behaviors without using a condom and a spermicide containing nonoxynol-9 or octoxynol.

Also refrain from unprotected oral-genital sex; fisting (insertion of a hand or fist into someone's rectum or vagina); or rimming (placing your mouth or tongue on or into another person's anus) unless you are certain neither you or your partner is infected. *Any* activity that exposes a person to blood, semen, vaginal secretions, menstrual blood, urine, feces, or saliva should be considered a high-risk behavior unless partners are in a mutual sexually exclusive relationship and neither is infected. The AIDS virus (HIV) and other STD organisms can enter the mucous membranes of the mouth, vagina, or rectum and through even microscopically small breaks anywhere on the skin.

7. **If you decide to have penile-anal intercourse, using condoms and a spermicide with nonoxynol-9 or octoxynol as an ingredient can provide good protection against many STDs.** Because the rectum produces no natural lubrication, the tissues are more easily subject to small tears or breaks than the vagina; use a water-based lubricant.

8. **If you decide to have penile-vaginal intercourse, using condoms and a spermicide with nonoxynol-9 or octoxynol as an ingredient can provide good protection against many STDs.** Condoms don't provide protection when an infectious area is not covered. For example, a herpes sore on the scrotum would not be covered. For how to use condoms properly, see Chapter 16.

9. **If you decide to engage in fellatio (oral sex on a penis), using a condom provides good protection if either of you is infected.** Put the condom on before touching the penis with your mouth, lips, or tongue.

10. **If you decide to engage in cunnilingus (oral sex on a vulva), placing a dental dam over the vulva provides good protection if either of you is infected.** Dental dams are thin sheets of latex rubber used by dentists to isolate an infected area of the mouth during dental work. You may have to search for dental dams; try a medical supply store.

11. **One way some people increase sexual stimulation is by using vibrators,**

dildos, or other "sex toys." These can provide pleasure and satisfaction and be one safer alternative to riskier activities as long as these items are not shared with another person until thoroughly washed with soap and water. Apply plenty of lubricant and use them gently to avoid irritating skin or breaking vaginal or rectal tissues if they're used for penetration.

12. **Rubbing bodies together without vaginal, anal, or oral contact is also an erotic and a "safer" activity if no semen or vaginal fluids come into contact with mucous membranes or broken areas of skin.**

13. **Mutual masturbation is both a pleasurable and a "safer" activity as long as semen or vaginal fluids touch only healthy, unbroken skin.** But remember that HIV and most other STD organisms are microscopically small and not visible to the naked eye; it doesn't take a visible sore or cut to permit entry into one's body.

14. **Showering or bathing together can be a highly erotic "safer" sex activity as long as semen or vaginal fluids touch only healthy skin.**

15. **Mutual touching, caressing, hugging, and massaging are other erotic and "safer" sex activities as long as neither person has open cuts or sores on the body, mouth, or lips.**

16. **Intimate talk and sharing sexual fantasies is safe and can be highly erotic for both partners.**

What's a Person to Do?

Until you have established a relationship that is based on trust and is mutually sexually exclusive, you must take responsibility for protecting your own health and the health of your partner. As you make new friends, if the relationship becomes potentially sexual, begin at the bottom of the "Safer Sex" guidelines with Number 16 and *gradually* work your way up through the different activities. For example, you might begin your new relationship by developing communication and sharing fantasies, and then add mutual touching or massage.

Linger at each stage and savor the increasing intimacy and building of trust. Many people have already learned that using "safer sex" activities can actually enhance sexual pleasure and contribute to building an intimate loving relationship while also protecting the health of both partners.

Surprising to many, there appear to be some positive aspects related to taking sex slowly and being cautious. Restricting sexual intercourse to a mutual sexually exclusive relationship often means getting to have sex more often—which may be rewarding for some people. In The Kinsey Institute's recent study of college students, for example, those in sexually exclusive relationships had an intercourse frequency of 86 times in the year before the survey while those in nonexclusive relationships averaged only 49 times. Since it takes time for partners to learn what touches and activities are especially arousing and satisfying to each other, sex may also be "better" in exclusive relationships.

I'm confused about who might have AIDS. After a divorce several years ago, I had a lot of "one-night stands." I have remarried and have had sex only with my husband since I met him three years ago. He also fooled around until we met, but now is faithful.

In articles about AIDS, one risk listed is having multiple partners (which we've both had), but neither of us is homosexual, nor have we had sex with homosexuals. Is there a chance that one of us could have AIDS?

In part that depends on how much you know about the sexual partners you and your husband had before you became a sexually exclusive couple. Can you be *sure* that none of your sexual partners were users or former users of intravenous drugs, recipients of a blood transfusion or blood products, or bisexual males? What do you know about the sexual partners they had contact with before you or your husband? Most people don't ask for or volunteer this kind of personal information during a "one night stand." In fact, research shows that when asked about these things people often lie.

Unless you both are absolutely certain that none of your previous sexual partners (and their other sexual partners) engaged in high-risk behaviors, there is at least some risk that one or both of you were exposed to HIV or to some other STD that might cause an infection but have no symptoms.

If you and your husband always used condoms and spermicidal foam containing nonoxynol-9 in those sexual contacts, then the risk of having been exposed to HIV would be greatly reduced but not completely eliminated.

I have had sexual partners who simply cannot maintain an erection when they wear a condom. After numerous attempts, the problem persisted. I have herpes simplex and wish to protect my partners as much as possible from contracting it, and I want to protect myself from AIDS and other STDs. Even using thinner prophylactics, which are advertised as "more sensitive," does not seem to help.
   Why are some men able to perform normally with condoms, while others aren't? And what suggestions do you have for dealing with this problem?

You are to be commended for your sensitive and responsible attitude toward the use of condoms to protect yourself and your partners. It is important to remember that condoms can *only* provide protection against transmitting herpes if the sore is completely covered.

It is true that some men have difficulty maintaining an erection while using a condom. Some experts believe this may be caused by the reduction in sensitivity resulting from the layer of latex covering the penis. Others, however, believe erection problems are psychologically based, related to anxiety about performance or the belief that the condom will somehow affect the erection.

Some experts recommend that couples put on the condom as part of their sexual foreplay. This practice reduces interruptions in lovemaking and may allow more spontaneity later.

While you are experimenting with more sensitive condoms, make sure you use only the latex variety. Research has shown that condoms made from natural materials (such as animal intestines) may not be as effective in inhibiting the transmission of the AIDS virus or other STD organisms. The addition of a spermicide containing nonoxynol-9 or octoxynol probably increases protection.

Finally, use only a water-based lubricant (such as K-Y Jelly) with the condoms. Any oil-based lubricant—including Vaseline, Crisco, butter, Nivea, Vaseline Intensive Care and baby oil—can cause the condom to quickly erode during intercourse.

THERE IS NO ONE DISEASE CALLED VD

How can a person tell whether they have VD or just something else? I recently had sex with a guy I'd been dating and began having vaginal itching. Should I be alarmed? There are no sores. What are the signs of VD and how long does it take for these symptoms to show up?

There is no single disease called VD (venereal disease). In the past this phrase was a blanket classification that included all sexually transmitted diseases (STDs). Now more than 50 diseases are called STDs and each has its own different infectious organism, symptoms, tests, and treatment. Vaginal itching can be a sign of infection and you must have a medical examination and complete testing to diagnose which organism is involved and what treatment will be successful. Delaying proper diagnosis and treatment risks progression to PID and later infertility.

I just had a knock-down, drag-out fight with my father-in-law. He claims that in his day (he's 62), people had higher morals. He says that nobody slept around (had sex before marriage) and that we can all thank the Woodstock generation for the current spread of disease. I told him that somebody must have been sleeping around because they sure did have STDs in the 1940s.

At the same time, I have to admit that the epidemic proportions of sexual diseases indicates that people are, indeed, sleeping around more these days. Are there other reasons why more people are contracting STDs?

You are right: People did "sleep around" in your father-in-law's day. Kinsey's interviews of more than 12,000 men and women in the 1940s and 1950s showed that sex before marriage and extramarital sex are nothing new. It is also true that more unmarried adults and teenagers are having intercourse with more partners now than in the 1940s. These changing sexual patterns are only one reason the incidence of STDs is higher than ever before.

There are other reasons, too. Diagnosis and treatment are better, so more people go to physicians. More STD organisms like chlamydia and the viruses that cause herpes and genital warts have been identified. Reporting is more systematic. The Centers for Disease Control are collecting more statistics on how many people are infected and how many new cases are contracted each year. Another factor is that the popularity of the Pill and IUD led to a dramatic drop in condom use.

Some researchers speculate that there might also be a connection between the increase in STDs and increased mobility. The availability and lower cost of air travel and the fact that most Americans have cars makes travel easier and more feasible. People then can have sex with partners far from home and either spread a disease or have a higher risk of being infected.

Because STDs continue to be associated with "immorality" and "sin," as your father-in-law apparently believes, there is still a reluctance to generously fund programs designed to inhibit the spread of STDs. Public schools in the United States have not provided adequate education to help students understand and prevent transmission and spread of STDs, even though we know that many students are sexually active. This differs dramatically from some European countries, where such education is included in schools as a matter of course. Until recently in the U.S. it was even unacceptable to say the word *condom* on TV, let alone advertise them in mainstream magazines.

As you can see, there are a number of likely reasons why the incidence of many STDs has increased over the last three decades. But your father-in-law should also realize that sexual intimacy, and the diseases that may accompany it, did not begin with Woodstock. In fact, from ancient times to the present sharp increases in the rates of STDs have been more directly associated with wars than with cultural events.

I am 32, married, and have two beautiful children. When I was 19, I had my first sexual experience with a man I loved dearly. Afterwards, I felt itchy and sore. A week later the itch was worse, there was a greenish discharge, and I noticed a swollen-type sore on my vaginal lips. I was terrified and thought I had VD.

I was young, came from a strict family, and was too afraid to go to a doctor. When my boyfriend next returned from the service, he didn't mention anything. I assumed that men know more about such things than women and he would say something if he had VD. He never did. Later I took some antibiotics on my own.

Two years later I finally went to a doctor and told him I had a vaginal infection. He did tests, said it was a yeast infection, and gave me a cream which did clear up the discharge. He also mentioned I didn't have VD, even though I had been too embarrassed to tell the truth.

Now I regret being so stupid and not going to the doctor sooner. I worried myself constantly then, and after all these years I still worry and am embarrassed about it. I hope young people today don't wait out of fear like I did. Did I have VD? How long does VD stay in your body? I've heard that once VD gets in your body it can't be cured.

It's not possible from your description to say whether you had one of the 50 or so STDs in your youth. Having a sore on the labia could be a symptom of several different STDs, such as yeast, syphilis, or herpes. But you probably would have known whether or not you had syphilis by the time you got married (since many states require a blood test for syphilis before granting a marriage license) and if it were herpes, you would probably have had another attack.

At this point, the only way for you to be completely free of this worry is to consult a physician and have whatever tests are appropriate.

You're right to be concerned about today's young people. Unfortunately, most don't act any more responsibly than you did when you became sexually active. Individuals must accept responsibility for maintaining their health if they are sexually active. Because testing can be done anonymously in most communities (and without charge at most public STD clinics), there really is no valid excuse for not being tested and treated.

I always thought that most sexually transmitted diseases could be passed along during oral sex. However, recently a friend visited a VD clinic and claims they told him that the chances of contracting a disease during oral sex are "highly unlikely." Is the clinic right, or am I?

You are. There are no data on the frequency, but there is plenty of clinical evidence that many STDs can be transmitted through oral-genital contact. Gonorrhea, herpes, human papillomavirus (warts), Candida albicans (yeast), and syphilis are among them. This is why many STD specialists routinely take throat cultures of their patients.

The mucous membranes of the mouth are similar to those of the genitals, so if the mouth comes in contact with an infected area—a penis with herpes lesions, for instance—it can definitely become infected as well.

I'm a 54-year-old male. With all the different STDs around, is it possible for a couple to get tested for everything in one shot and get a clean bill of health, once and for all?

I've met someone who says he was tested for VD and is OK. Is that true?

Each STD has its own tests or test so one test could not give anyone a "clean bill of health." It's important to understand that tests only evaluate a person's health up until the moment of testing. Someone who claims to be "safe" because of a negative test result might have become infected sometime after the testing. For that reason, the idea of having an identification card (often suggested by some groups) supposedly indicating a person is "safe" is not only unscientific, but potentially dangerous if it leads sexual partners to lower their guard and reduce or abandon preventative efforts.

Is it possible for me to run a test myself to identify the presence of a sexually transmitted disease?

No. All of the tests that reliably report whether a person has one of the many STDs require trained medical personnel to collect proper samples, sophisticated equipment, and expertise at interpreting the results. During a detailed medical examination, it only takes a few minutes to collect samples of blood, tissue or fluids needed for most STD tests. Samples are taken from all body areas that might be involved, not just the genital area. It usually takes several days to get the results and as with any type of disease testing, the results are not always absolutely clear. In some cases, a second test is needed, or a patient may be referred to a specialist who can more accurately interpret symptoms and test results.

There *is* something you can do on your own, however. Write to the American Social Health Association *(see page 490)* and ask for a brochure that describes the symptoms of the various STDs. *But if you suspect you've been exposed to an STD, sending away for pamphlets should not be your first priority. Make a doctor's appointment **today** or go to an STD clinic.*

Are there any harmful effects on a baby whose mother has a venereal disease? Can the baby be born with the same disease?

Maternal infection with an STD during pregnancy or delivery can have harmful effects such as spontaneous abortion, stillbirth, prematurity, and infection of the fetus or newborn. Among the many STDs that can cause fetal or neonatal illness or death are AIDS, syphilis, gonorrhea, chlamydia, genital herpes, and human papillomavirus (all discussed later in this chapter).

These are all good reasons for early and regular prenatal care which should include tests for all obvious infections and any diseases for which the mother may be at risk. The health and safety of both the mother and fetus or newborn are also good reasons to use condoms during pregnancy if there is *any* chance the pregnant woman believes she could contract an STD from her sexual partner.

Is it true that once you've had a sexually transmitted disease you are immune from catching it again?

No, that is definitely not true. STDs are not like chicken pox and mumps which you can only catch once.

IF THE DOCTOR SAYS YOU HAVE...

The following are medical conditions or syndromes you may be told that you have. Although you might not think of them as STDs, they can be caused by STD organisms or by bacteria from your own body that have grown out of control or been transferred to the genitals from the anus.

This is why the diagnosis and treatment of these infections can be complex and why you may need a number of tests and examinations before your physician can identify exactly which organism is causing your problem and how best to treat it. If the first treatment doesn't clear up the infection, ask to be tested for other organisms.

These are listed in alphabetical order to make it easier for you to look up the words your physician may use. *(To see where these various sites of infection are located in the body, look at the illustrations in Chapters 2 and 3.)*

- **Bacterial vaginosis** means infection of the vagina that does not involve swelling or discomfort. There may be an unpleasant odor, and sometimes a slightly increased vaginal discharge; many women have no symptoms. Causes include infection by Gardnerella vaginalis and other bacteria which have replaced the normal vaginal organisms.

- **Cystitis** means infection of the bladder and most often affects women. It is relatively rare in men because the longer length of their urethra makes it more difficult for infectious organisms to travel to the bladder. Symptoms in women include pain or burning on urination (felt inside the body), frequency and urgency of urination, or blood in the urine. Infectious organisms include Escherichia coli and other bacteria found in the gastrointestinal tract, staphylococcus, and herpes simplex virus.

  Some preventive measures include urinating, even if just a few drops, soon after sexual intercourse and keeping the urine more acidic (which is thought to help kill bacteria) by drinking cranberry juice. Certain sexual positions—vaginal penetration from behind, for instance—can increase the chances of bacterial transfer, so try other positions. Also, those who have anal sex should make absolutely sure their partner's penis is washed thoroughly before having vaginal intercourse.

- **Ectocervicitis** means infection of the outer surface of the cervix. Symptoms can include vaginal discharge and those listed under vaginitis (see below).

The following organisms can be involved: herpes simplex virus, Chlamydia trachomatis, Trichomonas vaginalis, Candida albicans, and cytomegalovirus.

- **Endocervicitis** means infection of the inside of the cervical canal. Symptoms may include vaginal discharge but often there are no symptoms; this is usually diagnosed in the female partner after urethritis symptoms send a male partner to his doctor. Chlamydia trachomatis, Neisseria gonorrhoeae, and herpes simplex virus are the infectious organisms usually involved.

- **Endometritis** means infection of the lining of the uterus. Symptoms are similar to PID (see below). Infectious organisms include Neisseria gonorrhoeae, Chlamydia trachomatis, Mycoplasma hominis, Escherichia coli, Gardnerella vaginalis, other bacteria, and perhaps some viruses. With careful testing, several different organisms are often found to be present at the same time.

- **Epididymitis** means infection of the epididymis. Symptoms may be similar to urethritis or include pain, swelling, and tenderness in the scrotum (almost always on only one side), and fever. This infection can be caused by Chlamydia trachomatis, Neisseria gonorrhoeae, and other bacteria.

- **Infectious prostatitis** means infection of the prostate gland. Symptoms include inflammation (swelling), difficulty in urinating, increased frequency and urgency of urination, pain and burning at urination, and dribbling following urination. The causes are not very well understood. In some cases STD organisms seem to be involved, but their role is unclear. Men often do not have symptoms for many years.

  The causes of prostate infection are sometimes difficult to diagnose and often even more difficult to treat. Most drugs simply do not reach the prostate gland. Long-term, low-dose medication may be necessary. It is also important to be rechecked even after symptoms disappear and after all the medication has been taken to make sure that the infectious organism is truly controlled.

- **Nongonococcal urethritis** (NGU) is the term used to describe any inflammation of the urethra (urethritis) *not* caused by gonorrhea. NGU affects both men and women and is one of the most common STDs. NGU is an infection of the urethra caused by bacteria-like organisms. The two most common bacteria involved in NGU are Chlamydia trachomatis in both women and men, and Ureaplasma urealyticum in men.

  No one is sure how many people are affected. But studies have shown that in the United States and Great Britain NGU is twice as prevalent as gonorrhea. On college campuses, the incidence of NGU is five times greater than that of gonorrhea.

  About 30 percent of infected men have no symptoms. NGU symptoms in men are similar to those for gonorrhea and other urinary-tract infections: a slight discharge from the penis and discomfort while urinating. The majority of women with NGU have no symptoms, although if the organism has also infected the genital tract some report vaginal discharge or pelvic pain. A sore throat can signal that the organism causing NGU is present there, a result of oral-genital sexual activity.

  Even though NGU can be difficult to diagnose, if it is caused by Chlamydia trachomatis it can be cleared up in 80 percent of cases by taking the antibiotic drug tetracycline for eight to ten days. Most of the remaining 20 percent respond to taking tetracycline for a longer time. Erythromycin can be substituted for pregnant women or for people allergic to tetracycline.

• **Pelvic Inflammatory Disease (PID)** is a term that is used to describe bacterial infection of the Fallopian tubes, the uterus, and/or the ovaries. Scarring resulting from PID can cause infertility. In 1980 it was estimated that approximately 857,000 American women experienced a new episode of PID. The rate of PID has been increasing. In the United States, England, and Sweden the estimated numbers of new cases each year range from 10 to 14 in each 1000 women of reproductive age, with the most cases occurring in women 15 to 24 years old.

   PID can be caused by Neisseria gonorrhoeae, Chlamydia trachomatis, other sexually transmitted organisms, and infections related to using an IUD (intrauterine device) and childbirth. PID can also be caused by Escherichia coli; bacteria from the rectum, which may be transferred to the vagina by improper wiping after defecation; or by having vaginal intercourse after anal intercourse without first thoroughly washing the penis. Use of the Pill for contraception has been shown to provide some protection, particularly if it is taken for more than a year.

   Many women with PID have *no* symptoms, but if symptoms develop they may include tenderness around the abdomen, lower abdominal pain or cramps, cervical discharge, bleeding between menstrual periods, and tenderness when the cervix is touched. In acute PID, a woman may also experience irregular and unusually painful menstruation, pain during intercourse, severe abdominal pain, vomiting, nausea, and headache. Treatment usually involves antibiotics to fight the infection, but some acute or chronic cases also require surgery to remove the infected area.

• **Proctitis** means infection of the anus and rectum. Symptoms include rectal pain and bleeding, mucous discharge, and diarrhea. This can be caused by STD organisms either as the result of spreading from the genitals (in women) or directly from receptive anal intercourse.

• **Salpingitis** means infection of the Fallopian tubes. Symptoms are similar to PID and causes include Neisseria gonorrhoeae, Chlamydia trachomatis, Mycoplasma hominis, Escherichia coli, Gardnerella vaginalis, other bacteria, and perhaps some viruses. Several different organisms are often present at the same time. Salpingitis can also result in infertility.

• **Urethritis** means infection of the urethra. The name is the same for both men and women. Symptoms in men may include discharge from the urethra, pain, burning and discomfort at urination, and itching at the tip of the penis. Symptoms in women may include urgency to urinate, burning or pain felt inside the body before urine comes out and during urination, and low abdominal pain. Males are more likely to have symptoms than are females, but many men and even more women have no symptoms.

   Organisms involved include Neisseria gonorrhoeae, Chlamydia trachomatis, Ureaplasma urealyticum, herpes simplex virus, Candida albicans, Escherichia coli, other bacteria and rarely Trichomonas vaginalis.

- **Vaginitis** means infection of the vagina that, unlike bacterial vaginosis, does cause swelling and/or discomfort. Symptoms may also include increased vaginal discharge that may have an odor, swelling, itching, burning, or pain in the vagina; and pain with intercourse. Symptoms may worsen during or immediately following menstruation. Organisms involved include Trichomonas vaginalis and Candida albicans.

- **Vulvitis** means infection of the external female genitals. Symptoms may include burning or pain felt at the urinary opening or on the outside of the genitals after urination begins; increased vaginal discharge; irritation, burning, or itching of the vulva; and sores or lesions on the vulva. Organisms that can cause this include herpes simplex virus, Candida albicans, and possibly human papillomavirus.

SEXUALLY TRANSMITTED DISEASE ORGANISMS

Now we will discuss some specific STD organisms and the diseases they cause.

Bacteria

Gonorrhea

Neisseria gonorrhoeae is the organism that causes gonorrhea, commonly called "clap" and one of the oldest known diseases. Gonorrhea means "flow of seed," probably because the characteristic discharge from the penis was misinterpreted to be semen rather than the symptom of an infection. Symptoms of gonorrhea in men were described in the writings of ancient China, Egypt, Rome, and Greece and in the book of Leviticus in the Bible. More than 400 years before the birth of Christ, the ancient Greek physician Hippocrates appeared to have recognized that gonorrhea was sexually transmitted, because he wrote that a disease with similar symptoms resulted from "the pleasures of Venus."

As with most STDs, accurate information on the number of people who become infected each year and the total number of cases in most countries is not known. However, it appears that in the United States, gonorrhea has shown a slight decline since its last peak in 1975. In Sweden, the rates have decreased considerably more than in the United States, probably as a result of universal sex education in schools and the greater acceptability and availability of condoms.

Gonorrhea is almost exclusively transmitted through unprotected sexual activity (or during birth from mother to baby). There is no evidence that transmission occurs from toilet seats or other similar objects. The risk to a man who has intercourse with an infected woman one time is estimated to be 20 percent; that is, he has a one in five chance of catching the disease. If he has intercourse with that same woman four times (or with four different women who have gonorrhea), his chances increase to 60 to 80 percent (six to eight out of ten). Researchers believe that the risk for a woman to become infected by a man is higher, probably because women retain the infected semen in their vaginas.

This organism usually infects the urinary and genital tracts, with the rectum, the throat, and the eyes infected less frequently. Serious illness results if the bacteria spread up the genital tract to infect the Fallopian tubes or epididymis, or if they enter the bloodstream.

Infection of the urinary tract is the most common form of gonorrhea in men. Symptoms appear within one to fourteen days, with the majority of men developing symptoms two to five days after infection. The most prominent symptoms are first, difficult or painful urination, followed by the development of a discharge from the urinary opening. Without treatment these symptoms usually disappear after several weeks, and in 95 percent of men within six months. More serious illness results when the bacteria ascend into the internal reproductive organs and cause infection of the epididymis (epididymitis), the prostate (prostatitis), or the seminal vesicles (seminal vesiculitis).

In women, the most common site of infection is the cervix, although 90 percent of these patients will have Neisseria gonorrhoeae in the urinary tract as well. Only women who have had hysterectomies are likely to experience urinary-tract infection alone. Infection of the Skene's and Bartholin's glands is also common.

A large proportion of women do not develop any symptoms and have what may be called a "silent" or asymptomatic infection. In those women who do develop gonorrhea symptoms, these are likely to appear within ten days of infection and include increased vaginal discharge, painful or difficult urination, bleeding from the vagina between menstrual periods, and heavy menstrual bleeding. Genital gonorrhea during pregnancy can result in spontaneous abortion, premature delivery, and infection of the amniotic sac (which surrounds and protects the fetus during pregnancy), and infection of the newborn.

If untreated, the infection can travel into the female reproductive organs and cause PID. This occurs in about 10 to 20 percent of infected women. Long-term effects resulting from damage particularly to the Fallopian tubes include infertility and ectopic (tubal) pregnancy—a life-threatening situation.

Infection of the anus and rectum is involved in 35 to 50 percent of women with infection of the cervix and usually has no symptoms. Forty percent of homosexual men with gonorrhea are infected only in the rectal area as a result of receptive anal intercourse with an infected partner. Men are more likely to have symptoms that include constipation, discomfort or pain, urgency to defecate, bloody stools, and discharge.

In a few rare cases, the bacteria invade the bloodstream and cause arthritis and skin diseases.

Treatment involves one large dose of antibiotic, such as ampicillin, amoxicillin, ceftriaxone, or spectinomycin—depending on the type of gonorrhea bacteria discovered. This should be followed by seven days of medication (either tetracycline or erythromycin) for chlamydia, which is also often present.

The best protection against either infection or transmission of gonorrhea is following the "Safer Sex" guidelines, earlier in this chapter.

How does one get tested for gonorrhea? Is it something that the physician performs automatically when she does a PAP test?

No, physicians don't routinely perform gonorrhea tests with every Pap smear, although perhaps they should. Basically, gonorrhea tests involve taking a sample of penile or vaginal discharge. In the Gram-stain test, a sample of discharge from the cervix or the urethra is treated with a special stain that makes the gonorrhea bacteria visible when looked at through a microscope. In a culture test, which is more accurate for females, bacteria are placed in a laboratory dish containing a special material that encourages gonorrhea bacteria to grow. If present, they will multiply and can be identified.

If I suspect I have gonorrhea, can I treat myself with penicillin pills I happen to have? I've heard that penicillin will cure it. I'd rather not see a doctor.

Do *not* attempt to treat yourself. Penicillin doesn't work on some strains of gonorrhea bacteria. You must see a doctor to find out which strain of gonorrhea has caused your infection, to determine the appropriate treatment, and to treat any other STD organisms that might be present.

Syphilis

Syphilis, caused by the organism Treponema pallidum, is a disease whose symptoms can take a vast variety of forms, does not resolve without treatment, can last for many decades in the body, and inevitably leads to death. If diagnosed it can be treated with penicillin and cured. It has great historical importance because of the many influential individuals it affected—from kings to statesmen to artists. Before penicillin, syphilis was a very common disease that infected all segments of Western society. Some of its symptoms are described in biblical and other ancient writings. The current medical name comes from a 1530 poem about an infected swineherd named Syphilis.

The first European epidemic arose in the late 1400s around the time Columbus returned from America, which led people to believe that the disease had been acquired from the natives in the New World. There is, however, little evidence suggestive of syphilis among early native Americans; other similar disease organisms prevalent in tropical climates may have mutated to become the syphilis bacteria. It is more likely that the return of Columbus and the rapid spread and increase in the severity of syphilis were a coincidence.

A more likely cause of the epidemic was widespread warfare in Europe during this period, involving the movement of large numbers of soldiers and the inevitable camp followers, providing an ideal environment for the rapid spread of an STD. (Similarly enormous increases in STDs were associated with World War I and World War II; the conflict in Vietnam may have been a major factor in the rise in STDs during the 1960s and 1970s.)

As we have seen today with the AIDS epidemic, people prefer always to blame a new STD on someone else. Just as Americans pointed to Africa and Haiti, for example, when trying to explain the origin of AIDS, so syphilis was called the "French disease" by the Italians and the "Italian disease" by the French during its initial epidemic.

In the United States, the number of syphilis cases rose during World War I and World War II, declined during the 1950s, then rose again in the 1960s.

Factors thought to be involved in this increase included decreases in governmental funding for STD control and a shift from public health clinics to private doctors' offices for treatment. In 1987 the number of cases per year increased a dramatic 27 percent in both men and women.

Syphilis is most often transmitted by sexual contact. It can be acquired during vaginal intercourse, anal intercourse, or oral sex with an infected partner. The chance of contracting syphilis from one contact with an infected sexual partner is estimated as one in three. Syphilis is usually infectious and transmissible only during the first few years an individual has the disease. However, it can be transmitted from an infected mother to her fetus for many years, although after approximately eight years the risk of maternal/fetal transmission is nearly zero.

Unlike gonorrhea, syphilis spreads throughout the body shortly after it enters. If the infection is not treated, it typically goes through three stages. The primary stage is characterized by the appearance of a sore or lesion called a chancre at the site where the bacteria entered the body. The chancre appears between 10 and 90 days after exposure. This is usually a single sore that is rounded, rubbery, and painless. Most often located on the genitals or near the anus, the chancre can also appear on the lips, tongue, tonsils, breasts, or fingers. Even if untreated at this stage, the chancre heals in a few weeks.

The secondary stage usually begins within a few weeks or months of the initial infection. It is characterized by a general illness including one or more of the following symptoms: rash, low fever, feeling of general discomfort, sore throat, headache, swollen glands, weight loss, patchy or thinning hair loss, and general aches and pains. Contact with the rash can result in transmission of syphilis from an infected to a healthy individual. In some cases there are also signs of brain or spinal cord disease during this phase. If untreated, the symptoms of the secondary phase also disappear, and a period of time passes (up to thirty years). During this time the bacteria are still infecting the body but there are no outward signs of disease; this is called the latency period.

The final or tertiary stage is characterized by very serious disability that may involve paralysis, severe psychiatric and mental illness, and then death.

Treatment of the primary or secondary stages involves one large dose of benzathine penicillin (given in two injections, one in each buttock), followed by daily injections for seven to twelve days. If the patient is allergic to penicillin, then tetracycline capsules are taken four times a day for fifteen days. Treatment during the latency stage may require a longer period of antibiotic therapy. The earlier syphilis is treated, the fewer health consequences result. This is why it is important that *all* genital sores be checked by a physician as soon as they appear.

See the "Safer Sex" guidelines for ways to prevent transmission of this organism.

I've read that the most sensitive test for syphilis is one done on scrapings from a lesion. Approximately two years ago, I had a blood test for syphilis, which was negative. However, when the test was administered, the lesions had disappeared.

Could I still have syphilis even though that blood test was negative and I've had no symptoms? If this is possible, how can I be sure I don't have syphilis?

If you have had no further symptoms since your initial negative blood test, it is highly unlikely that you have syphilis. However, if you continue to worry, or if you think you've been exposed to syphilis since your last test, ask your physician or an STD clinic about having one of the blood tests described below.

Syphilis progresses through stages, and the most sensitive tests vary according to which stage a patient is suspected to be in. During the primary syphilis stage or whenever a lesion is present physicians will do a "dark-field" examination using a fluorescent antibody technique on the tissue specimen taken from the chancre and embedded on paraffin (DFA-TP). This is the most accurate test to determine whether a sore is due to primary syphilis or some other cause (like herpes).

Blood tests are the most accurate way to diagnose the secondary stage of syphilis. Some excellent blood tests include the VDRL slide test, unheated serum reagin test (USR), rapid plasma reagin card test (RPR), automated reagin test (ART), reagin screen test (RST), FTA-ABS test, and the MHA-TP test. These tests can also be used to check whether treatment has been successful.

Detection of syphilis in a late stage of the disease process can also be done with the FTA-ABS test, but determining whether the nervous system has been affected requires examination of a sample of cerebrospinal fluid (the liquid that surrounds the spinal cord and the brain).

Gardnerella Vaginalis

Gardnerella vaginalis is an organism that is one of the most common causes of vaginal infections. These infections are often referred to as bacterial vaginosis or nonspecific vaginitis—misleading because men can also contract and transmit Gardnerella vaginalis.

Many bacteria and other organisms are often present in the healthy vagina. One researcher has suggested that Gardnerella vaginalis constitute about 1 percent of the vaginal organisms in normal women. They pose no problem unless their numbers greatly increase. Gardnerella vaginalis has been found in the vaginas of 40 percent of women with nonspecific vaginal infections.

In males there are usually no symptoms. This increases the likelihood that a man will unknowingly infect his partners. Women infected with Gardnerella vaginalis may experience an unpleasant vaginal odor and discharge, but often the infection has no symptoms.

Gardnerella must be cultured in a laboratory to be accurately diagnosed, and may have to be detected indirectly by indicators such as the vaginal fluids having a higher-than-normal pH level (more alkaline/less acidic). Examination of vaginal fluid under a microscope reveals cells that are clues to the existence of these bacteria. It is very important not to douche before being examined; this makes diagnosis difficult or impossible.

Treatment recommendations vary, with some researchers reporting that metronidazole (Flagyl is one brand name) is effective in 90 percent of cases. Others report that clindamycin and ampicillin are sometimes effective. However, sulfonamide creams often prescribed for vaginal yeast infections are *not* effective against Gardnerella vaginalis. Even with treatment, recurrence is common and up to 80 percent of women have been reported to develop another bout of bacterial vaginosis within nine months of metronidazole treatment.

There is disagreement about how to treat the male sexual partners of infected women. Even though most men are found to have these organisms in the urethra (without having symptoms), treating the male partners with metronidazole does not appear to prevent the women from becoming reinfected later.

I need information about the vaginal disease Gardnerella. How do these infections get started in the first place? Is it uncleanliness? Why do they keep coming back?

It is not yet clear what causes gardnerella to multiply and become an infection, but poor personal hygiene is not thought to be involved. Being sexually active, having more than one sexual partner, use of an IUD, childbirth, and having a cervical infection are factors associated with increased risk of gardnerella infection.

Reasons why bacterial vaginosis recurs so often include reinfection by an infected partner; bacteria which are inactivated but not killed, and so grow again; failure of the normal protective vaginal organisms (lactobacillus) to reestablish themselves after treatment; and infection by other organisms which were not killed by the first treatment.

Chlamydia

Chlamydia trachomatis is a bacterium that is also a parasite—in order to survive, it must live inside the cells of another organism—in this case the cells of humans. It is a major cause of infection in the male and female urethra, the male epididymis, and the female cervix, uterus, and Fallopian tubes. Thus it is a common factor in the development of PID. PID and epididymitis often lead to female and male infertility, and increased risk of ectopic (tubal) pregnancy in women.

Chlamydia is frequently found to co-exist with other infectious organisms. Because chlamydia has been difficult to identify, treatment of other more easily identifiable organisms may not cure chlamydia, and so the infection continues.

Unfortunately, chlamydia often are able to flourish in the body for years without any symptoms while still damaging the reproductive tract. For example, only about one out of three women with chlamydial infection of the cervix have any symptoms. Many cases of chlamydial infection of the Fallopian tubes, which result in scarring and damage, show no symptoms that this damage is occurring. Although in the industrialized world chlamydia is primarily a sexually transmitted organism, in the developing world nonsexual means of transmission are prevalent. Trachoma (an infection of the eyes that can result in blindness) is contracted in these countries during the birth process or early in life from physical contact. Chlamydia can also be transferred with the hands from the genitals to the eyes.

By the late 1980s chlamydia had become the most common sexually transmitted bacterial infection in both North America and Europe. It was estimated that by 1986 there were at least 4 million new cases developing each year in the United States. Of these, almost 60 percent are thought to be in women. Exact figures are not possible since chlamydial infections are not reportable to national health agencies in the United States, and until quite recently there was no readily available test that could be done by physicians quickly in their offices.

About 40 percent of nongonococcal urethritis (NGU) in men is caused by chlamydia. Chlamydial infections of the urethra are now twice as common as those caused by gonorrhea. Chlamydial infections are probably more easily transmitted from men to women than from women to men. When the female sexual partners of men with NGU caused by chlamydia are tested, between 60 and 70 percent of them have chlamydial cervicitis.

Happily, the future looks brighter because a new test for chlamydia has been developed. Called the Abbott Testpack, it evaluates a swab from the cervix (like a Pap smear), can be done in a doctor's office, and the results are available in thirty minutes. Although it identifies only about 75 to 80 percent of those who are infected, when the test is positive it is rarely wrong. Having several tests done over a period of time may raise the rate of detection of the organism for those women who are in a high-risk group and whose first test result is negative.

Women who are at low risk can be fairly comfortable about accepting a negative result as correct. Dr. Robert Jones, a chlamydia expert and STD researcher at the Indiana University School of Medicine, recommends that all sexually active women who have had more than one partner or who have changed partners have this new chlamydia test done each year when they get their annual Pap smear.

Based on how common this infection appears to be and the permanent damage it can cause, all female partners of men with NGU should be examined for signs of chlamydial infection and treated with tetracycline or doxycycline for seven to fourteen days. Also, the male partners of women with PID and cervicitis should be treated. In men without symptoms, researchers have found chlamydia in 2 percent to 31 percent of every group studied. If chlamydial infection is found in either the man or the woman, both partners should be treated at the same time and then retested to make sure the organism is gone.

A friend of mine was recently diagnosed as having chlamydia. She was upset and thought her husband had been unfaithful to her, but her doctor said you could be infected with the chlamydia organism for five to fifteen years without knowing it. This would mean that her husband had gotten it from an old girlfriend before they were married, and it was dormant all these years. Is this true?

Nearly any sexually active person might have a chlamydia infection without knowing it, and it may be difficult to determine exactly when a person became infected. If symptoms do occur, they are similar to many other STDs and most often include burning or increased frequency of urination and discharge from the urethra or vagina. It is also not unusual for these symptoms to disappear without treatment. Given all this, it is clearly possible to have chlamydia without knowing it and without knowing exactly where or when you got it.

Can a mother spread chlamydia to her baby? If so, is it serious?

Yes, infected women can transmit this organism to their babies at birth, and even babies delivered by Caesarean surgery may be infected if the amniotic sac ("bag of waters") has broken before delivery. Several studies of pregnant women around the United States found from 2 to 26 percent carried chlamydia in their cervix. In adolescent pregnancy clinics, up to 37 percent of pregnant teens have been identified as infected with chlamydia. Most of these teens and women have no symptoms.

If the disease transmitted at or before birth is not treated, 11 to 20 percent of the infants develop chlamydial pneumonia, 18 to 50 percent are infected with conjunctivitis (inflammation of the eyes that can lead to blindness), and infection of the nose, throat, and vagina are also possible. Chlamydia infection transmitted at birth and left untreated is a major cause of blindness (trachoma) in developing countries. Although chlamydia cannot be transmitted by casual contact, if an infected mother touched her genitals and then touched her infant's eyes, the chlamydia could be transferred.

Yeast and Protozoa

Candida albicans

Candida albicans is a yeast that lives in the vaginas of an estimated 20 percent of healthy reproductive-age women. Like syphilis and gonorrhea, this is also not a new disease. In 1849 J. Wilkerson, an English physician, reported that vaginal candidiasis was caused by a yeast.

When the vaginal environment is normal, this yeast produces no symptoms. Certain conditions appear to stimulate overgrowth of the yeast in some women, causing vulvovaginal candidiasis. These conditions include pregnancy, use of high-estrogen-content birth control pills, diabetes, and taking antibiotics (particularly broad-spectrum types like tetracycline and ampicillin) to treat some other infection or illness.

Vaginitis caused by Candida albicans is the second most common vaginal infection in the United States, following bacterial vaginosis, and is three times more frequent than infections caused by Trichomonas vaginalis (see below). Since infection by this yeast is more prevalent in wet, hot tropical climates, factors that encourage similar conditions around the genitals may contribute to its increase in Western societies (such as wearing tight, restrictive, poorly ventilated clothing and nylon underwear). The more widely known athlete's foot and jock itch are caused by similar organisms, which also increase in warm weather. Candida albicans can also commonly exist in the mouth and throat, with or without symptoms.

Whether or not an infection develops, women whose vaginal environments include Candida albicans seem to belong to one of three groups. The first group is made up of women who never develop symptoms throughout their lives; the second are women who suffer from infrequent outbreaks; and the third group suffers from repeated or continuing recurrences of infection. In 20 percent of the male partners of women with recurrent vaginal candidiasis, Candida albicans has been found on the penis. Infection may be passed back and forth between partners unless both are treated at the same time.

The most common symptom of vulvovaginal candidiasis is itching. Other symptoms include soreness, irritation, burning, swelling, pain with intercourse, and external discomfort when urinating. If a discharge is present, it can vary from watery to thick and is sometimes described as having the consistency of cottage cheese. This discharge does not have a disagreeable odor. Itching, soreness and inflammation of the vulva are the most common symptoms but the presence of sores or lesions is not at all unusual.

Treatment usually involves imidazoles such as Monistat, Mycelex, and Femstat or Nystatin (Micostatin and Nilstat). These medications are placed into the vagina in the form of a cream, suppository or tablet and are used from one to three, or seven to fourteen days. In general, physicians advise against treating Candida albicans unless there are symptoms. Prevention of recurrence may involve wearing looser, well-ventilated clothing and absorbent cotton underwear.

I'm slightly confused over several diseases which have similar if not almost exact symptoms. What is Moniliasis?

Moniliasis is a less preferred name for candidiasis or candidosis and is one of a large group of infections caused by a yeastlike organism (Candida albicans). Frequently, when this disease occurs in a woman's vagina it is called a yeast infection. Candidiasis is found in both men and women of all ages and, although infections can be sexually transmitted, sexual contact is *not necessary*. For example, diaper rash and thrush (a mouth infection) are candidial infections seen in infants.

I need to know an effective treatment for yeast infections. I had a D&C several years ago and since then I have been plagued by this condition. When I urinate it comes out in big blobs even if I used a medicated douche just a few hours previously. The stuff is so bad it gets all over me, my clothes and if we make love it gets all over him and then he is sore and miserable for days.

My husband and I have been treated with Monistat, Flagyl, Gyne-Lotrimin, medicated douches, suppositories and we've practiced abstinence. Nothing works. It has practically destroyed our love life. I am 39 and my husband of 20 years is also 39. Neither of us fool around.

My doctor says she'll try anything—she's almost as frustrated as we are.

Researchers estimate that 75 percent of all women will get at least one yeast infection (candidiasis) during their reproductive years and about half of those will have a recurrence. A few women get an infection every month as their hormones change at ovulation, and the condition is common in pregnant women when levels of estrogen and progesterone are high.

It sounds as though you've already tried the traditional approaches to the problem, including simultaneous treatment of both you and your husband. The best bet at this stage is to ask your doctor for another set of tests that includes both slides and cultures. Several causes of vaginitis need to be checked; some causes only appear in cultures that must be done at a well-equipped laboratory. Have your doctor also test you for cervicitis, infection of the cervix. And all vaginitis patients should also routinely receive a Pap smear and a gonorrhea test. She also should check for diabetes and candidiasis in your digestive tract or your husband's mouth. The fungus has also been shown to live on diaphragms and cervical caps. So, if you use one of these for contraception, ask your doctor to sterilize it.

If the doctor finds the infection is indeed caused by a Candida albicans organism, ask her about trying Nizoral, an oral drug.

New evidence has indicated that for some women with recurrent and severe yeast infections (or cystitis) spermicides containing nonoxynol-9 may be a factor. If you've been using such a product and are in a mutual sexually exclusive relationship, consider trying a different contraceptive method for awhile to see if ceasing use and effective treatment prevents recurrence.

Trichomonas vaginalis

Trichomonas vaginalis is a protozoan (a one-celled animal) first identified in 1836 by Alfred F. Donne, a French physician. It can cause a vaginal infection called trichomoniasis. In 1974 it was estimated that between 2.5 and 3 million women contract trichomoniasis each year (based on the fact that an estimated 2 million cases of trichomoniasis were treated in U.S doctors' offices). Since then the rate of infection appears to be declining in many other Western countries.

Trichomonas is found in 30 to 40 percent of male sexual partners of women with the infection. In men, most who are infected exhibit no symptoms and the infection often disappears by itself. On the other hand, when the female partners of men diagnosed with trichomonas are evaluated, at least 85 percent are found to also have the infection.

Fifty percent of women have no symptoms; for those who do, symptoms of infection can include one or more of the following: vaginal discharge seldom having an unpleasant odor, vaginal irritation, itching, pain during intercourse, and mild burning or pain during urination. The discharge can be gray or yellow-green. Some women exhibit symptoms only during or right after menstruation. Trichomonas is one of the organisms that cause NGU in men. A slight discharge, often only noticeable in the morning before first urination, is the most common symptom. Others include mild irritation of the urethra and itching.

The most successful control of the infection involves treatment of both the woman and her male partner at the same time with metronidazole (Flagyl is one brand name) or tinidazole. Unless both partners are treated, recurrence in the woman is likely. If the male partner can't be treated, then the seven-day multidose regimen (rather than the single-dose treatment) is recommended for the woman. Vaginal treatment alone is often not a permanent cure, because any organisms living in the urinary tract can eventually reinfect the vagina. However, the official warning on the medication says that Metronidazole should not be used during the first months of pregnancy and taking it at any time during pregnancy should be considered a risk.

Lately I've seen trich (trichomoniasis) listed as an STD but in the past I was told it was just a type of vaginal infection. Now I'm not sure if I really understand what a sexually transmitted disease is. Can a monogamous couple who is careful about their hygiene (we won't even use each other's washcloths, much less anyone else's) catch this? I've been told that foreplay alone can cause trich, even in a monogamous relationship.

Trichomoniasis is the name of the infection caused by Trichomonas vaginalis. It is one of the common infections transmitted by sexual contact, which is why it is now listed as an STD. The infection is not directly the result of foreplay, but foreplay can increase the symptoms if an infection is present.

Although the organism is primarily transmitted by sexual contact, nonsexual transfer is possible. Trichomonads have been shown to survive in urine for three hours, in semen for six hours and on wet cloth for 24 hours (so direct contact of the vagina with infected semen on towels, washcloths, or bedclothes could be infectious). The organism can also live for about forty-five minutes on a toilet seat and longer in the toilet-bowl water, but these would have to come in direct contact with the vulva or penis to cause infection. Although transfer via body secretions on objects is theoretically possible, it is highly unlikely. No well-documented cases have ever been reported.

My wife and I have both been diagnosed as having trichomoniasis. Neither of us has ever fooled around outside the marriage. We never had any real symptoms. If my wife became pregnant, would the baby be in danger?

Infection of the newborn with Trichomonas vaginalis is rarely detected and is thought to cause few if any problems. About 5 percent of girl babies born to mothers with trichomoniasis contract the infection during delivery; the organism can live in the high-estrogen environment of a newborn's vagina for only three to six weeks, because after this time the influence of the mother's estrogen during pregnancy disappears and the organism cannot survive in the normal low-estrogen infant vagina. Unless a vaginal infection in a baby becomes obvious, and this is rare, the infection will disappear on its own. Recently trichomonas has been suspected in a few cases of pneumonia in the newborn.

Ectoparasites: Lice and Scabies

Pubic Lice

There are 400 species of sucking lice that are ectoparasites—parasites that live on the surface of the body. Three of these species infest humans, and one of these is the sexually transmitted pubic lice or "crabs." Based on the sales figures for treatments, it is estimated that more than three million cases of louse infestation occur in the U.S. each year. Most are due to head and pubic lice.

What is the difference between lice and crabs? How do you get each? How do you get rid of them?

Crabs is slang for pubic lice (Pthirus pubis), and these creatures indeed resemble tiny crabs when viewed with a magnifying glass. These "crabs," however, prefer pubic hair to the seashore so they can feed on human blood.

After a first infestation, it takes at least five days for the allergic reaction to begin. This results in intense itching, which leads to scratching, redness, irritation, and inflammation. Small blue spots may appear on the skin from crab louse bites; these will disappear after several days. Pubic lice can also be found in other hairy places, such as the armpits, beard, and eyelashes.

The other two types known to infest humans are body lice and head lice. Head and body lice are transmitted by sharing combs, towels, toilets, bedsheets, and other personal articles. Although pubic lice can be picked up from objects, they are primarily transmitted by sexual contact. Both adult lice and their eggs (called *nits*), can be seen by the naked eye upon close inspection.

Several nonprescription medications that kill lice and eggs are available at drugstores. The ones reported to be most effective contain pyrethrins and piperonyl butoxide; two brand names with these ingredients are RID and Triple X. Read the instructions for use and follow them carefully, but application of the medicine on the lice and their eggs should be maintained for at least one hour to be most effective. Consult a physician for treatment near the eyes.

The most commonly used prescription medication is Kwell (gamma benzene hexachloride in a lotion, shampoo, or cream) but this is not recommended for pregnant women, small children, or people with large areas of sores or scratched skin. In one study, 96 percent of patients using this medication were cured of louse infestation. Whatever the treatment, a careful reexamination is necessary after four to seven days to make sure that all adult lice, as well as any eggs, have been killed. You can do this yourself. A magnifying glass will help.

It's also important to wash the infected person's clothing, bed linens, and towels in hot water (125 degrees Fahrenheit). Dry cleaning is also effective. Nonwashable items that have been in close contact with the infected areas can be sprayed with standard disinfectants containing pyrethrin-piperonyl butoxide (Raid and Black Flag are two brand names).

If for some reason the above steps do not work for you, do not simply increase treatments. Go to a physician for a more complete diagnosis. Other types of infections and skin problems have symptoms similar to the itching produced by the crab louse.

Scabies

The source of the word *scabies* is thought to be the Latin *scabere*, "to scratch." The itch mite was discovered by Bonomo in 1687, and thus scabies was the first disease in humans to have an identified cause. But it wasn't until the 1800s that this fact was generally accepted by the medical community. Each mite has four pairs of legs and walks rapidly on human skin until it finds a suitable location to burrow in. This burrow is its home for its thirty-day lifespan. Here the female mite lays eggs for the next generation of mites, which take about ten days to mature. Infested individuals have an average of eleven adult female mites on their skin. Like crabs, the symptoms of scabies are caused by a kind of allergy to the mites: this takes several weeks to develop.

The most effective treatment for scabies is Lindane cream or lotion (Gammexane, Kwell, Quillada, Scabene). It is applied in a thin layer over the entire body from the neck down and left on for eight to twelve hours. Then a thorough shower or bath is taken to remove the medication.

Lindane is not recommended for infants, young children, and pregnant women. For these individuals the centuries-old treatment with a sulfur ointment is safer. This medication is applied to the body for three nights in a row. Twenty-four hours after the last treatment the individual bathes thoroughly. Following both treatments, underwear and bed linen must be well laundered.

One of my bunkmates at camp told us she once had scabies and I'm wondering if this is something I should worry about. I would hate to catch this. I'm not even sure what scabies is but I don't want it.

Scabies is a contagious disease that can be spread through sexual and nonsexual physical contact. Close personal contact is usually involved, but nearly any physical contact—even shaking hands—can spread scabies. However, unlike most STDs, which require actual sexual contact to be transmitted, scabies can be spread when two people simply sleep in the same bed together overnight. So if you are not sleeping in the same bed, you are not at great risk of catching scabies from someone sleeping in a separate bunk bed.

The major symptom of scabies is intense itching, a red rash, discolored lines on the skin where the mites have burrowed, welts, and blisters filled with pus or water. However, in people who bathe regularly signs of infestation are very difficult to see. The itching usually gets worse at night but should not be scratched as this spreads the infection. Scabies most often infests the hands and wrists but can also appear on the genitals, buttocks, feet, and in the armpits. It does not, however, appear above the neck.

Viral Infections

Four common STDs are caused by viruses: herpes, genital warts, AIDS, and hepatitis B. The ones discussed in this chapter are herpes, genital warts, and AIDS, the three STDs we are most often asked about. Unlike bacterial infections, sexually transmitted viruses are either difficult or, in the unfortunate examples of AIDS and herpes, as yet impossible to cure. As scientists work toward finding a vaccine, a cure, or an effective treatment for AIDS and herpes, we are certain to learn more about all types of viral infections and the immune system in general and, hopefully, develop effective treatments and cures for many other diseases as well.

Herpes simplex virus (genital herpes)

Despite what Americans might have been led to believe, herpes infection is far from a new disease. The word *herpes* meant "to creep" in ancient Greek and was used in medicine to describe a spreading skin eruption. At the beginning of the second century A.D., the Roman poet Juvenal described sores of the genitals that may have been caused by the herpes virus. Around the same time, the Roman physician Herodotus described the cold sore. In 1736, the physician to the French king Louis XV wrote a description of genital herpes as accurate as any we have today. In 1814 Thomas Bateman, a British physician, described the course of a herpes outbreak from the prodromal phase to the opening of the sores. Then in 1887 British surgeon Jonathan Hutchinson reported that herpes was likely to recur. Although herpes was understood at the beginning of the twentieth century to be caused by a virus, not until the early 1960s did researchers in Germany and the United States discover there were two types, one most often associated with the face and one with the genitals.

The medical name for genital herpes is herpes simplex virus-2 (HSV-2); the type of herpes that most often causes sores of the mouth and lips is herpes simplex virus-1 (HSV-1). Although each type is most likely to be found in one location or the other, both can infect either site. These and other similar herpes viruses are found in all human populations and, in each, a large number of people are infected.

Since genital herpes is not a disease that must be reported to government health agencies, there are two ways to try to estimate the number of individuals who have been infected. The first is to obtain information on how many people go to doctors for treatment of a new infection and the second is to test for antibodies against the disease in the blood of different populations. For example, the percentage of people in different socioeconomic groups who have the antibodies in the United States ranges from 20 percent to 60 percent; this means that 20 to 60 percent of individuals tested were at some time infected with the genital herpes virus. When populations of pregnant women have been tested, approximately 30 percent had herpes antibodies in their blood indicating that they had been infected at some time. But the estimate of the number of people who actually come for treatment each year is much lower. Based on the disparity between these two figures, it is clear that many people have the infection without any symptoms. One fact that seems quite clear is that the prevalence of herpes infection in both the United States and much of Europe has been increasing since 1960, particularly among white middle-class men and women between 15 and 35 years of age.

The first time a person has an outbreak of genital herpes it is called a primary infection. This primary outbreak often has the most severe symptoms, including some that affect the rest of the body. Local genital signs can include many painful sores (sometimes in more than one location), itching, painful or burning urination, and a discharge from the vagina or urethra, depending on where the outbreak occurs. Most women also develop an infection of the cervix during their first episode of herpes outbreak.

About 40 percent of men and 70 percent of women also have symptoms that affect the whole body—such as fever, headache, a feeling of general discomfort, and muscle pains. More than half report general symptoms and about one-third have headache, stiff neck, and a mild sensitivity to light. The general body symptoms appear and then disappear within the first eight or nine days.

The attack can range in severity from mild to debilitating, but it is believed that many cases are so mild that the individual does not seek medical care. Studies have shown that during the first episode of genital herpes pain lasts an average of nine to thirteen days, and the lesions take an average of fifteen to twenty-three days to heal. Painful sores are reported by 99 percent of women and 95 percent of men. Pain and irritation from the sores gradually increase over the first week and reach their peak between seven and eleven days.

Herpes sores begin as red rounded cone-shaped bumps that develop into groups of small blisters filled with a clear, very infectious fluid. These blisters then break, leaving a painful, open, moist sore. If these sores or lesions are not on mucosal tissue they will develop a crust and then heal. In addition to the genitals, lesions on the buttocks, groin, or thigh may also develop (more frequently in women than men) usually in the second week of the disease. These symptoms then decline. In a primary infection, sores are widely spaced and may appear on both sides of the genitals.

After the first outbreak, the virus goes into a state called latency. During this time, the virus is located in nerve cells and is neither active nor infectious. For reasons that are still unclear, the virus becomes active again, causing new outbreaks in the years following the first occurrence. These episodes are called recurrent infections and are characterized by only the local symptoms (sores, pain, etc.) in a milder form and usually appear on only one side. The duration of recurrent outbreaks is briefer: symptoms can vary in severity from one outbreak to another for the same person and are likely to be more severe in women than in men.

About 50 percent of people have symptoms that precede each recurrent outbreak. These feelings are called the prodromal phase and can vary from mild tingling sensations occurring thirty minutes to forty-eight hours before the sores appear at the location to shooting pains in the buttocks, hips, or legs one to five days before the attack. Approximately 90 percent of individuals who have a primary outbreak experience recurrences and about 50 percent of these have five recurrences or more each year during the first two years, with men having slightly more than women. It is no longer believed that infection with herpes is related to the development of cervical cancer (see the section on human papillomavirus).

Transmission occurs when an infected area is shedding the virus and comes in close contact with the mucous membranes of another individual (particularly those of the genitalia, mouth, lips, or throat) or small breaks in the skin. Since the virus is easily inactivated at room temperature or by being exposed to air, it is unusual for the disease to be spread by objects like toilet seats or clothing.

Herpes is only infectious and can only be transmitted when the virus is shedding; this occurs mostly from the time bumps appear on the skin to when the sores develop a crust. But to be safe, unprotected sexual activity should not occur during the entire period from the time an infected person first feels the tingling that precedes the eruption of a sore until the lesions are fully healed. Occasionally viral shedding has been identified when no sores were present.

The herpes virus can also be transferred from mother to fetus either during pregnancy or birth. Although initially there was a great deal of concern about transmission during pregnancy and delivery, it has become clear that this is a relatively rare occurrence and caesarean sections are now recommended only for those women who have an active outbreak at the time of delivery. A recent major study indicated that having a *recurrent* episode of herpes during pregnancy had no negative effect on the health or birth weight of the newborn or on the length of the pregnancy. *Primary* herpes infection during pregnancy is a more serious condition resulting in a significantly higher rate of transmission to the fetus. All women who have herpes should seek prenatal care and delivery services from an obstetrician experienced in the management of pregnant women with primary and recurrent herpes.

Diagnosis of herpes is done primarily by physical examination. If the findings of the examination are not clear, then a sample from the sores will be cultured in a viral laboratory. This viral isolation technique is the most sensitive and specific method of identifying HSV and requires one to four days. Other tests are available and new evaluations are being developed.

The medically accepted medication in the United States for the treatment of genital herpes is acyclovir. This antiviral agent taken in pill form is most effective in reducing the severity of the primary outbreak and can also be helpful in preventing recurrent attacks. Treatment decreases the duration of the sores and the length of time the virus sheds. When taken daily on a long-term basis it is also quite effective in decreasing the number of recurrent outbreaks for many people and is prescribed for those who have frequent, more severe recurrences. Acyclovir in the form of a cream minimizes the discomfort of the sores in a primary outbreak but is not effective if there is cervical, urethral, or throat infection. The European acyclovir cream appears to be more effective than the preparation now available in the United States.

Use of condoms, *if the sores are fully covered,* helps prevent transmission of herpes. The addition of a spermicide containing nonoxynol-9 may enhance protection because this compound has been shown to effectively inactivate herpes virus in the laboratory. See the "Safer Sex" guidelines earlier in this chapter.

Herpes virus can be spread from one part of the body to another, so always carefully wash your hands after touching a sore or putting on medicine. Be particularly careful about touching your eyes after touching a sore or the area around it.

Good sources of up-to-date information on herpes treatment are clinics for sexually transmitted diseases (often called STD or VD clinics) or local public health officers. The clinic staff is generally more supportive and concerned about the impact of herpes on a patient's life than are some general physicians. Of course, visits are confidential. HELP (Herpetics Engaged in Living Productively) is an organization that helps people cope with herpes. For the address of the HELP chapter nearest you, write them at P.O. Box 100, Palo Alto, CA 94302. Or write the American Social Health Association (P.O. Box 13827, Research Triangle Park, NC 27709) and ask for information about living with herpes. For more information, call the Herpes Resource Center Hotline 12:00 - 4:30 p.m. Pacific Time, 415-328-7710; if you're in California, call 1-800-982-5883. Or call the STD National Hotline, sponsored by the American Social Health Association, at 1-800-227-8922.

My husband and I have genital herpes. We are concerned for our small children, that they could contract herpes from us. When we have an outbreak and apply medication, will our hands carry the virus even after proper soap and water washing? Are linens safe after being laundered? Should they have a different bar of soap? What about the bathtub and toilet seat?

The general guideline for herpes sores is to keep them covered by light clothing so there is no contact with another person's mucous membranes or skin. That's easier to accomplish if the sores are on the genitals instead of on the mouth or hands.

The herpes virus theoretically can live for as long as three days on more absorbent surfaces so it is possible to contract herpes from towels, sheets, washcloths, or similar items that have been in contact with an active herpes lesion (sore). Thus it is not a good idea to share washcloths, towels, glasses, toothbrushes, or anything else that could have been in contact with a sore with your children. If they are too young to help do this, consider getting them their own easily identified items. Perhaps you could use a liquid soap dispenser instead of bars.

Most normal household hygiene is sufficient to reduce the risk of spreading the herpes virus. Sheets, for example, should be virus-free after washing in detergent and hot water. Theoretically it is possible to become infected through contact with bathtubs or toilet seats, but in reality it's unlikely. The herpes virus is readily inactivated at room temperature or by drying. To become infected by touching an object like a toilet seat, the virus would have to come into direct contact with your genital area or a break in your skin.

Wash your hands with a detergent soap carefully and thoroughly each time you have touched a herpes sore; this will also help avoid spreading the virus to new locations on your own body.

I eat out a lot and have thought about this a lot. What about people who work in restaurants, if they should have herpes. I'm sure they taste the food; I've seen them do it. I've seen waiters and cooks with sores on their faces. Would you not catch herpes from them if it was in the active stage?

Most lesions or sores are not caused by a herpes virus. Although I don't have exact figures, I would guess that the vast majority of noticeable skin lesions are caused by noninfectious conditions, such as acne.

I could not find any confirmed reports of herpes being transferred via food service, but this would be an unlikely way to transfer the virus anyway. Call your local department of public health if you have concerns about a particular restaurant.

I'm a 51-year-old woman who contracted herpes from the unfaithful man I was married to. I have outbreaks on the genital area (maybe once a year or more) usually due to stress in my life or job.

I have recently met a wonderful man. Believe it or not, he's a physician. He's got a few problems of his own, but herpes is not one of them. I must tell him soon but for some reason I'm putting it off. We've made jokes about it and I imagine I'm afraid I'll lose him or he'll think bad of me.

My GYN doctor laughs about my herpes and says "Half my office staff has it!!" Am I overly concerned? Do I have to tell my friend?

It's easy to confuse STDs and moral issues. Having an STD doesn't mean you are a "bad" person. You are not alone in reacting as you did to the herpes diagnosis; like you, some people avoid forming new social and sexual relationships. But it is now clear that it is possible to lead a full life, including sexual activity.

You should tell any potential partner about your herpes, if for no other reason than allowing him or her to share in the responsibility of protecting his or her own health by practicing safer sex techniques (see guidelines). Both of you need to work together to prevent spreading the virus. Most herpes patients say their partners respond sympathetically, especially if they learn of the herpes in advance of any sexual contact. Many point out that herpes affects only certain intimate activities at certain times, not the total relationship or other expressions of love and affection.

An organization called HELP (Herpetics Engaged in Living Productively) suggests that being honest about herpes is the most ethical approach. It's also legally prudent, since lawsuits have been filed by people whose sexual partners did not disclose a preexisting herpes infection.

I want to say that the herpes simplex virus on the lips has nothing whatsoever to do with sex! I have been plagued by these "cold sores" on the lips for 35 years. Why it has the same name as the herpes in the vagina, I'll never know. Sex is not involved at all with the kind of virus I have on my lip. No one I've ever known has caught a cold sore from me.

Telling someone to go to "a clinic that specializes in STDs" wouldn't work, because they would know nothing about cold sores!

There are two types of herpes simplex viruses, HSV-1 and HSV-2. HSV-1 more commonly appears on the lips as "cold sores" and HSV-2 usually appears on the genitals, but both viruses can appear in either (or both) locations. In fact, these two viruses are so similar that people who already have had HSV-1 have less severe reactions if they are exposed to HSV-2.

A person with a sore on the lip caused by HSV-1 can transmit HSV-1 to another person's mouth, genitals, or any other body area where the virus can enter. It has been found that from 5 to 15 percent of patients with a first episode of herpes sores on the genitals are infected with HSV-1, the herpes you have. There is no question that this virus can be sexually transmitted, although it can also be transmitted in nonsexual ways.

I suggest that people go to an STD clinic if they suspect they have a herpes virus sore—no matter where the sore is located—because testing for either HSV-1 or HSV-2 can be difficult. These clinics are more likely to have access to specialized equipment and the personnel are more experienced at interpreting test results.

In addition, most STD clinics or specialists are highly committed to teaching patients how to live with the herpes simplex virus without infecting others. Because HSV-1 on the lips also can be transmitted to others when the virus is active, even you might find information from such a specialist helpful. You should not, for example, kiss anyone, even in a nonsexual context, while you have a "cold sore." You should also not share washcloths, towels, glasses, cups, or toothbrushes with others.

Last fall while attending college I was diagnosed as having a primary herpes infection. The doctor didn't give me one bit of information about herpes. Instead, she tried to prescribe Tylenol with codeine even though she was aware I was pregnant. I refused to take the medicine. I miscarried at 20 weeks of pregnancy.

I have since read that most doctors recommend an abortion for a woman who has a primary herpes infection during pregnancy. I was never told this. I was already 18 weeks along when I read about it. Why don't doctors do a better job of educating their pregnant patients about herpes?

Most doctors try to keep up with current information about herpes and pass it along to their patients. Unfortunately, there isn't a great deal of definitive information on herpes and pregnancy, and even experts disagree about how best to manage the situation.

There is currently no conclusive research to support recommending abortion for all pregnancies during which a woman exhibits a primary herpes simplex virus infection (the first herpes outbreak).

There are known risks associated with having an HSV infection during pregnancy. The spontaneous abortion (miscarriage) rate for women with a primary infection may be as high as 50 percent (and the percent of newborns with low birth weight as high as 35 percent) compared with a 10 percent rate for spontaneous abortions in general.

Some studies have found the rate of premature births also increased from 17 percent without HSV to 35 percent in the presence of a primary HSV infection. Recent studies showed that women with recurrent HSV, however, had no greater risk of premature delivery or low newborn birth weight than did women without HSV.

Pregnant women with a primary infection need to know they have an increased risk of spontaneous abortion and may have an early delivery. They should see an obstetrician with experience managing pregnancy in herpes-infected women. More research is needed on the risks and benefits of acyclovir treatment during pregnancy.

Human papillomavirus (HPV)/genital warts

In ancient times, warts of the anal and genital (anogenital) area were both well-known and common. These warts originally were thought to be a symptom of syphilis or gonorrhea. After the bacterial causes of these STDs were identified, it was then believed that genital warts resulted from irritation or genital secretions. The fact that viruses cause warts was established in the early twentieth century, but until the 1970s it was thought that all warts were caused by one virus. Scientists now know that there are at least sixty types of papillomaviruses, twenty of which can infect the genital tract. Until the middle of this century most scientists did not believe that genital warts were infectious, but when an outbreak occurred among the wives of American soldiers returning from the Korean war it became clear that indeed they were an STD.

Genital and anal infections with papillomavirus and herpes virus are now considered two of the most common STDs in the United States. Genital warts are most common in men and women between 20 and 24 years of age. As with herpes, the number of people infected with human papillomavirus (HPV) who don't have any obvious symptoms is probably much higher than those who are aware that they have genital warts. Therefore, all assessments of the number of infected people in the United States probably grossly underestimate the actual figure. However, some idea of the prevalence of infection with HPV has been obtained by pooling studies conducted in different health care environments. When women seeking health care at various family-planning and university health care clinics have been tested for the HPV virus, 5 to 19 percent were infected; in STD clinics, as many as 27 percent of patients were infected with HPV.

The number of cases of warts on the external genitals is increasing in both the United States and the United Kingdom. Because many sufferers never visit a physician for diagnosis and internal warts are not included, these cases represent only a small percentage of the total number of infections.

The majority of HPV infections are not readily visible. For example, among college women having routine gynecological examinations, eight times as many had evidence of infection with HPV on the cervix than had visible genital warts. In a German study, 31 percent of healthy males between 16 and 79 years old who were evaluated by taking smears from the glans penis showed evidence of infection with HPV. Based on these and other data, researchers have estimated that 1 percent of Americans have visible genital warts, 2 percent have warts that can only be seen under magnification, and 7 percent have infections that cannot be seen. Based on the fact that the United States has 122 million people between 15 and 49 years of age, it is conservatively estimated that more than 12 million Americans are infected with HPV.

Anogenital warts come in a variety of shapes and sizes, from so tiny that they cannot be seen even under magnification to very large. Their shape and size probably depend on the type of papillomavirus causing the infection. In men, warts can appear on all parts of the penis, foreskin (if the man is uncircumcised), scrotum, or inside the urethra, where they can cause bleeding and discharge, diminish the flow of urine, or produce no symptoms at all. In women, HPV can be found on the vulva, labia majora or minora, inside the vagina, or on the cervix. Warts around the anus are found in both sexes and have also been discovered in the rectum.

Direct sexual contact between infected and uninfected partners is the most common way in which genital warts are transmitted. In a recent study that investigated the male sexual partners of women diagnosed with genital warts, nearly 70 percent were found to be infected also. As with most STDs, the more partners people have had the more likely they are to be infected. Although HPV was, until recently, considered more of an embarrassment and inconvenience than a threat, several of the types that infect the genital tract have now been associated with precancerous or invasive lesions or tumors of the cervix, vulva, anus, and penis.

As with genital herpes, proper use of a condom can reduce the risk of transmission if all the warts and infected areas are completely covered.

Infection with HPV can be treated and often eliminated. The sexual partners of people diagnosed with this viral infection should always be examined. The earlier treatment begins, the better the result. Before treatment starts, laboratory tests should be done for all other STD organisms that often coexist with HPV. Anyone with genital warts or another form of HPV infection should avoid sexual contact that involves the unprotected affected area until treated and retested to make sure the virus is gone.

Several methods are used to treat HPV and none has been found to be superior to the others. Treatments include painting the warts with substances that destroy them or removing the warts (see below). The best overall treatment strategy is to eliminate all the visible signs of infection and then keep having regular exams to check for any recurrence.

HPV-related Cancer. Infection with HPV is associated with genital-tract cancer in men and women, particularly cancer of the cervix. Scientists believe that these viruses stimulate the first step in what is now seen as a multistep process that may lead to most genital cancers. One piece of evidence that supports a link between HPV and cervical cancer is the finding that current wives of men whose previous wives had cervical cancer are at increased risk for developing this cancer. The supposition is that these men have carried HPV from the first marriage partner to the second. Another finding provides additional support. Women who report only one sexual partner in their lives but whose husbands had six or more sexual partners appear to have about four times the risk for abnormal cervical cells than do women whose husbands reported fewer than six partners.

This is another good reason why genital warts should be treated immediately. Once you have been diagnosed with an infection of HPV, you should have regular and frequent examinations to check for changes in your genital tissues. Remember, cancer diagnosed early can almost always be cured.

I have what seems to be a pimple on one of the outer vaginal lips. It recently occurred to me that it might be a wart. Now I'm worried. Could I have venereal warts? What do venereal warts look like?

The only way to know whether any pimple is an anogenital wart is by seeing your physician. Anogenital warts can vary quite a bit in size, color, and appearance. They usually begin as soft moist pink or red swellings that grow rapidly. Frequently several may appear in the same area and have a cauliflower-like appearance or look like small fungi. They can be white, gray, pink, or brown. They can be round or flat, bumpy or smooth. Some look much like the kinds of warts that appear on the hands. They can also be so small you cannot see them. Condyloma acuminatum means "pointed nob" and refers only to warts that have one particular shape, so it is not correct to use this name for all genital warts.

In women, high bumpy genital warts usually first appear near and on the inner labia (minora) and can spread quite rapidly. About 20 percent of women also develop warts on the perineum (the space between the vagina and anus), around the anus, and inside the vagina. Low bumpy warts (papular) grow on the outer labia (majora) and the perineum. Papillomavirus infections of the vulva that can only be seen by magnification take the form of microwarts (flat lesions). The virus in the form of microwarts can also infect the cervix. About half of the women who have vulvar warts also are infected on the cervix.

Condylomata acuminata are the most common genital warts found in men. They are soft, fleshy and project out from the skin. These warts most often appear first on or around the foreskin (if not circumcised) and on the glans penis (head of the penis). They can also grow on the shaft of the penis, the scrotum, and the anus. Low bumpy warts (papular) are also found on the shaft of the penis or other dry areas. Genital warts can also infect the urethra and, although many produce no symptoms, urethral bleeding or discharge is not uncommon. Flat condylomas, which usually come in continuous groups, are usually not visible to the naked eye without magnification.

Last fall, my husband contracted condyloma from another female with whom he had been sleeping. In January he had outpatient surgery at a urologist's office. I was told by a friend that this is considered a venereal disease.

Is this true? How contagious is condyloma? Can I be exposed to this disease even though he had the surgery done? I am not sure if he is still sleeping with his "lady friend" or not. He tells me that he does not see her but I am not sure.

I am embarrassed about this and really do not want to ask my family doctor. I should probably tell you that my husband is 48 and I am 49, so we are not youngsters in the sense that he really should have known better than to get himself involved with another woman.

Anogenital warts are highly contagious, and anyone who has had sexual contact with a person who has had anogenital warts must be checked to see if she or he has contracted the disease. If you had sex with your husband between the time he contracted anogenital warts and the time he was treated, there is a good chance that you were exposed to and may have become infected with the papillomavirus which causes genital warts. For example, studies have shown that at least two-thirds of the sexual partners of individuals with genital warts are also infected. Anogenital warts can incubate for many months before appearing.

Also, a single treatment is not always sufficient to eradicate the warts. Before you assume that your husband is no longer contagious, he needs to be carefully checked to make sure that all of the warts were removed and that none have reappeared.

Although these warts may appear in easy-to-see locations (on the penis or scrotum in men and the vulva in women), they also can occur inside the urethra in men, deep inside the vagina or on the cervix in women, or inside the rectum in both sexes.

This means that you will need a thorough examination which *must* include laboratory evaluation of cells from the cervix before you can be certain that you do not have this disease. This is too important to let embarrassment stand in the way of action. You are not the first patient to ask to be checked for anogenital warts and it is important that you are thoroughly examined.

If you don't want to go to your family doctor, go to either an STD clinic or a specialist; they are most experienced in diagnosing and treating papillomavirus infections.

Until it is determined that both you and your husband are not contagious, refrain from sexual activity, or at least use a condom to reduce the amount of contact between genital areas. Using a spermicide containing the ingredient nonoxynol-9 (which has been shown to destroy viruses in the laboratory) inside the condom and inside your vagina will add to your protection.

I have just been diagnosed as having venereal warts. I'm very distressed by this as they fall under the STD category. My husband and I have been married for five years and have each been completely faithful. Can you explain? Please be honest and direct. I can't seem to get a straight answer from my physician (male).

Although most cases can be traced to direct sexual contact with an infected person, indirect transmission of the wart virus via towels or clothing may also be possible. The incubation period (the time between exposure to the virus and appearance of the warts) varies greatly—from as short as a few weeks to as long as two years. Moreover, warts can disappear and reappear spontaneously, or remain unnoticed for years unless they cause pain or other symptoms or are spotted during a medical examination. It is possible that you or your husband were exposed to the wart virus before you married and your current infection is just the first time they've been noticed.

The primary issue now should be treating the genital warts and rechecking to see that both you and your husband are completely free of them.

I've read all about the symptoms and now I'm sure I have genital warts and I'm so embarrassed I could just die. There's no way I'm going to go to a doctor and let him see these things. How can I treat them myself?

Although in Britain there is a new wart treatment that men can apply at home, this is not yet available elsewhere. In the U.S. there are several treatments for anogenital warts and all require a physician. For warts in open areas such as the penis or vulva, a doctor applies podophyllin, an extract from the rhizome of a plant that grows in North America and the Himalayas. In one study only 38 percent of men were permanently cured after one or two applications.

Podophyllin is a toxic chemical and requires close medical supervision. Pregnant women should not use podophyllin, since it may harm both the fetus and the woman. It also should not be applied to warts on a woman's cervix or to very large warts. Experts also advise against continuing the treatments for longer than one month.

For warts in the urethra, anus, cervix, or other internal locations (or if podophyllin is not successful or cannot be used) there are other treatments: cryotherapy (freezing) is often successful in treating limited anogenital warts. Since this treatment is painful, a local anesthetic should be given as well. Electrocautery (burning) with local anesthetic is appropriate for infection of the shaft of the penis, labia majora (outer lips), and around the anus. Laser treatment can be used to treat warts at any site and is the most successful with more rapid healing, but only when done by a specially trained and highly experienced practitioner with additional skill in colposcopy (visualization through a special magnifying instrument). Surgery with scissors has been successful for removing warts around and inside the anus. You can't perform any of these procedures on your own. Depending on the location and size of the warts, many of these removal techniques can be done in a doctor's office.

A relatively new treatment for genital warts that continue to recur is alpha-interferon injections. Researchers have found that for recurring warts the most successful treatment is a combination of surgical removal procedures (such as laser surgery) combined with alpha-interferon injections directly into the warts themselves. This is thought to more completely destroy the original wart, as well as any warts not visible at the time of treatment. This treatment takes time and does have some side effects. (Topical interferon treatment—on the skin—has not been successful.)

Even after successful treatment, any changes in the area should be promptly examined and both men and women should have regular examinations to identify any recurrence early. Annual Pap smears to detect changes in the cells of the cervix are even more essential for a woman who has had a papillomavirus infection.

I've recently noticed some small warts on my private parts. Are they dangerous? I would like to become pregnant one day. Could the warts be harmful to
the baby?

First, get a definitive diagnosis from an STD clinic or specialist. If what you have
is caused by a HPV, it is important you begin treatment right away. Researchers
strongly suspect that there is a link between having warts on the cervix and a
higher risk of developing cervical cancer later in life. For this reason you will
need to have a regular schedule of pelvic examinations and Pap tests designed to
evaluate the status of your cervical tissue. You should follow this testing
schedule religiously for the rest of your life so that any changes can be
diagnosed long before they become cancer.

Babies born to mothers with active genital warts or papillomavirus infection
have been known to develop warts in the throat. These don't usually appear
until several weeks after birth, which suggests that transmission mostly occurs
during delivery. Caesarean birth rather than a vaginal delivery is *not* currently
recommended as a preventive measure for women with active genital warts or
papillomavirus infection. A woman who has had genital warts should make sure
she tells her obstetrician so that she is carefully and regularly examined for any
outbreak during pregnancy.

Treatment during pregnancy with podophyllin can be dangerous to both
mother and fetus, so other techniques for removal are the only therapy
recommended—removal can be accomplished by laser surgery, electrocautery, or
cryotherapy.

Acquired Immunodeficiency Syndrome (AIDS)

During the 1960s and 1970s physicians noticed isolated cases of individuals
whose immune systems appeared to have stopped protecting them against
disease. Their immune systems became crippled and infections that usually
were easily defeated by the body now attacked with unheard of power, leading
to devastating illness and finally death. This condition was not thought of as a
separate disease because no one physician saw enough cases to realize that this
lack of immunity signaled the existence of an unidentified infectious organism.
Acquired Immune Deficiency Syndrome (AIDS) in the United States and Europe
may have been reported as early as 1952 but was not recognized as such.

Then, in June 1981, a Los Angeles physician and researcher reported to the
United States Centers for Disease Control (CDC) that he had seen five cases of a
rare form of pneumonia in young homosexual men. Until then this type of
pneumonia, Pneumocystis carinii, had only occurred in patients whose immune
systems had been suppressed, usually by therapy for problems like cancer. It
was unusual even under those circumstances and virtually unheard of in young,
previously healthy individuals. The next month, a report described another
relatively rare disease in twenty-six homosexual men in New York City; called
Kaposi's sarcoma, it is a kind of cancer that had formerly almost always been
seen only in elderly men of Mediterranean origin; four of these homosexual men
also had Pneumocystis pneumonia.

By 1982 in Europe it became apparent that the unusual cases of Kaposi's
sarcoma noticed there since the late 1970s were the result of the same problem.

In the United States it was clear that the outbreak of AIDS was not limited to a few cities or populations; by the end of 1982 over 800 cases had been reported in more than thirty states. Once it was known that AIDS was caused by an infectious organism, the suspicion that it might be sexually transmissible was confirmed when a study of the first 216 cases in southern California found that forty of the men could be linked sexually to one another.

What Causes AIDS? By 1984, the disease organism that causes AIDS was identified in France and the United States. After much scientific discussion, the virus was finally named Human Immunodeficiency Virus (HIV). It is a special kind of retrovirus called a lentivirus. Retroviruses use the genetic material in the cells they invade to reproduce. *Lenti* means slow; lentiviruses cause infections that take a long time to reveal themselves. This means that months or years may pass between the time the virus invades the body and the time the person has any symptoms of a disease. In the case of HIV, once the virus has entered the body it invades certain cells of the immune system and may reside in these cells for years without any obvious effect; then, in response to some stimulation that is still not clear, the virus uses the genetic material in those cells to reproduce large numbers of itself, destroys and exits the cells, and spreads out to infect many more immune-system cells. Eventually, the immune system and its ability to fight off diseases is disabled or destroyed.

What Does It Mean To Be HIV Seropositive? When a disease organism invades the body, the immune system responds in a number of defensive ways. One response is to develop antibodies against the disease organism; these help the immune system identify and fight the organism. In most cases, the antibodies help cure the disease and then remain to defend quickly against the same disease in the future (this is called immunity). The problem with the AIDS virus (HIV) is that it attacks the cells of the immune system itself, whose job it is to fight and defeat this and other diseases.

Viruses are more difficult to identify as the cause of a particular disease than are bacteria and other organisms because they are so small; therefore the easiest way to find out if a person has been infected with a virus is to test the individual's blood for the presence of antibodies against the virus.

Being HIV seropositive (*sero* = "blood") means that a person's blood has been tested for the presence of the specific antibodies against HIV (the virus that causes AIDS) and the antibodies were found. Being HIV seronegative means that no antibodies were found. When a person is HIV seropositive, we know that the AIDS virus is in the body because the immune system has produced antibodies to it. Scientists also use the term "seroconversion" to mean that the immune system has produced the antibodies associated with a particular disease organism once the organism has entered the body. Seroconversion to HIV infection can begin in as few as five days and be completed by between the second and seventh week after infection. In rare cases seroconversion can take up to a year or more to show up on an HIV antibody test.

Testing for HIV itself rather than for its antibodies is difficult, time-consuming, and expensive. So the vast majority of tests to discover whether a person is infected with HIV are really tests to detect antibodies the immune system has made in an attempt to fight the virus.

What Does It Mean To Have AIDS? Since the AIDS virus (HIV) attacks, disables, and then kills important components of the immune system, the immune system is ultimately unable to destroy the virus. And eventually the virus damages the body's defenses to such an extent that the individual is vulnerable to other disease organisms (opportunistic infections) to which he or she might be exposed; AIDS patients may die from these illnesses even though they don't ordinarily kill.

The course of infection with HIV, which results in AIDS and finally death, is a complex one that is similar in many respects to untreated syphilis—it often starts with some very mild symptoms, disappears for years, and then reappears in a devastating and deadly form.

The majority of individuals first respond to HIV infection with no symptoms at all or with mild symptoms like those for flu or mononucleosis. If mild symptoms do appear, they may include fever, muscle and joint pains, a general feeling of discomfort, tiredness, lack of appetite, nausea, diarrhea, sore throat, or a rash. Headache, stiff neck, eye pains, sensitivity to light, irritability, or depression are also not uncommon. These symptoms may last for two to three weeks and then usually disappear.

After infection, whether the initial period involved symptoms or not, a period of time elapses when the infected individual usually experiences no symptoms. These individuals are called asymptomatic carriers of HIV. In adults, it is now estimated that this asymptomatic carrier state—from infection to the development of AIDS—lasts an average of seven to nine years, although there are healthy-appearing infected individuals who have been symptom-free (asymptomatic) for as long as twelve years. A group of 6700 homosexual and bisexual men from San Francisco have been studied over a number of years. Of those who had been infected for seven years or more, 36 percent of the original asymptomatic carriers have developed AIDS. Another 40 percent are experiencing some symptoms, and only 20 percent are still symptom-free.

Many individuals with no other symptoms do have swollen glands at several different places in the body; these last for more than three months. This condition, called lymphadenopathy, does not appear to predict when the person will progress to having AIDS—several studies have shown no difference in the timing of the appearance of AIDS between asymptomatic carriers with or without this condition. Although an individual has no symptoms and is likely to look and feel perfectly well, he or she can infect others. Specifically, this means that they can spread the AIDS virus (HIV) to other individuals in the following ways: intimate sexual contact, exposure to their blood, or during pregnancy and delivery of the fetus and during nursing of the newborn.

It is not yet clear what factors are responsible for progression from the symptom-free state to developing AIDS. Such factors as infection with other disease organisms, genetic factors, the virulence of the particular strain of HIV, and life style (for example, whether or not one smokes or drinks alcohol) have been suggested. After a variable period of being HIV-seropositive, the beginning of AIDS may be signaled by a variety of symptoms, including long-lasting fevers, night sweats, weight loss, diarrhea, and/or the appearance of other illnesses such as shingles or yeast infections. (The term ARC—AIDS-related complex—is no longer favored to describe the syndrome at this stage).

Following this period, the AIDS patient may experience a great variety of serious problems, which can include any of a number of opportunistic infections, tumors, and nervous system disorders. The AIDS virus has been shown to be capable of directly affecting the skin and mucous membranes, the gastrointestinal tract, the kidneys, heart, lungs, and nervous system. Once a diagnosis of AIDS has been made, most individuals die within two years and few survive longer than three years. The length of survival is dependent on such factors as age, sex, and in what way the disease was acquired. It is not known what percentage of individuals who are infected with HIV will eventually progress to AIDS and die; current estimates range from 30 to 100 percent.

How Is HIV Transmitted? The AIDS virus (HIV) can only be spread in four ways—through intimate sexual contact, exposure to infected blood or needles, and from an infected mother to her fetus during pregnancy or delivery, or to the newborn through breast feeding. Unprotected penile-anal intercourse and penile-vaginal intercourse are the sexual behaviors that have been clearly demonstrated to present the highest risk of sexual transmission. (See the "Safer Sex" guidelines earlier in this chapter for more detailed information.) All these activities are only associated with the risk of infection if one of the individuals involved is already infected with HIV. In industrialized nations, it appears that male-to-female transmission is more likely than female-to-male.

Sharing of needles by intravenous drug users is a major route of transmitting HIV not only from one user to another but, secondarily, through intimate sexual activity with their sexual partners.

Although at the beginning of the epidemic many individuals became infected with HIV through contaminated blood transfusions or blood products, now that careful testing of donated blood is routine, that risk has been almost completely eliminated.

After almost a decade of the AIDS epidemic, there is *no* evidence that this disease can be transmitted by casual contact, insect bites, or the handling of food and water. Even among close family members who have shared food, kitchen utensils, toilets, and even toothbrushes and razors with an AIDS patient, no cases of transmission have occurred. So the risk of transmission in less intimate circumstances like schools, workplaces, swimming pools, restaurants, and theaters appears to be zero.

How Is AIDS Treated? Each seropositive person must find out exactly how to prolong his or her own wellness and how to protect others from infection even though the infected person does not feel sick or have any AIDS symptoms. Keeping well can involve taking better care of your health (including giving up smoking and use of drugs and alcohol, eating a healthy diet, and sleeping enough); taking medicine like AZT (zidovudine), which may prolong health in a symptomless HIV-infected person; and practicing safer sex to protect yourself from another exposure to HIV or other STD while at the same time protecting others from your infection. Finally, knowing you are HIV positive permits you to keep up-to-date on new treatment options for prolonging life and perhaps some day for curing the infection.

To date HIV infection and AIDS cannot be cured. However, within three years of the identification of the virus AZT had been developed and was being tested as a treatment. This antiviral substance appears to interfere with the replication of HIV in the cells the virus has invaded. In the original clinical study of AZT in AIDS patients, it appeared to prolong life and reduce the number of opportunistic infections. These patients were also more likely to gain weight than those who had been given a placebo. New studies indicate that AZT can prolong the period before the emergence of AIDS in HIV-asymptomatic carriers. Treatment of persons with AIDS also involves therapy for any opportunistic infections as they arise.

What Does This Mean For You? In April 1990, 132,510 people in the United States had been diagnosed with AIDS, and it was estimated that between 1 and 1.5 million were already infected with the AIDS virus.

If you believe that this virus only infects people who are not like you, I will offer just a few statistics. In a recent study of college students from nineteen universities around the United States who had visited their student health clinic for any reason, one in 500 was found to be HIV-positive, meaning they were infected with the AIDS virus. Furthermore, most experts agree that the proportion of heterosexuals infected with HIV is increasing and will continue to increase in the coming years. In 1989, 5 percent of new cases of AIDS in the United States were attributed to heterosexual transmission. Thus, AIDS *cannot* be thought of as restricted to the so-called high-risk groups such as homosexual men or intravenous drug users. The best thing you can do to avoid infection with HIV (as well as other STDs) is to identify and acknowledge any factors that may put you at risk and take steps to protect yourself. *(Read the "Safer Sex" guidelines earlier in this chapter for more you can do.)*

Getting More Information. Telephone hotlines, organizations, and information clearinghouses can be excellent sources of updated information about AIDS. There is no need to leave one's name or any identifying information. Many of the hotlines are equipped to refer callers to AIDS testing sites and counseling agencies; some of them will send literature if requested.

National AIDS Hotline 1-800-342-AIDS
American Foundation for AIDS Research (AmFAR) For those who are HIV-positive and want to be involved in research 1-800-992-2873
Drug Abuse Hotline 1-800-662-4357
National Gay and Lesbian Crisis Line 1-800-SOS-GAYS
Project Inform, a central clearinghouse for information on experimental drugs and treatment 1-800-822-7422
Spanish AIDS/SIDA Hotline 1-800-344-7432
STD National Hotline 1-800-227-8922
TDD Teletype AIDS information for the deaf 1-800-243-7889

I am completely confused about AIDS. Can a person have AIDS and infect other people without knowing they are sick?

Yes, and this is one reason that the AIDS virus (HIV) continues to spread. When responsible people do finally find out that they are infected, they usually stop engaging in behaviors that place others at risk for becoming infected—but this is often *after* they have already unknowingly passed the virus to others.

The only way to find out if you have been infected with HIV is to have a blood test. If the test is positive, a person is said to be HIV-seropositive. This means that he or she can be infectious to others and that persons who have been in contact with their semen, vaginal secretions, or blood may also be infected.

Can you tell by looking if a person has AIDS?

You certainly cannot tell just by looking at a person whether he or she is infected with HIV. It usually takes years before any evidence of illness appears. Moreover, until a blood test finds HIV antibodies in a person's blood, even the *person* does not know he or she is infected with HIV and can infect others.

Once an AIDS patient has become very ill, he or she will look sick, but even then he or she often will look just like any other extremely ill person. Remember it's the opportunistic infections that usually are the cause of AIDS death; all individuals with severe pneumonia look alike, even though only some have pneumonia because their immune systems were impaired by the AIDS virus.

We recently discovered that my younger brother is a homosexual and has been for a while. AIDS seems like such a serious disease, I'm afraid for my two teenage daughters, my husband and myself. When I showed my brother an article about AIDS he just said not to worry. Our doctor won't say much either. What can we do about this?

It sounds from your letter as if you believe all homosexual men are infected with the AIDS virus (HIV). Being homosexual does not mean that a person is infected with HIV or that he or she will develop AIDS.

Also the risk of catching the AIDS virus by casual contact is extremely low, virtually nonexistent. This means that even *if* your brother were to be diagnosed as being infected with HIV, participation in the usual family activities wouldn't endanger the health of you or your family. Studies of households where one person has AIDS revealed that sharing food, drink, kitchen utensils, and even toothbrushes does not transmit the virus from the AIDS patient to the other household members.

I'm a 42-year-old-man, recently divorced after 21 years of marriage. I'm not especially eager to jump into the singles scene thanks to AIDS—talk about party-poopers! I think I'd rather enter a monastery than risk my life for a couple of thrills. Say I do meet the perfect woman and decide it's worth the risk. Is there a way she could be tested so I know I'm starting with a clean slate? (I'd be willing to be tested too if it gives her peace of mind.)

Yes, there is a way you both can start with a "clean slate." You would both wait six months or longer since your last sexual contact with someone else, then you both would be tested. During this waiting period, you both should avoid any sexual activities that might put you at risk of infection (that means following the "Safer Sex" guidelines) and neither should share needles with anyone if you use intravenous drugs. You both would also establish your commitment to a sexually exclusive relationship. In other words, neither of you would engage in sexual activity with anyone else.

Then if you both get negative test results, the chances of being infected with the AIDS virus are reported to be extremely low and you can assume you're both free of HIV infection. Of course, that "safety" lasts only as long as neither of you have sex or share needles with anyone else.

My girlfriend and I are both 45 years old and enjoy giving each other great pleasure by oral sex. With all the talk about AIDS going on, do we have any reason for out-of-the-ordinary concern? Neither of us uses drugs or engages in sex beyond ourselves.

If neither of you have ever been exposed to the AIDS virus (HIV), then there is no risk of becoming infected with the virus or developing AIDS regardless of the sexual activities you engage in as a mutually sexually exclusive couple (no other partners). Oral sex does not "create" the AIDS virus.

Moreover, most researchers currently think that the incidence of transmission of the AIDS virus from an infected partner by oral sex is low or practically impossible.

My wife and I are in our 50s, have been married for 35 years and enjoy a good sex life. I have always wanted to try anal sex, and we've read some sex books which say it's OK as long as it is gentle and sanitary precautions are taken.

But now we are afraid to try this because we've heard that anal sex causes AIDS. That's hard to understand, since I thought the activity had existed for centuries, while AIDS is a new disease.

Will my wife and I get AIDS if we try this once?

No. Anal intercourse itself cannot "create" AIDS in one or both of you. AIDS is caused by a virus that can only be contracted from a person who is already infected with HIV. So if neither of you has had sex or shared a needle with anyone else since 1980 or had a blood transfusion or received a blood product (such as treatment for hemophilia) before March 1985, you can try this new activity with no fear of the AIDS virus. *(For information about anal sex see Chapter 7.)*

My husband and I desperately want a child but because he had a vasectomy nine years ago we're looking into artificial insemination. Is there a high risk of getting AIDS from sperm banks, or do they screen donors thoroughly? I know it takes several weeks for the AIDS virus to show up and wonder if some virus is getting through undetected. Has it been proven that freezing semen kills the AIDS virus? Or should we even be considering artificial insemination?

Based on what scientists know about HIV, it is unlikely that anyone will guarantee semen and sperm as being 100 percent safe from the risk of infection with HIV. But the small risk can certainly be further reduced by good screening, testing, and by using frozen semen.

Basic screening criteria for donors should include a complete history of the man and his sexual partners. If a man has used intravenous drugs, or has had multiple sexual partners, a male sex partner, or contact with a prostitute, his semen should not be used. If he has had contact with a partner who used intravenous drugs or who has had an STD, reputable clinics will not use his sperm.

Semen donors should have blood tests for syphilis and hepatitis-B antigen. The semen should be tested for Neisseria gonorrhoeae, Chlamydia trachomatis, Mycoplasma hominus, Ureaplasma urealyticum, streptococcal species, cytomegalovirus and Trichomonas vaginalis—all infectious organisms that can be present in semen. The donor should also have a blood test for the AIDS virus (HIV) antibodies six months after his semen is collected, tested, and frozen. This is not a 100-percent guarantee, but it dramatically lowers the risks.

The American Fertility Society and the CDC have recommended that only frozen sperm be used for insemination. Freezing the donated semen allows time for lengthy cultures and other tests to be done before any of the semen is used. Freezing also permits time for testing the blood of the donor for HIV six months after the donation. If he is free of HIV antibodies at that point, then the frozen semen is currently considered to be as safe as possible to thaw and use.

Freezing is being recommended only because it allows time for adequate testing of the donor and the semen, not because freezing destroys disease organisms. However, some physicians are reluctant to use frozen sperm because it has a slightly lower rate of producing a pregnancy, sometimes requiring several more inseminations than does fresh semen.

A reputable fertility specialist will be as concerned as you are that donated sperm be free of STDs. Be wary of any clinic or physician who advises you not to worry about STDs or who refuses to give you a list of screening questions and tests used to select sperm donors. In fact, get up, walk out, and select another physician or clinic. Write to the American Fertility Society (*address is in Chapter 15*) for their published guidelines and recommendations for fertility clinics.

I read you could catch AIDS from blood products. Can I catch AIDS from this? (The reader enclosed a label from a multivitamin bottle.)

Just because the label refers to vitamins as being "good for the blood" does not mean that vitamins are considered a blood product.

A "blood product" is something made *from* blood, not *for* the blood. It is a compound distilled from whole blood (such as those used to treat leukemia patients) or blood used for transfusions during surgery. Today all blood products in the United States are made only from blood that has first been tested for the AIDS virus (HIV).

In other words, vitamins are not made *from* blood, and thus you cannot get AIDS from vitamins.

The use of "poppers" is common practice among some homosexuals. Recently I heard a rumor connecting poppers with an increased risk of AIDS. Is this true? What are the risks if a person used poppers two or three times a month?

"Poppers" (amyl nitrite, butyl nitrite, or isobutyl nitrite) are inhaled, supposedly because they enhance orgasm. They can be dangerous to some individuals. Research compiled for a federal government study concluded that "the use of nitrites does not cause AIDS." Some researchers speculated that using nitrite vapor might be linked to an increased incidence of Kaposi's sarcoma (a usually rare type of skin tumor) among people who already have AIDS, but it is not clear whether this is true. One study suggested a link, but other larger studies have not supported this.

Regardless of what research concludes about poppers, a person should follow safer sex guidelines to reduce the risk of exposure to HIV (the virus that causes AIDS). Drugs and alcohol may reduce one's ability to follow safer sex practices responsibly.

My mother and I can't come up with an answer to this question: If AIDS can be passed by using the same needle, can it be passed by a mosquito or other insect?

According to the CDC, the AIDS virus cannot be transmitted by mosquitoes or any other insects because of the manner in which insects metabolize (process) blood. Moreover, researchers have not been able to link any case of AIDS to this type of transmission, nor have they been able to find evidence of AIDS infection in any insect.

Dr. Jonathan Mann, former Director of the World Health Organization's special program on AIDS, described in detail why AIDS cannot be transmitted through mosquitoes and other insects.

1. The HIV virus can only live in very specific kinds of mammalian cells. So it does not thrive inside insects—unlike malaria, which does thrive in a particular type of mosquito.
2. The amount of blood that might be carried on a mosquito's mouthparts from one person to the next is extremely tiny. This, combined with the fact that there are only a very small number of HIV particles present in the blood of infected persons, makes transmission of the virus by this means even more unlikely.

But there is even stronger evidence from Africa that mosquitoes, bedbugs, and lice do not transmit the disease: First, the people with AIDS in Africa are primarily between the ages of 20 and 40 (the age group most likely to have STDs). If the AIDS virus was transmitted by mosquitoes, then equal numbers of children and old people would also be infected, since all ages are equally likely to be bitten by mosquitoes. Second, if mosquitoes or other insects could transmit the disease, we would expect people of all ages living together in crowded spaces with an infected person to also be infected. Research has shown that people living in the same household as an AIDS patient are no more likely to be infected than those in households without an AIDS patient (as long as they are not having sex with the infected person).

Mosquitoes cannot transmit the AIDS virus!

What is really meant when you say that frequent contacts increase the chance of getting AIDS? Does it take once or do you need a buildup that makes contact so much more dangerous each time?

An amazing number of supposedly intelligent people are incredibly dumb about these issues.

Simply put, the more sexual partners you have, the greater your chances of having sex with someone who is infected with the AIDS virus (HIV). Thus, the more likely it is that you will become infected yourself. Also, the more sexual contacts you have with a person who is infected, the greater your chances of actually getting the virus.

Remember that HIV can be transmitted to you through sexual activity *only* if the activity is with an infected partner. One study estimated that there is only a one in 5 billion chance of becoming infected with HIV in a single sexual encounter *if* a condom is used, intercourse is with a person who is at low risk, and that person has been tested recently and found not to be infected with HIV.

At the other end of the spectrum, having unprotected sex (not using condoms) just *once* with a partner who is infected with HIV carries a one in 500 chance of your being infected. According to the study, two out of three people who continue having unprotected sex with an HIV-infected person for five years will themselves become infected with HIV.

Certainly, these statistics are just that—statistics. Individuals have become infected after just one sexual contact with an HIV infected person. The most important point is to take all the precautions you can by using safer sex practices to protect yourself *(see "Safer Sex" guidelines in this chapter)*.

Are older people more likely to get AIDS than younger people? What I mean is, are more AIDS patients over age 40?

No. According to the November 1989 data from the CDC, nearly one-half (46 percent) of all AIDS cases were between ages 30 and 39. Another 20 percent were between 20 and 29 years old.

Only 31 percent of AIDS cases reported to the CDC involved individuals aged 40 or older. This disease is affecting young people in age groups usually thought of as being in the healthiest time of life.

At a recent gathering, the topic of AIDS testing was discussed and an interesting fact was disclosed by a nurse who was there. She said that if you are tested for AIDS, your name goes on a national computer whether or not the results are positive. Is this true? If it is, it would certainly put the chill on being tested.

As far as we know, there is no such national computer file. It is not clear what is being done by individual communities and states. Health professionals are greatly concerned that people will avoid being tested for the AIDS virus (HIV) precisely because they are concerned that their names may be listed somewhere. This is why public health officials have established AIDS testing centers with procedures that assure the anonymity of the people tested.

At confidential AIDS-testing sites, a person is not required to give a name, Social Security number, or any other identifying information. Thus, the government couldn't put names on a computer even if it wanted to. The basic requirements are that the person being tested must personally visit the site for the blood to be drawn and must pick up the test results in person about two weeks later. They do ask for general information, such as age, but you make up a number or false name to use for coding your blood sample.

These are often called Alternative Test Sites, and many also offer counseling and educational services. When you call for an appointment, ask in advance whether a center provides anonymous testing; if they don't, call another center.

At blood banks and plasma-donation centers, however, donor records are not considered to be as confidential as those of the Alternative Test Sites. These facilities are not currently required to report the names of individuals who test positive for the AIDS virus, but there is no guarantee that these records would remain confidential if laws are passed requiring disclosure. It is *not* appropriate to donate blood in order to get tested for HIV. If you want to know whether you are infected with HIV, go to an anonymous test center.

I am concerned about AIDS. When I was 14 weeks pregnant my doctor told me I had syphilis. I was devastated. And two weeks before I delivered I found out I had gonorrhea. I was so embarrassed and ashamed, I just wanted to die. My husband and I have been separated for several months now and I recently learned from my mother-in-law that my husband had sexual relationships with men before I met him. Do you think I could have gotten AIDS from him? Or would it have shown up on the other tests? I am 19 years old and have a beautiful seven-month-old daughter who came out of this terrible mess just perfect.

The tests for each STD are specific to only one disease, so no information about AIDS would show up in tests for syphilis or gonorrhea. It's important that you be tested specifically for HIV because your husband's behavior places you at increased risk.

Currently the two most common types of tests available to detect infection with the AIDS virus (HIV) are the ELISA and the Western blot, both are blood tests. These tests detect *antibodies* to HIV, not the virus itself.

The first test done is usually the ELISA (enzyme-linked immunosorbent assay). If your ELISA test results found no HIV antibodies, you would be considered seronegative, meaning that you were not infected with HIV. If your results were positive, the laboratory would do a second, more sophisticated test called the Western blot. This test looks for a series of protein bands associated with the virus. If none of these specific protein bands are present, the test results are considered negative and you would be considered seronegative. If the bands were present, you would be considered seropositive (meaning that your blood has HIV antibodies indicating you are infected with the virus).

The accuracy of these two tests in combination compare favorably with other medical diagnostic tests. However, some false results do occur. The NIAID (National Institute of Allergy and Infectious Diseases) is using a test called the Polymerase Chain Reaction Test, which actually tests for genetic material from the virus. So far, this test is only used for research, is very expensive, and takes a long time. It is expected that more accurate tests which detect the virus directly will be more widely available in the near future.

I had sex with someone this week that may be considered in the AIDS high-risk group. He was bisexual. I'd like to be tested immediately, but I'm wondering if it's too soon. How long does it take to get test results, and how do I know that everything will be kept confidential? Also, where do I go for testing. I'm sure not going to my family doctor.

The antibodies to the AIDS virus, which is what the tests look for, generally take at least two to twelve weeks to appear after infection occurs. In rare cases, it takes more than a year for the antibodies to appear. This is called the "window period." It wouldn't be useful for you to be tested the same week you suspect you were exposed, but do go for testing—have the first test three months after the suspected exposure and a second at six months.

Blood tests for HIV antibodies are widely available either free or inexpensively from state, county or city departments of health or at clinics. You can call the National AIDS Hotline (1-800-342-AIDS) to find the site nearest you that provides anonymous testing. Each person taking any test for HIV infection should ask the following questions of the clinic or test site: Are test results fully protected for confidentiality and anonymity? Does the clinic do both the ELISA and the Western blot tests automatically if needed? Does the clinic offer counseling and educational services? If all these services are not provided and all these conditions not met, call another testing site.

It generally takes two weeks to get test results. If a positive result on this first test is found, a second, more sophisticated test must be done.

Last December, in the course of regular blood work, I decided to be checked for any and all venereal diseases, including AIDS. (I've always been a curious health nut and I'd recently had sex with an old friend who I realized later had been quite promiscuous recently.)

Well, even though I'm not a homosexual, do not use any drugs and do not frequent prostitutes, the test came back positive. I felt that I was dead. Two weeks later I had the more definitive Western blot test, and it was negative. Six months later I had the Western blot again, and it was again negative. Thank God!

Recently a woman has appeared in my life, and she has given me joy. We have not engaged in intercourse. Is there any chance whatsoever that somehow she could be in danger if our relationship eventually leads to intercourse?

Your concern is commendable. The ELISA test is oversensitive in the direction of being positive, meaning that it's not unusual to get a positive result when, in fact, there is no HIV present. There are several reasons for false positive results on the ELISA. The test results may be wrongly influenced if the person has an antibody to the white blood cells in which the virus is grown to produce the test, has had previous blood transfusions (even with uncontaminated blood), has alcohol-induced liver disease, or has some tropical diseases such as malaria.

So far, false positives are said to be rare with the Western blot test, which is much more expensive, but more specific; that's why most testing sites do one if the ELISA result is positive. This is why it makes sense to go to an anonymous testing center rather than a family doctor for HIV testing.

If your personal risk factors have remained low and you have had two negative Western blot tests six months after the exposure you mentioned, your likelihood of carrying the AIDS virus would be very low, according to current scientific understanding. And that means the risk to your partner would also be equally low. However, the HIV status of your new friend needs to be evaluated as well. If she is also free of HIV then all you need to do is keep your AIDS risk factors low in your future behavior. Go to a counselor if you continue to have trouble putting your false positive test behind you.

Further Readings

Boswell, J.; Hexter, R.; and Reinisch, J. M., eds. *Sexuality and Disease: Metaphors, perceptions, and behavior in the AIDS era*. New York: Oxford University Press, in preparation.
(A scholarly collection of writings on the public perception of and policies regarding AIDS.)
Brandt, A. M. *No Magic Bullet: A social history of venereal disease in the United States since 1880*. New York: Oxford University Press, 1985.
(Written for educated readers.)
Cass, V. *There's More to Sex than AIDS: The A to Z guide to safe sex*. Richmond Victoria, Australia: Greenhouse Publications, 1988.
(An encyclopedic guide to various sexual behaviors and how to make them "safer" in the age of AIDS.)
Holmes, K. K.; Mårdh, P-A.; Sparling, P. F.; Wiesner, P. J.; Cates, W., Jr.; Lemon, S. M.; and Stamm. W. E. *Sexually Transmitted Diseases*. 2nd ed. New York: McGraw-Hill Information Services Company, 1990.
(This is a highly technical scientific book, but anyone who has been diagnosed as having a specific STD or STD organism will find all the information they need about tests and treatments.)
Shilts, R. *And the Band Played On: Politics, people, and the AIDS epidemic*. New York: St. Martin's Press, 1987.
(A fascinating account of the history of the discovery of AIDS and responses to the epidemic.)
Voeller, B.; Reinisch, J. M.; and Gottlieb, M., eds. *AIDS and Sex: An integrated biomedical and biobehavioral approach*. New York: Oxford University Press, 1990.
(A research-based collection of writings on data and methods used by medical and behavioral scientists concerned with AIDS.)

Appendix One

Locating, Selecting, and Evaluating Professional Services

It is difficult enough to admit to oneself that there is a problem with a relationship or with sexual functioning. It can be even more difficult to talk to someone else about such personal subjects. Embarrassment about such matters is common, but may be reduced if you have the information you need, such as what to expect when you see a therapist or physician.

The purpose of this appendix is to help you find professionals who have been trained to make discussing sensitive personal problems easier and more comfortable for you. It also explains how to find medical specialists who are trained to assess physical problems that can affect the sexual or reproductive aspects of your life. Also included are suggestions to help you get the most information possible from interactions with these professionals so that you can make informed decisions about your health care.

Remember, as a patient or client you are entitled to get the information you need to choose the medication, therapy, treatment, or surgery that is best for your particular needs and life style. You also have the responsibility to ask questions about how a medication or treatment will affect your health and well-being, including how it might change your sex life.

I. HOW TO LOCATE THE APPROPRIATE HEALTH PROFESSIONAL OR SERVICE WITH EXPERTISE IN SEX PROBLEMS

A. When you feel your problem or difficulty probably does not involve medical or physical factors, you should locate a sex therapist or marriage counselor.

Steps to locate a sex therapist or marriage counselor

- If you are comfortable doing so, ask friends, family members, or co-workers who have gone to a counselor whether they can recommend someone, or ask your family physician or clergyman for a recommendation.

- Look in the yellow pages of your telephone book under:
  Human Services Organizations
  Marriage, Family, Child and Individual Counselors
  Mental Health Services
  Psychologists
  Psychiatrists (may be listed under Physicians & Surgeons—Medical - M.D. or separately under Psychiatrists)
  Social Service Organizations
  Such listings often state specialties, certification status, and qualifications.
- Write to one of the following groups and ask for a list of certified counselors and therapists in your area (there may be a nominal fee):

  American Association of Sex Educators, Counselors and Therapists (AASECT)
  11 Dupont Circle N.W., Suite 220
  Washington, DC 20036

  American Association for Marriage and Family Therapy (AAMFT)
  1717 K Street N.W., Suite 407
  Washington, DC 20006

- Call your local Community Mental Health Center and ask for recommendations, or call the nearest medical school or large hospital and ask if they have a sex dysfunctions clinic.

B. **When you suspect your sexual or relationship problems may include medical or physical factors, locate a sex therapist who works closely with medical professionals or a physician with special training in sexual medicine and experience in diagnosing problems with sexual functioning.**

Steps to locate a medical sex dysfunctions specialist
- If you are comfortable doing so, ask your family physician, friends, family members, or co-workers to recommend a clinic or therapist.
- Look in the yellow pages of your telephone book under:
  Marriage, Family, Child and Individual Counselors
  Mental Health Services
  Physicians & Surgeons—Medical - M.D.
  Psychologists
  Psychiatrists (may be listed under Physicians & Surgeons—Medical-M.D. or separately under Psychiatrists)
  Such listings often state specialties and qualifications.
- Write to the groups mentioned above (AASECT and AAMFT) and ask for referrals near you.
- Call the nearest medical school, university, or large hospital and ask if they have a special clinic for diagnosing and treating sexual problems (dysfunctions). If your town does not have such a facility, most libraries have telephone directories of nearby large cities and will help you find the telephone number. Or call your county or state Medical Society and ask for telephone numbers of qualified clinics or physicians.

II. GATHER INFORMATION ABOUT THE HEALTH CARE PROFES-SIONALS AND SERVICES YOU HAVE LOCATED

Call the counselors, therapists, physicians, and/or clinics you've located. You may want to call several:

- Be prepared with a pen and paper so you are ready to take notes during the telephone conversation.
- Briefly state what you think the problem is and/or any symptoms.
- Ask if the professional or clinic has experience treating problems like yours.
- Ask the fee for an initial appointment.
- Ask the fee for an initial appointment.
- Ask if the professional or clinic can provide information about their qualifications, the services available, and standard fees. Ask if they are certified by any government agency or national organization. Many have informational brochures they will send you.
- Review your notes of the telephone conversations and any information you've received. You are looking for someone with a doctoral (Ph.D.), medical (M.D.), social work (M.S.W.) or master's (M.A. or M.S.) degree from an accredited university or college.

III. SELECT ONE PROFESSIONAL OR CLINIC AND CALL TO MAKE AN APPOINTMENT FOR AN INITIAL MEETING

- State that you are looking for help but do not want to begin the diagnostic or therapy process until you make a final decision on whom to hire.
- If you want to have your spouse or partner accompany you to the meeting, ask about that.

IV. EVALUATE THE HEALTH CARE PROFESSIONAL OR SERVICE AT YOUR FIRST APPOINTMENT

- Take along a pen and paper to write down any medical or scientific words you may hear. Ask the professional to write them down or spell them out for you. Then you can read more about your diagnosis, tests, and treatments later.
- Notice whether there are diplomas and certificates displayed on the office walls. If there are, read them.
- When you meet the professional, briefly state what you think the problem is or what symptoms you have.
- Ask what special training the person has had to qualify him or her to treat your problem. This information, combined with any diplomas and certificates displayed, should give the impression that the person is well-educated and has kept up-to-date by attending educational seminars and training programs in his or her specialty. In the United States, any mental health professional or physician, whatever his or her degree, is permitted to call him or herself a sex therapist. This is why carefully checking credentials and special training is important.
- Ask about membership in state and national professional organiza-

tions and whether the person is licensed by your state. Some professionals are not accustomed to being asked such questions, but a reputable professional will not mind providing this information. Moreover, giving informative answers to questions like these in a patient manner can be an early clue that the person will be easy to work with and supportive of your concerns.

- Ask if the person regularly does referrals to other professionals if special tests are needed and who those specialists are. Good working relationships with specialists such as endocrinologists, psychiatrists, psychologists, urologists, gynecologists, or surgeons are often necessary for adequate diagnosis and treatment.
- Ask how many cases similar to yours the person has diagnosed and treated and what the outcomes were for these other cases.
- Ask what the person might recommend as diagnostic tests and typical treatment for problems such as yours. In many cases an exact answer may not be possible, but the person should at least try to explain what may be involved. You are looking for someone who does a good job of explaining and teaching.
- Ask what you might expect in the way of number of appointments, length of treatment, and fees.

You have the right to full and clear answers to all your questions. If you don't get them, select another professional.

Your final selection of a counselor, therapist, or physician should be based on whether you feel comfortable with the professional and with the treatment methods and goals proposed. It is all right to "shop around" for a health care professional or service. It is no different than making an effort to find an honest, reliable mechanic for your car. If you are not sure about the first professional you see, make an appointment and interview another.

If after several appointments you find yourself disappointed with the professional you've selected, think about changing to someone else. Even competent professionals vary greatly in their personalities, treatment methods, and style of interactions with clients. It is not unusual for mismatches to occur. For example, you may prefer someone whose interactions with you are either more reserved or more informal.

The relationship between a therapist and client or physician and patient needs to be a working partnership. A particular professional may be exactly right for one person or couple and wrong for a different person or couple—just as at work you find you get along with some co-workers better than with others. Ask to have copies of your records and test results to give to the new professional. (Unfortunately, in some states such records must be transferred directly to the new therapist or physician without the patient seeing them.)

V. HOW TO FIND A MEDICAL SPECIALIST

At various points this book has suggested seeing a specialist in a particular field of medicine, such as endocrinology, or a physician who has specialized expertise in dealing with a particular problem, such as adolescent concerns.

A. **Steps to locate specific medical specialists:**

- If you are comfortable doing so, ask your family physician for a referral.
- Look in the yellow pages of your telephone book under Physicians & Surgeons—Medical - M.D. to see if there are such specialists in your area.
- Call the nearest medical school or large hospital, ask if there is such a specialist on staff and how to make an appointment; public libraries can often help you find these telephone numbers. For example, say "do you have a gynecological endocrinologist on staff who specializes in menopause? How do I make an appointment?"
- Look in the *Marquis Directory of Medical Specialists*. This reference book is updated every two years and should be available at your local public library.
- Call your county or state Medical Society and ask for telephone numbers of the particular type of specialist you are looking for.

B. **Call the specialists you've located:**

- Have a pen and paper ready to write down answers to your questions.
- Briefly state to the person answering the telephone what you think your problem is and any symptoms. (You will probably not be speaking directly to the specialist at this point.)
- Ask if the specialist has experience in treating problems such as yours.
- Ask what the fee is for the first appointment.
- Ask about the specialist's credentials. Most specialized fields of medicine require training beyond medical school and/or special examinations for professional certification; only after meeting such criteria is the physician certified as belonging to the specialty. These are often referred to as "Boards"; for example, in urology a physician who has satisfactorily completed advanced training and passed special written and oral examinations is called a Diplomat of the American Board of Urology or in gynecology, a Fellow of the American College of Obstetrics and Gynecology. **In the United States any M.D. is permitted to practice any specialty without specialized training, and this is why it is important to determine a physician's training and certification.**

C. **When you decide on a specialist, call to make an appointment:**

- Ask what records or other information you should bring with you or have sent from other doctors you have seen.

D. **Before your appointment:**

- Collect any records you have been asked to bring.
- Make a list of all prescription and nonprescription (over-the-counter)

medications you take, the dosages, and how often you take them—
even aspirin, vitamins, or ordinary cold medications.
- Write down everything you recall about your problem (what the
symptoms are, when you first noticed symptoms, how long you've
had the problem, whether symptoms are worse with any particular
activity or at different times of the day or month). Write down
anything you don't want to forget to tell the doctor.
- Make a list of all the questions you want to ask the doctor.

E. When you go to the appointment:

It is common to be upset or anxious about seeing a physician, especially
if a frightening or embarrassing condition is involved or you do not feel
well. Below are some suggestions to help make visiting a physician
more reassuring and informative.
- If you feel comfortable, bring a relative, friend or partner with you.
They are likely to be less anxious and may help you remember to ask
questions and get information.
- Take along your records and lists.
- Also take along a pen and paper so you can write down what the
doctor says. Ask to have words spelled out, so you can look them up
later at the library if you want to find out more about your diagnosis,
proposed treatments, or medications.
- When a professional suggests tests ask for their names, costs, and
what each is looking for.
- Before you leave the office, check your list of questions to make sure
they have all been answered in a way *you* can understand.

F. If a diagnosis is made (the doctor says what is wrong and what may have caused the problem):

- Ask what led him or her to decide on that particular diagnosis—
especially ask what the results were of any tests you had. Write them
down or get copies.
- Ask how certain he or she is of the diagnosis and whether any of the
test results are questionable or borderline.
- Ask if there are any other possible causes of your problem.

G. If recommendations for medication are made:

- Write down the name of each medication, the dosage, and the
schedule you are to follow for taking it.
- Ask if there are any side effects you should watch for, including
changes in your sex life, if this is important to you.
- Ask what might happen if you decide not to take the medication.
- Make sure you clearly understand how and when to take the medication and what might happen if you forget to take it.
- Keep track of *any* changes you notice while you take the medication
on a calendar or date book and report them to your doctor. This is
essential for your physician to evaluate the effectiveness of treatment
and to spot side-effects early.

H. If treatment or surgery is recommended:

- Ask for a description of the procedure, how long it will take, the costs involved, and the recovery time.
- Ask about any side effects (including those which might affect your sex life) and if any risks are involved.
- Ask how many other treatments or surgeries like the one proposed for you the doctor has performed and his or her success rate.
- Ask to speak with other patients to see if they are pleased with the results.
- Ask what other options are available to treat the problem and the side effects, costs and other details about those other options.
- Ask what will happen if you decide not to have the treatment or surgery.
- Say that you will need time to make a decision about the recommendations, then really *do* take the time to go home, calm down, and honestly consider your choices.
- In the case of surgery, radiation treatments, experimental treatments, or any other recommendations that appear to involve a degree of risk, seek a *second medical opinion*. Responsible professionals will not discourage you from doing this.

VI. GETTING A SECOND MEDICAL OPINION

This means locating a different, similarly qualified physician to assess your situation. However, the second physician should usually *not* be in practice with or specifically recommended by the first physician or specialist you've seen. For example, when surgery has been recommended, do *not* seek your second opinion from a surgeon unless you already know surgery is absolutely necessary and you are trying to compare surgical techniques or success rates. The same is true for other types of specialized treatments, such as radiation therapy. This is because a surgeon is likely to recommend surgery and a radiation specialist will recommend that treatment— not necessarily because one or the other is best, but because that's what they are most familiar with.

Most health insurance plans will pay for second opinions and, in fact, many *insist* on having a second opinion before authorizing payment for surgery or other costly medical treatments. If you have health insurance, call your company and ask for suggestions as to how to proceed with getting a qualified second opinion.

Go through the steps outlined in V.-A and B above to locate a specialist for a second opinion. Or if you happen to know a nurse or other person who works in health care, ask about the reputation of the physician who recommended a particular treatment or surgery and ask if he or she can suggest competent physicians for a second opinion.

When you select a physician for the second opinion:

- Call and state what the first doctor said your problem was and that you are seeking a second opinion.

• If you had tests or X-rays done by the first physician, mention this and ask how to arrange for copies of the results to be sent for review before your appointment.

ONCE YOU'VE MADE A DECISION it is essential that you keep your physician informed about the effects of any treatment, medication, or surgery—even long after it is completed. There is no way he or she can know how effective any treatment has been or if you need additional treatment if you don't keep the physician informed.

VIII. LIST OF SOME SPECIALISTS MENTIONED IN THIS BOOK; others are included in chapter introductions or where the topic is covered in the text.

• **Adolescent specialist or clinic** (a professional or center that specializes in treating the physical and emotional problems of adolescents).

If you can't find such a specialist locally, write to:

Society for Adolescent Medicine
Suite 101, 10727 White Oak Avenue
Granada Hills, CA 91344
(Enclose a self-addressed, stamped envelope for their reply)

• **Endocrinologist** (a specialist in the body's endocrine gland system). In the context of sexual problems, this usually involves the analysis of hormone levels and evaluation of using replacement hormones. They may be located at departments of endocrinology at hospitals or medical schools.

• **Pediatric endocrinologist** (a specialist in the endocrine system and the development of children, including sexual development). They may be located at either a department of endocrinology or a department of pediatrics.

• **Gynecological endocrinologist** (a specialist in the hormonal and reproductive systems of women). They may be located at either a department of gynecology or a department of endocrinology. Some of these, for example, specialize in treating post-menopausal women.

• **Reproductive endocrinologist** (a specialist in those aspects of the hormone system and organs necessary for reproduction). They may be located at a department of endocrinology or at a fertility clinic.

• **Gynecologist** (a specialist in female reproductive and sexual organs and women's sexuality). They may be located at either a department of gynecology or a department of obstetrics.

• **Urologist** (a specialist in the urinary and genital system, usually of males, and in men's sexuality). They may be located at a department of urology.

• **Sexologist** (a specialist with primary training and certification in fields such as gynecology, urology, psychology, or psychiatry who also has post-graduate training in biomedical sexology). These professionals are usually faculty members of an accredited university, medical school, or hospital who conduct research.

• **Venereologist** (a specialist in sexually transmitted diseases who has certification in some other branch of medicine, such as urology, gynecology, or infectious diseases, [a subspecialty of special medicine], but they also often have additional training in microbiology). They may have a home base in many different departments, but most medical schools and large hospitals have STD clinics which you can call.

• **Plastic/Cosmetic/Reconstructive surgeon** *(see Chapter 4).*

IX. IF PROBLEMS ARISE

Regardless of which type of professional you see or their stated credentials and qualifications, *you* are the best judge of whether you have been helped or not. If at any time during the diagnostic and treatment process you are not satisfied with the treatment you are receiving, discuss your feelings with the professional involved. Some medications and treatments do take a while before you will be able to notice progress. Although you need to give the professional a chance to explain, if the situation does not improve in a reasonable amount of time, try someone else. Sometimes it is necessary to try a series of treatments or medications before the right one for you is found. If you have confidence in the health professional you have chosen, stick with him or her.

As part of their ethical guidelines, every professional organization *prohibits* sexual interactions of any kind with clients or patients. If a counselor, therapist, physician, or other medical practitioner touches you in a sexual way or implies that sexual interactions are part of therapy, leave the office and report the incident. The steps to follow are discussed in Chapter 17.

Further Readings

Clayman, C. B., ed. *The American Medical Association Guide to Prescription and Over-The-Counter Drugs.* New York: Random House, 1988.
(Contains information about the most common prescription drugs as well as some over-the-counter medications.)

The Merck Manual of Diagnosis and Therapy, Rahway, NJ: Merck & Co., Inc. (Updated editions issued regularly).
(A guide to symptoms and standard treatments for many diseases and conditions.)

Physician's Desk Reference. Oradell, NJ: Medical Economics Company, Inc. (A new edition is issued every year.)
(A listing of prescription medications, side effects, and related information; ask a librarian to explain how to look things up in this book if you have difficulty.)

Appendix

Abbreviations

AIDS	Acquired Immunodeficiency Syndrome
AMA	American Medical Association
BBT	Basal Body Temperature
BPH	Benign Prostatic Hypertrophy
CDC	Centers for Disease Control
COPD	Chronic Obstructive Pulmonary Disease
D and C	Dilation and Curretage
DES	Diethylstilbestrol
DPA	Dual Photon Absorptiometry
FAS	Fetal Alcohol Syndrome
FDA	Food and Drug Administration
FSH	Follicle Stimulating Hormone
GIFT	Gamete Intrafallopian Transfer
hCG	Human Chorionic Gonadotropin
HIV	Human Immunodeficiency Virus
hMG	Human Menopausal Gonadotropin
HPV	Human Papillomavirus
HRT	Hormone Replacement Therapy
HSV	Herpes Simplex Virus
IUD	Intrauterine Device
LH	Luteinizing Hormone
NGU	Nongonococcal Urethritis
NIAID	National Institute of Allergy and Infectious Diseases
NIH	National Institutes of Health
NPT	Nocturnal Penile Tumescence
OTC	Over-the-Counter (Non-prescription medicines)
PC	Pubococcygeal Muscle
PCOD	Polycystic Ovarian Disease
PID	Pelvic Inflammatory Disease
PMS	Premenstrual Syndrome
PROST	Transfer of a Pronucleus
PSA	Prostate Specific Antigen
REM	Rapid Eye Movement (sleep)
STD	Sexually Transmitted Disease
TBT	Transcervical Balloon Tuboplasty
TEST	Transfer of an Embryo
TSS	Toxic Shock Syndrome
TURP	Transurethral Resection
VD	Veneral Disease (see STD)
WHO	World Health Organization
ZIFT	Zygote Intrafallopian Transfer

BIOGRAPHIES

JUNE MACHOVER REINISCH, PH.D., has served as director of The Kinsey Institute since 1982 and is a professor in the Departments of Psychology and Psychiatry at Indiana University. She was born in New York City in 1943 and attended City and Country School and the Farm and Wilderness Camps, both of which had a major impact on her view of life. After graduating from Great Neck North High School and receiving a Bachelor of Science (cum laude) from New York University, she spent several years in business including managing the Cafe Au Go Go in Greenwich Village and serving as a vice president for Daedalus Productions, which managed such recording artists as Sly and the Family Stone and Peaches and Herb. She returned to academia in 1969 and while receiving her doctorate in developmental psychology "with distinction" from Columbia University she also studied with Dr. John Money of the Psychohormonal Unit at Johns Hopkins Hospital in Baltimore. Following graduation, she was a member of the Departments of Psychology and Psychiatry at Rutgers University in New Jersey.

Dr. Reinisch's scientific work has focused on the study of sexual and psychosexual development with a special interest in behavioral endocrinology and behavioral teratology. This includes the investigation of the effects of drugs and hormones administered by physicians to pregnant women on the physical and behavioral development of their offspring. Since heading The Kinsey Institute, an additional major focus of her research has been the high-risk sexual behavior of women, adolescents and young adults as it relates to sexually transmitted diseases and the AIDS crisis. She has been awarded research grants from the National Institute of Mental Health, the National Institute of Child Health and Human Development, The National Institute on Drug Abuse, The National Institute of Education, and The Ford Foundation. Reports of her scientific work have been published in such journals as *Science, Nature, The American Psychologist, The Journal of Personality and Social Psychology,* and the *Archives of Sexual Behavior.* She is a fellow of the American Psychological Association, The American Association for the Advancement of Science, and the Society for the Scientific Study of Sex. Among her awards are the Morton Prince Award from the American Psychopathological Association and the medal as the 9th Dr. S. T. Huang-Chan Memorial Lecturer in Anatomy, Hong Kong University.

Dr. Reinisch has traveled extensively in Asia, Europe, North Africa, and Central and South America and gives many scientific and public lectures each year both in the United States and abroad. She believes that teaching should be a major responsibility for every scientist and is committed to presenting research findings in a way the general public can understand and find useful to apply to their own lives. This commitment is also obvious in her participation in radio and television interviews as well as in *The Kinsey Report* newspaper column written for the institute and distributed by United Feature Syndicate throughout the world.

RUTH A. BEASLEY was born in Indiana and has worked at The Kinsey Institute since 1971. During those years she has headed the library and other collections, acted as coordinator of training programs for health professionals, collaborated for five years with Dr. Reinisch on *The Kinsey Report* newspaper column and served as assistant director while working toward her doctorate in Library and Information Science. She has recently retired and begun work as a free-lance writer.

HOW TO USE THIS INDEX: Look under the word or phrase you normally use; the numbers are pages and illustrations about that topic. For example "Missionary position, 123, 125, il. 79" means look on pages 123 and 125 and an illustration is on page 79. If a word is followed by "See", all the pages about that topic are under the word after "See"—"Birth-control pills, See Oral contraceptives" means that you must look under "Oral contraceptives" to find the pages. If a word is followed by a list of page numbers and the "See also", more information can be found under the additional word or words—"Genitals, male" has both page numbers and "See also Penis; Testicles." You can find other page numbers under "Penis" and "Testicles." If a "See" or "See also" has a colon (:)—"Desire, sexual: low or inhibited", look under "Desire, sexual" and then down the list of subtopics for "low or inhibited" to find the pages you need.